W9-CEG-665

Fourth Edition

Reading, Writing, and Learning in ESL

A Resource Book for K-12 Teachers

Suzanne F. Peregoy
San Francisco State University

Owen F. Boyle
San Jose State University

PEARSON

Boston   New York   San Francisco
Mexico City   Montreal   Toronto   London   Madrid   Munich   Paris
Hong Kong   Singapore   Tokyo   Cape Town   Sydney

To our students, the spark and flame of our continued learning.

Series Editor: Aurora Martínez Ramos
Series Editorial Assistant: Erin Beatty
Senior Marketing Manager: Amy Cronin Jordan
Senior Editorial-Production Administrator: Beth Houston
Editorial-Production Service: Walsh & Associates, Inc.
Composition and Prepress Buyer: Linda Cox
Manufacturing Buyer: Andrew Turso
Cover Administrator: Linda Knowles
Interior Design: Glenna Collett
Electronic Composition: Monotype Composition

For related titles and support materials, visit our online catalog at www.ablongman.com

Between the time Website information is gathered and then published, it is not unusual for some sites to have closed. Also, the transcription of URLs can result in typographical errors. The publisher would appreciate notification where these errors occur so that they may be corrected in subsequent editions.

Library of Congress Cataloging-in-Publication Data

Peregoy, Suzanne F.
    Reading, writing, and learning in ESL: a resource book for K–12 teachers/ Suzanne F. Peregoy, Owen F. Boyle.—4th ed.
        p. cm.
    Rev. ed. of: Reading, writing & learning in ESL. 3rd ed. 2000.
    Includes bibliographical references and index.
        ISBN 0–205–41034–0
        1. English language—Study and teaching—Foreign speakers. I. Boyle, Owen. II. Peregoy, Suzanne F. Reading, writing & learning in ESL. III. Title.

    PE1128.A2P393 2005
    428'.0071—dc22

                                    2004044264

Printed in the United States of America

10 9 8 7 6 5   08 07 06

Photo credits: Suzanne F. Peregoy, pp. 1, 17, 33, 63, 68, 73, 89, 107, 118, 137, 156, 222, 248, 264, 268, 296, 314, 333, 346, 357, 368, 376, 386; Linda J. Russell, pp. 127, 206.

CONTENTS

5 Emergent Literacy: English Learners Beginning to Write and Read   156

6 English Learners and Process Writing   206

7   Reading and Literature Instruction for English Language Learners   264

x

xi

PREFACE

Reading, Writing, and Learning in ESL: A Resource Book for K–12 Teachers, Fourth Edition, is a comprehensive, reader-friendly resource book that provides a wealth of teaching ideas for promoting oral language, reading, and writing development in English for K–12 English learners. The book provides up-to-date language acquisition theory, classroom organization, teaching strategies, and assessment procedures for effective English learner instruction. As such, it is an ideal text for preservice and in-service ESL and bilingual methods classes. It also makes an excellent staff development tool.

Our purpose in the fourth edition remains the same as in the earlier editions: We wish to open a window on classrooms in which English learners are actively involved in learning about themselves, their classmates, and the world around them. In these classrooms, students pursue topics of their own choosing, using oral and written English to discuss and confer with their classmates, read, write, report, and share in the ongoing process of learning. Gradually, they advance their knowledge of English, expanding their discourse repertoires and refining their control of grammar, pronunciation, spelling, and mechanics. Ideally, they will use their growing academic, linguistic, and sociocultural competence to create better worlds for themselves and those around them.

NEW IN THIS EDITION

The fourth edition has been thoroughly updated and revised, including:

Companion Website: As a companion to this text, the website (www.ablongman.com/peregoy4e) offers additional learning resources, Internet links, and online communications among students and instructors, as well as additional resources for instructors.

Technology: We have added Internet resources specific to the content of each chapter.

Standards and Assessment: Discussion of curriculum standards and assessment has been integrated into a new section on policy. Standards-based instruction is also integrated into the discussion of effective English learner instruction.

Language Theory: We have added discussion of language as symbol and instrument of power, social standing, and personal identity because these affect English learners in school.

Secondary School Material: We have added material for middle and high school, including an illustration of sheltered instruction (SDAIE) in a social science class as well as six essay samples, holistic scoring, and a graph that suggests strategies for working with students who write at various levels.

Working with Student Errors: This new section provides detailed information on working with student errors in writing.

Comprehension and Metacognition: Discussion of reading comprehension and metacognition is expanded and discussed throughout chapters.

Extensive and Narrow Reading: The role of extensive reading and narrow reading is discussed.

New Suggested Readings: New annotated references have been added at the end of each chapter, totaling more than thirty new resources.

xiv

FEATURES OF THE BOOK

We have included several features to make this book easy to use:

- Each chapter begins with a **short introduction and guiding questions** so that the reader knows at a glance the focus and general content of the chapter.
- Each chapter includes numerous **classroom examples and vignettes** about teachers and students, giving life to the text and illustrating important ideas as they apply to classroom life.
- Each chapter ends with an **annotated bibliography of recommended readings** and a list of **discussion questions and activities** for readers to carry out that are aimed at extending and applying the content of the chapter.

ORGANIZATION OF THE TEXT

The book consists of ten chapters, sequenced as follows:

- Background information on English learners, including the impact of culture on learning, is provided in Chapter 1.
- An overview of first and second language acquisition theories as these relate to students, classrooms, and teaching practices is provided in Chapter 2.

- A coherent model of effective English learner instruction and assessment is developed and described in Chapter 3.
- Teaching and assessment strategies in oral language development are presented for beginning and intermediate English learners in Chapter 4, early literacy development in Chapter 5, writing in Chapter 6, reading and literature study in Chapter 7, and content learning in Chapters 8 and 9.
- Chapter 10 presents an in-depth view of reading assessment and its application to instructional decision making.

$\mathcal{U}$SING THE COMPANION WEBSITE FOR THIS BOOK

www.ablongman.com/peregoy4e

We are pleased to announce the Companion Website for *Reading, Writing, and Learning in ESL: A Resource Book for K–12 Teachers*. The purpose of the website is to enrich the learning opportunities provided by the book itself. Open the website by typing in the above URL. The opening page gives you three options to click on: **About the Book,** which provides general information; **Learning Resources,** which provides a collection of resources matched to the content of each chapter; and **Collaborative Network,** which allows you to discuss chapter content online with other students. The contents of Learning Resources and Collaborative Network are listed for you below.

Learning Resources

You will find a menu bar toward the top of the page that will allow you to choose any other chapter you wish. For each chapter, you will find the following:

- *Introduction and objectives* for the chapter.
- *Essay questions* (with hints to help you) that you may answer and send to your instructor or use for studying.
- *Internet resources* pertaining to the chapter's content.
- *Suggested activities* for each chapter.
- *Internet activities* for each chapter.
- A *site search* to help you find other places in the website where a particular topic from this chapter might be addressed.
- A link to *contact the publisher* to provide feedback about the site.
- A *syllabus manager* section.

Collaborative Network

This section of the website offers online communications through:

- *i-Chat:* In this area for virtual classroom discussion, you can schedule your own i-Chat sessions. You may even create your own chat room where your online study group may converse privately. Here you may also offer us feedback and ideas on how we can enhance this technology for your studies or classes.

- *Message Boards:* This area serves as a virtual bulletin board where you may post questions or comments to a wide audience. Others who visit the site are invited to respond to your questions or comments—and you are invited to respond to those who have posted before you.

We hope you will use and enjoy the companion website and that you will offer us suggestions for improvement!

xxi

Acknowledgments

Because this book culls from our own learning experiences, past and present, we wish to acknowledge, first of all, the following individuals who played a significant role in our professional development: Drs. Marilyn Hanf Buckley, Lily Wong Fillmore, Martha Haggard Ruddell, Robert Ruddell, and Sid Tiedt.

Next, we would like to acknowledge our university students, most of whom are prospective teachers or practicing teachers. They have helped us learn along the way and provided invaluable information for this edition. We also deeply appreciate the teachers who have welcomed us into their classrooms and shared materials with us, including Linda Chittenden, Debbie Dee Clark, Audrey Fong, Jennifer Jones, Jay Kuhlman, Anne Phillips, Reina Salgado, Juana Zamora, Cathryn Bruno, Don Mar, Angela Campbell, Juana Feisel-Engle, Peggy Koorhan, Gloria Lopez-Guiterrez, Rosemarie Michaels, Elda Parise, Debi Quan, and Pam Thomas.

We also wish to give special heartfelt thanks to the following reviewers. Francesco Bonavita, Kean University; Andrea Clemons, Loyola Marymount University; Marilee Coles-Ritchie, Utah State University; Lynn Cortina; Lori Elliot, Georgia State University; Carla Paciotto, Western Illinois University; and Patricia Pettigrew, California State University, San Marcos. They were remarkably helpful and thoughtful in helping us improve our book. Thank you for suggestions that expanded our thinking about teaching English learners.

ENGLISH LANGUAGE LEARNERS IN SCHOOL

In this chapter, we address the concerns of teachers when they first encounter students who are new to English in their classrooms, discussing such questions as the following:

1. Who are English language learners?
2. How can I get to know my English learners when their language and culture are new to me?
3. How do cultural differences affect the way my students respond to me and to my efforts to teach them?
4. How can I ease newcomers into the routines of my class when they understand very little English?
5. How do current policy trends affect English learners?
6. What kinds of programs exist to meet the needs of English language learners?

First, come with us into Buzz Bertolucci's classroom. It is the first day of school in Mr. Bertolucci's first grade. All the children are seated on the rug and have just finished the opening routines with the calendar. After introducing the children to each other through a song, Buzz places a Big Book of *The Gingerbread Man* in front of the class. With its large print and colorful illustrations, the 30-inch-tall Big Book not only captures the children's attention but also helps them understand the story's events. Mr. Bertolucci reads the book to the entire class, points to the pictures, puts on a gingerbread man mask, and acts out words such as "Run, run as fast as you can. You can't catch me. I'm the Gingerbread Man!" The entire book is "read" and acted out by members of the class on this, their first day of school. When the story is finished, one of the school cooks enters the room and hands a note to Mr. Bertolucci. He reads it to the class: "I jumped out of your book and ran to the cafeteria. Come and meet me! The Gingerbread Man." Teacher and children leave for the cafeteria but cannot find the Gingerbread Man there. They ask the cooks if they've seen the Gingerbread Man, but they haven't. Finally, one cook suggests that they look in the oven, and there they find another note from the Gingerbread Man: "I've gone to the janitor's storeroom by the bathrooms. See you there!" The class finds the janitor and asks if he's seen the Gingerbread Man, but he replies that the Gingerbread Man has gone to the nurse's office. When they meet the nurse, the children learn that the Gingerbread Man has gone to the counselor's office and then to the principal's office. Finally, the principal reports that the Gingerbread Man has returned to their classroom. When the children return to the classroom, each one finds a Gingerbread Man cookie at his or her desk.

As the children eat their cookies, Mr. Bertolucci reads *The Gingerbread Man* again. He has introduced his children to literature in an involving way. In addition, he has introduced the new children to their school and to the many people and places in the school they will need to know. He has also presented the literature and its simple theme in a concrete and interesting manner. His children will look forward to the next book he reads in class, and they will look forward to reading and writing themselves.

It may surprise you to learn that more than half the children in Mr. Bertolucci's class are new to the English language, coming from homes in which languages such as Spanish, Cantonese, and Japanese are spoken. Such linguistic variety was not always the case, but changes in the neighborhood over the past ten years have been dramatic. Mr. Bertolucci has responded to these changes by keeping many of his favorite teaching routines, such as the Gingerbread Man, but modifying them to meet the needs of his English language learners. You may be facing similar changes in your school, given today's immigration patterns. In this book, we will show you how to develop and modify oral language, reading, and writing instruction to meet the needs of your students who are new to English. But first we want to introduce you to the great diversity among the children who are called English language learners, to help you better understand and integrate them into your classroom and school. We use the terms *English language learners* and *English learners* to refer to non-native English speakers who are learning English in school. Typically, English learners speak a primary language other than English at home, such as Spanish, Cantonese, Russian, Hmong, and French. English learners vary in their proficiency in their primary languages. Of course, they vary in English language proficiency as well. Those who are beginners to intermediates in English are often referred to as **limited English proficient (LEP),** a term that is used in federal legislation and other official documents. We will use the terms **English learners, English language learners, non-native English speakers,** and **second language learners** synonymously throughout this book to refer to students who are in the process of learning English as a new language. Our main concern is with those who are at the beginning or intermediate stages of English language acquisition. The terms **English as a Second Language (ESL)** and **English for Speakers of Other Languages (ESOL)** are often used to refer to the acquisition of English as a non-native language. We continue to use the former term because it is widely used and descriptive, even though what we refer to as a "second language" might actually be a student's third or fourth language. A synonym for ESL that you will find in this book is **English Language Development (ELD).**

WHO ARE ENGLISH LANGUAGE LEARNERS?

Students who speak English as a non-native language live in all areas of the United States. The number of English language learners has steadily increased in recent decades, nearly doubling between 1992 and 2002 when survey results estimated that 4,747,763 English language learners were enrolled in U.S. public schools in grades pre-K through 12. During that time, English learner enrollment increased at almost eight times the rate of total student enrollment (Padolsky, 2002a, 2002b). Many English learners are sons and daughters of immigrants who have left their home countries to seek a better life. Some recent immigrants have left countries brutally torn by war or political strife in regions such as Southeast Asia, Central America, the Middle East, and Eastern Europe. Others have immigrated for economic reasons. Still others come to be reunited with families who are already here or or to seek educational opportunities they may find in the United States. Finally, many English learners were born in the United States, and some of them, such as Native Americans of numerous tribal heritages, have roots in American soil that go back for countless generations.

Whether immigrant or native born, each group brings its own history and culture to the enterprise of schooling (Heath, 1986). Furthermore, each group contributes to the rich tapestry of languages and cultures that form the basic fabric of the United States. Our first task as teachers, then, is to become aware of our students' personal histories and cultures, so as to understand their feelings, frustrations, hopes, and aspirations. At the same time, as teachers we need to look closely at ourselves to discover how our own culturally ingrained attitudes, beliefs, assumptions, and communication styles play out in our teaching and affect our students' learning. By developing such understanding, we create the essential foundation for meaningful instruction, including reading and writing instruction. As understanding grows, teacher and students alike can come to an awareness of both diversity and universals in human experience, as shared in this poem by a high school student who emigrated with her parents from Cambodia (Mullen & Olsen, 1990).

You And I Are The Same

You and I are the same
but we don't let our hearts see.
Black, White and Asian
Africa, China, United States and all other
countries around the world
Peel off their skin
Like you peel an orange
See their flesh
like you see in my heart
Peel off their meat
And peel my wickedness with it too
Until there's nothing left
but bones.
Then you will see that you and I
are the same.

by Kien Po (Kien Po, You and I Are the Same, 1990, San Francisco: California Tomorrow. Reprinted with permission of the author.)

HOW CAN I GET TO KNOW MY ENGLISH LEARNERS?

Given the variety and mobility among second language groups, it is likely that most teachers, including specialists in bilingual education or ESL, will at some time encounter students whose language and culture they know little about. Perhaps you are already accustomed to working with students of diverse cultures, but if you are not, how can you develop an understanding of students from unfamiliar linguistic and cultural backgrounds? Far from a simple task, the process requires not only fact finding but also continual observation and interpretation of children's behavior, combined with trial and error in communication. Thus, the process is one that must take place gradually.

Getting Basic Information When a New Student Arrives

When a new student arrives, we suggest three initial steps. First of all, begin to find out basic facts about the child: What country is the child from? How long has he or she lived in the United States? Where and with whom is the child living? What language or languages are spoken in the home? If the child is an immigrant, what were the circumstances of immigration? Some children have experienced traumatic events before and during immigration, and the process of adjustment to a new country may represent yet another link in a chain of stressful life events (Olsen, 1998).

Second, obtain as much information about the student's prior school experiences as possible. School records may be available if the child has already been enrolled in a U.S. school. However, as you are not likely to receive a cumulative folder forwarded from another country, you may need to piece the information together yourself, a task that requires resourcefulness, imagination, and time. Some school districts collect background information on students when they register, as well as administer English language proficiency tests. Thus, your own district office is one possible source of information. In addition, you may need the assistance of someone who is familiar with the home language and culture, such as another teacher, a paraprofessional, or a community liaison, who can ask questions of parents, students, or siblings. Keep in mind that some children may have had no previous schooling, despite their age, or perhaps their schooling has been interrupted. Other students may have attended school in their home countries. Students with prior educational experience bring various kinds of knowledge to school subjects and may be quite advanced. Be prepared to validate your students for their special knowledge. We saw how important this was for fourth-grader Li Fen, a recent immigrant from mainland China who found herself in a regular English language classroom, knowing not a word of English. Li Fen was a bright child, but naturally somewhat reticent to involve herself in classroom activities during her first month in the class. She made a real turnaround, however, the day the class was studying long division. Li Fen accurately solved three problems at the chalkboard in no time at all, though her procedure differed slightly from the one in the math book. Her classmates were duly impressed with her mathematical competence and did not hide their admiration. Her teacher, of course, gave her a smile with words of congratulations. From that day forward, Li Fen participated more readily, having earned a place in the class.

When you are gathering information on your students' prior schooling, it's important to find out whether they are literate in their home language. If they are, you might encourage them to keep a journal using their native language, and if possible, you should acquire native language books, magazines, or newspapers to have on hand for the new student. In this way, you validate the student's

5

INTERNET RESOURCES: We suggest you explore the companion website for this book and discover its contents. You will find information including chapter summaries, essay questions you can answer and send to your instructor, numerous Internet resources, and links to other valuable resources pertaining to each chapter. The address is: www.ablongman.com/peregoy4e.

language, culture, and academic competence, while providing a natural bridge to English reading. *Make these choices with sensitivity, though, building on positive responses from your students.* Bear in mind, for example, that some newcomers may not wish to be identified as different from their classmates. We make this caveat because of our experience with a 7-year-old boy, recently arrived from Mexico, who attended a school where everyone spoke English only. When we spoke to him in Spanish, he did not respond, giving the impression that he did not know the language. When we visited his home and spoke Spanish with his parents, he was not pleased. At that point in his life, he may have wanted nothing more than to blend into the dominant social environment, in this case an affluent, European American neighborhood saturated with English.

The discomfort felt by this young boy is an important reminder of the internal conflict experienced by many youngsters as they come to terms with life in a new culture. As they learn English and begin to fit into school routines, they embark on a personal journey toward a new cultural identity. If they come to reject their home language and culture, moving toward maximum assimilation into the dominant culture, they may experience alienation from their parents and family. A moving personal account of such a journey is provided, for example, by journalist Richard Rodriquez in his book *Hunger of Memory* (1982). Even if English learners strive to adopt the ways of the new culture without replacing those of the home, they will have departed significantly from many traditions their parents hold dear. Thus, for many students the generation gap necessarily widens to the extent that the values, beliefs, roles, responsibilities, and general expectations differ between the home culture and the dominant one. Keeping this in mind may help you empathize with students' personal conflicts of identity and personal life choices.

The third suggestion, then, is to become aware of basic features of the home culture, such as religious beliefs and customs, food preferences and restrictions, and roles and responsibilities of children and adults (Ovando, Collier, & Combs, 2003; Saville-Troike, 1978). These basic bits of information, though sketchy, will guide your initial interactions with your new students and may help you avoid asking them to say or do things that may be prohibited or frowned upon in the home culture, including such common activities as celebrating birthdays, pledging allegiance to the flag, and eating hot dogs. Finding out basic information also provides a starting point from which to interpret your newcomer's responses to you, to your other students, and to the ways you organize classroom activities. Just as you make adjustments, your students will also begin to make adjustments as they grow in the awareness and acceptance that ways of acting, dressing, eating, talking, and behaving in school are different to a greater or lesser degree from what they may have experienced before.

Classroom Activities That Let You Get to Know Your Students

Several fine learning activities may also provide some of the personal information you need to help you know your students better. One way is to have all your students write an illustrated autobiography, "All About Me" or "The Story of My Life." Each book may be bound individually, or all the life stories may be bound together and published in a class book, complete with illustrations or photographs. Alternatively, student stories may be posted on the bulletin board for all to read. This assignment lets you in on the lives of all your students and permits them to get to know, appreciate, and understand each other as well. Of particular importance, this activity does not single out your newcomers because all your students will be involved.

Personal writing assignments like the one mentioned lend themselves to many grade levels because personal topics remain pertinent across age groups even into adulthood. Students who speak little or no English may begin by illustrating a series of important events in their lives, perhaps to be captioned with your assistance or that of another student. In addition, there are many ways to accommodate students' varying English writing abilities. For example, if students write more easily in their native tongue than in English, allow them to do so. If needed, ask a bilingual student or paraprofessional to translate the meaning for you. Be sure to publish the student's story as written in the native language, because you will thereby both validate the home language and expose the rest of the class to a different language and its writing system. If a student knows some English but is not yet able to write, allow her or him to dictate the story to you or to another student in the class.

Another way to begin to know your students is to start a dialogue journal with them. Provide each student with a blank journal and allow the student to draw or write in the language of the student's choice. You may then respond to the students' journal entries on a periodic basis. Interactive dialogue journals, described in detail in Chapter 5, have proven useful for English learners of all ages (Kreeft, 1984). Dialogue journals make an excellent introduction to literacy and facilitate the development of an ongoing personal relationship between the student and you, the teacher. As with personal writing, this activity is appropriate for all students, and if you institute it with the entire class you provide a way for newcomers to participate in a "regular" class activity. Being able to do what others do can be a source of great pride and self-satisfaction to students who are new to the language and culture of the school.

Finally, many teachers start the school year with a unit on themes such as "Where We Were Born" or "Family Origins." Again, this activity is relevant to all students, whether immigrant or native-born, and it gives teacher and students alike a chance to know more about themselves and each other. A typical activity with this theme is the creation of a world map with a string connecting each child's name and birthplace to your city and school. Don't forget to put your name on the list along with your birthplace! From there, you and your students may go on to study more about the various regions and countries of origin. Clearly, this type of theme leads in many directions, including the discovery of people in the community who may be able to share information about their home countries with your class. Your guests may begin by sharing food, holiday customs, art, or music with

Example 1.2 A Few Important Books on Multicultural Teaching

Banks, J. A. (2003). *Teaching strategies for ethnic studies* (7th ed.). Boston: Allyn and
   Bacon.
Garcia, E. (2001*). Understanding and meeting the challenge of student cultural diversity*.
   (3rd ed.). Boston: Houghton Mifflin.
Igoa, C. (1995). *The inner world of the immigrant child*. New York: St. Martin's Press.
Nieto, S. (2004). *Affirming diversity: The sociopolitical context of multicultural education*
   (4th ed.). Boston: Allyn and Bacon.
Tiedt, P. L., & Tiedt, I. M. (2002). *Multicultural teaching: A handbook of activities, infor-
   mation, and resources*. (6th ed.). Boston: Allyn and Bacon.

students. Through such contact, through theme studies, through life stories, and
through reading about cultures in books such as those listed in Example 1.2 you
may begin to become aware of some of the more subtle aspects of the culture, such
as how the culture communicates politeness and respect, or how the culture views
the role of children, adults, and the school. If you are lucky enough to find such
community resources, you will not only enliven your teaching but broaden your
cross-cultural understanding as well (Ada & Zubizarreta, 2001).

   Not all necessary background information will emerge from these classroom
activities. You will no doubt want to look into cultural, historical, and geographical
resources available at your school or community library. In addition, you may find
resource personnel at your school, including paraprofessionals and resource teachers, who can help with specific questions or concerns. In the final analysis, though,
your primary source of information is the students themselves as you interrelate
on a day-to-day basis.

HOW DO CULTURAL DIFFERENCES AFFECT TEACHING AND LEARNING?

   The enterprise of teaching and learning is deeply influenced by "culture" in a
variety of ways. To begin with, schools themselves reflect the values, beliefs and
practices of the larger society. In fact schools represent a major socializing force for
all students, albeit a somewhat foreign one for many English learners. In addition,
teachers and students bring to the classroom particular cultural orientations that
affect how they perceive and interact with each other in the classroom. As teachers of English learners, most of us will encounter students whose languages and
cultures differ from our own. Thus we need to learn about our students and their
cultures while at the same time reflecting on how our own culturally rooted
behaviors may facilitate or interfere with teaching and learning (Trumbull,

Rothstein-Fisch, & Greenfield, 2000). In this section we define basic aspects of culture in the classroom as a starting point for looking at ourselves and our students in this light.

In order to learn about your students through personal interactions, you may need to hone your skills in observing and interpreting their behavior. Such skills are especially important when you first meet your students, whether at the beginning of the school year or when they first enroll in your class. One procedure to help focus your observations is to keep a journal in which you jot notes at the end of each day concerning how your new student is doing. Does she understand basic school rules such as hand raising? Is he starting to form friendships? What activities does your new student seem to be happiest doing: small-group activities, individual seatwork, listening to stories, drawing pictures? In which activities is the student reluctant? By noticing activities that are most comfortable for students, you can make sure that your newcomer has frequent opportunities to participate in them. In this way, you build a positive attitude toward what may as yet be an alien environment: school. From there, you may gradually draw the student into other school routines.

Culture in the Classroom Context

When you make observations in your classroom, you are actually using some of the tools used by anthropologists when they study another culture through ethnography (e.g., introspection, interviewing, observation, and participant observation). As the teacher, you are automatically both participant and observer in the classroom culture. However, you will need to step back at times to reflect introspectively on how your classroom operates. In addition, you may want to take time to observe your students during independent and small-group activity. In this way, you will have the opportunity to give full attention to how your students are functioning socially in your classroom.

In order to make the most of your introspective reflections and observations, you may need some concepts to guide interpretations. In other words, it's one thing to notice that Nazrene "tunes out" during whole-class lessons but quite another to figure out why, so that you can alter your instruction to reach her. To provide you with some interpretive touchstones, we suggest you consider for a moment some of the aspects that constitute culture, because these represent potential sources of overt conflict or silent suffering if your classroom rules and structures conflict with those already culturally engrained in your students.

Definitions of Culture and Its Content

Culture may be defined as the shared beliefs, values, and rule-governed patterns of behavior that define a group and are required for group membership (Goodenough, 1981; Saville-Troike, 1978). Thus defined, culture comprises three essential aspects: what people know and believe, what people do, and what people make and use. Every child is born into the culture of a particular group of people, and through the culture's child-rearing practices every child is socialized, to a greater or lesser extent, toward becoming first a "good boy" or "good girl" and ultimately a "good man" or "good woman" in the eyes of the culture. Thus, culture may be thought of as the acquired knowledge people use both to interpret experience and generate behavior (Spradley, 1980).

For the purposes of understanding your students, we summarize in Table 1.1 cultural content with questions outlined by Saville-Troike (1978). The content of culture may be categorized into various components, including (1) family structure; (2) definitions of stages, periods, or transitions during a person's life; (3) roles of children and adults and corresponding behavior in terms of power and politeness; (4) discipline; (5) time and space; (6) religion; (7) food; (8) health and hygiene; and (9) history, traditions, holidays, and celebrations. Table 1.1 provides a number of questions that you might ask yourself about these aspects of culture. As you read the questions, try to answer them for your own culture as well as for a different cultural group in order to get a sense of similarities and differences across cultures.

When students in our university classes discuss the questions in Table 1.1 according to their family traditions, interesting patterns emerge. Although many students identify with middle-class, European American cultural values, such as punctuality, some also add special traditions passed down from immigrant grandparents or great-grandparents, including special foods and holiday traditions. Other students come from families who have been in this country for centuries, yet maintain particular regional traditions such as herbal healing practices. In addition, some students have maintained strong religious traditions, such as Buddhist, Catholic, Greek Orthodox, Judaic, Muslim, and traditional Native American beliefs. From these discussions, we find that each individual actually embodies a variety of cultures and subcultures.

One student found the cultural questions an interesting way to look at her own family. Her parents had met and married in Germany, her father an Egyptian and Coptic Christian, her mother a German Catholic. From there they moved with their three young children to the United States. Najia reflected, with some amusement, on how different her German relatives were from her Egyptian relatives. For example, her German relatives visited once or twice a year, making plans well in advance and staying a short, predetermined amount of time. Her Egyptian relatives, in contrast, "couldn't seem to get enough of each other." They loved long visits, with as many of the family together as possible. Najia's German mother emphasized orderliness and punctuality in the home, with carefully scheduled and planned meals. The family ate at the specified hour, and all were expected to be there on time. With such differences concerning time and space, Najia wondered that her parents were able to make a highly successful marriage. She attributed their success in part to their individual personalities: her mother, an artist, is by nature easy-going and flexible; her father, an electronic engineer, is an organized thinker and planner. As individuals, they seemed compatible with many of each

TABLE 1.1   Cultural Content and Questions

Cultural Content	Questions
Family structures	What constitutes a family? Who among these or others live in one house? What are the rights and responsibilities of each family member? What is the hierarchy of authority? What is the relative importance of the individual family member in contrast to the family as a whole?
The life cycles	What are the criteria for defining stages, periods, or transitions in life? What rites of passage are there? What behaviors are considered appropriate for children of different ages? How might these conflict with behaviors taught or encouraged in school? How is the age of the children computed? What commemoration, if any, is made of the child's birth and when?
Roles and interpersonal relationships	What roles are available to whom, and how are they acquired? Is education relevant to learning these roles? How do the roles of girls and women differ from those of boys and men? How do people greet each other? What forms of address are used between people of differing roles? Do girls work and interact with boys? Is it proper? How is deference shown and to whom and by whom?
Discipline	What is discipline? What counts as discipline and what doesn't? Which behaviors are considered socially acceptable for boys versus girls at different ages? Who or what is considered responsible if a child misbehaves? The child? Parents? Older siblings? The environment? Is blame even ascribed? Who has authority over whom? To what extent can one person impose his or her will on another? How is behavior traditionally controlled? To what extent and in what domains?
Time and space	How important is punctuality? How important is speed in completing a task? Are there restrictions associated with certain seasons? What is the spatial organization of the home? How much space are people accustomed to? What significance is associated with different locations or directions, including north, south, east, west?
Religion	What restrictions are there concerning topics discussed in school? Are dietary restrictions to be observed, including fasting on particular occasions? When are these occasions? What restrictions are associated with death and the dead?
Food	What is eaten? In what order and how often is food eaten? Which foods are restricted? Which foods are typical? What social obligations are there with regard to food giving, reciprocity, and honoring people? What restrictions or proscriptions are associated with handling, offering, or discarding food?
Health and hygiene	How are illnesses treated and by whom? What is considered to be the cause? If a student were involved in an accident at school, would any of the common first aid practices be considered unacceptable?
History, traditions, holidays	Which events and people are sources of pride for the group? To what extent does the group in the United States identify with the history and traditions of the country of origin? What holidays and celebrations are considered appropriate for observing in school? Which ones are appropriate only for private observance?

11

other's cultural ways. Najia's reflections are a reminder that people's behavior combines both cultural and individual differences.

Sociolinguistic Interactions in the Classroom

One particularly important aspect of culture that can affect teaching and learning has to do with the ways you use language during instruction. Because teaching and learning depend on clear communication between teacher and students, the communicative success of teacher–student interactions is crucial. Early on, difficulties may arise from lack of a common language. However, communication difficulties may persist even after students have acquired the basics of English if the student and teacher are following different sociocultural rules about how to use language (Cazden, 1986). For example, if the home culture values strict authority of adults over children and if children are only supposed to speak when spoken to, then these same children may be reluctant to volunteer an answer in class. You might quite logically interpret this reluctance as disinterest or lack of knowledge, when in fact the student may simply be waiting for you to invite him or her to respond. On the other hand, some students may not want to answer your questions because displaying knowledge in class amounts to showing off, causing them to stand out like a sore thumb (Philips, 1983). Some students consider enthusiastic knowledge display impolite because it could make their friends appear ignorant. These examples illustrate how cultural values affecting language use may impede teacher–student communication in either English or the home language.

Language use differences can be especially confusing in the realm of teacher questioning. Research has shown that teachers often do not allow much "wait time" after asking a question in class (Rowe, 1974). It turns out that what is considered enough wait time in normal conversations varies across cultures, as do rules concerning how and when to interrupt and the number of people who may speak at once (Bauman & Scherzer, 1974; Ochs & Schieffelin, 1984; Schieffelin & Eisenberg, 1984; Shultz, Erickson, & Florio, 1982). In addition, students must learn what the teacher's rules are regarding who can speak with whom and when (Mehan, 1979). These rules may vary with the activity structure (e.g., teacher-led lesson versus small-group projects). Another aspect of teacher questioning that may be problematic is that teachers typically ask questions with a particular answer in mind, in order to assess what students know or have learned. For some students, these "known-answer" questions might be considered odd or of dubious purpose (Heath, 1983; Mehan, 1979), resulting in student reluctance to participate in such interrogations. You might want to reflect on your own questioning practices in terms of wait time, question types, and the actual phrasing you use. If your questions are greeted with blank stares, try altering your questioning style. Another possibility is to introduce question/answer sessions with a brief explanation of what you are trying to accomplish and why. That way, if students are unaccustomed to your question types, you will at least help them understand your purpose for asking them.

INTERNET RESOURCES: Visit the National Clearinghouse for English Language Acquisition (NCELA) web site at http://www.ncela.gwu.edu to explore the extensive resources, online library, databases, frequently asked questions, classroom ideas, and more all aimed at improving teaching and learning for English language learners. This site will also link you to current K–12 education policy briefs such as the No Child Left Behind legislation. Click on the State Resources and Census News in the left-hand margin of the home page to find out how many English learners are in your state, what primary languages they speak, and what kinds of programs serve them. Or choose one of the frequently asked questions to answer and discuss with your classmates. Check out our companion website for more links, activities and ideas: www.ablongman.com/peregoy4e.

Culturally Related Responses to Classroom Organization

There are other cultural differences that may interfere with student participation in learning activities in the classroom. One of these is the social organization of lessons (Mehan, 1979). Within the constraints of time and adult assistance, teachers typically utilize whole-class, small-group, and individualized formats for instruction. It is important to recognize that these formats represent distinctly different types of **participation structures** (Philips, 1983), each with its own rules about when to speak and how. Students may experience various degrees of comfort or discomfort with these various formats, based on both cultural and individual differences (Au & Jordan, 1981). For example, the use of small groups for cooperative learning has become a major thrust toward increasing learning for all students but especially for ethnic minority students (Kagan, 1986). The rationale is that many ethnic minority cultures instill strong values of group cooperation, and, therefore, such instruction will build on home experience. In addition, cooperative groups provide students with practice in getting along with people different from themselves to the extent that groups consist of students with different backgrounds. We are convinced that cooperative group learning is a valuable tool for teachers, for the reasons described. However, it is important to keep in mind that some students may feel that the teacher, as the academic authority, is the only proper person to learn from in the classroom. One way to accommodate such students is to balance your use of group work with necessary teacher-directed instruction. When you do ask students to work in cooperative groups, you need to explain your reasons for doing so, thereby showing that group learning is valid academically. In fact, parents may need to hear your reasons as well. We knew one child who was functioning beautifully in cooperative groups, yet during parent conferences, his father politely asked when we were going to start teaching! Cultural differences in teaching practices thus present challenges to teachers, students, and parents alike.

In summary, we know that different students may be more comfortable with some instructional formats than with others and that their feelings stem from both cultural and individual preferences. We suggest you *use a variety of formats to meet the multiple needs of your diverse students*. Your best route is to be aware of how you create the participation structures of learning (i.e., grouping formats) in order to observe and interpret student responses with thoughtful sensitivity, making modifications as needed.

Literacy Traditions from Home and Community

As you approach the teaching of reading and writing to English learners, you will want to be aware of the literacy knowledge your students bring with them. Literacy knowledge will stem not only from prior schooling but also from experiences with the ways reading and writing are used in the home and community (Au & Jordan, 1981; Boggs, 1972; Heath, 1983). It is helpful to become aware of how reading and writing are traditionally used in the community because these traditional literacy uses will influence your students' ideas, beliefs, and assumptions about reading and writing. You will want to build on these ideas and make sure to expand them to include the functions of literacy required by U.S. schools and society. Let us make this concept more clear through some examples.

Gustavo, age 7, entered the first grade of an urban elementary school in February, halfway through the academic year. He had come from rural Mexico, and this was his first time in school. He didn't even know how to hold a pencil. At first, he was so intimidated that he would refuse to come into the classroom at the beginning of the school day. With persistent coaxing from the teacher and her assistant, he reluctantly complied. Once in, Gustavo was anxious to fit into the normal class routines. He loved to wave his hand in the air when the teacher asked a question, although at first he didn't know what to do when called on. That part of the routine took a little time to master.

One day, as we were chatting with Gustavo, he began to tell us all about his little town in Michoacán, about the travails of the trip *pa' 'l norte* (to the north), and then about an incident when his 2-year-old sister became critically ill. His mother, he recounted, knew what medicine the baby needed, but it was only available in Mexico. So they had to "find someone who could write" to send to Mexico for the medicine. They did, and Gustavo's baby sister recovered.

What does this story tell us about the concept of literacy that Gustavo offers for the teacher to build on? First, we can surmise that Gustavo has not had extensive opportunities to explore reading and writing at home. He probably has not been read to much, nor has he been provided with paper and pencils for dabbling in drawing and writing—the very activities so highly recommended today as the foundation of literacy development. On the other hand, he is well aware of how important it is to be able to write—it was a matter of life and death for his sister! Furthermore, he is aware of the inconveniences, not to say dangers, of illiteracy. Thus, Gustavo, at the tender age of 7, brings a deeper understanding of the importance of literacy than many children whose rich early literacy experiences allow them to take such things for granted. Gustavo's motivation and understanding provide the foundation for the teacher to build on. Gustavo needs daily exposure to the pleasures and practical functions of print through stories, poems, rhymes, labels, letters, notes, recipes, board games, instructions, and more. With practice and hard work, his proudest moment will come when he himself writes the next letter to Mexico.

In contrast to Gustavo, students who immigrate when older often bring substantial experience and skill in reading and writing in their home language. These experiences and skills provide a good foundation for learning to read and write in English. Students who read in their home language already know that print bears a systematic relationship to spoken language, that print carries meaning, and that reading and writing can be used for many purposes. Moreover, literate students know that they are capable of making sense of written language. Such experience and knowledge will transfer directly to learning to read and write in English, given English language development and appropriate literacy instruction (Cummins, 1981; Hudelson, 1987; Odlin, 1989). Thus, when students arrive with home language literacy skills, teachers do not have to start all over again to teach reading and writing (Goodman, Goodman, & Flores, 1979; Peregoy, 1989; Peregoy & Boyle, 1991, Peregoy & Boyle, 2000). Rather, they can build on a more sophisticated base of literacy knowledge, adding the specifics for English as needed, a topic developed fully in subsequent chapters.

How Can I Ease Newcomers into the Routines of My Classroom When They Know Little or No English?

As you begin to know more about your students, you will be better able to offer them social and emotional support. Only when new students become comfortably integrated into your classroom's social and academic routines will optimal second language acquisition and academic learning occur. Thus, you'll need to give special effort and attention to those who are newcomers to the country. Adapting from Maslow's hierarchy of human needs (Maslow, 1968), we discuss basic strategies for integrating new children into your classroom. Two basic needs you will want to consider are (1) safety and security and (2) a sense of belonging. By paying close attention to these basic needs, you lay the foundation for meeting your students' self-esteem needs and for their growth in language and academic abilities.

First Things First: Safety and Security

When English language learners first arrive in school, a "first things first" approach is helpful, following Maslow's views. Thus, the first concern must be with creating a feeling of safety and security. To address this need, there are several things you can do. First, it is helpful to assign a "personal buddy" to each newcomer, if possible one who speaks the newcomer's home language. The buddy must be a classmate who already knows the school and is comfortable there. The buddy's job is to accompany the newcomer throughout the day's routines to make sure he or she knows where to find such essentials as the bathroom, the cafeteria, and the bus stop. The newcomer needs to learn not only where things are but also the various rules for using them. For example, each school has its own rules about how to line up and collect lunch at the cafeteria, where to sit, how to behave, and when to leave. Furthermore, there are culturally specific rules about how to eat particular kinds of food, rules that we take for granted but that may be totally foreign to a new arrival. Perhaps you yourself recall feeling tentative and intimidated the first time you ate in the school cafeteria. If so, you will have some idea of the anxiety that can accompany the first days of school for a youngster who is new not only to the school but also to the entire culture it represents. The personal buddy helps the new student through these initial days, helping alleviate anxieties and embarrassments that are bound to occur.

Another way to address the safety and security needs of newcomers is to follow predictable routines in your daily classroom schedule. Most teachers follow a fairly stable schedule within which instructional content varies. Predictability in routine creates a sense of security for all students, but it is especially important for students who are new to the language and culture of the school. In fact, your predictable routines may be the first stable feature some students have experienced in a long time, especially if they have recently immigrated under adverse circumstances.

Creating a Sense of Belonging

An additional way to promote security and create a sense of belonging is to assign your student to a "home group" that remains unchanged for a long time. In classrooms in which student seating is arranged at tables, the home group may be defined by table. The purpose of the home group is to develop minicommunities of interdependence, support, and identity. If such groups are an ongoing aspect of classroom social organization, with rules of caring, respect, and concern already in place, then the home group provides an ideal social unit to receive a newcomer.

Regardless of how you organize your classroom, it is always important to seat new students toward the middle or front of the classroom, in a place where you can observe them closely and where they can observe the classroom interactions of other, more experienced students. We don't recommend placing new students at the back or other far reaches of the room. In our experience, students who speak little or no English tend to be placed at the periphery of the classroom where they sometimes blend into the woodwork and are forgotten. Even if you feel a child can't understand a word you are saying, you can integrate the child into the class by simply looking his or her way while speaking. We encourage conscious integration of newcomers into the social fabric of the classroom so as to avoid unconscious marginalization.

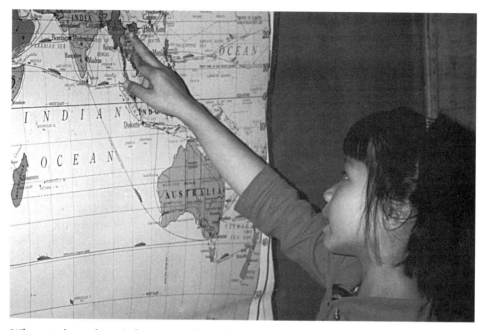

When students share information about their home countries, they grow in self-esteem while broadening the horizons of their peers.

17

By paying close attention to the social and emotional needs of your new students, you will be laying the foundation for the early stages of language acquisition. For example, the one-on-one attention of the personal buddy offers numerous opportunities for your newcomer to learn many basic English words and phrases at the "survival" level. In addition, repetition of classroom routines provides non-English speakers with ideal language learning opportunities because the words and phrases that accompany such routines are constantly repeated within a meaningful, concrete context. If you count up the number of times a child hears such functional phrases as "It's lunch time now" and "The quiet table may line up first," you will get an idea of how valuable such **context-embedded language** can be for rapid learning of basic English expressions. Finally, integrating newcomers into cooperative groups provides further social and academic language learning opportunities, as discussed in detail in Chapter 3. Thus, by attending to the security needs of your limited English proficient students, you also lay a firm foundation for English language acquisition.

As English language acquisition progresses and students begin to become a part of the social fabric of your class, they are well positioned to grow in self-esteem through successful participation in both the social and academic aspects of classroom life. Thus, Maslow's theory provides a useful way to look at the initial needs of newcomers. As the social-emotional foundation is laid, all the other aspects of personal growth may begin to interweave and support each other, with social and academic competence creating self-esteem and reinforcing feelings of security and belonging. In the process, English language development will be further enhanced.

CURRENT POLICY TRENDS AFFECTING THE EDUCATION OF ENGLISH LEARNERS

Whether you are new or experienced in the field of education, media reports have no doubt introduced you to various reform efforts in education, many of which have been promoted by federal and state education policy. Because disparate needs and interests are served by education policy, and because there are always divergent points of view as to how any problem may be solved, the arena of educational policy is filled with controversy and debate. In this section, we briefly discuss education policies affecting English learners across the nation and offer additional resources on this complex topic.

Academic Standards and Assessment

The implementation of academic standards and assessment permeates all levels of education today. If you are in a teaching credential program, for example, chances are your coursework is organized to teach and assess what you should know and be able to do to be an effective teacher. Similarly, standards have been delineated for K–12 students that specifically define the knowledge and skills that students must attain for promotion and graduation in subjects such as reading, math, science, social science, and English language arts. In addition, standards have been developed that specifically address English language development for students new to English (e.g., Teachers of English to Speakers of Other Languages, 1997; California State Department of Education, 2002). Teachers generally need to become familiar with the standards of the content areas they teach, as well as with standards specific to English learners. In this section, we introduce you to basic issues in standards-based reforms. In chapter 3, we discuss how teachers implement standards-based instruction in their classrooms.

The standards and assessment movement traces its origins to *A Nation at Risk* (National Commission on Excellence in Education, 1983), a national report funded by the U.S. Congress that called for improvement in education across the country. Among the outcomes of the report was the development of the National Assessment of Education Progress (NAEP), a large scale, national assessment program that permits comparisons among states on student achievement in reading, writing, and mathematics. By conducting periodic assessments of students in grades 4, 8, and 12, NAEP is able to provide the public with a "report card" on how well students are doing across the nation. NAEP findings have been used to spur education reforms, such as the reading instruction reforms of the 1990s, aimed at increasing student achievement. The current focus on rigorous academic standards, assessment, and accountability can all be traced back to the reforms called for in *A Nation at Risk*.

In recent years the push for high academic standards and achievement has gained momentum. In order for students to achieve high academic standards, Congress encouraged national education organizations and state departments of education to develop rather detailed descriptions of curriculum content to be taught across the grades in subjects such as reading, mathematics, social science, science, and English language arts. Standards documents are generally structured to include (1) content standards that delineate what students should know and be able to do, (2) benchmarks that specify expected knowledge and skills for each content standard at different grade levels, and (3) progress indicators that describe how well students need to do in order to meet a given content standard (Laturnau, 2003). Criteria for achievement are thus built in to the standards.

High-Stakes Testing

Hand in glove with the use of curriculum standards is the implementation of high-stakes, standardized testing to measure how well standards are being met. Serious consequences may be applied when standards are not met, supposedly to motivate achievement and increase accountability (Ananda & Rabinowitz, 2000). For example, performance on a high school exit exam may determine whether a student will receive a high school diploma, regardless of passing grades in all required high school coursework. Similarly, standardized test performance may play a part in deciding grade retention or promotion of students in elementary, middle, and high school. School funding may depend on raising test scores. Furthermore, teachers and principals may be held directly accountable for student achievement (Afflerbach, 2002). Low-achieving schools, for example, may be subject to restaffing measures, in which teachers and principal are moved elsewhere and a totally new staff brought in.

The teeth in the jaws of high-stakes testing have been sharpened by the *No Child Left Behind Act of 2001* (NCLB Act), federal legislation reauthorizing the *Elementary and Secondary Education Act* (ESEA) originally passed in 1965 to improve academic performance among lower-achieving, "economically disadvantaged" students. While standardized tests have long been used to identify students who qualify for educational assistance, the new law raises standardized testing to a higher pitch, requiring states to implement "accountability systems" covering all public schools and students. All students in grades 3 through 8 are to be tested by rigorous standards in reading and math. In addition, states are to establish and meet "progress objectives" ensuring that *all* groups of students reach academic proficiency within 12 years. In order to monitor the progress of "all groups," "test results are to be broken out by poverty, race, ethnicity, disability and limited English proficiency" (U.S. Office of Elementary and Secondary Education, 2002, p. 1). Schools that meet or exceed their progress objectives will be eligible for an "achievement award," whereas those who fall below must improve or be subject to "corrective action," such as restaffing. The Act thus places tremendous pressures on schools serving groups who tend to score lower on standardized tests than their middle- and upper-class, white counterparts.

Over the decades *socioeconomic status* has proven to be one of the strongest predictors of standardized test performance. Children from low-income families consistently score lower than those in more affluent circumstances, and racial, ethnic, and language minority students are overrepresented in the lower income brackets. Unfortunately, it is not clear that mandating achievement will improve learning or even raise test scores, especially with the high-pressure atmosphere it creates. For example, we have heard young children anxiously voice concern that their test performance might cause their favorite teacher to be moved to another school.

Equally problematic is the danger that test scores may be used inappropriately either to retain students or to sort them into less challenging instructional programs. Even worse, high-stakes testing may actually increase the already high dropout rate among racial, ethnic, and language minority students. Because of the lifelong consequences of educational decisions based on high-stakes testing, it is essential that these tests be proven both fair and valid for all students, especially those living in poverty. Therefore, constant scrutiny is needed to monitor the effects of high-stakes testing to ensure that all students are provided meaningful and equitable access to a high-quality education, one that welcomes them in rather than pushing them out, one that broadens their life choices rather than narrowing them (Escamilla, Mahon, Riley-Bernal, & Ruteledge, 2003; Valdez Pierce, 2003).

In addition to issues related to socioeconomic status, testing and progress mandates such as those in NCLB pose special problems for many students new to English. First of all, *English proficiency* affects student performance and may render test results inaccurate if not totally invalid (Abedi, 2001; Abedi, Leon, & Mirocha, 2001). If performance is low, it may not be clear whether the cause is limited English knowledge, insufficient content knowledge, or a combination of both. In addition to English language proficiency, other factors may affect English learners' preparedness for successful performance, including the amount, quality, content, and continuity of prior schooling relative to the content and format of the test.

Furthermore, the NCLB actually requires an *accelerated learning pace* for English learners in order to close the achievement gap between them and the general student population. With research showing that it takes five to ten years to development academic language proficiency (Thomas & Collier, 1997, 2002), this progress mandate is ill-informed and highly unrealistic for many English learners. Finally, it is important to remember that English proficiency is necessary but not sufficient for academic achievement in an English language curriculum. It takes more than knowledge of the language to make progress in school. Quality instruction, a safe and supportive school environment, student motivation and parental support are also factors that come into play.

In summary, in recent decades we have witnessed a tidal wave of movement calling for high educational standards and assessment. In the past, curriculum content has been generally similar in schools across the country, but states and local communities have always retained control over the specifics. However, the national standards and assessment movement is leading toward a standardized, uniform national curriculum. Whether these reforms will finally help or hinder learning among *all* students remains to be seen. More problematic is the implementation of high-stakes testing, the effects of which have the potential to create larger divisions between rich and poor, between those with power and those without.

Education Policy Specific to English Learners

While English learners are affected by general education policy, they are also subject to policies specific to their English proficiency status. Federal law requires schools to identify and serve students in need of educational support based on English language proficiency. The purpose of such educational support is twofold: (1) to promote English language development and (2) to provide meaningful instruction so that students may learn academic content appropriate to their grade level. Schools are free to choose the kind of program that will best meet the needs of their students, including whether students' primary language will be used for instruction or not. Since 1968 when the ESEA Title VII Bilingual Education Act was passed, bilingual education programs have been developed throughout the country, utilizing such languages as Spanish, Vietnamese, Chinese, Japanese, French, and Portuguese. In addition, bilingual programs have served numerous Native American languages such as Navajo, Cherokee, and Crow. However, with the passage of the NCLB Act, the bilingual education provisions of ESEA Title VII have *not* been reauthorized for the first time in history. The current reauthorization of the ESEA thus effectively eliminates federal support for (but does not prohibit) bilingual instructional programs.

Instead of supporting bilingual instruction, the comprehensive NCLB Act places heavy emphasis on English language proficiency, not only for students but also for teachers, who must be certified as proficient in written and oral English. While leaving schools choice of program type, the Act requires them to use instructional methods that research has proven effective. In order to increase accountability, the Act requires states to establish standards and benchmarks for English language proficiency and academic content. Academic content standards are to be aligned with those established for the general K–12 student population.

The elimination of federal support for bilingual education represents the culmination of several decades of heated debate, not just among lawmakers and educators, but among the general public as well. Arguments against bilingual education have often centered on the effectiveness of bilingual instruction in teaching English, with no attention given to potential benefits to bilingualism or to primary language use and maintenance. Proponents and opponents both cite research and statistics to support their cases regarding the effectiveness of bilingual instruction (cf. Crawford, 1999; Faltis & Hudelson, 1998; Lessow-Hurley, 2000; Ovando,

2003; Ovando, Collier, & Combs, 2003). However, research seldom provides absolute, unequivocal findings. Instead, results have to be interpreted based on the research method, including background information on students and teachers in the study, the type of program implemented, the extent to which teachers follow the program model, and many other variables. Because it is difficult to control for these variables, research results are usually open to criticism on either side of the debate. In the final analysis, research findings tend to play a smaller role than attitudes, values, beliefs, and ideology in the effectiveness debate. We offer additional resources on bilingual education in Example 1.4.

In addition to the effectiveness issue, anti–bilingual-education sentiment is fueled by the belief that, in order to unify diverse groups, in public life English should be used exclusively. The use of languages other than English in hospitals, social service agencies, schools, voting booths, and other public venues is considered anathema by members of the "English only" movement, promoted by groups such as U.S. English and English First. Resentment against immigrants and resources allocated to serve them adds fuel to the "English only" movement. These sentiments have found their way into a variety of ballot initiatives in states such as California and Arizona aimed at (1) eliminating bilingual education, (2) restricting public services to immigrants, and (3) requiring English as the "official language" to the exclusion of all others. Whether such initiatives are upheld in the courts or not, they send a chilly message that finds its way into our classrooms as we attempt to create positive learning environments for English learners (Gutierrez, Asato, Pacheco, Moll, Olson, Horng, Ruiz, Garcia, & McCarty, 2002).

In summary, English learners are subject to both *general* education policy and to policy *specific* to their English learner status. Educational reform in the U.S. has become extremely politicized in recent decades. Now more than ever, state and

22

Example 1.4   **Useful Resources on Bilingual Education**

Crawford, J. (1999). *Bilingual education: History, politics, theory and practice* (4th ed.). Los Angeles, CA: Bilingual Educational Services.

Cummins, J. (2001*). Negotiating identities: Education for empowerment in a diverse society*. (2nd ed.). Los Angeles: California Association for Bilingual Education.

Faltis, C. J., & Hudelson, S. J. (1998*). Bilingual education in elementary and secondary school communities: Toward understanding and caring*. Boston: Allyn and Bacon.

Lessow-Hurley, J. (2000). *The foundations of dual language instruction* (3rd ed.). New York: Addison-Wesley Longman.

Moraes, M. (1996). *Bilingual education: A dialogue with the Bakhtin Circle*. Albany: State University of New York Press.

Ovando, C. (2003, Spring). Bilingual education in the United States: Historical development and current issues. *Bilingual Research Journal, 27*(1), 1–24. (Available online at http://brj.asu.edu.)

LA CUCARACHA   BY LALO ALCARAZ

federal legislators are mandating not only the content of the curriculum, but at times even the method of instruction. Greater and greater emphasis is being placed on English as the primary language of instruction. These trends are leading to greater uniformity and standardization in curriculum and instruction. The current emphasis on detailed and specific curriculum standards and concomitant high-stakes testing has placed tremendous pressure on students, teachers, and principals to get students to test well. These trends existed prior to the passage of NCLB and are likely to continue when the ESEA comes up again for reauthorization. Now as never before educators need to form a strong voice in the political processes that create education policy.

WHAT KINDS OF PROGRAMS EXIST TO MEET THE NEEDS OF ENGLISH LANGUAGE LEARNERS?

If you are fairly new to the enterprise of educating English language learners, you might be interested in the kinds of programs in place throughout the country to serve them. We offer such information in the following sections so that you will have an idea of what some school districts are doing. If your school has just begun to experience growth in English learner populations, these general descriptions may provide a starting point for considering a more formalized English language support program. It is important to reiterate that *federal law* requires that all English learners be provided with an educational program that provides them (1) *access to the core curriculum* and (2) *opportunities for English language development.*

23

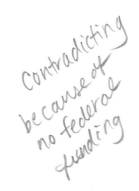

Districts are given substantial latitude in selecting program types and choosing whether to use the students' home language for instruction. *State laws govern program requirements at a more specific level.* Thus, as you consider program development for your English learners, you will want to seek information from your state and local offices of education.

Bilingual Education Programs

English language learners find themselves in a wide variety of school programs, from those carefully tailored to meet their specific linguistic and cultural needs to programs in which very little is done differently to accommodate them. Perhaps the simplest distinction among programs is whether two languages or one is used for instruction. Bilingual education programs are defined as educational programs that use two languages, one of which must be English, for teaching purposes. Bilingual education programs have taken many forms, but two goals are common to all: (1) to teach English and (2) to provide access to the core curriculum through the home language while students are gaining English language proficiency (Lessow-Hurley, 2000).

The following are brief sketches of some of the most prevalent bilingual program models. As you read these descriptions, think of them as skeletons that may vary considerably in the flesh as differences in communities, students, teachers, and administrators affect program implementation. In addition, bear in mind that some program models may overlap and that a single model may be called by a different name from the one given here.

In the program model descriptions we indicate whether the program serves language minority students, language majority students, or both. In the United States and other English-speaking countries, **language minority students** are those who speak a language other than English at home. In other words, their home language is a minority group language such as Cantonese, Crow, or Spanish. **Language majority students** are those whose primary language is English, the predominant national language or majority language. In this book, we are concerned with language minority students who are learning English in school, thus the term English learners. However, a discussion of bilingual program models would be incomplete without some mention of the immersion model developed in Canada, in which language majority students learn a minority group language in school. The extensively researched Canadian immersion model, discussed subsequently, has been highly successful and has influenced instructional development in second language teaching throughout the world (Lessow-Hurley, 2000).

Transitional Bilingual Education. Transitional bilingual education programs are designed to serve language minority students who are limited English proficient. Primary language instruction is provided for one to three years. The purpose of primary language instruction is to build a foundation in literacy and academic content that will facilitate English language and academic development as stu-

24

dents acquire the new language. After the transition to English instruction, no further instruction in the home language is offered. The goal is to develop English language proficiency for limited English proficient students as soon as possible.

Maintenance Bilingual Education. Maintenance bilingual education is designed to serve language minority students who are limited English proficient. It differs from transitional bilingual education in that primary language instruction is provided *throughout* the elementary grades and in some cases continues in middle and high school. English language instruction is also provided throughout the grades. The purpose of the maintenance model is to help language minority students develop and maintain their primary language as well as become fully proficient in oral and written English. Thus the program goals include full bilingualism and biliteracy for English learners.

Immersion Education. Originally developed in Canada, immersion programs are designed to teach a minority language to language majority students. For example, in Canada, native English-speaking students often learn French as a second language. In the United States, native English-speaking students learn languages such as Spanish or Cantonese. In immersion programs, students receive subject matter instruction through their second language to develop second language proficiency while learning academic content. Special techniques are used to help them understand, participate, and learn in the new language. Language, content, and literacy instruction take place in the students' new language in the early grades, with the gradual introduction of English language arts as students progress up the grades. The ultimate goal is full bilingualism and biliteracy in English and the minority language for native English-speaking students. Immersion programs are therefore *bilingual* programs designed to serve language majority students. Canadian immersion programs have been extensively studied and evaluated by the Ontario Institute for Studies in Education (Genesee, 1984, 1987; Swain & Lapkin, 1989). The success of the Canadian immersion model has influenced program development in two-way immersion described below as well as structured English immersion, and sheltered instruction (cf. Krashen, 1984) discussed in a subsequent section.

Two-Way Immersion Programs. Two-way immersion programs, also called developmental bilingual education (Christian, 1994), combine elements of Canadian immersion and maintenance bilingual education to serve *both* language majority and language minority students. Two-way immersion programs group more or less equal numbers of native English-speaking students and native speakers of a minority language together for instruction. In the early grades the non-English language (e.g., Spanish) is used for instruction in an immersion approach, that is, second language acquisition through content instruction in the second language. This procedure provides second language development for English speakers and intensive primary language development for the native speakers of the

25

minority language early on. Instruction through English, including reading and writing, begins with about 20 minutes a day in kindergarten and is gradually increased as students move up the grades until approximately equal time is given for each language (Reynolds, Dale, & Moore, 1989). As English language instruction increases, native English speakers develop their primary language (English) skills, and native Spanish speakers develop their second language (English) skills. At the same time, both groups develop skills in the minority language. Alternatively, some two-way programs use both languages from kindergarten on up the grades in approximately equal proportions. In any case, the goal is full bilingualism and biliteracy for *both* language minority and language majority students. For example, the English speakers acquire Spanish or Cantonese and the Spanish or Cantonese speakers acquire English. Both groups develop and maintain their home languages. Emphasis on primary language maintenance for language minority students is a goal shared by the maintenance bilingual education model. The two-way program model has been carefully developed, researched, and evaluated in school districts throughout the United States with positive results (cf. Christian, 1994; Lindholm, 1990; Lindholm & Gavlek, 1994; Lindholm-Leary, 2001; Peregoy, 1991; Peregoy & Boyle, 1990).

Newcomer Programs. Newcomer programs are designed to support the initial adjustment of immigrant students to the language, culture, and schooling of their new country. All students in newcomer programs are recent arrivals from other countries. Newcomer programs emphasize the integration of academic and personal-social support to help students adjust (Chang, 1990). Newcomer programs may make use of students' home languages for instruction, but they also emphasize systematic English language instruction. Newcomer programs are short-term, often only one year, and are intended to prepare students to succeed in regular schooling situations, where they may continue to receive bilingual instruction, English language development, and sheltered English content instruction, also referred to as Specially Designed Academic Instruction in English (SDAIE). (Full discussion of SDAIE is provided in Chapter 3.)

English Language Instructional Programs

Bilingual education programs serve only a small percentage of eligible students. Much more common are instructional programs that make use of only one language, English, for teaching. In many urban and suburban areas today, classrooms include students from several language groups, making bilingual instruction difficult to implement. Among program types that use only English for instruction are the following.

Sheltered English or Specially Designed Academic Instruction in English (SDAIE). In these programs, students are taught subject matter entirely in English. Subject matter instruction is organized to promote second language acquisition while teaching cognitively demanding, grade-level-appropriate material.

Special teaching techniques are used to help students understand English instruction even though they are still limited in English language proficiency. Sheltered instruction, or SDAIE, is most effective for students who have already achieved intermediate English language proficiency. Primary language support may be provided separately according to district resources and student needs.

ESL Pull-out. In these programs, English learners receive the majority of their instruction in regular classrooms alongside their monolingual English-speaking peers. However, they are "pulled out" of the classroom on a regular basis to receive additional help from an ESL teacher or aide. The help they receive consists of English language development activities as well as reinforcement of subject matter being taught in the regular classroom. The goal is to help students get by while becoming proficient in oral and written English.

English Language Development (ELD). In these programs, English learners are taught all subject matter using English as the language of instruction in a class taught by a teacher with special knowledge of second language development. The majority of students in such classes are usually non-native English speakers with various levels of English language proficiency. At the elementary school level, English language development teachers are responsible for teaching students English language and literacy skills as well as the full elementary school core curriculum, including mathematics, science, and social studies. The goal is full English language, literacy, and academic development. At the secondary level, English language development teachers are primarily responsible for English language and literacy development; content is taught by subject matter specialists using sheltering or SDAIE techniques. The term *English Language Development* (ELD) is sometimes used synonymously with ESL, English as a Second Language, and ESOL, English for Speakers of Other Languages.

27

Structured English Immersion. In these programs English learners are taught all content through English using sheltering techniques to make instruction understandable. It is important to distinguish structured English immersion from the Canadian immersion model described earlier. Specifically, structured English immersion does not promote primary language literacy, whereas the Canadian model does. Therefore, the goal of structured English immersion is language, literacy, and content learning in English only; whereas the Canadian model aims for full bilingualism and biliteracy.

English Language Learners in the "General Education" Classroom

Although various bilingual and monolingual English support programs have been designed specifically for English language learners, many students find themselves in classrooms where little, if any, special assistance is provided. These students face a "sink-or-swim" situation. Increasingly, however, sound practices in second language teaching are reaching the general education or "regular" classroom teacher. In this book, we offer information and ideas for developing language and literacy skills in English as a non-native language. We believe that these ideas can be applied by teachers, regardless of the type of program: bilingual, ELD, or English only. Just as our students bring diverse backgrounds, so also will programs exhibit diversity as we all join forces to move our students toward educational success and integration into the larger society.

Quality Indicators to Look for in Programs Serving English Learners

We have seen that English learner programs vary widely. However, there are certain basic elements recognized by professionals in English learner education that any quality program should include. These elements are summarized in the following statement on the education of K–12 language minority students in the United States issued by TESOL (Teachers of English to Speakers of Other Languages), the international, professional organization for educators working with English learners (TESOL, 1992).

> TESOL supports programs which promote students' growth in English language proficiency, enhance cognitive growth, facilitate academic achievement, and encourage cultural and social adjustment. Such programs include:
>
> • comprehensive English as a Second Language instruction for linguistically diverse students which prepares them to handle content area material in English.
> • instruction in the content areas which is academically challenging, but also is tailored to the linguistic proficiency, educational background and academic needs of students.
> • opportunities for students to further develop and/or use their first language in order to promote academic and social development.
> • professional development opportunities for both ESOL and other classroom teachers which prepare them to facilitate the language and academic growth of linguistically and culturally different children.*

28

$\mathcal{S}$UMMARY

In this chapter, we have highlighted the rich diversity among students who are learning English as a second language in school. In our descriptions, we focus on children's different experiential backgrounds and strengths, while pointing out particular challenges they face in school. Because we believe strongly in building on each student's prior knowledge and experience, we suggest a variety of ways you can get to know your English learners, even though you may not yet share a

---

*Copyright 1992 by Teachers of English to Speakers of Other Languages (TESOL), Alexandria, VA. Reprinted with permission of TESOL.

common language. These activities include personal writing topics, interactive journal writing, and writing by students in their home language. Knowing that cultural differences can create an initial source of miscommunication, we have pointed out various components of culture defined by anthropologists, while suggesting ways to recognize and honor cultural differences among students in the classroom. We have also discussed how classroom organization and language use may be more or less comfortable for students as a result of both cultural and individual differences. We suggest cooperative group learning as one strategy for integrating students into the classroom fabric and promoting English language acquisition. Because we are convinced that social and emotional security form an essential base for learning, we have also provided a variety of ways to promote newcomers' sense of belonging from day one, using Maslow's hierarchy to give attention to their social-emotional needs. Finally, we offered an overview of the kinds of classrooms and programs in which English language learners find themselves. In the next chapter, we will present the details of second language acquisition, maintaining our emphasis on students' experiences and reactions to the processes and motivating factors that lead to learning their new language, English.

As we come to the conclusion of this chapter, an experience comes to mind that happened thirty years ago during the summer after my (Suzanne's) first year teaching second grade in a Spanish/English bilingual maintenance program in Guadalupe, California. I had gone to my mother's home reservation, the Flathead Indian Nation in northwestern Montana, to visit relatives and enjoy the summer celebrations. From there we proceeded to the Crow Fair in southeastern Montana, where people gathered from all over the United States and Canada for singing, dancing, stick games, fry bread, beadwork and turquoise jewelry, and festivities at what is billed as the "biggest tipi encampment in the world." You meet a lot of new people at Crow Fair. One afternoon while relaxing in the shade with my relatives near the Little Bighorn River, we met a family from Canada: mom, dad, and three teenagers. The father, a lanky, long-haired man in his late 40s, asked me what my work was. I replied that I was a bilingual teacher in California and that my second-graders were mostly immigrants from Mexico. I was proud of my work. He paused reflectively and then asked, "Why aren't you helping your own people?" These words stunned me. My words stuck in my throat and would not form themselves into a meaningful reply. Into the silence, my grandmother intervened, "They are *all* her children."

In today's world, these words take on even greater meaning, as the diversity among our students increases daily. Few teachers will go through their careers without encountering students different from themselves in language, culture, race, religion, social class, or land of birth. For teachers of English learners, such differences are a given, representing the challenge and reward inherent in our professional lives. Facilitating English learners to speak, read, write, and learn in a new language has become the task of an increasing number of teachers each day. Without a doubt, it is a task that calls for new learning, not only about theories of language and learning, but also about other people, other cultures, and about ourselves.

29

The essence of our message throughout this book calls for creating a welcoming classroom climate, one that provides each student with a variety of ways to be an active participant and successful contributor. We do not downplay the challenge of creating classroom unity out of student diversity, but we believe strongly that it can be done. Teaching linguistically and culturally diverse students presents an exciting learning opportunity for all of us. Is it easy? Certainly not! The opportunity for any learning and growth, our own and that of our students, is accompanied by great challenge and risk. Successful teaching with culturally diverse students calls for a willingness to go the extra mile, to observe ourselves critically, to question our assumptions, and perhaps to try doing things a little differently: teachers continually learning with open eyes, open minds, and open hearts!

In recalling his younger years, novelist John Steinbeck (1958) spoke of just such a teacher:

> In her classroom our speculations ranged the world. She breathed curiosity into us so that each day we came with new questions, new ideas, cupped and shielded in our hands like captured fireflies. When she left us, we were sad; but the light did not go out. She had written her indelible signature on our minds. I have had lots of teachers who taught me soon forgotten things; but only a few who created in me a new energy, a new direction. I suppose I am the unwritten manuscript of such a person. What deathless power lies in the hands of such a teacher.

May you be such a teacher!!

SUGGESTIONS FOR FURTHER READING

Becker, H. (2001). *Teaching ESL K–12: Views from the classroom with commentary from Else Hamayan.* Boston: Heinle & Heinle.

This is a good introductory book for teachers and administrators alike. It discusses topics including ESL curriculum, program models for secondary and elementary schools, assessment issues, special education, and parent involvement. The discussion with commentary offers a unique look at ESL programs. From the back cover of the text: "Teaching ESL K–12 shows the kind of meaningful professional conversation that teachers can have as they relate their 'wisdom of practice' to the social discourse of research and policy-making."

Díaz-Rico, L. T., & Weed, K. Z. (2002). *The cross-cultural, language and academic development handbook: A complete K–12 reference guide.* (2nd ed.). Boston: Allyn and Bacon.

This 334-page book outlines all the basic information considered essential for the California English learner credential. Chapters cover information on second language acquisition and teaching; assessment; culture and cultures in contact; program models; and language program policies and issues. This resource is both comprehensive and up-to-date in its presentation of theory, research, and practice.

Ferguson, C. A., & Heath, S. B. (Eds.). (1981). *Language in the U.S.A.* New York: Cambridge University Press.

If you are interested in learning more about the rich language diversity in the United States, including Native American languages, immigrant languages, American English dialects, and language use in education, law, and medicine, this book is a must. Each chapter is written by a specialist on the topic. The book is readable and fascinating.

Garcia, G. (Ed.). (2003). *English learners: Reaching the highest level of English Literacy*. Newark, DE: International Reading Association.

This edited text contains articles from top teachers and researchers in second language literacy. There are three sections: "Teaching English Learners to Read: Current Policy and Best Instructional Practice"; "Teaching English Language Development: Rethinking and Redesigning Curriculum"; and "Optimizing Culture as a Bridge to Literacy Learning." This is an excellent, informative collection of articles.

Meyer, L. (2000). *Theory into practice: 39*(2), entire issue. Columbus: Ohio State University.

This themed volume brings together an exciting array of articles that portray issues and insights related to the diversity of children and languages in U.S. schools. Articles address immigrants learning English and "learning America," loss of family languages, Native American languages and tribal sovereignty, barriers to meaningful instruction for English learners, and English learners learning to read English. In addition there is an eye-opening dialogue among for bilingual, African-ancestry teachers, and finally an article on two-way immersion in the United States. Lily Wong Fillmore's article on the loss of family languages has won a national award.

Ovando, C. J., Collier, V. P., & Combs, M. C. (1985). *Bilingual and ESL classrooms: Teaching in multicultural contexts*. (3rd ed.) Boston: McGraw-Hill.

A detailed introduction to issues in bilingual and ESL classrooms, including discussion of students, language, culture, academic achievement, program models, and curriculum options. The new edition contains a new chapter on authentic assessment by Lorraine Valdez Pierce and a chapter on bilingual special education by Theresa Ochoa.

Wong, H. K., & Wong, R. T. (1998). *How to be an effective teacher: The first days of school*. Mountain View, CA: Harry K. Wong Publications.

If you look up this book on Amazon.com or Barnes & Noble.com, you'll find that it is one of the bestsellers in education, and it deserves to be so. This is a "How To" book that is incredibly thorough and wise. We wish we had the book when we started teaching; by the time we came to the book we had taught in public schools for many years and at many levels. Nonetheless, we still learned a great deal about setting up and running a classroom.

31

ACTIVITIES

1. As you look at Table 1.1, try to answer as many of the questions as you can regarding your own family traditions. For example, when you think of family, are you thinking about your mother and father and perhaps a sister or brother or are you thinking of hundreds of cousins, uncles, and aunts who get together every year for the holidays? Compare your answers with those of another adult. What are the similarities and differences?

2. Take the opportunity to visit a school near you that enrolls newly arrived students from other countries. Obtain permission from the principal to visit one of the classrooms. As you observe, try to find out where the students are from and what kinds of special help they are receiving. Use a checklist containing questions such as: What language(s) do the students speak? What assistance are they receiving? Is there a paraprofessional who speaks the students' language(s) or does the teacher use the language? Are there special materials available in the students' home language? What kind of program would you design for these students to promote language development and content-area learning if you were the teacher?

3. Meet with a teacher who specializes in teaching English as a second language. Ask his or her views about the effects of students' cultural and prior educational backgrounds on their school performance. What accommodations does the teacher make to help students adjust? What kinds of programs does the teacher consider best for English learners and why? What kinds of materials or activities has the teacher used with success with English learners?

4. Talk with a child who is learning English as a non-native language. Ask what it is like to learn English in school; what the hardest part is; what has been fun, if anything; and how long it has taken so far. Ask the student to tell you what program, materials, and activities seem to work best for her or him.

5. Begin an informal study of an ethnic group that you would like to know more about. Begin charting information about the group by listing and noting specific information from Table 1.1, such as the family structures, life cycles, roles of men and women in the culture, discipline structures, religion, values, and the like. In addition, after you've gathered descriptive information, look for literature to read by members of that group in order to get a sense of the culture from an inside view.

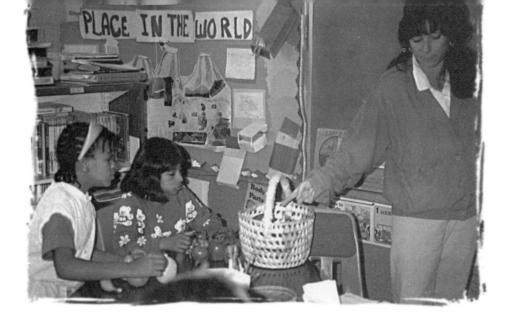

SECOND LANGUAGE ACQUISITION

In this chapter, we describe theories about how people acquire a second language, focusing on children and young people learning English in school. The following questions are discussed:

1. What do we know when we know a language? What are some ways experts have defined language proficiency and communicative competence?
2. How does language function as a symbol and instrument of power, social standing, and personal identity?
3. What theories have been proposed to explain first and second language acquisition?
4. What factors have researchers identified as important in acquiring a second language?
5. What are some important social, emotional, cultural, and educational factors that influence English learners' language acquisition experience in school?

We know a young Nicaraguan girl, Judith, who came to California at the age of 7. Her parents struggled to make a living for their seven children, and Judith was very protective of them, always looking to lighten their load. Once we asked about her younger brothers and sisters, but Judith admonished us never to mention the topic to her mother, who was still grieving the loss of an infant. Judith was virtually non-English-speaking in the third grade; her English grew very slowly in her fourth and fifth grades, though her native language remained fluent: She could make up extensive and complex Spanish stories on the spot, given a patient audience. For a long while we didn't see Judith, but then we happened to visit her school one day. We entered the main office to check in, and there answering the telephone in fluent English was Judith, now a sixth-grader, who had earned the prestigious job of student assistant. What a transformation! We greeted her at once and complimented her on her efficient office management skills. And then we just had to comment: "Your English is so good! How did you do it?" With hardly a moment's reflection, she replied: "I waited." And wait she had, a good four years, though much more went into the process than her answer implied.

Judith's story gives a glimpse of second language acquisition from the inside view. In this chapter, we look at how researchers and theorists have described the process. As you read on, you will find that Judith's brief answer carried the weight of truth. There is, of course, more to be said in order to understand what it is like to learn the language of the school and the larger society as a non-native language. In the following few sections, we first discuss what you know when you know a language, in order to highlight the complex territory English language learners must cover to become proficient. We next present an overview of first and second language acquisition theories. Finally, we discuss various factors that impinge on the process, including the nature of the language learning situation, the effects of age, the importance of social interaction and "comprehensible input," and the treatment of learner errors.

WHAT DO YOU KNOW WHEN YOU KNOW A LANGUAGE? DEFINING LANGUAGE PROFICIENCY AS COMMUNICATIVE COMPETENCE

In general, language proficiency may be defined as the ability to use a language effectively and appropriately throughout the range of social, personal, school, and work situations required for daily living in a given society. In literate societies, language proficiency includes both oral and written language. For our purposes as educators, we want our students to become competent in four language processes: listening, speaking, reading, and writing.

Our definition of language proficiency emphasizes not only the grammatical rules governing sounds, word forms, and word orders to convey meaning (phonology, morphology, syntax, and semantics) but also knowledge of social conventions of language use (e.g., how to start and end a conversation smoothly; how to enter a conversation without interrupting other individuals; how and when to use informal expressions such as slang as opposed to more formal ways of speaking; how, whether, and when to establish a first-name basis in a formal relationship). Thus, as you can see, judgments concerning language proficiency are deeply rooted in social and cultural norms. For this reason, the term *communicative competence* is often used instead of *language proficiency* to emphasize the idea that proficient language use extends beyond grammatical forms to include language functions as well as the social conventions of language to achieve communication (Canale & Swain, 1980; Wallat, 1984).

Classroom Example of Language Use in Social Context

It is important to note that when people use language, they must coordinate all language subsystems (i.e., phonology, morphology, syntax, semantics, pragmatics) simultaneously in a way that is appropriate to the social situation in order to communicate effectively. Let's look at a brief conversation as an example. In Ms. Baldwin's second grade class, the children have planted a vegetable garden, and a group of eight students is now getting ready to go outside to care for their plants.

TEACHER: Let's get ready to go out to the garden. Who remembers what our vegetables need?

CLASS: Water.

TEACHER: That's right. So I will turn on the hose and each of you will get a turn to water one row. What else do we have to do?

CLASS: Pull the weeds.

TEACHER: OK, anything else?

With this brief example, we can look at how various language subsystems operate simultaneously for communication to be achieved. First of all, the social context, as noted previously, is a second-grade classroom situation, with the teacher in charge of a group of students. The social situation constrains how talk will occur. For example, the conversational structure in this exchange is particular to classroom settings, with the teacher initiating the dialogue and the students responding, often as a group. The children know from experience that in this situation they are free to call out their answers. They are not required to raise their hands to be called on, as they are at other times. The teacher initiates the conversation with two utterances that serve to organize and regulate the behavior of the children as they get ready to go out into the garden. When the teacher asks, "Who remembers what our plants need?" her question serves two pragmatic functions. First, the question focuses children's thoughts to regulate their behavior when they go out to the garden. At the same time, the question serves an academic teaching function, which is to review plant knowledge learned recently. We have thus defined the **social context** and examined the **pragmatics** of the utterances

> **INTERNET RESOURCES:** You might explore the ERIC Clearinghouse on Languages and Linguistics site: http://www.cal.org/ericell/digest/subject.html. The site contains, among others, short articles on important topics by key writers and researchers. A few categories explored are: assessment, English as a second language, language diversity, technology and language learning, bilingual education and two-way immersion, and second language learning. You might explore one of these topics in preparation for a paper or a presentation in class. Or you might try an activity on our companion website: www.ablongman.com/peregoy4e.

in the conversation. All of the teacher's utterances are aimed at essentially the same functions: organizing the children's behavior and reviewing plant care concepts. The children's responses serve to display that they know what to do when they go outside. This sequence, teacher initiation-student reply-teacher evaluation, is typical of classroom conversations (Mehan, 1979).

Now let us look at how these utterances are formed to convey meaning. Languages convey meaning by the systematic and coordinated use of rules governing sounds, including intonation, pitch, and juncture **(phonology)**, word formation **(morphology)**, and word order **(syntax).** Each language in the world uses a finite set of sounds that make a difference for meaning: **phonemes.** Phonologists demonstrate phoneme differences by examining word pairs with minimal sound differences, such as pin/bin. Because a pin is different from a bin, that is, they have different meanings, we can conclude that the two sounds, /p/ and /b/, are phonemes of English, because the sound differences make a difference in meaning. In our classroom conversation above, the children responded to the teacher that they were going to "pull the weeds." If they had said "pull the seeds," varying the response by only one phoneme, it would still make sense but would change the meaning completely, in a way that would be disastrous for the garden! If the children had said "pull the tzekl," they would have used a combination of sounds that is not English at all. Each language allows certain sound sequences but not others. If the children had said "weeds the pull," they would not have made any sense, because they would have violated English word-order rules, or syntax. At the level of morphology, if the children had said "pull the weed" instead of "pull the weeds," it would not have been quite right because they needed the plural form with the -s suffix rather than the singular to convey meaning accurately. Prefixes, suffixes, and "root words" are the building blocks, or **morphemes,** from which words are formed. All three rule-governed systems, phonology, morphology and syntax, work together simultaneously to help create meaningful sentences.

So far we have discussed language forms as they combine to convey meanings. The study of linguistic meaning, per se, is yet another area of study, called semantics. When linguists study meaning in different languages, they often analyze the lexicon, or vocabulary of the language, examining, for example, synonyms, antonyms, kinship terms, and other aspects of the meanings of words in different contexts. Words and their meanings reflect the physical and cultural realities of the people who use the language. The ways in which languages serve to put meaning at the service of human communication are remarkably complex and interesting though not yet fully understood. Beyond lexical analysis, another way to study meaning is to analyze how languages convey information about actions indicated by the verb, including who or what instigates the action, who or what is affected by the action, where the action takes place, and a number of other cases that describe the meaning relationships among the elements in a sentence (Fillmore, 1968). For example, consider these two sentences:

Diego Rivera painted that mural.

That mural was painted by Diego Rivera.

The action in both sentences is conveyed by the verb *painted*. The agent is *Diego Rivera*, and the object is *that mural*. Both sentences yield the same semantic analysis, even though they differ grammatically. Our examples provide a simple illustration of a complex and interesting linguistic theory, just to give you a taste of one way linguists have attempted to characterize how languages operate to convey meaning. The exciting part is that thousands of person hours have been spent trying to understand how language works, but even though it is not yet well understood, children the world over have no trouble acquiring their native tongues, and many become bilingual or multilingual!

This discussion of linguistic subsystems is intended to give you an idea of the complex nature of language proficiency. Figure 2.1 summarizes the subsystems of language, with pragmatics as the overarching aspect. This depiction illustrates our view that all language subsystems serve the purpose of communication, for the prime impulse to use language is the need to communicate.

Literal and Figurative Language

Beyond literal meanings conveyed by words and their sequence in utterances, most of us use figurative language such as metaphors and idiomatic expressions every day. I remember my father sometimes saying, "That guy's a real bird." I knew that the person described was a bit wacky, but I did not expect him to have wings. Similarly, when someone says, "That car of mine is a real lemon," we understand that the car breaks down a lot. We do not expect it to produce lemonade.

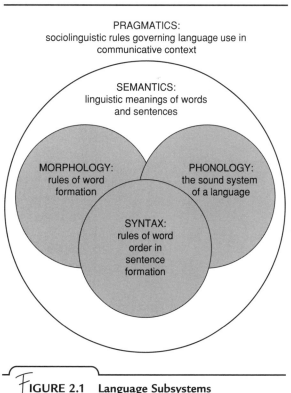

FIGURE 2.1 **Language Subsystems**

In these examples, *bird* and *lemon* are used metaphorically. Young children and second language learners have to grapple with these nonliteral uses of words as they become proficient speakers of their new language.

We are reminded of our experience teaching ESL to a group of men from Mexico and Central America who were working in the agricultural fields of California's central coast. We decided to bring in some practical material on cars and car buying, so we brought in a book on cars we had at home. We started with a chapter called "How Not to Pick Lemon." We hadn't really given any thought to the title, but the minute we held up the book to introduce the chapter, we had to start by explaining the title. As it happened, all of our students were lemon pickers! They certainly understood the literal meaning of the phrase, and we had a great laugh as we explained its figurative sense. This topic turned out to be one that engaged the most interest that semester. In fact, we ended up giving the book away to one of the students.

Idioms, like metaphors, are fixed expressions whose meaning does not correspond literally to the words that comprise it. Like metaphors, idioms present challenges to young children and second language learners. As you read the idioms below, visualize the literal meaning as well as the figurative one.

- He's got himself in a real pickle now!
- Everything's coming up roses.
- No sweat!

THE FAR SIDE®   By GARY LARSON

"Hang him, you idiots! Hang him! . . . 'String-him-up' is a figure of speech!"

Related to idioms are pat phrases or sayings such as the following:

- The coast is clear.
- There's a pot for every lid.
- Butter wouldn't melt in her mouth.
- If wishes were horses, beggars would ride.

In addition to using figurative language, it is possible to say something but mean its opposite, as in irony or sarcasm. For example, if you have just received notice that your insurance rate has gone up, you might say, "Oh great!" But you really mean "Oh no!" or "Oh how awful!" or perhaps something much more colorful. These examples of nonliteral language illustrate how very complex linguistic communication really is.

In summary, language proficiency represents a large and complex array of knowledge. As we have seen, appropriate language use involves both social and grammatical knowledge. People adjust their linguistic style from formal to informal, oral to written, according to their needs and purposes. Fully developed language proficiency, or communicative competence, thus includes the development of a repertoire of oral and written language skills from which to choose to achieve communication across a range of social situations, including academic situations.

Students learning English as a new language face a complex task that must take place gradually over time. Simultaneously, many will also develop and maintain proficiency in their home language, including literacy skills, thereby becoming bilingual and biliterate. For children living in bilingual communities, maintenance of the home language represents a vitally important aspect of communicative competence: bilingual communicative competence (Grosjean, 1982; Romaine, 1989). Consider, for example, the fact that the home language may be a child's only means of communicating with parents or grandparents. As a result, the home language becomes the primary vehicle for the transmission of cultural values, family history, and ethnic identity—the very underpinnings of self-esteem (Wong Fillmore, 1991a, 1991b). In addition to the important social and emotional advantages of home language maintenance, research suggests that primary language development supports second language development (Cummins, 1980, 1981) and that bilingualism itself may lead to cognitive flexibility (Hakuta, 1986). Although we focus on second language literacy in this book, we want to underscore the importance of the first language as an integral part of our students' lives, socially, emotionally, cognitively, and educationally.

LANGUAGE, POWER, SOCIAL STANDING, AND IDENTITY

The fact that words may be listed and defined in a dictionary, or that pronunciation and grammar rules may be catalogued, can draw attention away from the dynamic nature of language. Russian theorist Mikhail Bakhtin suggests that when people communicate via language, they engage in more than an exchange of words: they engage in an exchange of consciousness as meaning is negotiated and understanding achieved or not achieved (Bakhtin, 1981; Moraes, 1996). Words take on different meanings based on the social and power relationships between speakers. And that meaning is intrinsically related to the social, cultural, political, and historical contexts in which a conversation takes place.

In this section, we briefly discuss how language acts as an instrument of social, cultural, and political power. In this context we bring up the volatile topic of dialect. Finally, we discuss how the mother tongue is deeply connected to personal identity and self-esteem, and how adding a new language involves the forging of new identities (cf. Norton, 1997). Understanding these ideas helps us recognize and honor students' home languages and ways of speaking, while facilitating development of English as an additional language or dialect. Dialect issues are especially relevant because English Language Development classes may include native English speakers who are learning Standard English as a second dialect.

Language as an Instrument and Symbol of Power

Languages don't live in a vacuum. They live, breathe, proliferate, change, and die according to the vicissitudes of the lives of their speakers. For example, the Latin of ancient Rome is no longer spoken, even though it can be studied in its written form. As the Roman Empire spread to parts of Europe, northern Africa and central Asia, Latin gradually became the dominant language in commercial, legal, and administrative affairs. After Rome fell, Latin had gained such a strong hold in parts of Europe that it remained the primary language spoken even after the Romans lost power. In those areas, Latin gradually evolved into what we know today as the Romance languages: Italian, Spanish, Portuguese, Rumanian, and French. The spread of not only spoken Latin but also the Roman alphabet to the outlying provinces of the Roman Empire was one of many sociocultural effects of Rome's political domination on the diverse groups of people it conquered.

It is estimated that 4,000 to 8,000 different languages are spoken in the world today (Fromkin, Rodman, & Hyams, 2003). Mandarin, English, Hindi, and Spanish have the largest number of speakers. Some languages have very few speakers, and are therefore at risk of extinction. The languages of the world have been classified into 100 or so overarching language families based on linguistic similarities. Most European languages, including English, belong to the Indo-European language family, which also includes several Germanic and Gaelic languages and all modern languages that have descended from Classical Latin, Greek, and Sanskrit. Other language families include Afro-asiatic, Amerindian, Austroasiatic, Malayo-Polynesian, and Niger-Congo. Some languages, called isolates, do not seem to fit into any known language family, such as Euskara, the language of the Basque people of the Pyrenees Mountains in France and Spain (Crystal, 1997). Another isolate is Kutenai, the American Indian language of some of my (Suzanne's) ancestors, which is still spoken by a small number of people in Montana, Idaho, and

British Columbia. The world's linguistic diversity is truly immense, and it reflects the tremendous diversity of cultures throughout the world.

Language or Dialect?

One reason that numerical estimates of the world's languages vary so widely is disagreement over whether to classify a particular linguistic system as a "language" or a "dialect." Generally, we say that when there are systematic differences in the way different groups of people speak the same language, they are using different dialects or varieties of that language. Systematic differences in phonology, morphology, syntax, semantics, and pragmatics have been found, for example, in the English spoken by certain groups of African Americans, American Indians, European Americans, and Latino Americans in the United States. (Fromkin & Rodman, 2003). Mutual intelligibility is often cited as a criterion to test whether two language varieties are dialects of the same language. However, this test does not always work. For example, the so-called dialects of Chinese are not all mutually intelligible, yet they are generally called dialects, except for Mandarin, which is the official language of Mainland China. By the same token, languages such as Spanish and Portuguese are mutually intelligible. Yet they are classified as separate languages. In these cases, political status rather than mutual intelligibility plays the deciding role in distinguishing language from dialect, thus the assertion that a language is "a dialect with an army and a navy."

To illustrate how a "dialect with an army and a navy" assumes power, let's consider Spanish as an example. In this case we will look at a particular dialect of Spanish, Castilian, which became Spain's standard language beginning with several events in 1492. In that year, not only did Columbus claim the "New World" for Spain, but also the Moors were driven out of Granada, culminating the 700-year struggle to regain the Peninsula from its Muslim conquerors; all Jews were expelled from Spain, except those who were willing to convert to Christianity; and Antonio de Nebrija compiled a Castilian grammar, one of the first modern language grammars ever published. Language, religion, nationhood, and empire coalesced all at once under Ferdinand of Aragon and Isabella of Castille. Isabella's dialect (not Ferdinand's) became the standard, rather than Galician or Catalonian or some other Hispanic dialect. As Spain spread its empire to other parts of the world, Spanish supplanted numerous indigenous languages while continuing to evolve. What Rome had done to Spain, Spain was now doing to people in the Americas.

Today the Spanish Empire no longer exists. However, as its linguistic legacy, Spanish is spoken by some 310 million people mostly in South America, Central America, North America, and Spain (Katsiavriades, 2000). A correlate of that legacy, however, is the loss and extinction of many indigenous languages, a process that continues today. Because Spanish continued to evolve in the Americas, the standard varieties of Spanish of countries like Argentina, Mexico, and Puerto Rico are different from each other and different from the Castilian spoken in Spain.

41

In a similar fashion, English spread worldwide with the imperial expansion of Great Britain and the national growth of its former colonies, including the United States. As with Spanish, there are many varieties of English within and across nations. This historical discussion illustrates several points: (1) how languages migrate, evolve and change over time; (2) how language connects with power and may be used to consolidate the political hegemony within nations and empires; and (3) how political status plays a major role in determining dialect or language status.

The Role of a Standard Language. When a dialect comes into power as a standard, its status is usually reinforced by its widespread use in three major arenas: (1) in written media, such as newspapers, magazines, books, and articles; (2) in oral broadcast media, such as radio and television; and (3) in academic settings in both oral and written forms. Connoting higher social and educational status, the standard language becomes an instrument of power for those who use it. At the same time, facility in the standard language may offer access to broader social, economic, and political opportunities. For these reasons, fluency in the standard language is an important educational goal. Optimally, students will maintain fluency in the home language as well, keeping communication lines open with family, friends, and community (Wong Fillmore, 1991a, 1991b), while forging a personal identity that accommodates both languages and cultures.

Misuse of the Term Dialect. When language scholars use the term "dialect," they use it as a descriptive term to refer to regional and social variations within a particular language. However, in everyday usage, it often carries a negative, pejorative connotation. Judgments are made about people based on how they speak. To some people the term "dialect" may imply inferiority. Even worse are judgments that the speaker is using "bad grammar" or "lazy pronunciation," when in fact the language they are using is a rule-governed, fully developed linguistic communication system. The fact is that each of us speaks a particular variety or dialect of the language we are born into, and all language varieties are legitimate and equal as communication systems. The social and political reality, however, is that certain dialects carry more prestige and power than others. For example, the ability to use Standard English may offer access to economic, social, and political opportunities, which are otherwise denied. For these reasons, we want all students to develop fluency in Standard English, adding to the home language rather than replacing it.

Making judgments about students' grammar and usage tends to be second nature for many of us. However, it is crucial not to slip in to negative, stereotypical judgments based on students' language. This is where ongoing self-reflection and self-awareness are essential. Finally, we must recognize the validity and importance of diverse community languages and language varieties. When students sense that you as the teacher truly recognize and value their home language and culture, they are more likely to feel positive about school and learning. At the same time, you build students' sense of identity and self worth while creating the affective foundation for students' academic success. Because you as the teacher may represent the new language and culture, your positive attitude may also help students identify more positively with their new language and culture as well.

Personal Identity and Ways of Speaking: The Case of Ebonics

James Baldwin (1924–1987), the brilliant African American novelist and essayist, was eloquent in his use of language. Baldwin grew up in New York City and lived much of his adult life in Paris. He drew on his experiences at home and abroad to develop his essays on racism, language, and power. In 1979, he published an article in the *New Yorker* on the topic of "Black English," now sometimes referred to as Ebonics (Baldwin, 1979/1998). In the article, he talks about how one's language is intricately connected to one's identity:

> It [language] is the most vivid and crucial key to identity: It reveals the private identity, and connects with, or divorces one from the larger public, or communal identity . . . To open your mouth . . . is (if I may use Black English) to "put your business on the street": You have confessed your parents, your youth, your school, your salary, your self-esteem and, alas, your future. (p. 68)

In so few words, Baldwin crystallizes what we have taken several paragraphs to try to explain! But why does he say "and, alas, your future"? We interpret this statement as a reference to the way language functions as a gatekeeper, keeping some people down and preventing their access to social mobility and power. This is where access to standard language forms comes in, as noted earlier.

So what is Ebonics? Ebonics, or African American Language, is a variety of English spoken at least some of the time by many African Americans in the United States. Ebonics has been widely studied, and its particular rules of grammar, pronunciation, and discourse have been described by linguists (e.g., Baugh, 1999; Dillard, 1972; Labov, 1972; Perry & Delpit, 1998; Smitherman, 1986, 1998a,b). Like all other languages, Ebonics has a history that mirrors that of the people who speak it, in this case the descendants of African men and women who were captured to work as slaves on American soil. Because its features draw on and reflect aspects of the Niger-Congo languages spoken in West Africa, some call Ebonics Africanized English (Smitherman, 1998b). Baldwin (1979/1998) suggests that when the slaves were given the Bible by their White masters, the formation of the Black church began, and "it was within this unprecedented tabernacle that Black English began to be formed." Baldwin tells us, "This was not, merely . . . the adoption of a foreign tongue, but an alchemy that transformed ancient elements into a new language" (Baldwin, p. 69). Clearly, Ebonics is a rich and expressive communicative resource, a fully formed language, and hopefully, a source of solidarity and pride for its speakers.

In summary, as human beings each of us is born into a family and community whence we acquire basic ways of acting, believing, and making sense of the world around us. The language or languages we use and particular ways speaking are part and parcel of this sociocultural learning. As children we are all socialized

43

through language, and in the process we acquire it. Because the language we speak is so intricately interwoven with our early socialization to family and community, it forms an important element of our personal identity, our social identity, our racial identity, our ethnic identity, even our national identity.

Significantly, our first language is often referred to as the "mother tongue." We identify deeply with our mother tongue and with our family's ways of speaking: If you denigrate my language, you attack my mother, my father, my family, my neighborhood. As children growing up we become aware, sometimes painfully, of the social status of our ways of speaking. Yet the home language remains an integral part of our identity and may be the only way to communicate with parents and grandparents. As a result, the home language is essential for communicating cultural values, family history, and ethnic pride. Teachers can assist students by recognizing and honoring their home languages and ways of speaking. Finally, it is essential to realize that adding Standard English as a new language or dialect involves much more than learning grammar, vocabulary, and syntax. It also requires the expansion of one's personal, social, racial and ethnic identity to make room for the new language and all that it symbolizes and implies. Developing a bilingual, bicultural identity is a dynamic, challenging, and sometimes painful process that continues well into adulthood.

Languages in the Attic

One way to recognize and honor students' home languages is through an activity we use in class called Language in the Attic (Murray, 1992), which can be adapted for use with secondary and elementary age students. You might want to try this yourself. You start by drawing a family tree on a plain piece of paper, with your name in the center. On one side you list your father's name, and then the names of his parents. On the other side you list your mother's name and the names of her parents. Beside each family member, list the language or languages that each one speaks or spoke. Try going back as many generations as you can. What you end up with is your linguistic family tree. Looking at your language family tree, try to answer the following:

1. What circumstances led to maintenance or loss of your "languages in the attic"?
2. What family feelings have you discovered about your ancestral languages?
3. How have education, literacy, and employment in your family contributed to language maintenance or loss?

As you and several classmates share your linguistic family trees, try to identify interesting patterns in language maintenance, shift, and change.

1. How do these patterns reflect social, cultural, economic, and political realities in the lives of your parents and forebears?
2. How do men's and women's or boys' and girls' experiences differ?

Other activities include: (1) making a graph of all attic languages in your class to see how numbers compare; (2) identifying the number of languages that came from each continent in the world; and (3) researching and identifying the world language families represented in the class (cf. Crystal, 1997, or search the Internet with key words *language families*). Finally, don't miss the opportunity to highlight and share feelings of wonder and pride in the linguistic diversity of your particular group of students.

LANGUAGE ACQUISITION THEORIES

As we proceed with our discussion of how youngsters acquire a second language in school, we must take a moment to summarize basic language acquisition theories related to first and second language development. Our purpose is to acquaint you with those aspects of theory and research that are helpful to teachers in understanding both first and second language learners. It is important to note that neither first nor second language acquisition is yet fully understood. As a result, many controversies and disagreements prevail among experts. For this reason continued interdisciplinary research in psycholinguistics, sociolinguistics, and education is needed to help us better understand processes of language acquisition and use. The issues are complex enough to keep many researchers busy for decades, if not centuries, to come. With that, let us summarize some basic theories.

45

First Language Acquisition Theories

Our favorite first language learner is our young granddaughter, Hope. When Hope visits us, we enjoy playing hide-and-seek, reading books to her, and just listening to her talk. Recently, while playing a board game with Hope, Grandpa pronounced the *r* in rabbit as a *w*, saying, "It's a wabbit!" Hope was tickled by this. She immediately grinned with knowing amusement and giggled, "Him don't say it right!" At 3 Hope was confident enough about her own knowledge of phonology to point out the phonemic impropriety of an adult's pronunciation. At the same time, she remained oblivious to her own grammatical infelicities. We didn't correct Hope's grammar because we assumed that with time she would outgrow that phase to become mature in her language use, and eventually she did. Many parents and grandparents have similar stories to tell.

How do language acquisition theories explain observations such as these? Three basic theories of first language acquisition have been put forward over the years: behaviorist, innatist, and interactionist (Lightbown & Spada, 1993). We now discuss each briefly.

Behaviorist Theory. You are probably familiar with behaviorism as a major learning theory emphasizing stimulus, response, and reinforcement as the basic elements of learning. For language acquisition, behaviorists hypothesized that children learned their first language through stimulus, response, and reinforcement as well, postulating imitation and association as essential processes. For example, to learn the word *ball,* the child would first associate the word *ball* with the familiar spherical object, the stimulus. Next the child would produce the word by imitation, at which time an adult would praise the child for saying *ball,* thereby reinforcing the child's correct verbal response. Behaviorists assumed that the child's mind was a *tabula rasa,* a blank mental slate awaiting the scripture of experience.

Behaviorist concepts of imitation and reinforcement could not account for typical child utterances like "Him don't say it right," which were clearly not imitations of adult speech. Moreover, behaviorists could not explain how any novel utterance was produced, even those that were grammatically correct. Yet most utterances we produce in conversation or writing are in fact original. That is, they are not pat phrases we have learned by hearing and repeating. In addition, child language researchers noticed that parents typically reinforce their children for the meaning of their utterances, not for grammatical correctness. These and other concerns were boldly pointed out as Noam Chomsky (1957) engaged in a heated debate with behaviorist B. F. Skinner (1957), attacking behaviorist theory as inadequate to explain observations of child language development.

Innatist Theory. Chomsky was able to garner some very strong arguments against the behaviorist explanation of language acquisition, using examples from children's developing grammars, such as our example from Hope. Skinner and his behaviorist colleagues were experts in psychology, applying their theories to verbal behavior. Chomsky, on the other hand, was a linguist with a genius for analyzing syntax. In fact, his early work on syntax and transformational grammar revolutionized the field of linguistics (Chomsky, 1957, 1959). Chomsky's explanations of grammatical rules and transformations became the subject of psychological research on language use in the interdisciplinary field of psycholinguistics.

As Chomsky pondered the complex intricacies of children's development of grammar, he concluded that language acquisition could only be accounted for by an innate, biological language acquisition device (LAD) or system. Infants must come into the world "prewired for linguistic analysis." Specifically, Chomsky claims that infants universally possess an innate "grammar template," or universal grammar, which will allow them to select out the many grammatical rules of the language they hear spoken around them, as they gradually construct the grammar of their mother tongue.

From the innatist perspective, children construct grammar through a process of hypothesis testing. For example, a child may hypothesize the rule that *all* plural nouns end with an *-s.* Thus, when they come to a word such as *child,* they form the plural as *childs,* or when they come to the word *man,* they say *mans* for the plural. Gradually, they will revise their hypothesis to accommodate exceptions to the plural rule. Thus, children create sentences by using rules rather than by merely repeating messages they have heard, as assumed by behaviorists. This application of rules accounts for the generative nature of language. With a finite set of rules, people can generate an infinite number of novel utterances. Children acquire the rules, according to Chomsky, with little help from their parents or caregivers. But as Harvard psychologist Howard Gardner recently stated (Gardner, 1995, p. 27), the Chomskyan view is "too dismissive of the ways that mothers and others who bring up children help infants to acquire language." Gardner argues that, "while the principles of grammar may indeed be acquired with little help from parents or other caretakers, adults are needed to help children build a rich vocabulary, master the rules of discourse, and distinguish between culturally acceptable and unacceptable forms of expression." This interest in the role of people in the social environment provides the focus of the next theoretical perspective on language acquisition that we discuss, the interactionist perspective. In response to Chomsky's emphasis on innate grammar mechanisms centered in the infant, interactionists have brought back an interest in the role of the social environment and the influence of parents and caregivers on children's language acquisition.

Interactionist Theory. According to the interactionist position, caregivers play a critical role in adjusting language to facilitate the use of innate capacities for language acquisition. This is in sharp contrast to the innatist view that adapting language has little effect on a child's acquisition process. The interactionist view thus takes into consideration the importance of both nature and nurture in the language acquisition process.

Interactionists study the language mothers and other caregivers use when caring for infants and young children, with special attention to modifications they make during these social interactions to assist children in communication. One strategy often observed between English-speaking, middle-class mothers and their toddlers is conversational scaffolding (Ninio & Bruner, 1978), as illustrated in the following conversation:

CHILD: Birthday cake Megan house.
MOTHER: We had birthday cake at Megan's house. What else did we do at Megan's house?
CHILD: Megan dolly.
MOTHER: Megan got a doll for her birthday, didn't she?

In this conversation, the mother repeats the child's meaning using an expanded form, thereby verifying her understanding of the child's words while modeling adult usage. In addition, the mother assists or scaffolds the toddler's participation in the conversation through prompting questions at the end of each of her turns. In this way, scaffolding provides conversational assistance as well as focused linguistic input tuned to the child's own interests and language use at that moment. By preschool age, this kind of scaffolded conversation is no longer necessary. Whether scaffolding is actually necessary for language acquisition has not been verified. In fact, ways in which infants and young children are spoken to varies across cultures (Ochs & Schieffelen, 1984; Schieffelin & Eisenberg, 1984). Nonetheless, caregivers generally facilitate children's vocabulary development, their ability to use language appropriately in social situations, and their ability to get things done through language.

Children's language develops over time, not within a single interaction. As children develop language, they must construct the meanings of thousands of words. Adult assistance in this process is illustrated in the following dialogues, as British linguist M. A. K. Halliday and his wife (1984a, 1994) interact with their son, Nigel. This transcript captures Nigel's "ongoing construction" of the concept of cats as it transpired over a period of eight months. In these dialogues, we witness Nigel's semantic development as he both contributes and receives information to help him construct the concept cat.

Nigel at 2; 10; 22 (2 years; 10 months; 22 days)
NIGEL: And you [that is, "I"] saw a cat in Chania Falls.
MOTHER: Yes, you saw a cat in Chania Falls.
NIGEL: And you picked the cat up. Mummy, do cats like meat?
MOTHER: Yes, they do.
NIGEL: Do cats like bones? Do cats like marrow?

Nigel at 2; 10; 26
NIGEL: Can I stroke the cat? You ["I"] want to stroke the cat . . . you want to scratch it . . . it's drinking its milk . . . it's moving its tail out . . . it's moving its tail outside . . . it's scratching . . . it's putting it's its tail up what's this?

MOTHER: I don't know; I suppose its elbow.

NIGEL: It's wagging its tail . . . it's lapping it with its tongue . . . you can go near its elbow . . . you *can* go near its elbow . . . but you can't go too near its face . . . because it thinks you might take away its milk . . . it was just a bit frightened . . . it thinked that you might take away its milk . . . has it finished its milk?

Nigel at 2; 11; 5

NIGEL: [*thinking about "The House that Jack Built"*] What is a rat?

FATHER: It's a sort of big mouse.

NIGEL: Does the rat go when the cat has killed it?

FATHER: No, it doesn't go any more then.

NIGEL: Why did the cat kill the rat?

FATHER: Cats do kill rats.

NIGEL: Why do they?

FATHER: [*formula*] You'll have to wait to understand that till you're a bit bigger.

NIGEL: No, I can understand it now.

FATHER: Well, cats just like to eat rats and mice.

NIGEL: Why do they like to eat them?

FATHER: They just do.

Nigel at 2; 11; 15

NIGEL: Why did the cat go out? Mummy, why did the cat go out?

MOTHER: It gets fed up, having its tail squashed.

Nigel at 3; 0; 26

NIGEL: How do the cat's claws come out?

FATHER: They come out from inside its paws. Look, I'll show you.

NIGEL: Does it go with its claws?

FATHER: Not if it's going along the ground.

NIGEL: And not if it's climbing up a tree?

FATHER: Yes, if it's climbing up a tree it does go with its claws.

Nigel at 3; 2; 7

NIGEL: Will the cat eat the grape?

FATHER: I don't think so. Cats like things that go, not things that grow.

Nigel at 3; 5; 12

NIGEL: Cats have no else to stop you from trossing them . . . cats have no other way to stop children from hitting them . . . so they bite. Cat, don't go away! When I come back I'll tell you a story. [He does so.]

Nigel at 3; 6; 12

NIGEL: Can I give the cat some artichoke?

MOTHER: Well, she won't like it.

NIGEL: Cats like things that go; they don't like things that grow.

Nigel at 3; 6; 14

NIGEL: I wish I was a puppet so that I could go out into the snow in the night. Do puppets like going out in the snow?

FATHER: I don't know. I don't think they mind.

NIGEL: Do cats like going out in the snow?

FATHER: Cats don't like snow.

NIGEL: Do they die? [He knows that some plants do.]

FATHER: No, they don't die; they just don't like it.

NIGEL: Why don't puppets mind snow?

FATHER: Well [hesitating] . . . puppets aren't people.

NIGEL: Yes, but . . . cats also aren't people.

FATHER: No, but cats are alive; they go. Puppets don't go.

NIGEL: Puppets do go.

FATHER: Yes, but you have to make them go; like trains.

NIGEL: Trains have wheels. Puppets have legs.

FATHER: Yes, they have legs; but the legs don't go all by themselves. You have to make them go.*

In this excerpt we can see that Nigel has initiated the discussions about cats for his own purposes, controlling the topic for the most part. In addition, Nigel is a major conversational contributor in the dialogues as he constructs his knowledge about cats, about "things that go," and about some differences between animate and inanimate things. Halliday (1994) says: "Interpersonally, it (the dialogue) evolves into a dynamic modeling of question, answer, challenge, contradiction, and the like that is the essential component of the resources out of which all conversation is constructed" (p. 79). Most important, this is not talk for talk's sake, but a serious effort over time to build a concept through interaction between parent and child.

As we saw with Nigel, interactions do not necessarily lead to immediate understanding. Rudimentary understandings must be developed and refined over time, often through misunderstandings. For example, during recent salary negotiations between hockey players and club owners, there was a lot of talk about "salary caps." When a sportswriter's young son heard that the strike had been settled, he asked his father, "Will the players have to wear their salary caps now?" An explanation followed! On another occasion, Labov (1981) heard a child explain why his sister wasn't in school that day: "She had diapperhea." Children are constantly constructing meaning as they interact with people and the world around them, and through these interactions, they gradually sort out the nuances and construct the multiple meanings of words and phrases. The interactionist perspective acknowledges the important roles of both the child and the social environment in the language acquisition process.

---

*"Listening to Nigel: Conversations of a very small child," by M. A. K. Halliday, 1984, Sydney, Australia: University of Sydney, Linguistics Department. Reprinted with permission of author.

Summary of First Language Acquisition Theories. Table 2.1 summarizes the behaviorist, innatist, and interactionist perspectives on language acquisition by comparing (1) the focus of linguistic analysis, (2) how each theory accounts for the process of acquisition, (3) the role of the child, and (4) the role of the people in the social environment. Of the three approaches, the behaviorist approach, which places primary weight on children imitating what they have heard, has proven least adequate for explaining observed facts in child language development. The innatist view, in contrast, places primary weight on the child, and particularly on innate, biological mechanisms to account for language acquisition. The interactionist perspective, acknowledging both the child's role and that of caregivers in the social environment, emphasizes the importance of social interactions aimed at communication as the essential ingredient in language acquisition. To the extent that more research is needed on both the biological and social mechanisms in language acquisition and use, innatists and interactionists are likely to add important information to the overall understanding of language acquisition now and in the future.

TABLE 2.1 Comparison of Behaviorist, Innatist, and Interactionist Theories of Language Acquisition

Acquisition Aspects	Behaviorist Perspective	Innatist Perspective	Interactionist Perspective
Linguistic focus	Verbal behaviors (not analyzed per se): words, utterances of child and people in social environment	Child's syntax	Conversations between child and caregiver; focus on caregiver speech
Process of acquisition	Modeling, imitation, practice, and selective reinforcement of correct form	Hypothesis testing and creative construction of syntactic rules using LAD	Acquisition emerges from communication; acts scaffolded by caregivers
Role of child	Secondary role: imitator and responder to environmental shaping	Primary role: equipped with biological LAD, child plays major role in acquisition	Important role in interaction, taking more control as language acquisition advances
Role of social environment	Primary role: parental modeling and reinforcement are major factors promoting language acquisition	Minor role: language used by others merely triggers LAD	Important role in interaction, especially in early years when caregivers modify input and carry much of conversational load

51

Second Language Acquisition Theories

Theories about how people learn to speak a second (or third or fourth) language are directly related to the first language acquisition theories described above. There are two reasons why. First of all, because first language acquisition is a universal achievement of children the world over, researchers and educators interested in second language acquisition and teaching have often used first language acquisition as an ideal model, one that may inform us about how a second language might be taught. Until Chomsky, however, ideas about how a first language was acquired were not fully developed and researched. Behaviorists, for example, did not analyze closely the speech development of young children, but rather extended general learning theory principles to language development.

With the advent of Chomskyan linguistics, however, a whole generation of psycholinguists was inspired to go out and tape record the speech of infants and young children to analyze and describe the process of acquiring their mother tongue. The focus of the research was to describe the grammatical development of young children. Chomsky's contribution to the study of child language was his new way of looking at syntax. Researchers applied his methods of describing syntax to the problem of describing children's "interim" grammars at different ages and stages of language development. As a result, a remarkable amount of information was generated about first language acquisition in languages as diverse as Turkish, Mohawk, Spanish, and Japanese. This information provided a natural resource for second language acquisition researchers, not only in terms of theory, data collection, and data analysis, but in terms of framing the research questions themselves. One of the first questions was simply: Is a second language acquired in the same way as the first? If so, what are the implications for classroom instruction? Because first language acquisition is so successfully accomplished, should teachers replicate its conditions to promote second language acquisition? If so, how? These questions are not fully answered yet, but remain pertinent today.

Even as information began to accumulate from the study of child language, however, behaviorist views predominated in educational practice, heavily influencing methods of second language teaching in schools, emphasizing drill and practice of grammatical forms and sentence structures. Meanwhile, as researchers began to go into people's homes to tape record children's speech, the impact of the social environment in various cultural milieus emerged as an interesting variable in language acquisition and use. In fact, some early language acquisition researchers were thwarted in their data-collecting efforts when they discovered that their tape-recording procedures conflicted with cultural norms about how to talk to children! Sociologists and anthropologists were ready to combine their interests and insights about culture and language to inform what became the interactionist viewpoint on language acquisition.

The study of first language acquisition has now emerged as a necessarily interdisciplinary field involving anthropology, psychology, and education as well as linguistics. As you can imagine, careful attention to social and cultural conventions is essential in investigating how a second language is learned, given the intimate connections between language and culture. In the following section, we will introduce you to how second language acquisition is described and explained from the three perspectives examined for first language acquisition: behaviorist, innatist, and interactionist. We will also discuss their implications for teaching, and then offer a picture of our own understandings of second language acquisition in classrooms. See if you can identify the theories that we have taken to heart in our viewpoint!

Behaviorist Perspective in Second Language Acquisition. Behaviorist theories of language acquisition have influenced second language teaching in a number of ways that persist today in many classrooms. If you have taken a foreign language in high school or college, you are probably familiar with the methods informed by behaviorist learning theories. One behaviorist language teaching method popular in the 1960s is the audiolingual method, in which dialogues are presented on tape for students to memorize, followed by pattern drills for practicing verb forms and sentence structures. Students are first taught to listen and speak, and then to read and write, based on the assumption that this is the natural sequence in first language acquisition. (This sequence has been disputed, as you will see in Chapter 4.) For behaviorists, the processes involved in second or foreign language learning consisted of imitation, repetition, and reinforcement of grammatical structures. Errors were to be corrected immediately in order to avoid forming bad habits that would be difficult to overcome later. If you were taught with this method, you may remember the "drill and skill" practice, often carried out via audiotapes in a language laboratory. How well did this instruction work for you? When we ask our students this question in classes of 40 or so, only 1 or 2 report successful foreign language competence acquired through the audiolingual approach.

Innatist Perspective in Second Language Acquisition. Just as Chomsky's theories inspired psycholinguists to record and describe the developing grammars of young first language learners, they also influenced research on second language learning. One such theory put forth to account for second language development was the **creative construction theory** (Dulay, Burt, & Krashen, 1982). In a large-scale study of Spanish-speaking and Chinese-speaking children learning English in school (Dulay & Burt, 1974), English language samples were collected using a structured interview based on colorful cartoon pictures. Children were asked questions about the pictures in ways that elicited the use of certain grammatical structures. Children's grammatical errors were then examined to determine whether they could be attributed to influence from the first language or whether they were similar to the types of errors young, native English-speaking children make. Data analysis showed that the majority of errors were similar to those made by native English-speaking youngsters as they acquire their mother tongue. Based on these results, the authors proposed that English language learners creatively construct the rules of the second language in a manner similar to

53

that observed in first language acquisition. Dulay and Burt therefore concluded that second language acquisition is very similar to first language acquisition.

Dulay and Burt also used their findings to refute the hypothesis that learner errors will generally be predictable from a contrastive analysis of the learner's mother tongue and the developing second language. Contrastive analysis is a procedure for comparing phonological, morphological, and syntactic rules of two languages (the learner's mother tongue and his or her second language) in order to predict areas of difficulty in second language development. For example, Spanish creates the plural by adding an *-s* or *-es* ending to a noun (e.g., *casa, casas; lápiz, lápices*). This rule is similar to English pluralization. Thus, by contrastive analysis, it would be predicted that plurals in English will not be difficult for native Spanish speakers to learn. When the rules of two languages are quite different, contrastive analysis predicts learner difficulty. For example, Cantonese has no plural marker. The idea of plural is conveyed by context. Thus, it would be predicted that Cantonese speakers would have difficulty forming plurals in English. Although predictions based on contrastive analysis sometimes held true in their data analysis, Dulay and Burt found that most English language learner errors among their subjects were best described as similar to errors made by children acquiring English as a first language.

Krashen's Five Hypotheses. Continuing in the innatist tradition, Stephen Krashen (1982) developed a series of hypotheses about second language acquisition that have taken root in the field of second language teaching due in part to Krashen's desire to address classroom second language learning. Krashen's five hypotheses are: (1) the acquisition-learning hypothesis, (2) the monitor hypothesis, (3) the natural order hypothesis, (4) the input hypothesis, and (5) the affective filter hypothesis. Each of these is discussed here.

The Acquisition-Learning Hypothesis. One of Krashen's first assertions was that there is a distinct difference between acquiring and learning a second language. Acquisition, Krashen asserts, is a natural language development process that occurs when the target language is used in meaningful interactions with native speakers, in a manner similar to first language acquisition—with no particular attention to form. Language learning, in contrast, refers to the formal and conscious study of language forms and functions as explicitly taught in foreign language classrooms.

Krashen goes on to make two claims about the acquisition-learning distinction that have generated considerable controversy in the academic community: (1) that learning cannot "turn into" acquisition and (2) that it is only acquired language that is available for natural, fluent communication. Krashen's critics have pointed out that it would be extremely difficult, if not impossible, to detect which system, acquisition or learning, is at work in any instance of language use (McLaughlin, 1987). Furthermore, the two terms require much finer definition in order to be subjected to experimental study. These criticisms notwithstanding, Krashen's emphasis on second language acquisition by using the new language for relevant communicative purposes has had substantial, positive influence on class-room practice, especially in regard to the move away from the drills and pattern practice aimed at language learning.

The Monitor Hypothesis. Krashen has suggested that the formal study of language leads to the development of an internal grammar editor or monitor. As the student produces sentences, the monitor "watches" the output in order to ensure correct usage. In order for a student to use the monitor three conditions are necessary: sufficient time, focus on grammatical form, and explicit knowledge of the rules. Thus it is easier to use the monitor for writing than for speaking. Krashen maintains that knowing the rules only helps learners polish their language. The true base of their language knowledge is only that which has been acquired. From this assumption, he recommends that the focus of language teaching should be communication, not rote rule learning, placing him in agreement with many second language acquisition and foreign language teaching experts (cf. Celce-Murcia, 1991; Oller, 1993).

The Natural Order Hypothesis. According to the natural order hypothesis, language learners acquire (rather than learn) the rules of a language in a predictable sequence. That is, certain grammatical features, or morphemes, tend to be acquired early, whereas others tend to be acquired late. Figure 2.2 illustrates this view.

A considerable number of morpheme studies support the general existence of a natural order of acquisition of English grammatical features by child and adult non-native English learners. However, individual variations exist, as do variations that may result from primary language influence (Lightbown & Spada, 1993; Pica, 1994).

The Input Hypothesis. Central to Krashen's view of second language acquisition is the input hypothesis. According to the input hypothesis, the acquisition of a second language is the direct result of learners' understanding the target language in natural communication situations. A key element of the input hypothesis is that the input language must not only be understandable, thus the term **comprehensible input,** but should contain grammatical structures that are just a bit beyond the acquirer's current level of second language development, abbreviated as $i + 1$, with i standing for input and +1 indicating the challenging level that is a bit beyond the learner's current level of proficiency. Krashen suggests that acquirers are able to understand this challenging level of language input by utilizing context, extralinguistic information such as gestures and pictures, and general background knowledge. In other words, input can be made comprehensible as a result of these extra cues. Moreover, acquisition is facilitated by a focus on communication, not grammatical form.

In summary, according to Krashen, language is acquired (not learned) by

English morphemes acquired early:

| -ing: Verb ending | John is going to work. |
| -/s/: Plural | Two cats are fighting. |

English morphemes acquired late:

| -/s/: Possessive | We saw Jane's house. |
| -/s/: Third person singular | Roy rides Trigger. |

FIGURE 2.2 Acquisition of English Morphemes

understanding input that contains linguistic structures that are just beyond the acquirer's current level of competence ($i + 1$). Speech is not taught directly, but emerges on its own. Early speech is typically not grammatically accurate. If input is understood and there is enough of it, $i + 1$ is automatically provided. According to Krashen, we do not have to deliberately program grammatical structures into the input. Although Krashen's theory is particularly concerned with the grammatical structures contained in the input, vocabulary is also an important element in $i + 1$. Krashen emphasizes free-choice reading on topics of interest to students as an excellent way to acquire both vocabulary and other aspects of language.

The Affective Filter Hypothesis. Krashen's fifth hypothesis addresses affective or social-emotional variables related to second language acquisition. Citing a variety of studies, Krashen concludes that the most important affective variables favoring second language acquisition are a low-anxiety learning environment, student motivation to learn the language, and self-confidence and self-esteem. Krashen summarizes the five hypotheses in a single claim: "People acquire second languages when they obtain comprehensible input and when their affective filters are low enough to allow the input in [to the language acquisition device]" (Krashen, 1981, p. 62). For Krashen, then, comprehensible input is the causative variable in second language acquisition. In other words, listening to and understanding spoken language is the essential ingredient in second language acquisition. For this reason, Krashen urges teachers not to force production, but rather to allow students a **"silent period"** during which they can acquire some language knowledge by listening and understanding, as opposed to learning it through meaningless rote drills.

In summary, Krashen's second language acquisition theories have been influential in promoting language teaching practices that (1) focus on communication, not grammatical form, (2) allow students a silent period, rather than forcing immediate speech production, and (3) create a low-anxiety environment. His notion of comprehensible input provides a theoretical cornerstone for sheltered instruction, or Specially Designed Academic Instruction in English (SDAIE), described in Chapter 3. These practices have benefited students in many ways. More questionable theoretically, however, are his acquisition/learning distinction and the notion that comprehensible input alone accounts for language acquisition. The importance of output, that is, speaking and writing, cannot be ignored in a balanced view of language acquisition (Swain, 1985). Finally, evidence indicates that some grammatical forms may not develop without explicit instruction (Harley, Allen, Cummins, & Swain, 1990).

Interactionist Perspective in Second Language Acquisition. The idea that comprehensible input is necessary for second language acquisition also forms a basic tenet of the interactionist position. However, interactionists view the communicative give and take of natural conversations between native and non-native speakers as the crucial element of the language acquisition process (Long & Porter, 1985). Their focus is on the ways in which native speakers modify their speech to try to make themselves understood by English-learning conversational partners.

Interactionists are also interested in how non-native speakers use their budding knowledge of the new language to get their ideas across and to achieve their communicative goals. This trial-and-error process of give-and-take in communication as people try to understand and be understood is referred to as the **negotiation of meaning.** As meaning is negotiated, non-native speakers are actually able to exert some control over the communication process during conversations, thereby causing their partners to provide input that is more comprehensible. They do this by asking for repetitions, indicating they don't understand, or responding in a way that shows they did not understand. The listener's natural response is then to paraphrase or perhaps use some other cue to convey meaning such as gesturing, drawing, or modified speech (sometimes referred to as "foreigner talk," which is somewhat analogous to caregiver speech in first language acquisition).

In addition to the importance placed on social interaction, some researchers have looked more closely at output, or the speech produced by English language learners, as an important variable in the overall language acquisition process (Swain, 1985). We have seen that the language learner's output can serve to elicit modification of input from conversational partners to make it more comprehensible.

The three theoretical perspectives bear certain implications for instruction, as outlined in Table 2.2. As you read the chart, you will see how the three theoretical perspectives compare in terms of the source and nature of linguistic input to learners, ideal classroom composition vis-à-vis native speakers and second language learners, student output, pressure to speak or produce output, and treatment of learner errors.

57

Beyond Social Interaction in Second Language Acquisition Theory

Social interaction with native speakers represents an important theoretical cornerstone in explaining second language acquisition. However, placing second language learners and native speakers in a room together does not in itself guarantee social interaction or language acquisition. We also need to look closely at the larger social and political contexts in which our students live and learn because they can affect relationships between native speakers and English learners. Who are the native speakers? Who are the English learners? Are the two groups from the same social class or not? Are they from the same ethnic group or not? Will the two groups want to interact with each other? To what extent will particular English learners choose to interact with particular native English speakers and adopt their ways of speaking? How will English learners cross the linguistic, social and cultural boundaries needed to participate socially among native speakers?

Stereotypes, prejudices, and status and power differences may make interaction difficult. Furthermore, natural tendencies to affiliate with one's own linguistic, social, and ethnic group (Sheets & Hollis, 1999) may also work against the kind of social interaction that facilitates language acquisition. Two-way immersion programs described in Chapter 1 represent one of the few educational alternatives that explicitly promote equal status between language minority and language

TABLE 2.2 Instructional Implications of Second Language Acquisition Theories

Instructional Components	Behaviorist	Innatist	Interactionist
Source of linguistic input	language dialogues and drills from teacher or audiotape	natural language from the teacher, friends, or books	natural language from the teacher, friends, or books
Nature of input	structured by grammatical complexity	unstructured, but made comprehensible by teacher	unstructured, but focused on communication between learner and others
Ideal classroom composition	all target language learners of similar second language proficiency	target language learners of similar second language proficiency so i +1 can be achieved	native speakers together with target language learners for social interaction aimed at communication
Student output	structured repetitions and grammar pattern drill responses	output is not a concern; it will occur naturally	speaking occurs naturally in communication with others
Pressure to speak	students repeat immediately	"silent period" expected	no pressure to speak except natural impulse to communicate
Treatment of errors	errors are corrected immediately	errors are not corrected; students will correct themselves with time	errors that impede communication will be corrected naturally as meaning is negotiated; some errors may require explicit corrective instruction

58

majority students, with both groups learning the native language of the other while developing full bilingualism and biliteracy. Even in multilingual classrooms, however, you are in a position to promote positive social participation through heterogeneous grouping discussed in Chapter 3. To the extent that linguistically, culturally, and academically diverse students are able to work together to accomplish learning tasks, thinking through procedures and problems as a group, they create the moment-to-moment sharing of linguistic and cognitive resources that can lead to not only academic learning, but also respect and rapport amongst each other (Gutierrez, Baquedano-Lopez & Alvarez, 2001). As you begin to address intergroup relations in your classroom, you might want to select one or two multicultural education resources from Example 1.1 (Chapter 1) for closer study and discussion with your colleagues at your school or in your university classes.

LEARNING A SECOND LANGUAGE IN SCHOOL: PROCESSES AND FACTORS

We have just reviewed the complex nature of language proficiency and some theoretical perspectives on the process of language acquisition. What does this mean for students learning English as a second language in school? In this section, we discuss essential processes and factors influencing English learners in school, particularly the social context of second language acquisition, age and the interplay of social and cognitive factors in the second language acquisition process, social versus academic language use, comprehensible input and social interaction, and the treatment of language learning errors in the classroom. As we discuss these factors, you will see how theory has affected our views.

Second Language Acquisition Contexts: Formal Study versus Immersion in a Country Where the Language Is Spoken

One factor that affects second language acquisition is the social context in which the second language was learned. Have you ever studied another language, or do you know someone who has? How did you learn it? And how well did you learn it? When we ask our students this question, we hear a wonderful variety of second language learning stories. Most of our students have had the experience of studying a foreign language in high school or college. They often recall specific foreign language teaching techniques for learning the grammar, pronunciation, and vocabulary, usually of a European language such as French, German, or Spanish. Many also remember activities such as choral repetition of sentence patterns, memorization of vocabulary items, and perhaps in-class opportunities to put these together in writing or simulated conversations.

Under these learning conditions, some basic knowledge of the language may have developed. However, few people report reaching a substantial level of communicative competence unless they spent time in a country where the language was spoken. The opportunity for foreign travel or residency often bears fruit for second language development based on the seed of classroom instruction. In contrast, students who have come to the United States as immigrants have a very different language learning story to tell. Many hold vivid memories of entering elementary or high school knowing not a word of English and feeling frightened and baffled at the world around them. They struggled for months, perhaps years, to become acclimated to the new language and culture. All too often, immigrant students are overcome by these demands and drop out of school. Yet others learn English well enough to be successful in university classes, though perhaps retaining a foreign accent. Reflecting on your own language learning experiences and talking with other people about how they learned a second language can provide insights into the process of second language acquisition. What can we learn from different language learning stories?

Perhaps the first thing we can see is a distinction between studying a foreign language for one period a day in school and learning a language through immersion in a social environment, including the school, where the target language is used regularly for day-to-day communication. Differences between these two language acquisition contexts directly affect the language learning process. Students immersed in an environment in which the new language is spoken have the advantage of being surrounded with opportunities to hear and use it. The larger social environment features the new language, not only in the classroom but also everywhere else—in shopping malls, at the theater, on television, in newspapers, and more. As a result, classroom learning can be solidified and expanded to the extent that learners interact within the larger community (Dulay, Burt, & Krashen, 1982). In addition, students learning the language of their new country are likely to be motivated, because success in acquiring strong English skills is important for day-to-day functioning and full participation in society.

In a social immersion situation in which learners live in a country where the target language is spoken, second language acquisition is facilitated by the rich language exposure available and by the inherent **need to communicate.** At the same time, students are challenged to the highest levels of oral and written acquisition because they will need nativelike skills in order to qualify for future education and employment opportunities. In contrast, foreign language study tends to be limited in opportunities and necessity to use the language for functional communication. Similarly, the expectations for accomplishment are correspondingly lower. When students enter your class knowing very little English, they have the benefits of an immersion situation because the new language is used both in school and in the larger environment. At the same time, some may feel pressured by their need to learn the new language as quickly as possible.

Age and the Interplay of Sociocultural, Cognitive, and Personality Factors

Another factor that affects the second language acquisition process is the age of the learner when second language acquisition begins (Collier, 1987, 1987/1988; Harley, 1986). For native-born children who speak another language at home such as Spanish, Navajo, Crow, or Cantonese, second language acquisition of English may begin during early childhood or upon entry to elementary school. For immigrants, the process may begin at any age, depending on how old they are when they arrive in their new country. Age on arrival bears heavily on second language acquisition processes and eventual levels of attainment. Why is this so?

The influence of age on second language acquisition stems from the complex interplay of sociocultural, cognitive, and personality factors. Consider for a moment the language story told by Montha, a university student who came to the United States from Cambodia at age 12, the eldest of six children. She had been educated in Cambodia and was literate in Khmer when she arrived, but her education took place entirely in English after she moved to the United States. The family spoke Khmer at home, but nowhere else did she use or hear her home language, because she and her family were the only Cambodians in the area. Montha remembers how difficult it was to fit in at school, where she knew neither the language nor the customs of her schoolmates. She felt frightened and isolated, because there were no other Cambodians in her neighborhood or school. To exacerbate the situation, at age 12 she was self-conscious and concerned about being different. Nonetheless, she gradually found her way into school social groups and began to acquire English. Reflecting on her language learning, Montha feels that her younger sisters and brothers seem to have had an easier time. For one thing, as the eldest daughter, she was expected to help her mother daily with household chores, whereas her sisters were permitted to play with other children in the neighborhood. In addition, as an adolescent, she was not permitted to date or to go out with friends in cars, an accepted pastime of many American teenagers. For these activities, she had to wait until she had graduated from high school and no longer lived with her parents.

From this brief example, we can see how age interacted with social and cultural factors to constrain Montha's language learning opportunities. First of all, she entered the American social scene at an age when cultural expectations of teenagers differed considerably between her home culture and that of the larger society. Remaining at home to help her mother, she was restricted from certain aspects of social participation that could have helped her learn English. In contrast, her siblings were young enough to be permitted to play with English-speaking neighborhood children, and this type of play was acceptable to Montha's parents. In other words, Montha's siblings, by virtue of their age, were permitted a broader range of age-appropriate social activity acceptable to both Cambodian and American parents, and this, very likely, facilitated language acquisition.

Despite these external social and cultural restraints, Montha did become proficient in English, no doubt a result in part of certain personal attributes, including unflagging determination and persistence in achieving her goals. At this point in her life, she was dedicated to becoming a teacher of English learners, and was working on passing the basic skills test required to enter the teaching credential program. Another personal attribute was her particularly sensitive and empathetic attitude toward others, which certainly played a role in her desire to teach and may also have motivated her English language acquisition. Given that there were no other Cambodian families in her school or neighborhood, her social contacts required English, and Montha was a person who thrived on social relationships.

Montha was a successful English learner who went on to earn a baccalaureate degree at a state university. That she had developed literacy and academic skills in her first language no doubt contributed to her success in high school and college, given the fact that well-developed academic skills and strategies transfer between a bilingual's two languages (Cummins, 1981). Montha's journey was nonetheless a difficult one. Academic development in her primary language ceased on her arrival, and she had a great deal of academic English to acquire before she could qualify for the university. Once there, she struggled to earn the grades that would allow her to go on for a teaching credential. In addition, she had difficulty passing the timed reading, writing, and math examinations required for the teaching credential. Without her persistent nature and her commitment to helping children reminiscent of her former self, she would most likely not have been able to push through and become a teacher. But she did!

Montha's English developed fully, though she retained some pronunciation features that set her apart from native English speakers. She also maintained fluency in Khmer and a strong ethnic identity. As a postscript, Montha tells us that her mother never did learn English. Being an adult, her mother was not required to attend school daily as her children were. Nor did she seek work outside the home as her husband did. Thus, she did not find herself in social contexts that could have provided the exposure and motivation needed for English language acquisition. These days, her mother takes a great deal of pride in Montha's accomplishments as a bilingual teacher and serves as a valuable resource when Montha needs a forgotten phrase in Khmer or some detail of a cultural tradition to include in her curriculum at school. Montha's case highlights how her age on arrival interacted with sociocultural, cognitive, and personality factors in her language acquisition process and in her journey to becoming a bilingual teacher.

Differences in School Expectations of Younger and Older Learners

Another factor affecting second language acquisition is the level of cognitive-academic functioning normally expected at different ages, especially in school. A general task for all English language learners is to gain enough English proficiency to carry out school tasks about as well as their monolingual peers. For kindergarten and first-grade children, the linguistic performance gap between English language learners and their English-speaking age mates is relatively small. After all, monolingual children are still developing both language and concepts during the primary grades. Furthermore, learning for all young children is best derived from direct experience, manipulation of concrete objects, and social interaction with adults and peers. As kindergarten teachers know, younger children learn more by talking while doing than by listening to a long verbal explanation from the teacher. The same holds true for young English language learners. Thus, learning contexts that are age-appropriate for younger monolingual children tend to be optimal for young English language learners as well.

For older immigrant students, the classroom situation presents greater demands on second language proficiency than for younger newcomers (Ovando, Collier, & Combs, 2003). They have further to go and less time to catch up than their younger brothers and sisters, as we saw in Montha's case. From middle school on, and sometimes earlier, we expect students to be able to learn from lecture-style verbal instruction at least some of the time. Furthermore, subject matter grows increasingly complex and abstract. Thus, students who are older on arrival have a larger language gap to fill before they will be able to function academically in English at a level commensurate with their monolingual peers. On the other hand,

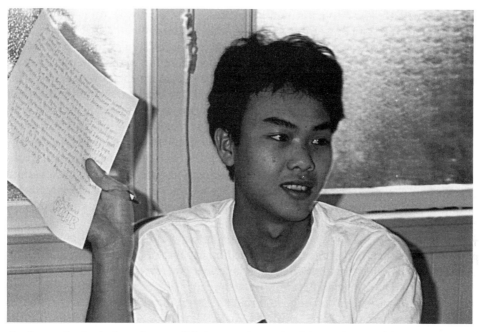

Students who begin learning English in secondary school face substantial linguistic and academic challenges.

precisely because they are older, they bring the advantages of a well-developed cognitive and conceptual system. Moreover, they may have had sufficient schooling in their home country to be facile in literacy and numeracy skills. If so, they stand a good chance of academic success, provided that their new school offers systematic support for both second language development and continued content area learning. Other students may have had little schooling, or their educational opportunities may have been interrupted by war, political turmoil, or the struggles involved in leaving their home country. In such cases, students will have much work ahead of them in both language and content area learning.

Teacher Expectations for English Learner Achievement

Neither we as teachers nor our students have any control over their age on arrival. Yet when students enter school with little or no knowledge of English, they are faced with the dual challenge of learning a new language and trying to fit into school routines both socially and academically—no small task! What do we know about second language acquisition processes that can facilitate these adjustments? First, we have seen that the process of acquiring a second language is facilitated when learners and speakers of the target language have the opportunity and desire to communicate with each other. Thus, students need opportunities to interact with fellow students and negotiate meaning by sharing experiences through activities such as group work, drama, readers' theater, art, and writing. Making use of natural cognitive and linguistic processes similar to those involved in acquiring their first language, English language learners take the language they hear spoken around them and use it gradually to acquire the new language—its vocabulary, sound system, grammatical structure, and social conventions of use.

In the earliest stages of second language acquisition, students grapple with understanding their teacher and peers and with somehow making themselves understood. As they begin to talk, learners grow in the ability to use their new language with fluency and ease, though as yet imperfectly. Eventually, as opportunities for higher-level thinking and problem solving are provided, students acquire the formal language competence necessary for more advanced instruction in mathematics, science, social studies, literature, and other subjects. Thus, students must learn to engage in complex social and cognitive transactions through their second language, both orally and in reading and writing.

When we say that students must become capable of complex social and cognitive transactions through their second language, we are putting forward the goal of full English language and literacy development. That is, we are expecting them to attain the same level of English language proficiency as their native English-speaking counterparts. For English language learners, this means acquiring the essentials of English phonology, morphology, syntax, semantics, and pragmatics and being able to integrate them for use in a wide variety of social contexts. Ultimately, we want our students to be at ease in English with their peers, potential employers, insurance agents, bank representatives, university recruiters, and the full range of social contacts that occur in daily life. Moreover, we want them to be capable of using both oral and written language in formal ways for academic purposes. This latter goal is one of the main charges of schooling for all students and represents access to the employment and social mobility available in U.S. society. If, in addition to English language skills, students have been able to develop their primary language, they will enjoy further options afforded by their bilingualism. In other words, teachers' expectations of English learners must be high, and social and academic support must be provided for these goals to be achieved.

Language Used for Social Interaction versus Language Used for Academic Learning

Some experts make a distinction between language used for basic social interaction and language used for academic purposes (Cummins, 1980). **Basic Interpersonal Communication Skills (BICS)** are language skills needed for social conversation purposes, whereas **Cognitive Academic Language Proficiency (CALP)** refers to formal language skills, including listening, speaking, reading, and writing, used for academic learning. Research shows that students may demonstrate basic social competence in a second language within six months to two years after arrival in a new country. In other words, they can speak English well enough to interact with their peers, talk on the telephone, and negotiate meanings with adults. However, the ability to demonstrate academic competence in the new language orally and in writing at a level commensurate with that of their native-speaking peers may take five years or more (Cummins, 1979; Thomas & Collier, 1995). Current preliminary research findings suggest that students with no prior schooling and no primary language support may take much longer, as much as seven to ten years, to acquire academic skills in their new language (Thomas & Collier, 1995). In other words, newcomers may need substantial time and educational support to develop English skills such as those needed to understand academic lectures, to make and defend logical arguments orally or in writing, to read school texts efficiently, and to write effectively for academic purposes.

Let's take a moment to consider some aspects of academic language use that students must control with increasing sophistication as they progress from elementary through middle school and high school. Reading and writing are two obvious aspects of academic language use, particularly reading and writing essays that compare and contrast, persuade, describe, and summarize content-area material. However, academic learning involves a variety of cognitively demanding oral language uses as well. For example, students need to be able to follow their teacher or peers' oral explanations of complex concepts and procedures in science, mathematics, and the social sciences. They need to understand such explanations well enough to apply them in carrying out their own experiments, in solving mathematical problems, and in debating issues and explaining their views of topics in social science and history. Academic language use, whether oral or written, requires a growing reservoir of background knowledge pertinent to any given discipline, along with knowledge of the conventions of how to organize information orally and in writing. If we assume that the basis for these academic skills is ideally established among monolingual students by fifth or sixth grade, it is not surprising that acquiring such skills takes English learners five to seven years, or longer. We provide strategies to promote oral and written academic language development in Chapters 3 through 9.

Information on how long it takes for students to acquire English sufficient for academic purposes is important to us for two reasons. First, it reminds us that, even though students may appear fairly proficient in English during basic social interactions, they are still likely to need special support to be able to learn and display their knowledge of complex academic material through their second language. Second, it gives us a direct index of the long-term nature of the language acquisition process. We usually have students in class for just one year, and it is helpful to know that we are unlikely to witness full-blown language development in our students during that short time.

Although we may not control the timetable of language development, there are numerous strategies we, as teachers, can utilize to promote that development. Thus, throughout this book, we will point out ways to assist English learners to develop the kind of linguistic competence that will facilitate their academic success.

65

Learning to Use English in Socially and Culturally Appropriate Ways

Academic language use is a major goal for all students. Equally important for students new to English is explicit instruction in socially and culturally appropriate ways of using English, oral and written. Early childhood teachers are quite accustomed to this type of socialization because it is a natural part of the curriculum. Reminding children to say "please" and "thank you," asking for a toy instead of grabbing it, waiting a turn instead of interrupting: All of these are second nature for teachers of young children. And all of them reflect social and cultural conventions of English in this society. Similarly, teachers help students learn the special classroom rules for taking turns, talking, listening, and responding to other points of view. Writing party invitations and "grace notes" to show gratitude or sympathy are other examples of language bound by social and cultural guidelines that are taught in school. The elementary curriculum provides many opportunities to help students learn socially and culturally appropriate language use.

If you teach English learners who arrived in this country in middle or high school, the social and cultural conventions of both oral and written language use continue to be of utmost importance. Older students typically have extensive social and cultural repertoires for primary language use. They may also know various conventions for English, but they need to add new ones as they become increasingly proficient. Explicit instruction with role-playing is often helpful as students learn both the phraseology and social protocol appropriate to everyday situations, such as using the telephone, eating at a restaurant, applying for a job, meeting new friends at a party, going to the doctor or dentist, and asking the teacher for help after school (cf. Jones, 2003). Making small talk is another aspect of communicative competence that can be quite difficult and thus merits explicit instruction. Appropriate phrases and ways of expressing emotions such as gratitude, impatience, empathy, enthusiasm, and even anger are all needed as students develop full communicative competence in English. We recommend that you use the TESOL standards (TESOL, 1997) to help you build social and cultural language competence into your pre-K–12 curriculum.

Comprehensible Input and Social Interaction

As noted earlier, comprehensible input refers to language used in ways that make it understandable to the learner even though second language proficiency is limited (Krashen, 1982). Paraphrasing, repetition of key points, reference to concrete materials, and acting out meanings are some of the ways speakers can help convey meaning and thus make language more understandable. When we pair two communication channels, the verbal and the nonverbal, words and meanings become discernible to the learner, as for example, when a picture of the digestive system is displayed and pointed to during an explanation of the digestive process. In this way, language is not only understood but also forms the raw material from which learners may gradually construct the new language system for themselves. During the earliest stages of language learning, face-to-face social interactions between learners and speakers of the target language provide optimal language learning opportunities.

Language learning opportunities are richly present during social interactions because participants are likely to be focused on communicating with each other, and they will naturally make use of all their resources to do so—facial expression, dramatization, repetition, and so forth (Wong Fillmore, 1982, 1985). Furthermore, the non-English speaker can communicate at a rudimentary level through actions, nods, and facial expressions. As communication is worked out or negotiated, a great deal of understandable language is generated, thereby providing comprehensible input from which language may be acquired. Take for example an interaction we observed between two boys, Marcelino, new to English, and Joshua, a native English speaker. They were coloring a drawing they had created of a helicopter. When finished, it was to be posted on the bulletin board with drawings of other transportation vehicles.

JOSHUA: Here, Marcelino. Here's the green *[hands Marcelino the green crayon]*.

MARCELINO: *[Marcelino takes the green crayon and colors the helicopter.]*

JOSHUA: Hey, wait a minute! You gotta put some red stars right here. OK?

MARCELINO: Huh?

JOSHUA: Red stars. I'm gonna make some red stars . . . right here. *[Joshua draws four red stars, while Marcelino continues coloring with the green crayon.]*

MARCELINO: OK.

In this interaction, the hands-on, context-embedded activity conveyed much of the meaning. Marcelino understood the purpose of the task and was able to interact with Joshua with minimal English to negotiate division of labor. With much of the meaning conveyed by the situation and the concrete materials, Joshua's language provided comprehensible input. Thus, Marcelino is apt to retain for future use words such as *green* and *red,* and phrases such as "Wait a minute." Working one-on-one with a partner also permitted Marcelino to convey his need for Joshua to clarify his concern over the red stars. While focused on the task of coloring the helicopter, Marcelino participated in the conversation with his minimal but functional vocabulary. At the same time, he was afforded quality English input from Joshua through conversation pertaining to the hands-on activity. Interactions such as this provide important elements for language acquisition—a functional communication situation, comprehensible input, and social interaction around a purposeful task.

As the teacher, the language you use can be a valuable source of comprehensible input, whether you are working with the whole class, small groups, or individuals. In Chapter 3, we show how you can tailor your talk and your lessons to make them optimally understandable to students, thereby enhancing content

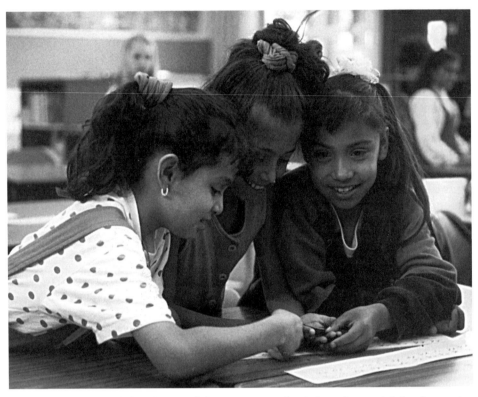

Working in groups while using English promotes academic learning, social development, and second language acquisition.

learning and second language acquisition. This kind of instruction is often referred to as sheltered instruction or Specially Designed Academic Instruction in English (SDAIE). Finally, it is important to note that written language also affords comprehensible input when students read, provided the material is relatively easy to understand (Krashen, 1993), a topic addressed in Chapter 7.

What about Language Learning Errors?

As we have seen, the question of learner errors in language acquisition is a topic of great interest and controversy. How should we treat second language errors in the classroom? Should we correct students' errors or not? If we do correct, when and how do we do so? We will give you our ideas on this complex issue, but you will need to decide for yourself how you will proceed on a case-by-case basis.

There are several considerations to think about in deciding whether to correct learner errors. Your first consideration is the English language development stage of the learner. Many errors are developmental and will eventually be replaced by conventional forms without your intervention. You will recall that certain morphemes develop early, such as the *-ing* form of the verb and the plural -/s/. Other morphemes develop late, such as the -/s/ for the third person plural. The latter error continues to appear in some English learners' speech many years after they begin to learn English. For students in the early stages of second language acquisition, errors that impede communication may be corrected in a sensitive and natural way, especially those involving vocabulary. Consider the following example from a third-grade English Language Development classroom in which five English learners are playing a board game with the teacher standing nearby. Natalia, a native Russian speaker, has been in this country four months and is a beginner in English.

NATALIA: I putting the marker on the points.
TEACHER: Those are called dots. You're putting the marker on the dots.
NATALIA: The dots.

The teacher focused on the vocabulary item *dots,* and her gentle yet explicit correction was well received. However, the teacher did not correct Natalia's use of *I* instead of *I am* or *I'm.* Why? First, lack of the verb or its contraction does not make a difference in meaning. Second, this is a common beginner error, and appropriate verb use is likely to develop with time. Third, it is doubtful that correction of this grammatical form would result in Natalia's being able to produce it in another context. Corrections that focus on meaning tend to be easier to learn than those that focus on grammar alone. As a rule of thumb, you may provide words and word forms to beginning English learners to help them make themselves understood, thereby maintaining a communication focus.

As second language acquisition proceeds, there may be some grammatical errors that persist and become permanent or *fossilized* (Selinker, 1972). We have seen, for example, that the third person singular, present tense verb marker *-s* develops late, and sometimes not at all. A possible explanation for its tardy appearance may be that the "person" and "tense" information conveyed by the *-s* can be understood through context. Because English requires that the subject be explicitly stated, subject—verb agreement is redundant, and the tense can be inferred from context, as illustrated by the following sentence pairs. Notice that the grammatical errors do not impede communication.

Renae bakes cookies for me.   Renae bake cookies for me.
The cat sits in the sun.   The cat sit in the sun.

What should you do if such grammatical errors persist among intermediate and advanced students? Our view is that grammatical errors are best dealt with in the context of student writing. For one thing, writing can be looked at and analyzed in a leisurely way, whereas speech goes by very quickly and unconsciously and then disappears. A student may not be able to perceive that a spoken error occurred unless it was tape recorded. Even then, the student may not hear the

69

error. On the other hand, a written error is visible and preserved. It can be pointed to and discussed. When patterns of error recur in a student's writing, specific mini lessons can be tailored for the student so that he or she may self-edit. Details of this process are discussed in Chapter 6 on editing during process writing.

In summary, the way you treat English learner errors will depend on your own judgment, taking into consideration the student's English language developmental level, the prevalence of the error type, the importance of the error type for communication, and your specific goals for the student in terms of English language development. There is not sufficient research on the specifics of English language development to give you error correction recipes. Even if there were, individual differences would obviate their usefulness. Finally, you should keep in mind that error correction is not the major source of English language development; meaningful experiences, using the language for a variety of oral and written purposes, play a much larger role. Nonetheless, grammatical refinements in speech and writing may require explicit instruction. Thus the error correction guidelines and examples we provide are suggestive, not prescriptive. Your own trial and error will provide you with further information, as you work with English learners to promote their school success.

Summary

70

In this chapter, we discussed second language acquisition as children experience it in school. First, we defined language proficiency, pointing out grammatical and social aspects of both communicative competence and communicative performance. Next we summarized behaviorist, innatist, and social interactionist theories of first and second language acquisition. We then examined a variety of factors that researchers and theorists have noted as important in second language acquisition: the language learning environment (immersion versus foreign language), age, cognitive development, the cultures of the home and school, and ways in which all of these interact to motivate and give purpose to second language acquisition. Finally, we discussed comprehensible input, social interaction, learner errors, and differences between social and academic language development.

Suggestions for Further Reading

Ellis, R. (1994). *The study of second language acquisition*. Oxford: Oxford University Press.
This book, over 800 pages long, is "everything I wanted to know about the study of second language acquisition." It is written in an accessible style and contains sections with chapters on learner language description; explaining second language acquisition, external and internal factors; explaining individual differences in second language acquisition; and classroom second language acquisition. This text should be on all of our bookshelves.

Ellis, R. (1997). *Second language acquisition.* Oxford: Oxford University Press.

This book, one in the Oxford Introductions to Language Study series, is 147 pages long. Short chapters include topics such as describing and explaining L2 acquisition, the nature of the language learner, interlanguage, social aspects of interlanguage, individual differences in L2 acquisition, and instruction in L2 acquisition. This excellent, short book also contains a glossary and annotated bibliography.

Fromkin, V., Rodman, R., & Hyams, N. (2003). *An introduction to language* (7th ed.). Boston: Thomson Heinle.

This classic text, in its seventh edition, is an excellent introduction to language study. Clearly written chapters include topics such as: brain and language, morphology, sentence patterns, language in society, language change, and writing.

Harley, B., Allen, P., Cummins, J., & Swain, M. (Eds.). (1990). *The development of second language proficiency.* Cambridge: Cambridge University Press.

This book presents a series of articles and the results of a major five-year research study on second language proficiency in various groups of school learners. It includes chapters on topics such as the nature of language proficiency, communicative competence, classroom treatments, and bilingual proficiency.

Lightbown, P., & Spada, N. (1999). *How languages are learned.* Oxford: Oxford University Press.

This excellent, friendly text, completely revised and updated, relates complex issues in a clear and concise manner. Chapter topics include learning a first language, theories of second language learning, factors affecting second language learning, learner language, second language learning in the classroom, and popular ideas about language learning. Using a scale from "strongly agree" to "strongly disagree," the text begins with twelve provocative questions regarding language learning; the questions provide an excellent advanced organizer for a course and for this book. A chapter reviewing classroom research is particularly excellent because it analyzes research based on language acquisition theories such as behaviorism and interactionism. This is a short book, 135 pages, that presents valuable information in a very accessible manner.

McLaughlin, B. (1985). *Second language acquisition in childhood* (Vol. 2). Hillsdale, NJ: Erlbaum.

A thorough critical review of research on children learning English and other languages subsequent to entering elementary school. Issues related to bilingual instruction are discussed, as well as program types and academic achievement of students schooled in a second language.

Activities

1. If you have studied another language, share your language learning story with the group. As other group members share their language learning stories, use the stories for discussing the effect of differences such as age, culture, and language learning situation on second language acquisition among the people in your group.

2. Reflecting on your own experiences studying a foreign language, what do you recall as the hardest part? Why was it hard? What was easy? Why was it easy? How proficient did you become? What affected your degree of proficiency? Can you identify a theory underlying the teaching approach (e.g., behaviorist, innatist, interactionist)?

3. After reading this chapter, which language acquisition theory do you favor? Or do you favor a combination of the different views? Do you think any one theory seems to account for all the variables in language acquisition? Discuss these issues with someone else who has read the chapter.

4. Taking each of the language acquisition theories in turn—that is, behaviorist, innatist, and interactionist—think of how each view might help

you organize your classroom for maximum language learning. Compare and contrast each of the views in terms of a classroom context. For example, look at Table 2.2, which delineates the different theories, and determine what a classroom that strictly followed one theory might be like: Would desks be in rows or circles? Would the teacher always be in the front of the class or moving around the class most of the time? Would students have many choices of classroom activities or would the teacher determine almost all lessons? Finally, describe what theory or combination of theories accounts for the kind of classroom you think is ideal for second language learners with varying degrees of English language proficiency.

5. Think of your own experiences learning or using a language. What were the contexts in which you felt you were most successful in learning a language? Did you learn best in a classroom context, or, if you have visited a country where you had to learn at least some basics of a second language, how did you go about doing it? What helped? What didn't help? If you were to need to learn a language for something important like getting a job, how would you go about it?

6. If you are currently learning a language, you might try keeping a journal of your language learning and language acquisition experiences. For example, how do you feel as a language learner under different kinds of circumstances? How do you react, positively or negatively, to circumstances in which you aren't fully proficient in the language? What humorous situations have you experienced as a result of learning a new language?

CLASSROOM PRACTICES FOR ENGLISH LEARNER INSTRUCTION

In this chapter, we describe effective classroom practices for English learners, addressing the following questions:

1. What is standards-based instruction and how can it be used with English learners?
2. What is sheltered English, or Specially Designed Academic Instruction in English (SDAIE), and how can it be organized and delivered effectively for beginning and intermediate English learners?
3. How can cooperative group work be organized to promote second language acquisition and academic learning?
4. How can thematic instruction be utilized to promote content learning and language and literacy development for English learners?
5. How does the scaffolding metaphor apply to teaching English learners? How can scaffolding enhance the learning experiences of English language learners?
6. How should English learners be assessed?

Recently, we observed the presentation of a thematic unit on Egypt over a period of seven weeks and were impressed with the way the teacher, Jamie Green, had integrated her intermediate-level English learners into her ninth-grade history class. We noticed many different ways she had developed lessons to make them both interesting and comprehensible to her students. Her classroom was like the inside of an ancient pyramid: Brick walls and ceilings had been created from butcher paper, hieroglyphics were posted on the paper walls, and Egyptian scenes, both ancient and modern, adorned the bulletin boards.

When Jamie began the unit, she asked her students to share anything they knew about Egypt. As the students brainstormed words such as *pyramids, tombs,* and *desert,* she created a cluster, or graphic word web, with the words (see Figure 3.1), drawing a picture next to each word. She then gave students ten minutes to share in small groups all that they knew about Egypt. When they reported their ideas back to the class, Jamie added the new information to the cluster. She then said: "I'm going to show you a short film about Egypt, and I want you to look for interesting things to discuss and add to our cluster." After the film, she asked students to list other items for the cluster and added them.

She then handed out a K-W-L worksheet (Ogle, 1986) and told the groups they would be listing what they knew about Egypt in the first column and what else they wanted to know about Egypt in the second column, as shown in Figure 3.2. She told them they would be able to choose their own study question after conferring with her, so that it was very important to decide on something they really wanted to explore and place it in the "want to know" column. The "L" column would be used later for summarizing what they had learned about their topics.

In subsequent weeks, students worked in their groups exploring and reporting some of their findings to others in the class. As they made these brief reports, students in the class helped one another by suggesting additional reading material. For example, when one group explored mummies, another student told them about a "neat book" she had seen about mummies in the library. Thus students served as resources for one another. Later, groups prepared their projects as exhibits for a family night, when parents would visit their Egyptian museum and students would act as docents, explaining their projects and displays.

In this complex unit, Jamie was able to implement a number of prac-

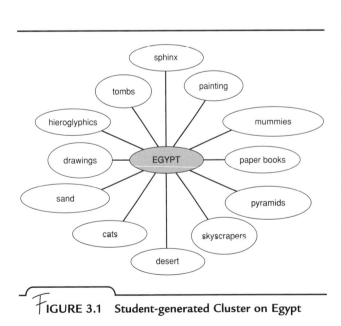

FIGURE 3.1   Student-generated Cluster on Egypt

K (Know)	W (Want to Know)	L (Learned)
Pyramids were tombs where pharoahs were buried.	How did the pharoahs live and how did they rule the people so they would build pyramids?	
Mummies were the way they preserved the pharoahs.	How did they make mummies and why did they do it?	
Hieroglyphics were the way they wrote.	Can we learn how to write in hieroglyphics?	

FIGURE 3.2   One Group's K-W-L Egypt Worksheet

tices that are recommended for effective English learner instruction. She developed her instruction around a theme, beginning by assessing and building students' background knowledge. She evaluated what students knew about the topic by creating a cluster of ideas and by having them list what they knew about the theme in the K-W-L sheet. In addition, she involved students in collaborative groups where they could share their knowledge and determine their own projects. At every step, she supported student comprehension and learning through direct experience and by accompanying verbal explanations with pictures, graphs, gestures, and careful use of language. By giving students an opportunity to make their own choices about projects, she motivated them to learn something important to them. In addition, students had an authentic purpose for their projects as they exchanged information with one another and finally as docents with their parents. Through subsequent discussions you will be able to identify many other strategies Jamie used to scaffold her students' language, literacy, and content learning.

In this chapter and subsequent ones, we discuss the numerous strategies that Jamie, an experienced teacher of English learners, used with her intermediate English speakers, strategies such as scaffolding, collaborative grouping, informal assessments, writing reports, and sharing projects to promote English language and literacy development. In this chapter, we focus on general principles of English learner instruction for beginning and intermediate learners. Many aspects of English learner instruction amount to what you already know as good, sound teaching. What may be new to you, however, are the strategies associated with tailoring your language use to make instruction understandable to students who are new to English, and creating lesson participation opportunities that take into account each student's prior knowledge and functional English abilities.

STANDARDS-BASED INSTRUCTION AND ASSESSMENT

In Chapter 1 we introduced you to standards-based reform efforts of the last decade or so. These reforms have resulted in the development and widespread use of standards in every curriculum area. In this section, we discuss how teachers use curriculum standards to help them plan instruction and evaluate learning. As noted earlier, standards-based instruction consists of three components: (1) content standards that delineate what students should know and be able to do; (2) benchmarks that specify expected knowledge and skills for each content standard at different grade levels; and (3) performance standards or progress indicators that describe how students will show they have met the standard (Laturnau, 2003). Assessment criteria are thus built in to teach standard.

Ideally, standards-based instruction will help you focus on high expectations for all students, while motivating you to tailor instruction to meet individual student needs. It also encourages multiple modes of assessing learning, including careful observation as students carry out particular tasks, such as writing an essay or conducting an experiment. Finally, standards-based instruction and assessment potentially will permit students to attain and demonstrate their knowledge and skill in a variety of ways. These are all worthy goals for effective English learner instruction.

If you are new to curriculum standards, you might find them a bit daunting at the beginning, especially if you have to contend with various sets of standards in several curriculum areas. If you are an experienced teacher at your grade level or subject, the content is likely to be familiar, but perhaps stated in more detail or from a different point of view than what you are used to. Also, don't be surprised to find a variety of formats and wording across different sets of standards: Standards documents are not yet standardized!

Your first task then is to study the standards you are expected to use for your grade level and subject. It is helpful to meet with other teachers to deepen your understanding and to share ways to teach and assess students according to the standards. Some schools provide staff development days for this purpose. As you gain experience in using the standards, you may discover new ways to meet them or perhaps the need to modify them. If so, you will want to discuss your ideas with your teaching colleagues and principal.

For teaching English learners, we recommend that you familiarize yourself with the *ESL Standards for Pre-K–12 Students* (TESOL, 1997). These standards were developed to be used side by side with curriculum standards in subjects such as math, science, and social studies. Focusing on the instructional and assessment needs of English learners, the TESOL standards are set up to help your students achieve the high standards required in all subjects. Therefore, they take into consideration different levels of English language proficiency—beginning, intermediate, and advanced—and provide ideas for helping students with limited formal schooling. Example 3.1 provides a list of instruction and assessment resources created by teachers showing how they have integrated the TESOL standards at different grade spans: pre-K to 2, grades 3 to 5, grades 6 to 8 and grades 9 to 12.

Each TESOL standard is structured around three overarching goals held for all students, prekindergarten through 12th grade: (1) to use English to communicate in social settings, (2) to use English to achieve academically in all content areas, and (3) to use English in socially and culturally appropriate ways. For each goal at each of the four grade spans, three standards are provided. Each standard includes several descriptors that detail the content of the standard and sample progress indicators that tell what students might do to show progress in meeting the standard. Here is an example to show how each standard is structured (p. 91), taken from the standards for grades 4 to 8.

Goal 2, Standard 3

To use English to achieve academically in all content areas:

Students will use appropriate learning strategies to construct and apply academic knowledge.

Descriptors (2 of 12 are shown here)	*Sample Progress Indicators (2 of 13 are shown here)*
• focusing attention selectively	• scan several sources to determine the appropriateness to the topic of study
• apply basic reading comprehension skills such as skimming, scanning, previewing and reviewing text	• skim chapter headings and bold print to determine the key points of the text

Example 3.1   **Resources for Using the TESOL Standards for Pre-K–12 Students**

Agor, B. (Ed.). (2000). *Integrating the ESL standards into classroom practice: Grades 9–12.* Alexandria, VA: Teachers of English to Speakers of Other Languages.

Irujo, S. (Ed.). (2000). *Integrating the ESL standards into classroom practice: Grades 6–8.* Alexandria, VA: Teachers of English to Speakers of Other Languages.

Samway, K. D. (Ed.). (2000). *Integrating the ESL standards into classroom practice: Grades 3–5.* Alexandria, VA: Teachers of English to Speakers of Other Languages.

Smallwood, B. A. (Ed.). (2000). *Integrating the ESL standards into classroom practice: Grades Pre-K–2.* Alexandria, VA: Teachers of English to Speakers of Other Languages.

TESOL. (1997). *ESL Standards for Pre-K–12 Students.* Alexandria, VA: Author. (Available online at http://www.tesol.org/.)

TESOL. (2001). *Scenarios for ESL standards-based assessment.* Alexandria, VA: Author.

For each standard, a classroom vignette is provided to illustrate how teaching and assessing the standard might look in "real life." The result is a teacher-friendly document that is firmly based in second language acquisition theory and clearly tied to classroom practice and student learning. The TESOL standards are very helpful for English Language Development alongside the other content standards (e.g., math, science, social studies) that you are asked to use in your school district. Next we show how you can plan your standards-based curriculum in such a way that it meets the language, content, and social/affective needs of your English learners through "Sheltered Instruction."

SHELTERED INSTRUCTION OR SPECIALLY DESIGNED ACADEMIC INSTRUCTION IN ENGLISH (SDAIE)

Content instruction, whether it relates to a piece of literature, a science experiment, or the study of ancient civilizations, can provide not only academic learning but language and literacy learning opportunities for English learners (Brinton, Snow, & Wesche, 1993). However, such instruction must be specially tailored so that students will *understand* your instruction and be able to *participate* in learning activities. Over the last two decades, educators have developed strategies to foster second language development and academic learning by using the second language for instruction in special ways to make it comprehensible to second language learners. The result was called **sheltered instruction** (Northcutt & Watson, 1986; Schifini, 1985), a term that some educators are replacing with **Specially Designed Academic Instruction in English** or **(SDAIE)** (California State Department of Education, 1994). Like sheltered instruction, SDAIE highlights *grade appropriate, cognitively demanding core curriculum* for English learners who have achieved an intermediate or advanced level of English language proficiency. For the purposes of this book, we do not draw a distinction between the two terms. Rather, we refer to them synonymously as sheltered instruction or SDAIE, defining and discussing exactly what we mean. The strategies we describe for English learner instruction can be applied for English language, literacy, and content development in bilingual or English-only instructional settings.

Planning and Organizing Sheltered Instruction or SDAIE

Sheltered instruction or SDAIE provides (1) access to the core curriculum, (2) English language development, and (3) opportunities for social integration into your multicultural classroom community. When you organize your content teaching using English in ways that make it understandable to your English learners, you provide comprehensible input for language acquisition and content learning. In sheltered instruction you modify your language: You make your instructional talk more understandable by speaking clearly, repeating key points, defining essential vocabulary in context, and pairing your talk with nonverbal communication cues such as pictures, graphs, objects, and gestures.

When you combine comprehensible input with social interaction opportunities in which English learners process information verbally and nonverbally, you promote deeper understanding and retention of the material. When students "represent" the information, orally or in writing, you foster second language production skills, or output, and further reinforce comprehension and learning. Well-designed learning activities thus offer excellent language and literacy development opportunities simultaneously with effective content learning. To the extent that you establish positive relationships to form a community of learners, you also promote social development and self-esteem among your students (Gibbs, 1994). Figure 3.3 summarizes the basic elements for planning and implementing English learner instruction: goals and objectives, flexible grouping, instructional features, and multidimensional assessment. These elements are not as discrete as they appear, but rather overlap and influence each other.

When planning English learner instruction, you need to include content, language, and social/affective objectives. Using your district's **content area standards** as a guide, you begin by establishing **content objectives,** often within the larger framework of a unifying theme. These objectives must be cognitively demanding, grade appropriate, and not watered down. In order for your students to learn such material, you will need *to build in multiple opportunities for your English learners to understand and process the material,* including individual and small-group activities. Because of the time it can take to understand cognitively demanding, grade-appropriate material in a non-native language, you may need

to adjust the amount of material you cover. To do so, you must carefully review and evaluate your curriculum to select those aspects that are essential and that will best prepare your English learners for continued academic development and success. In adjusting the amount of material you cover, you *adjust the cognitive load, but not the cognitive level or grade-appropriateness of the content* (Meyer, 2006).

As you decide on individual and group activities that will facilitate content learning, you need to review and analyze them carefully in terms of the amount and kind of English needed for students to understand and participate. In your analysis, you need to *identify both language learning opportunities*

FIGURE 3.3 **Sheltered Instruction (SDAIE)**

and language demands inherent in your lesson sequences. With your analysis in mind, you next establish **language objectives,** taking into consideration the functional English language abilities of each student in relation to your planned activities. You may refer to the TESOL standards to help you decide on language objectives. If your state or school district has its own English language development standards, you may use them to guide your planning. For students who are beginners, for example, your objectives may focus on comprehension rather than production. If the lesson requires specific vocabulary and grammatical structures, such as the past tense, these may become the basis of your lesson's English language objectives. You need only a few language objectives, aspects that you will focus on and assess. Because grammatical development takes place over time, you might specify grammatical objectives in terms of exposure or practice on particular structures. Your language objectives may focus on the use of oral language, reading, and/or writing.

In addition to creating language objectives, you need to plan **language-related lesson modifications,** including how you will modify your instructional delivery to support English learners' comprehension. Comprehension can be supported, first, by planning ways to accompany your instructional talk with visuals, direct experience, and other nonverbal means to convey lesson content. Second, you need to plan verbal means to get your point across, including how you will phrase your talk, what vocabulary you will use, and how to rephrase information and define new words in context if needed. This detailed attention to your own language use may be difficult at first. With practice, however, it will become a natural part of your instructional planning process.

Another language-related lesson modification that you must plan for is student participation, based on individual English language abilities. When you analyze the language demands of your learning activities, you need to build in ways for novice English language learners to participate. For example, a newcomer may not yet speak much of the language but will be able to draw or carry out important nonverbal aspects of a group project. Language-related lesson modifications thus require your attention to each student's functional English abilities with corresponding planning for everyone's inclusion and active participation to promote language acquisition and content-area learning.

Finally, you need to examine your individual, whole-class, and small-group activities to identify social interaction opportunities that serve as the basis for your **social/affective objectives.** Social/affective objectives concern interpersonal relationships, empathy, and self-esteem. For example, such objectives might refer to students working cooperatively to carry out a project, listening and responding sensitively to each other's responses to a piece of literature, and accepting opinions divergent from their own while maintaining their own point of view. Social/affective objectives will reflect what you value in student behavior. Your values will, of course, reflect your particular cultural point of view, and that is fine. In reality, you create your own classroom culture, which will be somewhat different from anyone's home culture, including your own. It is important to be conscious of what

INTERNET RESOURCES: The site of the TESOL organization (Teachers of English to Speakers of Other Languages) is invaluable to educators: http://www.tesol.org/. We suggest you find the Pre-K–12 Standards in the site and develop a mini-lesson based on a Standard that interests you. With the lesson you develop, discuss specific objectives based on the Standard and discuss how you will assess and determine the lesson's success. Also, see our companion website: www.ablongman.com/peregoy4e.

you value so that you can *explicitly state, and discuss as needed, the social/affective behaviors you wish students to develop and display.*

Because social interaction is conducive to both language acquisition and subject matter learning, **classroom organization** for English learners provides frequent opportunities for students to work together in pairs or groups. When you organize groups, it is important to vary group membership according to your particular academic, language, and social/affective objectives. Heterogeneous groups are usually preferable for language, social, and academic development. At times, however, you may call together a small group of students who need specific instruction on a particular skill or topic, usually on a short-term basis. However, be careful to *avoid inflexible, long-term ability grouping,* which has been shown to have negative effects on student learning and self-esteem (Eder, 1982).

In order to ensure both lesson comprehension and learning, you need to support instruction by selecting from a repertoire of teaching/learning strategies. We provide you with specific strategies in Chapters 4 through 9. In this chapter, however, we discuss general approaches that are recommended for English learners: theme-based instruction to increase the meaningfulness of lessons over time; language-related instructional modifications to ensure lesson comprehension and student participation; cooperative group work; and scaffolding to facilitate successful participation at a challenging level. Finally, we discuss English learner assessment, including assessment techniques designed to highlight student strengths in relation to your instructional goals, including portfolios and performance-based assessment.

Sheltered Instruction or SDAIE: A Science Example

Let's look at an example of a science lesson on owls from Ms. Bloom's fourth grade, a mixed group of native and non-native English speakers. After reading the example, look carefully at the Sheltered Instruction (SDAIE) checklist in Figure 3.4, adapted from Schifini (1985), the Los Angeles County Office of Education (n.d.), and the California Code of Regulations (Commission on Teacher Credentialing, 1995), to identify the techniques used by the teacher.

Ms. Bloom greeted her fourth-graders, who stood lined up at the door after mid-morning recess. She put her finger to her lips and quietly announced that

1. **The teacher organizes instruction around grade-appropriate content, often theme based (e.g., literature, math, science, integrated themes, social studies).**
   a. Instruction provides "access to the core curriculum"
   b. Content is academically demanding
   c. Language objectives are established according to students' English language proficiency in relation to language demands of lesson
   d. Language and content learning are integrated
   e. Content is presented from multicultural perspectives
2. **The teacher designs appropriate learning sequences.**
   a. Assesses and builds upon students' interests and prior knowledge, including cultural knowledge
   b. Explains purpose of activity
   c. Helps students develop learning strategies for reading, writing, thinking, problem solving
   d. Provides multiple opportunities for students to process information verbally and nonverbally (draw, dramatize, discuss, review, question, rehearse, read, write about)
3. **The teacher modifies language used during instruction.**
   a. May use slightly slower speech rate
   b. Speaks clearly, repeating if needed
   c. Defines new words in meaningful context
   d. Paraphrases in simple terms when using more sophisticated forms of expression
   e. Limits use of idiomatic speech
4. **The teacher supports verbal explanations with nonverbal cues.**
   a. Gestures, facial expressions, action to dramatize meaning
   b. Props, concrete materials
   c. Graphs, pictures, visuals, maps
   d. Films, videotapes, overhead projector, bulletin board displays
5. **The teacher plans ways to ensure participation of all students, keeping in mind English proficiency of each student.**
   a. Monitors lesson comprehension and clarifies concepts as needed
   b. Reviews main ideas and key vocabulary
   c. Plans for students to actively participate in learning activities verbally and nonverbally according to functional English abilities
   d. Provides opportunities for students to contribute based on their modalities of strength: visual, auditory, kinesthetic, oral, written, pictorial
6. **The teacher provides a variety of flexible grouping formats to provide opportunities for social, linguistic, and academic development.**
   a. Heterogeneous groups
   b. Pair work
   c. Short-term skill groups
   d. Teacher-student conferencing
7. **The teacher provides a variety of assessment methods that permit students to display learning through their modalities of strength (e.g., oral, written, visual, kinesthetic, auditory, pictorial).**
   a. Performance-based assessment
   b. Portfolio assessment
   c. Learner self-assessment
   d. If used, standardized tests are modified to accommodate English learners (e.g., extra time to complete)

FIGURE 3.4   Effective English Learner Instruction Checklist

today was the special day they had been waiting for. Then she asked them to tiptoe to their seats at their cooperative group tables. They took their seats, but not too quietly, because their curiosity was piqued by what they found at the center of each table: a small oval object wrapped in aluminum foil, a slender, five-inch probing instrument, and a graphing sheet depicting what turned out to be different kinds of rodent bones. Ms. Bloom waited for all to be seated and quiet. Then she proceeded to give her instructions:

"Yesterday we visited the Natural History Museum and we saw a diorama of the life cycle of owls. Who remembers what Table Three wanted to know more about after visiting the museum? (Students at Table Three answer: 'We wanted to know more about what owls eat.') OK, so I promised you I would give you a chance to investigate, or find out for yourselves. At your table, you have something wrapped in foil. (Ms. Bloom holds up an example.) This is called an owl pellet, an owl pellet. After an owl finishes eating, it regurgitates the pellet, or throws it up out of its mouth. (Teacher dramatizes with a hand gesture.) After everyone understands what to do, I want you to take the pellet apart, examine it carefully, and together decide what information you can figure out about what owls eat. I want you to look, to talk together, and to write down your ideas. Then each group will share back with the whole class. Take a look at the instruction card at your table and raise your hand when you are sure you know what to do."

Students went ahead, and with some assistance from the teacher, they got started. Because the groups included more advanced and less advanced English speakers, they were able to help each other understand what to do. After sharing back what they found, each group graphed the kinds of bones they found and then discussed the original question further in light of their findings.

Even in this short example, you probably have noticed how Ms. Bloom made use of many techniques to facilitate English learner comprehension, participation, and learning, including the following: (1) organization of instruction around cognitively demanding content, in this case, science; (2) explanation of the lesson's purpose, with attention to understanding what was to be done; (3) building background for lesson content by visiting a museum; (4) careful use of instructional language, including definition and repetition of key words like *owl pellet* in context, developing meaning through direct experience with the actual object; (5) acting out or paraphrasing the meaning of words like *regurgitated*; (6) use of direct experience when examining the owl pellets; and (7) opportunities for students to help each other through cooperative group work. Perhaps you have found that you already include many of these sheltering techniques in your teaching. If so, keep up the good work.

As second language acquisition progresses, comprehensible input may be oral or written, but in either case it must be accompanied by sufficient nonverbal cues to make it understandable despite learner limitations in second language proficiency. In subsequent chapters, we provide strategies for using reading and writing in ways that make it comprehensible to students with limited English proficiency.

Sheltered Instruction or SDAIE: A Literature Example

Last week we were in Roberto Heredia's kindergarten classroom of beginning and intermediate English language learners. Roberto was reading the predictable book *The Very Hungry Caterpillar* (Carle, 1986). You may remember this simple pattern story about the little caterpillar who eats through page after page of luscious fruits and fattening foods until he turns into a chrysalis and then emerges as a beautiful butterfly.

Roberto features the story by posting a picture of a caterpillar next to the large class calendar. Next to the caterpillar, you see labeled pictures of the caterpillar's food as depicted in the story: one apple, two pears, three plums, four strawberries, five oranges, and the many rich foods that the caterpillar surfeited himself with that Saturday. Roberto also had paper cutouts on popsicle sticks of the caterpillar and all of the different foods he ate.

After the calendar routine focusing on the days of the week, Roberto read the story from the book. When the children asked to hear it again, he reread the story using the popsicle stick props of the caterpillar and foods. As Roberto read the first sentence, "On Monday the very hungry caterpillar ate one apple," the children chimed in eagerly: "But he was still hungry." As he read "Monday," he pointed to the word *Monday* on the calendar; when he read "hungry caterpillar," he waved the caterpillar cutout; and when he read what the caterpillar ate, he mimicked the caterpillar eating the paper cutout of the apple. The children begged for another reading, so Roberto read it one more time, holding up the caterpillar and food cutouts while the children chimed in.

The next day Roberto read the story using sentence strips in a pocket chart, pointing to each word as he did so. By this time, the children were completely familiar with the story and its predictable pattern. Roberto now prepared the children to write their own story using a caterpillar or one of the other animals in the wall dictionary and following the pattern in the original story. Children worked in groups to write their first story together, which they published in a booklet made by folding a piece of paper in a special way demonstrated previously. When the groups finished their books, they read them aloud to the class. A part of one group's story, "The Very Hungry Dinosaur," begins as follows:

On Monday, the very hungry dinosaur ate a green horse.

On Tuesday, the very hungry dinosaur ate two red cars.

On Wednesday, the very hungry dinosaur ate three brown houses.

On Thursday, the very hungry dinosaur ate four purple elephants.

Finally, because the children enjoyed the stories so much, Roberto had the children make the books into big books to be kept in the classroom library. On the next day, children made small individual stories, which they took home to read to their parents. Roberto's goal was to allow each of the beginning students to participate in English at his or her own level in an enjoyable manner with no pressures to perform. However, he found that almost all of the students, both beginners and intermediates, already saw themselves as successful English speakers, readers, and writers through the lesson.

Sheltered Instruction or SDAIE: A Secondary Social Science Example

Ed Broach, a social studies teacher in an inner-city high school, has been providing appropriate instruction for first and second language learners even before the ideas of sheltered instruction or SDAIE existed. An excellent teacher, he always made sure his students were, in his words, "getting it." How did he do this and how did the concept of sheltered instruction improve his teaching?

One of the units in Ed's core curriculum requires students to understand and explain how a bill in Congress becomes a law. Ed starts with a brief overview of the purpose for the unit. He then asks students to consider the word *law* giving them a few minutes to share with a partner any experiences they've had with laws in this country or elsewhere. He then creates a cluster on the chalkboard that categorizes aspects of the laws that students have experienced. In the process, Ed engages students in a discussion of the need for good, fair laws. Ed explains that they should keep this discussion in mind because they are going to have a chance in class to create a new law or change an old one, following procedures used by the United States Congress.

Next Ed provides each student with a list of important vocabulary words for the unit, such as *legislature, Congress, House of Representatives, Senate, bill*. Then, using an overhead projector, he shows students pictures of Congress and explains a flowchart that illustrates how an idea becomes a bill and how a bill becomes law. As he does so, he emphasizes terms on the vocabulary list. Next, he has students work in groups to check their levels of knowledge and understanding of these terms. With each word students discuss whether they recognize the word, whether they can use it in a sentence, and whether they can define the word and explain the term to others. Ed uses this information to determine additional concept and vocabulary development that might be needed. With this preparation, students are ready for a short film on the topic, which furthers student learning. Ed continues to check for student comprehension during and after the film. Next he sets up a mini-congress. Students work as congressional committee members to write up a bill and take it through all the steps required to enact it as a law. For example, one group decided to pass a law to change school disciplinary procedures. During group work, Ed circulates the classroom, making notes as he checks for student involvement and understanding. After the simulation game, Ed reviews and clarifies essential concepts by summarizing what students have just done as lawmakers.

Students are now ready to read a chapter in the textbook on the legislative process. Ed lets students know that the purpose of the reading is to strengthen their understanding of how a bill becomes a law. He is always careful to make sure students know what they must learn from their reading. If he thinks students will find the text difficult, he sometimes provides a study guide. After the reading assignment, Ed projects the original flowchart on the screen and asks students questions on each stage of the legislative process. Finally, he evaluates student learning in a variety of ways to discover what they know. First, he meets with students individually to review the portfolio they have kept throughout the unit. Students discuss what they know, and Ed clarifies concepts they may not have understood fully. He also checks each student's ability to monitor their own understanding, that is, their metacognition, by asking them what strategies they use when they don't understand a word or concept. Finally, he gives them a short test consisting of multiple-choice and essay questions.

Let's look at how Ed has modified his teaching to make it more effective for English learners. Originally he assigned the reading first and did the simulation game last, followed by the multiple-choice test with essay questions. Now he does several things differently: First, he spends more time *before* students read the text to set the purpose for the unit, key into their prior experiences and knowledge of the topic, and provide an overview of concepts and vocabulary using visual aids. Second, he has become more conscious of modifying according to student needs the pace and complexity of his own instructional talk. Third, he checks carefully for student understanding at every step. Fourth, he watches to be sure that groups are functioning smoothly and that everyone has a chance to participate. Fifth, he assesses student learning in a variety of ways: through checklists while students are in groups and through individual portfolio conferences, as well as by more traditional means. These modifications have worked well. In fact, Ed recently told us that he has to make his tests a little tougher these days because students were all passing his old ones so easily. Through sheltered instruction, Ed has taken excellence to yet a higher level, improving learning opportunities for all his students.

ROUP WORK

An important element of sheltered instruction or SDAIE is group work. When you provide opportunities for English learners to interact with their English-speaking peers, receptive and productive **language learning opportunities** abound (Wong Fillmore, 1982). Imagine, for example, a small group of students working together to create a mural or an art project. Language will be used naturally to accomplish the task at hand. In addition, the language that is used will be **context-embedded** (Cummins, 1981), or directly related to concrete objects in a here-and-now situation, in which the mural, the paints, the children themselves, and their actions convey as much meaning as the words themselves. As a result, your students' speech will be comprehensible and, therefore, usable as input for language acquisition. Moreover, if words are used that are not understood, collaborative group work permits learners to ask for repetition and clarification if needed. Thus, learners themselves have some control over fine-tuning the input made available in carrying out the collaborative project. English learners are also challenged to speak during group work, thereby providing excellent practice in articulating their ideas in English. Collaborative group work therefore provides opportunities for both social and academic language development, with proficient English-speaking peers providing good models for English learners. For these reasons, collaborative projects generate particularly rich language learning contexts, especially when groups include advanced or native English speakers. Of course, the teacher continues to be an important language model and source of input as well. Table 3.1 depicts several different kinds of collaborative groups you

TABLE 3.1 A Few Types of Collaborative Groups

Type	Procedure	Purpose
Buddy system	Pair students; one more capable is paired with a student less proficient in English. The buddy helps the student in and out of the class until the second language learner becomes proficient and knowledgeable about class and school routines.	Helps the new second language learner become a member of the classroom society. Helps the student become comfortable in the school.
Writing response groups	Students share their writing with one another, concentrate on what is good in the papers, and help one another improve their writing. The teacher begins by modeling good response partners and giving students specific strategies for improving their papers.	Writing response groups have several purposes: making students independent; helping students improve their writing; and giving students an audience for their writing and immediate response to their writing.
Literature response groups	Teacher first models response to literature, emphasizing the variety of acceptable responses. Students learn to value individual responses and support responses with what they have read. Students focus on individual feelings first and later on structure and form of literature.	To help students use their own background knowledge to respond to literature. To value students' individual responses and to help them become independent readers of literature.
Cooperative groups	Students are given specific roles and responsibilities for group work. Students become responsible for the success of one another and they teach and learn from one another, creating success for all members of the group.	Build individual and group responsibility for learning. Build success for all members of the group. Develop creative, active learners.

87

may want to try in your class. Writing and literature response groups are described in detail in Chapters 6 and 7, and cooperative groups are discussed in the next section of this chapter.

Organizing Group Work

There are many ways to organize group work to suit the purpose at hand; some are informal and student centered, whereas others are more structured and require students to learn the cooperative processes before academic work can actually begin. For the purposes of language acquisition, the specific structure of collaborative groups is less important than the quality of the opportunities they provide for interaction. To organize informal group work, for example, you might provide activity centers as a free choice in the afternoon, with three to six students permitted at each center. By offering games, manipulatives, and problem-solving activities at each center, you encourage informal collaboration among students. In addition, you might create specific tasks for small groups to work on together. For example, to introduce a unit on animals, you might divide the class into groups of three or four students and provide each group with a set of photographs of different animals. One task would be to categorize the photos and then explain and justify the criteria for their groupings. The task is rich in natural opportunities for the use of academic language related to higher-level thinking such as comparing, contrasting, categorizing, explaining, and justifying. Furthermore, because students carry out the task in small groups, everyone gets a chance to contribute in a low-risk, low-anxiety atmosphere. The relaxed atmosphere, or **low-anxiety environment,** is considered conducive to language acquisition (Krashen, 1981a; Dulay et al., 1982).

To the extent that the target language, English, is used during group work, students practice their new language and gain context-embedded input for further acquisition. In some situations, you may explicitly encourage the use of English for group activities. For example, if most students in the class speak the same native language as well as varying levels of English, students may tend to use the home language instead of English. If so, you may choose to encourage English explicitly as the designated language for activity centers. In multilingual classrooms, English becomes the one language common to all students, the *lingua franca,* and students consequently choose it as a matter of course. The ideal learning situation occurs when the class includes advanced and native English speakers with whom newcomers may interact during group work. However, research suggests that group interaction may promote second language acquisition even when all participants are non-native English speakers (Varonis & Gass, 1985).

Cooperative Learning Methods

In addition to informal group collaboration, a great deal of work has been carried out on more structured cooperative learning methods (Cohen, 1986; Dishon

This group of girls worked together cooperatively to prepare their oral presentation to the class.

& O'Leary, 1984; Johnson, Johnson, & Holubec, 1986; Kagan, 1986). Cooperative learning may be defined as an instructional organization strategy in which students work collaboratively in small groups to achieve academic and social learning goals. In cooperative learning, you establish **heterogeneous groups.** That is, members are either randomly assigned, or else you set up membership to ensure that each group includes a variety of students in terms of gender, ethnicity, language proficiency, and academic achievement (Cohen, 1986). You may also balance groups in terms of personality characteristics: shy/outgoing, quiet/talkative, and so forth. In addition to heterogeneous grouping, procedural roles are assigned to students in each group, such as recorder, observer, encourager, or reporter. These roles are rotated so that all group members have a chance to experience them. In this way, leadership and other roles are distributed among all students, rather than falling on certain ones all the time.

In addition to heterogeneous grouping and role distribution, cooperative learning procedures are set up to build **positive interdependence** among group members. That is, students come to share and support each other's learning in socially appropriate ways. This occurs because members of a cooperative group succeed only if every member succeeds. Thus, in order to be successful, all students must care about the work of all the other group members. To build positive interdependence, assignments are established that require group members to cooperate smoothly. For example, you may assign a group project with each group member responsible for one part. In this way, the final goal cannot be achieved without each member contributing. Furthermore, the quality of the final project depends on the quality of each member's contribution. Thus, individuals are accountable for their own learning as well as that of the group, and they develop autonomy in their group learning.

Phases of Cooperative Group Development

You may find that many of your students have had little or no experience in group interactions. Some researchers have found that math teachers rarely use group work, and that even social science teachers use group work sparingly (Ratekin et al., 1985). Additionally, some of your students may come from cultures that don't value group work as a vehicle for academic learning. Therefore, we recommend that you gradually implement group work in your classroom. One of the first steps you can try is to place students in partnerships in which they can work together early in the year on specific tasks such as keeping buddy journals or helping with certain cleanup duties. You may next want to place students in groups of three as your students become comfortable with group work. Finally, you may create cooperative/collaborative groups of four or five students.

Even this gradual and careful grouping will not guarantee effective group work. You will need to work with your students carefully and help them evaluate their own group success (Cohen, 1986; Cohen, 1994). Some teachers have students evaluate their group performance using checklists addressing questions such as (1) Did we stay on task? (2) Were we courteous and respectful to one another even when we didn't agree? (3) How can we be more successful next time? Such checklists help students develop an awareness of their group dynamics, increasing their chances for success.

Whether homogeneous or heterogeneous in membership, groups will go through phases on their way to working autonomously. In the first phase, let's call it the **get-along phase,** you may find students need a lot of help. They may not know how to get along or how to resolve conflicts. They need to know that they are responsible for the behavior of others in the group as well as themselves (Cohen, 1986). You will need to work closely with them to help them move to the next phase, **developing relationships,** in which students determine one another's strengths and decide who is best suited for various aspects of group work. During this phase you may need to help groups that are dominated by one or two individuals, especially if the groups include native and non-native English speakers. We recommend that you have a multiplicity of ways students can display their knowledge: through reading and writing, and also through drawing and completing scientific experiments. When groups are asked to perform a variety of tasks, it's more likely that all students in a group will be involved. Once students have developed a successful pattern of relationships, they can move to the phase of **production,** in which they begin to become efficient group workers who can bring their task to completion. Sometimes groups will reach a final phase of **autonomy**, in which they hardly need any help from the teacher, develop many of their own topics, and seem to move from one task to another without any help. Whatever phase your students are in, you will need to work with them closely to help them advance to more productive phases of group work, always working toward group autonomy. To do this you may have to resolve conflicts and clarify directions groups are taking in their work. Finally, help students self-monitor by using checklists or by having successful groups role play how they work together. Successful group work is accompanied by a teacher who gives clear directions and works with students to help them grow as group members (Cohen, 1986; 1994).

Jigsaw

In one cooperative technique, called jigsaw (Aaronson, 1978), one segment of a learning task is assigned to each group member, who then works to become an "expert" in that area. After researching their special areas, the experts from each group meet to compare notes and extend their learning. Finally, the original groups meet again, and the experts report back to their original groups. For example, Mary Ann Smith created "base groups" consisting of three students each to help her students learn about spiders. She then assigned each member in the base group different pages from a selection on spiders. One student in each base group was responsible for pages 1 to 3, another for pages 4 to 6, and the third student was responsible for the final three pages. When students had read the assigned pages, Mary Ann met with the specialists on each section. These students became "experts" on the information they read, discussing and sharing

91

their understanding of the reading with their expert peers and planning how they would teach the information to members in their base groups. All experts returned to their base groups and shared their special expertise with their peers. In this way, all group members were availed of the whole spectrum of information on spiders. In jigsaw processes such as this, students may then apply their knowledge to a group task or to an individual task, assuring individual accountability for all information.

A final aspect of the jigsaw process is the development of group autonomy: Groups become responsible for their own learning and smooth functioning. Thus, the teacher needs to step back at times to let students solve their own procedural and conceptual conflicts. In this way, students use their critical thinking abilities and social skills to accomplish the task at hand.

To summarize our discussion thus far, we have seen that English language learners, by virtue of their immersion in a new language and culture, have the benefit of natural exposure to the new language both in and out of school. In addition, they have real and immediate life needs that motivate them to learn. At the same time, they must reach high levels of proficiency in order to succeed. In order to learn their new language, they need comprehensible input and opportunities to use the new language in day-to-day social interactions. Teachers can provide high-quality comprehensible input for both social and academic language use in the classroom by using sheltering techniques and by creating opportunities for collaborative group work in which English will be used with peers. Another excellent strategy to use with English language learners is thematic instruction within an integrated language teaching model. The next section explains why and how.

THEMATIC INSTRUCTION

For many years, teachers have used **themes** or **topics** as focal points for organizing curriculum content (Enright & McCloskey, 1988; Pappas, Kiefer, & Levstik, 1990). One teacher we know, Reina Saucedo, uses corn as the central topic for a unit that integrates math, social studies, science, and language arts. She begins the unit with a feast of quesadillas, which are toasted corn tortillas filled with melted cheese. Next comes a discussion about corn as the basic ingredient for tortillas. From there, the class embarks on a study of corn, a native American plant originally cultivated by indigenous peoples in North, Central, and South America. Reina's students read, illustrate, and dramatize corn legends; sprout corn seeds and record their growth; and create a world map, citing locations where corn is grown and eaten today. Some students choose to research how corn is prepared in different countries, creating an illustrated international corn cookbook. The class learns about the nutritive value of corn, finding out, for example, that it combines with beans to form a complete protein. They also learn how to dye corn kernels and string them into necklaces to wear or to give as gifts. As a culminating activity they create a menu based on corn and prepare a nutritionally balanced meal for the class.

Though more prevalent in the primary grades, thematic instruction lends itself to virtually any content and any grade level. For example, an extensive cooperative theme project, "Building Toothpick Bridges" (Pollard, 1985), would be appropriate for upper-elementary grades through high school. In this integrated science-math-building project, students work in groups of six, forming "construction companies," to design and build a bridge out of toothpicks. The unit begins with readings on the history of bridge development, analysis of bridge designs, and information about how bridges work. Students may visit local bridges to examine their architecture and consider how they are structured to bear weight and constant use. Each construction company member assumes a role, selecting from project director, architect, carpenter, transportation chief, and accountant. The goal is to design and build the strongest bridge possible, staying within the company's projected budget. In the planning stage, companies design their bridges, estimating the quantity and cost of necessary materials. On certain days, the "warehouse" is open for purchase of materials, paid for by check. At the end of the project, the strength of the bridges is tested to the breaking point, and the strongest bridge wins a prize. The bridge breaking is an exciting media event, described by students in an article for the local newspaper. This collaborative project is a highly involving, fun project that integrates the use of oral and written language with a wide variety of science and math concepts. The theme-based collaborative project serves many purposes: to teach science and math concepts and applications, promote the use of library resources, provide students with a chance to work together cooperatively, and help them become better readers and writers as they negotiate meanings for themselves and others. Finally, the purposes in a unit such as this one are met seamlessly as the students engage in activities that are involving and meaningful.

In summary, we recommend the use of thematic instruction for English language learners for several reasons. First, thematic instruction creates a meaningful conceptual framework within which students are invited to use both oral and written language for learning content. The meaningful context established by the theme supports the comprehensibility of instruction, thereby increasing both content learning and second language acquisition. In addition, theme-based collaborative projects create student interest, motivation, involvement, and purpose. Moreover, as students work together on their projects, they naturally use both oral and written language to question, inform, problem-solve, negotiate, and interact with their peers. Through such engagement, both social and academic language development is challenged and promoted. But keep in mind that most students, whether English learners or native English speakers, need time and assistance to be integrated into project-oriented, collaborative classrooms. Nevertheless, when combined with opportunities for collaboration, thematic instruction creates optimal content, language, and literacy learning opportunities for both native and non-native English speakers.

Distinguishing Theme Units from Theme Cycles

In current discussions on thematic instruction, a distinction has been made between traditional thematic units and theme cycles (Altwerger & Flores, 1991; Harste, 1988). The crux of the difference between the two lies with the degree of student input and choice at every step in the learning process—topic choice, selection of materials and resources, organization of projects, grouping, and manner of presenting final products of learning, such as plays, reports, or murals. Traditionally, the teacher has been responsible for all these decisions. In the theme cycle, the teacher and students negotiate these choices together. When students have input and choice in the direction of their own learning, they become motivated to pursue ideas and information. They also become active questioners and learners. Furthermore, they begin to see themselves as capable of initiating and carrying out their own learning. Finally, they evaluate their own learning based on the extent to which they are satisfied with the answers they have found. For a more complete example of a classroom at work during a theme cycle see Chapter 8.

Even though clear distinctions can be drawn between theme units and theme cycles, we believe that, in practice, a continuum exists, depending on the degree to which students are free to choose and negotiate their own learning with the teacher. For that reason, we use the term *thematic instruction* to subsume both units and cycles. We define thematic instruction as a learning sequence organized around a theme or a topic offering students opportunities to use oral language, reading, writing, and critical thinking for learning and sharing ideas. The criteria for thematic instruction that follow reflect our own preference for student choice in the learning process. At the same time, we view the teacher as ultimately responsible for the quality of learning opportunities available in the classroom. Thus, the teacher does not abrogate this responsibility but uses careful judgment, reserving the right to have the final say on how the learning sequence will be implemented.

Organizing Thematic Instruction

We offer six criteria for organizing thematic instruction to promote language development, critical thinking, independence, and interpersonal collaboration for English language learners. Our criteria represent basic learning principles that we have adapted from Enright and McCloskey (1988).

Meaning and Purpose. The content of the thematic unit/theme cycle is interesting and relevant to the students. One way to ensure interest and relevance is to provide opportunities for the students themselves to guide the choice of the theme and the activities and projects undertaken during the course of study. As students make choices, they invest themselves in their own learning, thereby creating self-direction and purpose.

Building on Prior Experience. The thematic unit/theme cycle builds on students' prior experiences—both in-class experiences, such as previous instruction, and prior knowledge and experience students bring from home. In this way, students' varied cultural experiences can be incorporated into their schoolwork, providing understanding of themselves and others.

Integrated Opportunities to Use Oral and Written Language for Learning Purposes. The teacher is conscious of creating opportunities for oral language and literacy to be used for learning purposes established in concert with students. The teacher broadens the students' experiences with different forms and functions of print suited to student interests and goals.

Scaffolding for Support. Thematic instruction is provided in a classroom atmosphere that supports students' efforts and values their accomplishments. One way to support students is to use sheltering techniques and various kinds of scaffolds, discussed fully further on, to assist students in participating successfully, even if their English language/literacy proficiency is limited. Another way is to give students varied opportunities to display and share their learning.

Collaboration. Students are given many opportunities to work together on theme-related projects and activities. Collaboration in pairs and small groups provides students with opportunities to process complex information actively in a low-risk, low-anxiety situation. In this way, language and content learning is productive, and positive social relationships can be promoted. At the same time, language and literacy are used purposefully, promoting acquisition of both.

Variety. Variety permeates the learning process—in topics of study, in the ways that learning is shared with others, in the functions of oral and written language used, in roles and responsibilities, and in task difficulty. Variety and flexibility characterize learning groups—pairs, small groups, and the whole class. Thus, interest remains high.

The process of developing thematic instruction is dynamic, ideally involving input from the students themselves at all levels of decision making. The first step is to choose the topic or theme that will serve as the focus of interest. There are many sources for themes and topics, including state and local curriculum guidelines as well as personal interests and curiosities expressed by the students. Not least, your own special interests provide an excellent source of topics and themes, and you are likely to have or know of resources and materials to share with your students. Enthusiasm is contagious, and when you bring your own curiosity and joy for learning into the classroom, you reveal your personal self, thereby deepening your relationship with your students and modeling lifelong learning. Likewise, when you build on your students' interests and curiosities, you can catch their wave of enthusiasm and embark on exciting new learning adventures yourself.

95

Once a theme is chosen, the next step is to brainstorm ideas related to the theme. One way to conduct the brainstorming is to create a cluster or word web on the chalkboard as you and your students generate ideas around the theme. During brainstorming, it is important to accept and write down every idea contributed by your students. Based on the words generated during brainstorming, related ideas can be grouped together, resulting in a map of the major subtopics to be investigated. Under each subtopic, activities and projects are listed together, as shown in the map in Figure 3.5. It is helpful to post the thematic map in the classroom to keep the organization and planning available at a glance.

Another way to generate and organize learning activities and projects around a theme is to write the chosen theme or topic on a large piece of butcher paper and invite students to list "what we know already" and "what we wonder

96

FIGURE 3.5   Trees: An Integrated Thematic Unit

Source: From *Mapping the Writing Journey* (p. 28, Fig. 15), by Marilyn H. Buckley and Owen Boyle, 1981, Berkeley: Bay Area Writing Project. Reprinted with permission of the publisher.

about," as Jamie Green did with her theme cycle on Egypt. Students may then form interest groups around the "wonder topic" of their preference and, together with the teacher, establish a plan to find out more. In this approach, groups conduct research with teacher guidance as needed, each group presenting its findings to the class in some form: oral, written, pictorial/graphic, or dramatic. Students are encouraged to combine at least two or three of the presentational modes so as to "shelter" their presentations for their classmates. For example, an oral presentation to the class might explain a mural. Finally, the butcher paper list is reviewed and revised with a new category: "What We Know Now." This theme cycle (Altwerger & Flores, 1991) may then be repeated by adding "What We Wonder Now," as students pose new questions and choose new areas of investigation. The thematic units and cycles provide students with opportunities for functional and purposeful language use in the classroom, which we discuss in more detail next.

Functional Language and Literacy Uses in Thematic Instruction

From the standpoint of second language learning, one of the teacher's major responsibilities is to make sure a variety of functional language and literacy uses is incorporated into the projects and activities undertaken by the students (Heath & Mangiola, 1991). The following list describes different forms and functions of reading and writing to consider as you expand students' repertoires.

Forms of Print Used in Class	Sample Functions of Print Used in the Classroom
Lists	For organizing and remembering information
Order forms	For purchasing items for classroom activities
Checks	To pay for classroom book orders
Ledgers	To keep account of classroom responsibilities
Labels and captions	To explain pictures on bulletin boards or other displays
Personal journals	To generate ideas on a project, etc.
Buddy journals	To develop or promote a personal relationship
Record-keeping journal	To keep track of a project or experiment
Interactive journal	To converse in writing; to promote a personal friendship
Notes	To take information down so it will be remembered
Personal letters	To share news with a companion or friend
Business letters	To apply for a job; to complain about a product; to recommend a procedure

Narratives	To relate stories to others; to share tales about other persons or to illustrate themes or ideas
Scripts (e.g., reader's theater)	To entertain the class by acting out stories
Essay forms:	
Enumeration	To list information either by numbering or chronologically
Comparison/contrast	To show how two or more things are different and alike
Problem/solution	To discuss a problem and suggest solutions
Cause/effect	To show cause/effect relationships
Thesis/proof	To present an idea and persuade readers of its validity

In addition to exposing students to a variety of literacy forms and functions, you will want to make sure that scaffolding supports, described in a subsequent section, are available to facilitate student participation, even if English language proficiency is limited. Therefore, as the final step in developing a theme cycle, you will want to examine the project and activity plans and consider the students involved in each, using questions such as the following to guide your students' involvement:

1. Which aspects of the project can be carried out by students with minimal English proficiency (e.g., painting, coloring, short answers, use of the student's native language)?
2. Which aspects of the project involve literacy uses that may be supported by literacy scaffolds and/or by peer assistance (e.g., writing a story based on the repeated pattern of a predictable book such as *Brown Bear, Brown Bear, What Do You See?* [Martin, 1967] or *Fortunately* [Charlip, 1997]; writing a letter in cooperative pairs; paired reading)?
3. What special resources might be of help to a particular group (e.g., books, encyclopedias, films, community members, school personnel)?
4. How might this project lead to particular kinds of language and literacy uses (e.g., a letter to a company protesting its use of laboratory animals, the contribution of an article to the school newspaper, oral reading of the poems discovered in researching the theme, the use of a log to record plant growth)?

Creating Variety in Language and Literacy Uses

Your role in generating a variety of oral and written language uses is crucial for optimal language and literacy development through thematic instruction. To support students' successful involvement, you will want to consider the students' performance levels and find ways to stretch them. As you consider how to assist your students with their projects, two questions should be kept in mind: (1) How

98

can I assure successful participation by each student? and (2) How can I encourage each student to perform at his or her best?

We believe that both participation and motivation are promoted by encouraging students to make choices. For example, if your curriculum requires the study of your state's history, you might start with local history by posing the questions: Has our town always been here? What do you suppose it was like here 100 years ago? Your discussion may lead students to other questions, such as: What and who was here? How did people live, work, and learn? How did they dress? What did they use for transportation? What did they do for fun? Students may form interest groups by choosing which questions they want to work on. Further choices may be made as to the books and materials they will use to answer their questions. Perhaps some students will choose to interview longtime local residents. Finally, students may choose the format they wish to use for presenting their findings—publishing a factual book on local history, creating a mural to depict the town as it was 100 years ago, creating a diary that might have been written by a local child 100 years ago, or creating a series of letters that might have been written to a cousin in another state. Your job is to be on hand to listen to students and make suggestions as needed. By offering students choices, you broaden their horizons, while allowing them to invest more fully in their own learning, thus sparking interest and involvement as well.

Active participation is also enhanced when students work in groups to accomplish self-selected tasks. Groups provide support and motivation to get things done. Your English learners may prove more capable than anticipated when allowed to work in a small group. In any case, you will want to move from group to group to observe students' progress and interaction. If necessary, you may suggest ways to involve new English language learners. For example, if a student speaks virtually no English, you might pair him or her up with another student to illustrate the group's book or to copy captions for the illustrations. You need to be observant, intuitive, and imaginative when making such suggestions for newcomers and others with limited English proficiency. Therein lies the art of teaching: knowing when to encourage and when to stand back!

Finally, as students reflect on their new knowledge, they are in a position to evaluate their own learning. Through the process of posing their own questions, researching to find possible answers, and presenting their findings to their classmates, they can see for themselves how much they have learned. At the same time, they may wish to note those areas still open to question, thereby generating questions for their next theme study. The theme cycle thus replicates the knowledge generation process used in formal research.

SCAFFOLDING

Russian psychologist Lev Vygotsky (1896–1934) introduced a useful concept about learning and development when he pointed out that what the learner can do with assistance today, he or she can do alone tomorrow. Teaching, he urged, must aim not at today's but at tomorrow's development, or, as he called it, the **zone of proximal development** (Vygotsky, 1962). Thus, students need to be challenged, but with support and encouragement. With support and assistance, they can exercise their next level of development and, thus, progress in learning and development. The support and assistance that permits this performance has been referred to as **scaffolding.**

We are going to focus on scaffolding as it applies to language and literacy development. Before we proceed, however, we would like to provide our own general definition of scaffolding along with some concrete examples. Scaffolding is a metaphor based on the temporary structures put up around buildings so that construction can take place. In learning and development, students are constructing the ability to carry out complex processes, such as walking, talking, reading, writing, thinking, and understanding the social and physical worlds around them. Scaffolds are temporary supports, provided by more capable people, that permit learners to participate in the complex process before they are able to do so unassisted. Assisted participation offers practice and development of a skill as an integrated whole, rather than drill on smaller aspects of the skill one at a time. Once proficiency is achieved, the scaffold is no longer needed and may be dropped.

For a concrete example, consider a 12-month-old child who is just beginning to walk but still has a tendency to fall flat on her well-padded bottom. Her father offers his hand to help her make it across the room. She succeeds with pride and delight. For a while, she needs the hand-holding support from more capable others to scaffold this complex process of coordinated psychomotor activity. Before long, though, she is able to walk by herself, and the scaffold is no longer needed. If some day she chooses to do more "advanced walking," such as walking on a balance beam, the same hand-holding scaffold may assist her. Thus a similar scaffold may be applied later as more sophisticated versions of the complex process are attempted. In the sections that follow, we examine scaffolding as it has been applied to language and literacy acquisition in native and non-native languages.

Scaffolding: A KEEP Example

One educational program that has applied Vygotsky's ideas and the scaffolding metaphor is the Kamehameha Elementary Education Program (KEEP) in Honolulu, Hawaii. KEEP was established over two decades ago as a research and development center to meet the educational needs of native Hawaiian children descended from the original Polynesian inhabitants of the island chain (Tharp & Gallimore, 1988). These children, ethnic minority group speakers of Hawaiian Creole English, were not achieving well in school, particularly in reading (Au & Jordan, 1981). Through the concerted efforts of a team of psychologists, anthropologists, linguists, and educators, an innovative educational program was established, which became a laboratory and demonstration school.

Two especially interesting innovations were made. First, a communication feature of the children's home culture was incorporated into reading lessons. That is, discussion of stories was carried out through co-narration, or the joint narration of a story by two people. Co-narration, or "talk story," the researchers had found, was a feature of the native Hawaiian storytelling tradition to which the children were accustomed. In their home culture, co-narration of a story not only conveyed information; it also served to reaffirm the relationship between the co-narrators. With this familiar communication style incorporated into reading lessons, children were more inclined to feel at home and participate in lessons. In time, reading achievement scores increased and remained at national-norm levels for over a decade (Tharp & Gallimore, 1988, p. 116).

The second KEEP innovation over the decades has been the implementation of a teaching model based on the Vygotskian notion of assisted performance in the child's zone of proximal development. The teaching model emphasizes the teacher's ability to respond to the child's developmental level and to stretch the child's performance accordingly through modeling, feeding back, instructing, questioning, and other processes (Tharp & Gallimore, 1988). The teacher "scaffolds" the child's development to the next level.

To illustrate the complex nature of scaffolding, as carried out in a KEEP kindergarten, Tharp and Gallimore (1988, pp. 138–146) provide a detailed description of a language-experience activity (LEA) in which the teacher leads a group of six children in making peanut butter and jelly sandwiches. This experience will later serve as the basis of a dictated story, following traditional LEA procedures (Allen, 1976; Stauffer, 1970). The "instructional conversation" between the teacher and children during the sandwich-making creates natural opportunities for the teacher to model, question, and instruct, thereby scaffolding children's linguistic and cognitive performance.

Gathering the children at a small table, the teacher begins with an improvised chant about making peanut butter and jelly sandwiches. Placing the peanut butter and jelly jars on the table with a loaf of sliced bread, she introduces the activity with a statement and a question (Tharp & Gallimore, 1988):

TEACHER: We're gonna make our peanut butter sandwich. What is the first thing I'm going to need? [*Produces a jar of peanut butter, a jar of jelly, and a loaf of sliced bread in a bag.*]

J: Get the bread!
[*Child points to bread; reaches across the table and pats the bag of bread.*]

TEACHER: I need to get a piece of bread. What am I going to do with it? [*Reaches into the bag and retrieves a slice. J. nods approval.*]

J: Put this first . . . and put this second.
[*Touches peanut butter jar; touches jelly jar.*]

TEACHER: Put it . . . [*Hesitates*]

J: Oh, no. Put this first . . . and this second.
[*Touches jelly jar; touches peanut butter jar.*]

R: Get the knife first, no get the knife in and spread it.

JK: Put the jelly on the sandwich, then that on the sandwich.
[*Points to peanut butter.*]

TEACHER: I put the jelly on top of the sandwich?
[*Places jelly jar on top of sandwich.*]

CHILDREN: (chorus) No! No! No!
[*Two stand up; another points; they laugh and smile with surprise and amusement.*]

R: You open it.
[*Takes jelly jar from teacher and removes lid.*]

JK: Then you put it in.

TEACHER: Oh I need to twist the lid off the jar?

CHILDREN: Yes, yes and then you make like that.

R: First you have to do peanut butter . . .

J: No. That!
[*Gestures toward jelly, disagreeing about which ingredient is applied first.*]

R: [*Shakes head in disagreement.*]

TEACHER: I have to spread the peanut butter first? Are you sure?

R: Yeah, cause I tried it, that's that's [the truth] everybody's [looking at it].

TEACHER: How do I spread it? Do I take my finger, stick it in, and rub it all over the bread?

J: No this! You stick that in . . .
[*Picks up knife; makes spreading motion with knife over bread.*]*

At this point, the children get the idea that they are going to have to tell their teacher methodically, sequentially, and step-by-step exactly how to make this sandwich. The instructional conversation continues, with questioning, modeling, and feedback from the teacher. By requiring the children to organize the procedure logically and to provide explicit directions through language, not gesture, she is inviting them to perform in their zone of proximal development both cognitively and linguistically. Making language clear enough to stand on its own without gestures or reference to objects in the environment is a cognitive-academic skill required for school literacy.

The teacher facilitates the children's performance by asking questions that require them to reflect on their prior peanut butter and jelly experiences and then analyze and organize the task into a logical sequence. She then provides feedback on the efficacy of their communication by following their directions literally. When she makes her sandwich-making response obviously wrong, the children rephrase their directions for her with greater specificity. If a child seems to lack the language necessary to make instructions clear, the teacher elaborates the child's

---

*From *Rousing Minds to Life Teaching, Learning and Schooling in Social Context* (pp. 138–139), by Roland Tharp and Ronald Gallimore, 1988, New York: Cambridge University Press. Reprinted with permission of the publisher.

meaning, thereby modeling vocabulary and structure in context. For example, R says, "First you have to do peanut butter," and the teacher replies, "I have to spread the peanut butter first?" Embedded in her request for clarification is the more specific verb spread. A single reply by the teacher thus serves several purposes. Throughout the lesson, these means of assistance are not set up in the form of a drill but emerge naturally in the course of the fun and engaging sandwich-making activity.

What we have described was the oral language interaction phase of a language experience activity. The precision in organization and language that the teacher encouraged during the instructional conversation paved the way for the next step of the activity, in which the children write the recipe for peanut butter sandwiches by dictating it to the teacher. The means of teacher assistance during the instructional conversation were questioning, modeling, and feedback. This phase of the activity guided children's thinking and language toward forms acceptable for schoolwork and academic literacy, an important transition for students whose ways of using language differ from those of the school (Michaels, 1979; Heath, 1983).

Scaffolding in First Language Acquisition Research

Scaffolding techniques similar to those used in the KEEP kindergarten lesson were originally identified by researchers studying first language acquisition (Bruner, 1978; Ninio, 1980; Ninio & Bruner, 1978). Adults, it was observed, sometimes helped young children verbally elaborate on a topic, thereby facilitating communication at a more sophisticated level. For example, a young child may exclaim, "Mommy, kitty!" to which the mother replies, "Yes, kitty wants to play with you, doesn't she?" In her response, the mother provides a scaffold, elaborating on the child's topic and unconsciously modeling linguistic and conversational patterns through natural social interactions with the child.

Language games and routines such as book reading provide another, more complex type of scaffold. In book reading, for example, children become accustomed to a question-answer sequence, "What's that?" "That's a ___." (Ninio & Bruner, 1978). At first, the adult may provide the answer, but through repetition of the routine the child acquires the ability to either fill in the blank or make the entire response. With further repetition, the child may ask the question and let the adult answer. All of these stages provide language practice at a level that stretches somewhat beyond the child's unassisted capability. Reading aloud to children at home was subsequently found to be of such great importance to later reading success (Wells, 1986) that the practice has been widely encouraged, including among ethnic minority communities where the practice was previously less prevalent or nonexistent (Ada, 1988; Edwards, 1989), a topic discussed in depth in Chapter 5.

The importance of the repeated routine in the scaffolding process is paramount. As noted by Snow (1977) in her study of mothers' communication with their infants, "We think of routines as simple and unsophisticated . . . but their simplicity allows for the introduction, into slots created by the routine, of fillers considerably more complex in structure and/or content than could possibly be dealt with elsewhere" (quoted in Cazden, 1983, p. 9). The *routines themselves* scaffold performance at a higher level.

It is important to note that routines provide effective learning scaffolds only to the extent that they are sufficiently familiar and appropriate to students' prior cultural experiences. For example, researchers in the KEEP found that the traditional round-robin oral reading routine went against the social norms of the children's home culture. Using ethnographic information, KEEP educators modified the reading instruction routine, incorporating "talk-story" co-narration from the home culture, as described earlier. The new, culturally consistent reading instruction routine provided an effective scaffold, whereas the traditional routine did not.

Few classroom teachers have the luxury of a research team to inform them of the nuances of their students' home cultures. However, classroom teachers have something that research teams generally do not have—the benefit of a deep, ongoing reciprocal relationship with students over time. Through the special teacher–child relationship and through thoughtful and sensitive trial and error, you will be in a position to judge which scaffolding routines work with your students and which do not. In fact, as you systematically observe your students, as you reflect on what you know about their families, and as you interpret their responses to you and your teaching, you will be expanding your role from teacher to teacher-researcher. Throughout the next chapters of our book we will be giving more specific examples of how you can involve yourself in meaningful research that can add to your knowledge of second language students. Remember that most research has been done by university professors who do not often know the students well; this can limit their understanding. You are in a perfect position to see your own students' development within your classroom context, a context only you can know fully.

Scaffolding Applied to Second Language Acquisition

In our work with children learning a second language in school, we have found that teachers provide a variety of scaffolding routines for second language acquisition (Peregoy, 1991; Peregoy & Boyle, 1999a, 1999b). In one kindergarten, for example, we noticed that the teacher created two overarching scaffolds by offering (1) a stable physical space arrangement and (2) a daily schedule that remained the same throughout the school year. Within the stable physical and temporal routines, content and structure changed, becoming more complex as the year progressed. For example, in the library corner at the beginning of the year, children just looked at pictures in trade books. As the year progressed, however, they began to publish their own books, based on predictable pattern books such as *The Very Hungry Caterpillar* described at the beginning of this chapter. Soon, they were able to read these books aloud to each other at the library corner. The stability of the routines made the kindergarten predictable for children who were just learning a new language, freeing their attention for learning.

104

The predictable room arrangement and schedule helped students know what to expect each day. Rules of behavior also remained constant for different centers and different times of the day (e.g., story time, free choice at learning centers, recess, and lunch). Through the repetition of daily routines, the children came to understand classroom events and rules, even though their second language proficiency was limited. At the same time, as the routines were repeated, the language that accompanied them was also repeated and rapidly learned by the youngsters. In this way, their second language development was supported.

Observing the kindergarten, we noticed that within routine instructional events, the teacher actually embedded a succession of other scaffolds to assist children in performing at a level just a bit beyond their budding language capabilities. During roll call and calendar activities with the whole class seated at the rug, for example, children were encouraged to make a gestural response to indicate whether they would be having hot lunch or cold lunch. If a child had cold lunch, he or she would walk over to the jacket rack and point to his or her lunch box. Gradually, they were able to answer verbally, "Hot lunch" or "Cold lunch," modeling after native speakers in the class and prompted by the teacher's simple question, "Hot lunch or cold lunch?" In addition, from the first day of school, the teacher would repeat the classroom rules. For each rule, she had a corresponding picture to convey the meaning. Thus, for "Speak softly," she had a picture of an index finger over a pair of lips, and for the raise-your-hand rule, she had a picture of a hand waving in the air. These pictures made the language associated with the routines comprehensible, creating daily language learning opportunities within a functional classroom event such as roll call.

In summary, we have described ways in which parents and teachers may scaffold oral language performance in first and second language acquisition. For a toddler, oral language scaffolding permits the child to carry on a simple conversation about a bird or a toy or some other object of interest to a very young child. In the KEEP example about peanut butter sandwiches, the kindergartners are proficient in the kind of conversations with which a toddler would need help. Now they are being required to use language at a higher level, one that requires logical sequencing of information that could be used to instruct someone to create a gourmet sandwich. Their oral recipe is scaffolded by the teacher, who pretends not to know what to do. Furthermore, the oral recipe thus generated became a scaffold for the written product, which could now be dictated by the children. When language development is scaffolded, it must challenge learners to operate in their zone of proximal development, a notion similar to Krashen's idea of $i + 1$. These two examples illustrate different levels of challenge for toddlers and kindergartners.

Scaffolds for First and Second Language Reading and Writing

Although most research has examined scaffolding in relation to oral language acquisition, we have applied the metaphor to literacy acquisition as well, creating criteria for what we call **literacy scaffolds** (Boyle & Peregoy, 1990; Peregoy &

Boyle, 1990b). Literacy scaffolds are reading and writing activities that provide built-in teacher or peer assistance, permitting students to participate fully at a level that would not be possible without the assistance. In other words, literacy scaffolds make it possible for students to work in their zones of proximal development in reading and writing, thereby challenging them to reach their next level in literacy development. Criteria defining literacy scaffolds are as follows:

1. Literacy scaffolds are applied to reading and writing activities aimed at functional, meaningful communication found in whole texts such as stories, poems, reports, or recipes.
2. Literacy scaffolds make use of language and discourse patterns that repeat themselves and are, therefore, predictable.
3. Literacy scaffolds provide a model, offered by the teacher or by peers, for comprehending and producing particular written language patterns.
4. Literacy scaffolds support students in comprehending and producing written language at a level slightly beyond their competence in the absence of the scaffold.
5. Literacy scaffolds are temporary and may be dispensed with when the student is ready to work without them.

Perhaps the clearest example of a literacy scaffold is the interactive dialogue journal, in which student and teacher carry on a written conversation. Dialogue journals have proven useful for English language learners of all ages, from kindergartners to adults (Kreeft, 1984). Typically, the student makes a written entry in his or her journal, perhaps accompanied by an illustration, and the teacher then responds in writing with a comment or question that furthers the conversation. The dialogue journal thus duplicates, in written form, the scaffolding opportunities we saw earlier in the informal instructional conversations between adults and young children at home and at school. Specifically, the student initiates the topic to which the teacher responds. The teacher responds to the meaning of the journal entry, thereby encouraging further elaboration of the topic. In their responses, teachers may model written language patterns by incorporating and expanding upon the students' entry, just as adults sometimes do in conversations with young children. Thus, the dialogue journal affords the teacher regular opportunities for scaffolding through questioning, modeling, and feedback. However, the scaffolding is always embedded in the natural flow of the written conversation between the student and teacher. Thus, the focus remains on interpersonal communication between teacher and child.

Dialogue journals meet the literacy scaffold criteria in the following ways:

1. They are part of a functional communication activity—a conversation with the teacher.
2. They make use of a discourse pattern that repeats itself and is therefore predictable (i.e., a written conversation in which participants alternate turns).
3. They provide modeling of written language patterns by the teacher.

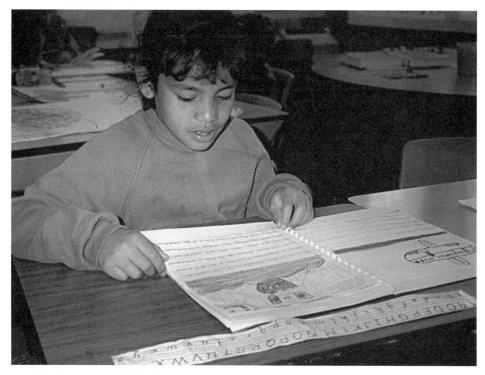

Reading her own published story, this little girl celebrates an achievement that was scaffolded by the process approach to writing.

4. The teacher's questions and encouragement help students comprehend and produce written language beyond what they might accomplish if unassisted.
5. Dialogue journals may be replaced with other forms of writing as students gain fluency, or other forms of journals can be used in addition to dialogue journals.

Other examples of literacy scaffolds include shared reading, patterned writing, mapping, directed listening-thinking activities, readers' theater, and interactive journal writing, described in Chapters 5, 6, and 7. We saw earlier how daily school routines may create a scaffold for language acquisition. Similarly, routines such as process writing and literature study circles create overarching scaffolds within which other scaffolding activities may be embedded to promote reading and writing development. These routines are presented in Chapters 6 and 7.

In summary, scaffolding helps students perform at a level somewhat beyond their unassisted capability. As teachers, we are constantly aiming to assist our students to their next developmental level in oral language and literacy, as well as in other areas of learning and development. In subsequent chapters, we provide many classroom examples to show you how to scaffold your students' oral language, reading, and writing development.

ASSESSMENT OF ENGLISH LEARNERS

Assessment of student learning is always a challenge no matter who your students are. In this section, we provide an overview of special issues in the assessment of English learners and principles for conceptualizing and organizing your classroom-based assessment procedures. These principles are applied in detail in the assessment sections at the end of Chapters 5 through 9, to provide specific ways to assess oral language, early literacy, reading, writing, and content-area learning. In addition, we provide an in-depth discussion of literacy assessment in Chapter 10, including case studies with instructional recommendations.

English Learner Assessment: Definition and Purposes

When we talk about assessment, we are referring to procedures used to evaluate student learning, achievement, or development. As teachers of English learners, we are primarily interested in assessing subject matter learning and English oral language, reading, and writing development. Bilingual teachers must also assess primary language development. Assessment serves three important purposes:

- Identification and program placement of students in need of special services
- Program evaluation
- Documentation of student learning and progress to
  (a) inform instructional decisions
  (b) communicate progress to parents

Student placement and program evaluation are generally initiated at the district level, whereas documentation of student learning and progress are the teacher's responsibility. Assessment procedures will depend on the purpose, as we shall discuss.

Whenever we assess students, we have to observe their performance on a particular task in order to infer or estimate their knowledge, skill, or competence in that area. Assessment procedures include data collection, data analysis, and interpretation of results. Assessment data may come from a variety of sources, including formal and informal measures. **Formal assessment** measures include standardized tests, such as group-administered standardized achievement tests in reading, language arts, and mathematics. Formal measures also include individually administered tests, such as those used to identify special learning needs. **Informal assessment** measures include such items as teacher-made tests, miscue analysis of oral reading, checklists, anecdotal observations, and student work samples. As a teacher of English learners, you will probably use all of these at different times with each of your students.

Formal assessment measures are designed according to rigorous testing theory and principles, including field testing to establish **validity** and **reliability.** A test is considered to have content validity if its items closely reflect the knowledge or skill it purports to measure. Suppose, for example that you want to measure the essay-writing ability of all sophomore students. A test that collects an essay sample will be more valid than one that simply consists of multiple-choice items on punctuation, because the essay sample more closely reflects the skill being evaluated, essay-writing ability. A test is reliable if it yields similar results when retaken, usually with the use of two equivalent forms to lessen the possibility of a learning effect between testing and retesting.

Formal and informal assessment measures have different purposes, strengths, and limitations. In general, **formal measures** are designed to compare individuals and groups with a previously established norm, whereas informal measures compare individuals with themselves and with small groups, such as other students in the class. Formal measures usually rely on short answers or multiple-choice items often elicited in a timed test situation, thus constituting **indirect measures** of student ability. In contrast, **informal measures** are generally based on student work samples and student interactions during naturally occurring classroom situations, that is, **direct measures** of student ability. Formal measures are relatively easy for the teacher to administer and score but tend to be anxiety-producing for many students. Informal measures, on the other hand, because they are based on student products and interactions that occur naturally, are easy to administer and are not especially anxiety-producing for students. However, considerable thought must go into collecting, organizing, and storing the information. In addition, analyzing the collection of student products requires time, effort, and thought from both the teacher and the student.

Currently, efforts have been made to combine some of the best features of both formal and informal assessment in what is called performance assessment (cf. Fradd & McGee, 1994). **Performance assessment** involves the direct observation and measurement of the desired behavior. For example, if problem solving using graphing is a curriculum goal, then assessment will consist of observing and evaluating students in the process of problem solving using graphs. Similarly, if the curriculum goal is for students to know how to write an autobiographical narrative, then assessment will elicit an autobiographical narrative to be evaluated. In this regard, performance assessment incorporates an element of informal assessment, that is, direct measure of the desired behavior. When performance assessment is used to compare student performance in different districts in a state, as with writing assessment, it incorporates an element of formal assessment, that is, cross-group comparison. In other words, data are collected in a systematic, standardized fashion so that valid group performance comparisons may be made. Assessment experts continue to struggle to find ways to meet the varying assessment demands for program evaluation as well as classroom use. This brief discussion has provided an overview of basic issues. Let us now consider how English learners are assessed, formally and informally, for the three purposes: student identification and program placement, program evaluation, and documentation of student learning and progress.

Identification and Placement of Students Needing Language Education Support Services

English learners are entitled by law to educational assistance that provides access to the core curriculum as well as English language development. The first order of business, therefore, is to identify students who need the support of a bilingual, English Language Development (ELD), or other kind of English learner educational support program. An established procedure for such identification involves two steps. First, a **home language survey** is sent to parents to find out whether a language other than English is spoken in the home. If a language other than English is used in the home, the child must be tested for English language proficiency. A standardized English-language proficiency test is typically administered to determine the student's English language knowledge.

The choice of an English language proficiency test is now being made by state departments of education in line with the current emphasis on uniform standards and assessment as discussed in Chapter 1. States may choose from an array of commercially published language proficiency tests, perhaps with oral language, reading, and writing subtests, such as the *Language Assessment Scales* (LAS) published by CTB-McGraw Hill or the *IDEA Language Proficiency Tests* (IPT) published by Ballard and Tighe. States may also develop their own language proficiency test, such as the *California English Language Development Test* (CELDT) published by CTB-McGraw Hill. Training in test administration is generally provided by the test publisher or developer. You can also find general information about language proficiency tests on the Internet at the National Clearinghouse for English Language Acquisition web site (AskNCELA, at http://www.ncela.gwu.edu/) or by using the test names as key words in an Internet search. If you are interested in the CELDT, we recommend the *CELDT Communications Assistance Packet for Districts/Schools* (California State Department of Education, 2003), available on the Internet.

Oral language proficiency tests are individually administered to collect a language sample that is subsequently analyzed and interpreted. Oral language sampling is usually accomplished by asking the student questions or by asking the student to tell a story about a picture or sequence of pictures. Analysis may be carried out by district language specialists, or the language samples may be sent back to the publishing company for analysis. Reading tests usually include passages with multiple-choice comprehension questions to answer. Writing tests elicit a writing sample for analysis.

Tests vary considerably in the kind of language elicited and in the methods used to analyze them. In each case, scores are finally interpreted to yield a level or phase of second language proficiency. Language proficiency tests vary in the number of levels they discriminate, but three categories emerge as important for program placement: Non-English Proficient (NEP), Limited English Proficient (LEP), and Fully English Proficient (FEP). School districts must provide language support services for NEP and LEP students, with eventual redesignation to FEP as the ultimate goal. The CELDT yields five language proficiency levels for each skill area: (1) listening/speaking, (2) reading, and (3) writing. A special scoring procedure is used to determine an overall score. These scores are used for program placement; to chart student's English language development progress; and to help determine when to redesignate the student as FEP.

Limitations of Standardized Language Proficiency Tests

Standardized language proficiency tests have certain limitations that can lead to inappropriate program placement. For example, the fact that a student's score is based on a single performance sample elicited out of the context of routine classroom activity may lead to inaccurate appraisal of language proficiency. In addition, test performance is easily affected by nonlinguistic variables such as lack of familiarity with the testing procedure, disinterest, and fatigue. Furthermore, to the extent that a student feels the pressure of a testing situation, performance may be affected by anxiety. Finally, different standardized language proficiency tests sometimes yield different levels for the same student. Use of a single test within a given state is helpful in this regard, but the problem persists if students move from one state to another. Because of these limitations, it is important for you to be aware of the possibility that a student has been inappropriately placed in your classroom based on language proficiency test performance. If you suspect a student has been misassigned to your classroom based on English language proficiency, you should check with your principal concerning procedures for retesting and reconsideration of the placement. Your judgment is extremely important and likely to be more accurate than the student's test performance.

Redesignation to FEP

Just as English learners have a legal right to alternative language support programs, they also have a legal right to exit these programs once they have gained sufficient English proficiency to succeed in the general education program. Redesignation to FEP is thus a critical matter requiring careful assessment of a student's ability to succeed educationally without special language support (Linquanti, 2001). Such assessment must be multidimensional, that is, based on multiple measures, including formal and informal measures of oral and written English, achievement test scores, and perhaps measures of academic performance in the primary language. In addition, it is important to include the judgment of teachers, parents, and any other resource personnel who have worked with the student.

Program Evaluation

School districts must comply with state assessment requirements, which usually include annual standardized achievement testing in reading, language arts, and mathematics. These tests are devised for comparing groups of students with each other or with a norm established by the publishing company. Norms are established by administering the test to a broadly "representative" group of students, mostly monolingual English-speaking, at particular grade levels, selected from different socioeconomic groups and geographical regions of the country. If a student scores in the 60th percentile, it means that 40 percent of the students in the norming population scored higher than the student and 60 percent scored the same or lower. English learners who take these tests are thus being compared to English proficient students on a test written and administered in English.

Sensitive and thoughtful teachers have seriously questioned the validity of standardized tests for English learners, and rightfully so. Students must be able to read English if a test written in English is to measure performance accurately. Beginning and intermediate English learners are at a distinct disadvantage in this regard by virtue of English language proficiency alone. Another disadvantage stems from the timed format of standardized testing. Research shows that reading in a second language is slower than native-language reading, even at advanced stages of second language development (Fitzgerald, 1995). Thus, second language test takers may score low, not because of lack of knowledge but because of the need for more time to finish the test. A final difficulty with standardized achievement tests is interpreting individual English learner performance. For English learners, the test publisher's norms are not appropriate unless the test was normed on English learners, which is seldom if ever the case. Furthermore, large-scale standardized achievement tests are technically not designed to reflect any individual's performance accurately, only group performance. Yet individual scores are reported to teachers and parents and are sometimes used to make decisions about a student's instructional program. In recognition of these problems, some school districts are limiting or modifying the use of standardized testing with English learners. At the very least, it is important to consider a student's English language proficiency when interpreting his or her score.

As a teacher of English learners, you need to be informed about language proficiency and standardized testing instruments and procedures used in your district. In addition, you need to understand the strengths and limitations of these tests. Moreover, it is important that you know how to interpret test results so that you can explain them to parents and consider them in your instructional planning. However, your greatest assessment responsibility will be the documentation of each student's learning and progress in order to make future instructional decisions and to communicate student performance and progress to parents.

Assessment of Student Learning and Progress

Classroom-based assessment for documenting student learning and progress requires a systematic approach. Current efforts in classroom-based assessment have moved beyond multiple-choice testing for mastery of discrete, behavioral objectives toward assessment procedures that rely heavily on focused observations and samples of student work collected during day-to-day classroom learning activities. Although it is important to have goals and objectives for your students, your assessment procedures should allow for students to display breadth and depth of learning beyond the limits of your stated objectives. Your students might surprise you with what they are able to do during classroom projects and group work when these are relevant and important to their lives and interests. In order to catch your students at their best, you need to become a careful observer and data collector. The following principles, based on Ruddell and Ruddell (1995), provide guidelines for your classroom-based assessment, often referred to as authentic assessment.

1. Assessment should be based on observations of students as they engage in authentic learning tasks.
2. Assessment should be tied directly to your instructional goals and teaching.
3. Assessment should be continuous, based on observations over a substantial period of time.
4. Assessment should take into consideration the diversity of students' cultural, linguistic, and special needs.
5. Assessment should be collaborative, providing opportunities for students to evaluate their own work.
6. Assessment should be multidimensional, that is, based on a variety of observations, in a variety of situations, using a variety of instruments.
7. Assessment should be based on current research and theory concerning language, literacy, and knowledge construction.

Keeping Cultural Considerations in Mind. We have already mentioned that a student's English language proficiency can affect test performance if the test is in English. Similarly, a student's cultural and experiential background might also interact with your assessment procedures to cloud or clarify the results. Because schooling practices tend to conform more or less to middle-class European American experiences and values, students from other cultural backgrounds may be misassessed by virtue of cultural and other experiential differences. For example, middle-class European American students are often accustomed to telling about events as a routine activity at home. You have probably heard someone say to a child, "Tell Aunt Rosie about your trip to the zoo," or "Tell me what you did at school today." In this way, adults prompt what researchers call **event casts** (Heath, 1983; Schieffelin & Eisenberg, 1984). Narratives of this type are thus familiar discourse routines for many children. However, in some cultures event casts are seldom if ever asked of children. Children with event cast experience may be more able to participate when similarly prompted at school, as might occur in retelling an experience orally or in writing, or in retelling a story as part of a reading comprehension assessment. This is but one example of the subtle ways in which students' prior cultural experiences may prepare them differently for school tasks.

There are many ways in which cultural differences might affect student performance in your class, as discussed in Chapter 1. As the teacher, you can optimize your students' chances for success by offering a variety of formats in which to display knowledge, including individual, small-group and whole-class instructional formats. In addition, you will want to provide students with a variety of opportunities to display knowledge through their modalities of strength: for example, visual, auditory, kinesthetic, oral, written, or pictorial. Finally, it is important to offer private knowledge-display opportunities, such as journal entries or individual conferencing, given that some students may be uncomfortable with public knowledge displays. As we mentioned earlier when discussing scaffolding, you will not always know which of your classroom routines are best suited to the cultural and personal experiences of each student. However, by providing a variety of routines, by observing how individual students respond, and by modifying your procedures accordingly, you become a culturally responsive teacher, increasing student comfort and success in your classroom. In so doing, you become a better evaluator of student learning as well.

Planning Systematic, Classroom-based Assessment. Most of your classroom-based assessment will make use of informal assessment methods. These methods include direct observation, teacher-student conferences, student journals or learning logs, writing samples, running records of oral reading, and teacher-made tests. In order to be systematic, it is important that you decide which of these methods you will use and when. In addition, you will need to decide how to record, interpret, and store the assessment results for each student.

One way to compile assessment results is the **portfolio.** A portfolio is a folder that contains a variety of samples of student work related to a particular curriculum area. Students and teachers together decide which pieces of work to include in the portfolio, in order to display the student's best work. In writing, for example, students may keep a working folder of drafts and rewrites. Periodically, perhaps every four to six weeks, they select their best piece or pieces from their working folder to be placed in the portfolio. By the end of the semester, students have a set of writing samples that will show their progress over time. Other items that may be included in a portfolio include interest inventories, lists of topics written or read about, running records of oral reading, unit tests, and any other classroom-based measurements that you believe will provide a rich and representative picture of your students' academic performance. Be sure to involve your students, not only in choosing items for inclusion in the portfolio, but also in devising ways to organize the contents that will make them easy for parents and others to read. For example, you may wish to include a table of contents and tabs to separate categories.

In summary, English learner assessment is vitally important for student placement, program evaluation, and documentation of student learning and progress. In Chapter 10, we provide in-depth discussion of individual literacy assessment. In addition, details on portfolios and other classroom-based assessments are provided in subsequent chapters as we discuss oral language, early literacy, writing, reading and literature, and content instruction. As always, it is important to consider the effects of English language proficiency and cultural differences in assessing English learners and interpreting their performance in classroom activities.

SUMMARY

In this chapter, we have described and illustrated three interrelated instructional approaches: sheltered instruction, or Specially Designed Academic Instruction in English (SDAIE); collaborative group work; and theme studies. We provided a detailed checklist of sheltering, or SDAIE, strategies and discussed how collaborative group work provides rich language and content learning opportunities as students discuss, debate, review, and otherwise negotiate meaning in their groups. Finally we showed how thematic instruction gradually builds learners' background knowledge each day, providing children with maximum opportunities for becoming proficient communicators, readers, writers, and learners in their non-native language. We also discussed the concept of scaffolding as an important metaphor to help us identify teaching strategies that promote language and literacy development. Finally, we discussed important issues in English learner assessment. The following chapters build on this instructional framework and provide over a hundred specific strategies for language, literacy, and content learning.

SUGGESTIONS FOR FURTHER READING

Celce-Murcia, M. (Ed.). (2001). *Teaching English as a second or foreign language* (3rd ed.). Boston: Heinle & Heinle.

This edited text, in its third edition, is thoroughly comprehensive, with sections on teaching methodology, language skills (listening, speaking, reading, writing), integrated approaches, "focus on the learner," and skills for teachers. We've relied on this excellent text for many years, and this edition adds nine new articles. Every teacher should have this one.

Echevarria, J., & Graves, A. (1998). *Sheltered content instruction: Teaching English-language learners with diverse abilities*. Boston: Allyn and Bacon.

One of the most important aspects of working with English language learners is their great diversity, and this text presents strategies and approaches to addressing this diversity. The book describes English learners with diverse abilities, gives theoretical and historical foundations concerning instruction and sheltered instruction in content areas, and develops strategies for teaching and learning. An excellent book with graphs, figures, and charts that are particularly clear and useful.

Fradd, S., McGee, P., with Wilen, D. (1994). *Instructional assessment: An integrative approach to evaluating student performance*. Reading, MA: Addison-Wesley Publishing.

An excellent, well-written book containing a wealth of information on the assessment of second language learners. The book contains case studies that highlight second language learning and many useful suggestions for monitoring and assessing students' performance. Chapters include discussions on second language performance, oral language assessment, assessing academic performance, and guidelines for instructional assessment. Highly recommended!

Herrell, A. (2000). *Fifty strategies for teaching English language learners*. Upper Saddle River, NJ: Merrill/Prentice Hall.

This practical book contains fifty strategies you can integrate into your classroom. At the beginning of the text each strategy is categorized according to its function: supports comprehensible input, encourages verbal interaction, supports contextualizing language, reduces anxiety, encourages active involvement, provides assessment information.

Richard-Amato, P. (2003). *Making it happen: Interaction in the second language classroom* (3rd ed.). White Plains, NY: Longman.

This textbook introduces a variety of approaches and classroom strategies for teaching English as a second language to students of any age. Examples of classrooms in different types of programs are provided.

Teachers of English to Speakers of Other Languages. (1997) *ESL standards for pre-K–12 students.* Alexandria, VA: Author.

This valuable resource provides goals, standards, and descriptors for English learners addressing grades Pre-K to 12. For each goal and standard, descriptors illustrate what to look for in student performance in class, with sample progress indicators provided. In addition, classroom vignettes are provided to illustrate how teachers can address the goals and standards in their teaching. This is a superb and readable set of standards.

Wink, J. (2000). *Critical pedagogy: Notes from the real world* (2nd ed.). New York: Addison-Wesley Longman.

If you have read about critical pedagogy but wondered how to turn its theoretical ideals into day-by-day practice in your classroom, this book is for you. Joan Wink invites us on a lively and engaging journey as she defines critical pedagogy succinctly and clearly, explains its origins, and then offers numerous examples of how theory can come alive through such classroom activities as problem posing, dialogue journals, and a useful problem-solving activity she calls "the mess." Finally, she wraps up with a discussion of why such pedagogy matters in the twenty-first century. This is a book that speaks to the heart and the mind, with a vision for a better future for all.

ACTIVITIES

1. Reread the vignette on *The Very Hungry Caterpillar* (pp. 84–85). Using the information in this chapter, discuss all of the things Roberto did to help his young, beginning English learners comprehend the story and write their own book. Do you find any strategies that have not been discussed in this chapter? Can you think of some strategies that Roberto should have used but didn't? How would you improve the lesson?

2. With a partner discuss the following ways of learning and rank each one from most to least helpful: learning from direct experience (including movies, pictures, and simulation games), learning from writing, learning from reading, learning in a large class lecture (in which there is little opportunity for questions and interaction), and learning in a small collaborative group (in which students can share their knowledge and help one another define terms). After you've ranked yours, share with your partner and discuss how each approach might be better depending on the situation. See how others in your class ranked the activities.

3. Think back to a memorable learning experience you had in elementary school. Jot down the experience as you remember it, making note of what you were learning about and what you were doing in the process of learning. Now analyze the lesson to see how many, if any, sheltering techniques were used. Were any techniques used that we now define as sheltering techniques? If sheltering techniques were not used, to what do you attribute the strength of your memory? What made the situation memorable to you? What implications can you draw for your own teaching?

4. Take a lesson plan from a published source or one you have written yourself. Critically review the plan to analyze its comprehensibility for English learners. What modifications or additions could you make to ensure comprehension and participation by English learners? Is the lesson thematically oriented? Does the lesson involve collaborative group work? Does the lesson shelter information for students in a variety of ways? How would you change the lesson

based on the information you now have concerning some of the ways teachers provide instruction of English learners?

5. Try a theme cycle with a small group of children. Begin by brainstorming the question, "What are some things we would like to know more about?" Next, as a group, choose one topic to focus on. Write the topic on a piece of butcher paper and create two columns for listing "what we know" and "what we want to know." With the children, decide which question to investigate and how. With student input, create a list of books, people, and places to obtain the needed information. Students may choose to work alone or in pairs to present the final product of their learning to the rest of the group. When finished, make a new butcher paper list of "what we know now" and "new questions we have now." Discuss the pros and cons of working with children within a theme cycle.

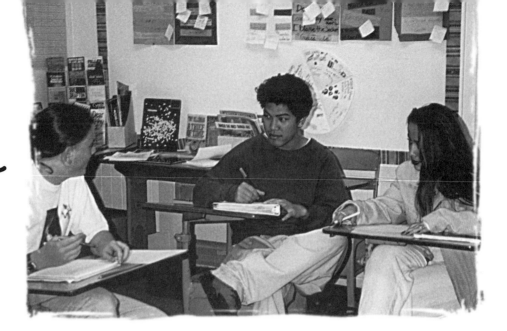

4

ORAL LANGUAGE DEVELOPMENT IN SECOND LANGUAGE ACQUISITION

In this chapter we discuss oral language development and its relationship to literacy and academic development. We also provide suggestions for promoting and assessing oral language development in second language acquisition. The following questions are addressed in the chapter:

1. What are the relationships among listening, reading, speaking, and writing? How do these relationships inform classroom teachers?
2. How do language form, communicative function, and social context combine to affect students' oral language performance in the classroom?
3. What are some characteristics of beginning and intermediate levels of second language oral proficiency in English?
4. What strategies will assist beginning and intermediate students in developing oral language proficiency?
5. How can structured observation tools, checklists, and anecdotal observations be used to describe and document oral language performance and development?

We look forward to visiting Lisa Garcia's third-grade classroom because her students are always so actively involved and because Lisa sees oral language as foundational to everything she does. When we enter her room we see children dancing and singing; we see them pantomiming snowflakes; we see them talking about books they have read or heard; we see them discussing the growth of the class bunny; and we see them preparing puppet shows. In addition, we know that when we enter the class, the children will expect us to be a part of the daily events. They often want to share their recent writing with us, or they will read or recite a pocket poem to us. In Lisa's class children get recognition for reading a favorite poem to anyone who enters the class or for reading the poem to someone in the schoolyard at recess time. The children carry favorite poems in their pockets, and when they recite a poem to someone, that person signs the poem.

Another reason we look forward to visiting Lisa's class is that something exciting and unpredictable happens every day. One day the children gave Lisa a surprise birthday party and presented a skit about their class. They laughed hilariously as one child played Lisa while others played themselves in the little drama. Because Lisa and her children value the social, dramatic, poetic, academic, and other functional uses of oral language in her classroom, they enjoy daily opportunities to forge understandings, create new meanings, and promote interpersonal relationships through talk.

119

ORAL LANGUAGE IN PERSPECTIVE

Walter Loban, a favorite professor of ours and a pioneer in researching oral language development of students from kindergarten through 12th grade (Loban, 1982), used to say:

We listen a book a day,
talk a book a week,
read a book a month,
and write a book a year.
        (Loban, 1980)

With this saying Loban highlighted the pervasiveness of oral language in our lives; it is so pervasive, in fact, that we easily take it for granted—until plagued with a case of laryngitis. Reading and writing also play vitally important roles in our lives, but oral language interactions account for the bulk of our day-to-day communications, remaining the primary mode of discourse throughout the world.

For students learning English as a second language in school, oral language development plays a key role as well. When students are working or playing together, their conversations are based on concrete, here-and-now topics of current interest. As a result, opportunity abounds for them to negotiate meaning through requests for clarification, reference to objects at hand, and other face-to-face communication strategies. At the same time, the language used becomes comprehensible and usable as input for second language acquisition. To optimize classroom oral language learning opportunities, we need to make time each day for students to talk to each other while working in a variety of situations, including paired reading, group research projects, group work at learning centers, brainstorming a writing topic, sharing news with the entire class, and just visiting quietly while carrying out tasks. While classroom oral language opportunities such as these may seem obvious to you, research indicates that teachers do from 65 percent to 95 percent of the talking in most classrooms (Lowery, 1980). Language development should be vocal and visible in classrooms where talk is valued as a learning tool.

Task-directed talk, including teacher talk during instruction, is useful in and of itself for second language acquisition if sheltering techniques are used, as discussed in Chapter 2. Talk is also important for helping students clarify concepts and arrive at their own understandings. As academic content increases in complexity, the use of small- and large-group discussion plays a vital role in promoting students' conceptual understanding and learning. Consistent with the value we place on oral language interactions, we incorporate opportunities throughout this book for students to develop their own thinking through talking and responding as they read, write, and learn in English, because it is the integrated use of oral and written language for functional and meaningful purposes that best promotes the full development of second language proficiency.

Integration of Listening, Speaking, Reading, and Writing

What does it mean to integrate listening, speaking, reading, and writing? In natural, day-to-day experience, oral and written language uses are not kept separate and isolated from one another. Instead, they often occur together, integrated in specific communication events. For example, when you are reading the Sunday newspaper, you may comment on an article to your roommate or spouse, engendering a discussion about it. Such discussion may lead you to reread parts of the article to clarify questions that emerged in the discussion. Similarly, when the phone bill arrives, you might have an extended discussion of its written contents to decide who owes what, or whether one or more members of the household needs to stop making so many long-distance calls. If your parents were immigrants and spoke little English when you were a child, you may have had the experience of translating for them and helping them fill out forms at the doctor's office. In each of these real-life situations, oral and written language uses intermingle as people go about the business and pleasures of life, and the intermingling of oral and written language occurs in literate societies across ethnic and social class boundaries (Heath, 1983; Vásquez, 1991).

Listening, speaking, reading, and writing also occur naturally together in learning events in school at all grade levels, even though traditionally they were taught separately. (See Chapter 3 for more discussion.) In primary grades, for example, the teacher may read a picture book aloud, taking time along the way to let children orally predict what will happen next, or to discuss the characters or plot. Older students may perform a play from a written script, engaging in lengthy discussion over the fine points of interpretation, with the final result being a dramatic oral performance of the play. When students write stories, they read what they write, ask others to read and comment on their writing, and perhaps read their writing aloud to celebrate its completion. In all these situations, a written text has been the subject of oral discussion and interpretation, demonstrating how oral and written language become naturally interwoven during a particular communication event. In school, you enrich each school day when you give children opportunities to interweave oral and written language for functional, meaningful learning purposes.

Relationships among Listening, Speaking, Reading, and Writing

Another way to look at the integration of the four language processes is to consider how they interrelate during language development. In first language acquisition, we know that all children, barring severe abnormalities, become grammatically competent speakers of the mother tongue by about age 5. Subsequent language development relates primarily to vocabulary acquisition and expansion of the functions for which language is used. Competence in reading and writing, on the other hand, is a much later development and one not universally achieved. Thus, oral language development occurs earlier and more fully than written in first language acquisition.

Various patterns emerge among students who are learning English as a second language in school. For young English learners with little literacy in the home language, basic oral language competence is likely to emerge earlier than competence in reading and writing (Fradd & McGee, 1994). For older students who know how to read in their first language, however, the pattern may be different. Some of these students may develop competence in written English earlier than oral English. In either case, a good deal of time is spent simultaneously developing both oral and written language abilities. We also know that English language learners do not need to be fully proficient in oral English before they start to read and write (Hudelson, 1984). Furthermore, second language knowledge can be developed from written input as well as oral, provided that the text is comprehensible to the language learner (Elley & Mangubhai, 1983). The relationships among listening, speaking, reading, and writing during development, then, are complex relationships of mutual support. Practice in any one process contributes to the overall reservoir of second language knowledge, which is then available for other acts of listening, speaking, reading, or writing. For this reason, it is important to provide abundant exposure to functional, meaningful uses of both oral and written language for all learners.

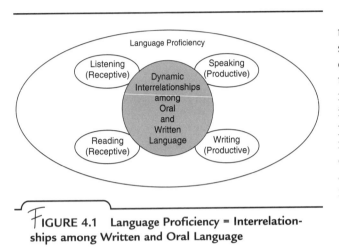

FIGURE 4.1   Language Proficiency = Interrelationships among Written and Oral Language

Figure 4.1 illustrates the interrelationships among listening, reading, speaking, and writing. More specifically, listening and reading are receptive uses of language: Messages are received by ear or by eye, and meaning is reconstructed based partly on prior knowledge. Listening and reading are not passive processes, however. Listeners and readers must actively take the speaker's words and recreate the message in order to comprehend it. Thus, when you assist students with listening comprehension, you are assisting them with reading comprehension. Conversely, speaking and writing are productive uses of language: the speaker or writer must *create* the message for an audience. When you assist students with spoken composition, therefore, you are assisting them with written composition. Moreover, reading can be one of the most important ways we develop oral vocabulary, and writing helps us learn how to compose in oral language. Thus, in our day-to-day lives oral and written language are interwoven like threads in a tapestry, each supporting the other to create the whole picture (Boyle, 1979).

We have spent some time discussing the integration of listening, speaking, reading, and writing in order to emphasize the importance of creating learning opportunities that involve using all four interrelated language processes. We have described two general reasons for this recommendation. First, in the course of day-to-day living, people move back and forth from oral to written modes during communication because both serve essential functions. The same holds true for the kinds of communication that promote learning in the classroom. Thus, the integration of listening, speaking, reading, and writing is functionally appropriate. Second, practical use of each language process provides both specific development of that process and overall language development in English. As teachers, we want to develop each student's abilities to the fullest as listeners and speakers, readers and writers.

Form, Function, and Social Context in Oral Language Use

As you begin to focus on your students' oral language use, you need to take into account language forms, functions, and social contexts. As you begin to facilitate students' oral language competence, you will want to consider how social context affects choice of language form for a given language function or purpose. The social context consists of the social setting, the speakers and the social and power relations among them. Language forms include choice of words, grammar, and pronunciation. Language functions are the communicative intentions or purposes of speakers' utterances (see Table 4.1). For example, consider a social setting consisting of parents, grandparents, and three teenage boys having dinner at home. One of the teenagers wants the salt, which is near his younger brother. He says, "Hey, gimme the salt, woudja?" If the salt were near his grandmother, he might say instead, "Grandma, can you pass me the salt?" He might even say "please." If this same family were having dinner at a formal banquet, the teenager might be a little more formal in his request of his brother, saying perhaps, "Could ya pass the salt over here please?" The teenager's choice of language form has varied according to formality of the social setting and his relationship with the person to whom he addressed his request. The social context in which language is used plays an important role in communication, setting parameters, of formality or politeness, for example, that guide linguistic choices.

The social context of language use places different cognitive and social demands on speakers that may affect the quality of their oral language performance. The same thing can happen, though perhaps less obviously, in one's native language. Consider, for example, the difference between a casual chat with a friend about a movie you have just seen and a formal job interview in which six interviewers are seated around a boardroom table facing you. The two situations differ considerably in the extent to which you "watch your language" and attempt to be clear, precise, and grammatically correct. For English language learners, the more formal and cognitively demanding situation can trigger noticeably more errors in pronunciation, grammar, and vocabulary than would generally occur in a less formal situation. This being the case, you can see why it is important to observe students in various social contexts or communication situations, formal and informal, in order to accurately assess their oral proficiency.

As we discuss students' oral language proficiency, we will refer not only to language forms, but to language functions. Table 4.1 illustrates **Halliday's functional categories** (1985) for oral language use along with corresponding classroom examples. You can develop specific activities in your classroom to expand students' ability to use language to carry out a variety of communicative functions. For example, Halliday's interactional function deals with getting along with others and can be translated into cooperative group work in your classroom. Group work enhances student's growth in language, building on conversational skills they already possess and easing adaptation to school routines. As teachers, we are charged with the task of developing students' abilities to use language effectively for heuristic (scientific discovery and problem-solving) and informational functions. Thus K–12 schooling serves to expand children's and young adults' repertoires in a variety of oral language functions.

While keeping in mind our philosophy concerning the integration of the four language processes serving a variety of communicative functions, we will spend the remainder of this chapter discussing English learners' oral language development. We begin with a discussion of oral language proficiency characteristics of

TABLE 4.1 Language Functions and Analogous Classroom Experiences

Functions	Classroom Experiences
Instrumental: I want; language as a means of getting things, of satisfying needs	Child clarifying instructions from morning routines; asking for supplies in play store or kitchen; asking for book in class library
Regulatory: Do as I say; controlling the behavior, feelings, or attitudes of others	Developing pantomimes and role-playing routines with partners or in groups; determining steps for completing projects
Interactional: Me and you; social interaction, getting along with others	Working in cooperative and collaborative groups on projects, art activities, and play
Personal: Here I come; pride and awareness of self, expressions of individuality	Sharing and telling about oneself; dictating language experience stories to others; sharing personal experiences
Heuristic: Tell me why; seeking and testing knowledge	Asking the teachers and students how something works; explaining the ideas in a story or retelling a story
Imaginative: Let's pretend; making up stories and poems; creating new worlds	Using wordless books to create new stories; using pictures to create stories; using creative dramatics to act out original ideas
Informative: I've got something to tell you; communicating information, description, ideas	Sharing ideas about what should be studied in a project or theme cycle; explaining what happened during a school event or describing a favorite television show
Divertive: Enjoy this; jokes, puns, riddles, language play	Telling riddles and jokes during special time devoted to this purpose

124

beginning and intermediate English learners. Next we provide descriptions of classroom activities that promote oral language development, followed by procedures for documenting oral language performance and development during classroom activities.

DESCRIBING ORAL LANGUAGE PERFORMANCE OF BEGINNING AND INTERMEDIATE ENGLISH LEARNERS

We have undertaken to provide instructional strategies for English language learners who are not yet fully proficient in English. We assume that fully proficient English language learners will be able to benefit from the same instructional program, provided you validate them personally and culturally in the educational process. Most of the reading, writing, and learning ideas in this book are appropriate or can be adapted for all students, not just beginning and intermediate English learners. Thus, you may use the strategies with fully proficient English learners and native English speakers as well, according to your judgment.

In keeping with our concern for English learners described as limited in English proficiency and in order to facilitate your use of this book, we have taken the larger category of LEP and divided it into two subcategories of English language learners: (1) beginning and (2) intermediate. We use these categories in this chapter in reference to oral proficiency and in subsequent chapters to describe second language reading and writing proficiency. We include non-English speakers in our beginner category because the strategies we suggest work as well for them as for children who have already begun to speak the new language. As you read on, bear in mind that these are broad, general guidelines, not levels set in stone. We designate activities as appropriate for beginning and intermediate English learners for your convenience. However, please keep in mind that no activity should be withheld from any particular student solely on the basis of perceived English language proficiency. It is all too easy to misjudge a child's language competence because language performance varies across situations and from week to week as a result of the dynamic and context-specific nature of language proficiency. Moreover, motivation tends to stretch children's performance. Therefore, we recommend that you allow students the choice to take part in more difficult activities according to their interests and desires. You may be in for some pleasant surprises!

Second Language Oral Proficiency of Beginning English Learners

The beginner phase of second language development starts immediately upon exposure to the new language. Early on, the child may neither understand nor speak a word of English. Soon, however, language comprehension develops as a result of opportunities for social interaction with speakers of the new language and the comprehensible input that is generated. Although it is important not to force beginners to speak, the fact is that very shortly, within perhaps a week to a few months, most students will naturally begin to speak on their own (Terrell, 1981). At this point, their speech is likely to be limited to simple phrases and expressions that have highly functional communicative payoffs, such as "OK," "No," "Wanna

125

play," "I wanna she go, too," and "I donno" (Wong Fillmore, 1983). As beginners develop, they are able to generate utterances according to simple grammatical rules, enabling them to carry out various tasks according to their own needs and purposes. The conversation in Example 4.1, described by Lily Wong Fillmore (1980), shows a young beginner's attempt to get an eraser back from her friend Cathy.

Kim-girl is at the table doing seatwork. Cathy, Sin Man, Suh Wah, and Chui-Wing are at the same table; they have been arguing over the possession of a pink eraser all morning. As you can see in the example, Kim-girl makes use of various formulaic expressions, such as "That's all," "Bye-bye," and "No way." In addition, in this conversation, she demonstrates her ability to use simple present-tense grammar for statements and questions when she says: "Can I eraser? Can I hab color? Se want 'raser. This Edlyn gip me." Her pronunciation shows some influence from her native language, Korean, in the use of se for she and gip for give. As a beginner in English, Kim-girl is resourceful in using her rudimentary English knowledge to try to get her eraser back. She also takes the opportunity for pattern practice with her litany of "Gip me" sentences. With limited formal language knowledge in terms of grammar, vocabulary, and pronunciation, Kim-girl is effective in achieving her communicative goal: the return of the eraser.

Your initial concern for beginners when they first arrive is to provide social-emotional support by assigning new students to a home group and a buddy, preferably one who speaks the child's home language. The buddy accompanies the newcomer everywhere throughout the school day, including to the bathroom, cafeteria, and bus stop. Meanwhile the home group assumes responsibility for the new child during routine classroom activities. Some teachers set up home groups

126

Example 4.1 — Beginning-Level Second Language Development

CATHY: Gimme 'raser! [*Takes Kim-girl's eraser.*]
KIM-GIRL: [*Looks up crankily. Turns to Lily Wong Fillmore and complains:*]
Can I eraser? Se took my 'raser. Se want 'raser.
This Edlyn gip me.
> [*She grabs microphone that has been placed right in front of her and says into it:*]
Gip me 'raser, yah!
Gip me pencil, yah!
Gip me chopstick, no!
Gip me crayon, yah!
Can I hab color? No way!
That's all! Bye-bye!

Source: From "Learning a Second Language: Chinese Children in the American Classroom," by Lily Wong Fillmore, in *Current Issues in Bilingual Education: Georgetown University Roundtable on Languages and Linguistics,* ed. by J. E. Alatis, 1980, p. 323, Washington, DC: Georgetown University Press.

of four to five students each at the beginning of the school year. These groups remain fairly stable throughout the year in order to create interpersonal support and cohesion. With such groups in place, much responsibility for caring for a new student may be transferred from the teacher to the home group. These assignments help meet the safety, security, and belonging needs of a new student and create the social interaction matrix from which language acquisition begins to grow.

At the beginner level, support for participation in lessons comes from three sources: the teacher, the other students, and the newcomers themselves. Early on, you may provide some tasks that do not require speech but rather invite a nonverbal participatory response. For example, if a group is working on a thematic project, the newcomer may be involved in drawing, painting, or coloring a mural with the assistance of the other group members. In this way, the child contributes actively to the group project, while interacting through concrete and context-embedded language. Drawing or painting a mural is actually a high-level cognitive activity. Information gleaned from the theme study must be synthesized and portrayed accurately and meaningfully. Thus art becomes a valid academic learning tool for English language learners, just as it can be for native English speakers. Working on the mural project can also promote language development because active involvement in a low-risk, small-group activity means that a good deal of talk will go on, providing excellent input for language acquisition.

When English learners work and play with native English speakers, language learning opportunities occur naturally and often.

Similarly, you and the other students can make use of sheltering techniques such as gestures, paraphrasing, and checking for understanding to help make lessons and routine activities more understandable to the newcomer. Finally, you can make sure that small-group activities take place frequently, in order to create numerous opportunities for social interaction. With this kind of support, beginners will gradually advance toward the intermediate phase described next.

Second Language Oral Proficiency of Intermediate English Learners

Intermediate English language learners are able to understand and speak English in face-to-face interactions, and they are able to speak with minimal hesitation and relatively few misunderstandings. Nevertheless, because their grammatical abilities (syntax, semantics, phonology) are still developing, you may notice features in their speech that are not typical of standard English. For example, students may at times confuse *he* and *she*. They may not conjugate verbs conventionally, saying things like, "My friend, she like to read a lotta books," using *like* instead of *likes*.

Even though these speech differences may nag at you for correction, we recommend that you control the natural tendency to constantly correct students' grammar in the middle of a conversation. Instead, make a point of noticing how much the child can now do with the new language. Show interest by asking questions that focus on the activity at hand, encouraging the student to tell you more. Build in and model appropriate grammar and vocabulary as you respond, thereby providing input that is tailored to the student's immediate linguistic needs and interests. You may be surprised to find that with patient listening your student is able to understand and discuss ideas at a fairly complex level. For example, intermediate students may be able to recall the details of a story, identify main ideas, predict what will come next, and, perhaps, summarize a plot. However, at this phase of development, students are likely to struggle to formulate their ideas in their new language, both orally and in writing. To get an idea of an intermediate English learner's oral language, take a look at how Teresa described the movie *Poltergeist* to us (Example 4.2). Teresa, a fifth-grader whose first language is Spanish, has been learning English since the third grade.

As you can see, Teresa is quite expressive in English and is able to provide a rather detailed account of the movie. She employs her developing vocabulary with a variety of grammatical rules, utilizing both past and present tense forms. Furthermore, she is able to coordinate her linguistic knowledge without hesitation much of the time. The aspects of Teresa's speech that indicate her intermediate level of English language development consist primarily of (1) her nonconven-

---

Example 4.2 **Intermediate-Level Second Language Speaker**

SUZANNE: Was it scary?

TERESA: No, it wasn't escary. But, well . . . First it was scary but then the other one no. Because there was . . . First a little girl . . . There was a television and the father was sleeping in the . . . in a . . . *sillón?* in like a chair. And then the little girl pass the television and she said, "Right here!" Then . . . then a hand get out of the television and she said, "Ouch!" And then a little boy was sleeping and the little girl sleep here and the boy here and then he see all the time a tree and then . . . then . . . there was outside a tree . . . a tree. But it look ugly in the night. It look like a face . . . And then he was escary. Then he tell his father and his father said OK. Just count 1, 2, 3 to not escare. Then . . . then . . . the . . . he . . . the little girl and the little . . . the two brothers go in with the mother and her father because they're still escare.

tional verb use (e.g., "hand get out," "little girl sleep," "it look ugly"), (2) nonidiomatic expressions (e.g., "he see all the time a tree," "the little girl pass the television"), and (3) occasional groping for appropriate vocabulary items (e.g., "*sillón, in like a chair*" and variations of the word *scare:* scare, scared, scary).

During the intermediate phase of second language development, you can support students' participation in learning activities by continuing with the sheltering techniques and small-group collaboration discussed earlier. In addition, now is the time to involve students in more linguistically demanding tasks. For one thing, intermediate English language learners know sufficient English to be able to serve as the buddy of a newly arrived non-English speaker. In terms of classroom learning activities, the intermediate student will be able to hold a speaking part in a story dramatization or readers' theater, or any other more formal language activity that permits rehearsal. In addition, during this phase, students may enjoy participating in small-group discussions of stories, science experiments, and other activities.

As intermediate-level English language learners progress, they may appear able to use English with nearly as much facility as their native English-speaking counterparts. Their speech may be fluent, and you might find them responding with enthusiasm during whole-class as well as small-group discussion. Their reading and writing may be relatively fluent as well. At this point, it is important to continue both sheltering techniques as well as group collaboration. More advanced intermediate students are capable of understanding steady streams of verbal instruction, but you still need to accompany your words with charts, graphic organizers, concrete objects, and pictures to convey meaning. These efforts will enhance learning for all students. In addition, intermediate students can benefit from hearing the teacher use technical vocabulary, provided that it is introduced with concrete experiences and visual support such as graphs and pictures that parallel your verbal explanations.

129

PROMOTING ORAL LANGUAGE DEVELOPMENT IN THE CLASSROOM

The classroom is a natural environment for a large variety of oral language learning opportunities, and you will find that the following chapters build on and integrate this oral language foundation with writing and reading. As the teacher, you can organize your classroom in ways that encourage the two most important elements of oral language development: **comprehensible input** and **social interaction.** Keep in mind that a predictable schedule helps students adjust to the classroom and provides easily acquired basic vocabulary with the repeated routines.

In addition to the basic routines of roll call, recess, snack, lunch, and dismissal, the use of routine instructional events also provides oral language learning opportunities. Some typical routine instructional events include circle time, journal time, literature study circles, process writing, projects, theme studies, and other lesson sequences in content areas such as math, science, and social studies. To the extent that these instructional events maintain the same structure while the content changes, they provide a familiar routine with repetition of familiar language that scaffolds student participation and learning (Boyle & Peregoy, 1991; Peregoy, 1991; Peregoy & Boyle, 1999.) For example, a literature study circle has a small-group discussion format centered on one book. The format remains stable throughout the year, but the content, that is, the book being discussed, changes. Another stable feature of the literature study circle is the discussion of literary elements and the informal turn-taking procedures. Thus students become familiar and comfortable with the literature study circle as an interactional format that supports their oral language use and development.

Whether you are engaging your students in literature study, process writing, or theme studies, it is always important to review your own instructional delivery to incorporate additional cues to convey meaning, especially nonverbal cues such as dramatization, gesture, pictures, graphic organizers, and concrete objects. As a teacher-researcher you can analyze and evaluate ways in which classroom activities and verbal/visual adaptations work with your English learners by keeping a daily log or by videotaping lessons for later analysis. Verbal strategies that help students understand your talk include paraphrasing, repeating key vocabulary in context, and summarizing main points. Social interaction can be promoted in the classroom by encouraging students to work in pairs and groups. These strategies for sheltering, scaffolding, and group work were described in detail in Chapter 3.

In addition to the oral language development opportunities available during managerial and instructional routines, there are a number of wonderful learning activities that showcase oral language use in ways that promote acquisition. Interestingly, many of these activities are based on the arts. This makes sense if you stop to consider that the arts employ nonverbal media of communication. When these media are combined with language use, a natural scaffolding is provided for comprehension and production of oral language. The activities described in the following pages can be integrated into literature study, theme studies, and process writing, or they can take on a life of their own. Because they provide opportunities for negotiation of meaning through social interaction, they facilitate oral language development. Each activity below can be easily adapted for beginning or intermediate-level students. In most cases we give examples of possible adaptations that make student participation easier or more difficult so that you may adjust the level to challenge your students appropriately.

Using Games in Second Language Classrooms

In our teaching at the elementary, secondary, and college level, we have used games such as simulation games, drama games, pronunciation games (Tatsuki, 1996), grammar games, story games, and writing games to improve student learning and to create an atmosphere of ease, creativity, and fun. We especially enjoy

130

and recommend drama warm-up activities like those in Spolin (1963/1983) described at the end of this chapter. We believe that any lesson that allows us to use a game improves student learning and attitude. Games create experiences with language and ideas, and "experience is the glue that makes learning stick." Throughout this book we give examples and recommend games for motivating, engaging, and getting feedback from students (Wisniewska, 1998). At the end of this chapter we recommend a classic book full of games for beginning, intermediate, and advanced English language learners (Wright, Betteridge, & Buckby, 2002). You can start with this classic book and easily adapt ideas for your own classes. For example, older students can make board games based on content they are studying. Younger students might create games based on the stories they are reading. Finally, with your guidance, students can make and play their own games based on a game such as Monopoly (Yang, 1992). You won't be disappointed if you try games.

Songs

Sing a song a day at least! Songs bring levity, laughter, and beauty into your classroom. Songs also promote a feeling of unity in the class, particularly important when differences among students prevail. In addition, all students can participate at some level, regardless of English language proficiency. Some songs may be related to a theme or topic of study, whereas others may be favorite tunes suggested by your students. Bear in mind that songs are language-based, so you will need to provide cues to meaning such as pictures, pantomime, or gestures. We recommend that you post song lyrics accompanied by pictures or rebus symbols to convey meaning. In addition, you may wish to copy lyrics for each student to illustrate and keep in a song book. Because songs are popular with all ages, this activity can be successful throughout the grades. Just make sure your students have some say in which songs they get to sing.

One final note: Although we suggest songs for English language development, you might also want to invite any and all willing students to share a song with the class in their home language by bringing a recording or by singing it. It can be a

131

INTERNET RESOURCES: The Randal Davis site on language teaching (http://www. esl-lab.com/research/articles.htm) contains helpful resources and links. Of special interest for oral language is an article on "Internet Multimedia Resources for Language Learning," which gives information for "educators interested in using audio-video technology, including video conferencing and streaming, in their classrooms." You might want to select an interactive "cyber listening lab" that contains an audiovisual player and a large archive of listening activities. Share some of the best activities or write a paper with an annotated bibliography for classmates. And remember to check our companion website, which gives other links on oral language: www.ablongman. com/peregoy4e.

fine cross-cultural experience for everyone. We remember the day an East Indian girl, Barjinder, sang a beautiful song in her native language. When she finished, the class sat in awed silence and then broke out in spontaneous clapping. Barjinder looked down with a smile, beaming with pride at her classmates' enthusiastic response.

Drama

Acting out stories and events in math, science, history, literature, or theme studies can be a highly motivating way for students to process and present information they have studied. Dramatic enactments in the classroom range from informal to formal. For drama at its least formal, you can provide props in a dramatic play center of your classroom. During free time, students create their own dramas within the context of the props. Changing the props from time to time is important to stimulate new interest and new topics for dramatic play. Another dramatization technique has been developed by early childhood educator Vivian Paley (Weinborg, 1989). In this self-expression process, children first dictate a story for you to write down. Later, a child dramatizes the story with help from friends as you read the story during group time. A third way to encourage informal dramatization is to make props available for enacting stories that are currently being read in the classroom.

A favorite book of ours, *Improvisations for the Theater* (Spolin, 1963/1983), outlines numerous drama techniques, beginning with simple pantomimes, progressing to brief, context-embedded dialogues, and moving on to one-act plays. For example, early in the year students might develop warm-up routines in which they mirror a partner's every move; later, they mime catching a ball that changes from a basketball to a soccer ball to a tennis ball. The nonverbal warm-up activities involve all students and create confidence and concentration, preparing them for later activities that require oral language use.

The next level of activities involves students in brief improvisations based on a situation for which they create a dialogue. For example, the teacher might say that the children are stuck in an elevator for 10 seconds, and then for 5 minutes, and, finally, for 2 hours. The students then create appropriate dialogue for each of the situations. Gradually, the activities lead students to where they can improvise little plays of their own. Drama activities provide students with a variety of contextualized and scaffolded activities that gradually involve more participation and more oral language proficiency; they are also nonthreatening and a lot of fun. The Spolin book and other books containing hundreds of developmentally appropriate activities are annotated at the end of this chapter.

Dramatizing Poetry

Poetry also provides an excellent springboard for dramatization (Gasparro & Falletta, 1994) and is effective with English learners of all ages. Selecting the right poem is essential. Poems that present minidramas or that express strong emotions, attitudes, feelings, or opinions work best (Tomlinson, 1986). One such poem that appeals to all ages is "The Crocodile's Toothache" (Silverstein, 1974), a hilarious dialogue between a crocodile and his dentist. For poem enactment, you begin by reading the poem aloud, modeling not only pronunciation but also dramatic intonation and stress. You may wish to have the poem copied on chart paper with some pictures to help convey meaning. During the first readings, you need to clarify difficult or unusual words, making sure that your students generally understand the poem. If you like, you may next invite all your students to read the poem chorally. Finally, in pairs or groups, your students prepare a dramatic rendition of the poem to be presented to the entire class. If you find that you and your students enjoy dramatizing poetry, you will want to start a collection of poems that fit in with content areas and themes you teach. In this way, poem dramatizations will become integrated into your curriculum.

Recently, we had the opportunity to observe fourth-grade English learners performing a skit on the California Gold Rush, a topic designated by the state curriculum framework. In this integrated curriculum project, students incorporated songs, poems, and dramatizations in ways that promoted oral and written language development. The teacher began by providing a variety of experiences to give the students a feel for the Gold Rush era. The class visited historical museums where they learned about people arriving from all over the world by horse, by foot, by wagon train, and by ship to try their luck in the California foothills. Students sang songs of the era, such as "Sweet Betsy from Pike," and read poems and newspaper articles from the period. They saw films depicting gold panning, sluice boxes, and tent towns. They learned that miners wore denim jeans, giving the Levi Strauss Company its start as a factory outlet in San Francisco. They also made sourdough bread and sourdough pancakes. They even had the chance to pan for gold at a nearby park. The "gold" (painted rocks) had been planted beforehand by their industrious teacher. After these experiences, the children decided they wanted to write a play about a family moving to California to join the Gold Rush. The teacher divided the class into four groups, and each group put together a script for a short drama. Next the groups gathered props for their skits. The teacher set aside an hour a day for one week for rehearsal. Finally, each group performed its 10-minute skit for the rest of the class as a culminating event. As it happened, the student teacher had arranged to videotape the skits, adding to students' excitement and pride.

In developing their skits, these fourth graders used oral language for a variety of functions. In addition, they used written language to scaffold their oral performance of songs, poems, and the skit itself. First, they synthesized large amounts of information and selected aspects they wished to portray in their skit. They did this through informal discussion in small groups, proposing and evaluating ideas and then making decisions by consensus. Next they created a basic story to tell in their skit, selected characters to play different roles, and wrote out dialogue. Some groups incorporated songs and poems learned during the theme study. One group read aloud a letter written to a relative back home to convey the character's inner feelings. During rehearsal, students used a great deal of directive language to organize, practice, and perfect the skit. Finally, each group gave a formal performance of their skit. As a follow-up, the students critiqued the performances, including oral performance aspects such as diction, volume, and pace. Because the skits had been videotaped, the children were able to see and hear themselves over again. As you can see, the oral language development opportunities in this theme study were rich and varied, while optimal oral performance was scaffolded by group support, the chance to work from written scripts, and multiple rehearsals.

As you develop instructional sequences with and for your students, you can begin to make note of the oral language opportunities inherent in them. From there, you can look for ways to incorporate more such opportunities, increasing the variety of functions and interactional formats available such as pairs, small groups, and whole-class performances. It is important to point out that performances should take place only after students have had plenty of practice prior to the spotlight. Be sure to allow student choice in such events.

Show and Tell

Show and tell, a strategy teachers have used for years, involves children bringing a favorite object, such as a teddy bear, to the class and telling the class about it. The situation is context-embedded because all the children can see the prized possession, making it easier for the audience to understand the child's words. This is a beginning activity for young language learners that can be expanded to more advanced, context-reduced oral language use by simply asking children to place the favorite object in a paper bag so that it is not visible to classmates. Then the owner of the object begins describing the object to the class. Because the object is not visible, the speaker must be more specific about the object to assist classmates in guessing what it is. Later in the year, students can work with more difficult objects that are not in a bag but in their imagination, or they can have pictures in front of them that they describe to others. The variations of show and tell can scaffold children's early speaking with objects on hand and can induce more accurate descriptions when their comfort and language levels are more advanced.

One Looks, One Doesn't

In an activity called "One Looks, One Doesn't," you place a transparency of a picture on an overhead projector after telling students that one of them may look at the transparency while the other one looks away. The student who looks at the transparency describes it to his or her partner, who attempts to draw a picture of it. Because the describers can see their partner drawing the picture, they can adjust their language to assist the drawer; thus, the task is both easy and fun for the students. After five minutes or so the picture is revealed to all of the students and they get to see how accurate their communication was. This activity can also be developed for different levels of language use and proficiency. For example, the

134

first transparencies used might be quite concrete, such as a picture of a red car with a number of people in it; later transparencies can be more abstract or complex, such as a picture of a fantasy scene with wizards and goblins.

Another way you can change the complexity of the task as students become more proficient in their oral language is to ask the describer and drawer to place a book or some other object between them so that the describer cannot see what the artist is doing. This then tests the accuracy of the describer and the listening accuracy of the artist. The first activity, in which the two could see one another, is similar to an oral language conversation and is context-embedded because the individuals conversing can check to see if the person they are talking to is understanding them; the second approach is closer to a written message, context-reduced, and causes the communicator to be more specific and accurate to make sure that the response to the communication is effective. The following list gives directions for making transparencies from magazine pictures without special equipment.

1. First wet your finger and touch the border of the page. If your finger shows a chalky substance, then any picture in the magazine will make a transparency.
2. Next, buy clear adhesive shelving paper at a grocery or hardware store.
3. Cut out the picture you want and cut a little larger piece of the shelving paper, removing the backing.
4. Place the picture face down on the adhesive shelving paper and rub firmly with a spoon or plastic scissors handle until the picture adheres clearly.
5. Finally, drop the picture in warm water for about five minutes; then clean the moist magazine paper off the transparent shelving paper. The picture will adhere.
6. Seal your newly made transparency by backing it with another piece of clear shelving paper.

Tape-Recording Children's Re-Creations of Wordless Book Stories

Working with partners, students can use a wordless picture book to create and tape-record a story based on the pictures. Then they can play the story as they show the pictures to the rest of the class. You might have all the students share the same book at first, later on preparing different books to present to one another. Because listeners can see the pictures as each original rendition of the wordless book is being presented, story comprehension is scaffolded. Following is a list of some of our favorite wordless books for older and younger students. In Chapter 7 we present more information on wordless books for students of all ages.

Briggs, R. (1978). *The Snowman.* New York: Random House.
Carle, E. (1971). *Do You Want to Be My Friend?* New York: Harper.
Day, A. (1989). *Carl Goes Shopping.* New York: Farrar.
Goodall, J. (1985). *Naughty Nancy Goes to School.* New York: Atheneum.
McCully, E. (1984). *Picnic.* New York: Harper.
Tafuri, N. (1988). *Junglewalk.* New York: Greenwillow.
Turkle, B. (1976). *Deep in the Forest.* New York, Dutton.

*Wiesner, D. (1988). *Free Fall*. New York: Lothrop.
*Wiesner, D. (1991). *Tuesday*. New York: Clarion.

Taping and Dubbing a Television Show

One activity students enjoy is taping and dubbing their favorite television show, such as a cartoon, a sports event, or a situation comedy. We have found that older students enjoy using soap operas and action/adventure stories to share with one another. You begin by taping the show and showing it to the students without the sound. Alternatively, the original program may be played all the way through with sound first if you think it will help your students understand the original story. Then your students create their own script for the show and dub it either on the original videotape or onto an audiotape to play along with the video. Students work with partners or in small groups to re-create their own television show, which is then played back for their classmates. It's especially fun to see the different ways each group has treated the same visual story. It can also be interesting at this point to play the original show to compare it with the meanings students have imputed in their scripts. If you have questions about your particular use of a television show, check copyright laws.

This taping and dubbing activity allows students to choose some of their favorite television programs, negotiate the meaning of the pictures, and create their own drama to present to the class. Because they are familiar with the show, they are able to use its story structure to create their own play. Moreover, in small groups children assist one another in understanding and re-creating their own stories. Because the scene is visual, it provides an additional channel of communication for English learners. Perhaps most important, script development of this sort is highly motivating, thus promoting functional and fun involvement in a multimedia language and literacy event. When this dramatic activity is used in classrooms, students and teacher often laugh heartily at the outcomes of each group's drama, motivating them to create more scripts!

Choral Reading

Have you ever been to a large gathering where there is community singing and found that you couldn't remember all the words to the song? You may have been able to succeed in the group singing because you could fake it: When you weren't sure about the next word you could often sing the word a split second after others around you. In a sense you were experiencing the way a group singing scaffolds an unsure singer. Choral reading, a strategy involving students reading together, scaffolds English language learners reading in a classroom in the same way. By involving students in selecting the readings, you can ensure that students of all ages are afforded the benefits of choral reading.

---

*Books for older students.

When you use choral reading with English learners and other students, you need to select materials that are age appropriate and a little beyond what your students can read on their own, that is, in their zone of proximal development (McCauley & McCauley, 1992). Next, you read the materials to students several times while showing the words to a poem or story. Then students can practice through repeated reading before they perform. During this practice phase, the students may brainstorm different ways to act out or pantomime the actions in the reading. Finally, students read the story together and act out the actions.

One of the powers of choral reading is that you can select books and have children select books for varying degrees of language and reading ability. Books and poems that lend themselves to more concrete actions and

These first-graders put in a lot of effort preparing to present a choral reading to the fifth-graders of a favorite book. Their rehearsals had a real purpose, motivating them to perfect their reading through repetition and practice.

that have repeatable patterns, such as *The Very Busy Spider* (Carle, 1984), will be easier for students to understand. As students develop ability they can still be challenged with more difficult books. We recently observed one first-grade class performing a choral reading of *Madeline* (Bemelmans, 1939). When they read each part of the story, they acted out the actions. For example, when the children in the story brushed their teeth, the choral readers brushed with much vigor; when the children ate, the performers pretended to eat as well. Dramatization, when combined with choral reading, allowed these English learners to be actively involved and reinforced the meaning of the story phrase by phrase.

Research indicates that choral reading helps children learn the intonation of English stories and improves their diction and fluency (Bradley & Thalgott, 1987). In addition, choral reading raises the enthusiasm and confidence of early readers (Stewig, 1981) and helps them expand their vocabulary (Sampson, Allen, & Sampson, 1990). Finally, children find great joy in choral reading and are eager to try it over and over with some of their favorite books. Choral reading need not be limited to young children. Poems, song lyrics, and picture books that appeal to older learners can serve as the basis for this enjoyable, low-anxiety oral language activity. You may select passages from literature such as *The House on Mango Street* (Cisneros, 1994) or poetry selections suggested in the district curriculum. Finally, consider asking your students to suggest song lyrics.

Riddles and Jokes

Riddles and jokes can be a lot of fun for students at the intermediate English proficiency level. You will need to consider the extent to which the age and cultural backgrounds of your students will affect their understanding of the humor, though. You might read some riddles and jokes that you think are appropriate for the age, language level, and cultural backgrounds of your students, modeling for them what they will do when they have practiced their own riddles and jokes in small groups. Then you can set aside a day for your students to share the jokes. As an alternative, you might make riddles and jokes a part of your regular classroom routine, inviting student participation on a volunteer basis. The activity allows students to have fun with something they enjoy doing, helps them become more comfortable speaking in front of the class, and gives them a chance to rehearse before making their presentation.

In summary, there is a variety of oral language development opportunities available through drama, songs, poetry, riddles, and jokes. The activities described in this section facilitate oral language development in at least three ways: (1) They encourage students to work in groups on motivating projects, (2) they provide various scaffolds for oral language performance, including informal rehearsal, written scripts, and choral readings prior to spotlighted performances; and (3) they focus on fun uses of oral language, reducing the anxiety sometimes associated with using a non-native language. Finally, although these activities may be implemented solely for the sake of language development and community enjoyment, some can and should be integrated into academic projects in content-area learning, at least some of the time.

ORAL LANGUAGE DEVELOPMENT THROUGH CONTENT-AREA INSTRUCTION

In addition to integrating drama, music, and poetry into your academic curriculum, each of the content areas presents specific oral language demands and learning opportunities. In this section, we discuss mathematics, science, and social studies to illustrate how content-area instruction provides both content learning and academic language development if comprehension and learning is supported with sheltering strategies. Our discussion concerning second language development and content instruction applies to learners of all ages but is especially pertinent for upper elementary, middle, and high school.

Oral English Development and Use in Mathematics

To tailor your mathematics instruction to the language and learning needs of your English learners, consider the particular cognitive-linguistic demands that mathematics instruction places on your students. Mathematics is a formal and sys-

138

tematic approach to using numbers and number concepts for solving problems in daily life and other areas, including research in the physical, social, and biological sciences. Most elementary math concepts (e.g., addition, subtraction, multiplication, and division; fractions and mixed numbers; inverse operations; and patterning and probability) can be illustrated through demonstration and manipulation of concrete objects such as unifix cubes, beans, buttons, and patterns blocks. Using concrete objects is one way to make math concepts meaningful and more accessible. In fact, current mathematics pedagogy emphasizes extensive use of manipulatives to promote discovery of basic mathematics concepts, in a sequence that goes from concrete to pictorial to abstract (National Council of Teachers of Mathematics, 1989; Reys, Suydam, & Lindquist, 1991). Another way to make math concepts more meaningful and understandable is to embed them in real-life situations that your students have experienced.

All students, regardless of age or home language, must develop both the concepts and the academic language that mathematics uses to convey these concepts. Mathematical language, whether conveyed in English, Spanish, Chinese, or any other language, is specific, precise, and logical. As with all content instruction, English learners are best prepared to benefit from math instruction if they have attained at least an intermediate level of English language proficiency. However, English learners' prior math background, the difficulty of the material, and the extent to which the concepts can be conveyed nonverbally also affect the ease with which English learners learn math. Where feasible, primary language support for conceptual understanding may be helpful for many. Let us take a look at some aspects of English as used in mathematics that English learners, as well as others, need to control for successful learning.

Mathematical language includes unique vocabulary, sentence structures, semantic properties, and text structures, both oral and written, as discussed in full by Dale and Cuevas (1987) and summarized here. You generally teach these aspects of mathematical language through oral instruction or oral instruction supported by writing words, formulas, and equations on the chalkboard. Math vocabulary includes words that are specific to the discipline, such as *numerator, denominator, addend,* and *sum*. In addition, math vocabulary includes words students may already know but must now learn with a new meaning, such as column, table, rational, and irrational. As you consider the cognitive-linguistic load present in mathematics instruction, you need to keep in mind that certain difficult vocabulary may require review, preferably in the context of solving problems related to your students' daily experiences. For example, students need to learn that addition can be signaled by any of these words: *add, plus, combine, and, sum,* and *increased by*. Similarly, subtraction may be signaled by such words as *subtract from, decreased by, less, minus, differ,* or *less than*. These addition and subtraction examples come from Crandall, Dale, Rhodes, and Spanos (1985), cited in Dale and Cuevas, 1987.

One of the best ways to promote cognitive processing of math concepts is through pair work and small-group problem solving. Here we have an ideal situation for development of cognitively demanding oral language use. As students discuss how to approach a problem, they become conscious of problem-solving strategies. If you teach such strategies, you will help students develop both metacognitive skills and the kind of language we employ to guide our own thinking efforts, the heuristic function of language, in Halliday's terms. Word problems provided in written format can be analyzed and discussed orally and converted to appropriate mathematical formats to be solved. As you can see, mathematics requires substantial linguistic processing in order for students to understand and apply mathematical concepts and operations to problem solving.

Oral English Development and Use in Science

Science abounds with cognitively demanding oral language uses, provided that it is taught using a process-oriented inquiry approach (Kessler & Quinn, 1987). Within such an approach students work in pairs or groups to define a problem, state a hypothesis, gather data, record observations, draw conclusions relating data to the hypothesis, and explain and summarize findings. Scientific inquiry requires students to use academic language to convey the thinking involved in observing, classifying, comparing, measuring, inferring, predicting, concluding, synthesizing, and summarizing. In fact, researchers concerned with quality education for English learners have found that process-oriented science classes provide excellent language and content learning for students learning English (De Avila & Duncan, 1984; Kessler & Quinn, 1984; Mohan, 1986; Thomas & Collier, 1995).

The success of inquiry-based science projects for English learners is attributable to three major factors: (1) Students investigate real science problems that engage their natural curiosity about the world, such as plant growth, the solar system, electricity, and magnetism; (2) students are actively engaged in investigations involving hands-on activities, actual observations, and lab work rather than solely reading facts and theories in a textbook; and (3) students carry out investigations in groups that promote talking out their thinking and planning. What we see, then, is that inquiry-based science provides many opportunities for higher-level thinking through use of context-embedded oral language aimed at solving scientific problems, creating ideal opportunities for both language and content learning.

You will increase motivation and facilitate comprehension of science concepts if you connect these concepts to students' prior knowledge. For English learners, prior knowledge is apt to reflect different cultural assumptions from your own. You will want to bear in mind that every culture has its own theories and beliefs about many domains of science, such as classification of plants and animals and explanations for the movements of celestial bodies. Kessler and Quinn (1987) point out that miscommunications may arise with English learners when your students start with different assumptions from yours about the world. For these reasons, you will need to find ways to identify your students' prior knowledge, beliefs, and assumptions about phenomena you are studying. Students' observations and thinking may conflict with previous notions about the physical world, and these conflicts are most likely to come to light during group discussions. Such "sociocognitive conflict" is a natural part of scientific learning that we all go through, however, and should be considered as positive (Kessler & Quinn, 1987). We recall writer Eudora Welty (1983) telling about a short story she had written in which she described the moon rising in the west. Her editor promptly advised her to be more accurate in her settings, creating both sociocognitive conflict and an immediately relevant learning opportunity for Welty!

There are certain kinds of academic language use associated with science that all students, including English learners, need to learn. Vocabulary related to a particular scientific domain is necessary for precision in identifying and describing concepts (e.g., *periodic table, element, ion*) as well as naming materials and tools (e.g., *microscope*). In addition, students need to develop the ability to put together logical descriptions of experimental procedures and findings. Logical descriptions require careful sequencing of information held together by cohesive ties such as *however, therefore, because,* and *in conclusion.* Research shows that using cohesive ties in both oral and written language is especially difficult for English learners, a topic addressed in detail in Chapter 8 (Goldman & Murray, 1989, 1992). Oral discussions in pairs or groups will assist students in conceptually organizing their results for a clear presentation, oral or written.

As you can see, full participation in inquiry-based science requires at least an intermediate level of English proficiency, although beginners may benefit as well, particularly if sheltering strategies are used and if primary language support is provided by the teacher or paraprofessional. In addition to rich oral English learning opportunities, science projects offer natural and necessary math applications. We describe strategies for integrating oral language, literacy, and content areas, including strategies for reading and writing research reports, in Chapters 8 and 9.

141

Oral English Development and Use in Social Studies

In some ways, the concepts, generalizations, and understandings required for social studies depend heavily on oral and written verbal descriptions and explanations. This is especially true for a discipline such as history, which concerns people and places no longer available for direct viewing. Nonetheless, social studies topics may be made more concrete for students through films, pictures, videotapes, and museum visits. In addition, students may study their own communities and family histories as a personally relevant social science project through which they can learn social science inquiry methods, such as survey, interview, and observation. Finally, students will benefit from group discussions to help them understand and communicate what they have learned. In addition to research efforts carried out through oral language interactions, students need access to information that may be available only in written form. Literacy skills are thus essential. We provide many strategies for content-area reading and writing in Chapters 8 and 9. Here we will briefly review some of the oral language development opportunities inherent in the study of the social sciences.

The social sciences present oral language opportunities in a variety of ways. Chances are you will be presenting information orally to students some of the time through a lecture format. If you use pictures, graphs, flowcharts, gestures, and other visual supports to convey meaning, you will increase students' concept development while providing oral language development opportunities. All of the sheltering strategies presented in Chapter 3 are appropriate not only for social studies instruction but for other content areas as well.

Social studies also provides opportunities for students to present simulations or reenactments of historical or political events. We saw earlier how fourth graders wrote and presented a play depicting the Gold Rush, incorporating songs and poems. Playing the part of legislators, students may debate a proposed bill or dramatize the process of enacting legislation. In addition, groups of students may select particular topics to study in depth, as in the jigsaw cooperative group procedure described in Chapter 3. As experts, they then present their findings to the class. When students make presentations to the class, they should always support their talk with visuals they have prepared to convey meaning. Through presentations such as these, presenters organize information and rehearse it for effective oral delivery. Listeners benefit in content and language development from the sheltered delivery provided by their peers. As you gain practice in analyzing the social studies content you teach, you need to find (1) ways to present the content through visuals, dramatizations, and other multimedia and (2) ways to increase students' use of oral language to discuss, analyze, synthesize, and summarize information; i.e., their academic language use.

In summary, we have briefly described oral language development demands and learning opportunities inherent in mathematics, science, and social studies. Our discussion is intended to illustrate ways of looking at the content you teach in terms of the oral language required for learning. If you are a content-area teacher, you know your subject area in depth. As you review your lesson plans, you will want to think about the kinds of oral and written language required for your English learners to understand the concepts and to demonstrate their learning. In all content areas, sheltering strategies should be used along with hands-on, direct experiences for inquiry and discovery. In addition, students should be given time and opportunity to process information orally in pairs and groups. They also need time and opportunity to rehearse for oral presentations. Given such time and opportunity, your students will advance in English language development while learning subject matter with greater understanding and retention than would otherwise be possible.

CLASSROOM ASSESSMENT OF ENGLISH LEARNERS' ORAL LANGUAGE DEVELOPMENT

In Chapter 2 we described formal, standardized language proficiency tests, which serve the purpose of program assignment. In this section, we describe ways to document and assess students' oral language progress through classroom observation using checklists, anecdotal observations, and a structured oral language observation instrument called the Student Oral Language Observation Matrix (SOLOM). The SOLOM focuses your attention on five oral language traits: comprehension, fluency, vocabulary, grammar, and pronunciation. Checklists can be constructed to include any of a variety of oral language behaviors that you wish to document, including particular grammatical structures, vocabulary, conversational interactions, and presentational skills. Anecdotal observations consist of on-the-spot narrative accounts of student oral language use during particular classroom activities. Each of these observation techniques allows you to evaluate your students' use of oral language forms as they are used to serve communicative functions in particular social contexts in the classroom. We discuss the SOLOM oral language performance checklists and anecdotal observations below.

The Student Oral Language Observation Matrix (SOLOM)

Teacher judgment is one of the most important and accurate measures of English learners' oral language development. One observational instrument that teachers can use to assess their students' oral proficiency is the Student Oral Language Observation Matrix (SOLOM), shown in Figure 4.2. With this tool, your observations of student oral language use during day-to-day classroom activities stand in place of formally elicited language samples used by the commercial tests such as the language assessment scales and others described in Chapter 3. As the teacher, you will be able to observe your students periodically over the year in a variety of naturally occurring classroom situations. As a result, your cumulative observations of student oral language use will be much richer, more natural, and more educationally relevant than a standardized test (Goodman, Goodman, & Hood, 1989). In addition, your students will be focused on the classroom task, alleviating the anxiety factor typical of testing situations. By combining your focused observations over time with the descriptive evaluations in the SOLOM, you will be able to document student progress in English oral language development.

While you observe students during day-to-day classroom activities, the SOLOM observation matrix is organized to focus your attention on general oral language traits, that is, comprehension, fluency, vocabulary, grammar, and pronunciation. Thus, you are, in fact, evaluating student language on several analytic dimensions. Your ratings are ultimately subjective and require substantial linguistic sensitivity to be accurate and meaningful. However, we believe that you can develop such sensitivity through guided experience in language observation and analysis. Research, in fact, supports teacher efficacy in rating students' second language oral proficiency, using procedures similar to the SOLOM (Jackson, 1980; Mace-Matluck, 1980, 1981).

To use the SOLOM, you observe a student during a classroom activity that promotes oral language use, such as group work. You may spend five minutes or so listening to the speech interactions among the members of the group, paying particular attention to the student or students you wish to evaluate. During the observation itself, or shortly afterward, you fill out one observation form per student according to the descriptive traits outlined for you on the form. If

143

	1	2	3	4	5
A Comprehension	Cannot be said to understand even a simple conversation.	Has great difficulty following what is said. Can comprehend only "social conversation" spoken slowly and with frequent repetitions.	Understands most of what is said at slower-than-normal speed with repetitions.	Understands nearly everything at normal speed, although occasional repetition may be necessary.	Understands everyday conversation and normal classroom discussions without difficulty.
B Fluency	Speech is so halting and fragmentary as to make conversation virtually impossible.	Usually hesitant; often forced into silence by language limitations.	Speech in everyday conversation and classroom discussion frequently disrupted by the student's search for the correct manner of expression.	Speech in everyday conversation and classroom discussions generally fluent, with occasional lapses while the student searches for the correct manner of expression.	Speech in everyday conversation and classroom discussions fluent and effortless, approximating that of a native speaker.
C Vocabulary	Vocabulary limitations so extreme as to make conversation virtually impossible.	Misuse of words and very limited vocabulary; comprehension quite difficult.	Student frequently uses the wrong words; conversation somewhat limited because of inadequate vocabulary.	Student occasionally uses inappropriate terms and/or must rephrase ideas because of lexical inadequacies.	Use of vocabulary and idioms approximates that of a native speaker.
D Pronunciation	Pronunciation problems so severe as to make speech virtually unintelligible.	Very hard to understand because of pronunciation problems. Must frequently repeat in order to make himself or herself understood.	Pronunciation problems necessitate concentration on the part of the listener and occasionally lead to misunderstanding.	Always intelligible though one is conscious of a definite accent and occasional inappropriate intonation patterns.	Pronunciation and intonation approximate that of a native speaker.
E Grammar	Errors in grammar and word order so severe as to make speech virtually unintelligible.	Grammar and word-order errors make comprehension difficult. Must often rephrase and/or restrict himself or herself to basic patterns.	Makes frequent errors of grammar and word order that occasionally obscure meaning.	Occasionally makes grammatical and/or word-order errors that do not obscure meaning.	Grammatical usage and word order approximate that of a native speaker.

FIGURE 4.2 SOLOM: Student Oral Language Observation Matrix

SOLOM PHASES: *Phase 1: Score 1 = non-English proficient; Phase II; Score 12–18 = limited English proficient; Phase III:*
Score 5–11 = *limited English proficient; Phase IV; Score 25 = fully English proficient.*
Based on your observation of the student, indicate with an "X" across the block in each category that best describes the student's abilities. The SOLOM should be administered only by persons who themselves score at level "4" or above in all categories in the language being assessed. Students scoring at level "1" in all categories can be said to have no proficiency in the language.

Source: Courtesy of California State Department of Education.

you are using the SOLOM to document student progress over the course of the year, you need to make sure that the social context of your observations is similar each time in order to ensure comparability of performance. For example, you may wish to make cooperative group work your primary observation time. To get a richer picture of your student's oral proficiency, you should observe several different contexts such as formal presentations in front of the class, cooperative group work, and individual conferences with you when discussing schoolwork. These contexts are not test contexts, but rather involve students as they carry out routine classroom activities. As a result you are evaluating authentic oral language used for real, day-to-day classroom purposes.

Figure 4.2 explains how to score the SOLOM. As you can see, each trait (i.e., comprehension, fluency, vocabulary, pronunciation, grammar) receives a rating from 1 to 5, according to the descriptors. After writing an X on the appropriate descriptors, you tally the ratings for all five traits. The SOLOM yields four phases of English language proficiency: Phase I, 5–11, non-English proficient; Phase II, 12–18, limited English proficient; Phase III, 19–24, limited English proficient; and Phase IV, 25, fully English proficient. You will notice that both Phases II and III are described as limited English proficient.

For an example of a SOLOM evaluation, let us return to Teresa, the fifth-grader whose *Poltergeist* narrative we offered as an example of an intermediate English speaker earlier in this chapter (Example 4.2). Teresa, a fluent Spanish speaker who came to California in the third grade, is fluent in oral and written Spanish. She has been enrolled in a bilingual program since her arrival, and she has been learning English for two years. We have reproduced Teresa's narrative below for you to read again, this time with some additional conversational interchanges lasting a total of 85 seconds. As you read through the transcript, consider how you might evaluate Teresa's oral language performance based on the SOLOM descriptors for comprehension, fluency, vocabulary, grammar, and pronunciation.

SUZANNE: But at least you got to see *Poltergeist*.

TERESA: Yeah.

SUZANNE: Was it scary?

TERESA: No, it wasn't escary. But well . . . at first it was scary but then the other one no. Because there was . . . First a little girl . . . There was a television and the father was sleeping in the . . . in a . . . *sillón?* in like a chair. And then the little girl pass the television and she said, "Right here!" Then . . . then a hand get out of the television and she said, "Ouch!" And then a little boy was sleeping and the little girl sleep here and the little boy here and then he see all the time a tree and then . . . then . . . there was outside a tree . . . a tree. But it look ugly in the night. It look like a face . . . And then he was escary. Then he tell his father and his father said OK. Just count 1, 2, 3 to not escare. Then . . . then . . . the . . . he . . . the little girl and the little . . . the two brothers go in with the mother and her father because they're still escare. Then the other night . . . the little boy was . . . everyday he was counting and counting and he get up to . . . up to 2,000. He say 2,000, 2,001 and the hand of the tree get up like that . . . and the hand of the tree get up like that...And the . . . then the other escare that . . . because he broke the window. The tree. And the hand. And he get the boy and he said, "Mommy, mommy help me!" And then . . . But the tree was . . . I think the house was . . . it was haunting because there was a lot of the . . . of the . . . in the movie there came out many . . . um . . . many men but they are bad. They was ugly.

SUZANNE: Ooh, were they skeletons?

TERESA: Yeah.

SUZANNE: Or were they ghosts?

TERESA: They look like a ghost. They were a ghost and . . .

At this point another student interrupted. Discussion of the movie ended.

Now let's evaluate Teresa's oral language based on this sample. First, take a look at the descriptors for comprehension. Because Teresa does most of the talking, we do not have a great deal to go on to evaluate her comprehension. Based on her responses to questions and her comprehension of the movie itself, we give her a 4: "Understands nearly everything at normal speed, although occasional repetition may be necessary." For fluency, we have some trouble deciding between a 3 and a 4. Reviewing the transcript, we try to decide *how frequently* Teresa's speech is disrupted because of lack of fluency. Many of Teresa's repetitions and restarts are similar to those of native English speakers. In and of themselves they do not disrupt communication. However, there are three instances in which Teresa seems to be searching, somewhat unsuccessfully, for a way to express herself. The first time is at the beginning when she says, "No, it wasn't escary. But well . . . at first it was scary but then the other one no. Because there was . . . First a little girl." It takes her five tries to get into the narrative. After that, however, she is off and running until she says, "Then . . . then . . . the . . . he . . . the little girl and the little . . . the two brothers go in with the mother and her father . . . ." Here again she is disfluent. She seems to have been searching for a word meaning "brother and sister." The closest word in English, though not commonly used in conversation, is *siblings*. Teresa apparently uses a direct translation of *los hermanos,* the brothers.

In Spanish *los hermanos* can mean "the brothers," but it can also mean "the brothers and sisters," or "the brother and sister." Therefore it has a broader range of meaning than "the brothers" in English. As a result, when Teresa uses the direct translation, her meaning becomes confused. The third example of disfluency occurs at the end when she says, "And the . . . then the other escare that . . . because he broke the window. The tree. And the hand. And he get the boy and he said, 'Mommy, mommy help me!'" These three instances of disfluency go beyond repetitions and restarts found in natural, spontaneous speech of native and nonnative speakers alike. We decide that these disruptions are infrequent enough to rate this oral language sample as a 4: "Speech in everyday conversation and class-

146

room discussions generally fluent, with occasional lapses while the student searches for the correct manner of expression."

For vocabulary, we are again torn between 3 and 4 to describe Teresa's oral performance. As with the fluency trait, it is the word *frequently* that we have to consider carefully. We decide on 4: "Student occasionally uses inappropriate terms and/or must rephrase ideas because of lexical inadequacies." For example, she uses the word *sillón,* rephrasing it as *chair.* Although her vocabulary is not rich, we think that it is usually adequate for her purposes, thus the 4.

For evaluating pronunciation we rely on the audiotape because our written transcript conveys only a few aspects of her pronunciation. We rate the sample as a 3: "Pronunciation problems necessitate concentration on the part of the listener and occasionally lead to misunderstanding." Teresa is not "very hard to understand" as in the descriptor for a 2, nor "always intelligible" as in the descriptor for a 4. The 3 rating thus fits very well. For grammar, we find ourselves trying to decide whether Teresa's grammatical errors are frequent—3—or occasional—4. We decide on a 4, primarily because her grammar and word order errors do not obscure meaning for us. She demonstrates one error consistently: the omission of the -s on third person singular verbs, such as *he see* and *it look like.* In a similar vein, she says, "a hand get out." Teresa uses the present tense form for indicating both present and past tense, a fairly typical strategy that often persists rather late in second language acquisition, but which does not seriously impede communication. She also uses non-native English word order at times, such as "he see all the time a tree" and "there was outside a tree." For us, these errors do not impede communication, so we are comfortable with the 4 rating.

Now that we have rated Teresa's oral language performance on the SOLOM traits, we add the scores for a final rating.

Comprehension:	4
Fluency:	4
Vocabulary:	4
Pronunciation:	3
Grammar:	4
Total:	19, or Phase III: limited English proficient

Let's talk for a moment about the rating process for the SOLOM. You must have noticed that we had difficulty choosing between ratings on some dimensions. You might have rated Teresa's sample differently yourself. In fact, when we ask our students to fill out the SOLOM for Teresa's narrative, there are always some variations in trait scores and the resulting total score. For one thing, the taped narrative, though very useful as an introduction to the SOLOM, lacks the major strength inherent in the tool: *in-person observation of natural language use in your own classroom.* If you were getting ready to make instructional or programmatic decisions for Teresa, you would need several in-person observations upon which to base your SOLOM ratings. Another factor influencing ratings is the extent to which raters are accustomed to the non-native speech patterns of English learners. The

147

important thing in using the SOLOM is to apply the descriptive criteria as consistently as possible. It is also important to notice that a broad range of scores, from 14 to 24, yields a "limited English proficient" label, though divided into Phase II and Phase III. Thus the SOLOM offers additional descriptive detail and analysis within the category "LEP," highlighting the fact that "LEP" actually covers a rather broad range of second language development. In summary, the SOLOM provides a general index of oral language proficiency that is based on actual oral language use during day-to-day classroom activities such as group work, teacher student conferences, and classroom presentations. By building a set of observations over time, you will obtain a developmental picture of oral language progress.

What instructional implications can be drawn for Teresa? First, Teresa has sufficient English oral language proficiency to benefit from academic instruction delivered in English, provided that sheltering or SDAIE techniques are used to ensure lesson comprehension. Moreover, substantial exposure to academically demanding material in English is precisely what she needs to challenge her to higher levels of second language development. However, Teresa still needs the educational support of a bilingual or English language development program. She will benefit from reading, writing, and making oral presentations in English with scaffolding provided by the teacher and other students who are more advanced in English language development. At the moment, she struggles when reading in English, though she is fluent, successful, and enthusiastic when reading in her home language, Spanish. We would encourage her continued Spanish literacy use and development, while providing structured opportunities for her to read and use a wide variety of English language materials supported by opportunities for buddy reading, story mapping, literature discussion, and other strategies for intermediate-level students described in Chapters 6 through 9.

In summary, oral language assessments based on the SOLOM may be used as one source of information, among several, to inform decisions to reclassify students to the category of fully English proficient, as discussed in Chapter 3. In addition, SOLOM data may be collected periodically and placed in a student's language development portfolio. For this purpose, the descriptive statements and total score are more useful for documenting student progress than the designations of NEP, LEP, and FEP. By including periodic SOLOM observations in the student's portfolio, you form a developmental picture of oral language progress over time that will provide a solid basis for instructional decisions.

Checklists and Anecdotal Observations

The SOLOM provides a general index of oral language proficiency. Two other assessment tools, checklists and anecdotal observations, may also be used to provide additional information about your students' ability to use oral English for a variety of purposes. Checklists can be useful because you can tailor them to your specific evaluation needs. In addition, checklists are convenient to use because they list the behaviors to look for and merely require a checkoff. However, when you devise a checklist, you need to try to include any and all potential behaviors, as well as leaving a place for "other" so that you can list unexpected behaviors. Another benefit of checklists is that evaluations are based on holistic observations of students in the course of day-to-day classroom language use, as is the case with the SOLOM and anecdotal records.

An anecdotal record is a running account of an observed oral language event, written on the spot, describing the event and quoting the participants as closely as possible to convey how the interaction unfolds in real time. Anecdotal observations require considerable effort and focused attention because you must observe and interpret the flow of a social interaction while simultaneously recording it. The benefit of anecdotal observations is that you record interactions as they occur, rather than filling in a checklist. They are thus much more open-ended and provide much richer detail of student behavior. As you make your written account, you provide some on-the-spot analysis, but you also have a narrative record to review later, at which time you might see and understand something that was not evident to you during the observation. A drawback to anecdotal observations is that they start with a blank page. It takes some practice and training to know what to look for and how to "see" when observing, because what you see depends a great deal on how well you understand what you are observing. In addition, the quick pace and complexity of student interactions can be difficult to capture on a page. Some teachers, particularly those interested in conducting their own classroom research, have chosen to use videotapes to back up their on-the-spot observations.

We offer two oral language observation forms in Figures 4.3 and 4.4. These two forms combine the use of checklists and anecdotal observations. If your instructional program requires that you document your student's oral language development with greater specificity than standardized tests or the SOLOM provide, we recommend that you consider these two forms and modify them according to the goals and objectives of your program. Both forms focus your attention on participation structures or interaction patterns. These are the grouping structures within which students interact during your observation. Your form will need to reflect the actual grouping structures that you use in your classroom. Each form also lists a number of language functions often served during classroom interactions. As we observe English learners, we want to see how well they are able to achieve communicative goals and purposes through their developing English skills. Each of the two forms offers examples of classroom language functions that you might look for as your students interact. The language functions in Figure 4.3 are based on Buckley (1981), whereas those in Figure 4.4 are based on Halliday (1975), described earlier in this chapter. You may want to add, elaborate, or modify classroom language functions to suit your curriculum. Finally, each form includes linguistic elements or language forms to call your attention to grammar, pronunciation, vocabulary, and your students' ability to coordinate these as they produce different oral discourse structures such as conversations, debates, and formal presentations to the class.

Although both forms address (1) participation structure, (2) language functions, and (3) language forms, the two forms are designed to be used differently. The form in Figure 4.3 is a modified checklist in which you determine on the spot whether the student is performing at a beginning, intermediate, or advanced level.

149

For each category, there is room for you to jot notes that describe aspects of student performance that support your judgment. The form in Figure 4.4 is set up for you to record a running record of the entire interaction. To use this form, you first fill out the name, subject, and date and then circle the participation structure you are observing. Next, you write a narrative that describes what is happening, who is saying what to whom, and what is accomplished during the interaction. The descriptors listed under language functions and language forms serve as reminders of forms and functions that your student might use during the interaction. After the observation, you review the narrative and make an overall evaluation of the student's performance in terms of language forms and functions within this particular type of grouping format or participation structure.

In summary, the detail with which you document oral performance among the English learners in your classroom will depend on the goals and objectives of your instructional program. General observations such as those prompted by the

150

Classroom Involvement	Beginning Level	Intermediate Level	Advanced Level
Functions: Informal talk Reporting Discussing Describing Explaining Questioning Debating Evaluating Persuading			
Interaction patterns: Partners Small groups Large groups			
Linguistic elements: Vocabulary Syntax Organization Ideas Audience sensitivity			

Other
Comments: Student Name_____   Date_____

FIGURE 4.3   Informal Chart to Follow the Oral Language Development of Your Students

Source: Based on *Oral Language Guidelines*, by M. H. Buckley, 1981. Unpublished.

Student Name_____   Subject _____   Date _____

Activity	Anecdotal Observations
Participation structure: Formal presentation ⟨ individual / group Structured cooperative group work Informal group work Pair work	

Language functions:
 	
    Heuristic
        Hypothesizes
        Predicts
        Infers
        Considers
        Asks
        Reports
    Informative
        Describes
        Explains
        Synthesizes
        Summarizes
        Clarifies
        Responds
        Retells
    Instrumental
        Requests
        Asks for
    Regulatory
        Directs
        Commands
        Convinces
        Persuades
 	
    Personal and interactional
 	
    Divertive and imaginative	

Language forms:
 	
Vocabulary: particular to domain and
        general vocabulary
Sentence structures:
        declarative
        question
        command
        exclamation
        grammatical correctness
Morphology:
Phonology:
Discourse:
	Overall Evaluation:

151

FIGURE 4.4   Oral Language Observation Chart

Source: Based on *Learning How to Mean: Exploration in the Development of Language*, by M. A. K. Halliday, 1975, London: Arnold.

SOLOM may suffice. If greater specificity is needed, language observations structured along the lines of the forms just discussed may be implemented. In that case, you will probably need to develop forms that are tailored to your program, your students, and your classroom organization patterns. Systematic observations carried out periodically are appropriately placed in a student's portfolio and will provide a record of oral language development over time.

Summary

In this chapter we focused on oral language development in second language acquisition. We began by describing how listening, speaking, reading, and writing are intertwined in daily use. We also noted that each of these language processes supports the others during language development. We showed how natural oral

152

Strategy / Grade Level	K	1	2	3	4	5	6	7	8	9	10	11	12
Drama	←———————————————————————————→
Dubbing TV shows			←———————————————————————→
Jokes				←————————————————————→
One looks/one doesn't		←——————————————————————————→
Riddles				←————————————————————→
Scaffolds:													
Create advertisement				←————————————————————→
Create board game			←———————————————————————→
Create comic books			←———————————————————————→
Create popular song			←———————————————————————→
Draw scene/char.	←———————————————————————————→
Dress up figures	←——————————————→
Make wanted posters			←———————————————————————→
Pictures/collages	←———————————————————————————→
Select music for story	←———————————————————————————→
Turn poem into song					←————————————————→
Show and tell	←————→
SOLOM	←———————————————————————————→
Songs	←———————————————————————————→
Wordless book stories	←———————————————————————————→

FIGURE 4.5 **Grade Levels at Which Strategies May Be Used**

language functions can be connected to your classroom routines, and we discussed the importance of integrating oral language with reading and writing activities. Strategies for oral language development were described, as well as oral language demands and opportunities inherent in academic subjects such as mathematics, science, and social studies. Next we described developmental oral language characteristics of English learners by presenting an oral language observation instrument, the SOLOM, followed by examples of speech from beginning and intermediate English speakers. Finally, we offered ideas for structuring your observation and evaluation of students' oral performance by using modified checklists and anecdotal observation records.

We believe that by integrating drama, poetry, and songs into your curriculum, by creating a secure climate where all students want to share, and by providing opportunities for students to process and present academic material in small groups and in front of the class, you will assist English learners with oral language development.

In Figure 4.5 we summarize the strategies discussed in the chapter. The chart provides a general grade-level guideline for using strategies in the chapter, but only you can make the best decision concerning whether children are prepared to work with various strategies in your classroom.

$\mathcal{S}$UGGESTIONS FOR FURTHER READING

Crandall, J. (Ed.). (1987). *ESL through content-area instruction: Mathematics, science, social studies.* Englewood Cliffs, NJ: Prentice Hall.

This edited book offers in-depth discussion and analysis of how to use content-area instruction to promote English language development in mathematics, science, and social studies. For each discipline, special vocabulary and language structures are discussed. In addition, teaching strategies and successful programs for English learners are described for mathematics, science, and social studies.

Ernst-Slavit, G., & Wenger, K. J. (1998). Using creative drama in the elementary classroom. *TESOL Journal, 7*(4), 30–33.

The authors discuss using drama with elementary students, and secondary teachers could easily use the guidelines here to use drama in their classrooms and, more specifically, to help students act out familiar stories. The authors list several benefits students derive from drama: a defined context for language use, extended oral communication repertoires, improved reading and writing, expanded listening skills, emboldened risk taking, and advanced problem-solving skills. Moreover, they give specific examples of how to set up a story-telling classroom.

McCauley, J., & McCauley, D. (1992). Using choral reading to promote language learning for ESL students. The Reading Teacher, *45*(7), 526–533.

An excellent article on choral reading that gives a rationale, procedures for using poetry in particular, and several examples of second language children adapting poetry and drama together. In order to adapt choral reading to English language learners, the article shows how to add gestures and acting out to make the material more comprehensible for novice and more advanced English learners.

Richards, J., & Renandya, W. (Eds.). (2002). *Methodology in language teaching: An anthology of current practice.* Cambridge: Cambridge University Press.

This is one of the best books of its type. It contains 41 short articles on topics ranging from speaking and listening to reading and writing, grammar and pronunciation, and assessment and technology. Articles are written by known experts in specific aspects of second language learning. If you could buy only one book, this might be the best choice.

Silverstein, S. (1974). *Where the sidewalk ends.* New York: Harper & Row.

A book full of poems children love to hear, act out, and read over and over again. The poems range from nonsense poems to fantasy to more serious. Our own classes have loved, among others, "Ickle Me, Pickle Me, Tickle Me Too," "Captain Hook," "Listen to the Mustn'ts," "I'm Making a List," and "Boa Constrictor."

Spolin, V. (1963/1983). *Improvisations for the theater.* Evanston, IL: Northwestern University Press.

This is a classic drama text for actors that we have used from the first year we began to teach. It starts with silent improvisations such as asking pairs to act out being mirrors of one another. It moves to small talking parts in which, for example, strangers are stuck in an elevator for 10 seconds, then 5 minutes, and finally for 2 hours. It ends with students acting out plays. The book contains over a hundred meaningful activities for the classroom. This book is our favorite, but Viola Spolin also has several other very useful books available through the same publisher.

Wright, W., Betteridge, D., & Buckby, M. (2002). *Games for language learning: New edition.* Cambridge: Cambridge University Press.

Games for Language Learning is in its 24th printing since 1983 and there's a reason why: It is an excellent resource for teachers who want to add to their repertoire in language learning and have fun at the same time. The authors provide activities ranging from controlled to guided to free, thus giving appropriate amounts of direction for students at beginning, intermediate, and advanced levels of language. There is a brief but very useful introduction to using games in classrooms.

154 ACTIVITIES

1. Discuss with a partner or in a group the various oral language activities you have been involved in throughout your schooling. Were your teachers anxious to have you involved in group work or were you required to sit still and be quiet most of the time? Did you put on plays, puppet shows, or readers' theater after reading books, or were you in a class in which the book was read and the teacher asked questions about the book? Were you involved in panel discussions? Did you give formal speeches in class? What effect did your involvement or noninvolvement in oral language activities have on your overall interest in school and your capacity to learn?

2. It has been said that very young children learn through their talking, that through talking they are able to think (Buckley, 1981). You will hear young children talking even when they are playing by themselves. Children will talk aloud while they play with dolls or Legos or other toys. What would be the effect on children's language growth of organizing a class to be silent most of the time? What kind of classroom organization provides children with the greatest opportunities for language growth? In terms of language acquisition, are input and output equally important? Whose input and output?

3. If possible, observe a classroom in which students are involved in literature circles or literature response groups. How involved are the English language learners in this activity that relies mainly on language? Does the silence of some students mean that they are not involved? Would they be more involved if the same group of students were preparing a puppet show about a story they had read or if they were creating a poster advertising the story? Observe a class that uses various scaffolds for students and determine whether beginning English learners are more involved when scaffolds such as murals, drawings, or collages are used. What seems to involve intermediate and advanced English learners the most?

4. Help intermediate and advanced English learners set up a debate about a topic that particularly concerns them and have them present the

debate in front of the class. Help students learn formal rules of debate and assist them with practicing before they present it. Provide students with a chart of specific guidelines for debating, preferably making the debate more like a discussion than a competition with winners or losers. Debates may be carried out in teams. Let students evaluate themselves based on the guidelines you provided at the beginning.

5. Demonstrate for students literature study circle responses and discussions. Read a story to the students first and then model a possible discussion concerning the literature. If possible, make or get a videotape of a successful literature circle discussion and show it to your students. Create guidelines for a literature study circle with your students and discuss with them what might work best. Next, read a story and ask students to discuss the story using the guidelines you have created. For more advanced students, let them read a story they've selected and discuss it in their groups. After the first group discussions, ask students to discuss how the group worked together and how they could make their group discussions even better.

6. Observe an elementary school and a high school serving English learners. Arrange to observe a sheltered science lesson (or other content area) in each. When you observe, make a note of how the teachers use language and nonverbal cues to convey lesson content. In addition, make a note of how students interact during whole-class instruction and small-group work. After your observations, compare the elementary and high school lessons in terms of (1) the teachers' talk and sheltered instructional delivery, (2) the cognitive demands of the lesson content, and (3) the opportunities for oral language development made available through the lesson. What conclusions do you draw concerning the challenges teachers and students face? What are the similarities and differences between the elementary and secondary school lessons?

7. Make a focused observation of one English learner during small-group work when free talk is appropriate. Based on your observation, fill out the SOLOM observation chart. Discuss your evaluation with the teacher to see how your evaluation compares with the teacher's judgment. If there are discrepancies between your evaluation and that of the teacher, what might be some sources of these differences? Based on your experience, what are some of the advantages and disadvantages of the SOLOM?

EMERGENT LITERACY: ENGLISH LEARNERS BEGINNING TO WRITE AND READ

In this chapter, we discuss English learners' early literacy development, home–school relationships, classroom strategies to involve your students in reading and writing, and assessment procedures to document their progress in the early stages of reading and writing development. The following questions will guide your reading for the chapter:

1. What does research tell us about the early literacy development of English learners?
2. What are the "emergent literacy" and "reading readiness" perspectives, and how do they influence early literacy instruction?
3. How can teachers and parents work together to enhance home–school relationships and promote early literacy development?
4. How can you organize your classroom to maximize early literacy development for all students?
5. What classroom strategies can you use to provide a firm foundation for English learners' early literacy development?
6. How can you assess early literacy development?

A few years ago, we spent some time in a two-way Spanish immersion kindergarten observing and helping the teacher. Children were immersed in a print-rich environment where they drew and wrote daily in journals, listened to predictable stories and poems, rewrote stories, and played in literacy-enriched dramatic play centers that included a post office, restaurant, office, and grocery store, as well as blocks, arts, and writing areas. We were very interested in how these kindergartners would approach the task of writing in a classroom such as this, where children were invited to draw and write to their hearts' content but were not given much explicit instruction on writing.

During English language arts one day, I (Suzanne) asked a group of six children (native Spanish speakers, native English speakers, and bilinguals) to write a story in English to take home to my husband. I passed out the paper, which was lined on the bottom half and plain on the top, and the children began writing without hesitation. As they wrote, I made note of how each child approached the task, and as they finished, I knelt down to ask each one to tell about their story. Lisa had written the words "I love my mom" in legible script and had illustrated her story with hearts and a picture of herself next to her mother. Rosa had drawn a picture of her seven family members and had filled several lines with block letters evenly spaced. Osvaldo was the last child to finish his work. He had filled the lined half of the page with indecipherable letters and punctuation and was now busy drawing. Three times I asked him to tell me about his story and three times he simply replied, "I don't know yet." The fourth time I interrupted his drawing, he explained in desperation, "I won't know what my story is about until I finish my picture!" His story (see Figure 5.1) was about a boy kicking a soccer ball, a shiny black and white triangular sphere that nearly flew off the page to hit me in the face of my ineptitude!

157

FIGURE 5.1 Boy Kicking a Soccer Ball

These kindergarten children had never been told how to write or what to say. Yet somehow they were quite comfortable with this request to write a story someone else would read. The forms of their writing varied from wavy lines to apparently random arrays of block letters to conventional print. The topics of their stories came from their own interests and experiences. They knew their stories had a purpose of a sort: My husband would enjoy reading them. Yet the children seemed more focused on their own purpose: personal expression of a message from within. It was clear that all six children knew at least something about both the forms and functions of print. Furthermore, they were all confident that they could write a story, one that would at least have meaning for themselves. They differed, however, in the extent to which they were able to approximate conventional writing forms to convey their meaning. Indeed, they differed in their understanding of whether print has anything to do with meaning at all! For Osvaldo, the writing had no meaning until the picture was complete.

When I returned to the classroom after spring break, Osvaldo asked, "How'd your daddy like the story?" In typical kindergarten fashion, he had created an equivalence between "husband" and "dad." But his question revealed something more than his developing understanding of human relationships. It illuminated his sense of audience! Osvaldo provides us with a rich example of the many aspects of writing children must eventually coordinate: forms, functions, and illustrations as well as the need to shape these in a way that will please one's audience. In the early stages of literacy development, young children typically understand and control some aspects of the task better than others. And they must grapple with these complexities while still constructing their understanding of the social and physical world around them: Virtual reality is complex.

The kindergarten children just described were demonstrating early literacy development in an emergent literacy environment. In this chapter, we examine early literacy development as it has been researched over the past two decades. In so doing, we will briefly contrast two viewpoints on children's literacy development: the emergent literacy viewpoint and the reading readiness viewpoint. We will spend some time discussing the main tenets of the emergent literacy perspective, illustrating our points with samples of children's writing and reading, and describing how teachers implement such a perspective in early childhood classrooms. Finally, we describe ways to assess English learners' early reading and writing development. In our discussion we also address a pressing concern of many teachers: *How do I help older English learners who have not yet learned to read or write in any language?*

What Does Research Tell Us About the Early Literacy Development of English Learners?

A large body of research investigates early literacy development in a *first language*. As a result, we now have a substantial amount of exciting and interesting information about young children's early literacy development in English, Spanish, and other languages (e.g., Chi, 1988; Clay, 1975; Ferreiro & Teberosky, 1982; Harste, Woodward, & Burke, 1984; Teale, 1984; Teale & Sulzby, 1986). However, relatively little research documents early literacy development in English as a second language, particularly among students who have not had literacy instruction in their first language. Nevertheless, the research we do have shows that *English reading and writing development processes are essentially similar for both English learners and native English speakers* (Edelsky, 1981a, 1981b; Goodman & Goodman, 1978; Hudelson, 1984; Urzúa, 1987). That is, in reading, all learners gradually come to use their developing English language knowledge, their world knowledge, and their understanding of print conventions to make sense of written text. Similarly, in writing, they use their developing English language knowledge, world knowledge, and understanding of print conventions to put their ideas on paper. For all learners, literacy development is a complex process that takes place over a lengthy period during which they demonstrate gradual approximations to mature versions of reading and writing. In both reading and writing, all learners must learn the forms of print in English, including the letters of the alphabet and how these are sequenced into words, sentences, and paragraphs to create letters, stories, recipes, and other forms of written communication. At the same time, all learners must learn to select from this rich array of written discourse forms to achieve the communicative functions at hand, whether to direct, inform, persuade, entertain, complain, or console. Finally, written language use takes place in a social context and serves personal and social purposes. Furthermore, literacy learning is achieved through interpersonal relationships in the varying social contexts in which literacy instruction takes place. Literacy development thus evolves through social interactions involving written language from which children develop ideas about the forms and functions of print. They also become aware of the ways print is used in different social contexts for a wide variety of purposes.

While many aspects of reading and writing development are essentially similar for English learners and native English speakers, there are important differences as well. Two important differences are a student's English language proficiency and ability to read and write in the primary language (Hudelson, 1987). Students at the beginning stages of English language development are still acquiring basic knowledge of English while learning to read and write English in school. Research shows that English learners can benefit from English literacy instruction well before they have developed full control of the language orally. In other words, oral and written English can develop more or less simultaneously (Hudelson, 1984, 1986; Goodman, Goodman, & Flores, 1979; Urzúa, 1987), provided that instruction is carefully organized to be meaningful and relevant, a topic we discuss throughout this chapter.

If your English learners are literate in their primary language, they may bring knowledge, skills, and attitudes about reading and writing that transfer to the task of English reading. In fact, research and theory consistently support the benefits of teaching children to read and write in their primary language first, not only because it is easier to read and write a language you already know, but also because

159

> **INTERNET RESOURCE:** Try using the Enchanted Learning site, http://www.sedl. org/sed/diversity.html, to create separate lessons for beginning- and intermediate-level English learners. Within each lesson create a variety of choices among areas such as games, dictionary, and activities using different languages. Have fellow students help you evaluate the efficacy of the lessons and discuss whether your objectives could be met with individual students. See also our companion website, which contains links on emergent literacy: www.ablongman.com/peregoy4e.

literacy skills transfer from the primary language to English, as English language proficiency develops (Cummins, 1981; Peregoy, 1989; Tragar & Wong, 1984). In summary, research shows that English language proficiency and primary language literacy contribute to the ease with which English learners develop English reading and writing skills. Other factors may contribute as well, including cultural factors that affect classroom communication, teacher perceptions of student abilities, student motivation, and teacher-student relationships as discussed in earlier chapters.

In our discussion of early literacy in this chapter, we focus on beginning and intermediate English learners who are new to reading and writing in English as a second language. Most of our discussion applies to beginning readers and writers under age 7. However, we also discuss early literacy instruction for a special group of English language learners: older children and adolescents who have never learned to read or write in any language. Our teaching recommendations for non-native English speakers draw heavily on first language research, applied with caution and sometimes modified to accommodate linguistic and cultural differences. If you are a bilingual teacher, you should note that many of the teaching strategies we describe for beginning literacy in English can be used to teach beginning reading and writing in the primary language, with occasional modifications based on the writing system of the primary language you are teaching.

CONTRASTING THE EMERGENT LITERACY AND READING READINESS PERSPECTIVES

Ideas about when and how young children should be taught to read and write have always been subject to a variety of influences. This is not surprising if you stop to consider that two very different sources of advice, a culture's traditional child-rearing practices and scientific thought of the day, have played a part in forming views of how young children should be educated. In this section we will discuss two theoretical perspectives that have influenced literacy instruction: reading readiness and emergent literacy. We then elaborate on the emergent literacy perspective, the perspective we believe offers the most effective teaching practices for native English speakers and English learners alike.

Reading Readiness Perspective

The **reading readiness** perspective held sway in many parts of the world during much of the twentieth century. Based on maturationist theories of development (see Gesell, 1925) and the standardized testing movement of the 1930s and 1940s, reading readiness proponents adhere to the belief that children are not developmentally ready to read until they reach a mental age of 6.6 years (Morphet & Washburn, 1931). In practical terms, this translated into the postponement of reading until first grade. Writing instruction was also postponed until first grade and aimed at proper letter formation rather than composing or communicating. Kindergarten was to serve the purpose of socialization and oral language development, not literacy.

Reading readiness practices in kindergarten were further influenced by the testing movement of the 1920s and 1930s. Test developers created tests of specific subskills that correlated with reading achievement, including auditory discrimination, visual discrimination, left-to-right eye progression, and visual motor skills. Some educators fell into the trap of assuming a causal relationship in the correlations, believing that early reading success *resulted* from subskill acquisition, rather than just being somehow *linked* with it. As a result, it became common practice to teach these "readiness skills" in kindergarten to "get children ready to read" in first grade. Reading readiness subskill activities were translated into corresponding kindergarten objectives as shown in the following list. When basal reader publishers incorporated readiness subskills into workbooks as part of their reading series, reading readiness theories became effectively established in classroom practice nationwide.

The list below provides examples of reading readiness subskills and corresponding learning objectives for kindergartners (Morrow, 1983, 1993).

Reading Readiness Subskills	Sample Objectives
auditory discrimination	• identify and differentiate familiar sounds (car horn, dog barking, siren) • identify rhyming words • identify sounds of letters
visual discrimination	• recognize colors • recognize shapes • identify letters by name
visual motor skills	• cut on a straight line with scissors • color inside the lines of a picture • hop on one foot
large motor skills	• skip • walk on a straight line

Several years ago we had a personal experience that called our attention to reading readiness practices in school. When our neighbor's child, Aretha, entered kindergarten, she could already read and write stories. She used to sit at a little

161

table in the living room and churn out pages of imaginative stories that often began with "Onc upn atym." Occasionally, she would ask her mother or father how to spell a word, but she usually used her own spelling. Perhaps because her parents were teachers, she loved to play school and "teach" her little brother how to read using her mother's kindergarten materials. By first grade, Aretha was already a writer and could read books from the second- and third-grade classes.

But when Aretha's mother and father met with her kindergarten teacher during parent conferences, they were astounded to hear that Aretha was not ready for first-grade reading instruction. The teacher explained that Aretha was still having trouble with some basic kindergarten tasks: cutting with scissors and hopping on one foot. Aretha's parents could not see the connection between these motor skills and learning to read. Moreover, they knew Aretha could already read and write. To remedy the situation, Aretha's father asked the teacher to listen to Aretha read a book. After Aretha successfully and fluently read out of two textbooks, her teacher concluded that Aretha was indeed ready for reading instruction. Though well-meaning and conscientious, Aretha's teacher held some false assumptions about reading that blocked her ability to recognize Aretha's capabilities and potential, a reminder that we must always examine and reexamine our assumptions about learning and teaching.

In summary, reading readiness is a traditional view of literacy instruction that assumes that children must be able to perform certain auditory, visual, psychomotor, and linguistic tasks in order to show the maturity needed for reading instruction. Children like Aretha would be tested to see if they could tie their shoes, skip properly (one of the things Aretha had trouble with and still does at 19), trace pictures, hear the difference between similar words such as *pin* and *tin*, and so on, all as prerequisites for reading instruction. Problems with the reading readiness perspective came to light when children like Aretha proved they could read without having developed some of the so-called prerequisite readiness skills. For English learners, the language-related prerequisites for reading were often especially inappropriate, such as hearing the difference between initial consonants in two otherwise identical words (e.g., *pin–bin, chair–share*), or the expectation that oral language should be fully developed before reading instruction could begin. For native English speakers and English learners alike, many reading readiness subskill prerequisites turned out to be unnecessary hindrances to literacy development.

Emergent Literacy Perspective

The basic tenets of the reading readiness perspective were called into question as a result of research in the 1960s on children who learned to read before receiving reading instruction in school (Durkin, 1966). These early readers had not been drilled on auditory and visual discrimination tasks, nor did they wait until they could hop proficiently on one foot before they engaged in reading. On the other hand, they didn't learn to read by age 2 while hiding alone in a closet either, as philosopher Jean-Paul Sartre (1967) claimed to have done. Rather, these early readers set their sights on doing what they saw other people doing, and they engaged the adults at home in answering their questions about print and reading. Gradually, they figured the rest out for themselves. The percentage of children who learn to read without formal instruction is quite small. However, by investigating these children's literacy development processes, researchers documented the need for a theory of early literacy development that could accommodate their findings. The stage was set for a new perspective: the emergent literacy perspective.

According to the **emergent literacy** perspective, pioneered by Marie Clay (1975) in New Zealand and Emilia Ferreiro and Ana Teberosky (1982) in Latin America, children begin to develop written language knowledge from the moment they are first exposed to reading and writing at home during their preschool years, possibly from the time of birth (Clay, 1982). Literacy development is viewed as somewhat parallel to oral language development in process (Peregoy & Boyle, 1993). That is, as children are immersed in social environments where people are reading and writing for a variety of purposes, they take note of how the written word is used around them in lists, notes, letters, storybooks, road signs, product labels, magazines, and other environmental print. From this highly functional written input, children gradually construct knowledge of the functions and forms of print. Of course, little ones want to get into the act as well and will take to pencil, paper, and books readily. You may have seen preschoolers pick up a storybook and "read" it to their stuffed animals, turning the pages and pointing out the pictures as they go along. Given the opportunity, children will also try out writing on paper with drawing, scribbling, and various other forms of writing that gradually begin to approximate conventional writing. Thus *comprehensible input, social interaction, and children's gradual approximations to mature reading and writing are important factors in early literacy development*, just as they are in oral language development.

An important aspect of the emergent literacy perspective is that literacy development begins at a very young age at home amid day-to-day family and community activities. As a result, with literacy learning no longer considered the sole province of the school, family involvement in early literacy is highlighted. Whereas advocates of reading readiness discouraged parents from teaching their children to read, emergent literacy educators encourage parents to involve their children in naturally occurring literacy events at home such as reading stories and making grocery lists, emphasizing the importance of home–school relationships in early schooling.

To summarize, we have examined two viewpoints on beginning reading and writing development: reading readiness and emergent literacy. The reading readiness perspective was based on the best scientific knowledge available in the first half of the century. However, literacy research in recent decades refutes the major assumptions of the reading readiness perspective and calls into question many of its practices, especially practices that withheld from children opportunities to engage in authentic, purposeful reading and writing, however rudimentary their efforts might be. Emergent literacy research has led to the following teaching recommendations, which we consider applicable to native English speakers and English learners alike.

163

1. Acknowledge that all children bring literacy knowledge to school, while recognizing that children vary in their sophistication in literacy concepts and skills.
2. Immerse children in a variety of functional reading and writing experiences that display the purposes of literacy while demonstrating and modeling the processes of reading and writing.
3. Enrich dramatic play centers with functional print, including lists, tablets, prescription forms, phone books, and other props, to encourage children to experiment with reading and writing during play.
4. Accept and celebrate children's progress in their gradual approximations to conventional literacy.
5. Encourage children to read and write at home and to talk to their parents about their reading and writing.

Specific strategies to implement these recommendations for English learners are described in the remainder of this chapter.

Differences between Oral and Written Language Development

The emergent literacy perspective emphasizes similarities between oral and written language acquisition. Although there are many similarities between oral and written language acquisition, there are also some significant differences, summarized in Figure 5.2. First, oral language is universally achieved, whereas literacy acquisition is not. No one has posed an innate "literacy acquisition device" comparable to Chomsky's "language acquisition device." Thus, there are some cultures that never developed literacy, and there are some individuals in literate cultures who do not learn to read and write.

Oral Language Development	Written Language Development
Every culture develops oral language.	Not every culture develops written language.
Every child learns the language of his or her community with rare exception.	Not every child learns the written language of his or her community.
Oral language is learned with little explicit instruction.	For most children written language must be learned with a lot of explicit instruction.
Oral language is the primary vehicle for meeting our basic needs.	Written language is not the primary vehicle for meeting our basic needs.

FIGURE 5.2   Some Significant Differences between Oral and Written Language Acquisition

Another difference between oral and written language development is that oral language is learned with relatively little explicit instruction, whereas written language development requires substantial explicit instruction and practice. For example, young children self-correct as they move from saying, "Him don't say it right" to "He doesn't say it right." No one needs to teach them. In contrast, almost all students need explicit instruction on particular reading and writing conventions. One reason explicit instruction is needed is simply that it saves time to tell a third-grader to spell -*tion* at the end of words instead of the more logical -*shun* that the child has been using or to break long words into parts or to use letter/sound cues to promote early independence in reading. Speaking of explicit instruction, we are reminded that emergent literacy pioneer Marie Clay is also the developer of Reading Recovery (Clay, 1975), an early intervention program that provides explicit phonics instruction integrated with meaningful reading and writing for first-graders experiencing difficulty learning to read.

Differences between oral and written language acquisition tend to be differences in degree rather than kind (Snow, 1983). For example, the fact that literacy acquisition is not universally achieved in literate societies may be partially attributable to the difference in degree of functionality between oral and written language. You can't get by in life very well without talking because oral language is used so often to meet basic needs. Written language is certainly functional, but it does not have the immediacy of oral language. No child is required to read the word *Cheerios* in order to get breakfast. As teachers, we need to increase and highlight the functions of literacy in our classrooms. As literacy uses proliferate, your students will be motivated to read and write. In addition, the more you read and write in the classroom, the more your students will be able to see how it is done and why. You are a powerful model. As students work with the medium of written language, they will develop many conventions on their own. When necessary, though, you should feel free to use explicit instruction, especially when children ask you for it. And they will!

HIGHLIGHTING LITERACY FUNCTIONS IN YOUR CLASSROOM

It takes some thought and imagination to create and highlight literacy functions in your classroom. When you create a variety of literacy purposes for your students, you broaden their understanding of literacy functions and motivate them to learn how to read and write. If your students have little prior experience with reading and writing, it is all the more important that you explicitly talk about how these can be used for different purposes, such as a card to send birthday wishes to a friend far away, a list to help you remember what to buy at the store, a journal to keep a record of the events of a trip to visit relatives, and a personal phone book to keep your friends' numbers handy. Table 5.1 cites additional examples of literacy functions that children use at home and at school.

TABLE 5.1 Written Language Functions and Classroom Experiences

Functions	Classroom Experiences
Instrumental I want	Order forms in play store
Interactional me and you	Message board for notes from teacher to children; class post office; dialogue journals
Personal Here I come	Books about self and family with captioned pictures; individual language-experience stories
Heuristic Tell me why	Question box; single-concept books; science experiments; learning logs; response journals
Imaginative Let's pretend	Story reading; readers' theater read-along books and records; comic strips
Informative I've got to tell you	Message boards and bulletin boards; notes to pupils paralleling school messages to parents; class newspaper; content textbooks; resource books
Regulatory You should	Daily schedule posted; directions for feeding the class pet posted; behavioral rules posted

EXPLORING THE VISUAL FORM OF WRITTEN LANGUAGE

One fascinating aspect of early literacy development is young children's explorations of the visual form of the writing system they see used around them, whether alphabetic as in English, logographic as in Chinese, or syllabic as in the Cherokee writing system developed by Chief Sequoyah in the nineteenth century (see Crystal, 1997). Just as children acquire the oral language forms spoken around them, they also experiment with the written forms that they see others using. Figure 5.3 illustrates 4-year-old children's attempts at writing in English, Arabic, and Hebrew, each of which uses a different alphabetic writing system, in which letters represent language sounds (Harste, Woodward, & Burke, 1984). Although not yet conventional, each child's writing is recognizable as a precursor of the conventional form of the corresponding alphabet. These examples of young children's early attempts at writing show us their efforts to represent the visual aspects of the alphabetic writing system they have seen used around them. Their writing approximates the mature writing systems, but not well enough yet to be clearly decipherable.

Research suggests that children learning logographic writing systems, in which written characters represent words, may also go through similar stages, from scribbling to inventive character forms to standard character formation (Chi, 1988). Figures 5.4 and 5.5 show young Taiwanese writers' approximations in constructing characters of the Chinese writing system. Figure 5.4 shows early iconic pictographic writing in which the child's writing looks like the actual item. That is, for the word *bed* the child draws a picture of a bed. Below each item is the Chinese character for the word. Figure 5.5 gives an example of more advanced, invented pictographic writing that closely approximates conventional Chinese characters (Chi, 1988).

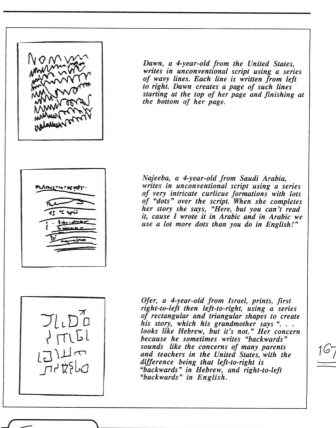

Dawn, a 4-year-old from the United States, writes in unconventional script using a series of wavy lines. Each line is written from left to right. Dawn creates a page of such lines starting at the top of her page and finishing at the bottom of her page.

Najeeba, a 4-year-old from Saudi Arabia, writes in unconventional script using a series of very intricate curlicue formations with lots of "dots" over the script. When she completes her story she says, "Here, but you can't read it, cause I wrote it in Arabic and in Arabic we use a lot more dots than you do in English!"

Ofer, a 4-year-old from Israel, prints, first right-to-left then left-to-right, using a series of rectangular and triangular shapes to create his story, which his grandmother says ". . . looks like Hebrew, but it's not." Her concern because he sometimes writes "backwards" sounds like the concerns of many parents and teachers in the United States, with the difference being that left-to-right is "backwards" in Hebrew, and right-to-left "backwards" in English.

FIGURE 5.3 Emergent Writing in English, Arabic, and Hebrew

Source: Reprinted by permission of Jerome C. Harste, Virginia A. Woodward, and Carolyn L. Burke, *Language Stories and Literacy Lessons*, 1984, Portsmouth, NH: Heinemann, a division of Reed Elsevier Inc.

Development of Alphabetic Writing: Connecting Symbols and Sounds

The examples of children's emergent writing in Figures 5.3, 5.4, and 5.5 illustrate youngsters' attention to the visual aspects of writing systems. In this section, we take a look at two studies that show how children working with alphabetic writing systems gradually connect the visual symbols with the sounds they represent in order to make their written messages decipherable to others. Elizabeth Sulzby, an emergent literacy researcher, examined the writing of 24 English-speaking kindergarten children (Sulzby, 1985). She identified six categories of writing strategies that the children used, but cautioned that these categories did not necessarily represent developmental sequences. The categories were:

FIGURE 5.4   Chinese Iconic Pictographic Writing. These pictographs were written by a 5-year-old Chinese boy. Beneath his pictographic writing is the conventional Chinese character and the meaning in English.

Source: Original data, reprinted with permission, courtesy of Dr. Marilyn Chi.

FIGURE 5.5   Pictographic Invented Writing. This 5-year-old Chinese boy is using symbols that look like the conventional Chinese character, as shown in parentheses.

Source: Original data, reprinted with permission, courtesy of Dr. Marilyn Chi.

1. Writing via drawing
2. Writing via scribbling
3. Writing via letterlike forms
4. Writing via reproducing well-learned units or letter strings
5. Writing via invented spelling
6. Writing via conventional spelling

As shown in Sulzby's research, when children first begin to use letters, they may not use them to represent sounds. Eventually, however, children represent sounds with letters. At this stage, they create their own invented spellings, which are logical and readable but not yet fully conventional. When children create invented spellings, they are demonstrating advanced emergent literacy. It is through children's invented spellings that we see them really working through the sound/symbol puzzle inherent in writing English (Gentry, 1980).

In our own research in the two-way Spanish immersion kindergarten described at the beginning of this chapter, we analyzed journal entries made by eight Mexican American children who were native Spanish speakers writing in Spanish (Peregoy & Boyle, 1990a). We identified seven developmental scripting strategies in Spanish that correspond very closely with those found by Sulzby in English. Our categories, shown in Figure 5.6, are distributed along a continuum from least advanced to most advanced: scribble writing, pseudo-letters, letters, pseudo-words, copied words and phrases, self-generated words, and self-generated sentences. Like Sulzby, we found that these were not discrete developmental sequences. In fact, some children used two or more scripting strategies in the

169

WRITING TYPE	DEFINITION	EXAMPLE
scribble writing	wavy lines or forms that don't look like letters, but look a little like writing	
pseudo letters	forms that look like letters, but aren't	
letters	recognizable letters from the alphabet; often seen in long rows	
pseudo words	letter or pseudo letters that are spaced so they appear to be words	
copied words	words that have been copied from displays in the classroom	
self-generated words	words students created that are close enough to conventional spelling to be recognized	
self-generated sentences	conventional or nearly conventional sentences that communicate ideas	

†IGURE 5.6   **A Continuum of Developmental Scripting Strategies**

Source: From "Kindergartners Write! Emergent Literacy of Mexican American Children in a Two-Way Spanish Immersion Program," by Suzanne F. Peregoy & Owen F. Boyle, 1989–90, *The Journal of the Association of Mexican American Educators*, p. 12. Reprinted with permission of the publisher.

same journal entry. You may want to adapt Figure 5.6 as a teacher-researcher and chart the developmental progress of your own emergent writers.

In our emergent writing research in the Spanish immersion kindergarten, we were able to document ways in which native Spanish-speaking Mexican American children took control of their own Spanish literacy development in a constructive manner similar to that reported in other studies (Ferreiro & Teberosky, 1982; Sulzby, 1985). They used drawing to assist them with the task of developing ideas for writing, and they wrote about topics related to home and school, including topics initiated during circle time. In addition, these kindergartners used the print that surrounded them in and out of the classroom as a form of input for scripting. They took note of words in the wall dictionary, labels from around the room, alphabet charts, and their own names, and incorporated these into their journal writing. Several of the children made significant progress in constructing literacy in the emergent literacy kindergarten. However, some children made relatively little progress, the result, in part, of the teacher's extended absence because of illness that year. More research is needed on children whose literacy progress proceeds very slowly in emergent literacy classrooms.

Finally, it is important to note that the children in our study varied in prior literacy experiences gained at home. In some cases the children's parents had attained less than a sixth-grade education, whereas other parents were high school graduates. One child, whose mother we met at school, was already being encouraged to write at home. Therefore, it is not surprising that he was the most sophisticated writer in our study. We regretted that we were unable to visit each child's home to find out what kinds of literacy materials were available and how the family incorporated literacy events into day-to-day activities.

In summary, in this section we examined ways in which young children explore the visual forms of written language. As they experiment with written language, they may gradually reconstruct the spelling system well enough to convey written messages without having to explain their meaning. To achieve accuracy in conventional spelling and other aspects of written language generally requires formal instruction. In the next section, we take a closer look at some of the concepts about print that students need to develop in order to use the alphabet for reading and writing.

Print Concepts That Emerge in Emergent Literacy

We have suggested that children begin to develop their own literacy knowledge through exposure to meaningful, functional literacy events in a process similar to oral language development. What are some basic literacy concepts and insights that develop during the emergent literacy phase? In addition to an ever-broadening understanding of the many communicative functions and personal purposes served by written language, emergent readers and writers must grasp the following ideas about print:

1. Print carries meaning. It conveys a message.
2. Spoken words can be written down and preserved.
3. Written words can be spoken, that is, read out loud.
4. In English, words are read from left to right, top to bottom.
5. In English and other languages that use alphabets, the speech stream can be divided into sounds, and these sounds are represented by letters or groups of letters. This is the alphabetic principle.
6. The speech stream has a linear sequence in time that corresponds to written language's linear sequence on the page.
7. Sound/symbol correspondences are consistent, but in English there are many exceptions.

As you read this list, you probably noticed how abstract all this sounds. It is abstract! You could never teach children these things by trying to have them memorize these statements! It is through immersion in a literacy-rich environment with lots of stories read aloud and lots of opportunities for children to write on their own that they begin to understand the marvelous truths about print, its relationships to spoken language and its power to communicate across time and space.

The first four of the preceding list of print concepts probably seem extremely obvious to you. For young children, however, there is still a great mystery to the printed word, and children have to come to understand gradually that print can convey meaning and that it does so by representing language. You will recall our friend Osvaldo, the kindergartner whose writing had no meaning until his picture was complete. Osvaldo did not yet grasp the specific relationship of print to meaning and language. On the other hand, he did understand that writing should convey a message, and he was interested in knowing how his story was received!

The last three print concepts, which sound technical to many who hear them for the first time, all relate to the alphabetic principle, that is, the idea that language sounds are represented by letters and letter sequences. The first alphabet was created over 3,000 years ago by the great Semitic trading people of the Mediterranean, the Phoenicians. Theirs was a brilliant discovery, one that is reconstructed daily by children learning to read and write. What does it take to reconstruct the alphabetic system that children see in use around them? Let's consider the idea that the speech stream can be divided into sounds. If this idea seems obvious to you, it is probably because you read and write and have therefore had many opportunities to work with the **graphophonemic units,** or letter–sound correspondences, of your language. A phoneme, you may recall, is the smallest unit of sound that makes a difference in meaning in a language, and a **grapheme** is the letter or letter combination, such as *d* or *th*, that represents that sound (Stahl, 1992). The streamlike nature of speech is more evident when you listen to someone speaking a foreign language. Then it's hard to discern individual words, much less individual sounds: It's all a flow of sound. Young children are confronted with the speech stream in a similar manner, except that they are further distracted from listening for sounds by their attention to the meaning of the speech stream. Young children do, however, know how to play with language sounds, an ability that develops around age 4 or 5. Evidence that children can divide the speech stream comes from word play, such as spontaneous rhyming. For example, you may have heard children who take a word like *cake* and generate a litany of rhymes: *take, lake, Jake, rake.* They do this for fun, but it shows that they understand the concept of a speech sound because they have replaced the initial consonant, a single speech sound, in each word to create a new rhyming word. In so doing, they are demonstrating **phonemic awareness,** or awareness of individual sounds that constitute spoken words. In fact, one way to assess a child's level of phonemic awareness informally is to ask him or her to tell you words that rhyme.

Research suggests that phonemic awareness is an important aspect of early reading development in English and one of the best predictors of native English-speaking children's future success as readers (Adams, 1990a, b). This makes sense when you consider that the alphabet is a graphic system that relates letters to speech sounds. As students learn the relationships between speech sounds and the letters in written words, they gain access to one of the main cueing systems in reading (along with syntax and semantics): phonics or graphophonics (Goodman, 1967; Stahl, 1992). Key research suggests that once children grasp (1) the idea that words consist of different phonemes and (2) that letters represent these phonemes, they can benefit from phonics instruction (Ehri & Wilce, 1985; Frith, 1985; Juel, Griffith, & Gough, 1986; Perfetti et al., 1987). However, phonics instruction should address sound/symbol correspondences that students have not acquired already through meaningful experiences with print and through their own personal efforts at reading and writing.

You can no doubt see how important the concept of speech sounds is to the development of the alphabetic principle. Phonemic awareness should not be considered a prerequisite for literacy instruction, however. Indeed, we believe that exposure to written language promotes phonemic awareness by showing children how oral language sounds are divided, sequenced, and represented by letters and letter sequences. Reading poems, stories, and song lyrics aloud while students read along is one way. Giving them opportunities to write is another. Your students' emergent writings demonstrate the extent of their understanding of the alphabetic principle as well as other concepts about the forms and functions of print. In fact, one of the best ways for learners to work on phonics is through their own writing using invented or temporary spelling. Just as children's oral language "errors" (e.g., "he goed" for "he went") represent logical, developmental hypotheses about grammar, so also children's and older students' invented spellings (e.g., *bar* for *bear*) represent their logical, developmental hypotheses about how to spell. You need to be well prepared to explain invented or temporary spelling to parents as a high-level cognitive process in which students "think through" how sounds and letters relate to one another. Invented spelling represents an important step on the way to conventional spelling while providing individualized phonics practice that will assist both reading and writing development.

Invented or Temporary Spelling: Children Working Out Sound/Symbol Correspondences

We have talked about invented spelling at some length. Now let's look at two children's writing samples to examine the logic inherent in their invented spellings. Sam is a 7-year-old Farsi/English bilingual who is proficient in English, whereas Martha is a 6-year-old native English speaker. In Figure 5.7, we see a note Sam wrote to his mother, a university student. Because she is not always home when Sam gets out of school, the two of them post notes, messages, and letters on the refrigerator door to keep one another apprised of events of the day or coming events.

Sam uses some interesting spelling strategies. For example, he spells *Friday* "Firiday," because that's how he hears it. Notice that each of the words he invents or constructs is decipherable by sounding out the word phonetically with a little help from the context. So we get "shering" for *sharing*, "scelitin" for *skeleton*,

FIGURE 5.7 Sam's Writing

173

"girag" for *garage*, "owt" for *out*, and so on. We know how he pronounces the word *envelope* because of his spelling, "onvilope." We also get Sam's original spelling for *take*, which we might not expect: "tace." Most important, we see in Sam's writing a consistency as he constructs the sounds he hears in English into his own individual, sophisticated, and logical spelling system. Incidentally, we thought that the words at the end of the letter, *Berrloe'lh Berrbill,* were made-up or Farsi words, but his mother told us they were from a favorite book of his—another indication of the effects of a highly literate environment.

In Figure 5.8 we see evidence of 6-year-old Martha's approach to the task of representing her words through invented spellings. For the most part, the consonants she uses are consistent with the sounds she wishes to represent. She has learned the conventional sound/letter correspondences and uses them effectively. In contrast, spelling vowel sounds presents a challenge to Martha. English has numerous vowel sounds, but few vowel letters to represent these sounds, just *a, e,*

FIGURE 5.8   Martha's Writing

In the figure, the child's handwritten text reads:

thar wus a lost dog and hee Koodint finde a hom but hee finlee fawnd a onr

Foow

174

i, o, u, and sometimes *y* and *w.* Even conventional spelling does not offer a one-to-one correspondence between English letters and sounds. Let's see how Martha is handling this challenge. In her story in Figure 5.8, she consistently uses *"ee"* to represent the long *e* sound as in "hee" for *he* and "finlee" for *finally.* Her double vowel strategy is used inconsistently, however. For example, she uses double *o* in "koodint" for *couldn't,* even though it doesn't have a long *o* sound. In addition, Martha uses a different approach to long vowel sounds, writing "finde" for *find,* "hom" for *home,* and "onr" for *owner.* In these words, she lets the vowel "say its name." Finally, Martha hears the diphthong, two vowel sounds combined, in the word *found,* which she spells "fawnd". Even though Martha's vowel spellings are inconsistent, they portray the sounds well enough for the words to be decipherable. Invented spellings as sophisticated as Martha's and Sam's show us how children are working out orthographic representations of language sounds. If you can decipher the message, the child has done an effective spelling job even if it is not completely conventional.

Although Sam and Martha provide interesting examples of invented spelling for us to analyze, their efforts also demonstrate a clear understanding that writing has meaning and purpose. Their messages make sense and serve particular functions: Sam is communicating with his mother; Martha is writing a piece of fiction. Martha is an avid storywriter, in fact, and she uses a number of literary devices in her stories, including openings such as "Wuns upon a time." In addition, her characters tend to have a problem that they solve, evidence of a rudimentary plot. We mention these aspects of the children's writing to highlight that spelling is but one aspect of written language that learners must begin to control as they develop literacy. They will need time, practice, and instructional support to proceed to conventional reading and writing, important topics we develop in Chapters 6 through 9. In addition, we discuss spelling development and instruction later in this chapter.

ℰMERGENT LITERACY IN ENGLISH AS A NON-NATIVE LANGUAGE

Very little research addresses the emergent English literacy development of English learners who have not received literacy instruction in their primary language. Although more research is needed, we believe that English learners will develop emergent literacy concepts following patterns similar to those documented for native English speakers (Hudelson, 1984, 1986). Therefore, the teaching strategies we offer in subsequent sections of this book emphasize immersing students in meaningful, functional uses of reading and writing combined with explicit instruction to assist them in becoming independent readers and writers. National panels reviewing research on the teaching of beginning reading recommend phonemic awareness, phonics, reading fluency, and comprehension as the cornerstones of the curriculum. Students should receive beginning reading instruction in the primary language, if possible (Snow, Burns, & Griffin, 1998). Complex topics like phonemic awareness have yet to be investigated in English as a second language. However, there will be differences early on in English learners' ability to perceive and produce English speech sounds, depending on the extent of their English language proficiency. For this reason, *English learners should not be involved in phonics instruction that isolates sounds and letters from meaningful use of text.* That is to say that any phonics instruction should take place in the context of whole texts such as poems, songs, and predictable stories for which understanding and enjoyment have been developed, prior to focusing on individual words and sound/symbol patterns. In so doing, both language and literacy acquisition are served first, and children receive explicit phonics instruction subsequently.

As with young English learners who are new to literacy, there is very little research on older English learners who have little prior literacy experience in either the primary language or English. However, Else Hamayan (1994) has given us an interesting report on her experiences teaching ESL to Southeast Asian refugee adolescents in the Philippines in a program designed to prepare families to relocate to North America. For various reasons, the adolescents in her class had never received literacy instruction, and their families were nonliterate as well. Thus, the students had very little experience with functional print. In dialogue journal entries to share with her, Hamayan's students tended to copy print materials they found at home, such as their parents' ESL exercises. They seemed to focus on form, without any idea that print served to communicate a message. Hamayan concluded that their lack of experience with print left them in the dark about its functions and purposes.* Based on her experiences with these students,

---

*Alternative explanations for these students' approach to writing in dialogue journals might be their unfamiliarity with the genre or their belief that the most important thing was to produce correct forms for the teacher.

Hamayan suggests that older nonliterate students need to be introduced gradually to the numerous ways reading and writing are used for communication, that is, written language functions. In addition to constant exposure to literacy functions, Hamayan suggests explicit teaching of reading and writing strategies in order to help them learn as quickly and efficiently as possible. As Hamayan says, "Although an exclusive use of structural approaches falls short of the needs of children from low-literacy backgrounds, explicit attention to the rules and the structure of written language can help learners become literate and develop higher-order thinking skills and learning strategies" (Hamayan, 1994, p. 290). Hamayan's recommendations echo the ones we make here for younger learners. Because of their age and more advanced cognitive development, older learners may be able to learn some aspects of literacy more quickly than younger children. However, as yet we have insufficient data to draw detailed conclusions about the differences between younger and older learners whose first exposure to literacy is in their second language. If you have such students, you might consider documenting your teaching strategies and corresponding student progress over time. Sharing your experiences in class or at conferences can increase your own understanding while making a worthwhile contribution to the field!

In summary, we have contrasted the reading readiness and emergent literacy perspectives of early literacy development. We elaborated on the emergent literacy perspective, discussing research findings and implications for instruction, including the importance of immersing students in a variety of functional literacy events and providing opportunities for them to construct reading and writing in their own way, gradually approximating conventional written language. We went on to discuss in some detail several early insights learners must achieve in the emergent literacy phase of reading and writing development, most of which related to the alphabetic principle. In our discussion, we emphasized that emergent readers and writers are also expanding their understanding of how print can serve a vast array of communicative functions and purposes. Thus a crucial role for teachers is to illustrate the usefulness of reading and writing for many purposes in classroom and community. Finally, we discussed implications for English learners, noting that more research is needed on the emergent literacy paths taken by English learners, including those who are older when introduced to literacy for the first time.

HOME AND SCHOOL ENVIRONMENTS THAT NURTURE EMERGENT LITERACY

In literate societies, young children's literacy development begins well before kindergarten, and this holds true across ethnic and socioeconomic lines. In many countries, children are exposed to environmental print in the form of road signs, billboards, announcements in store windows, and magazines in doctor's offices, to name just a few. In addition, you will find literacy materials of various kinds in most homes: magazines, newspapers, CD or tape labels, TV guides, books, and paper and writing tools. Many teachers have been led to believe that immigrant families, poor families, and other minority group families neither use literacy at home nor value education in general. A growing body of research now refutes this belief. Although it is true that families vary in the ways children are involved in literacy at home, literacy nonetheless serves numerous functions in most homes, including homes of families living below the poverty level (Chall & Snow, 1982; Taylor & Dorsey-Gaines, 1988), families in which English is not the primary language (Delgado-Gaitán, 1987; Díaz, Moll, & Mehan, 1986; Vásquez, 1991), and families with low educational levels (Heath, 1983; Purcell-Gates, 1995). Perceptive teachers will find ways to recognize and build on children's home language and literacy experiences, thereby transforming deficit myths about English language learners and other language minority students (Díaz, Moll, & Mehan, 1986; Flores, Cousin, & Díaz, 1991).

How Do Home Environments Promote Early Literacy?

Parents and other family members provide a powerful model for children every time they pick up a newspaper or magazine; every time they put pen to paper, whether to post messages on the refrigerator, make grocery lists, write letters, or note appointments on their calendar; and every time they cut out grocery coupons or discuss the call-waiting feature announced in the recent phone bill. In so doing, family members model the forms and functions of print for children. These natural, functional, daily uses of written language provide a good foundation for literacy because children see that written language is a wonderful tool. They want to own the mystery of such powerful magic.

Another way families promote literacy development is by answering children's questions about print. Children often initiate literacy events when they ask, "What does that sign say?" The question triggers a response, "That's a stop sign. It means we have to stop at the corner to let other cars go by." I (Suzanne) can remember at age 7 sitting in the front seat as my father was driving home from the store. I saw a big, yellow YIELD RIGHT OF WAY sign, and I asked my dad what it meant. He explained it, but I remember being confused by the concept. Luckily, I didn't need to understand that sign for another ten years, when I finally got my driver's license! Sometimes children ask parents how to spell a word as they write at home. At other times, children will beg to have a story read. In each case, children *invite* modeling, scaffolding, and explicit instruction from parents and siblings, thereby providing a natural means of language and literacy development at home.

Children also show interest in writing from an early age. As soon as a toddler can grasp a pen or crayon, the impulse to write will appear. This impulse often takes on grand proportions if children gain surreptitious access to a "blank" wall in the house. Perhaps you are one of those early writers/artists who wrote on walls as a child, or less joyful, perhaps you were the parent who had to repaint the wall!

177

Providing children with writing materials early on may not only encourage literacy development but also save your walls!

A favorite story of ours illustrates another way parents and siblings promote early literacy development: reading aloud to children. When the writer Katherine Anne Porter entered school as a child, her teacher discovered that she knew how to read upside down! It turned out that her mother had always read stories across a small table, and Katherine taught herself to read upside down! Reading aloud to children is, indeed, a powerful learning experience that can begin very early in a child's life. We recommend holding the book right side up, though, so that children can see that reading in English is done left-right, top to bottom.

What do we know about the literacy concepts children bring to school if a language other than English is spoken in the home? First, we know that for early literacy concepts to develop, exposure to literacy events is what matters most, not the language of the written materials or the language in which the discussion around written materials takes place. Many non-English-speaking parents have feared that using their native language at home might be harmful to their children's acquisition of English. This turns out to be untrue (see Wong Fillmore, 1991a, 1991b; Cummins, 1981). In the case of early literacy in particular, when children are involved in functional literacy activities at home—in, say, Spanish or Cantonese—they begin to form important concepts about how print works in form and function. In the process, they begin to have expectations about print and they want to read and write. These understandings will transfer to English literacy when they go to school. Similarly, with oral language use, it is important that parents talk to children in extended and elaborated ways in the language they know best, because doing so helps young children build knowledge of the world that will serve them in school and transfer to English once the second language is developed.

A small percentage of English learners may come to school with extremely limited literacy experience. However, even parents who are not highly educated often expose their children to the functions of print. You may recall the story of Gustavo in Chapter 1. Gustavo at age 6 understood deeply the importance of the written word because his mother had to find someone who could write a letter to Mexico to obtain medicine essential for his baby sister's health. His mother could not write, but the importance of writing was certainly understood. Parents of English learners, whether immigrants or native-born, vary in their own literacy development; some are highly educated, others are not. However, nearly all value literacy and education (cf. Delgado-Gaitán, 1987). In fact, many have risked their lives to come to this country for the specific purpose of obtaining a better education for their children.

Some children who are learning English in school come from cultures with strong oral storytelling traditions in the home language, be it Navajo, Spanish, Hmong, or African American English. It is important to note that oral traditions also offer excellent foundations for literacy development. We know, for example, that fables and folk tales have predictable story structures, as do television soap operas, which you can watch in Spanish, Chinese, English, and other languages in some areas of the country. Children become familiar with the narrative structures of these genres and with the characters themselves, potentially creating a familiar foundation when they encounter similar stories in print at school. It can be a challenge to find out about the oral traditions of the children in your class, but these stories can provide a rich multicultural resource for early literacy development.

In summary, families promote early literacy in many ways: by modeling a variety of day-to-day literacy uses; by answering children's questions about print and its meanings; by providing children with literacy materials, including paper, pencils, books, and magazines that allow them to play with reading and writing; and by telling stories and reading aloud to children.

Family Literacy Programs

Numerous research studies have shown that children who are read to at home tend to achieve better when they go to school (Wells, 1986). Furthermore, the active involvement of parents in children's schooling has a positive impact on their school adjustment and performance (Epstein, 1986; Topping & Wolfingdale, 1985). These research findings have led many educators to become involved in family literacy projects aimed at promoting story reading and other kinds of literacy activities among families, particularly low-income, minority, and immigrant families. Some family literacy projects offer classes for parents in English language and literacy with a focus on promoting parent involvement in their children's schooling. The best family literacy programs assess and acknowledge the language and literacy used at home and build from there.

We have seen family literacy projects of various kinds. A number of projects emphasize teaching parents to read storybooks to their preschool and kindergarten children. Some projects teach specific read-aloud techniques such as asking children to predict what the story will be about or to predict what will happen on the next page, or asking children at the end why they liked or disliked the book (Edwards, 1989). Story reading seems to be beneficial in a variety of ways. Perhaps most powerful is the cozy, loving laptime moments that story reading creates. It also provides parents with a chance to exercise their own reading skills, while boosting parental self-esteem in knowing that they are strengthening their child's chances for success in school. Finally, by modeling story reading for children, parents provide a rich source of numerous emergent literacy concepts.

A special kind of family literacy project has been instituted in the last decade as a result of federal funding (ESEA Title VII): Family English Literacy. These programs serve the parents of children who are learning English in school. The parents themselves are English learners, and the Family English Literacy programs assist parents in learning to speak, read, and write in English. The functional focus of English language use involves parents in reading with their children as well as listening to their children read; talking about homework and school concerns with their children; and engaging children in literacy-related home activities such as cooking, writing notes, and marking the calendar for special events.

179

Among the most promising Family English Literacy projects are those that make a particular effort to learn about, acknowledge, and build on the literacy activities already present in the home (Auerbach, 1991). In such projects, parents use the English literacy class to identify their own needs and concerns in a safe forum for dialogue about family and community issues. At the same time, they learn how to advocate for their children in school. Most important, family literacy projects help forge comfortable connections with the school among parents who previously may have felt alienated from educational institutions, while helping immigrant and other parents take control of their own lives and those of their children.

One particularly interesting family literacy project was undertaken in the Pajaro School District in California several years ago (Ada, 1988). In this project, educator Alma Flor Ada invited Spanish-speaking parents to come to the library to study children's literature as a focus for developing their own literacy skills. Many of the parents had never advanced beyond the second or third grade in Mexico and were therefore unsure of themselves in school settings. Children's literature provided a natural, nonthreatening, and inviting means to literacy. As parents attended the sessions, they began to see that there were many ways in which they could become involved in literacy activities at home with their children. They felt validated to know that using Spanish and talking about Spanish language children's literature would have a positive effect on their children's school experiences, including literacy development in English. As a culminating project, parents and children wrote stories about significant events in their lives. Through this project parents had the opportunity to reflect on their relationships with their children, with the school, and with their as yet unwritten futures. In so doing, they took a more active and aware stance in creating and re-creating their own life stories.

Promoting Parent Involvement in English Learners' Schooling

Promoting involvement among your English learners' parents can be quite a challenge, especially if you don't share a common language. Cultural differences may also impede the school relationships you wish to achieve, if parents' prior experiences with schools were minimal or if their school experiences emphasized separate, autonomous roles for home and school. We offer some suggestions here that we have gathered over the years.

Make Parent Involvement a Schoolwide Goal. If parent involvement is a school priority, then resources can be provided for increasing home–school communication. For example, school notices can be translated into your students' home languages. Because schools often have numerous different primary languages within the student population, it is essential to have the support of the administration in providing translators. If possible, a community liaison worker can be hired to make phone calls or visit the homes, if needed, to make sure parents receive important information.

Teachers sometimes report difficulties in getting parents to come to school, whether for Open House, parent conferences, or other school functions. If children are bussed some distance to school in cities or rural areas, it is often quite difficult for parents to get to the school. In addition, some parents work long hours and are unable to attend school functions because of work schedules. Nonetheless, you can make a special effort to help parents feel comfortable at school by providing notices in the home language that explain the purpose of the school function and what will be happening. We have often been told that the best way to get parents to come to school is to provide a social event that includes food and the opportunity to see their children performing songs, dances, or plays. Because each community is different, you may wish to brainstorm parent involvement ideas with paraprofessionals, community liaisons, teachers, and the principal at your school, especially those who are members of the particular cultural groups you serve.

Taking School Activities Home. In addition to translating notices sent home and making efforts to bring parents to school, you can forge home–school connections and promote language and literacy development through carefully structured take-home activities. We know of one teacher who lets children take home a teddy bear for one day. The next day at school, the child reports to the class what the teddy bear did at home. Similarly, you can implement the use of a "literacy backpack." You will have to buy one or more small backpacks, depending on how many you want to have in use at one time. You place literacy materials in them to be taken home for a specified number of days. One week, you might insert colored markers and several sheets of paper; another week, you might put in a copy of the storybook you have been reading to the class. You need to make sure that the rules on caring for the items and the due date for return are clear. To promote parent involvement, children can be asked to show their parents what they wrote or drew, or to read a story to their parents, or to otherwise talk about activities. Children who have taken the backpack home may also report to the class what they did with the materials at home.

Another item to put in the literacy backpack is storybooks with audiotapes that your children have been reading in class, a routine that has been researched and found effective with young English learners (Koskinen et al., 1995). In this home–school literacy project, the teachers sent home a tape recorder as well as the storybook and audiotape. They found that 12-inch tape recorders with color-coded buttons, which they marked with colored dots for "play," "stop," and "rewind," worked best. They sent home letters explaining the project translated into the home languages of the parents. Whenever possible, teachers explained the use of books and audiotapes during parent conferences. In this project, five backpacks at a time were available to take home to keep for three to five days. Thus it took several weeks for each child to have a first turn. Children were given instructions on how to select a book, how to check it out and return it, and how to use the tape recorder to read along with the story. The children were responsible for teaching their parents how to use the tape recorder with the storybooks. Projects such as these take considerable time, money, and organization, but the rewards in literacy development and home–school relations make them worthwhile. Financial support is sometimes available from parent-teacher groups, professional organizations, local merchants, or fast-food chains.

In summary, as children become involved in using literacy in their homes and communities, they will begin to form ideas about the forms and functions of print—the beginnings of emergent literacy. You can build on these early concepts by offering all children a wide variety of functional literacy experiences, including shared reading, journal writing, shared writing, and immersion in literacy-enriched play centers, as described subsequently.

Classroom Strategies to Promote Early Literacy

In the previous section, we discussed early literacy development and ways to link children's home and school experiences in natural, fun ways to support their developing concepts of the forms and functions of print. Our discussion focused primarily on early childhood classrooms. In this section, we describe classroom strategies that will continue to support early reading and writing development for young English learners. In addition, we make suggestions for adapting these strategies for older English learners whose first exposure to literacy begins later, whether in upper-elementary, middle, or high school.

Early Literacy Goals

Any student, regardless of age, who is just beginning to read and write in English needs to develop (1) awareness and appreciation of the variety of purposes reading and writing serve in everyday life, (2) understanding of relationships between print and oral language, including the alphabetic principle, (3) knowledge of print conventions, such as left-to-right, top-to-bottom sequencing, (4) knowledge of specific sound/symbol correspondences, or phonics, and (5) ability to recognize a growing number of words on sight. During early literacy development, learners need to begin to coordinate all these understandings to read and make sense of simple texts.

All five goals are served by holistic teaching strategies, while explicit skill instruction further reinforces phonics and sight word development. We define **holistic strategies** as literacy events involving reading and writing whole texts such as stories, poems, songs, and recipes, that serve real, day-to-day purposes. Holistic strategies, or what we defined as literacy scaffolds in Chapter 3, are especially important for English learners because they provide rich and meaningful print experiences, with comprehension scaffolded by the teacher or other students. Holistic strategies should be used extensively every day. These strategies may then be supplemented by explicit phonics and sight word instruction. Phonics and sight word instruction should be based on words that students have already seen and heard many times in stories, poems, songs, letters, recipes, and other texts used previously. When you offer numerous meaningful, functional print experiences, your students increase their awareness of why we read and write, that is, the functions of print. When you offer explicit phonics instruction, you increase students' knowledge of how print works, that is, its form. Both are important aspects of early literacy development.

Creating a Literacy-Rich Classroom Environment

In the early grades, especially kindergarten, you can promote literacy development in many ways. First, you can enrich activity centers with literacy props that encourage children to learn about literacy through play. Some centers reflect familiar aspects of the child's home and community, such as the kitchen and grocery store; others introduce new themes, such as science centers, that are precursors of later academic subjects. For literacy development purposes, each center should be enriched with literacy props. For example, the kitchen can be supplied with calendars, note paper for grocery lists, cookbooks, and recipe cards for boys and girls to enjoy. The other centers can be similarly enriched. With an eye toward literacy opportunities, you can create a plethora of functional literacy opportunities for children to explore and enjoy.

The following list illustrates some ways to enrich your classroom with functional literacy opportunities in several different centers. Figure 5.9 on page 185 gives a sample floor plan showing how you might organize your classroom for children's optimal use of functional literacy opportunities.

Books, Books, Books

Books—not just those that the teacher reads aloud daily, but also books children make themselves—take on new life in early literacy classrooms. Here is a list of the many different kinds of books found in exemplary emergent literacy classrooms (Tease, 1995):

- individually written, child-made books
- published trade books
- children's journals
- poetry books
- books related to theme studies
- holiday books
- Big Books
- dictionaries and encyclopedias
- alphabet books
- phone books

- recipe books
- teacher-made books
- photo album books with pictures labeled
- sign language books
- author of the month books
- collections of songs or poems children have learned at school

With so many books in the classroom, you'll need to find a way to organize them so that children can find them easily and put them away after use. Book-shelves are often organized with labels by subject, author, title, or size (tall, wide, and small). In each case, alphabetical order may provide the sequence. Some teachers put books in color-coded bins according to topics, authors, or level of reading difficulty. Single-book display racks showcase a special theme book, the author of the month, or a current story or poem. All good literacy programs build on children's fascination with books.

Using Daily Routines to Highlight the Forms and Functions of Print

Daily classroom routines can enhance children's awareness of the forms and functions of print. Give some thought to the routines of your classroom so that you may highlight for your students how literacy serves everyday purposes. At the same time, call attention to the actual processes of reading and writing as you go about daily activities.

Morning Message. One classroom routine is the "morning message," in which you preview the day's activities for your students. By writing the day's activities down on the board as you say the words, you model the organizational/ mnemonic function of writing as well as the form (i.e., the left-to-right, letter-by-letter sequence corresponding to your spoken words).

Classroom Rules and Procedures. Another routine that lends itself to a functional literacy learning opportunity stems from classroom rules and proce-dures that you and your students establish together at the beginning of the year. As decisions are made, you write down on a large chart the rules and procedures for such duties as table cleaning, floor sweeping, pet care, and any other routine chores. In this way, your students will see the spoken words written on the board. Each duty can be simply illustrated with a broom, an animal, a table, or other appropriate picture to support student understanding of the chart. By highlighting print uses during day-to-day routines, you make literacy so natural and unintim-idating that children begin to read without even knowing it.

Wall Dictionary. Another way to incorporate a literacy learning opportunity into your daily routines is to post the alphabet at children's eye level, creating a wall dictionary (Figure 5.10). The first entries in the dictionary are the children's

Kitchen Center	Recipe cards
	Notepads and pencils
	Cookbooks
	Cupboard items labeled for putting away
Science Center	Information about class pets posted: name, when and what
	to feed the pet, whose turn to feed the pet
	Books about science display (e.g., hamsters, rocks)
	Labels on display items
Block Center	Turn-taking chart to limit block use to two or three children
	Books about architecture or about props in the block center
	(e.g., transportation, farm animals)
Grocery Store Center	Products on labeled shelves
	Receipt books
	Tablets to make grocery lists
	Cash register
Writing Center	Paper of various sizes and colors
	Pens, pencils, markers
	Stationery, envelopes
	Postcards

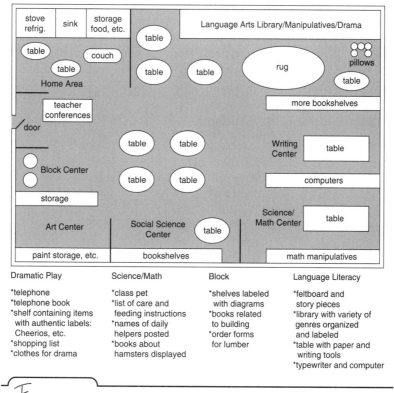

Dramatic Play

*telephone
*telephone book
*shelf containing items
  with authentic labels:
  Cheerios, etc.
*shopping list
*clothes for drama

Science/Math

*class pet
*list of care and
  feeding instructions
*names of daily
  helpers posted
*books about
  hamsters displayed

Block

*shelves labeled
  with diagrams
*books related
  to building
*order forms
  for lumber

Language Literacy

*feltboard and
  story pieces
*library with variety of
  genres organized
  and labeled
*table with paper and
  writing tools
*typewriter and computer

FIGURE 5.9 Classroom Floor Plan Optimizing Functional Literacy Opportunities

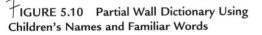

A a	B b	C c	D d
Anna	Barbara	Cathy	Don
an	be	cat	Dan
and	bear	can	
are	but	car	dad
animal	bat	colt	did

FIGURE 5.10   Partial Wall Dictionary Using Children's Names and Familiar Words

186

names on tagboard posted below the appropriate letter of the alphabet. If possible, post a photo of each child next to his or her name. During roll call children can place their name tags on the wall dictionary under the appropriate letter: María would place her tag under the letter *M*, for example. For each of us, there is a magic in our names and those of our friends. To be able to write their own name early in school creates a power over print for children. Later on, favorite words from songs, poems, stories, and theme studies may be added to the wall dictionary. As words accumulate, you may invite children to read, chorally or individually, all the words that begin with *M*, or one word that begins with *M*. Or you might ask children to find all the animal names posted. You can no doubt think of other games to play using the wall dictionary. The wall dictionary provides many opportunities for children to become aware of both the alphabet and its sound/symbol correspondences. In addition, the wall dictionary helps students develop a sight vocabulary that they will use in reading and writing. Finally, the wall dictionary familiarizes students with the concept of alphabetical order.

Reading Aloud to Students

Reading aloud is beneficial for students of all ages. When you read aloud to your students, you involve them in the pleasure function of print, you model the reading process, and you develop general knowledge as well as literary notions about story plots and characters. Keep in mind, however, that following a story line places heavy cognitive-linguistic demands on listeners in terms of attention, comprehension, and memory. You can help your students listen and comprehend by stopping at certain places in the book to discuss a picture as it relates to the story or to review the plot. You may also focus comprehension by asking prediction questions as you go along. If the book is short and simple, repeated readings will assist comprehension. As you try these techniques, you will find out which ones work best with your particular group of students. Their purpose is to facilitate comprehension for your beginning and intermediate English language learners so that they may enjoy the read alouds.

In reading aloud to students you will want to select age-appropriate books that they will be able to understand. At the same time you will want to gradually move to books that are more demanding for your students, books that increase in length, language level, and plot complexity. If you are new to the act of reading aloud to an audience, we recommend that you practice story reading at first. You can get ideas for oral reading from professionally recorded audio or videotapes. For example, if you listen to Danny Glover reading *How the Leopard Got His Spots* or James Earl Jones reading *Bringing the Rain to Kapiti Plain* (Aardema, 1981), you will get an idea of how professional actors use intonation and other techniques to convey the enthusiasm and wonder that oral readings can bring to a story. Such oral readings greatly enhance anyone's ability to listen.

You will also find reading aloud more fun if you choose some of your own favorite books. Your natural enthusiasm will be contagious. Big Books or oversized books are an excellent choice, because you can point to the words as you read aloud. In this way you model the reading process, promoting development of print concepts, the alphabetic principle, phonics knowledge, and sight vocabulary. Most important, the reading-aloud moments should be a special time when students feel comfortable to simply sit and enjoy listening to stories. Finally, encourage children to bring books they enjoy for you to read to the class; this will give them a sense of ownership during reading-aloud time. Below is a list of some of our favorite books to read aloud for readers of different ages.

Ahlberg, J., & Ahlberg, A. (1981). *Peek-A-Boo.* London: Puffin.

Ahlberg, J., & Ahlberg, A. (1986). *The Jolly Postman.* Boston: Little, Brown.

Anno, M. (1983). *Anno's USA.* New York: Philomel Books.

Brown, M. W. (1947). *Goodnight Moon,* illustrated by C. Hurd. New York: Harper & Row.

Bruchac, J. (1989). *Iroquois Stories.* Cassette tape. Greenfield Center, NY: Good Mind Records.

Bryan, A. (1991). *All Night, All Day: A Child's First Book of African-American Spirituals.* New York: Atheneum.

Carle, E. (1986). *The Very Hungry Caterpillar.* New York: Philomel Books.

Connolly, J. (Ed.). (1985). *Why the Possum's Tail Is Bare and Other North American Indian Nature Tales.* Seattle: Stemmer House.

Delacre, L. (1989). *Arroz con Leche: Popular Songs and Rhymes from Latin America.* New York: Scholastic.

de Paola, T. (1985). *Tomie de Paola's Mother Goose.* New York: Putnam.

Galdone, P. (1979). *The Three Bears.* New York: Clarion.

Garcia, M. (1978). *The Adventures of Connie and Diego/Las Aventuras de Connie y Diego.* Chicago: Children's Book Press.

Griego, M., Bucks, B., Gilbert, S., & Kimball, L. (1981). *Tortillitas para Mamá and Other Nursery Rhymes, English and Spanish.* New York: Holt, Rinehart & Winston.

Kitchen, B. (1984). *Animal Alphabet.* New York: Dial.

Lobel, A. (1970). *Frog and Toad Are Friends.* New York: Harper.

McKissack, P. (1986). *Flossie and the Fox.* Chicago: Children's Book Press.

Myers, W. (1990). *The Mouse Rap.* New York: HarperCollins.

Prelutsky, J. (Ed.). (1983). *The Random House Book of Poetry for Children,* illustrated by A. Lobel. New York: Random House.

Say, A. (1995). *Grandfather's Journey.* Boston: Houghton Mifflin.

Sendak, M. (1963). *Where the Wild Things Are*. New York: Harper.

Steptoe, J. (1987). *Mufaro's Beautiful Daughter: An African Tale*. New York: Lothrop.

Yep, L. (1989). *The Rainbow People*. New York: Harper & Row.

Shared Writing and Reading through the Language Experience Approach

The language experience approach to writing and reading, discussed fully in Chapter 6, is a literacy approach based on student's dictations that can be used with learners of any age, preschool through adult. A good way to start is to invite your students to dictate stories or ideas as a whole class. As they dictate the words, you write them down on chart paper, inviting students to read the words back as you point them out. This simple use of language experience models functional writing and reading, illustrates the relationship of print to speech, helps develop sight vocabulary, and illustrates sound/symbol correspondences. Finally, the fact that students themselves generate the content ensures a text that is appropriate to their age, experiences, and interests. You can later use these texts as the basis of phonics and sight word instruction. By writing down things students say each day you will be helping them learn to read and write.

188

Dialogue Journals

Dialogue journals provide an excellent introduction to literacy for English learners of all ages (Kreeft, 1984). As you may recall, in dialogue journals students write regularly on the topic of their choice, and you respond to the content of their entries, not the form. By doing so, you show interest in the students' ideas, ask questions that encourage elaboration, model form and function in writing, and deepen your personal relationship with students. For emergent readers and writers, dialogue journals offer students the chance to work out sound/symbol relationships in the context of an authentic communicative interaction with their teacher. English learners also work on overall English language development through journals, as evident in the following examples from a first-grader working on the phrase "What I like to do is _____." We offer some clarifications of the child's words in italics.

Dec. 1:   I like to do is sing for egg de I like to do is it a pizza? *(I like to do is sing for egg day. I like to do, "Is it a pizza.")* Teacher responded: You should teach us an egg song.

Dec. 8:   I like to do is sing de He like to do is paly happy sing paly? *(I like to do is sing day. He like to do is play happy sing play.)* (Teacher did not respond that day.)

Dec. 15:   I like to play whaat butterfly de vey like to do is play a round bks Butterfly is like to it flsr *(I like to play with butterfly day they like to do is play around bikes. Butterfly is like to eat flowers.)* Teacher responded: I have never played with a butterfly before. It sounds like fun.

Students of all ages enjoy dialogue journals, in part because of the personal attention they receive from the teacher. Journals also provide ongoing writing samples from which to assess students' literacy development over time.

Alphabet Books

We have already mentioned using print in functional and meaningful ways to develop children's appreciation of the purposes and pleasures of print. All of these activities, such as wall dictionaries, language experience stories, rhyming games, the alphabet song, and shared reading, help children develop the alphabetic principle. With the **alphabetic principle,** children come to know that there is a relationship between letters and sounds in the English language. Alphabet books provide yet another avenue for teaching both the alphabetic principle and the alphabet itself. Alphabet books display capital and lowercase letters in interesting ways and can help students become aware of the alphabetic principle while learning the names of the letters. Many of the books teach not only the letters, but concepts as well. Interestingly, alphabet books are available for all ages, from Bruna's *B Is for Bear* for the very young to *Ashanti to Zulu: African Traditions* for older students. The best books use enjoyable illustrations that convey meaning and can also help learners begin to make the connection between specific letters and the sounds they make in words the children already know. We've listed some of our favorites below.

Alphabet Books

*Anno, M. (1975). *Anno's Alphabet.* New York: Crowell.
*Base, G. (1986). *Animalia.* New York: Abrams.
Brown, M. (1974). *All Butterflies.* New York: Scribner's.
Bruna, D. (1967). *B is for Bear.* Sydney, Australia: Methuen.
Dr. Seuss. (1963). *Dr. Seuss's ABC.* New York: Random House.
*Dragonwagon, C. (1987). *Alligator Arrived with Apples.* New York: Macmillan.
Duke, K. (1983). *The Guinea Pig ABC.* New York: Dutton.
Eisele, B., Eisele, C. Y., Hanlon, S. M., Hanlon, R. Y., & Hojel, B. (2002). *My ABC Storybook.* White Plains, NY: Pearson Education.
Gag, W. (1933). *The ABC Bunny.* New York: Coward-McCann.
Garten, J. (1964). *The Alphabet Tale.* New York: Random House.
Kitchen, B. (1984). *Animal Alphabet.* New York: Dial.
McNaught, H. (1988). *The Sesame Street ABC Book of Words.* New York: Random House.

*Books older students enjoy.

*Musgrove, M. (1976). *Ashanti to Zulu: African Traditions*. New York: Dial.

Oxenbury, H. (1972). *Helen Oxenbury's ABC of Things*. New York: Watts.

Rankin, L. (1991). *The Handmade Alphabet*. New York: Dial.

Red Hawk, R. (1988). *ABC's: The American Indian Way*. Albany, CA: Sierra Oaks.

*Van Allsburg, C. (1987). *The Z Was Zapped: A Play in 26 Acts*. Boston: Houghton Mifflin.

HELPING STUDENTS RECOGNIZE AND SPELL WORDS INDEPENDENTLY

As students progress in their emerging understanding of the functions and forms of print, they have already begun to develop some rudimentary word recognition abilities. You can help them become more effective and efficient in recognizing words by increasing their sight word vocabularies and providing explicit phonics instruction. In this section, we briefly review some of the most useful teaching strategies for these purposes. For a much more comprehensive discussion of word recognition instruction, we recommend Bear, Invernizzi, Templeton, and Johnston (2003), described in the resource list at the end of this chapter. This book was written with native English-speaking students in mind, so you will have to consider the language and cultural needs of your students as you select from the teaching strategies provided.

Using Big Books to Teach Sight Words and Phonics

Although we discuss the use of Big Books more fully in Chapter 7, we want to point out a few ways you can use them, as well as poems and song lyrics written in large format on chart paper, to develop word recognition and phonics knowledge early in children's reading and writing development. First, these large-format texts allow children to follow the words that you point to as you read. Second, you can create a window or frame that allows children to focus on only one word at a time in the book. By framing only one word, you provide practice in actually recognizing the word on sight. You can also use predictable books with repetitive patterns and phrases to teach or reinforce sound/symbol correspondences, including consonants, vowels, and letter sequences found in rhyming words. In addition, you may invite children to write their own stories following the pattern in predictable books that they have heard several times. In writing their own stories, your students will have a chance to put their phonics and sight word knowledge into meaningful practice.

The sight word and phonics strategies just described are also applicable to older students who are new to literacy. The key is to find short texts with age-appropriate content. There are a number of predictable books that are appropriate for older students, such as *Fortunately*, by Remy Charlip (1987). In addition, poems and song lyrics are good sources of predictable texts. Songs lyrics, poems, and predictable books can be written in large letters on tagboard or chart paper and used in the same way that Big Books are used with younger children.

Increasing Students' Sight Word Vocabulary

Students begin to develop a sight word vocabulary as a result of immersion in meaningful, functional encounters with print, including writing in dialogue journals, seeing the morning message printed and explained, using wall dictionaries, repeated reading of rhyming poems and predictable books, and shared writing through language experience dictations. All beginning readers and writers need daily opportunities such as these to develop literacy. In addition, you'll need to provide them with explicit instruction in strategies they can use to recognize words they have not encountered before or do not recognize easily when reading.

Certain words occur very frequently in any English text, such as *a, and, the, I, we*. If your students have not learned these words through holistic strategies, you may wish to provide practice with these and other words from stories and themes you are studying by using flash cards in a game. Students can do this in pairs or small groups. It is important that your students know the meanings of the words on the flash cards, however, and it may be helpful for the words to be illustrated on the back of the cards. To demonstrate the meaning of articles, prepositions, conjunctions, and other function words, you need to use them in full sentences. If readers do not learn how to recognize sight words automatically, they will plod their way through print and lose the meaning along the way. Below we give a brief list of high-frequency words adapted from Mason and Au (1990). Students may keep their own word banks or dictionaries with these words along with other words they choose to include.

1. the	11. at	21. was	31. but	41. which
2. of	12. he	22. this	32. what	42. their
3. and	13. for	23. from	33. all	43. said
4. a	14. on	24. I	34. were	44. if
5. to	15. are	25. have	35. when	45. do
6. in	16. as	26. or	36. we	46. will
7. you	17. with	27. by	37. there	47. each
8. is	18. his	28. one	38. can	48. about
9. that	19. they	29. had	39. an	49. how
10. it	20. be	30. not	40. your	50. up

Phonics

The purpose of phonics instruction is to help students recognize words independently, *not* to have them state rules or generalizations. A substantial amount of research on native English readers supports the importance of phonics instruction

(Adams, 1990a, 1990b; Anderson et al., 1985; Bond & Dykstra, 1967; Chall, 1983; Ehri, 1991). Although there is little research, if any, on phonics instruction for English learners, we believe that English learners will also benefit from phonics instruction, judiciously applied. The following principles, developed for native English speakers, apply well to phonics for English learners:

1. Provide ample time for students to read and write for meaningful purposes, allowing students to develop their own understanding of sound/symbol correspondences.
2. Informally assess phonics and word recognition skills your students already use in writing and reading, then focus your teaching on new skills that will promote independence.
3. Always teach phonics and other word recognition skills within a meaningful context; enjoy the story or poem for meaning first, then teach the skill.
4. Generally, teach spelling patterns rather than rules.
5. Remember that phonics and other word recognition strategies are a means to an end: comprehension.

Through thoughtful phonics instruction students can begin to read words that they would otherwise be unable to recognize. Bear in mind, however, that phonics strategies work best during reading when combined with meaning cues provided by the context of the passage. If a student comes across a new word while reading, phonics strategies will provide a tentative pronunciation, while the sentence context will provide the meaning or gist, thereby facilitating comprehension. In fact, mature readers use several cueing systems simultaneously during reading: graphophonic, syntactic, and semantic, for example. We discuss these more fully in Chapter 7.

Word Families

In addition to helping students with phonemic awareness through your daily use of print, it is important to teach students **word families,** sometimes referred to as **onsets and rimes.** The onset is the initial consonant in a word or syllable, followed by a vowel-consonant sequence, the rime (Stahl, 1992). Thus, in the word *gain* the letter *g* is the onset and the letters *-ain* represent the rime. Adams and others (Adams, 1990a, b; Cunningham, 1995; Ruddell & Ruddell, 1995; Stahl, 1992; Trieman, 1985) have found that "letter sound correspondences are more stable when one looks at rimes than when letters are looked at in isolation" (Stahl, 1992). Thus you can help students learn words associated with the -at rime by simply placing letters in front of the *-at* to make words such as *cat, rat, bat, sat, mat, fat, hat,* and *pat.* Or you can make a word wheel containing the rime *(-at)* in the center and the onset *(c, r, b)* on the outside; as children turn the wheel, they create the different words. Likewise, other rimes, such as those found in Stahl's list, which follows, generate nearly 500 words (Stahl, 1992). Knowledge of rimes, along with the consonants that provide the onsets, give students a powerful word recognition strategy that they can use in combination with meaning and grammatical cues to make sense of text.

-ack	-ain	-ake	-ale	-all	-ame
-an	-ank	-ap	-ash	-at	-ate
-aw	-ay	-eat	-ell	-est	-ice
-ick	-ide	-ight	-ill	-in	-ine
-ing	-ink	-ip	-ir	-ock	-ok
-op	-or	-ore	-uck	-ug	-ump
-unk					

One mistake teachers sometimes make is to identify a student's inability to pronounce a word with a lack of phonics knowledge, or to consider non-native pronunciation of a word as a reading error. If we give you a word such as *icosahedron,* you might not be able to pronounce it, not because you don't know phonics or can't read, but because you may never have encountered the word before, orally or in writing. Too many students are sent to reading labs for phonics instruction because they can't pronounce a word and have been misdiagnosed as needing phonics instruction. For the purposes of reading and writing, vocabulary instruction highlighting word meaning is a close ally to sight word and phonics instruction because we want students to be able to *access the meaning of the word,* regardless of pronunciation.

A general sequence of phonics instruction often recommended for native English speakers is the following:

1. single consonants at the beginning of words
2. short and long vowels
3. letter patterns and word families (onsets and rimes)
4. digraphs (two consonants together that make one sound such as *th, ch, ph*) and blends (two consonants together that blend their sounds, such as *cl-, bl-, tr-, cr-, pr-*)
5. syllabication

This sequence is probably useful for English learners whose first exposure to literacy is in English. When you focus on any of these elements, we recommend that you base your instruction on words taken from poems, stories, song lyrics, and other texts you have used in class many times. For example, if you have read *Brown Bear, Brown Bear* (Martin, 1967), you would hold up the book, point to the words *brown* and *bear,* and proceed to talk about the letter *b* and the sound it represents. Next, you might ask your students to tell you other words that begin with the letter *b,* perhaps permitting them to peek at the wall dictionary. In this way you ensure that students understand the words themselves and that they are aware of how letters are related to words in meaningful, whole texts.

An important consideration for English learners is the extent of literacy skill in their first language. In general, students who are literate in their primary language will already possess knowledge of the functions of print. However, they will need to learn the forms of English print, as well as some of its functions, to the extent that they differ from the students' prior print experiences. Bear in mind that students who read a language with an alphabet similar to that of English (e.g., Spanish, French, German) are apt to need less phonics instruction because of transfer of alphabetic knowledge, especially with consonants. The English vowels and their spellings present difficulties for most readers, however, native and non-native English speakers alike.

Besides the many ways students can learn phonics through literacy events such as reading aloud and journal writing, we recommend using games to help reinforce the learning of individual sound/symbol correspondences when more practice is warranted. We also recommend that you spend a brief time each day going over sound/symbol correspondences you feel students should already know, both to evaluate their phonics knowledge and to determine whether more explicit instruction is needed on word analysis and recognition.

Finally, your students can learn phonics through their own explorations using computers. New software programs are coming out daily that can assist children with learning to read independently, programs that sound out any word children point to as they are reading an animated text. Other programs will read texts in different languages to help English language learners. One other kind of program that is a favorite of ours is "Kids Write," which allows students to write down any word or story and will pronounce the word they have written.

194

Invented or Temporary Spelling and Word Recognition

We advocate that students write from the first day of class, and we suggest that you accept their temporary or invented spellings. Awareness of word structure and phonics is often best developed through students' own attempts at writing. One study of invented spelling among native English speakers (Clarke, 1989) compared groups of children who used invented spelling with groups of children who were in traditional spelling programs. Results showed that the children who were in the invented spelling groups were better in decoding and comprehension. In addition, "low readiness" students performed significantly higher on spelling and word recognition tests. Many teachers who have used invented spelling techniques testify to the efficacy of encouraging invented spelling and confirm research findings such as these. However, just as with anything else you do in your classroom, you will want to be aware of the progress students are making and adjust your program accordingly.

Developmental Levels in Student Spelling

One way to assess students' progress is to analyze their spelling according to developmental characteristics. We suggest using four developmental levels: *prephonetic, phonetic, transitional,* and *conventional,* as defined briefly here and discussed more fully below.

Prephonetic spelling: Letters or letterlike forms do not represent speech sounds.

Phonetic spelling: Letters represent sounds; words are decipherable.

Transitional spelling: Conventional spellings are mixed with phonetic spellings.

Conventional spelling: Most words are spelled conventionally.

Prephonetic spellers use letters or letterlike forms or even numbers or scribbles that do not as yet represent speech sounds. In other words, prephonetic spellers do not demonstrate understanding of the alphabetic principle, the idea that a letter or letter sequence represents a speech sound. Oswaldo's soccer story at the beginning of this chapter illustrates prephonetic spelling. The examples in Figure 5.11 also illustrate the kind of spelling found at this stage.

Prephonetic spellers need rich exposure to functional uses of written language, the kind provided by reading big books, by writing language experience stories, by discussing word spellings on the word wall, and by generally talking about how print works as you use written language for functional purposes in day-to-day classroom activities. As students develop an understanding of the alphabetic principle, they become able to associate English speech sounds with letters of the English alphabet. When they begin to use this knowledge in spelling, they are on their way to becoming phonetic spellers.

Phonetic spellers use letters and letter sequences to represent speech sounds, thereby demonstrating their grasp of the alphabetic principle (see Figure 5.12). However, they use many spellings that are not conventional. Martha's story a few pages back about the lost dog represents advanced phonetic spelling. Students who are developing the ability to spell phonetically vary a great deal in their approach. Early on, some students may represent a whole word such as *mother* with just one letter, *m*. Gradually they begin to represent each speech sound with one letter. At this point, most phonetic spellings students produce are more

195

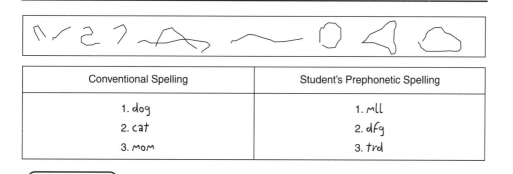

Conventional Spelling	Student's Prephonetic Spelling
1. dog	1. mll
2. cat	2. dfg
3. mom	3. trd

ƒIGURE 5.11 **Examples of Prephonetic Spelling**

Conventional Spelling	Student's Phonetic Spelling
from	frum
clown	cleeown
cat	kat
city	sity
bake	bac

FIGURE 5.12   Examples of Phonetic Spelling

logical and consistent than many conventional English spellings because English orthography is not based strictly on a one-to-one correspondence between sounds and letters. In other words, some letters consistently represent just one sound, but others do not. Similarly, some speech sounds are represented in several different ways and/or with several letters, such as long vowel sounds. Figure 5.12 shows examples of phonetic spelling.

Phonetic spellers should be recognized and praised for their thoughtful spelling. They should also be encouraged to write more. They will benefit from the kind of exposure to interesting uses of written language recommended above for prephonetic spellers. Moreover, phonetic spellers can benefit from basic, formal spelling instruction such as the spelling patterns in the simple word family words provided earlier in the discussion of phonics. In this way you can build on what they already know and move them to the next level of spelling development.

Transitional spellers (see Figure 5.13) extend their knowledge beyond the phonetic aspects of spelling and begin to include conventional spellings that are not strictly phonetic. These students are in the transitional phase moving toward conventional spelling. The term *transitional* indicates that they are making the transition from purely phonetic spelling to conventional spelling. Transitional spellers remain adept at phonetic spelling, but they also use a growing number of conventional spelling patterns, such as using the silent *e* for long vowel sounds as in *lake,* or two vowels for long vowel sounds as in *beat.* Sam's note to his mother a few pages back provides a good example of transitional spelling.

Students at the transitional level of spelling may be spelling 60 percent to 90 percent of words correctly in their writing. They are on their way to becoming good spellers. They need to continue reading and writing each day for a variety of purposes. In addition, they will benefit from instruction on new spelling patterns as they begin to write longer, more complex words. In this way they will continue developing toward conventional or standard spelling.

Non-native English speaking students may vary somewhat in the developmental patterns just described. Young English learners whose only literacy instruction has been in English are likely to display the developmental patterns noted above. Nonetheless, their phonetic spellings are apt to reflect both their pronunciation and grammar in English, that is, their phonological, morphological, and syntactic

One day we went to the beech. We played volly ball and we swam arond in the ocean. My friends brought lots of food too. We ate enchaladis and tamalez and we had differen kinds of samiches.

FIGURE 5.13   Examples of Transitional Spelling

development in English. For example, a first grade English learner recently wrote, "My ma se go st an by de food." ("My mama, she go to the store and buy the food.") The child's pronunciation and grammar are reflected in his spellings. He should be complimented for his ability to convey his idea rather well in English with enough sound/symbol regularity to make it decipherable to his teacher.

Non-native English speakers who begin literacy instruction in English when they are a little older may demonstrate similar English pronunciation and grammar features in their spellings. If they are literate in a primary language that uses an alphabet similar to English, such as Spanish, students may spell using sound/symbol correspondences from their first language. Literacy knowledge in their first language provides them with a starting point for spelling in English. A literate Spanish speaker new to English might write, for example, "I laic to see de circo," for "I like to see the circus." In this case, the word *like* was spelled using Spanish spelling rules. On the other hand, the student is already using the conventional spelling for the words *I, see,* and *to*. The word *circo* is borrowed entirely from Spanish.

The important thing to remember, whether students are native or non-native English speakers, is to recognize the logic of their phonetic spellings and commend for this accomplishment. Phonetic spellers are showing you their ability to hear sounds in words (phonemic awareness) and their knowledge of representing those sounds in a systematic manner, using conventional English sound/symbol correspondences (phonics) at least some of the time. These abilities permit them to spell in ways that make their writing decipherable. Their next challenge is to learn the conventional spellings of words that are not spelled exactly as they sound.

Conventional spellers spell nearly all words conventionally, that is, the way they are spelled in the dictionary. However, even students at the conventional level of spelling development must gradually learn how to spell longer, more complex and more difficult words, a process that takes place over a period of many years. You can expose them to more complex spelling patterns used in English through word study and through vocabulary development in the content areas, including literature study.

We recommend three sources of words that you may use for spelling instruction: (1) misspelled words that recur in the student's own writing, such as journal entries, (2) words related to themes or topics you are currently studying, and (3) words that illustrate particular spelling patterns pertaining to individual speech sounds and to word structure and word formation. At the level of individual sound/symbol correspondences, for example, it is necessary to learn the sounds represented by each consonant letter of the alphabet. Moreover, it is necessary to learn that some consonant letters represent more than one speech sound, such as the letter *c* in *can* and *city*. Likewise, students need to learn that some individual speech sounds are represented by two letters, called *digraphs,* such as *sh, ch, th.* In terms of relating spelling to word formation, it is necessary to learn, for example, that the consonant is doubled at the end of certain words such as *cut, bid,* and *let* when you add *-ing* to make *cutting, bidding, letting.* Thus, you'll want to select words that teach students basic spelling patterns in English, beginning with simple spelling

197

patterns such as those found in the word families presented previously and moving on to more complex spelling patterns related to word structure and formation, including prefixes, suffixes, root words. Of course, students who constantly read will learn new words and new spellings.

Selecting words from students' own writing and from the content of your curriculum is fairly straightforward. However, when it comes to word lists based on spelling patterns, which are rather numerous and complex, we recommend that you avail yourself of published resources on the topic rather than staying up late at night pulling together your own lists. Published lists provide a point of departure for you to modify according to your students' needs and your instructional goals. One resource is provided by published spelling series that your school district may adopt. In addition, we note professional books in the resource list at the end of this chapter that have helped us understand English spelling instruction better.

Using ideas and information from the resources above, you may wish to construct word lists to inform your instruction that evaluate the kinds of spelling patterns and conventions students know or don't know. Note the spelling list in Figure 5.14, given in November and then in March to a 6-year-old student. With this list the teacher was able to evaluate the student's knowledge and progress and to develop a curriculum for the student.

In summary, spelling is an important skill for writing. It is also influential in early reading development. As students learn the various spelling patterns of English, they can apply this knowledge to word identification during reading and writing. Although developmental spelling details and terminology may vary, the continuum we have offered provides a basic outline for describing students' spelling

Word Given	Fall/November	Spring/March
monster	mistr	monster
united	unti	vonited
dress	trste	dress
bottom	botm	boutom
hiked	htiel	hiked
human	hanin	humin
eagle	ell	egole
closed	kuost	klosd
bumped	bode	bumped
type	top	tipe

FIGURE 5.14   Spelling List Displaying 6-Year-Old Student's Development

development in English whether they are first language learners or second language learners. Attention to students' spelling and thoughtful instruction thus yield benefits to students' literacy development.

Summary of Early Literacy Instructional Strategies

In summary, our view is that through authentic, meaningful literacy events students will begin to develop understandings of both the forms and functions of print. Holistic teaching strategies are essential for English learners because they provide many opportunities for students to access the meanings and functions of written language while exposing them to the formal aspects of print. Therefore we described several holistic strategies as well as a number of specific word recognition and phonics strategies that we believe promote early independence in reading and writing. As teachers in student-centered classrooms we need to make decisions about how much and what kind of phonics and other skills instruction students may or may not need based on their progress in reading and writing. We strongly advocate continuous use of holistic, meaningful, and functional reading and writing throughout the year in combination with carefully selected skill-based instruction. In Chapters 6 through 9 we provide additional early literacy strategies under the heading of beginning activities for English language learners.

EVALUATING EMERGENT LITERACY DEVELOPMENT

Evaluating students' emergent literacy development requires us to focus on what students know, with an eye to moving them to the next developmental level. To document your English learners' emergent literacy development, we recommend keeping a portfolio that includes both reading and writing information for each student. For writing, you may select samples from a student's journals as well as dictated stories. For reading, you may include a list of favorite stories. You may also wish to keep a checklist of your students' knowledge of letters/sounds and sight words and any other word recognition strategies you have taught. In addition, you may wish to use a holistic checklist such as those in Figures 5.15 and 5.16 to document reading and writing development.

Figure 5.15 presents a scale of writing development in which Levels 1 through 6 represent emergent writing behaviors, Level 7 represents transitional writing, and Levels 8 through 11 represent a developmental progression of more mature writing. Figure 5.16 provides developmental descriptors for reading in a manner similar to the writing development scale. Levels 1 through 5 represent emergent reading behaviors, and Levels 6 through 8 represent transitional reading. Levels 9 through 11 represent developmental progressions of more mature reading.

You can use these reading and writing development descriptors to document and evaluate how students are progressing. Although these levels appear to represent steps of a staircase, it is important to note that they should not be considered as lockstep sequences. Students will develop in individual ways, perhaps

Level 11: Child uses a variety of strategies for revision and editing.
Child uses a variety of literary techniques to build suspense, create humor, etc.

Level 10: Child willingly revises and edits.
Child writes creatively and imaginatively.
Child writes original poetry.
Child writes clearly. The message makes sense.
Child uses commas, quotation marks, and apostrophes.

Level 9: Writing includes details, dialogue, a sense of humor, or other emotions.
Spelling becomes more conventional.
Child willingly revises.

Level 8: Child writes a story with a beginning, middle, and end.
Child uses different forms for several different purposes (narrative, expository, persuasive).
Revisions include adding to the story or piece.
Child uses basic punctuation purposefully and consistently.

Level 7: Child writes the start of a story.
Child uses both phonics and sight strategies to spell words.
Child writes several short sentences.
Child rewrites a familiar story or follows the pattern of a known story or poem.

Level 6: Child invents spellings.
Story is a single factual statement.
Message is understandable (decipherable).

Level 5: Child labels or makes statement about drawings.
Letters have some connection to sounds.
Child writes lists.
Child separates words with space or marker.

Level 4: Letters don't match sounds, but child can explain written message.
Child writes strings of letters.

Level 3: Child copies words he or she sees around the room.
Child writes letters and mock letters in a line across the page.
Child writes in left-to-right sequence, top to bottom of page.

Level 2: Child copies words he or she sees around the room.
Child writes mock letters, but these may not be in any conventional sequence.
Child pretends to write.

Level 1: Child attempts to write in scribbles or draws patterns.

FIGURE 5.15   Scale of Writing Development

Source: Adapted from L. Lamme and C. Hysmith, "One School's Adventure into Portfolio Assessment," *Language Arts, 68,* 629–640, December 1991. Copyright 1991 by the National Council of Teachers of English. Reprinted with permission.

200

Level 11: Child reads fluently from a variety of books and other materials.
Level 10: Child seeks out new sources of written information.
Child voluntarily shares information with other children.
Level 9: Child uses context clues, sentence structure, structural analysis, and phonic analysis to read new passages in a functional, effective, and strategic manner.
Level 8: Child reads unfamiliar stories haltingly, with little adult assistance.
Level 7: Child reads familiar stories fluently.
Level 6: Child reads short texts word by word.
Level 5: Child memorizes text and can pretend to read a story.
Level 4: Child participates in reading by supplying rhyming words and some predictable text.
Level 3: Child talks about each picture (attends to pictures, less so to the story itself).
Level 2: Child watches pictures as adult reads a story.
Level 1: Child listens to a story but does not look at pages.

FIGURE 5.16 Scale of Writing Development
Source: Adapted from L. Lamme and C. Hysmith, "One School's Adventure into Portfolio Assessment," *Language Arts, 68,* 629–640, December 1991. Copyright 1991 by the National Council of Teachers of English. Reprinted with permission.

skipping some levels and intermixing various levels as well. When we use these developmental checklists, we put a check beside each description that pertains to the student's behaviors exhibited during a particular observation period. We are thus able to document what the child can do and set goals for development to the next levels. By making observations over time, we will be able to document their progress, communicate their progress to parents and others, and adjust our instruction.

As students advance beyond emergent literacy, we will introduce them to the idea of editing for publishing, as described in Chapter 6. At that time, we will begin to help them focus on conventional spelling. For now, though, we applaud everything the child produces. Our goal is to allow students the freedom to create as they write—to create the message of their choice while re-creating the medium, the spelling system. We also want them to have many choices in reading as they develop into mature readers.

SUMMARY

In this chapter, we described current viewpoints on emergent literacy in contrast to traditional reading readiness views. We described the early insights about the forms and functions of print that learners who are new to the written word must develop, regardless of their age. In addition, we focused on current efforts to forge stronger connections between families and schools, including descriptions of programs to assist the parents of English learners in learning English themselves. We provided a variety of strategies for developing early reading and writing and suggested several ways to assess and document emergent literacy development. Figure 5.17 summarizes the teaching strategies described in this chapter, showing the many age levels to which they may be applied, provided the content is age appropriate.

Most of the strategies in Figure 5.17 will be used in the early grades, of course, but you may find older English learners who have not been to school or did not learn how to read in their primary language. As a result, these older students may be able to profit from some of the strategies teachers normally use with younger learners. Through ongoing evaluation you can make appropriate decisions about which strategies will be most useful to you and your students as you help them become readers and writers. Nevertheless, to bridge a possible gap between home and school you will probably want to start by reading aloud to students of all ages to give them a strong sense of good stories and to start them on the road to becoming competent readers. A good teacher will continually evaluate children's

Strategies / Grade Level	K	1	2	3	4	5	6	7	8	9	10	11	12
Alphabet books													
Assessment													
Formal													
Informal													
Dialogue journals													
Drawing													
Experiments													
Invented spelling													
Labeling													
Language experience													
Name charts													
Play centers													
Reading aloud													
Shared reading													
Wall charts													
Word recognition													
Sight words													
Phonics													
Context													
Dictionary													

FIGURE 5.17   Grade Levels Where Strategies May Be Used

progress and assist them as needed with such skills as sight word recognition and other word analysis skills. But the heart of beginning literacy instruction is reading aloud to children and sharing the wonder and magic in reading and writing for ourselves and others.

Suggestions for Further Reading

Adams, M. (1990). *Beginning to read: Thinking and learning about print*. Cambridge, MA: MIT Press.
A thorough discussion on beginning reading, this controversial book reviews the literature and research and makes recommendations for integrated approaches to teaching word analysis. We believe that anyone who wishes to advocate for or against phonics instruction should read this excellent, thoughtful book first.

Antunez, B. (2002). Reading and English language learners. WFSU Reading Center. WFSU.org. Retrieved May 31, 2003, from http://readingrockets.org/wfsu/article/php?ID=409
This excellent seven-page article provides a clear overview of how to teach reading to primary grade English language learners using current research and policy guidelines. It begins with the recommendation to teach beginning reading in children's primary language, if possible. Then it illustrates how to incorporate five components of beginning English reading in a developmentally appropriate manner: (1) phonemic awareness, (2) phonics, (3) vocabulary, (4) reading fluency, including oral reading skills, and (5) reading comprehension strategies. Each section includes special considerations to keep in mind for young English language learners.

Bear, D. R., Invernizzi, M., Templeton, S., & Johnston, F. (2003). *Words their way: Word study for phonics, vocabulary and spelling instruction* (3rd ed.). Upper Saddle River, NJ: Merrill/Prentice Hall.
This resource book is based on invented spelling and spelling development research. It provides detailed information and ideas for teaching and assessment in the area of word study. Activities include concept sorts, playing with sounds, developing the concept of *word,* alphabet games and matching, word banks, studying consonants, word families, short vowel sounds, word pattern sorts, and more advanced spelling strategies for students.

Bolton, F., & Snowball, D. (1993). *Teaching spelling: A practical resource*. Portsmouth, NH: Heinemann.
A companion to their excellent book, *Ideas for Spelling* (Heinemann, 1993), this volume offers detailed information on content of the spelling curriculum, including assessment; exploring sound/symbol relationships; the structure of words, creating new words, and shortened words such as abbreviations and contractions; and the possessive apostrophe. Other topics include alternative spellings and games for playing with words.

Hamayan, E. (1994). Language development of low literacy children. In F. Genesee (Ed.), *Educating second language children: The whole child, the whole curriculum, the whole community* (pp. 278–300). Cambridge: Cambridge University Press.
This chapter describes the author's experiences teaching literacy in English to nonliterate, adolescent English learners in a Southeast Asian refugee camp in order to help prepare them for relocation to North America. The author provides a thorough discussion of teaching strategies, such as dialogue journals, along with the students' responses to her efforts. A combination of holistic and structural (e.g., phonics) instruction is recommended along with a special emphasis on promoting understanding of the purposes and functions of reading and writing.

Johnson, D., with Sulzby, E. (1999). Critical issue: Addressing the literacy needs of emergent and early readers. North Central Regional Educational Laboratory. Retrieved July 20, 2003, from http://www.ncrel.org/sdrs/areas/issues/content/cntareas/reading/li100.htm
This 14-page online article summarizes an enormous amount of information on emergent and early literacy, creating a developmental picture

for native English speakers from birth to age 8 years. Numerous Internet links are embedded throughout the article, creating an incredibly rich resource on the topic. The breadth, depth, and quality of the discussion are superb. The authors offer suggested program goals, action options, implementation pitfalls, and a word on different points of view in the emergent/early literacy dialogue. Links are provided to specific schools where new literacy efforts have been implemented. Finally, contact information is provided for six professional organizations concerned with emergent/early literacy. Teachers of English learners will find the information immediately applicable to their classrooms. In addition, links are provided to other web sites specific to emergent/early literacy development of English learners. This site is a treasure trove of online resources!

Morrow, L. M. (Ed.). (1995). *Family literacy: Connections in schools and communities.* Newark, DE: International Reading Association.

This book contains 20 articles describing projects that have been successful in promoting home–school relationships and increasing language and literacy development opportunities for young children from various cultural backgrounds in urban, suburban, and rural settings.

Peregoy, S. F., & Boyle, O. (2000). English learners reading English: What we know, what we need to know. In L. Meyer (Ed.), *Theory Into Practice, 39*(4). Ohio State University.

This article looks at some basic elements of reading in a second language. Headings include: "Diversity among English Learners;" "Good Readers Reading in English;" "English Language Proficiency;" "Background Knowledge: Text Content;" "Background Knowledge: Text Structure;" "Phonemic Awareness and Phonics;" "Experience in the Primary Language;" "Types of Writing Systems;" "Writing Systems Similar to English;" "Writing Systems Different from English;" "Students with Minimal Literacy Experience;" and "Instructional Implications."

Snow, C. E., Burns, M. S., & Griffin, P. (Eds.). (1998). *Preventing reading difficulties in young children.* Washington, DC: National Academy Press. A national panel of experts was given the task of "conducting a study of the effectiveness of interventions for young children who are risk of having problems learning to read." This book is the report that reviewed research and gave advice on teaching reading. Chapters address the process of learning to read, who has reading difficulties, predictors of success and failure in reading, preventing reading difficulties before kindergarten, instructional strategies for kindergarten and the primary grades and recommendations for practice and research. English language learners are discussed throughout the chapters. Panels that make recommendations about reading always find their critics, and this book is no exception. However, whatever your perspective on reading, this is a book you should read.

Strickland, D. S., & Morrow, L. M. (Eds.). (1989). *Emerging literacy: Young children learn to read and write.* Newark, DE: International Reading Association.

This book contains a collection of articles on emergent literacy by top researchers and practitioners. Articles on topics such as "Oral Language and Literacy Development," "Family Storybook Reading," "Literature for Young Children," "Reading to Kindergarten Children," and "Emergent Writing in the Classroom" give an excellent overall view of many different facets of emergent literacy research and practice. If you could read just one book on emergent literacy, this is the one to read because of its overall perspective.

ACTIVITIES

1. Identify two or three "excellent" kindergarten or first grade teachers serving English learners. To help you in your search, ask a teacher, principal, or supervisor to make recommendations and help you get permission to observe. Spend an hour or so in each class taking note of the phys-

ical arrangement of the classroom, the kinds of reading and writing activities children do, and the kinds of things the teacher says and does to engage children in reading and writing. How would you evaluate what you see going on? What do these excellent teachers do similarly? What do they do differently? Can you identify their literacy philosophy based on what you see happening in the classroom (e.g., emergent literacy or reading readiness)?

2. Think about the "ideal" emergent literacy environment for children entering school for the first time. How would you organize your classroom for these children? When and under what circumstances would children be reading and writing? What kind of activities would take place to create a risk-free environment where children can develop completely and confidently?

3. Observe a classroom in which there are many second language learners. Compare and contrast their growth in English-writing with young English-speaking children. Do you notice similar kinds of invented spelling or do the English learners seem to be developing along very different lines from native English speakers? Do you see areas in which a teacher's knowledge of second language learning would be especially helpful for classroom instruction with these children? What knowledge would that be?

4. What important differences do you see between the emergent literacy and reading readiness views regarding young developing readers and writers? How would each of these views affect the reading and writing instruction of children in kindergarten or later grades? What information would you give to a teacher who has traditionally taken the reading readiness view of her new kindergarten children?

5. How would you evaluate the writing and reading of English learners in kindergarten and first grade? What is the importance of knowing their prior literacy experiences in their first language and second languages? What differences might you find among children who have been read to a lot before entering kindergarten and those who have not been read to much? If English learners have prior literacy experiences in their first language before entering your class, how will those children be different from English learners who have had little or no literacy experience? What will these differences mean for classroom teachers at different grade levels?

6. What insights does the emergent literacy perspective offer concerning older second language emergent readers and writers? What expectations would you have of these students based on your knowledge of their reading and writing in their first language? How would you teach these students based on this knowledge of their prior literacy experiences?

7. Make yourself available as a literacy tutor for an older, preliterate English learner. With some advice and guidance from the teacher, try a combination of holistic and skill-based literacy strategies with your student. For example, you might keep a dialogue journal, read aloud and/or invite the student to dictate stories to you that may be published. Based on these texts, help your student come to understand how print in English reads from left to right, top to bottom. In addition, help your student associate letters and sounds, including word family patterns. Keep a daily log of your experiences and your student's responses and progress. What worked? What didn't work? What did you learn from this experience?

6

ENGLISH LEARNERS AND PROCESS WRITING

In this chapter, we look at how English language learners benefit from the process approach to writing instruction. We address the following questions:

1. What does research tell us about writing in English as a non-native language?
2. What is process writing, and how can it be used with English learners?
3. Which classroom contexts and teaching strategies can best assist second language writers?
4. What does the writing of beginning and intermediate English learners look like, and how can it be assessed?
5. IIow can wc work with errors in student writing?

When we went to school, our teachers taught writing just as their own teachers had before them: They gave us topics to write about and then read our papers with red pens twitching in their hands to find errors. Our favorite teacher would hand out a mimeographed tome containing the 162 errors she would be looking for whenever we wrote. Consequently, writing was a little like crossing a minefield and hoping we wouldn't get red-penned on our way. We always wore out the eraser before the graphite portion of our No. 2 pencils. The assumption was that students' writing just needed correcting to make it better and that good thinking came automatically. Some teachers would roll out the tanklike opaque projector, project our papers on the screen, and discuss only the things that were wrong with the writing. Crossing that minefield with short, fearful steps, we learned to write short, correct sentences that fended off red pens but were often empty of thought. Our teachers would reluctantly take home student papers on Friday nights, put off reading them until Sunday evening, and then anesthetize themselves with a glass of red wine to help them endure the dreary reading.

By the 1960s many teachers saw that this concentration on correctness was not working, and many of them moved to what was called creative writing. In the creative writing approach, teachers avoided correcting student writing for fear of stifling creativity. Some would give two grades for writing, one for content and the other for grammar, spelling, and mechanics. Everyone knew that creative content would pull the higher grade. We were often allowed to select our own topics. For our teachers, this meant that instead of reading dreary papers, they read papers that were novel and interesting. We certainly thought so anyway. But some papers contained so many errors that the wonderful ideas were impossible to discern.

Following this confusion about teaching writing, researchers such as Janet Emig (1971) began to look at what students and professional writers actually did when they wrote. They found out that good writers concentrated on ideas first rather than on correctness. When writers concentrated on correctness while drafting ideas, their writing suffered. Gradually, process writing developed from this research and from teacher practice. The creative writing emphasis of the 1960s evolved into writing in phases. In the prewriting phase, writers engaged in thinking and concentrating on forming their ideas with a particular audience in mind. In the next phase, drafting, writers tried to get their ideas down on paper. In the revising phase, writers tested whether they had accomplished their task and made changes accordingly. If they had accomplished their task, then they would correct it in preparation for publication or for sending it to their intended audience. Thus, process writing allowed writers to manage the writing task by breaking it into manageable parts or phases. Writers could now focus on topics they cared about and on each phase of the process: prewriting, drafting, revising, editing, and publishing. Student papers improved so much that many teachers found themselves sharing favorite student papers with one another.

One such teacher is our friend Paul, who has taught immigrant kindergartners in an inner-city school for twenty years. Each year, on the first day of school, he invites the children to write. He shows a few examples of student writing from previous years, including drawings, scribble writing, and invented spelling, written in whichever language the child has chosen. Given the invitation to express themselves freely, his students begin to write. Some scribble, some draw pictures, some copy letters and words from the board, some write their names, and a few write messages. Whatever they write, however, Paul listens to their stories and praises their accomplishments, letting them know they're "on their way and getting better every day."

Paul doesn't expect each student to construct elaborate messages upon entering kindergarten, nor does he believe in teaching children each little skill before allowing them to begin writing. Rather, he assumes that the best way for them to learn is to express themselves with pencil and crayon from the start—to learn to write by writing. This view, original twenty years ago, has now grown into the highly researched fields of emergent literacy and process writing.

The process approach to teaching writing has gained prominence among educators from kindergarten to college over the last decade. In recent years, the process approach has also been successfully applied with second language writers. In this chapter, we describe theory and research supporting the rationale for using process writing with English language learners. We describe ways in which students may collaborate to practice and improve their writing. In addition, we provide general descriptions of beginning and intermediate second language writers and outline various teaching strategies to facilitate their progress. Samples of student writing are interspersed to give you a sense of what students are able to do in writing and to illustrate how their writing reflects both written language knowledge and general second language development. Finally, we conclude with procedures for assessing writing progress.

RESEARCH ON SECOND LANGUAGE WRITING

Current research confirms the similarity of writing processes for both first and second language writers. For example, second language writers make use of their budding knowledge of English as they create texts for different audiences and different purposes, just as first language writers do (Ammon, 1985; Edelsky, 1981a, 1981b). As students develop control over the language, their writing gradually begins to approximate standard English (Hudelson, 1986). In addition, at the early stages, children writing in a second language often support their efforts with drawings (Hudelson, 1986; Peregoy & Boyle, 1990a), just as their first language counterparts do (Dyson, 1982). It makes sense that the task of English writing should be similar for both first and second language learners. After all, the problems writers face are either specific to the conventions of written English, such as spelling, grammar, and rhetorical choice, or they relate to more general aspects of the writing process, such as choosing a topic, deciding what to say, and tailoring the message to the intended audience—elements that go into writing in any language.

While the processes of English writing are essentially similar for both first and second language writers, there are some important differences in what the two

INTERNET RESOURCE: The National Writing Project has over 100 sites throughout the world and consists of teachers and researchers from K-University backgrounds. You could explore this site for articles and ideas about teaching: http://www.gse.Berkeley.edu/Research/NWP/nwp.html. Another excellent site for intermediate and advanced writers who need help with grammar and spelling is the OWL Online Writing Lab: http://owl.English.purdue.edu./handouts/esl/. The site contains interactive lessons and teacher handouts on lessons as varied as subject/verb agreement to appositives. Select a lesson to teach to your students or classmates. And remember to explore our companion website: www.ablongman.com/peregoy4e.

groups bring to the task. First of all, students new to English are apt to experience some limitations in expressive abilities in terms of vocabulary, syntax, and idiomatic expressions. In other words, second language proficiency plays a role in writing. In addition, English learners may not have had the exposure to written English that comes from reading or being read to. As a result, they may not have a feeling for the way that English conventionally translates into written form. The more they read or are read to in English, however, the easier it will be for them to write (Krashen, 1982).

Some students know how to write in their native language, and this knowledge facilitates the English writing task. For example, they are apt to display a sophisticated understanding of the nature and functions of print as well as confidence in their ability to produce and comprehend text in their new language (Hudelson, 1987). In addition, to the extent that their native language alphabet is similar to the English alphabet, first language letter formation and spelling strategies will transfer partially to English writing (Odlin, 1989). Finally, research demonstrates that students can profitably engage in reading and writing in their second language well before they have gained full control over the phonological, syntactic, and semantic systems of spoken English (Goodman, Goodman, & Flores, 1979; Hudelson, 1984; Peregoy & Boyle, 1991). In fact, providing students with opportunities to write not only improves their writing but also promotes second language acquisition.

Given the similarity between first and second language writing processes, it is not surprising that effective teaching strategies for first language writers tend, with some modifications, to be effective for second language writers as well. One such strategy is the process approach to writing instruction. In fact, process writing has been enthusiastically embraced by bilingual and ESL teachers, and researchers have pointed out the importance of teaching English learners composing, revising, and editing processes (Krapels, 1990; Silva, 1990). We provide ways for both beginning and intermediate English learners to take part in writing. However, full participation in all phases of the process approach described next requires at least some English language proficiency, either advanced beginner or intermediate, depending on your students' ages and prior academic and literacy experiences in English or their primary language.

WHAT IS PROCESS WRITING?

Process writing is an approach to teaching writing that has been researched in depth over the past several years with both first language learners (Calkins, 1986; Emig, 1981; Graves, 1983) and English language learners (Kroll, 1990). As mentioned previously, in process writing, students experience five interrelated phases: prewriting, drafting, revising, editing, and publishing. During the prewriting phase, students choose a topic and generate ideas, often through brainstorming and oral discussion. Once they have chosen and explained their topic, they begin drafting. As they compose their first draft, they are encouraged to let their ideas flow onto the paper without concern for perfection in form or mechanics. After completing the first draft, students reread their papers and, with feedback from the teacher or their peers, get ready to revise. Revisions are aimed at conveying the writer's ideas as effectively as possible. Finally, the paper is edited for correct punctuation, spelling, and grammar in order to be presented for publishing. Table 6.1 describes the purpose of each phase of the writing process and provides examples of strategies to use with each.

The process approach thus breaks the writing act into manageable parts and puts oral language, reading, and writing at the service of the student's communi-

210

TABLE 6.1   Writing Process Phases and Strategies

Phase	Purpose	Strategies
Prewriting	Generating and gathering ideas for writing; preparing for writing; identifying purpose and audience for writing; identifying main ideas and supporting details.	Talking and oral activities; brainstorming, clustering, questioning, reading, keeping journals in all content areas.
Drafting	Getting ideas down on paper quickly; getting a first draft that can be evaluated according to purpose and audience for paper.	Fast writing; daily writing; journals of all types; buddy journals, dialogue journals, learning logs.
Revising	Reordering arguments or reviewing scenes in a narrative; reordering supporting information; reviewing or changing sentences.	Show and not tell; shortening sentences; combining sentences; peer response groups; teacher conferences.
Editing	Correcting spelling, grammar, punctuation, mechanics, etc.	Peer editing groups; proof reading; computer programs for spelling, etc.; programmed materials; mini-lessons.
Publishing	Sharing writing with one another, with students, with parents; showing that writing is valued; creating a classroom library; motivating writing.	Writing may be shared in many formats; papers placed on bulletin boards, papers published with computers, papers shared in school book fairs, etc.

cation goals. As a result, process writing allows students to concentrate on one task at a time and to experience the value of peer feedback in developing their ideas for effective written expression (Boyle, 1982a, 1986b). Because their writing is published, students learn to tailor their message for a particular audience and purpose. Moreover, as students share their polished pieces, a great deal of excitement and enthusiasm is generated about writing. Not least important, students evolve into a community of writers who know how to listen to what others have to say and to critique each other's writing in a positive and sensitive manner.

Using the process writing approach, teachers encourage students to write daily and to select a few papers for revising, editing, and publishing. They also respond positively to the message of the student's writing first and later to the form of the writing when it is deemed appropriate to do so. Moreover, they concentrate first on what the student is doing right before addressing errors in the papers. When students are doing something right, we should encourage them to continue. Finally, teachers provide opportunities to write for different audiences for different purposes, and to write in many domains or genres, including stories, letters, biographical pieces, and persuasive essays (Boyle, 1983; Boyle & Buckley, 1983).

To give you a feeling for the process approach, we invite you to try the procedure described below, a writing activity based on a personal memory that works well with any age (Caldwell, 1984). After trying it, you may wish to use it with your own students. As you follow the procedure, notice how the five phases of process writing are included: prewriting, drafting, revising, editing, and publishing.

211

Experiencing Process Writing: "I Remember"

TEACHER: I want you to think of five things that have happened to you. Write down each of the five things, beginning with the phrase *I remember*. When you have finished, share your ideas with a partner. [*gives students time to share*]

TEACHER: Now, write down one name associated with each of the five things you selected. [*waits a few minutes*]

TEACHER: Can you name our five senses? [*Students generate the five senses: touch, sight, smell, hearing, and tasting.*]
Write down the most important sense that goes with each of your "I remembers." [*waits a few minutes*]

TEACHER: Now, select the "I remember" you would most like to write about. Share the memory with your group. [*waits about 15 minutes*]

TEACHER: Next, write the part of the memory that makes it memorable or very important to you; share it with your group.

TEACHER: Now, writing as fast as you can for 10 minutes, see how much of the memory you can get on paper. Don't worry about punctuation or spelling; you can think about that later, if you like what you've written.

TEACHER: [*ten minutes later*] Share your papers with your group and ask them to make suggestions that will make your paper clearer.

Questions for Discussion

1. In what ways did the exercise help your writing?
2. In what ways do you suppose the process approach might help English language learners with their writing?

Students' Responses to "I Remember"

The "I remember" activity ties well into literature study because published authors often make use of their own personal and family memories as the basis of their fiction. For example, in the foreword to *Mirandy and Brother Wind* (McKissack, 1988), author Patricia McKissack briefly relates the "I remember" family story that inspired the book, which is one elementary students enjoy. Mildred Taylor offers a similar note to her readers in *Roll of Thunder, Hear My Cry* (Taylor, 1976), which middle school students may read, and Richard Rodriguez writes of his childhood recollections in *Hunger of Memory* (Rodriguez, 1982), a book appropriate for high school students. When students read literature, it is important to discuss the authors and make explicit the connection between professional and student authors. Authors are real people who face the same essential challenges when writing as do the students themselves. By discussing authorship in the context of their own reading and writing experiences, students come to see themselves in a new light and gain a deeper understanding of the relationship between reading and writing.

Using literature in this way, teacher Anne Phillips read her second graders the autobiographical piece *When I Was Young in the Mountains* (Rylant, 1989) to introduce the "I remember" process writing activity. Figure 6.1 shows Peter Aguirre's first draft based on the "I remember" procedure.

Writing such as Peter's does not happen by chance. Peter has heard and read numerous stories, he has been taught to use descriptive words, and he has used the writing process as outlined in the "I remember" activity. After generating his first draft, he listened to advice from his group, which suggested that he needed an introduction to make clearer why he was cutting down a tree in his backyard. In addition, he added information at the end of the story to make the milk and sandwich scene fit. He then worked with his teacher to edit his story for publication. In the final draft, he corrected most of his original errors and, incidentally, added a few new ones. Ms. Phillips then asked the students to create a cover for their story and write a dedication, just as their favorite published authors do. For his story, Peter drew a picture of "the old tree" and dedicated it to his pet parrot. Example 6.2 shows Peter's final draft.

Abel, a classmate of Peter's who immigrated from Mexico, produced the following final piece during the "I remember" activity (Example 6.3). He dedicated his story to "Mrs. Grazvawni because she help me with my story."

212

As English learners write about their memories, we find that they bring a wealth of experience to personal writing topics. One reason personal writing is so useful with English learners is that it provides a bridge between their previous experiences and those of the classroom. In this way, they are validated for what they know, and their teacher and classmates come to understand them better.

Years ago, when Vietnamese students first began to arrive in U.S. classrooms, one well-meaning teacher shared her frustration over a new student in her classroom: "Truc has come along okay with her English, but she never seems to get anything down in writing. She never has anything to say." The resource teacher, however, was able to elicit several pages of writing from Truc during their weekly sessions together. Truc shared the horrors of war, her family's perilous escape by boat, the death of loved ones, and what it felt like to be in a new country with twelve people in a one-bedroom apartment.

Why, we asked, was Truc so reluctant to write in her regular class? In further conversations with her teacher, we found out that writing topics were always assigned. Students almost never chose their own. Truc had difficulty generating ideas under these circumstances. In contrast, she was able to write much more fluently with the resource teacher because she was free to choose her own topic. She may have felt more comfortable in the small-group situation afforded by the resource program. However, there can be no doubt that a great deal of power resides with the freedom to choose

213

The Old Tree

It was a scorching hot summer day in the back-yard. The smell of lilacs filled the air. I came out in my shorts, put on my shirt, picked up the hatchet, and faced the old persimon tree. "Goodbye tree," I said "I'll miss you." The tree seemed to droop a little bit but it had to go. I started chopping, and finally the old tree fell to the ground with a smash. I stared at it for a long time. And afterwards I had a salmon sandwich and milk. The End

FIGURE 6.1   First Draft of "The Old Tree"

Example 6.2   Final Draft of "The Old Tree"

The Old Tree

   My favorite memory was when my Dad tought me how to chop down a tree and today was my first test. It was a scorching hot summer day in the backyard. The smell of lilacs filled the air. I came out in my shorts put on my shirt, picked up the hatchet and faced the old persimon tree. "Goodbye tree," I said "I'll miss you. The tree seemed to droop a little but it had to go. I started chopping, and finally the old tree fell to the ground with a smash. I stared at that tree for the longest time. Then it hit me. I went inside the house. Mom asked what I was sad about. "I miss the tree" I said. "Don't worry" she said I'll fix you some milk and a sandwich.

The End.

Example 6.3   Abel Writing His "I Remember"

My Favorite Memory

   I was in Mexico. It was cold. I was with my uncle. My horse was big and black. I rode slow in the street. I gave grass to him to eat. My uncle jumped in the river; it felt good and cold.

Abel, age 7

214

one's own topic: power in choice, power in knowing something about the topic, and power in having something to say (Boyle, 1985a).

   All students bring rich personal experiences into the classroom. If they are given the opportunities to voice these experiences orally and in writing, you will find that they will often have valid topics to write about and plenty to say.

HOW PROCESS WRITING HELPS ENGLISH LEARNERS

   The process approach to writing is especially valuable for English learners because it allows them to write from their own experiences. As they share their writing during writing groups and publishing, their teachers and friends get to know and appreciate them. Thus, personal relationships are enhanced. In addition, second language writers benefit from cooperative assistance among students during both revising (Samway, 1987; Urzúa, 1987) and editing (Peregoy & Boyle, 1990a). As a result, there are numerous opportunities for supporting both clear self-expression and correctness. Cooperative groups not only promote better writing but also provide numerous opportunities for oral discussion within which a great deal of "comprehensible input" is generated, promoting overall language development. Furthermore, the supportive interaction that takes place in effective response groups helps students appreciate and accept each other, another positive factor for second language learning (Cohen, 1986). Finally, by setting editing aside as a separate phase, process writing frees English learners to focus on their ideas first and focus on corrections last. Yet through the editing process they grow in their awareness of English grammar, punctuation, and spelling.

In summary, you can help students with their writing by assisting them with strategies for generating, drafting, revising, editing, and publishing. By introducing students to the writing process, you can show them that they will need to concentrate on various aspects of writing at different times in the process. They must first generate ideas, then form them for different audiences and different purposes, and then revise and edit them to prepare them for publication and sharing. When good literature is combined with opportunities to write often, when strategies are offered to solve problems in writing, and when writing is shared and published, your students will grow both in writing and overall English language development (Boyle, 1985b).

COLLABORATIVE CONTEXTS FOR PROCESS WRITING

When you use the process writing approach, writing ceases to be a solitary activity and becomes a highly interactive group endeavor. Of course, individuals ultimately own their own work. However, throughout the phases of the writing process, they have worked with the whole class, in pairs, and in small groups, brainstorming ideas, focusing their topics, considering ways to express themselves, revising their papers, getting ready for publication, and, finally, sharing their polished pieces with the entire class. Thus, the process approach calls for group collaboration and support at every phase: prewriting, writing (drafting), revising, editing, and publishing.

Although cooperative groups are useful during any phase of process writing, group work is particularly crucial during revision and editing. Groups that help the writer during revision are called **peer response groups,** and those concerned with editing are called **peer editing groups** (Beck et al., 1984; Liu & Hansen, 2002). For both kinds of groups, students need explicit guidelines on what kinds of things to say and how to say them so as to benefit their group members. Thus, students need to learn both the social rules of group work and specific elements of good writing and editing in order to be effective participants.

Response Groups

After students have chosen a topic and produced a first draft of their papers, they are ready to work in response groups. The purpose of response groups is to

TABLE 6.2   Initiating Peer Response Groups

A	By responding to students' content rather than to the form of their writing, you model response to writing.
B	By teaching students specific strategies such as show and not tell, you give them the vocabulary and means to truly improve their writing in peer response groups.
C	By sharing sample papers with students on the overhead projector, you can model responding to writing and give the students an opportunity to practice response.
D	By sharing papers before and after revision, you can show students the effects of response groups' efforts.
E	By taping or videotaping successful response groups or having successful groups show how they work together, you can assist all children in learning how to be successful response group members.
F	By continually sharing good literature with children, you can help them recognize good writing.

give writers a chance to try out their writing on a supportive audience. Response groups usually include three to five people, although other configurations are possible. Each student gets a chance to read his or her paper aloud to the group for feedback, which the writer considers when making revisions to improve the paper (Calkins, 1994; Campbell, 1998; Graves & Hansen, 1983; Healy, 1980). At this point, comments should focus on expression of ideas, not on mechanics, as those will be addressed later during editing. Responding to another's writing is a very high-level task, both cognitively and socially, involving careful listening to the author's intent and critical thinking about possible questions and suggestions. Clearly, students need explicit instruction in how to respond effectively and sensitively. Unfortunately, we have seen many groups falter or fail simply because they were not clear about the purpose or function of response groups. How can this be taught? Table 6.2 outlines general procedures for preparing students to work in response groups (see also Berg, 1999). We now describe how teachers can prepare students to be responsive peer group partners.

Before asking students to respond in groups, we suggest that you **model the responding process** by displaying an anonymous first draft paper on an overhead projector and commenting on it yourself (see also Liu & Hansen, 2002). This may be done with the whole class or with a smaller group. First, find one or two things you like about the paper. The golden rule is: "Find something positive to say first." Next, you need to model questions you would ask the writer if there were parts you didn't understand. You might also look for flow of ideas, sequence, organization, and other elements of good writing such as those listed in Table 6.3. Next, place another paper on the overhead and invite students to respond to it following the procedure you have just modeled. This procedure gives students a chance to practice responding before they work with one another and boosts their chances of success in collaboration.

TABLE 6.3   Elements of Good Writing

Element	Description of Element
Lead	The opening of a paper, whether the first line, the first paragraph, or the first several paragraphs, must capture the reader's interest and/or state purpose clearly.
Focus	The writer must choose a single focus for his or her writing, omitting information that does not directly contribute to the point of the piece.
Voice	Voice in a paper is that element that lets you hear and feel the narrator as a real person, even if the narrator is fictitious. Voice should remain consistent throughout a piece.
Show not tell	Good writers learn to create pictures for their readers rather than just make flat statements that tell. Examples also help to show, not just tell.
Ending	A good ending will suit the purpose of the piece to provide closure on the topic, but may take the reader by surprise or leave the reader interested in hearing more.

Later on, as a variation, you might role-play a good response partner and a poor response partner. Contrasting constructive and sensitive responses with those that are unhelpful or unkind may help beginning responders become effective in their response groups. Students need to see what a good response partner is like and hear the kinds of questions that partners use to assist writers. Once students have practiced as a class with your modeling and guidance, they will be ready to act positively in their groups.

Reading and discussing quality literature also provide students with ideas about how to respond to other's writing. When your students read and share literature, ask them to select writing that is particularly vivid or interesting to them. You might ask them to point out good examples of "showing and not telling," sentence combining, or sentence models (these strategies will be discussed in detail later in this chapter) to try themselves. Ask your students to underline or highlight their favorite parts of a story to share with one another. By sharing good writing by students and professionals alike, you heighten your students' awareness of the author's craft.

Finally, don't forget the power you exert daily as a role model. The way you respond to students' papers will directly influence their ways of responding to others. If you comment in a positive manner, celebrating what they have done well rather than concentrating on mistakes in grammar, punctuation, or spelling, you will find your students doing the same. Your own daily interaction with students is, without a doubt, your most powerful means of modeling response!

In Figure 6.2 we make further suggestions to help students become good responders within the context of an "author's circle," in which writers share their drafts in small groups. Your students now know something about how and what to say in their response groups. As they get ready to move into their groups, you

Directions to Students: You may wish to use the following questions to guide your response to your friends' papers and to help others respond to your writing.

Examples for Authors:
1. Decide what kind of help you would like on your paper and tell your group.
2. Read your paper aloud to your group; you may want your group to have copies of your paper also.
3. Ask your group what they liked best about your paper; ask them to discuss other parts of the paper.
4. Ask your group to respond to the areas you said you wanted help with and discuss their advice, knowing that you will make the decision about whether to change something or not.

Examples for Responders:
1. Listen very carefully to authors while they are reading their papers.
2. Respond to the questions the author asks and try to be helpful.
3. Point out sentences, descriptions, or other things you liked about the paper.
4. Point out one thing that might not have been very clear to you in the paper.

FIGURE 6.2 Guidelines for Author's Circle

may wish to supply them with a list of questions to help them remember what to say. The sample feedback sheet in Figure 6.3 is one way to guide students until they are confident with their ability to help one another. Another way to guide students' responses is to give them specific tasks each time they meet in their groups, such as looking for "show and not tell" sentences in their writing or for sentences that need combining or shortening. The writing strategies you have taught can become the springboard to successful response groups. Remember, however, that keeping a writing group together is a lot like keeping a good relationship together: It needs constant communication and caring among the group members.

Thus prepared, your students are now ready to work in their response groups. You may assign students to groups or let them choose for themselves. A good way to start is with an author's circle, in which one student reads his or her paper aloud

Some questions you may wish to use to assist your students with responding in peer groups:

1. What did you mean when you said _____?
2. Could you describe that scene so we could see it and hear it?
3. What is the most important part of your story? What do you want the reader to think when he or she has finished reading it?
4. What part of the story would you like help with?
5. What part of your story do you especially like?
6. What do you want to do next with this piece?

FIGURE 6.3 Sample Feedback Questions

while others listen. The author takes charge of this group and may begin by telling the response group what kind of feedback would be most helpful. When the author is finished, the others respond to the writing, concentrating on making positive comments first, with questions and suggestions later. After one student has been responded to, others may take the role of author, reading their papers and eliciting input from their groups. It is important for students to know that the purpose of response groups is not to count errors or look for mistakes in writing but to provide support to the writer. Because you have carefully explained the procedure, your students will know how to begin. As they all experience the roles of responder and author, their understanding and expertise in responding will grow.

Once the students are settled in their groups, you may move around the room and provide help as needed, but resist the temptation to take over or dominate the interactions. Your students will become more independent if you let them solve their own problems. In order to reinforce positive group functioning, you may wish to tape-record or videotape the work of a successful group and share it with the class. In addition, you may occasionally review the attributes of a good responder or invite a successful group to share its response to a paper with the entire class. Finally, you may periodically ask students to evaluate strengths and weaknesses in their group work and ask them to suggest ways of improving.

One kind of teacher research project you may wish to carry out is to chart student writing growth in response groups. Two interesting questions to ask might be: Do second language students only learn errors from one another in response groups or do they seem to learn correctness from one another? and Would it be better for the teacher to play a more active role in correctness? We do not have definitive answers to questions such as these, but we agree with Hirvela (1999): "Whatever the language skills being taught—listening, speaking, reading, or writing—collaboratively oriented tasks enrich and extend the learning process when developed with proper care."

A Sixth Grade Class Works in Response Groups. Students in Sam Garcia's sixth grade class selected their own response groups and responded to one another following the described model. The responders used some of his feedback questions and worked on papers together. Here is an example of one group working with an English learner's paper (Example 6.4). Notice that the responders first concentrate on the content rather than correctness; they also concentrate on what they like about the paper before making suggestions.

When Christa finished reading her paper, the students in her group made suggestions after Christa asked what more she should say.

LISA: I liked the part about the food.

CHRISTA: I should say more about her cooking?

LISA: Yeah—like what's good about the tamales. What else did you eat?

JOE: I like the part about her talking. What accent did she have? You might say that.

219

Example 6.4   Student Describing Trip to Grandma's House

Student's Paper

I went to my grandma's house. She live in the country. We drive for 12 hours. We get on the highway to get ther. She cook so good. We ate tamales and ice cream. She only talk Spanish but she have kind of funny ascent and my sisters and all we love to hear her talk. We love it when she tells about the old days. Like when she talk about other places.

We staying 3 days. Granpa let us help on the farm. I love to visit he's home. I help to cook and help with the animals.

                                                                    Christa, 11 years old

LAURA: Maybe you could spell words like she said them, like *Roll of Thunder*.
CHRISTA: That's good, but she talked different.

The group discussed the paper for about 10 minutes, pointing out other improvements such as naming what animals were on the farm. When they had finished and were ready to work on another paper, Josie volunteered to help Christa with the accent. The session with Christa ended when Martha asked her why she selected that story to tell. Christa replied, "My granma and granpa are gone, and I wanted to remember them; so I wrote this." Christa indicated that her group helped her a lot. She said that she would be able to write a clearer picture of her "granma": "You'll see and hear her now."

Peer Editing Groups

The purpose of peer editing groups is to read over final drafts to make corrections on grammar, punctuation, and spelling. Peer editing groups work well if used at the appropriate time in the writing process, after students are satisfied that their writing says what they want it to say. When students are still revising, it is inappropriate to concentrate on correctness, like placing frosting on a cake that contains baking soda but no flour, sugar, or eggs. However, once students are satisfied with what their papers say, it is time to edit for correctness.

Correct spelling, grammar, punctuation, and other mechanics are best learned within the context of the students' own writing (Cooper, 1981). We generally address these elements within the context of particular pieces of writing. Students can use computers, if available, to correct their spelling. Allow them to help one another rather than play the major role yourself. You don't need to improve your proofreading skills—they do. Therefore, make them responsible for correctness. One way to begin peer editing groups is to teach a mini-lesson on an element of grammar or punctuation and then post this element on the chalkboard to focus on during editing. Every so often, teach a new editing element, thus gradually building student knowledge of mechanics. Also useful are editing checklists that students use to help remember elements of grammar, punctuation or spelling as they edit their own paper, or those of their peers. In this way, students apply their mechanical skills directly to their writing, thereby using these skills for purposes of clear communication.

Another possibility is to tutor particular students as "experts" on topics such as capitalization, punctuation, spelling, or subject/verb agreement. Then, when students have editing questions, they go to the "experts" in the class, not to you. This builds self-esteem in your class and also builds independent learners. After all, your

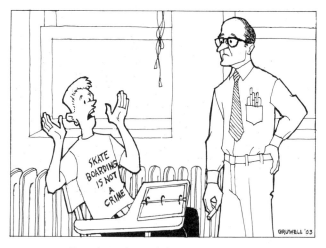

"I can't REvise; I ain't even VISED yet!"

main concern in teaching should be to create independent learners, thus making yourself obsolete. Finally, when students select their own topics, when they work in response groups, and when their work becomes important to them, you will find that they are more willing to work in editing groups. Most important, when they know that their work will be published in your class, you will find a renewed enthusiasm for the work that goes into revising and editing.

Publishing Student Writing

One way to develop a spirit of meaningful collaborative writing is to encourage **publishing projects.** Some teachers like to have classroom newspapers with the students as columnists. Others have students publish newspapers for special holidays. Still others have them write newspaper articles describing calamities such as tornadoes, earthquakes, or wars. Newspapers are easy to produce and involve students in learning different sections of regular newspapers. They can learn about creating headlines for articles they write; they can learn the difference between editorials and features; and they can learn to write sports, entertainment, and other sections. Publishing projects involve your students in collaborative group work as they organize, write, revise, edit, and publish. Not least important is student enthusiasm. We have seen many resistant students become very enthusiastic about writing after learning that their work would be published in the classroom newspaper for all to see.

Other publishing activities you may want to try include poetry anthologies, short-story collections, and individual publications of student writing. Your English learners will become very excited when they know that what they write will be read by others in booklike form. You can create a classroom library by having students publish books that will remain in your room, but you will find that students will value their published books so much that they are often unwilling to let them go. If you explain that their writing will be read by future students, you will get more cooperation. You can also ask students to donate one of their books to the school library or to make copies or second editions of their books.

Another successful publishing activity involves older students sharing their publications with younger children. Third-graders, for example, might read their books to a first-grade class. They might also discuss with the first-graders how they got their ideas for writing and how they developed the idea into a book. Similarly, high school students can share their writing with younger students. This kind of sharing creates great enthusiasm in the older students, who enjoy a real audience for their writing, and helps younger students see writing as a valuable enterprise practiced by their "elders."

Have you ever noticed that when you take a group picture, the first thing you look at when the developed picture returns is yourself? Why? Did you forget what you looked like? Something similar happens when students publish their writing. They continually return to their own books and reread them. It's not that they don't know the contents of the book but that they find deep satisfaction in reviewing their accomplishments. One way we informally evaluate classrooms we visit is by noticing the number of students who line up to read their books to us. In classrooms in which books are regularly published, students enthusiastically share their writing with others and demand opportunities for more publishing. If you create a publishing center and library, you will find students are motivated to write, revise, and edit their papers.

In summary, we have outlined the process approach to teaching writing, an approach that supports writing success and celebrates English learners' accomplishments through sharing and feedback each step of the way. As students begin to see themselves as authors, they develop pride and ownership in their writing. As the process writing cycle is repeated, as students continually write for real and functional purposes, and as they learn to provide valid feedback to their peers, they grow into more proficient and caring writers. By giving your English learners chances to work on meaningful collaborative writing tasks and by having them share their writing through publishing classroom books, you can be assured of their involvement in the revising and editing phases of the writing process. All of

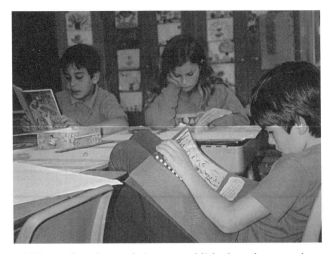

Children often choose their own published works to read during quiet reading time.

these benefits are especially important for English learners because process writing facilitates progress in written expression and promotes second language acquisition as well.

DEVELOPMENTAL PHASES IN SECOND LANGUAGE WRITING

Second language writers, like their first language counterparts, progress developmentally as they gain control over the writing process. To become truly effective writers, they must coordinate a broad range of complex skills, including clarity of thought and expression, knowledge of different genres to suit different purposes, and the ability to use conventional spelling, grammar, and punctuation. Such coordination depends, among other things, on students' English language proficiency, cognitive development, and writing experience. Because good writing exhibits numerous traits, because these traits vary according to the kind of writing and its purpose, and because individual development of these traits is apt to be uneven, it is not easy to characterize developmental levels. For example, one youngster may write very short pieces with correct spelling and punctuation, whereas another writes elaborate, action-packed stories without any punctuation or capitalization. Both are beginners, but neither writer has consistent development in all aspects of good writing. Such variation is to be expected.

Despite the complexities in establishing developmental characteristics, developmental descriptions are necessary as a starting point from which to guide your teaching decisions. In this section, we discuss in detail two general developmental phases, beginning and intermediate second language writing. These phases are defined in terms of the matrix shown in Table 6.4 and are analogous to the oral language matrix (SOLOM) you saw in Chapter 4. Though we include advanced second language writing characteristics, we restrict subsequent discussion to beginning and intermediate phases, consistent with the rest of the book. For these phases, we offer examples of student writing and suggest strategies you may introduce to help your students progress. Because you know your own students well from daily contact, you will be able to use your intuition as well as your analytical skills to decide finally which strategies will be most helpful. As a final note, please feel free to use or adapt any of the strategies for any student, according to your own judgment.

In Table 6.4, we describe beginning, intermediate, and advanced second language writing on five trait dimensions: fluency, organization, language use, style, and mechanics. Our concept of an advanced second language writer is defined in terms of an effective first language writer of the same age. In general, if a student's writing tends to be characterized by the trait descriptions listed for beginners, then we suggest that you start with strategies for beginners described in the next section. Similarly, if a student's writing tends to be characterized by the trait descriptions listed for the intermediate phase, we suggest you use the corresponding

TABLE 6.4   Writing Traits Matrix

Trait	Beginning Level	Intermediate Level	Advanced Level
Fluency	Writes one or two short sentences.	Writes several sentences.	Writes a paragraph or more.
Organization	Lacks logical sequence or so short that organization presents no problem.	Somewhat sequenced.	Follows standard organization for genre.
Grammar	Basic word order problems. Uses only present tense forms.	Minor grammatical errors, such as -s on verbs in third person singular.	Grammar resembles that of native speaker of same age.
Vocabulary	Limited vocabulary. Needs to rely at times on first language or ask for translation.	Knows most words needed to express ideas, but lacks vocabulary for finer shades of meaning.	Flexible in word choice; similar to good native writer of same age.
Genre	Does not differentiate form to suit purpose.	Chooses form to suit purpose, but limited in choices of expository forms.	Knows several genres; makes appropriate choices. Similar to effective native writers of same age.
Sentence variety	Uses one or two sentence patterns.	Uses several sentence patterns.	Uses a good variety of sentence patterns effectively.

224

strategies described for that phase. Bear in mind that your students are apt to vary in phase from one trait to another, and you will need to use your own judgment as to which strategies you will use.

DESCRIPTION OF BEGINNING WRITERS

Beginning second language writers, similar to beginning first language writers, are new to the coordinated efforts that go into creating a good piece of writing in English. They may find writing laborious, producing very little at first. If so, organization is not a problem, because there is little on paper to organize. If beginners do produce a great deal, logical organization is apt to be lacking. Like their first language counterparts, beginning second language writers may use invented spelling that might include elements from the spelling system of their first language. In addition, during the beginning phase, second language writers may not have a good sense of sentence boundaries or of the conventional word order required in English. Thus, they are apt to make errors in grammar, vocabulary, and usage. In addition, they may exhibit grammatical and other infelicities that may or may not be common to native English beginning writers.

When you evaluate your beginning second language writers, you need to take the time to notice and emphasize what they do well. This may not be natural or easy because errors call our attention like a flashing red fire alarm, whereas well-formed sentences go unnoticed as we focus on their meaning. When a child draws a picture, we don't compare it with Michelangelo's work. Instead, we delight in the accomplishment. Similarly, with beginning writers, we need to find specific elements to praise while pointing out areas to improve. Take for example, the following piece, a beginning-level student's paper referring to the cartoon character Bart Simpson:

> The puppy go to bart. He jump on bart. He look at bart. He see. He go.
>
> Kim, first grade

The child who wrote this paper worked laboriously to produce the final product. As a beginner, Kim uses one type of sentence only. She is able to use the present tense but has not developed the ability to use the past tense. This young beginning writer needs time and practice in both oral and written English. As a first-grader, Kim has plenty of growing time, and we suspect that she will improve steadily. Based on this writing sample, we would suggest two immediate strategies. First, additional effort during the prewriting phase of process writing might help her arrive at a more personally meaningful topic. Secondly, oral discussion of her topic combined with drawing would probably result in an elaborated message. Because she is new to English and because she is just a first-grader, we would not require her to alter her verb tenses. Such alteration would make little sense to her at this point and would not be likely to transfer to her next piece of writing. In sum, at this point we are aiming at fluency in writing and enjoyment in elaborated self-expression.

Not all beginning writers will be so young as first-grader Kim. Quite the contrary. Beginning ESL writers vary in age, interests, prior literacy experience, and second language proficiency. To repeat a point, the beauty of writing is that it accommodates many of the differences related to age, in that the topics are often selected and developed by the students. Thus, age and cultural appropriateness are, to an extent, built in by the students themselves through writing. Older beginning writers may bring a fairly sophisticated concept of the forms and functions of writing to the task, along with a well-developed conceptual system. Example 6.5 shows a writing example of a third-grade beginning English writer, Jorge. In this essay, Jorge attempts to describe the differences between two kinds of birds, mountain dwellers and valley dwellers, based on their portrayal in a cartoonlike picture.

Example 6.5   Jorge Describes the Differences between Two Kinds of Birds

> Tey are the same becaes the bofe of them haves two eggs and there head and there foot and they are not the same becaes they don't eat the same thing and ther beak and one place is the mountain and one is the valley. the end.
>
> Jorge, third grade

The assignment that led to this essay called for an expository type of writing. As a third-grader, Jorge had very little experience in writing, especially expository writing in English. He was a fairly fluent Spanish reader and had just begun instruction in reading English. Thus, the cognitive demand of this writing task was rather high. Nonetheless, he was able to convey similarities between the birds' eggs, their heads, and their feet, as well as differences in food, beak types, and dwelling locations. He used little capitalization or punctuation. His single, extended sentence consists of several clauses conjoined by "and," which is a characteristic of less mature writers. Furthermore, he ends his expository piece with a narrative formula: "the end." These characteristics are indicative of beginning-level writing, though more advanced than Kim's writing. Jorge needs opportunities to write daily for a variety of purposes that he perceives to be real and important. His ability to generate ideas, even within the constraint of a particular assignment, is excellent. With opportunities to create longer pieces of writing on topics that interest him and with the chance to publish and share, it is likely that Jorge will begin writing longer essays. Organization and punctuation are two areas on which he will need to work as he prepares his writing for publication.

STRATEGIES TO ASSIST BEGINNING WRITERS

We have discussed how effective writing requires the coordination of various kinds of skills and knowledge. One way to assist beginning and intermediate writers is to provide them with temporary frameworks that allow them to concentrate on one aspect of the writing process at a time. We refer to such temporary frameworks as **literacy scaffolds.** Just as scaffolding is temporarily provided to help workers construct a building, literacy scaffolds provide temporary frameworks to help students construct or comprehend a written message. In Chapter 3, we defined literacy scaffolds (Boyle & Peregoy, 1990) as instructional strategies that help students read or write whole, meaningful texts at a level somewhat beyond what they could do on their own. In general, literacy scaffolds include predictable elements as a result of repetition of language patterns and/or routines. Scaffolds are temporary and may be discarded when the student is ready to move beyond them.

226

Within this definition, the writing process itself is a powerful scaffold in that it breaks a complex process into smaller subprocesses, each of which is aimed at creating meaning. Other types of literacy scaffolds are described subsequently, including dialogue journals, buddy journals, and clustering. Each of these activities provides support for beginning-level writers. We recommend using the activities within the context of collaborative groups in which the students share and respond to one another's writing.

Oral Discussion

Oral discussion prior to writing, which obviously requires some oral English abilities, represents one kind of scaffold to literacy. When students share their ideas orally with the teacher or with their peers, they are facilitated in choosing and focusing their topic. Oral interactions help students organize their ideas and may also provide helpful vocabulary items for English learners. Informal oral language opportunities thus provide a safe arena for children to practice their language production. You don't want your English learners to answer as someone we know did when we asked how she liked school: "I hate school," she said. "I can't read. I can't write. And they won't let me talk." You can avoid that kind of judgment by encouraging your students to talk and share orally throughout the day. We describe several activities next that promote natural use of oral language and pave the way to literacy.

Partner Stories Using Pictures and Wordless Books

One activity that promotes second language development is the use of wordless books. Wordless books tell stories through their pictures and thus offer a unique opportunity for limited-English–speaking students to interact with a book. Using wordless books, students orally share their versions of stories in response groups, recognizing that the pictures might yield different interpretations. As a follow-up to wordless books, students may draw their own pictures for a book or a cartoon strip. Students may also try labeling pictures and developing a written story. Wordless books thus offer easy access to literacy events for both younger and older English learners. Whereas elementary students can simply enjoy the illustrations and stories, more advanced wordless books such as *Tuesday* (Wiesner, 1991) can challenge even college students and adults. A few additional wordless books you may want to try are listed here:

Alexander, M. (1970). *Bobo's Dream*. New York: Dial.
*Anno, M. (1978). *Anno's Journey*. New York: Putnam.
Anno, M. (1984). *Anno's Flea Market*. New York: Philomel Books.
Aruego, J. (1971). *Look What I Can Do*. New York: Scribner.
Hutchins, P. (1971). *Changes, Changes*. New York: Macmillan.

*Books for older students.

Mayer, M. (1967). *A Boy, a Dog, and a Frog.* New York: Dial.

Meyer, R. (1969). *Hide-and-Seek.* New York: Bradbury.

Wezer, P. (1964). *The Good Bird.* New York: Harper & Row.

*Wiesner, D. (1991). *Window.* New York: Clarion.

Concept Books: Creating a Teaching Library

Concept books, excellent for beginning writers, focus on and illustrate one concept or idea. For example, a student, after being introduced to a concept book, might illustrate a color, or the concepts *tall* and *short* or *above* and *below*. Students enjoy making their own concept books. Lisa, for example, made a book illustrating the concepts *little* and *big* by drawing and cutting out pictures to convey the ideas. One page featured a drawing of a little girl with the label *little*, and on the adjacent page was a picture of a big girl with the label *big.* The teacher, Ms. Shirley, kept a collection of concept books that students could use to learn a new concept. Students in her class had favorite concept books and used them as models for their own books. Some of the favorites were large books to illustrate the idea of big, and miniature books to illustrate the concept of small. Other favorite books were pop-up books and peek-a-boo books, in which the students had to guess the concept before they could see the entire picture. Concept books build vocabulary, provide opportunities for productive language use, and create opportunities for successful participation in classroom activities.

Peek-A-Boo Books for Younger Students and Riddle Books for Older Students

Another effective activity for younger English language learners, peek-a-boo books are excellent for beginning-level writers. Based on Janet and Allan Ahlberg's story *Peek-A-Boo!* (Ahlberg & Ahlberg, 1981), the stories allow young children to become actively involved in a nonthreatening "writing" activity. *Peek-A-Boo!* involves a repeated refrain: "Here's a little baby/ One, two, three/ Stands in his crib/ What does he see?" The page opposite the refrain contains a 3-inch-diameter hole, revealing only part of the picture on the next page. Beneath the hole is the phrase *Peek-a-boo!* When the page is turned, the entire picture is revealed, permitting the child to see whether his or her guess was correct. Children can use the repeated refrain and the peek-a-boo page to create their own first books. They write their own repeated refrain and create a page with the hole and peek-a-boo. On the following page, they can either draw their own pictures for others to guess, or they can cut pictures out of magazines to create their own book. Children then label the picture with a word, phrase, or sentence that describes the hidden picture. One child, Laura, created the following phrase: "Here's little Laura/ One, two, three/ Watching a movie/ What does she see?" Behind the peek-a-boo window, Laura had pasted a picture from her favorite movie and had written the title of the movie, *Home Alone,* below the picture. Peek-a-boo books offer children early access to writing stories because they are visual and because they contain repeated refrains that provide a simple pattern to build on. Children love these easily shared stories that involve them in oral discussions of their writing. For some children, the rhyming and peek-a-boo routine become like a mantra that they will repeat for days at a time. Peek-a-boo stories prepare children for future composing and sharing activities.

Riddle books are an extension of the peek-a-boo books but are adapted for older learners. Using the same format, with riddle books students create a word riddle beneath the cutout opening on the page and ask others to guess what is partially hidden. On the next page, the full picture is revealed and labeled appropriately.

Pattern Poems

Pattern poems are sentence-level scaffolds that make use of repeated phrases, refrains, and sometimes rhymes. The predictable patterns allow beginning writers to become involved immediately in a literacy event. One excellent resource for sentence-level writing scaffolds is Kenneth Koch's *Wishes, Lies and Dreams: Teaching Children to Write Poetry* (Koch, 1970). Full of sentence patterns that serve as springboards for writing, the book contains delightful poems written by Koch's high school and elementary multilingual students. Typically, students first write their own poems based on the patterns, sharing them with one another in peer response groups and in classroom publications. Two Spanish-speaking ESL second-graders with whom we worked created the following poems using the sentence patterns "I used to be . . . but now I am . . ." and "I am the one who . . ." The repetition of the pattern lends a poetic quality to the full piece of writing.

> JUAN: I used to be a baby.
> But now I am really big.
> I used to be a karate ninja.
> But now I am an orange belt.
> CHABELA: I am the one who like my teacher.
> I am the one who gots new shoes.
> I am the one who take care the baby.
> I am the one who plays on the swings.

To supplement poetry writing and reading, many teachers also introduce students to predictable literature that contains the same types of patterns and predictable features of Koch's poems. After hearing a story several times, students use pattern books as models for creating, publishing, and sharing books. Typically, they use the given patterns several times before they are ready to experiment with their own patterns and poems. Thus, the pattern offers a scaffold that students abandon naturally when it's no longer needed. Patterns like Koch's and pattern books offer easy and almost instant success to students' first attempts at writing in their second language. One pattern book frequently used with older, less advanced English learners is *Fortunately* (1997), by Remy Charlip. The book follows the fortunes and misfortunes of a boy using the pattern *fortunately* on one page and *unfortunately* on the next page. One high school student used the pattern to create the following story:

> Fortunately, I gotta job and I buy me a car
> Unfortunately, may car aint running too good
> Fortunately, I know this guy and he gonna fix it
> Unfortunately, it gonna cost a lot for fix it.
> Fortunately, I gotta job.

Arturo, age 15

From Personal Journals to Dialogue Journals to Buddy Journals

You will want to develop fluency in your beginning writers as a first priority. Fluency, the ability to get words down on a page easily, can only come with writing practice and continued English language development. Another word that is integrally related to fluency is **automaticity** (LaBerge & Samuels, 1976). Automaticity is the ability to engage in a complex activity without having to concentrate on each part of it. For example, when you first started learning how to drive a car, you had to concentrate on the steering, on the brakes, on making appropriate signals, and, perhaps, on using a clutch. At first this was difficult, but with practice you began coordinating all of these driving activities at once without having to concentrate on them. Writing and reading work in a similar way. For example, one child might first concentrate on making the letters, working laboriously just to write his or her own name. Only later will he or she go on to writing words and phrases. Other learners aim at getting a lot of "writing" on the page, but it will not as yet conform to conventional script.

Young beginning writers approach the task in different ways, however. You may recall our kindergartner Osvaldo, for example, who filled an entire half page with carefully written but undecipherable words. When asked what his writing was about, he replied that he did not know and returned with great sobriety to his task. We asked him two more times, with the same response, until he explained, "I won't know what I wrote about until I draw my picture." At that point, he created a fine drawing of a boy playing soccer. Writing does indeed involve the coordination of many resources, and the writing process helps students take one step at a time so that they are not overwhelmed by the task.

One of the most popular ways teachers help children develop fluency is through extensive prewriting activities, one of the most powerful being journal writing. By writing in journals daily, students develop fluency and generate ideas on which they might elaborate later. One friend of ours, who has used journals successfully for a long time, told us about a field trip she and her class took to a natural history museum. The students were to take notes in their journals; one fourth-grader was overheard saying to another, "Don't look. Don't look. She'll make you write about it!" Unlike these two fourth-graders, most students find journal writing nonthreatening and fun. In this section, we discuss ways to use journals for developing ideas, sharing thoughts and feelings, and exploring ideas.

Personal Journals. The first type of journal you may wish to share is a personal journal in which your students get used to writing their private thoughts. When these journals are used, you do not comment on them unless the writer asks you to do so. Students soon learn that the journals are for their own personal and private ideas. We recommend that you ask them to write in their journals three or four times a week at a regular time in the day. Some teachers ask their students to write in their journals at the end of the day, others like them to write after lunchtime or after a reading period. Whatever you decide, set a regular time aside for journals so that your students come to expect and anticipate journal writing. Journals can be constructed by folding pieces of paper in half, stapling at the fold, and decorating the cover.

Dialogue Journals. When students become accustomed to writing in their personal journals, you may want to move toward dialogue journals. First, describe dialogue journals (Kreeft, 1984), explaining to students that they can continue to write about the same topics and ideas as in personal journals except that you will respond to their writing regularly. Make sure you explain that you may not be able to respond to everything they write, but if they have something special to which they want you to respond, they can mark it with a colored marker. In your responses, respond to the content, not the form, of the writing. The purpose of interactive journals is to develop fluency and authentic conversation on paper. Moreover, you are making students' writing functional and purposeful by replying to them and elaborating on what they have said, in the same way that parents scaffold what children say to them in early oral communication. It is only polite to respond to what people say and not correct how they say it. Similarly, in journals, concentrate on positive things you can say. Encourage students to continue writing in their journals, but also let them know that some language or topics may be inappropriate for their journals if that is how you feel. If you respond to their journals, make suggestions positively if needed about what they might write about and encourage your students, they will look forward to writing in their journals while eagerly anticipating to your responses. Dialogue journals help develop fluency because they are meaningful, because they are responded to, and because they give writers the freedom to concentrate on what they are saying rather than on how students are saying it. Journals also provide ideas for topics students may write about more extensively later (Peyton & Reed, 1990).

Buddy Journals. A buddy journal is a written conversation between two students (Bromley, 1989, 1995). Buddy journals are a natural extension of personal and dialogue journals. Buddy journals involve students in meaningful, self-selected dialogues about issues that concern them. Moreover, they give them the immediate feedback they require for growth as well as a real audience and purpose for their writing. After modeling responses in dialogue journals, you can introduce buddy journals to students by explaining that they will be responding to one another instead of to you. Next, assign pairs to work with one another, explaining that they will have an opportunity to work with many other partners throughout the year. You might also provide guidelines for responding to the writing in the journals. Let students see that it is important to be helpful conversational partners in the journals. You might also ask your students to brainstorm potential topics to write about in their journals. Place these topics on the board and suggest that they can write about anything going on in the classroom or anything else they might want to share with one another. Older beginning English learners might share their thoughts concerning a movie or television show they had seen, while younger students might write to one another in buddy journals while reading *Harold and the Purple Crayon* (Johnson, 1955), as in the following dialogue:

> JOSEPH: I like the crayon magic and how he color thing.
> JIMMY: And the pies and things.
> JOSEPH: There's a "Harold and Circus" book to read.
> JIMMY: Yeah, it has purple coloring.
> JOSEPH: Let read it.

Journal writing is a valuable activity for English learners because it involves real and purposeful dialogue and because it is nonthreatening—it will not be corrected or graded. Finally, because journals are structured like an oral conversation and provide a real audience, students see journal writing as a meaningful activity, one worth the extra effort it may require of them. Table 6.5 summarizes several types of journals you may wish to use in your classroom.

Improvisational Sign Language

Using a dictated story or a story students already know, such as "Goldilocks and the Three Bears," "The Parsley Girl," or other folk tales, students can create gestures to represent characters and actions in the story. With her second language first-graders, Sheila Jordaine asked children to share stories with the whole class before creating their own. Children first dictated a brief story, which Sheila wrote on the blackboard: "Jill had a pet frog. She brought it to school." Next, they determined the symbols for each of the words. Because Jill was a member of the class, all they had to do when her name was read was point to her. They decided that bringing their hands toward them with the palms upward would stand for *had,* and they made an **A** with their hands, followed by petting their heads for *pet.* For the word *frog,* they got out of their chairs and hopped like frogs. For *she,* they simply pointed back at Jill, because *she* refers to Jill. In this way, they naturally learn anaphoric references. When they finished with their symbols, Sheila read the story, pointing to the words, while the children dramatized the story with signs.

TABLE 6.5   Types of Journals

Journal	Purpose	Procedure
Learning log	Develops sense of direction and success in the class; helps teacher evaluate student's progress; helps student articulate what is learned and ask questions for self-assessment.	After certain lessons each day you ask students to keep a daily log of their knowledge or confusions or any elaborations they may wish to make relating to the topics discussed in class. Journal is private or shared with teacher.
Buddy journal	Gets students used to the idea of writing each day; writing becomes a functional and meaningful activity, with almost immediate audience.	Students write and respond to one another about classroom topics and other topics; response is to content and not form of the message; often modeled by teacher in dialogue journal first.
Dialogue journal	Makes writing purposeful in school; gives students audience for their writing and models how to respond to the writing of others.	Journal is used daily or often; teacher responds to content or to something the student has highlighted for the teacher; writing is used as communication.
Project journal	Assists students with preparing for a project in English, science, etc.; students take notes of plants growing in science class in preparation for a report; they take notes of conversations in preparation for story they might write.	Students keep journal with a specific task in mind: plans for writing a story; notes for a social science paper; measurement for a math project.

233

The next day, the children decided to do a "real" story, "The Parsley Girl," to act out in signs.

The signing activity provides students with several cues for understanding stories. If the story is in a Big Book, the children have the words and pictures in front of them. In addition, the visual dramatization cue for comprehension gives them more information for understanding the stories they are reading. Finally, the activity involves all the students in a meaningful and functional process aimed at comprehension. Children in Sheila's class ask for improvisational signing performances throughout the year, even after they no longer need the extra comprehension support. Older students, even adults, also have a great deal of fun using the technique. For example, older students, who often know many folk tales, enjoy creating their own sign language in groups, acting the folk tale out and playing a charade-like game that requires other groups to guess the folk tale that is being presented in sign language.

Life Murals

Another activity that provides a scaffold for English learners is creating life murals. Using murals, students create drawings depicting significant events, people, and places in their lives and then write about them. For example, one child represented her family by drawing a house with people outside. In another picture she drew the inside of her own bedroom, a trifle messy, to show where she spent most of her time when she was at home. Other drawings depicted a church and school with her friends standing outside in the rain. She also drew a picture of her grandmother, who always read stories to her. When she finished her drawing, she explained these life symbols to her writing partner, and her partner did the same. Finally, she wrote about her life, using the mural to guide her.

Older beginning English learners also use life murals to scaffold their writing. One student in a tenth-grade class compared his life to a soccer game and created a mural showing him sometimes falling, sometimes missing the soccer ball, and sometimes scoring a goal. After creating the mural, he shared it with his group orally in preparation for writing. Then in writing he explained how his life was like a soccer game.

Life murals make writing simpler because they are based on very personal experience. Because they are visual, writers can easily get ideas from looking at one another's pictures and hearing their stories. After completing their murals and stories, students read them to their partners. Life murals provide an excellent beginning writing experience, with the drawings scaffolding learners' efforts to compose something more complex than journal entries.

Clustering

Clustering assists writers in developing vocabulary and preparing for writing (Rico & Claggett, 1980). The cluster in Figure 6.4 illustrates different words a student thought of when preparing to write about a personal experience. To create the cluster, Mai simply placed her name and the word *park* in the center of the circle and then quickly wrote all the other things that came to mind. She thought of different members of her family, of friends, and of a trip she took to an amusement park. When she completed her cluster, Mai shared it with members of her peer response group by telling them about how she got very wet on a log ride at the park. In fact, "They all got so wet that they had to buy tee-shirts to change into something dry."

Mai used the cluster as a prewriting strategy to begin thinking about her topic and what she wanted to say. Clusters represent one of the first steps, along with buddy journals, as beginning-level students begin to consider an audience for their

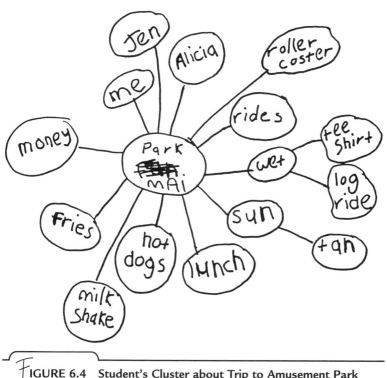

FIGURE 6.4   Student's Cluster about Trip to Amusement Park

writing. The cluster has several advantages: It is easy to create and there are no rules for what can go into a cluster—students decide for themselves; it fills the page and thus assists psychologically in helping the student create a piece of writing; and it is easy to share with others and thus helps the student create a story or experience orally. When English learners are ready to share their writing with their peers, clustering will help them do so. Finally, clustering is used successfully by students when they become older and more advanced; indeed, clustering is used by college and graduate students to improve their writing.

Freewriting

"Freewriting" is a strategy developed by Peter Elbow (1973) in which writers let their words flow freely onto the page without concern for form, coherence, or correctness. In the same way that journals provide opportunities for daily writing, freewriting assists with fluency. Using freewriting, students write quickly to get their ideas down on paper. After freewriting for several minutes, students may select a phrase or sentence they like and write about that for five minutes. They next select their favorite word, phrase, or sentence and write on it for five minutes. This process continues until students have discovered a topic or theme about which they might want to write. The freewriting helps develop writing fluency by allowing writers to concentrate on getting as many words on the page as possible without paying attention to correctness, and it also assists them with narrowing their topic. Through practice with freewriting, writers can be freed from the constraints of having to "get it right." They can instead pay attention to generating and shaping ideas. Along with the use of journals, freewriting assists students with fluency, with automaticity, and with developing ideas. Thus, it prepares them to move to the intermediate level, where they will pay more attention to refining and editing their ideas.

In summary, beginning-level English language learners can participate successfully in classroom writing events from day one, if you provide support. The scaffolds provided by picture books, symbol writing, concept books, clustering, freewriting, and dialogue journals give students the assistance they need to participate in the classroom. These activities, shared in pairs and collaborative groups, are meaningful activities, not an assortment of abstract skills. Through these activities, English language learners grow from beginning writers to intermediate writers—from writers learning to generate ideas to writers who shape ideas for different audiences and different purposes. They will move on from developing fluency to developing form in their writing and to revising and correcting their work. The strategies in the next section will help them develop into competent intermediate-level writers.

DESCRIPTION OF INTERMEDIATE WRITERS

Whereas your main concern with beginning second language writers will be helping them to generate ideas and develop fluency, your main concern with intermediate writers will be to add form to fluidity in expression. That is, you will want your intermediate writers to begin developing a variety of sentence structures and organizational patterns, from narrative to letter, essay, and more. To do this, you may offer strategies that build on the skills they learned as beginning-level writers, while continuing to share good literature. In addition, you and your students are now in a position to select aspects of spelling, grammar, and punctuation to be focused on during editing.

Intermediate-level writers have developed a general knowledge of simple sentence types and corresponding capitalization and punctuation conventions. However, they need strategies to improve their sentences in quality, style, length, and variety. In addition, as their writing increases in length, they will need to develop organizational strategies such as paragraphing and logical ordering of ideas. At this point, spelling may be fairly standard, though as yet imperfect, especially if students are using more advanced vocabulary. In addition, some intermediate writers may rely too heavily on one or two sentence patterns as a conservative strategy for avoiding errors. You will want to encourage these writers to try new forms that will improve their writing and strengthen their general knowledge of English. Finally, intermediate writers may still make fairly frequent errors in punctuation, grammar, and usage. In fact, they may make more such errors than beginners because they are producing more writing—a positive sign of writing progress. Recurrent errors may serve as the basis of an individual or group mini-lesson, so that students may correct such errors during editing.

In summary, intermediate writers have developed fluency in their writing. They are able to produce a large number of words on the page, but they still need to work on organization of longer pieces of writing as well as on sentence variety, grammar, and spelling. The essay shown in Figure 6.5 provides an example of intermediate second language writing, representing the writer's best effort after working in his peer response group.

Juan has worked very hard on developing a topic about which he clearly cares very much. Based on the writing traits matrix, his writing exhibits elements of intermediate phase writing. Of particular note, he has organized his essay into a beginning, middle, and end. His teacher gave him special help with this. He writes with considerable fluency but retains errors in his final draft. For example, his writing exhibits minor problems with spelling and verb forms. He misspells *both* as "bouth" and *said* as "sed." However, his inventive spellings are phonetically

The Frist Time I saw Her

The frist time I saw her she was seven year's old and so was I. We bouth in frist grade. One day I want to take her out but my mom sed I was to young.

I try letter's and poetry so she would like me. In third grade she started to like me. In forth grade we want to see the movie avalanche at the Kabuki theater. We bought popcorn with our money. We bouth enjoy the movie because it tell you about people from diffrent contry's and how it was hard moveing to America.

I had a good time with her. I want to go out to a movie with her again.

Juan 4th grade

FIGURE 6.5 Juan's Story: The First Time I Saw Her

accurate and thus more logical than conventional English spelling. He consistently uses 's to pluralize "year's," "drink's," and country's. He also keeps the *e* in moves, for "moveing." His spelling demonstrates substantial sophistication, requiring just a little more refinement to be perfect. Now would be a good time to provide a mini lesson on plural spellings for Juan. He may keep these spellings in a notebook so that when he edits his own work, he can refer to it if necessary. His overuse of the apostrophe with plurals reflects a previous mini lesson on the use of the apostrophe to indicate possession. He needs a review of this skill, along with a short explanation of the difference between plurals and possessives.

A different type of error occurs with verb forms. Juan does not yet consistently use the conventional present and past tense verb markers, writing *tell* instead of *tells* or *enjoy* instead of *enjoyed*. These tendencies are probably related to his developing English language knowledge. In our experience, verb agreement of this kind represents grammatical refinement that develops late in second language acquisition. We would not attempt to correct this error if Juan were a beginning English learner. However, because Juan's writing shows substantial fluency in English, he is probably ready for a mini-lesson on the *-ed* ending to indicate past tense. He may list this skill on his editing checklist to remind him to correct this element when editing his work. Juan needs daily opportunities to use the writing process approach. He has a lot to write about and enjoys sharing with his peers during response groups. He needs more opportunities to create finished pieces in which logical organization is needed to convey his message.

Example 6.6, illustrates an intermediate second language writer who is very close to moving into the advanced phase. The essay is a piece of expository writing, similar to the assignment required of Jorge that we shared with you earlier. For the essay, students were asked to compare ocean fish and bay fish based on information they could glean from cartoonlike drawings of the two kinds of fish.

Alberto's essay, a first draft comparing and contrasting ocean and bay fish, exhibits thoughtful and logical sequencing. The topic has been thoroughly covered in a manner that is clear and concise. At the same time, the essay lacks variety in

238

Example 6.6   Alberto's Essay Comparing Ocean Fish and Bay Fish

How the Ocean fish are alike to the Bay fish is that the Bay fish has same eyes like the Ocean fish. And they have same gulls as the Ocean fish. And they have same fins and 3 dots on its tail. And now how they are different is that the Bay fish have claws and the Ocean fish don't even have any teeth. An so the Ocean fish have big tails and the Bay fish have little tails. And the Ocean fish swim on the borrom of the ocean and the Bay fish wim at the top of the Bay. And the Ocean fish eat weed and the Bay fish eat little fish.

Alberto, fifth grade

sentence patterns. In general, comparisons call for more complex sentence patterns, which Alberto was not able to produce. Instead, he uses simple statements, beginning new sentences with *And*. To improve this essay, Alberto would benefit from a mini-lesson on sentence variety, which he could then apply in the revision process. In addition, the essay would be improved by an introduction and a conclusion, which Alberto could add rather easily during revision. In the next section, we offer a variety of ideas to help improve the writing of intermediate second language writers working in collaborative groups.

STRATEGIES FOR INTERMEDIATE WRITERS

Successful teachers of writing make sure that students have frequent opportunities to use writing for authentic purposes, often developing topics of students' own choosing and shaping pieces for particular audiences. In addition, teachers provide a variety of opportunities for students to publish their writing in a variety of ways for a variety of purposes. Just as beginning writers work on meaningful writing tasks, so must intermediate writers work on tasks that matter to them. Thus, the strategies we share here are used within the context of meaningful, functional writing assignments. In most cases, your students will have selected the topics they are writing about, and they will share their writing with one another, as well as with you. Without this meaningfulness, the following strategies will become empty assignments, no better than isolated worksheets. However, when the strategies help students develop and shape their own ideas, they become functional for students.

Show and Not Tell

A sentence that *tells* simply makes a flat generalization (Caplan, 1982; Elbow, 1973). For example, a young writer might write, "The party was fun," or "She has a nice personality," or "The Thanksgiving dinner was delicious." None of these sentences provides any descriptive detail about what the writer wants to convey. Was the party fun because of the food, the games, or the people? We don't know. In contrast, sentences that *show* give specific information for the reader about a party, dinner, or person. D. H. Lawrence once said that in good writing, characters should never merely walk up stairs; they should walk up 15 stairs or 40 stairs. "Show and not tell" is a powerful strategy because students can learn to use it after a very brief introduction and a little practice. They can apply it to improve their writing almost immediately. The following passage, from Jean Shepherd (1971), illustrates the "telling" sentence "In the morning, my father could be grumpy":

> He slumped unshaven, staring numbly at the kitchen table, until my mother
> set the coffee down in front of him. She did not speak. She knew that this was
> no time for conversation. He lit a Lucky, took a mighty drag and then sipped
> gingerly at the scalding black coffee, his eyes glaring malevolently ahead. My

old man had begun every day of his life since the age of four with a Lucky and a cup of black coffee. He inhaled each one alternately, grimly, deeply. During this routine, it was sure suicide to goad him. (p. 130)

"Showing" sentences such as Shepherd's make actions specific by illustrating in multisensory detail exactly what happened. After you introduce the concept to writers, ask them to identify showing sentences in literature they are reading. You can also assist them with the strategy by giving them telling sentences to rewrite with partners. The following examples were provided by English language learners in Shirley Vance's class:

Telling sentence: The band was noisy.
Showing sentences: As the band played I felt the drummer was banging on
                       my eardrums and the guitars yelled at me. I thought I
                       would never hear right again.

One of the most powerful reasons to use the show and not tell strategy, in addition to its ease of learning, is that English learners are able to transfer this knowledge to their own writing. They are also able to use it when they are working with peer response groups. They can pick out telling sentences, and they can make suggestions for showing sentences in their own writing and in the writing of others. Giving your students a concrete strategy that immediately improves their writing empowers them and motivates them to learn more.

Sentence Combining

Sentence combining simply teaches students to combine shorter sentences into longer ones while retaining the meaning. Researchers note that as writers mature they begin to write longer, more sophisticated sentences (Loban, 1968; O'Hare, 1973). Practice in sentence combining assists students in producing more mature writing. We suggest that English learners can benefit from sentence combining as well. You may use examples from students' own writing to assist them with sentence combining, or use sentence combining exercises found in books.

The essay on George Washington in Figure 6.6, by a student in a fifth grade class of language minority students, is typical of what intermediate writers often do when they become comfortable with basic short sentences. A peer response group suggested combining some of the short sentences into longer, more complex sentences. The essay, of course, needs more work than just sentence combining, and the students who worked on it discovered that they needed to help Lettie organize and delete some of the information in order to complete their task. Example 6.7 presents a revised draft of the essay.

There are, of course, many possible ways to combine the sentences. If you place some examples of sentence combining exercises on a transparency, your students can try the exercises and share results. Through sentence combining, students learn to play with sentence variations and choose the one that best suits

George Washington was the very first president. He had a wife name Martha. He had false teeth and wore a wig. His face is carved on Mount Rushmore. He died of pneumonia. He was an orphan at 15 years old. He was ill many times as a young man. He was very shy and polite. His wife Martha was a widow. He was a good leader. He was not selfish. He was a hero in the revolutionary war. He spent a horrible winter in Valley Forge.

Lettie, grade 5

FIGURE 6.6   Essay on George Washington before Sentence Combining

Example 6.7   **Revised Essay on George Washington**

George Washington was the very first president and he had a wife named Martha. He was an orphan when he was young and was ill and very shy and polite. He was a hero in the revolutionary war and spent a horrible winter in Valley Forge. His face is carved on Mount Rushmore.

their meaning. Moreover, developing writers can apply the strategy to their own writing.

An example of a teacher-made exercise follows:

Example:	1. The boy wanted something.
	2. He wanted to buy tickets.
	3. The tickets were for a rock group.
	4. The rock group was his favorite.
Combination:	The boy wanted to buy tickets for his favorite rock group.

Sentence Shortening

Sentence shortening, the opposite of sentence combining, assists students with changing wordy sentences into more concise sentences (Peterson, 1981). In the early phases of writing development, some students may write sentences that ramble on and on. You can give students long sentences to revise into shorter sentences that mean the same thing. Arturo Jackson introduces the idea to students in small groups by making a game out of sentence shortening. Using a transparency, he places a wordy sentence on the screen and challenges students to make the sentence shorter while preserving the meaning of the original sentence. Students rewrite the sentence in their groups and then report back the number of words in the reduced version. The object is to write the shortest sentence with no loss of meaning. He also discusses the revised sentences with students so that they can evaluate whether the shortest sentence is actually the best one. A few examples of original student sentences and their revisions follow:

Original Student Sentence:

That man who I know invented something that was entirely new.

(adapted from Peterson, 1981)

Student Group Revisions:

That man I know invented something.

I know a man who is an inventor.

Original Sentence:

The store over there across the street is owned by three sisters who live in the apartment above the store across the street.

Student Group Revisions:

The sisters live above the store across the street in an apartment.

There is an apartment above the store across the street. Three sisters live above it.

In the latter example, the student groups in the class determined that it was better to break the original sentence into two sentences. They felt that one-sentence versions didn't sound right. Arturo let their decision stand, and they learned that there are no rigid rules for rewriting sentences. They also learned to pay attention to the sound of sentences as well as the meaning. They were beginning to develop a sense of style in their writing.

Sentence Models

Sentence modeling, another helpful strategy for intermediate writers, is based on sentences from quality classroom reading materials or from writing produced by students themselves. You can introduce simple sentence models at first, then more complex models. Through the use of sentence models, students develop con-

242

fidence in their ability to write with power and variety. Sentence models help intermediate-level writers move from a few simple sentence structures to more complex structures, building the confidence that students need to make the transition from beginning to intermediate phases and beyond. The models that follow represent only a few examples of the kinds of sentences you may wish to share. When students are working alone or in peer response groups, they can try the models and immediately develop a more mature writing style. Through these procedures, English learners benefit in both English language development and writing.

A group of fourth-graders selected a model based on a favorite sentence in *Charlotte's Web* (White, 1952), consisting of a series of clauses that finish with a major statement (Seigel, 1983). They then developed their own sentences from the model:

> KIM: Leticia reaches in her purse, gets the lipstick, colors her lips, and gets the mirror to see how she look.
>
> NG: Jan runs fast, opens the car door, getting in to go to the rock concert.

All 26 students in the class, with help from their groups, were able to write good examples of the model. Later, in their own writing, the model and variations of it began to appear. The students could show off with the sentence, knowing also that they could punctuate correctly. Finally, they had fun using patterns occasionally introduced by their teacher and began lifting patterns of sentences they liked from their own reading. Using sentence models gave the students confidence to experiment and play with language.

Another more complex sentence model you may want to introduce to intermediate writers is the dependent clause in a pair or in a series. We have found that intermediate writers can follow this model and gain confidence through their success, impressing themselves and others. The model, which is particularly useful as an essay topic sentence or as a concluding sentence in an essay or narrative, contains the following form (Waddell, Esch, & Walker, 1972, p. 30):

> If . . . , if . . . , if . . . , then Subject Verb.
>
> Because . . . , because . . . , because . . . , Subject Verb.
>
> When . . . , when . . . , when . . . , Subject Verb.

Student Examples of the Model

Because it is rainy, because it is cold, because I feel lazy, I think I won't go to school today.

When I am home, when I am bored, when I have nobody to play with, I watch television.

If I was rich, if I could buy anything, I would buy my parents a house.

In the last example, the writer did not want to use a series of three and saw that she could use a series of two if she wanted. Using sentence models, students begin to experiment with the sentences and learn that sentences can be organized in a variety of ways. This gives English learners confidence in their ability to learn new English sentence structures. Using sentence models in their writing not only teaches students to develop variety in their sentences but also shows them how to punctuate.

Mapping

While "show and not tell" and sentence models work with form at the sentence level, mapping works with form at story or essay levels. A map is a visual/spatial representation of a composition or story and can assist students with shaping stories or essays they are writing (Boyle & Peregoy, 1991; Buckley & Boyle, 1981). Mapping has been used by students of all ages. The writer Henry Miller used to draw on the walls of his room making maps in preparation for writing his novels.

You can introduce students to mapping by having them work in groups; later they can learn how to map by themselves. Jackie Chi introduces the strategy by giving students a familiar topic and asking them to brainstorm words or phrases for the topic. Below are some words children in a third-grade class brainstormed based on the word *soap:*

hand soap	bathroom	kitchen	hands
powder	slippery	colors	sink
dirty	shiny	liquid	clean
clothes	face	showers	bubbles
bar	facial	bath	dry

After students have generated the words for soap, Jackie asks them to think of words that go together (categories) and to place words under the category names, as in the following example. She reminds them that they can add new words to the list and that some of their words may not fit in any categories.

Type of Soap	Places Used	Used For
liquid	kitchen	showers
powder	bathrooms	baths
bar	machines	hands

After they have placed their words into categories, Jackie asks students to use butcher paper and marking pens to make a map representing their words (Figure 6.7). She provides them with the simple structure in Figure 6.7 to start them out but asks them to be creative in developing maps. For example, they might want to draw pictures to illustrate their words. When each group has finished mapping, she has them share their maps. Later, she might ask students to map their own topics on a piece of paper and share them. They would use the same process Jackie introduced to them: brainstorm, create categories, draw a map. When it is completed, they can use the map to write a story about themselves. Lisa, age 7, developed the map in Figure 6.8 in preparation for a piece about her friends.

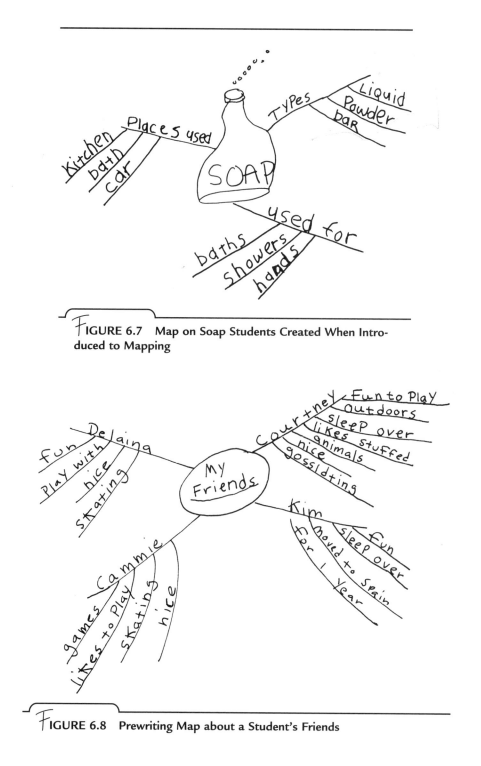

†IGURE 6.7   **Map on Soap Students Created When Introduced to Mapping**

†IGURE 6.8   **Prewriting Map about a Student's Friends**

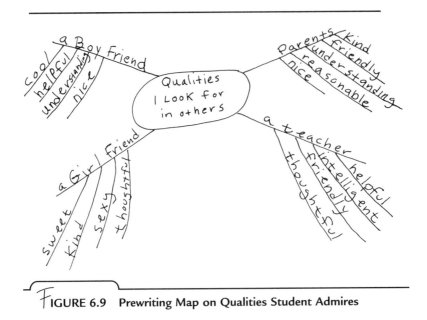

ꟻIGURE 6.9   Prewriting Map on Qualities Student Admires

246

The mapping procedure helps students generate ideas and think about how they might organize their ideas before they begin to write. It helps them think about the content and form their story or essay will take and allows them to try out different ideas before they commit them to paper. Because mapping is less intimidating than writing a whole story or essay, students gain confidence in their ability to compose. The map in Figure 6.9 and short paper in Example 6.8 are by a student who usually struggled with writing but, with the help of the map and

Example 6.8   Essay about Qualities Student Admires (based on map in Figure 6.9)

This composition is about the way I feel about others. For instance, how I feel about my parents, girl friend, teachers and friend. Sertain kind of people make me sick. I don't like some people that just think that there so perfect, and so fine. I think that you have to look for alot of qualities in a parent. They have to be understanding because if your parents arent understanding you mit as well not call parents. and they must be loveing, thoughtful, and exspecialy helpful, they help you when your sick they help you when your in troble they help you ever day of your life. . . .

Keno, age 12

his response group, was able to turn in a paper that far exceeded anything he had written before (Hudson, 1982). We present one of the five paragraphs he wrote.

In summary, intermediate strategies help second language writers organize their thoughts on paper, develop specificity in expression, and utilize a variety of sentence patterns with conventional punctuation and grammar. Moreover, these strategies help students expand the array of genres they can use, from letters to stories to essays to poetry. As your English learners use the strategies, they will develop confidence and become motivated to work on revision. The strategies also guide students in evaluating the writing of others and making constructive suggestions in their peer response groups. Without specific "how to's," students will falter in response, as we learned in class one day. After peer response groups had not gone well in our third grade class, we asked Joe to read his paper for class comment. When Joe finished his paper, Sarah raised her hand and commented, "That's a good paper." When we asked her to be more specific, she elaborated, "That's a *really* good paper." If students are not provided with specific strategies for revision, you might end up as Joe did that day: no farther ahead than if he had worked alone instead of with the group. On the other hand, if you explicitly teach English learners how to revise, you will give them the vocabulary to talk about writing, and you will model response to writing. The strategies we have presented have been proven to be successful with English learners; they have helped improve their writing and promoted their English language proficiency as well.

247

$\mathcal{A}$ WORD ABOUT WRITING WITH COMPUTERS

If you have a computer in your classroom, word processing programs can be particularly helpful to English language learners. For example, with a spelling checker they will have their own individualized spelling program. We have discovered that the invented spellings of beginning-level English language learners can be recognized by a good spelling program, which reads the invented spelling word and gives back the correct spelling of the word most of the time. For example, if we give our spelling checker the invented spelling of the words *wus, scelitin,* or *onvilope,* the checker gives the words *was, skeleton,* and *envelope.*

In addition to computer-assisted spelling, a teacher or paraprofessional can type language experience (student-dictated) stories into the computer so that students can see the writing as they speak the words. A good program allows you to type in large letters so that students gathered around a computer can see the words, or you can use the computer with an overhead projector so that the entire class can see the words as they are typed. Chavez (1990) found that when language experience was used with a computer, students became enthusiastic learners and felt validated because they could write about their own families and cultural experiences. Moreover, they grew in sentence and content maturity and developed their ability to respond to each other's writing. Other researchers report positive findings when English learners work with one another and when they

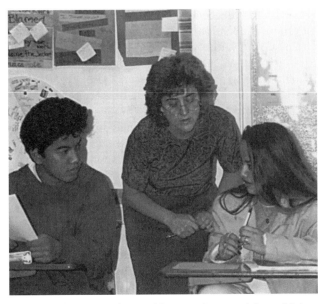

In responding to student writing, teachers model sensitivity and wording that students can use in peer response groups.

248

work with English-speaking students in groups using a computer (Merino, et al., 1990).

Finally, new computer programs contain prompting programs and voice synthesizers. *Prompting programs,* which guide writers by displaying helpful messages on the screen, have been developed to assist writers at different developmental stages. Those of us who write on computers are thankful if we have a prompt program that reminds us to save our work. Some prompt programs may give students the form for a business letter, book report, or newsletter. Others may ask them if they can identify the main idea in their statement. Research indicates that students are able to improve their writing using such prompting programs (Daiute, 1985). Voice, or *speech synthesizer,* programs read and pronounce students' words as they type them and let students reread them, listening to the words as they read. These programs can assist students with oral language, reading, and writing in a nonthreatening and natural way by "talking to them" (Rosegrant, 1988). New and truly excellent programs such as the synthesizers are coming out every day. The best way to keep track of what is available is through journals such as *The Reading Teacher* or *TESOL Quarterly,* which regularly discuss innovations in technology.

ASSESSING ENGLISH LEARNERS' WRITING PROGRESS

The best kind of assessment in any classroom comes from day-to-day informal observations of your students as they write and interact in their writing groups. Such informal assessment gives a much better picture of the student's overall achievement than any single paper, standardized test score, or other one-time performance sample. To accompany your observational insights, we suggest using portfolios and holistic scoring and involving students in evaluating their own writing. In this way, students become aware of their own progress. Remember that the best assessment of student writing is going to be the writing itself, not tests on grammar, spelling, or punctuation, for instance. Finally, when students become evaluators of their own writing and know how and what they need to do to improve it, they will improve.

Portfolio Assessment

Portfolio assessment involves keeping selected pieces of a student's writing in a special folder (Howard, 1990; Murphy & Smith, 1990). You and your student select which pieces should be saved to illustrate the student's writing abilities. Portfolios are useful for several reasons. First, through the use of portfolios you can assess students' growth by viewing all of their writing over the year and thereby assess your own teaching. Second, you can promote self-assessment in your students and motivate them to evaluate their own growth. Third, portfolio assessment motivates students to improve as they see their development throughout the year and helps them to see real growth when they compare what they wrote at the beginning of the year with what they accomplished by the end of the year. In summary, the keeping of writing portfolios assists students in evaluating themselves as writers and assists you in evaluating your own program. Look at the two pieces of writing in Figures 6.10 and 6.11, which are separated by one and a half years, and you can see that you would learn a great deal about Jorge's improvement as a writer.

Now imagine that you are Jorge's teacher and have received the essay in Figure 6.10 along with one he has just written for your class (Figure 6.11); both essays come from the same stimulus, drawing of two kinds of fish.

Clearly, the two papers might be viewed differently within the context of how far Jorge has advanced if they are found together in a portfolio. If you receive a piece of writing like Jorge's and can compare it with what he was doing last year, you can make certain decisions about what needs to be done next, about his strengths and weaknesses. You can also ask him to look at the two papers and see his own advancement. Portfolios allow you to contextualize the student's advancement and better evaluate what is needed and what has been accomplished.

Earlier, in Figure 6.5, we shared a piece of writing by Juan ("The First Time I Saw Her") as an example of an intermediate writer. However, Juan's portfolio shows that he didn't write at the intermediate level when he entered the class. Example 6.9 shows his writing in the second month of school, Example 6.10

FIGURE 6.10 Jorge's First Portfolio Sample: Writing about Fish

The fish are alike · because they both have three dots
on their tale and both have two lines on the and
They both both have pins this or and the both have
some eyes and the both live in the water and they have a
mow mouth · and the both have two a tale.
fish are different because some have thr tits thits
and some have big mouth and some have some
small tails and some have big trails and some
eat smaler fish and some eat things that are planted

FIGURE 6.11   Jorge's Writing about Fish: A Later Sample

Example 6.9   Juan: Second Month Sample from Portfolio

To day it was ranning. why? The only men who can tell us is faster dan a speeding bullet. More bigger dan a penut smaller dan my hand. It middy mouse. Yes hes baaaack beeter dan ever. Faster dan ever.

He' parner jast like! But! more dumer dan middy mouse. Its supper Juan. Yes he's back more dumer dan ever. Middy mouse can't belive I he's parnter.

Example 6.10   Juan: Fourth Month Sample from Portfolio

Dear Eney one
To day I got up. I whast to, I took a shower. I help my brother get dress, and I got dresset too. My mom left me some money. It was five dollars in cash. I went to the story to buy my brother a pice of candey. We got on the bus we came to school and played. Her I am writing this for you.

                                                    P.S. See you later!!!

Example 6.11 **Juan: Sixth Month Writing from Portfolio**

The first time I saw her she was seven year's old and so was I.

We bouth in first grade. One day I want to take her out but my mom sed I was to young.

I try letter's and poetry so she would like me. In forth grade we want to see the movie Avalanche at the Kabuki theater. We bought popcorn, and drink's with our money. We both enjoy the movie because it tell you about people from different country's and how it was hard moveing to America.

I had a good time with her. I want to go out to a movie with her again.

Juan, fourth grade

shows a piece from the fourth month, and Example 6.11 shows the sixth month of school.

In the three examples, we can see Juan moving from a beginning to an intermediate level. In the first example, Juan uses the pattern from the Mighty Mouse cartoons to create his own pattern in writing. The pattern gives him support while he is still at a beginning level in English. In the second example, Juan writes about more mundane matters in mostly simple sentences. He makes fewer errors in his writing, but he is held back in expression by his limited English. In the third, only four months after the first sample, Juan is beginning to express himself well and in a variety of sentences. His English language ability has grown, and he shows this growth through writing. He also shares matters that are important to him, and he shares them with feeling. In a four-month period, he has moved from copied patterns to familiar sentence models to individual sentence structures. He writes more, he writes better, and he is well launched as a writer. Through portfolio assessment, Juan and his teacher can share his success and determine his next step. These next steps will offer Juan more opportunities to write for different purposes and for different audiences. Moreover, he will be exposed to more sophisticated language in the stories he reads. All of these opportunities will assist him in becoming a better writer. If you ask Juan today what he wants to be, he will say, "A writer."

Students not only share portfolios with their teachers but also refer to them while working with their peers. When students have been working in peer response groups, they become critically perceptive of their own writing as well as that of their peers. As they look at their writing portfolios, they begin asking the same questions they ask of others in writing groups: What was I trying to say? Did I accomplish what I wanted to? How would I change it?

Some questions you might have students address in their own writing will reveal the strengths and weaknesses of your own program as well as the perceptions of your student writers. For example, you might ask them to think about one thing they like about a piece of writing. In contrast, you could also ask them to reflect on one thing they did not like about their writing. Students' answers to these questions reveal the depth of their understanding and help you assist them in going beyond such superficial responses to their writing as finding two spelling errors in a paper. Student self-evaluation is at the heart of portfolio assessment, helping you determine what you need to do next, while empowering the students in their own development.

Once students have collected a body of work in their portfolios, you can assist them with procedures for comparing their writing. Ask them to look over their writing and select what they think is the best piece of writing and what is their worst. Then, ask them to respond in writing to questions such as: Why did you select the piece? Why is it good or bad? If you decided to revise the piece, what specifically would you do with it? What have you learned about your writing by evaluating the pieces in your portfolio? What might you do differently when you write next as a result of viewing the writing in your portfolio?

Thinking and writing about the work in their portfolios helps students reflect on their writing and encourages them to share their thinking with others. Most important, perhaps, is the fact that students begin to see that some pieces in their portfolio are incomplete and that others may be worthy of revisions for publication. Moreover, students tend to see writing as the development of ideas rather than the correcting of papers. Portfolio assessment helps students become reflective and self-evaluative writers. When this happens, they can use the revision and editing strategies they have learned to improve their writing and to prepare it for sharing with others.

Holistic Scoring

Holistic scoring refers to the evaluation of a piece of writing as a whole, rather than to evaluation of separate aspects such as spelling, punctuation, grammar, style, or mechanics (Myers, 1980; White, 1985). Holistic scoring is usually used to evaluate a set of papers that have been written on the same topic with the same topic development and writing procedures. In this way, the papers can be compared readily in terms of quality. When teachers assess a paper holistically, they read papers swiftly and rate them on a scale, often from 1 to 6, with 6 as the best and 1 as the worst score. In the evaluation process, reader-evaluators agree on "anchor papers," or essays that typify each rating, 1 to 6. Usually, two readers evaluate each essay to increase the reliability of the score. Generally speaking, scores of 1 and 2 represent our category of beginner; scores of 3 and 4 represent the intermediate category; and scores of 5 and 6 are the advanced writers with the particular group you are evaluating. Holistic assessment has been used to assess a school's or even a whole district's progress in writing, and helps students evaluate their own writing.

Holistic scoring has several advantages over traditional methods of evaluating and grading papers in your classroom. First, you develop the anchor papers along with the students and then specify writing traits that make the papers low or high on the scoring scale. Second, holistic scoring helps students evaluate a paper based on its communication of ideas rather than on correctness alone. Third, holistic scoring provides models for good writing, making the traits of good writing explicit to students. Developing writers can apply these models and knowledge of good writing to their own composing, and they can evaluate their own writing holistically, thinking critically about what it needs to receive the highest evaluation.

Procedures for Using Holistic Scoring in the Classroom. We recommend using the following procedures for holistic assessment with your students, based on Miles Myers's work (Boyle, 1987; Myers, 1980). First, discuss with the students a topic they might want to write on and make sure all students can address the topic with ease. Topics such as "write a description of someone who is important to you," or "write about a favorite object you have," or "write about a person who has influenced you" are good topics because everyone can write about them. After they have selected the topic, give your students a half hour or so to think about the topic, take notes, brainstorm, or perform whatever prewriting strategy they use (Boyle, 1986). Let them know that, on the following day, they will have time to write an essay on the topic. On the next day, give them time to review their prewriting notes and to think about the topic before you ask them to write.

It is a good idea to ask another teacher from another school to have students write on the same topic using the same procedures. Then you can use those unfamiliar papers to discuss assessing and scoring the papers with your students. These papers can be used throughout the year to evaluate papers on other topics. Once you've received the other class's papers, you can go through them and, using a scale of 1 to 6, select papers you feel clearly represent each score on the scale. Simply place the papers on a table and begin ranking them after reading them quickly. After you have done this with all the papers, you will want to select representative papers to become model or anchor papers that the students will use to score their own writing. Be careful that you do not select a high paper that is so perfect that no other student will be able to get a 6. Likewise do not select a low paper that is too low.

Sample Holistic Essays, Rubrics, and Possible Teaching Strategies for Each Level. The six holistic anchor papers below were taken from the essays of two secondary school ELD classrooms. They are not meant to represent a holistic scoring done in your classroom, but to illustrate the results of two teachers' holistic scoring. The teachers, from different schools in different cities, were able to use their own students' essays as well as the essays of each other's classes. Once you have ranked papers, you can create a **rubric** that lists the qualities of papers receiving scores of 1 to 6, such as organization, vividness of description, originality of ideas, spelling, grammar, and punctuation. These rubrics you have developed can be used by you and by students to make writing qualities more explicit. The essays in Examples 6.12 through 6.17 represent each holistic score; level one essays received the lowest score in the session, and level six represents the highest score received.

Example 6.12 Level One Essay

The most important person I have my next door person she always call at me and tell about dog bark in other hose about cats to a lot. she only tell about those things and my mom don't like it or talk to me bout it.

Example 6.13 Level Two Essay

The most important to me is my uncle the way he tell me to go to school and tell me to read my books and do work teacher says. I was to go school and learn things I need to know and get a good work place. My uncle have good work and he is good person. What he told me is right and it help me do pretty good in school. I can think how I learn from my uncle. He my favorite person. What he say is right.

Example 6.14 Level Three Essay

The most important for my life is a man I met in my house. He was friend of papa and he smiled a lot. He tell me about his job and how he fix cars and do this with the engines and mechanical things. He tell he always do work on car when he was 14 like me. And I can learn to do something important like he work on. Alexander always tell he work hard to fix cars and help people drive and enjoy their drives. He would told me work hard, be a good person you will be successful and like life. He was important he told me the right things to do and he was always nice. I will work hard all my life.

Example 6.15 Level Four Essay

The person who is important is my best friend who taught me to play soccer better. Joseph treat me like a good friend and when he knew I could not play good he showed me how to do it. One thing he showed me was how to practice for along time he say to be a soccer player you had to practice so I practice every day. And I get better to practice and I made the team this year he is on the team too. When I don't play so good he told me that everybody make mistakes and errors a part of the game very good player and even start make mistakes too. And I will make mistakes like stars.

I want to be a star and practice helps meke me better. And Joseph practice with me and he show me how I can be better. We practice kicking the ball and passing the ball and I will be making the first team like Joseph makes it. He is one of the best players and he gives me time to practice and get better like him. Most people don't do that and that why he is important to me and will always be my friend and companion. He tell me the new word it means very good friend.

Example 6.16   Level Five Essay

I have not known anybody who has been as important to me as Larry. Larry who always wanted to help me. When I first come to this country he was the first person to help me. He told me how I should be in school and how I should raise my hand when I had the answer and to not talk if I don't raise my hand. He told me what shows on television I would like and he was right about that too. Larry was very popular with the other kids and I know I was lucky to have him as a friend. He didn't have to choose me as a friend. Lots of other kids were his friends also. I didn't know many words when I came to this country and he helped me because he could speak Spanish and he could also speak English. That was a great help to me.

Larry did other things that helped me. He introduced me to his friends and he made me part of the teams when we played baseball and he knew I was a good shortstop so I git to play that position sometimes. He showed me how to play other positions too and I got to pitch one time but I wasn't good at that. Because of Larry when I moved to this country it was a lot easier and now we are still friends after four years. Larry taught me how to be with other other people and how to help them and when someone new comes to our class I make sure I help him just like Larry helped me. That's why he is a very important person.

Example 6.17   Level Six Essay

Except for my parents Bob James is the most important person in my life. He is important to me for several reasons and I will relate a few of them. First of all, he has always treated me well even when I have not always treated him well. He accepts my mistakes, lets me know how I have offended him, and communicates with me so I will understand his feelings. Once I got so mad at him for ignoring me at school that I decided I wouldn't be his friend anymore; I decided I would not talk to him when I saw him. But he would not let me ignore him; he called me on the phone and asked me what was wrong and I told him that he ignored me in fornt of his friends. Right away he said that he didn't mean to and that he considered me a good friend. He also thanked me for being honest with him and we become good friends again.

Bob also would make good suggestions about what we should do, go to the movies go to the mall and other things. He always had good ideas and he knew how to have fun no matter what. We didn't just drive around in his car; once we visited all the churches in our town and we met ministers and priests and got to go inside the churches. The churches were interesting but what surprised us was how nice the people were. In every church they showed us around and seemed interested in us. They didn't treat us just like two kids who shouldn't be there. I guess Bob will be the best friend I will ever have and that he will always introduce me to interest and curious things.

Based on these essays, Figure 6.12 illustrated rubrics for each level of writing and possible strategies that might be used with beginning-level, intermediate-level and advanced intermediate-level writers. The *rubrics* discuss characteristics of essays, including fluency, organization, mechanical errors, sentence structure, grammar, and communication. The strategies are meant as possible suggestions for the students, not as recommendations for individual students. Your knowledge of students will determine appropriate strategies.

256

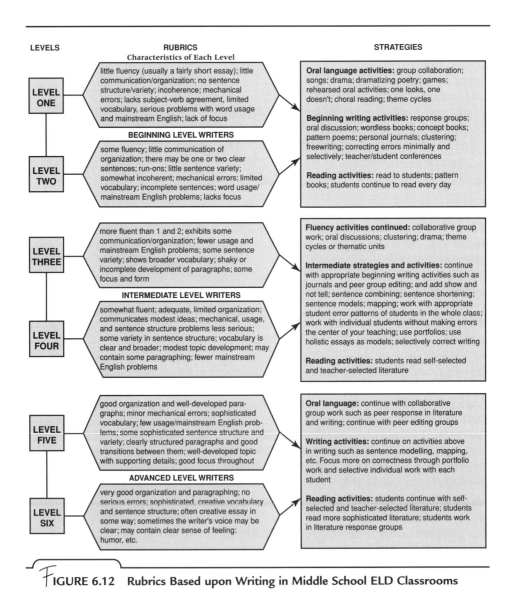

ꟻIGURE 6.12 **Rubrics Based upon Writing in Middle School ELD Classrooms**

Working with Errors in Student Writing

The goal of writing instruction is to promote student competence in writing effectively and correctly across a variety of genres: letters, stories, poems, essays, and reports. To help students achieve that goal requires explicit instruction, not only on generating and expressing ideas, but also on numerous details such as text structures, sentence styles, grammar, punctuation, and spelling. When teachers ask how to deal with errors in student writing, they are usually concerned with these mechanical details. We suggest that teachers take time each day to provide explicit instruction on mechanical details, taking into consideration English language proficiency (Echevarria, Vogt, & Short, 2000) and writing development needs that are common (1) to the whole class and (2) to individuals and small groups. These details might include, for example, subject/verb agreement, spelling words related to a theme topic, and perhaps a new sentence style or text structure. Once taught, these items may then be incorporated into peer editing and self editing checklists.

When choosing writing elements to focus on, you can assess specific needs of individuals and groups by evaluating the writing they produce in class. As students write daily, sometimes taking a piece through all five writing phases including publication, error patterns in their drafts provide information on specific instructional needs. After you have conducted mini-lessons addressing particular error patterns, these items are then incorporated into individualized or group editing checklists.

257

Balancing Goals: Fluency, Form, Correctness

Three important goals in writing development are illustrated in Figure 6.13: fluency, form, and correctness. **Writing fluency,** which is closely related to a student's general English proficiency, is the ability to generate ideas with ease while writing them down on paper. **Form** refers to sentence styles, paragraphing, and text structures; while **correctness** concerns the proper use of grammar, punctuation, and spelling. A good piece of writing displays its author's competence at all three levels. Because few students are writing experts, an instructional program that leaves out any one of these aspects lacks balance. Virtually all students need explicit assistance in all three. In the past, instruction often focused only on correctness, leaving students to find their own way into fluency and form. With the advent of the process approach, fluency sometimes took over completely, leaving minimal time for instruction on form and correctness.

The purpose of the model is to remind us to keep fluency, form, and correctness in mind for all students, while focusing attention on one aspect at a time. For example, students who have difficulty getting just a few words on the page need to focus on developing their writing fluency. Nevertheless, it is generally appropriate to assist them with correct use of capitals at the beginning of sentences and

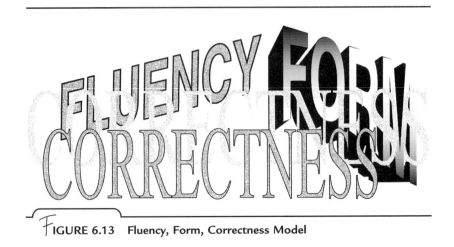

$\mathcal{F}$IGURE 6.13   Fluency, Form, Correctness Model

258

periods at the end. Once they are able to write fluently, the focus changes to form, to such matters as paragraphing, sentence models, and creating smooth transitions between paragraphs. The writer also will deal with correctness within the longer piece of writing. Finally, in preparing to share a piece of writing for publication or sharing, writers focus on correctness. Thus, the fluency, form, and correctness model reminds us to focus on one specific aspect of writing at a time, but not to the exclusion of others. In sum, all students will work on fluency, form, and correctness, but the specific details and relative focus will differ according to (1) the student's individual needs as an English learner and as a developing writer and (2) the phase the student is working on developing the particular piece, i.e., prewriting, drafting, revising, editing, or publishing.

Balancing Instruction: Scaffolds, Models, and Direct Instruction

The process approach incorporates an instructional model calling for scaffolds, models, and direction instruction (Cazden, 1983) as shown in Figure 6.14. Process writing provides a variety of **scaffolds** to assist students with all aspects of writing, including correctness. For example, as explained in Chapter 3, the writing routine itself provides a scaffold: Students know that they are going to edit their work for grammar, spelling, and punctuation after they are satisfied with the content. In addition, teacher and peer feedback will help them locate errors in their writing.

Models are provided in several ways. For example, the teacher may model a particular sentence pattern, including correct spelling, grammar, and punctuation. When teachers respond to student's journal entries, they model correctness as well. In addition, when teachers guide the class in editing a paper on the overhead projector, they model both the process and corrections involved.

FIGURE 6.14   Model for Working with Correctness

Direct instruction is essential for helping students revise and edit effectively and correctly. We might teach a lesson to the entire class, a small group, or an individual student based on assessed needs (Ferris, 1995, 2002). One possibility is to use programmed materials or games for students to use on their own or with others. As an alternative, we might suggest a computer program on spelling or some other aspect of writing. Most word processing programs contain spelling and grammar checking capabilities. Although these programs aren't perfect, they can assist students by pointing out potential grammar, spelling, and usage problems and suggesting possible solutions. Students make the final choice as to how to use the suggestions. Another possibility is to keep student workbooks on hand in class to provide specific help as needed. For example, if a student continues to have trouble with a particular sentence type, we may refer the student to the topic and page in the workbook for additional help.

As students learn writing conventions, they can become effective participants in responding to their peers' writing. Liu and Hansen (2002) make excellent suggestions for assisting students with grammar during peer response and editing:

1. The teacher should focus on only a few types of grammatical/stylistic issues per peer response activity to make grammar more manageable and effective.
2. The teacher should provide grammar reviews on what students have already been taught in class in order to reinforce instruction.
3. Based on learners' error patterns, the teacher should offer a mini-lesson on a particular pattern and then have the students focus on that pattern in responding to each other's papers.
4. During and after peer response activities, students should keep a journal that lists their own errors and ways to correct them, creating a personal self-editing or error log (Ferris, 2002). Students use these personal logs as they revise and edit their own papers in the future. They thus monitor their own error patterns and become self-sufficient in editing.

Finally, and above all, when it comes to working with errors in student writing, we must know our students well enough to make crucial decisions as to how many details the student can handle at one time, whether they respond better to blunt or delicate suggestions, and how much supervision they need in implementing corrections. We don't want to overwhelm them, but maybe just "whelm" them a bit. With all these considerations, it becomes clear that correcting student errors is more an art than a science, one that calls for capitalizing on "teachable moments," while at the same time systematically addressing the detailed conventions of good writing. By keeping in mind fluency, form, and correctness; by implementing effective teacher and peer response; by providing scaffolding, modeling, and direct instruction; we create optimum opportunities for students to learn to write effectively.

Summary

We have presented research indicating that second language writers are similar to first language writers in the ways they develop. They use their background knowledge to develop ideas and use the writing process in ways similar to those of first language learners. Process writing, consisting of prewriting, drafting, revising, editing, and publishing, makes writing easier for second language writers because it breaks the writing task into manageable phases. Students, instead of having to coordinate their budding ideas with grammar, spelling, and sentence styles, can concentrate on one area at a time. Once they have gathered and organized their ideas, they can focus on correcting their writing.

In presenting the writing process, we offered examples of writing from beginning and intermediate second language writers to show what these students are able to do in writing and to illustrate how their writing reflects both written language knowledge and general second language development. We also showed the strategies that successful teachers often use with English learners who are beginning or intermediate writers. Further, we suggested that you allow your students to work in collaborative and cooperative peer response groups in which they use language to share, discuss, and solve their writing problems. Finally, we advocated that you encourage your students to express themselves in writing, viewing their first attempts as small miracles. With this encouragement, your students will gain confidence in their abilities to learn and will continue to try.

In Figure 6.15 we have listed the grade levels at which we have seen teachers successfully using writing strategies. As your students gain confidence and proficiency in their writing, you may find that they can work easily with strategies designated in our figure to be beyond their grade level. We suggest you use the chart as a general guideline and adjust according to your judgment. With this in mind you can achieve the highest success with your students.

Small successes lead to larger successes, and all success, when you and the students recognize it, leads to further success. Thus, assess and evaluate student writ-

260

FIGURE 6.15   Grade Levels At Which Strategies May Be Used

ing not in terms of comparing it to an essay by an accomplished expert but in terms of current accomplishments and next levels of development. In other words use portfolios to keep in touch with what students know now and what they need to learn next. Moreover, view the assistance you can give them in terms of their development and how you can help them advance to the next level. Successful writing teachers build English learners' confidence, encourage them to continue to write, and point out what they have done well.

SUGGESTIONS FOR FURTHER READING

Calkins, L. M. (1994). *The art of teaching writing.* Portsmouth, NH: Heinemann.

A thorough approach to teaching the writing process by a top researcher. Calkins presents practical strategies for developing children's writing at every stage of the writing process. The book discusses the writing process at different grade levels and makes excellent suggestions for setting up writing workshops and for teaching mini-lessons. Although the book is not explicitly for ELD students, you can easily adapt the strategies for English language learners.

Ferris, D. R. (2002). *Treatment of error in second language student writing.* Ann Arbor: University of Michigan Press.

Every ESL writing teacher should have this book: It presents theory, practice, and advice in a much needed area, that of working with L2 writing errors. Chapters include "Why Is Error Treatment Necessary for L2 Writers?" "Perspectives on Error Correction," "Preparing L2 Writing Teachers to Treat Student Error," "Responding to Student Errors," and "Beyond Error Correction: Teaching Grammar and Self-Editing Strategies to L2 Student Writers", and it has useful and practical appendixes. We wish this book had been available when we first started teaching writing to L2 students. Although the book is primarily concerned with university student writing, the ideas are directly applicable to secondary-level and adaptable to elementary-level student writing.

Liu, J., & Hansen, J. G. (2002). *Peer response in second language writing classrooms.* Ann Arbor: University of Michigan Press.

A theoretically sound approach that is very helpful for practicing teachers. The chapters cover topics such as: effects of peer response, contexts of peer response, grouping students in peer response, and instructing students in peer response. For teachers who want to establish peer response groups in their classrooms, this book prepares you for the pros and cons and assists with setting up groups and maintaining them.

Raimes, A. (1983). *Techniques in teaching writing.* Oxford: Oxford University Press.

This book takes a more traditional view of teaching writing, one that is quite different from our own book. Nevertheless, the book has been used by second language instructors for many years and deserves to be read. One of its most valuable aspects is the question-and-answer section. In this section, Raimes answers questions such as, What do I do with the errors English learners make? How will students work in groups? and Who reads what students write? The book also contains specific strategies for teaching second language writers.

262 Activities

1. Collect one student's writing over a period of several weeks. Collect from journals, notes, letters, stories, or any other type of writing the student may do during the period of collection. At the end of the collection period, compare the student's writing as it developed over time. You might categorize such things as the topics the student wrote about, the genre of writing, the conditions under which the student did his or her best writing, and the kinds of advancements the student made in developing and organizing ideas, in grammar and spelling, or in any other aspect of writing that interests you. Report your findings to your classmates.

2. Observe classrooms where teachers approach the teaching of writing differently and evaluate the writing that takes place in those classrooms. For example, compare a classroom that uses peer response groups and encourage students to select their own personal topics with a class in which the teacher selects topics and spends a great deal of time correcting papers and returning them to students. What are some differences you find in the writing of the students in the two classes? Do students in different classroom circumstances write differently? Are they motivated differently? What recommendations would you make to your classmates based on your observations?

3. Observe English learners working in peer response groups and take notes on the kinds of questions they ask one another and on the kinds of responses that seem to lead to improved writing. Make a list of questions and responses that seem to be most useful to young writers to share with your class. If you identify a group that appears to work especially well, ask that group to role-play their peer response group in front of the rest of the class.

4. Observe how different teachers prepare students to work with the writing process. How is the writing process introduced? How are topics selected? How are students prepared to function in peer response groups? Does the teacher pre-

pare students explicitly for working in successful peer response groups? For instance, does the teacher remind students to be respectful of others' writing and to make comments concerning what they like about the writing to provide a positive context for any revisions they may ask about? Finally, what is the importance of publishing student writing in the classroom, and what are the varieties of ways teachers value and ask students to share their writing?

5. Collect writing from different grade levels and English language development levels so that you can compare and contrast how students' writing develops over time. For example, how does spelling develop from the first to the third grade? Do students naturally move from invented spelling to more standard spelling without a great deal of instruction, or do they need instruction in spelling in order to learn how to spell? When is it appropriate to intervene with the students' natural process to help them become better writers? Do students, as they develop in reading and writing, change sentence length and maturity naturally over time, or must these be explicitly taught in order for student writing to grow? Look at the writing you have collected from different grade levels and see what other categories you might evaluate.

7

READING AND LITERATURE INSTRUCTION FOR ENGLISH LANGUAGE LEARNERS

In this chapter we discuss the reading process, compare first and second language reading, and provide suggestions for promoting second language reading through a variety of contexts and strategies emphasizing the use of multicultural literature. The following questions are discussed:

1. What does research tell us about students reading in a second language?
2. Which classroom contexts and teaching strategies can best assist English language learners in reading and enjoying literature?
3. What are the characteristics of beginning and intermediate-level second language readers?
4. How may second language reading be assessed?

When Susan Jacobs was absent with the flu for a few days, her students complained about the substitute. "She didn't know any of the rules," one child said. "She made me clean up the sinks, and it was Juan's turn," said Julia. Others complained loudly, "She didn't know anything!!!" Susan asked the students what they thought should be done about the situation. The children told her not to be absent. Knowing she couldn't guarantee that, she asked her students for suggestions to improve things if she should be absent again.

Glad to have been asked, the students eagerly suggested that the substitute needed guidelines about how the classroom functioned, and, since they knew the rules, they could write a substitute handbook. One group decided to take charge of the guidelines for cleaning the room. Another group said they would make a list of some of the general rules of behavior. "We have to talk 'bout mailboxes on our desks and that it's OK to pass notes except when something's going on. But no airmail letters!!!" said Tina.

Thus charged, the children spent two weeks developing and refining the handbook, complete with classroom charts, to make it easier for the substitute to know procedures, rules, and student roles. Each group wrote one part of the handbook, revised it, and gave it to other groups for further clarification and revision. Finally, an editorial team edited the handbook and published it using a computer. They told Susan that all she had to do the next time she was ill was tell the substitute to read the handbook.

Because this happened early in the year, the students learned the classroom rules at a deeper level. Susan also allowed them to negotiate new rules that they thought would make the classroom work better. These new rules, added to the handbook, were to be followed by everyone, including Susan. Through the activity, children received validation for their own views on classroom management, learned the system more clearly, and became involved in a meaningful literacy event. Susan decided she would negotiate rules and create a substitute handbook with classes in the future.

You may wonder why we start a chapter on reading with an example of what seems to be a writing activity. We start this way because, although writing and

---

INTERNET RESOURCE: The SCORE site (Schools of California Online Resources for Educators Project: http://www.sdcoe.k12.ca.us/score/cyberguide.html) contains detailed lesson plans for K-12 classrooms. There are specific lesson plans and links to sites that expand lessons. Each "Cyberguide" delivers a "unit of instruction centered on a core work of literature."

Another excellent site, *The Children's Literature Guide: Internet Resources Related to Books for Children and Young Adults* contains lessons and links on literature: http://www.acs. ucalgary.ca/~dkbrown/. The links contain such categories as "Authors on the Web," "Stories on the Web," "Readers' Theater," "Recommended Books," and "Resources for Teachers." And don't forget our companion website: www.ablongman.com/ peregoy4e.

reading are the focus of Chapters 6 and 7, we view them as integrally related processes. When the students wrote their drafts for the handbook and considered the appropriateness for a substitute, for example, they became readers. When they shared revisions with one another, they became readers. When they worked with other groups and with the editorial team, they became readers. Though we concentrate on reading in this chapter, the emphasis will always be on reading and writing as interrelated processes working together to serve the larger purposes of communication and learning (Heath & Mangiola, 1991).

WHAT DOES RESEARCH TELL US ABOUT READING IN A SECOND LANGUAGE?

Over the past decade, researchers have looked at how people process print when reading in English as a second language (Carrell, Devine, & Eskey, 1988; Goodman & Goodman, 1978; Grabe, 1991; Hudelson, 1981). They consistently find that the process is essentially the same whether reading English as the first or second language. In other words, both first and second language readers look at the page and the print and use their knowledge of sound/symbol relationships, word order, grammar, and meaning to predict and confirm meaning. The linguistic systems involved in reading are commonly referred to as **graphophonics** (sound/symbol correspondences), **syntax** (word order), and **semantics** (meaning). In the process, readers use their background knowledge about the text's topic and structure along with their linguistic knowledge and reading strategies to arrive at an interpretation and to achieve their purpose for reading. If their interpretation does not make sense, they may go back and read again (see Peregoy & Boyle, 2000).

To see for yourself how you use graphic, syntactic, and semantic cues, try reading the passage in Figure 7.1. We made the task more difficult by deleting sev-

266

Once upon a time, long ago and far away, there lived a gentle queen. It was the deepest and darkest 1. _____ winters, and every day the gentle queen would spend 2. h _____ afternoons sitting with her needlework at the only window in the 3. _____. The castle window itself was framed in blackest ebony, 4. _____ anyone passing below could gaze upon the beautiful queen, 5. _____ as a picture, as she quietly worked at her 6. _____. One day, as she sat sewing, she pricked her finger 7. _____ her needle, and three rich, red drops of blood 8. _____ upon the glistening snow below. At the sight of the red blood upon the 9. _____ snow, the gentle queen whispered: "Oh, how I wish 10. _____ a baby daughter with hair as black as ebony, 11. _____ as red as blood and skin as white as snow." And so it came 12. _____ pass that the queen gave birth to such a 13 _____, whom she called Snow White.

Answers 1. of; 2. -er; 3. sunlight; 4. and; 5. pretty; 6. embroidery; 7. with; 8. fell; 9. white; 10. for; 11. lips; 12. to; 13. child

FIGURE 7.1   Passage with Some Words Missing

eral words and leaving a blank in their place. Think of the blank spaces as words you don't recognize. In some cases, we provided an initial letter or two as grapho-phonic cues. Were you able to fill in all the blanks? What kinds of clues did you use to help you create a meaningful whole? Even though this passage was not titled, the very first lines provided an important clue: "Once upon a time" signals the fairy tale genre. As you read on, you needed to predict words for each blank that fit grammatically and made sense. In order to do so, you used your internal-ized knowledge of the syntax and semantics of English. Your implicit linguistic knowledge allowed you to make two essential judgments: Does it sound right, and does it make sense? In this way, you gradually created a tentative envisionment of the story. A slightly different approach would have been to skim over the passage first to get a general idea of what it was about and then fill in the blanks. If you took this approach, you probably noticed that the story was "Snow White." This information would have facilitated the task because it would have activated your background knowledge about this familiar tale. You would still make use of your knowledge of the graphophonics, syntax, and semantics of English to predict and confirm specific words to put in the blanks.

Second Language Readers

A reader who speaks English as a second language uses essentially the same process that you did to read the passage. Yet the task is apt to be more difficult. Why? As you have probably predicted by now, the resources that first and second language readers bring to bear are different. The two most important differences are **second language proficiency** and **background knowledge** pertinent to the text being read. Take another look at the Snow White passage and consider it from the point of view of a student learning English. Limitations in language pro-ficiency will generally make it more difficult for a second language student to fill in the blanks. For example, you probably had no difficulty filling in *the* or *her* before *afternoons* in the second sentence. However, predicting words such as *a, the, in,* and *on* is often difficult for students who are still learning English. Formulaic expressions such as "Once upon a time" and "pretty as a picture" may be unfa-miliar and thus difficult to interpret fully. Thus, limitations in second language proficiency affect second language reading comprehension, causing it to be slower and more arduous. When English learners read texts that are fairly easy for them, their reading provides comprehensible input that promotes English language acquisition (Elley & Mangubhai, 1983; Krashen, 1993). With your assistance, they will be able to advance to more difficult texts.

English Language Learners and Background Knowledge

Although second language proficiency affects reading comprehension, another powerful factor in the equation is the reader's prior knowledge of the topic of a passage or text. In the Snow White example, you probably knew the

267

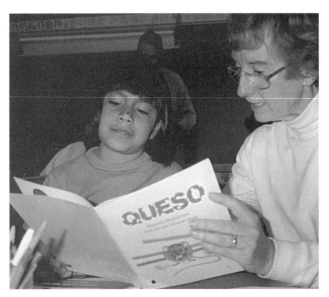

Providing students with the opportunity to read in their primary language helps boost success in second language reading.

268

story. This knowledge made it easier for you to fill in the blanks. Fairy tales also follow a particular narrative structure, beginning with the formulaic opening "Once upon a time," moving through a predictable plot sequence, and ending with "They lived happily ever after." Thus, your experience with fairy tales provides you with background knowledge not only about the content of particular stories but about common narrative forms and plot sequences. This background knowledge facilitates comprehension of written stories by helping you predict where the story is leading. To the extent that second language readers are less familiar with the topic and structure of a particular text, their comprehension task will be more or less difficult (Carrell & Eisterhold, 1988). By providing reading material on content familiar to your students and by building background prior to reading a text, you can offset reading comprehension difficulties stemming from limited second language proficiency.

English learners may experience reading difficulties related to limited second language proficiency and background knowledge that does not match the topic of a particular text. However, English learners who know how to read in their first language bring sophisticated literacy knowledge to the task of second language reading. They know that print is part of a systematic code that represents language and thereby carries meaning. If the student's home language uses a writing system similar to the English alphabet, the transfer from the home language to English reading is fairly straightforward (Odlin, 1989). Students still need instruction and practice in English reading, but they have a substantial head start over students who are preliterate or who must learn the *Roman alphabet* used for writing English.

Reading Processes of Proficient Readers

Learning to read involves gradually developing the ability to recognize words almost instantly. Good readers become so automatic in word recognition that they concentrate on meaning and are rarely aware that they are attending to almost every letter they see (Adams & Bruck, 1995). Try reading the passage below, observing your own process as you go along, to see if you can identify elements of the reading process we have been discussing (Buswell, 1922).

The boys' arrows were nearly gone so they sat down on the grass and stopped hunting. Over at the edge of the wood they saw Henry making a bow to a small girl who was coming down the road. She had tears in her dress and also tears in her eyes. She gave Henry a note which he brought over to the group of young hunters. Read to the boys, it caued great excitement. After a minute but rapid examination of their weapons, they ran down to the valley. Does were standing at the edge of the lake making an excellent target. (p. 22)

How aware were you that you were scanning the letters and words as you read? Research on eye movement suggests that good readers attend to almost every word on a page almost without realizing it; moreover, they also attend to almost every letter (Rayner & Pollatsek, 1989; Zola, 1984). You probably perceived the words in this passage quickly and somewhat unconsciously, except for certain tricky words that created problems in meaning. You may also have noticed that the word *caused* was misspelled as "caued;" we misspelled it intentionally to illustrate that when a letter is missing, your reading fluency can be slowed, because the information in almost every letter is important to you as a good reader (Bertera & Rayner, 1979).

Because this is a passage that plays tricks with a reader's normal expectations of a text, you probably had problems with certain words or phrases. You probably misread *bow*. We suggest that you did this because your experience with print has told you to use your background knowledge to predict what will come next. Because the text uses words such as *hunting* and *arrows*, your hunting schema or background knowledge has been activated, leading you to choose *bow* (rhyming with *so*) instead of *bow* (rhyming with *cow*). We also predict that you mispronounced the word *tear*. Your knowledge of syntax told you that the word should be pronounced *tear*, as in *teardrop*. English meaning is based largely on syntax, or word order, leading to the difference in meaning, for example, between a *Venetian blind* and a *blind Venetian*. In some languages, such as Latin or Turkish, word order is not as important. When you came to the phrase *Read to the boys* you had a 50 percent chance of getting it right, but may have pronounced it *read* (as in *reed*) instead of *read* (as in *red*). We also suspect you may have mispronounced the word *minute* in *After a minute but* because you are more familiar with the common phrase *after a minute* (as in 60 seconds). Finally, we guess that you hesitated but pronounced *Does* properly even though you've repeatedly seen the word at the beginning of a sentence pronounced as does (rhyming with was). No doubt you got this one right because you started adapting to the trickiness of the text and read more slowly and carefully.

The miscues or deviations from the print you made with the text further illustrate the need for readers to use linguistic and background knowledge while interacting with print to make the best prediction possible about what they are reading. This aspect of background knowledge is particularly important when thinking of second language reading because of the different background knowledge that second language readers may bring to a text.

269

ℰLEMENTS OF READING COMPREHENSION AND METACOGNITION: A CARTOON EXAMPLE

Let's look at a cartoon to further illustrate some features of reading comprehension. Because cartoons are largely pictorial, they provide a fresh way to examine the role of background knowledge, inferences, and metacognition (i.e., reflecting on your understanding) in the comprehension process. Because cartoons include captions and word balloons, they also require reading. Look at this "Far Side" cartoon and answer the following questions so that we can engage in a dialogue about our comprehension processes.

Comprehension Questions:

1. Who are the figures in the forefront of the cartoon?
2. Where are these figures? How do you know?
3. What do the written words tell us about the event the figures are attending?
4. What kind of movie are they going to watch: adventure, comedy, drama, horror, or mystery?
5. Is this cartoon funny to you? Why or why not?

270

THE FAR SIDE®   By GARY LARSON

You probably answered most, if not all, of the questions above with relative ease. Let's look at what enabled you to do so. First of all, your prior experience with cartoons would alert you to the idea that there must be humor here. In order to get the humor, you have to look more closely. For example, you would have to notice that the figures represent flying insects of some kind, that they are sitting in a movie theater, and that the title of the film has just appeared on the screen. You might have also inferred that the event is a horror movie. How were you able to do this? Essentially, you made use of your background knowledge to make inferences based on the picture and word cues in the cartoon. To get the humor, you have to make another inference, drawing a parallel between what constitutes a horror movie for people versus what might constitute a horror movie for flying insects. Once you understand the cartoon, you may or may not find it funny. Your response to the cartoon is ultimately personal, similar to your response to a poem or a piece of literature. These processes are similar to those you use to comprehend written texts as we explain next.

Background Knowledge and Inferences

A major element in reading comprehension is **background knowledge** about the genre and subject (see Anderson, 1999). In this case the genre is a cartoon. Your prior experience with cartoons lets you know that you have to interpret the pictures and words to find humor. If you are familiar with Larson cartoons, which have become almost a genre of their own, you may expect rather quirky humor. As you look at the cartoon, you need to engage your background knowledge to recognize the characters and setting: bugs in a movie theater. If you ever watched *Mystery Science Theater 3000* on television, the scene of bugs in a theater might be immediately familiar. If you are an entomologist, you might be inclined to respond to these bugs affectionately as a kind of "extended family." The curtain, screen, and seats helped you identify a theater setting. If you are a theater major, you might have identified the proscenium. As you engage your prior knowledge to interpret the pictures in the cartoon, you need to activate two main schema: flying insects and movie theaters.

Decoding and Vocabulary

Understanding the cartoon is not complete, however, until you decode and comprehend the words on the movie screen. For example, if *windshield* were an unfamiliar word, you might **decode** it by breaking it into parts and sounding it out. Comprehending the word is of course necessary also. We have to know what a windshield is, and the cartoon does not provide clues in this regard, thus the importance of **vocabulary knowledge.** We remember seeing something like "Entschuldigensiebitte" ("excuse me please") on a large sign in Germany. Although we often used this phrase in conversation, we didn't recognize it in print until we had broken it apart and sounded it out. We were surprised to find such a familiar phrase in such an unfamiliar print form.

Recognizing and understanding the words is still not sufficient, however, for understanding the cartoon. Background knowledge is required once again to notice that the words are the film title. This title follows a familiar formula for horror movie titles, but it is only familiar if you have had the experience of watching or have heard of such movies. You have to make an **inference** to conclude that the bugs are watching a horror movie. You make the inference by piecing together clues in the cartoon—the theater setting and the words on the screen—and then applying your prior knowledge of titles, especially horror movie titles. You do the same thing when you make inferences in reading: You use the literal information provided in the text combined with your background knowledge to interpret and draw conclusions about the meaning. Reflecting once again on the various kinds of background you bring, imagine the challenges you would face understanding the cartoon if you had recently arrived, for example, from a village in the Andes, from a large city in China, or from a small town in Russia. Can you see how your knowledge stems from your own particular social and cultural experiences? As you can imagine, humor often does not translate easily across cultures.

Metacognition: "Thinking about Thinking"

If we don't get the humor in a cartoon, we might have to rethink our comprehension process, using *metacognitive strategies* to repair our lack of understanding (Urquhart & Weir, 1998). **Metacognition** is the process of analyzing our own comprehension processes, or "thinking about thinking." We use metacognition to recognize and repair understanding when something we read does not make sense. Some metacognitive strategies include looking at the cartoon again more closely to see if we missed anything in the picture or in the words. Perhaps there was a caption that we overlooked or some other visual feature. Other metacognitive strategies include questioning ourselves while reading, asking for example, "Where are the bugs?" or "What is the cartoonist trying to say to us?" Explicit instruction on metacognitive strategies is valuable for students when taught in the context of reading literature and content area texts (Grabe & Stoller, 1997).

272

Text Structure

Another important aspect in reading is *text structure* (Meyer, Brandt, & Bluth, 1980). The cartoon structure, for example, tells us to look at the pictures, word balloons, and perhaps a caption to get the full meaning. In a similar way, if students recognize the compare/contrast structure of an essay, then they will expect to find objects compared and contrasted. For example, if two schools are discussed in an essay, they will expect the author to discuss how the schools are the same and how they might be different. In other words, the structure helps us make predictions about what will come next, what to expect.

In summary, we have presented three examples (a fairy tale, a passage, and a cartoon) to illustrate elements of reading comprehension. We have emphasized how several kinds of knowledge work together in the process: language knowledge, background knowledge, text structure, decoding, and vocabulary. We have also illustrated the role of cognitive processes such as inferencing and metacognitive strategies such as re-reading if needed for full understanding. Explicit teaching of cognitive and metacognitive strategies as students read literature and content texts will increase their academic learning. For English learners, it is especially important to consider their language proficiency and prior experiences relevant to any text they read so that you can prepare them to be successful as they read. Throughout this chapter and also in Chapters 8, 9, and 10, we will illustrate how to help students use and increase their abilities in the elements of comprehension as they read various kinds of texts such as stories, novels, news articles, encyclopedia entries, and textbook selections.

The learning contexts and strategies we suggest for second language readers in this chapter are those in which students are hearing, reading, sharing, and responding to high-quality literature. Just as collaborative work and sharing play an important role in second language writing development, so also do they play a crucial role in second language reading development. These learning contexts will include the whole class listening to and reading fine literature, small groups of students responding to stories they read, pairs of students reading to each other, and individual students reading on their own. Just as process writing helps create a community of writers, shared reading experiences will further develop your students into a community of readers and writers.

We think of the ideal reader as an independent reader—one who responds to literature individually and shares responses with others, listens to other viewpoints and adjusts interpretations, and uses information in a literary text to support interpretations, but remains open to the interpretations of others. An ideal environment for literature response gives students opportunities to work in collaborative groups. To provide such an environment, we offer several types of response groups that you may wish to try in your classroom.

WORKING IN LITERATURE RESPONSE GROUPS

Literature response groups, or literature circles, are analogous to writing response groups. The main difference is that in literature response groups students discuss the work of published authors, whereas in writing response groups they discuss the work of their peers. Literature response groups consist of three to six students who have read a piece of literature and are ready to discuss it together. Just as we recommend that you model how to work in writing response groups, we recommend that you model response to literature before asking students to respond in groups. However you decide to work with your own students, you can be assured that English learners, especially those at the intermediate level of English language development, can be very active participants in literature response groups (Samway et al., 1991; Urzúa, 1992).

If you have modeled response to writing already, you can easily make the transition to reading response groups because the two are so similar. You may wish to remind students to respond to the content of the literature (i.e., to the problems faced by characters and situations in a narrative). They need to be flexible in their interpretations and tolerant of differing views. For example, they may find that there are several valid ways to interpret what motivates a character to act in a particular way.

At first, some teachers provide groups with response sheets to scaffold their initial response to literature. These sheets provide the students with model questions they may ask of any story. Moreover, the sheets help them begin to develop

1. If you did (or didn't) like the book, was there one event, character, or aspect of the book that caused this reaction? What? Why?
2. Do your response group members share a common reaction to the book? What reactions are the same? What are different?
3. If you were faced with the same problems as the main character in the book, would you have responded in a similar manner? Why?
4. How was the main character feeling when we first met him or her? Have you ever felt like the character?
5. How do you feel about the ways the main character behaves with other characters?
6. Did any of the characters remind you of anyone you have known? Yourself?
7. Do you think the author was trying to teach us something? If so, what?
8. Would you change the ending of the book? If so, how?
9. Which character would you like to have met? What would you want to say or do when you met the character?
10. Did your feelings change toward the character(s) as the story progressed? What made your feelings change?
11. If you could step inside the book and be part of the story, where would you enter? Who would you be? What would you do? How would these things change the story?
12. What things would be different in this story if it took place in a different period of time or a different place?

FIGURE 7.2   Model Generic Response Sheet

their own questions. Other teachers ask students to make up their own response sheets based on a story that the children are reading and share that sheet as a part of their own literature activity. One model response sheet developed by teachers is provided in Figure 7.2. It is meant to guide students' response and to prepare them for more independent interpretations of the literature they read.

The response sheet in Figure 7.2 includes the following directions:

> This response sheet is recommended for self-paced reading scheduled by students working in literature response groups. Expectations for your responses have been set by your class and teacher. Be ready to accept and respect the opinions of others in your group. You may expect the same from them with regard to your views. Your job is to help one another understand the story you are reading and to share your own views of the story. *Remember, there is no one single interpretation of any story you are reading;* in fact, there will usually be many different views of stories. You may begin your discussion with the questions listed on this sheet, but feel free to develop your own questions as your discussion proceeds.

Steps That Prepare Students to Work in Response Groups

Some of the steps teachers take in preparing students to work efficiently in response groups are as follows:

1. They read good literature to students daily and ask for individual responses informally.
2. They share with students their own responses to characters' dilemmas.
3. They help students connect the characters and situations to decisions and circumstances in their own lives.
4. They encourage different views of the literature, including views that differ from their own.
5. They share their enjoyment of stories and literary language.
6. They emphasize personal response to literature over theoretical literary analysis.
7. They teach students vocabulary to talk about literature.
8. They may provide students with a model response sheet to assist them at first.

After your students have discussed a story in their response groups, you may invite them to extend their interpretations through dramatization, readers' theater, illustration, or some other re-creation such as those in the list that follows. For example, Mary Donal sets up literature centers with materials for carrying out literature extension activities, including art materials for illustration, props for dramatization, pencils and colored markers for writing, and idea cards for further responses to particular stories. Her students sign up for the centers at the beginning of the day. She wants all of her students eventually to try a variety of response extensions, including readers' theater, rewriting stories, and dramatization, instead of illustrating the story every time. By providing centers, she guides her students while giving them choices.

When students begin to respond independently to literature, they can choose from the following list. Additionally, they may respond to the literature in their response journals, perhaps using the same questions they used in group work to focus their reading. By providing students with tools to respond to literature, we motivate them to read on their own.

Ways to Extend Response to Literature

Readers' theater	Improvisational signing
Illustrations	Response groups
Response sheets	Journals
Storytelling	Creating big books
Story maps	Developing time lines
Puppet shows	Rebus books
Egyptian hieroglyphs	Board games
Animated films	Collages
Making dioramas	Mobiles
Creating songs	Posters
Murals	Mock court trials
Book jackets	Dressing up as characters
Creating radio scripts	Creating videos

275

How Response to Literature Assists English Language Learners

Literature response, whether involving the whole class, small groups, pairs, or individuals, offers English language learners the opportunity to enjoy good literature. The groups are informal, and there are many chances for students to help each other negotiate the meaning of stories. As story discussion becomes routine, English learners will become familiar with ways of talking about literature, as will their first language counterparts. The oral discussions thus provide opportunities for comprehensible input (Krashen & Terrell, 1983) and negotiation of story meaning through social interaction (Samway & McKeon, 1999). In many ways, first and second language learners are on an equal footing in that they may all be new to the ways of responding to literature promoted in literature response groups.

Being able to read literature well enough to discuss it in groups, however, requires the development of both reading ability and knowledge of how to talk about it in terms of character, plot development, and so forth. You may wish to research intermediate and advanced students' capabilities in terms of response groups and the strategies that may assist them in working together.

εXTENSIVE READING: THE FOUNDATION OF EVERY READING PROGRAM

Whether we call it extensive reading, narrow reading, or Uninterrupted Silent Sustained Reading, having our students read from self-selected books every day is a key to second language acquisition. Moreover, national tests indicate that one of the most important features of a school where students score high on reading tests is that its students do a lot of daily reading. We believe that the most important thing we can do for our students is promote a love for reading and create a risk-free environment that encourages daily reading of self-selected materials. While acknowledging the importance of teacher-selected books, especially in content reading, we also recognize that the extensive reading that students do will have a profound affect on their language acquisition. We will briefly define each type of reading, noting the general characteristics and advantages of each.

Uninterrupted Silent Sustained Reading (USSR) (see McCracken, 1971; McCracken & McCracken, 1972) has many different names such as DEAR (Drop Everything and Read) and OTTER (Our Time to Enjoy Reading) and is similar to *extensive reading* (see Day & Bamford, 1998; Krashen, 1993). They both recommend large amounts of mostly self-selected books in a friendly environment where students do not have to worry about being tested. Moreover, the books are at students' independent levels, that is, they can read them without difficulty (See Chapter 10 for a specific definition of independent level). Additionally, in both approaches teachers read with their students, thus modeling the importance of reading. One difference between the two is that in USSR there may be some sharing of books after reading, but postreading activities are not necessarily emphasized; with extensive reading, postreading is an integral part of the program. Follow-up activities might include role-playing the story, designing a poster to advertise the book, copying interesting words and useful expressions in a journal, writing a letter to the author, and sharing their views about the book with a small group of classmates (Renandya & Jacobs, 2002).

Research, practice, and teacher experience have shown that extensive reading is key to any reading program (Day & Bamford, 1998; Krashen, 1993). Advantages include building vocabulary, background knowledge, and interest in reading, and improvement of reading comprehension. Krashen has written about the "incidental learning" that comes from a wide variety of reading, and we like to think of the incidental erudition that comes from all of the reading we do: Even from reading mysteries we can learn about medicine, about law, about our government, and about our environment. One of the most important things we can do as teachers is provide students with daily opportunities and time to read and to honor the culture of reading.

To develop an extensive reading program you will need large amount of culturally appropriate materials at all levels and a risk-free environment. Additionally, Kim and Krashen (1997) in their work with adult learners give a suggestion we think could be invaluable to our students: "Tell them about the benefits of reading." Another approach we see as an adjunct to extensive reading is *narrow reading* (Krashen, 1981b). With narrow reading students read many texts on the same topic (Schmitt & Carter, 2000). Thus, they are given a chance to read materials that will build their vocabulary and background knowledge, making subsequent reading easier. In summary, through extensive reading of self-selected texts, second language readers can develop their vocabulary, background knowledge, comprehension, and love of books. Extensive reading should be a part of every reading program for ESL classrooms, for students with reading problems, and for students of all ages and capabilities. In the next sections, we discuss strategies for helping students move ahead in reading ability while developing their sense of literary elements.

DEVELOPMENTAL PHASES IN SECOND LANGUAGE READING

We view the developmental phases of second language readers as a continuum, and a fuzzy one at that. We don't see identifiable discrete stages, with crystal-clear categorization. In our experience, real students defy categorization. However, for the purposes of discussion, we offer two general categories of second language readers to guide your teaching decisions initially: beginning and intermediate. For each category, we provide some general descriptions of learners and strategies to help them progress. As with writing, your task will be to help students move from one developmental phase to the next by challenging them to ever higher levels of performance. As we describe strategies for beginning and intermediate second language readers, keep in mind that only you know your own students. Thus, you are in the best position to combine our suggestions with your own analysis and intuition as you plan for your class. Therefore, feel free to use any strategy, beginning or intermediate, with any learner, according to your own judgment.

Beginning Readers: Characteristics and Strategies

In general, beginning-level second language readers, like their first language counterparts, are just beginning to pull meaning from reading short texts. They may still be somewhat unfamiliar with the English alphabet and its unusual, if not unruly, spelling patterns. Chances are they recognize a number of sight words but they need more reading practice to develop a larger sight word vocabulary. Most beginners can read simple texts, such as predictable books, through word recognition strategies, language knowledge, and memorization. However, they may have difficulty processing information beyond sentence-level texts. Regardless of their age, beginners need more experience with written language. If they have never read before in any language, they need frequent reminders of the many ways we use reading and writing for practical purposes and enjoyment. If they are literate in their first language, they probably have some idea of what reading and writing are for, but their literacy concepts should be broadened. In summary, beginners need to be immersed in reading and writing for readily perceived purposes. They need practice to solidify sound/symbol correspondences in English and to remind them that English reads from left to right, top to bottom. Finally, they need enough practice to move them toward being able to read simple texts independently. In this section, we describe a number of teaching strategies that have proven useful for beginning readers.

Language-Experience Approach

The language-experience approach is one of the most frequently recommended approaches for beginning second language readers (Dixon & Nessel, 1983; Tinajero & Calderon, 1988). The beauty of this approach is that the student provides the text, through dictation, that serves as the basis for reading instruction. As a result, language-experience reading is tailored to the learner's own interests, background knowledge, and language proficiency. It builds on the linguistic, social, and cultural strengths and interests the student brings to school. Not least important, this approach works well for those older preliterate students who need age-appropriate texts dealing with topics that interest them.

The core of the language-experience approach builds on stories dictated by individual students, small groups, or the whole class. As a rule, the stories are writ-

278

Lan —
The big
fish eat
the little
fish.
Swimmy
swam away
and he scared
and sad.
Swimmy saw
the sea and he
was happy. The
little fish are
scared of the
big fish.
Swimmy
said, "Let's
make a big
fish."

FIGURE 7.3   Lan Huong's "Swimmy" Story

ten down verbatim, after which students read them back. Students are usually able to read their own stories with minimal decoding skills because they already know the meaning. Through this approach, students learn to see reading and writing as purposeful communication about their own interests and concerns. Moreover, they observe the process by which their own meanings, expressed orally, are put into print form. Important learning about the English writing system is thus conveyed indirectly, preparing students to write. Finally, when they read their own stories back, students are able to experience the success of independent reading. Lan Huong used the book *Swimmy,* by Leo Lionni, to relate her own version and then read the story to her friends; she created a watercolor for the illustrated page of a book she planned to "write" using the language-experience approach (Figure 7.3).

While dictation itself provides a useful literacy event for beginners, the language-experience approach (cf. Stauffer, 1970; Tierney, Readence, & Dishner, 1990) provides systematic follow-up to solidify learning. For example, students may underline words in the story that are most meaningful to them, write them on a word card, and place them in their word bank in alphabetical order. In addition, students may cut their stories into sentence strips and rearrange them again to form a coherent piece. The language-experience approach thus bears resemblance to Ashton-Warner's key-word approach (Ashton-Warner, 1963) and to Freire's generative-theme approach (Freire, 1970; Freire & Macedo, 1987). All three approaches base early literacy instruction on the immediate concerns of students. Thus, as an introduction to reading, the students' own stories become the core of instruction in composition, comprehension, word recognition skills, and general conventions of English print.

One first-grade teacher, Lydia Tanaka, sees language experience as an important part of her literature-based reading program. She reads daily to her students from Big Books and little books, she helps her students make their own Big Books based on predictable story patterns, and she responds to them weekly in their interactive journals. She also uses language-experience stories. The following example shows how.

After an earthquake, Lydia decided to let the children talk about the tremor and share their feelings. She started by asking them to share in groups and brainstorm their ideas for a dictated story. She told them that they were going to create a newspaper about the earthquake and that the front page story would be written by the entire class. When children finished brainstorming and talking in their groups, they began sharing with Lydia, who wrote their statements on the board.

CHABELA: I hear a sound first. Then it shook.
JOSE: Pictures in my house move and dishes too.
LISA: My dad looked at us. He said we better move. We got under tables.
KELLY: We turned on television.
JOE: We watched the world series and it happen.
SAMMY: Glasses broke.

Students continued in this manner until they had related the most important things about the earthquake. At this point Lydia read the group story to the students, pointing to each word as she read it. Next, the students read with her as she pointed to the words. Afterward, she framed individual words and asked the students to read them. Then she asked them to illustrate their story for the newspaper, working in pairs. The class selected one picture to be used for the front page, and the other pictures were presented with short captions on other pages. When the groups had finished their pictures, Lydia asked them to copy the group story.

The next day, students read their story to one another and underlined words in the story they were sure they knew. These words were then copied on separate index cards to be filed alphabetically for each child. Periodically, the child's knowledge of the word bank was checked to make sure the student hadn't forgotten words learned previously.

Lydia's class used the original story and others to create their own newspaper about the earthquake. They then used a computer so that they could publish the paper. Later, the English learners read individual articles to one another and took the newspaper home to read articles to their parents and friends. The initial group sharing of a critical event allowed children to express their fears about the earthquake, helped them become involved in an initial literacy experience, showed them that the words they speak can be written, and gave them a newspaper with words they knew and could share with others.

Lydia doesn't always have events as dramatic as an earthquake (although a year later children wanted to talk about a war), but she uses whatever her students are interested in at the time to develop language-experience stories. She is also quick to point out that these are not the only stories students hear in her class. She reads aloud daily from quality literature, they write in journals, and they hear and act out many stories from the first day of school.

The following text was dictated by Yukka, one of Lydia's first-graders. First she drew a picture, then started to write her story. After having some difficulty writing the story, Yukka asked a student teacher to write down what she wanted to say. We include Yukka's writing attempt along with the story she dictated.

YUKKA'S WRITING: I like horse becuss they hav lovely fer.
YUKKA'S DICTATION: They run fast. If I could have horse, he be brown. I ride him in park. I ride him to school and I leave him on the bus.

As Yukka gains experience, her writing will be coordinated enough to keep up with her vivid imagination. Meanwhile, dictation empowers her by providing an adult scribe to get her ideas down on paper. Knowing this, Lydia will encourage Yukka to continue her own writing while taking her dictated stories from time to time. Language-experience stories provide but one important part of Lydia's scheme for assisting children to become literate in their second language. She feels that students must do much more than just read their own stories; therefore, she provides a print-rich environment, full of literature to be heard and read throughout the day. This environment, supplemented with language-experience stories, will enhance the growth of students like Yukka throughout the year. By using English learners' experiences and language, Lydia scaffolds their learning to read and share experiences.

Providing Quality Literature for Beginners

For beginning readers, you will need to create a classroom designed to assist them in making decisions about selecting and responding to quality literature. This does not mean that you won't ever choose a book for students. In fact, you may first want to select a book your entire class reads in order to model response to literature. Overall, your goal will be to assist students with making choices about what they read, about what they do with what they select, and with their own responses to literature. You will want them to share their reading with one another and to accept different responses to the same literature. However, you'll give beginning level readers a little more early direction to assure success with their first encounters with a text or story. We have selected several literature-based strategies, sequenced from simpler to more complex, that work well for beginning level readers. These strategies all fit the criteria for literacy scaffolds discussed earlier, by working with meaningful and functional communication found in whole texts, by making use of repetitive language and discourse patterns, and by supporting students' comprehension beyond what they could do alone. All of these strategies are meant to provide temporary support to beginning-level students who will drop the scaffolds when they no longer need them.

Pattern Books

Pattern books contain stories that make use of repeated phrases, refrains, and sometimes rhymes. In addition, pattern books frequently contain pictures that may facilitate story comprehension (Heald-Taylor, 1987). The predictable patterns allow beginning second language readers to become involved immediately in a literacy event in their second language. Moreover, the use of pattern books meets the criteria for literacy scaffolds by modeling reading, by challenging students' current level of linguistic competence, and by assisting comprehension through the repetition of a simple sentence pattern.

One popular pattern book is Bill Martin's *Brown Bear, Brown Bear, What Do You See?* (Martin, 1967). The story, amply illustrated with colorful pictures, repeats a simple pattern children use to begin reading. In one first grade class, for example, Rosario Canetti read *Brown Bear* to a group of nine children with varying English proficiencies. Having arrived recently from Mexico, four of the children were just beginning to learn English as a second language. After hearing the book read once through, the children responded to the second reading as follows:

ROSARIO READS: Brown Bear, Brown Bear, what do you see?
[*Rosario turns the page and children see a picture of a red bird.*]
CHILDREN REPLY: Red bird!
ROSARIO READS: I see a red bird looking at me!
Red bird, Red bird, what do you see?
[*Rosario turns the page and children see a picture of a yellow duck.*]
CHILDREN REPLY: Yellow duck!
ROSARIO READS: I see a yellow duck looking at me.
Yellow duck, Yellow duck, what do you see?
[*Rosario turns the page and children see a picture of a blue horse.*]
CHILDREN REPLY: Blue horse lookin' at me.

The story continued in this way as other colorful characters were introduced: a green frog, a white dog, a black sheep, a goldfish, and finally pictures of children and a teacher. As a group, the children began to elaborate their responses to include the full pattern: "I see a _____ looking at me." A few children, however, just mouthed the words, participating in the story in a way that was comfortable for them with the support of the group.

After reading several pattern stories to the group, Rosario gives her students opportunities to read the books to each other during self-selection activity time. She also invites them to create their own Big Book versions of the story or to tell each other the story using flannel board pieces or their own drawings.

One group of Chinese first-graders in Audrey Fong's class created their own Big Book after hearing the pattern story *Meanies*. In the story, the question repeated is: "What is it that Meanies do?" This question is followed by an answer repeated three times: "Meanies drink their bath water [in normal voice]. Meanies drink their bath water [louder]. Meanies drink their bath water [shouting in disgust]." And the final phrase: "That's what Meanies do." Using the pattern, the children created their own book: "What is it that Goodies do?" A part of the story is shown here without the illustrations the children drew:

What do Goodies drink?

 Goodies drink 7-up.

 Goodies drink 7-up.

 Goodies drink 7-up.

That's what Goodies drink.

In the book, Meanies eat old bubble gum. The children created their own phrase:

What do Goodies eat?

Goodies eat cake and ice cream.

 Audrey Fong's kindergarten class

After becoming familiar with the story and language patterns in books like *Meanies,* children create their own illustrated books following the pattern. Pattern books' most important function is to offer immediate access to meaningful and enjoyable literacy experiences in the student's second language. That may explain why we've seen small second language children carry predictable books around with them all day like security blankets. A partial list of pattern books that have proven successful with older and younger English language learners includes the following:

Allard, H. (1979). *Bumps in the Night.* Garden City, NY: Doubleday.

*Barrett, J. (1970). *Animals Should Definitely Not Wear Clothing.* New York: Atheneum.

Brown, M. (1947). *Goodnight Moon.* New York: Harper & Row.

Carle, E. (1977). *The Grouchy Ladybug.* New York: Crowell.

*Charlip, R. (1971). *Fortunately.* New York: Four Winds Press.

de Paola, T. (1978). *Pancakes for Breakfast.* Orlando: Harcourt Brace Jovanovich.

Flack, M. (1932). *Ask Mr. Bear.* New York: Macmillan.

Galdone, P. (1975). *The Gingerbread Boy.* Boston: Houghton Mifflin.

Hoban, R. (1972). *Count and See.* New York: Macmillan.

Hutchins, P. (1968). *Rosie's Walk.* New York: Macmillan.

*Books older learners might like.

Keats, E. J. (1971). *Over in the Meadow.* New York: Scholastic.

Kent, J. (1971). The Fat Cat. New York: Scholastic.

Martin, B. (1967). *Brown Bear, Brown Bear, What Do You See?* New York: Holt, Rinehart & Winston.

Mayer, M. (1968). *If I Had....* New York: Dial.

Polushkin, M. (1978). *Mother, Mother, I Want Another.* New York: Crown.

Sendak, M. (1962). *Chicken Soup with Rice.* New York: Scholastic.

*Tolstoy, A. (1968). *The Great Big Enormous Turnip.* New York: Watts.

Illustrating Stories and Poems

Illustrating stories or poems they have read provides another way to develop English language learners' response to literature. Students can make a published book of a short story, folk tale, or poem and create pictures that illustrate the literature. Judy Bridges uses this activity because all of the students, even those who speak little or no English, become involved in the illustrations. The activity immediately integrates both older and younger English learners into the collective activities of classroom response groups. The illustrations also assist the students in expressing and defining their own individual responses to the literature and prepare them for verbally sharing in response groups. When students develop illustrations together, they help one another with a basic understanding by illustrating key events. Because they are shared easily, the illustrations provide a communication channel beyond words for assisting comprehension and response to stories.

Shared Reading with Big Books

Big Books, oversized books used to present literature to groups of students in an intimate and joyful way, simulate the kind of lap reading that may take place in the children's homes (Holdaway, 1979). If children have been read to in this way, they move readily from lap reading to large-group shared reading with Big Books. If they haven't been read to often at home, the large-book experience provides an interesting, nonthreatening introduction to reading. Because the books are oversized, all the students can share them in a more personal way than a smaller book would allow. As a result, all of the children become group participants in this delightful and engaging literacy event. Moreover, we've seen teachers use carefully selected Big Books successfully with older students.

Big Books may present predictable stories in patterns that students memorize easily after two or three readings. Then they can "read" the books themselves or to each other, demonstrating a good deal of literacy knowledge. Finally, you can use oversized books to share stories and discussions with students; to point out certain words in the stories that might be difficult to decode; to help them become familiar with reading from left to right, top to bottom; and to assist them with recognizing oral and written versions of the same word.

To use shared reading with Big Books, you will need to develop a small collection of oversized books. Many are available commercially. You and your students may also create your own Big Book versions of your favorite stories using large tagboard for each page and securing the page with ring clasps. Either way, select stories that are predictable at first, as these are well loved by all students and easy to understand and remember. When you introduce the story, be sure to read the title and the names of the author and illustrator. When your students create exact remakes of a story, they will include the author's name, too, but the students will be named as the illustrators. If they write new episodes based on a particular pattern, they will be credited with authorship. In this way, reading and writing are integrated, and important learning takes place.

When Thalia Jones introduces *Animals Should Definitely Not Wear Clothing*, a book appropriate for older and younger students, she starts by asking students to imagine what different animals would look like if they wore clothes. Sometimes, she starts by letting the students draw a picture of an animal wearing clothes to support their thinking and discussion and to help involve students who barely speak English. If necessary, she shows a picture or two of animals wearing clothes to help them start drawing. After this introduction to the topic and title, she reads the story using a pointer to underscore the words from left to right. She reads each word clearly and naturally and gives students time to look at the pictures of each outrageously bedecked animal. She leaves time for laughter, too, especially after their favorite picture, the one of the hen whose newly laid egg is caught in her trousers! When the story is over, Thalia allows students to read small-book versions of the story in pairs. At times, small groups listen to a tape of the story as each child follows along in the book. Finally, she invites students to make their own individual or group books based on the story. Students then make their own oversized books using pictures of animals wearing clothes, labeling each picture with a sentence that models the pattern in the original Big Book and often competing with one another to see who can create the most absurd illustration. As the weeks go by, Thalia occasionally rereads the Big Book and the students' own patterned books. All of the books are kept on hand in the classroom library to choose during free reading.

Big Books, full of rhythm, rhyme, and interesting sequences, motivate students to see reading as fun and interesting. If you are careful to select books with predictable patterns and imaginative language, your students will call for the stories again and again. Their initial engagements with print will be joyful and fun, motivating them to want to read more.

285

Directed Listening-Thinking Activity (DL-TA)

The Directed Listening-Thinking Activity (DL-TA) provides a scaffold by modeling how experienced readers make predictions as they read. Using DL-TA, you ask questions throughout a story, guiding students to make predictions and to monitor these predictions as subsequent text is provided (Boyle & Peregoy, 1990; Stauffer, 1975). Usually you ask more questions at the beginning of the activity, encouraging students to generate their own questions as the story proceeds. Eventually, students incorporate the DL-TA questioning procedure as a natural part of their independent reading.

Lisa Joiner uses DL-TA with her English learners early in the year as a part of the regular classroom time used for listening to stories; thus, the activity becomes a listening activity at first for her students. She likes to introduce the concept by using Crockett Johnson's magical crayon story *Harold's Circus* (1959). In the story, a little boy, Harold, encounters problems that he is able to solve by drawing something with his purple crayon. For example, he falls into deep water and draws a sailboat so that he can float away safely. Lisa makes overhead transparencies of the pages in the book in order to share it with the whole class. Before reading the book, she asks children to fold a large piece of paper in quarters and hands each child a purple crayon. Then she asks them to think about what they might draw with the crayon if it were magic and could make anything they drew become real. After the children share their ideas, she introduces the book:

> LISA: The story I'm going to read to you today is about a little boy named Harold, who has a magic purple crayon. Harold gets into little troubles at the circus and sometimes has to get out of trouble by drawing something with his magic crayon. What kinds of things do you think might happen to Harold at the circus?
>
> NG: Tiger eat him.
>
> JUAN: A elephant steps on him.
>
> TERRI: A snake swallow him.

The discussion goes on until most of the students have shared their own ideas. The children have fun seeing who can think of the worst thing and say, "Aaaah!!! Ugghh!!!" after each new comment. At this point Lisa quiets the children and introduces the DL-TA strategy.

> LISA: I'm going to ask you to draw what you think Harold will draw to get out of trouble. So listen carefully and, when I ask you to, draw a picture of what you think Harold will draw next. [*She reads the text on her overhead pointing at the words as she says them.*]
>
> LISA: One moonlit evening, mainly to prove to himself he could do it, Harold went for a walk on a tightrope. [*The picture shows Harold drawing a tightrope.*] It is easy to fall off a tightrope and Harold fell. By a stroke of luck, a comfortable-looking curve appeared beneath him. [*The picture shows Harold drawing a curve.*]
>
> LISA: [*Speaking to the children.*] I want you to draw what you think that curve was. Remember this is about a circus. Draw your guess on the upper left-hand corner of your folded paper.

The children draw their pictures and share them with partners before Lisa reads on and shows them the picture of what Harold drew—an elephant. Most of the children drew other things, so they laugh when they see that the curve Harold started to draw became the trunk of an elephant. Lisa continues to read the story, and the children get better at guessing and drawing pictures as they catch on to how the story works.

Through DL-TA activities like this, Lisa's children become actively involved in understanding a story that is shown to them on the overhead. They learn how to make predictions when reading, finding out that, as they do so, they get better at understanding what they read. They also see that reading stories like this can be fun, and they frequently ask Lisa to read stories like it again. At first they are only interested in "Harold" stories, but later they ask for other stories too. This activity is very sheltered in that pictures accompany the story, and the children themselves respond by drawing. In this way, they are involved through pictorial means in the higher-level processes of story comprehension. They also learn to use drawings on a folded piece of paper to make their own stories and to have others guess what might be on the next page. The stories become little mysteries that they share.

During the DL-TA, Lisa avoids making judgments about students' predictions, so students learn that it is acceptable to make predictions that may be inaccurate. In addition, they learn that, by making predictions, even incorrect ones, they are more likely to get involved in the action and understand the story. Moreover, they learn that good readers may make inaccurate predictions but that they improve as the story progresses. Finally, the children have fun making predictions with stories, as active, rather than passive, involvement engages them in story comprehension and in predicting and monitoring for their understanding while reading. DL-TA has the added advantage of being a strategy that can be used with younger and older students and with beginning and intermediate English learners. Moreover, it can be used with both narrative and expository texts, using the same basic procedures illustrated in Lisa's lesson.

Readers' Theater

Many teachers like to use readers' theater in their classrooms to assist students in responding to literature. Readers' theater is an excellent activity for beginning second language readers as well as intermediate readers (Busching, 1981; Sloyer, 1982). Beginning readers read and dramatize a script from a story they have read. Intermediate readers, as we describe later, create their own scripts to read and dramatize. For beginning English learners, select stories that have several characters so that more students can participate. In addition, the stories should be somewhat brief and have a simple structure with a clear beginning, middle, and end. Many folk tales are excellent for introducing readers' theater because they meet all of these requirements. For example, a story such as "Cinderella" has clear examples of character roles and requires several different parts. In addition, it has a clear beginning, middle, and end, with the slipper fitting only Cinderella's foot. A side benefit of "Cinderella," as well as other fairy tales or folk tales, is that variations exist among different cultures. This allows students to act out and understand different Cinderella stories. Some teachers like to use story maps or Venn diagrams (described in Chapter 9) to assist students in determining the variations in different versions of a folk tale.

Once an appropriate story has been selected, you may make performance suggestions to improve diction, dramatization, and expression. Because students have had a chance to rehearse and because they read from a script, they are able to read well during the performance. A good starter story for readers' theater is *Why Mosquitoes Buzz in People's Ears* (Aardema, 1975). The rhythm and rhyme of this delightful cumulative African tale are compelling, and the moral speaks to us all. Your students might want to create masks for the various animal parts in the story before they perform the script.

> *Partial Reader's Theater Script for Why Mosquitoes Buzz in People's Ears*
> NARRATOR: One morning a mosquito saw an iguana at a waterhole.
> MOSQUITO: Iguana, you will never believe what I saw yesterday.
> IGUANA: Try me.
> MOSQUITO: I saw a farmer digging yams that are almost as big as I am.

Once students have been introduced to the idea of readers' theater, they can act out other scripts of favorite folk tales or other stories. Let them select from the many stories that they have heard in your class or from a book or movie they know.

One third-grade class, after consulting with their teacher on their script, performed the story of "The Three Little Pigs" in front of the class. Later, the teacher told them that there was a book that presented the wolf's side of the story, *The True Story of the Three Little Pigs by A. Wolf* (Scieszka, 1989), and that maybe they would like to read that script. When they read the story, they were excited and presented it to the class.

When students do readers' theater, they have to analyze and comprehend the story at a deep level in order to present it again to the class, and they have to share their understanding with others. They also have to determine the tone of voice for the various characters and orchestrate their reading performance into a coherent dramatic production. In short, they have to respond to the story, accept various interpretations from their peers, and offer an effective presentation to the class. Readers' theater gives power over story interpretation to students. Later, as these beginning-level students become intermediate-level students, they will write their own scripts from favorite stories.

Story Mapping

Story mapping is an example of a scaffold because it helps students use story grammar or the basic structure of a story for comprehending and composing stories. For example, many stories have a basic skeletal structure consisting of a major character or two, a goal the character wishes to achieve, an obstacle that makes it difficult to achieve the goal, and a resolution of the conflict between the goal and

Someone	Wants	But	So

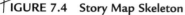

FIGURE 7.4   **Story Map Skeleton**

the obstacle. In the words of novelist John Gardner, "In nearly all good fiction, the basic—all but inescapable—plot form is this: A central character wants something, goes after it despite opposition (perhaps including his own doubts), and so arrives at a win, lose or draw" (Gardner, 1983). The simple story map in Figure 7.4, which is based on this skeletal structure, provides a four-part sequence for students to fill in (Boyle & Peregoy, 1990; Schmidt, n.d.).

Using the story map, one group of five second-grade ELD learners produced several story maps after their teacher read "The Three Little Pigs" to them. The children's responses are reproduced in Figure 7.5. Because this was the children's first experience with story mapping, the teacher involved the whole group in creating the maps together. In the process, the children first chose the Big Bad Wolf as the character to map, producing "The Big Bad Wolf wanted to eat the pigs, but they boiled him in hot water, so the pigs lived happily ever after."

Another version produced by the group resulted in "The three little pigs wanted to build strong houses to be safe from the wolf, but the wolf blew the houses down, so they boiled the wolf in hot water." Through the process of mapping the story, the children were able to focus on the different perspectives of the wolf and the three little pigs. By the time they created the second map, they had arrived at the type of analysis for which the story map aims.

Students may use the simple story map to focus their attention on important parts of a story. When they use story mapping, it soon becomes evident to students that stories have several characters whose goals often conflict, leading to interest

Someone	Wants	But	So
the wolf	wants to eat the pigs	but they boil the wolf in water	so the pigs live happily ever after
the pigs	want strong houses to be safe from the wolf	but the wolf blows all but one house down	so the pigs boil him in water and live happily ever after

FIGURE 7.5   **Second-Grade English Learners' Map of "The Three Little Pigs"**

and intrigue as the plot develops. Even a story as simple as "The Three Little Pigs" can be mapped in a variety of ways following the story map model. By sharing and discussing their maps, children deepen their story comprehension and gain awareness of how stories are structured, which assists them with subsequent reading and writing. Once introduced, story maps help English learners not only to understand and to remember key elements of a story but also to create an outline for writing their own stories.

Finally, the story maps provide a starting point for students to share their individual responses to the values and events they perceive in their transactions with the text (Rosenblatt, 1978, 1983, 1984). Through these transactions, English language learners can discuss various views and experiences presented in a story. Ultimately, these responses lie at the heart of literature study, and the maps provide a scaffolding for student explorations and transactions with stories. A different kind of story map was used by Lianna for the story *Bedtime for Frances* (Hoban, 1960) and is shown in Figure 7.6.

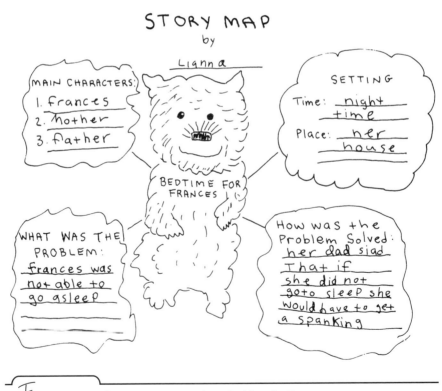

STORY MAP
by
Lianna

MAIN CHARACTERS:
1. Frances
2. mother
3. flather

SETTING
Time: night time
Place: her house

BEDTIME FOR FRANCES

WHAT WAS THE PROBLEM:
Frances was not able to go asleep

How was the Problem Solved:
her dad siad That if she did not go to sleep she Would have to get a spanking

FIGURE 7.6   Lianna's Map Based on *Bedtime for Frances*

INTERMEDIATE READERS: CHARACTERISTICS AND STRATEGIES

Intermediate second language readers will come to you with a rather large sight vocabulary and the ability to comprehend various kinds of texts, such as stories, letters, and some news and magazine articles. Generally, they are apt to speak English well enough to negotiate meanings orally with their peers during literature response groups. They have a fair amount of automaticity in their reading so that they also are able to read with a degree of fluency. They read extended texts but have some difficulty dealing with texts that contain new vocabulary. They will generally need less assistance than beginning-level students and less contextualization of lessons with visuals and other scaffolds. Nevertheless, you will want to provide them with the strategies used with beginning readers in addition to the new ones presented in this section.

Cognitive Mapping

Similar to a story map or a life map, a cognitive map is a graphic drawing summarizing a text. Intermediate-level readers can use maps to assist them with comprehending and remembering what they have read, and they can use mapping as a prewriting strategy to generate a plan for their compositions (Boyle & Buckley, 1983; Boyle & Peregoy, 1991; Buckley & Boyle, 1981; Hanf, 1971; Ruddell & Boyle, 1989).

Whereas story maps assist students by scaffolding comprehension and memory of a simple story such as a folk tale, cognitive maps assist them with comprehension and memory of more complex stories containing many characters, settings, and plots. To introduce cognitive mapping for narrative texts, we suggest you follow procedures similar to those you used to introduce mapping as a prewriting strategy. Another good way is to draw a map on the chalkboard or use a mobilelike map such as the one in Figure 7.7 showing the characters, setting, and plot. Once students have a clear understanding of the categories, you can ask them to generate information from a story they have read to be placed on the map, or you may choose a story with which all the students are familiar to introduce mapping for the first time.

After practicing group mapping, students can begin to create individual maps to summarize information from their reading. The map shown in Figure 7.8 was developed by a fifth-grader on the folktale "Beauty and the Beast." Many teachers use maps as a part of their individual reading programs. Because maps help students organize and remember stories, they prepare them to share in their literature response groups.

You will notice that the map in Figure 7.8 differs from the prototype used to introduce the concept to students. That is because students quickly move away from

291

the prototype after they have a clear understanding of what the process is about. They make maps with concentric circles, triangles, ladders, and different artistic shapes to illustrate concepts in their stories. Because mapping is easily learned and easily shared and because it is visual and spatial, second language teachers and their students find it a particularly useful strategy (Northcutt & Watson, 1986).

Directed Reading-Thinking Activity (DR-TA)

Directed Reading-Thinking Activity (DR-TA) is carried out in the same manner as the DL-TA (Stauffer, 1975). The only difference is that students read the text themselves silently after having made predictions during oral discussion. The activity is actually directed by the teacher, who invites predictions and confirmations on one portion of text at a time and then tells students how many paragraphs to read in order to find out whether their predictions are correct. This activity provides support at the beginning of a story to help readers get into the text. It also provides students with a model of active questioning during reading. Soon readers carry out the prediction process without teacher participation.

Leticia Palomino models DR-TA using the overhead projector and an index card to cover parts of a story. Uncovering the first paragraph, she asks students to read and predict what they think will happen next. She starts with simple stories such as "The Magician's Apprentice" and teaches students to ask questions beginning with *who, what, when, where, why,* and *how. Who* are the characters in the story? *What* happens in the story; *what* are the problems faced by the characters? *When* does the story take place? *Where* does it take place? *Why* did the boy want to be a magician? *How* will the problems be resolved? *What* will happen next? The following is a partial script of Ms. Palomino's students working with "The Magician's Apprentice." First read the part of the story that we have transcribed (Boyle, 1990) and then note the approach she uses to introduce the DR-TA strategy to her students.

292

FIGURE 7.7   Mobile Map Illustrating Story Parts

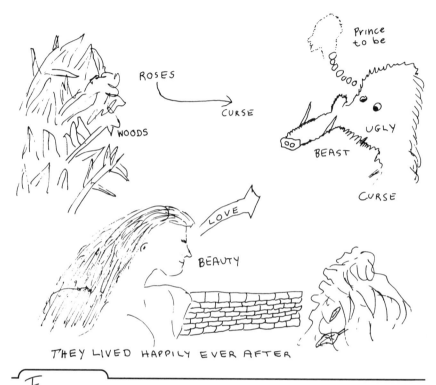

FIGURE 7.8   Map Student Created after Reading "Beauty and the Beast"

The Magician's Apprentice

Once upon a time there was a boy named Julio who wanted to be a magician. He read about magicians and watched magicians on television and bought magic tricks. When he became a magician, there was one trick he wanted to perform. He wanted to make a tiger disappear. One day a circus came to the boy's town. The great Magica the magician was with the circus. Magica was especially known for one trick. She could make a tiger disappear right in front of the audience.

The boy could not wait to go to the circus. That night he had a dream. He dreamed that the magician would teach him the tiger trick. The next day he was very nervous about going to the circus.

Ms. Palomino began by reading the title and asking the students what they thought would happen in the story.

STUDENTS: Magic tricks! Juggling! Balls in air! Disappearing things! Rabbits get lost!

TEACHER: Do you know what an apprentice is? [*The students stared at one another and waited for the teacher.*] That's what they call somebody who helps a person who is very good at what they do. Somebody who has experience. Like a good plumber might have a helper or a carpenter has a helper. Helpers are people who are learning to do something, and they are called an apprentice. So what do you think a story about a magician's apprentice will be about?

STUDENTS: 'Bout man helps magicians? About people helping magicians.

TEACHER: I'm going to read parts of the story and ask you questions. When I do, you guess about what you think will happen next in the story. OK? [*She begins reading after the students nod their understanding. She uncovers only the sections of the story she is reading.*]

TEACHER: Once upon a time there was a boy named Julio who wanted to be a magician.
Class, what do you think will happen to Julio in this story?

STUDENTS: Helps a magician. Rabbits disappear.

TEACHER: He read about magicians and watched magicians on the television and bought magician tricks. When he became a magician, he thought, there was one trick he wanted to perform.
What trick do you think Julio will do?

STUDENTS: Elephant disappear! Ball floats. Card tricks.

TEACHER: He wanted to make a tiger disappear. One day a circus came to the boy's town.
What do you think Julio will do when the circus comes to town?

STUDENTS: He'll go to the circus. He'll ride on a elephant. He'll see motorcycle riders. A magician.
Other students seem to agree with the magician idea.

TEACHER: The great Magica the magician was with the circus. Magica was especially known for one trick.
What trick do you think Magica was known for?

STUDENTS: Tricks. Tigers disappear. Tigers disappear!

TEACHER: She could make a tiger disappear right in front of the audience. [*Students laugh.*] The boy could not wait to go to the circus. That night he had a dream.
What did Julio dream, class?

STUDENTS: About the circus. About the magician. About tiger tricks.

TEACHER: He dreamed that the magician would teach him the tiger trick. The next day he was very nervous about going to the circus.

Ms. Palomino continued to read the story, and the students' guesses became more enthusiastic and more accurate. Notice that she did not correct students if they predicted incorrectly. In fact, she encouraged all guesses and made a point of

294

showing them that it really is not as important to guess correctly as it is to make plausible predictions and to check them against the text as new information appears. In this way, students gain experience in predicting and monitoring their comprehension as more mature readers do. After some practice with the DR-TA strategy, Ms. Palomino reminds the students to make predictions in their independent and group reading activities. She starts their independent reading with stories that are amenable to making predictions and monitoring comprehension and then moves them to more difficult texts, in which it may be a little more difficult to make predictions but even more important to do so. In her 20 years of teaching lower and upper grades, Ms. Palomino has used DR-TA with short stories, children's stories, and history texts using the same basic procedures.

Literature Response Journals

Literature response journals are personal notebooks in which students write informal comments about the stories they are reading, including their feelings and reactions to characters, setting, plot, and other aspects of the story; they are an outgrowth of learning logs and other journals (Atwell, 1984). You may wish to let students decide how often they will write in their journals, or you might set a schedule for them. The choice really depends on the purpose. For example, if several students are getting ready for a literature response group, you might suggest that students comment at the end of each chapter and finish the book by a certain date. On the other hand, if the response journal is based on voluntary, free reading, you may wish to leave the choice entirely up to the student. As a middle road, you might want to give students some general guidelines such as suggesting that they respond once a week or after reading complete chapters.

To help students get started in their response journals, it is useful to provide sample questions they can consider while they are reading, such as: What do you like about the book or characters in the story? How do you feel about some of the decisions characters make in the book? Would you make different decisions? What do you think the main characters should do at a particular point in the story?

In other words, the questions you suggest to students should invite their personal reactions and responses to the experience of the story rather than aiming at literary analysis. That can come later. The purpose of the journal is to encourage dynamic, experiential, and authentic involvement with literature. The following example shows a few brief responses by Sammy, a third grade intermediate-level reader, to a story he selected to read individually. Following Sammy's response is a high school student's response to *Romeo and Juliet* after seeing an excerpt of a film and reading and discussing the play in his group.

> The story about "The Japanese Fairy Tale" about a very ugly man of long long ago. He ugly becuss he give his pretty to the princess. He loveing her very much to do that. I wouldn't do that I don think so.
>
> Sammy

The plays about two gans or families that wants to fight all the time. The boy and girl love each one and they don't want the family to fight at all. I dont think they will live very happy.

Joseph

You or your other students may respond to the journals. Either way, be sure to respond to the intent, not the grammatical form. You might ask an occasional question about the literature or a character in the story or what might happen next. Or you might share a similar response to a piece of literature you have read. Whatever your comment, encourage the students in their search for meaning in the literature. To manage your own responding time, you might ask students to highlight sections to which they want you to respond. In this way, literature response journals may become interactive. Some questions you can give students to assist them with responding to the stories they are reading include the following. These questions may be used for journals, response groups, or independent reading.

1. What would you tell characters in the story to do if you could talk to them?
2. What was the most exciting or interesting part of the story for you?
3. Why do you think the author wrote the story?
4. If you wrote this story, what parts would you change?
5. Would you recommend the story to others? Why?
6. What way would you like to respond to the story? Mural, map, summary, etc.?

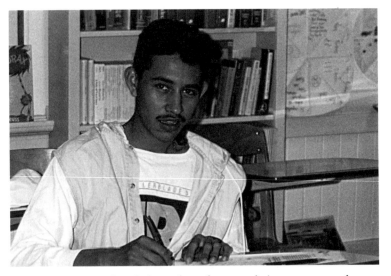

Literature response logs help students focus on their own personal reactions to characters, plot, setting, and other aspects of a particular piece of literature.

Developing Scripts for Readers' Theater

When English learners attain the intermediate level, they are ready to go beyond the readers' theater activities that asked them to read, interpret, and act out scripts provided for them. At this point, they can begin to develop and write scripts of their own, based on the stories they are reading. Developing their own scripts requires them to pick out the most important events in a story according to their own interpretations. In addition, they must identify the most important characters in a story as well as the conflicts and problems they face. Finally, students must interpret the resolution of these problems and think about the tone of characters' voices: Are they happy, sad, or indifferent? After these choices are made, students determine the dialogue that they will use for their script. You may want to have them create maps of the stories before they develop their scripts; the maps will help them make decisions about major events and the dialogue that goes with them. In order to create scripts, students must know a great deal about story structure. Thus, readers' theater at the intermediate level requires substantial sophistication.

Students must be sophisticated in their understanding of character motivation and conflict, and they must be able to show this sophistication in the scripts they write. They must have sophistication concerning the conflicts characters face and interpret these conflicts for their script. Finally, they need to understand the resolution of the story, its meaning and ramifications for various characters, and they must portray this in their script. Developing a readers' theater script provides students with a purposeful and meaningful activity for interpreting stories and involves them in activities that will enhance their comprehension of stories. Because they must negotiate meaning when developing scripts and because they act out the dramatic script, second language intermediate readers benefit from readers' theater, an activity that integrates oral and written language with a dramatic flair.

Adapting Stories into Plays and Scripts for Film and Videotape

Another way you can involve students in meaningful and motivational reading and writing activities is to have them adapt stories into scripts for making animated films or for interpreting stories from television. Animated films require students to develop a story first and then create a storyboard for the film. Storyboards are cartoon strips created by animators to portray the sequence of events both visually and with dialogue. Once they have developed the story, they create a storyboard for the film. Once students have developed the storyboard, they are ready to create cutout or clay characters to be moved on backgrounds for the animated effect. They then make the film, adding dialogue and music to the finished piece of animation. Just as readers' theater requires students to interpret stories at a sophisticated level and provides different channels for assisting students with negotiating meaning and developing scripts, so also the animated storyboard and film provide built-in sheltering to communication.

USING COMPUTERS AND CD-ROMS TO ENHANCE LEARNING

If you have computers available for your students, there are programs coming out every day that can assist your English language learners. Some animated programs tell colorfully illustrated stories in both English and another language. In addition, some programs highlight words as they say them. Thus, your students gain access to stories through visual as well as verbal information. Other programs allow your students to develop and animate their own stories, and help students to work together in collaborative groups to develop stories that can be played back by anyone in the class. Many computer stores sell CD-Roms that contain samples of the stories so that you can preview them in your home. You can also purchase sample programs inexpensively or read reviews in magazines such as *MacWorld*, which offers "free" CD-Roms containing parts of programs and games you can preview. We recommend that you try these programs before purchasing any at your school. You may also ask students to preview programs to help you develop your own school library for different grade and developmental levels.

298

ASSESSING SECOND LANGUAGE READERS' PROGRESS

Assessing second language reading progress is an ongoing process requiring a variety of information sources. Daily observations while students read in class provide one important source. The advantage of in-class observations is that they focus on students' reading in natural, routine situations involving authentic literacy tasks. These informal assessments will tell you much more than a myriad of standardized tests. Nothing takes the place of a perceptive and observant teacher who knows students and watches for their progress throughout the year. To augment your observations, you may wish to use individual assessment procedures from time to time to document student progress or to understand better a student experiencing reading problems. We describe several individual assessment procedures you can use, including miscue analysis and running records. In Chapter 10, we offer in-depth discussion of individual reading inventories, an analytic procedure for assessing student reading strengths and instructional needs. Here we focus on day-to-day classroom observations and interactions with students as they negotiate meaning through print. A teacher who recognizes and responds to the teachable moment easily takes the place of all the standardized tests and reading labs in the entire school district.

Assessing with Materials Students Bring to Class

One excellent and valid way to assess students' reading abilities is to ask them to bring something to the class to read. This casual approach to assessment is non-intimidating and affords you an opportunity to see what students select. Moreover, from this approach you might discover whether students have anything to read at home or whether they read at all outside of the school environment.

When using this approach, make sure the students understand that they can bring anything they want to school: a TV guide, a record label, a comic book, a magazine, or anything else. When they have brought in their selection, ask them to read it aloud. As they do so, evaluate their performance with their self-selected materials in comparison with materials you've heard them read in class. If the students do quite well with self-selected materials and poorly with school materials, you can begin to select materials more appropriate to their interests and level of reading efficiency. If they do poorly with self-selected materials, you will have a better idea of their proficiency and of how you can assist them with becoming better readers. Be careful not to make judgments too quickly when assessing students, however. Assess them with various materials from school and from home, and assess them informally each day to gain as much knowledge as possible before you draw conclusions about their reading abilities.

Informal Assessment

Informal assessment procedures may be used with individual students to evaluate their reading. They differ from most standardized tests in that they are individually administered to evaluate performance on specific reading tasks. If administered periodically during the year, they establish a profile of progress. We feel strongly that the informal assessment procedures presented here and in Chapter 10 are the ones that will help you to determine how your students are doing. As already noted, we suggest that the best informal procedure for assessing students' reading and writing is to watch English learners as they approach various reading, writing, and oral language tasks and accomplish authentic reading activities throughout the day. The informal procedures presented in the following sections, therefore, represent strategies for assessment to augment your daily informal assessment in the classroom.

Miscue Analysis

Miscue analysis is a reading assessment tool that focuses on the reader's **miscues,** or variations from print made during oral reading (Goodman, 1973; Goodman & Burke, 1972). Rather than carrying the onus of a terrible mistake, miscues provide a valuable source of information about how the reader is processing print. Some kinds of miscues actually indicate good comprehension. By analyzing a reader's miscues or deviations from text, it is possible to evaluate strengths and weaknesses and thereby determine what kind of instructional assistance might be appropriate. By studying the kinds of deviations a reader tends to make, you can infer which reading strategies children use and which ones should be taught to help them improve. Because miscue analysis is based on oral reading, teachers need to separate oral pronunciation style and/or errors from reading errors. Although the miscue analysis reveals the process of comprehending, a measure of overall comprehension of the text is also needed. This is accomplished by asking the reader for a summary, an oral retelling, of what was read.

Miscue Procedure*

1. Select a student whose reading you wish to assess. Then choose a reading selection somewhat more difficult than what the reader usually deals with easily in class. The selection should be about 500 words in length and should be a meaningfully complete piece. Use your own judgment if you think the selection should be shorter.
2. Gather and prepare materials for tape-recording the oral reading:
   (a) a copy of the reading selection for the student (original or copy)
   (b) a tape recorder and blank tape
   (c) a copy of the selection for you to write on (triple-spaced)
   (d) notes on the selection that you will use to probe the student's spontaneous retelling of the piece (i.e., what you think are important parts to remember in terms of characters, plot, theme, setting)
3. Find a quiet place to record the session. Start by telling the students that you are going to tape-record their oral reading in order to help you learn more about how students in their class read.
4. Turn the machine on "record" and ask the student to read the passage out loud all the way through. Tell the student: "Here is something I want you to read for me out loud. I can't help you read it, though, so if you come to a word you don't know, try to figure it out and then read on. When you have finished reading, I will ask you to tell me all you can remember about what you have read." After the reading is finished, ask the student to tell you all he or she can remember. Then follow up with questions as needed to see if the student can retell all the parts you consider important.
5. At the end, let the reader listen to his or her voice just for fun.
6. Later, listen to the tape to analyze the miscues.

The coding system in Figure 7.9 defines and illustrates how to mark miscues students may make while being informally assessed.

---

*Based on *Reading Miscue Inventory Manual: Procedure for Diagnosis and Evaluation,* by Y. M. Goodman and C. L. Burke, 1972. New York: Macmillan.

1. **Insertion:** The child inserts a word not in the text; place a caret where the insertion is made and write the inserted word above it.

   Example: The cat was *also* in the kitchen.

2. **Omission:** The child leaves a word out; circle the word the child omits.

   Example: Many people find it (difficult) to concentrate.

3. **Substitution:** Child replaces one word with another; place the child's substitution over the replaced word.

   Example: The *dog* doll was in the little girl's room.

4. **Word Supplied by Tester:** Child can't get word and tester supplies it; put supplied word in parentheses.

   Example: Joe ran to *(school)* school.

5. **Word Missed then Corrected by Reader:** Child says word wrong then immediately corrects it; place missed word above word and place a check by it.

   Example: The *rat* ✓ cat is sleeping.

FIGURE 7.9   Marking Miscues

An example of one reader's oral reading and miscues is shown in Figure 7.10. Juanita was asked to read a passage and the questions following it. The passage (Karlsen, Madden, & Gardner, 1976) is marked according to the information in Figure 7.9.

After reading and answering the questions, Juanita retold the story. What can we learn from her reading and retelling? How can the miscue analysis combined with comprehension questions assist you in determining a reading program for Juanita? Let's analyze Juanita's performance and make some decisions for assisting her.

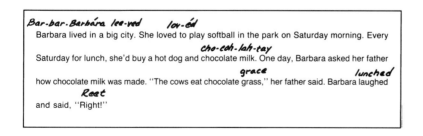

Bar-bar-Barbára *lee-ved*   *lov-éd*
Barbara lived in a big city. She loved to play softball in the park on Saturday morning. Every
                           cho-coh-lah-tay
Saturday for lunch, she'd buy a hot dog and chocolate milk. One day, Barbara asked her father
                              grace   *lunched*
how chocolate milk was made. "The cows eat chocolate grass," her father said. Barbara laughed
      Reet
and said, "Right!"

FIGURE 7.10   Miscue Analysis Passage

Interpreting Miscues. Juanita had trouble pronouncing the name Barbara, but this didn't impede understanding. She knew she was reading a girl's name. She pronounces *lived* in a nonstandard way, but this mispronunciation was not a problem because she understood the meaning. Again, the miscue is not one that stands in the way of meaning. The same is true of her pronunciation of *loved;* when she was asked what that meant, she answered: "It mean she like baseball." For Juanita baseball and softball are the same thing. Juanita also pronounces the Spanish word *chocolate (cho-coh-lah-tay)* for *chocolate;* clearly she is understanding the passage. When we get to the last sentence, however, we find that she has trouble with words that do impede comprehension. She says *grace* for *grass* and *lunched* for *laughed.* In the retelling, it becomes clear that at that point she is confused. Nevertheless, even the miscue of *lunched* for *laughed* indicates a degree of comprehension up to this point. She matches the word *laughed* with a word, *lunched,* that matches *laughed* syntactically and is contextually appropriate given the previous information concerning lunch.

Based on this analysis, we can see that Juanita has many strengths as a reader. First, she reads for meaning and tries to make sense of the passage. Second, she is able to pronounce most of the words according to her oral language equivalents. She misses a few words in the text but, with further reading, will probably learn these with teacher guidance. Through the miscue analysis, we are able to gain a great deal of information about Juanita, information that will help us determine whether she needs special assistance, whether she is reading for meaning or just for pronunciation, and whether we need to intervene in her progress as a reader.

In contrast to Juanita, who reads for meaning, you might find a student who pronounces every word perfectly but does not comprehend the passage well—a student who seems to be "barking at print." Miscue analysis is a powerful tool for you to use with students to identify strategies and patterns in their reading behavior as a basis for developing an appropriate program for reading.

Now let's take a look at a younger reader with more difficulties, Candy. Candy's teacher, Chris Belmont, told us that Candy was not understanding what she was reading and was having difficulty pronouncing words correctly. He asked us to evaluate her reading and to develop a plan for helping her become a more proficient reader. She had transferred from a nearby school district to his fifth-grade English Language Development class after being in the United States for three years. She had attended first grade and part of second grade in Guanajuato, Mexico, before coming to the United States. In the process of immigration, Candy missed out on several months of her second-grade year. Consequently, upon arrival in this country, she was placed in a second-grade class, one in which English was the primary language of instruction. By the fifth grade, when we met her, her oral English was fluent, she got along well with the other students, and she was eager to become a good reader. In fact, she could read second- and third-grade-level books in English quite easily, and she enjoyed reading poems in the reading textbook series selected by the district, though she had done very little writing yet.

302

Two aspects of Candy's language and literacy profile suggested that English reading instruction was an appropriate choice for her at this point in her schooling. First of all, her English proficiency was at the intermediate level, Phase III, based on her teacher's SOLOM observations. Second, her English reading abilities were already established, though not yet commensurate with her grade level. In other words, she was able to read simple, connected discourse in English but had trouble with longer, more complex pieces. For beginning English learners who are not yet literate in any language, we usually recommend literacy instruction in the primary language if possible. For Candy, we did not consider primary language literacy instruction to be necessary at this point. Nevertheless, we wondered if her present reading difficulties might have been avoided if she had enjoyed the benefit of full primary language literacy instruction earlier in her schooling.

With this background information in hand, we met with Candy, a charming, enthusiastic young girl, who was eager to hear what we would say about her reading. She told us that she had learned a lot from Mr. Belmont and she wanted to become the best reader in the class. She told us that she had trouble with long words. Clearly, Candy was an articulate, thoughtful, and reflective student with strong expressive abilities in English. We began by asking Candy to read a second-grade passage. She read the passage with several miscues, but was able to summarize what she read quite well. Next, we skipped to a more difficult text based on a traditional Mexican story about our Lady of Guadalupe. We taped Candy's reading of the text, but chose not to mark her errors on the spot because we did not want her to feel self-conscious. When she completed the text, we asked her to retell the story, but she insisted that she did not remember any of it. However, when we asked her questions about the passage, she was able to remember the main characters and essential parts of the plot. However, her understanding of the passage was sketchy. She told us she had not heard this story before, but she had seen a picture of Our Lady of Guadalupe on the calendar at home. Thus prior story knowledge did not assist her in her reading. We thanked her for coming and told her we would be back to see her the following week.

We then proceeded to evaluate her oral reading (Figure 7.11). Overall, we saw that Candy usually utilized her intermediate-level English language knowledge and reading skill to make sense of the text. She knows that the story is in English, so she reads John instead of Juan in the first line but corrects to Juan the second time the name appears. She also uses the Spanish cognate *misión* for *mission*. Neither miscue creates any comprehension problem. When examining miscues, it is most helpful to look for **persistent miscue patterns.** If a student makes the same kind of miscue repeatedly, the pattern often provides a direction for instruction. One pattern we see in Candy's oral reading is that she omits almost all -*ed* endings of words. She also has problems with **digraphs,** in which two letters stand for one sound, such as *th*- in *thousand* or *sh*- in *shining.* She seems to have difficulty with words beginning with a **blend,** in which two letters stand for two blended sounds, such as *bl*- in *blanket, sp*- in *spoke,* and *st*- in *stopped.* She even has trouble with *from,* which should be in her sight word vocabulary by now. When she comes to words

Long ago in Mexico, there lived an Indian farmer named Juan [*John*]

Diego. Juan Diego went to Mass every Sunday at the Spanish mission. [*misión*]

Then one day, something happened that would change the entire [*en the*] [*cage*]

history of Mexico. [*story*]

On December 9, (1531), Juan Diego rose at dawn to go to church. [*down*]

He put on his best white pants and shirt, covered himself with his [*wit*]

blanket, and began the long walk to the mission. He followed the rocky [*and*] [*misión*]

dirt road over the dry desert hills. When Juan Diego got to the hill [*dree*]

named Tepeyac, he heard a beautiful song coming from the sky. On the [*on*] [*skee*]

hilltop Juan Diego saw a large white cloud with gold light shining from [*shine*]

it. Juan Diego stopped and looked. Suddenly a lovely voice spoke: [*sop*] [*apok*]

"Juan Diego! Juan Diego!"

Before him stood a beautiful lady dressed in a blue satin robe that [*sashen*]

was covered with a thousand (glimmering) stars. Her skin was smooth [*tousan*]

and brown, and her long black hair was crowned with a (shimmering) [*aroun*]

halo.

FIGURE 7.11   Candy's Miscues on the Guadalupe Passage

304

with initial blends, she seems to lose the flow of meaning.

After identifying these miscue patterns, we needed to determine whether these types of miscues were preventing Candy from understanding the text. In other words, do these miscues make a difference in meaning? The unpronounced *-ed* ending does not appear to impede comprehension and reflects her present oral pronunciation. The same is true for her digraph errors, such as *tousand* for *thousand,* and *dey* for *they.* We therefore did not choose to address these miscue patterns in our suggested instructional plan. On the other hand, her consistent trouble with initial blends in words such as *blanket, stopped,* and *spoke* suggests some instruction on this element might help. Comprehension is an issue, indicated both by her difficulty in retelling the story and by the teacher's comments. Thus, we also wanted to build a strong focus on meaning, both within sentences and throughout the story. We explained our analysis to the teacher, reminding him that English learner pronunciation differences *per se* should not be considered a reading problem with either beginning or intermediate learners. Only miscues that impede meaning should be cause for concern. We then shared the following instructional recommendations:

1. Candy needs wide self-selected reading of materials at her current reading level and just a bit beyond.

Candy should read many trade books at about a third-grade level as well as some that are a little more difficult. We suggested three ways to promote successful comprehension and enjoyment of these stories: buddy reading, keeping a literature log with story map, and opportunities to talk about books informally with her peers and her teacher. Buddy reading motivates students to keep reading and provides assistance from the reading partner. By keeping a literature log and story map, Candy will have two scaffolds for understanding and remembering the story so that she will be confident in sharing it with others. The teacher may wish to create a set of important questions about plot and characters to guide the comprehension of some of these books to be addressed in the literature log.

2. Candy needs to be reminded to monitor her own reading. Does the text make sense? If not, she should reread the text to see if another way of reading will make sense.
3. Specific skill instruction is recommended on blends, one of the miscue patterns that seemed to make a difference in Candy's comprehension.
4. Because Candy had a similar problem with the words *dry* and *sky,* it should simply be pointed out to her that these words rhyme and are pronounced with a long *i* sound.

With these recommendations in mind, we decided to begin our next session with Candy by asking her about the words that gave her problems and found that it was easy for her to take the Guadalupe passage and tell us. We began our subsequent sessions by inviting Candy to bring favorite books to read to us. We also arranged with the teacher to begin a buddy reading program for her in class. She read short books, as well favorite parts of longer books. As she read to us, we emphasized that what she read should make sense to her. If it didn't, then she should re-read to see if reading some words differently made better sense. We then told her we would give her some strategies to help her read words accurately so that they would make sense. We began with work on blends, based on our hypothesis that these were creating problems for her. We gave her a series of cards containing blends such as *bl, fl,* and *cl* and asked her to pair them up with other parts of words. Figure 7.12 illustrates the game.

First, we made sure that Candy knew how to sound out the blends, and then we gave her a few examples of how the game worked. We did this by moving a blend such as *bl* next to the rest of a word such as *ue*, and then we pronounced the word we made, *blue.* Next we asked Candy to play the game, and we pronounced the words with her until she felt comfortable pronouncing the words on her own. Candy's performance supported our belief that she knew the meanings of these words and was a fast learner. We next moved from blends to digraph games and finally mixed the blend and digraph games together. Even though her digraph miscues did not indicate a need for instruction, we wanted to make sure she distinguished digraphs and blends, which she did easily. She found the games fun and was happy to see how easy it was for her to learn something that helped her become a better reader. Next we offered her a selection of books to read that used many of the blends she had practiced. Finally, we

FIGURE 7.12   Blending Game

asked her to read the Guadalupe passage again, first reminding her that many of the blends and digraphs would be found in the passage. In reading the passage over again, she got 90 percent of the blends right and was able to give us a very brief, but correct, summary of the passage.

We worked with Candy for three weeks and saw immediate improvement. However, continued growth in reading comprehension would require the teacher to implement our recommendations in the coming months, specifically by providing wide reading with opportunities to summarize and talk about her reading. Nonetheless, by asking Candy to slow down and make sure she saw all of the words, by teaching her about blends and digraphs, and by providing her with opportunities to read with a buddy, keep a literature log, and talk about stories with others, we were able to start Candy toward success. With practice and continued evaluation of Candy's reading we are certain she will become a proficient reader.

As a fifth-grader, Candy will need to read expository material for information efficiently. This kind of reading must be addressed by the teacher for all his students, and we provide strategies for such reading instruction in Chapters 8 and 9. We wanted to base Candy's reading improvement program on stories at this point because she enjoys them immensely and can practice reading longer pieces in this favorite genre of hers.

Not every reader is as easy to work with as Candy. Many do not learn as readily as she did, many take much more evaluation, and many do not have Candy's cheerful attitude and motivation. But generally in our twenty-five years of working with English learners who are having problems, we follow a very similar pattern. We spend time asking the students about their reading and try to find out what we can about their reading background and instruction. Then we give them passages to read, summarize, and answer questions about to probe their level of comprehension. We next look at the miscues they have made to see if they interfere with their comprehension; if they do, we try to set up a program to assist them. Most of the time we try to work with student strengths to assist them. Candy's love of stories and her ability to learn quickly from explicit instruction were major strengths. Finally, if students are progressing well, we continue with the program we've designed. But more frequently, we try many different things before we are able to find the key to each student's learning. We always have resource books on reading that assist us in determining other strategies we might try if a child is not succeeding. (See additional readings at the end of this chapter.)

Informal Reading Inventories

An informal reading inventory consists of graded passages with comprehension questions. When you use passages from the inventory or if you use graded passages you have devised, you tape students as they read the passages aloud and then ask the students to answer the comprehension questions. The comprehension questions, usually both factual and interpretive questions, give you a good sense of what the student does with texts of varying difficulty. Some teachers also like to ask students to summarize the information to help them get a fuller picture of the student's reading abilities. When they do this, they prepare an outline of the major points in the text they expect students to retell.

When the student has completed the passages, you can listen to the tape and evaluate how the student has performed. You can make the comprehension check or summary check and then do a miscue analysis of the student's performance. In this way, if the student is having some comprehension problems, you can see if there are patterns of miscues that might explain the comprehension difficulty. You can also look for general patterns of miscues to see what the student's strategies for reading are. Usually you'll want to begin with a passage that is relatively easy for your student and then have the student read increasingly difficult passages. But only have students read two or three short passages at a time or they may tire. In this way you can get data on the relative reading level of your students and on what assistance they may need—for example, in determining main ideas—to move up to the next level of reading. You can then develop a plan for your students to help them with becoming more competent readers. Informal reading inventories take some time, but they are well worth it for the data you will get on your students' reading capabilities. We provide further discussion of informal reading inventories in Chapter 10.

Running Records

A running record is a shorthand transcription of a child's oral reading of a text, taken "on the spot," while the child is reading. Running records allow a teacher to evaluate student progress on a day-to-day basis without using copies of the text the student is reading. Instead the teacher stands behind the reader and marks words the student gets right with checks and takes notes similar to miscue notes to code a reader's deviations from the text.

According to Clay (1979, 1989), teachers use running records to guide instructional decisions about the following:

1. the evaluation of text difficulty
2. the grouping of students
3. the acceleration of a student
4. monitoring progress of readers
5. allowing different readers to move through different books at different speeds and yet keeping track of (and records of) individual progress
6. observing particular difficulties in particular students

Procedures for Running Records. Clay (1989) suggests that you can begin using running records effectively after about two hours of training. You will get better at it with practice and begin noticing more and more about students' reading behaviors. Clay also suggests that it's better to use regular graded books from the program you use; if this isn't possible, you can use graded sets of paragraphs that are available in Informal Reading Inventories discussed in Chapter 10. Teachers

1. Check each word that is read correctly. In the example below there are five checks because all words were read correctly.

   Joe went to the store.   ✓ ✓ ✓ ✓ ✓

2. When a student gives an incorrect response, place the original text under it.

   Student: sale
   Text: store

3. If a student tries to read a word several times, record all the attempts.

   Student: stare | st- | story
   Text: store

4. If a student makes an error and then **successfully corrects** it, write **SC**.

   Student: stare | st- | story | ("store") **SC**
   Text: store

5. When the student gives no response to a word, use a dash to record it. If a student inserts a word, the word is recorded over a dash. If a student can't proceed unless you give a word use a **T** to record that you **told** the word to the student.

   a. doesn't give response: Student: _–_
   b. inserts a word: Student: _star_
   c. student told word: Student: _T_

308

ꟻIGURE 7.13   **Some Guidelines Used for Recording Running Records**

Source: Based on *The Early Detection of Reading Difficulties*, by M. Clay, 1979, Auckland, New Zealand: Heinemann.

normally use passages of about 100 to 200 words at different graded levels to see how students work with varying texts. Often teachers use running records with students' self-selected books. Based on Clay's work (1989), we present some of the conventions of running records in Figures 7.13 and 7.14.

Starting with the brief list of running record conventions, many teachers adapt ways that are more efficient for them. In fact, Marie Clay encourages teachers to adapt running records to their own needs and wishes. But with running records, we do not have the text to mark so we have to write quickly to keep notes. Nevertheless, with practice, teachers become comfortable using the procedure.

Strengths of Running Records. The biggest advantage running records have over other methods of evaluating students is that they give you the ability to evaluate your students' reading competencies during classroom instruction. With training and practice you can become used to the conventions of running records (or create your own conventions) to check your students' abilities regularly and without a great deal of time and effort. In addition, we recommend books such as Johns and Lenski's *Improving Reading* (1994) or other books that will give you a good idea of what to do with students who are having difficulties with word recognition, main idea recognition, or the like. Another excellent book you shouldn't be without is Ekwall's *Locating and Correcting Reading Difficulties* (1993). We have worked with reading difficulties among students at every grade level and would not be without these wonderful resource books. With them you will have expert advice at your fingertips that will assist you with assessing and helping your students.

Student Self-Assessment

Throughout our book we have emphasized placing students in charge of their own learning. For example, they are responsible for their own writing and work in writing response groups to shape their narratives. Similarly, they take charge of their reading literature in literature response groups. Moreover, we shall see in Chapter 8 how students set purposes and monitor their comprehension. This kind of self-assessment has often been a missing element in the past. Now, however, there are many writers and researchers who build student self-assessment into their programs (Heath & Mangiola, 1991; Yochum & Miller, 1990).

You may be surprised at how much information students, even young children, can give you about their own reading abilities. They are often able to tell you the kinds of words that give them difficulty or the kinds of reading they find frustrating. We believe in asking them regularly about their interactions with any text they are reading. There are several advantages to this approach. First, students often know more than you

Jill thought it was	✓ ✓ ✓ ✓ ✓			
going to be a great	gonna ╱ ✓ ✓ ✓ ✓ going to			
day.	✓			
It was her birthday	✓ ✓ ✓ ✓			
and she had asked	✓ ✓ ✓ acked asked	ached	SC	
for a new bicycle.	✓ ✓ ✓ bissel	bi-	bisissle T	

In the example above, Jody got all of the first line correct. In the second line she changed *going to* to *gonna*, which would be appropriate for her dialect. In the fourth line she got everything correct, but in the next she tried *asked* twice before she got it right and self-corrected (SC). Finally, she was unable to get *bicycle* and had to be told by the teacher (T).

FIGURE 7.14   A Sample Running Record

or any test will reveal about their reading; you only need to ask them. Second, asking students can save you the time of using any elaborate methods to discover their reading abilities. Finally, and perhaps most important, asking students about their own reading processes helps them become more aware of what they are doing and what strategies or procedures work for them under what circumstances. For example, they may discover that they can read narrative texts rather quickly but that they need to slow down with more complex expository text. They learn that speed of reading and choice of reading strategies must be adjusted according to the demands of the tasks. This metacognitive aspect of reading may be the best gift you can give them in their development as readers. We strongly recommend asking students first; by doing so you place them in charge of their own advancement without abrogating your own responsibilities.

SUMMARY

In Chapter 7, we began with a description of the reading process of English language learners, emphasizing the interplay of linguistic knowledge, background knowledge, and reading strategies. We then provided a rationale for literature instruction, followed by specific contexts and strategies for implementing literature study with beginning and intermediate second language readers, using appropriate literature and other reading materials. We emphasize students' selecting their own books and responding to these books in literature response groups. We also suggested a variety of legitimate responses to literature that go beyond the usual discussion of stories: activities that allow second language learners to draw pictures that depict major themes and scenes in stories they are reading, that give them opportunities to dramatize stories in readers' theater or puppet shows. We emphasized variety in responding to the needs of all learners regardless of their language proficiency.

Finally, we described assessment procedures for second language reading development. Through using informal observations, miscue analysis, and running records you can become an expert "kid watcher," assisting children in making regular advancements in language and literacy (Goodman, 1978). In addition, by assisting students with self-assessment, you help them take charge of their own learning and assist you with instructional decisions. In the next chapters, we further our discussion of reading assessment with a thorough discussion of portfolios.

Our belief is that English learners need frequent opportunities to read self-selected literature. You can assist them best by constantly sharing good literature with them and by sheltering the literature and activities involving the whole class. One of the most powerful ways to help students of different cultural backgrounds is to give them choices in their reading and responding to literature. They will choose experientially and culturally appropriate materials for themselves with your help, and they will let you know what they like and what they have difficulty with if you create a secure classroom in which all students are involved in decision making, in choosing to be silent when they wish to, and in taking control of their own learning while trusting your guidance.

Finally, excellent literature is the core of all excellent reading programs. Literature is a human and humane experience because through good books, students may explore their own natures, become aware of potentialities for thought and feeling within themselves, acquire clearer perspectives, develop aims and a sense of direction, and compare their values with the values of characters they meet in books. Literature is the only subject in school that is fully and honestly involved in exploring what it means to be human; it is the written record of human experience.

In a sense, when we read, we discover not only the world around us, but ourselves. Through literature, we can extend our experiences, compare our ethical concepts, relieve emotional frustrations, discover beauty and grandeur in language and in ourselves, and nourish our imaginations. The goal of every literature program should be to enhance these experiences for students, to give them the ability to read literature with enjoyment and understanding, and to nurture a need for further reading. Literature is an intensely personal experience, and it is with this experience that the literature study should be mainly concerned.

Figure 7.15 gives grade levels for using various strategies to enhance students' love for literature. You may want to use the chart to think about your English learners' growth and development and to decide what strategy may be useful. But the chart is not meant to be a rigid one; only you can determine a student's needs and wants when it comes to their growth as readers. Indeed, only you with your student can decide what literature or literature strategies will extend their experi-

Strategy \ Grade Level	K	1	2	3	4	5	6	7	8	9	10	11	12
Adapting stories					→	——	——	——	——	——	——	——	→
Big books	→	——	——	——	——	→							
Cognitive mapping		→	——	——	——	——	——	——	——	——	——	——	→
DL-TA		→	——	——	——	——	——	→					
DR-TA		→	——	——	——	——	——	——	——	——	——	——	→
Developing scripts			→	——	——	——	——	——	——	——	——	——	→
IRIs	→	——	——	——	——	——	——	——	——	——	——	——	→
Illustrating poems	→	——	——	——	——	——	——	——	——	——	——	——	→
Language experience	→	——	——	——	——	——	——	——	——	——	——	——	→
Miscue analysis		→	——	——	——	——	——	——	——	——	——	——	→
Patterned books	→	——	——	——	——	——	——	→					
Portfolios	→	——	——	——	——	——	——	——	——	——	——	——	→
Reader's theater		→	——	——	——	——	——	——	——	——	——	——	→
Response groups	→	——	——	——	——	——	——	——	——	——	——	——	→
Response journals			→	——	——	——	——	——	——	——	——	——	→
Scripts to interprete plays					→	——	——	——	——	——	——	——	→
Story mapping		→	——	——	——	——	——	——	——	——	——	——	→
Running records		→	——	——	——	——	——	——	——	——	——	——	→

FIGURE 7.15 Grade Levels at Which Strategies May Be Used

ence and growth. Because literature can be such an intensely personal experience, we all have to pay special attention to our students as they make choices and build their knowledge.

For all students, including English learners, literature not only extends experience and gives chances for comparing values, but plays an important role in expanding the language of readers. Through literature, students become aware of the delight and magic of words; through poems, short stories, riddles, books, and jokes they can learn about the full range of language use. In our best literature exists the finest use of language. Thus, an excellent reading program for English language learners consists of the best literature. Anything less is a disservice to our students. As Mark Twain once said, "A man who reads poor literature has no advantage over a man who doesn't read at all."

SUGGESTIONS FOR FURTHER READING

Anderson, N. (1999). *Exploring second language reading: Issues and strategies*. Boston: Heinle & Heinle. This engaging book begins with a brief, clear introduction to models of the reading process and discusses eight strategies dealing with reading: (1) activate background knowledge, (2) cultivate vocabulary, (3) teach for comprehension, (4) increase reading rate, (5) verify reading strategies, (6) evaluate progress, (7) build motivation, and (8) select appropriate reading materials. The brief book (129 pages), well-written and organized, gives valuable, theoretically sound, and practical information in addition to providing a model for teaching.

Birch, B. (2002). *English L2 reading*. Mahwah, NJ: Erlbaum

Researchers who have developed models of the reading process can separated into three views: top-down views, bottom-up views, and interactive views (interactive views are a combination of bottom-up and top-down views). This book offers a valuable contribution to the bottom-up view of reading, including chapters on listening skills, processing letters, the English spelling system, phonics, morphophonemic writing, and vocabulary acquisition. An excellent book that discusses graphophonic and word-level details of L2 reading, with specific ideas relative to students' particular first language literacy skills.

Carrell, P., Devine, J., & Eskey, D. (1988). *Interactive approaches to second language reading*. Cambridge: Cambridge University Press.

A thorough discussion of second language reading theory and research is found in this collection of articles written by researchers and practitioners of reading. The sections in the book suggest its comprehensiveness: "Interactive Models of Reading," "Interactive Approaches to Second Language Reading—Theory," "Interactive Approaches to Second Language Reading— Empirical Studies," "Implications and Applications of Interactive Approaches to Second Language Reading—Pedagogy."

Custodio, B., & Sutton, M. J. (1998). Literature-based ESL for secondary school students. *TESOL Journal, 7*(5), 19–23.

This article describes how two teachers used literature-based instruction. The article states some advantages to the approach: It promotes literacy development, provides language models, and integrates language skills. The authors go on to explain why content-based instruction (CBI) is effective and suggest how it might be used in a middle school using historical fiction and in high school in a theme-based unit. They note the many advantages of using literature with ESL students and provide a list of multicultural literature that might be used with beginning, intermediate, and advanced students.

Dixon, C., & Nessel, D. (1990). *Language experience approach to reading and writing: LEA for ESL*. Hayward, CA: Alemany Press.

The book presents a clear and thorough discussion of the language-experience approach for English language learners, both readers and writers. It is particularly valuable because it contains views of how to use the approach with students at different developmental levels. It also contains a good example of one teacher's class in which language experience is being used.

Eskey, D. (2002). Reading and the teaching of L2 reading. *TESOL Journal, 11*(1), 5–9.

This article is informative, playful, and insightful. David Eskey pulls from researcher and practitioner information that makes clear the reading process for both first and second language readers. The article contains information, graphics, and humor that teachers will want to use in their own classrooms. The article illustrates Eskey's knowledge and understanding of both first and second language research and practice.

Kamil, M. L., Mosenthal, P., Pearson, P. D., & Barr, R. (Eds.). (2000). *Handbook of reading research: Vol. III*. Mahwah, NJ: Erlbaum.

The Handbook has for years been one of the books every reading teacher should have on his or her bookshelf. While most chapters focus on first language reading, there are articles also on second language reading, international issues in reading, and multicultural perspectives on reading policy. The book starts with five articles on reading research around the world: Australia and Aotearoa/New Zealand, United Kingdom, Central and Eastern Europe, Latin America, and the United States. Among the 47 chapters written by experts are 3 valuable ones for ELL teachers: "Second Language Reading as a Case Study of Reading Scholarship in the 20th Century" by Elizabeth B. Bernhardt; "Bilingual Children's Reading" by Georgia Earnest Garcia; and a "Multicultural Perspective on Policies for Improving Literacy Achievement: Equity and Excellence" by Kathryn H. Au.

Tierney, R., & Readence, J. (Eds.). (2000). *Reading strategies and practices: A compendium* (5th ed.). Boston: Allyn and Bacon.

This book contains everything you wanted to know about reading instruction. Although it is not aimed specifically at second language learners, you can adapt most of the strategies for use with your English learners. More than 60 strategies offer ways to assist response to literature and drama, ways to build vocabulary, approaches to cooperative learning, and teaching comprehension. This is the best book of its kind.

Urquhart, S., & Weir, C. (1998). *Reading in a second language: Process, product and practice.* London: Longman.

The authors do a thorough job of discussing research and practice in second language reading. They discuss oral language and its relationship to reading and writing, different theories of reading, the difficulties of testing and teaching reading comprehension; and the teaching of reading among other topics. The reference section alone is worth the price of the book.

Activities

1. Assess a student in reading using a reading miscue inventory or a running record. List the student's specific strengths and weaknesses (e.g., What are the student's decoding skills when reading in context? What is the level of comprehension?). Finally, discuss the kind of program, procedures, or strategies you would suggest for the student. What are the student's strengths that you can build on? For example, if the student is strong in listening comprehension, you may want to ask him or her to read along with taped stories to help develop automaticity.

2. Observe a class with students working in literature response groups. What are the advantages of creating literature response groups? Are there any disadvantages with which a teacher needs to be concerned? What would you do differently from the classroom you observed in order to implement literature response groups? Do you think there are times when teacher-directed discussions are more appropriate than literature response groups? When? Why?

3. Develop a readers' theater script for a story in elementary or secondary school, and discuss how you would use readers' theater. Observe how drama is used in the classrooms you visit: What does drama add to students' abilities to respond to literature? How would you use readers' theater differently for older and younger students? For example, would you have older students develop their own scripts? What other dramatic activities would you use with English learners who have limited proficiency versus

intermediate proficiency? How can you be assured that all of your students are involved in dramatic activities?

4. Working with a student who is limited in English proficiency, develop a series of language experience lessons. How does the student, within the context of language experience, develop as a reader over time? Does the student seem more or less enthusiastic about reading than a student who has been immersed in literature only? What are some of the shortcomings of a literature-based or language-experience approach to teaching reading? For example, how rich will students' English be if they are only reading from one another's language experience stories? Is it important to introduce patterned stories and other stories to students early on as they are learning to read? Why?

5. Observe several classrooms in which teachers feel that literature is central to students' learning to read. What are the variations in the ways different teachers implement literature programs? What are the views of the teachers, stated or unstated, toward literature study? What role does the teacher play—expert, facilitator, or equal participant in exploring literature? What effect do these different views of literature study have on the students' response to literature? What effect do these views have on students' enthusiasm for reading or independence in reading? Do students choose to read when given free time?

313

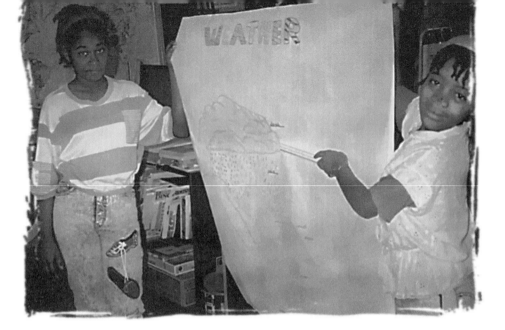

CONTENT READING AND WRITING: PREREADING AND DURING READING

In this chapter and Chapter 9, we discuss content-area reading and writing, that is, reading and writing in social science, science, mathematics, English, and other subject areas. We address the following questions:

1. What does research tell us about content instruction for English learners?
2. What characteristics of narrative and expository text structure are useful for students to know and why?
3. What kinds of classroom contexts and teaching strategies can assist students to use reading and writing in English as a learning tool?
4. How can teachers prepare students to read and monitor their own comprehension while reading?

The sea is a radiant water galaxy. It's a world of its own in a special way. Under its foam crested surface, there exists a universe of plant and animal life. With the tiniest microscopic beings to the most humungus creature that ever lived, the sea is alive!

Thus opens *Our Friends in the Water* (Kids of Room 14, 1979), a delightfully written and informative 79-page book on marine mammals: sea otters, whales, dolphins, seals, sea lions, walrus, manatees, and dugongs. What's different about this book is that it was conceived, written, and illustrated entirely by a fourth/fifth-grade class. It's a book by kids for kids! The work that went into this book is remarkable. The reverent wonder expressed in the opening paragraph is unmistakable. How did it all come about?

As explained by the children, the class expressed curiosity about marine mammals, and their teacher, Lynda Chittenden (1982), followed their wonder by facilitating a yearlong research project that culminated in the delightful publication. Living near the Pacific coast, the class was able to take a number of field trips. They visited a seal rookery, spent two days watching gray whales migrate south, and observed dolphins in training. They also put their imaginations to work to sense from within what it would be like to live as a marine animal in the water. One child's conclusion: "Today I learned how important it is to have blubber. Our class went swimming in a 40 degree pool. I did learn that I COULD swim in that temperature. But, I couldn't even breathe the first time I jumped in. Gradually I got better. I could swim two laps without flippers. But I still don't see how a whale could live in 33 degree water, even with layers and layers of blubber" (Steig Johnson's learning log quoted in *Our Friends in the Water,* Kids of Room 14, 1979, p. 16).

Sparked initially by general interest, the class was spurred on by the fascinating information that began to accumulate. The more they found out, the more they wanted to know. Manatees and dugongs, it seems, were the animals that gave rise to the mermaid legend and were probably what Christopher Columbus was referring to in his diary when he mentioned sighting "three mermaids" in the Caribbean! Thus engaged in the pursuit of knowledge, the class read books, invited marine mammal experts to visit their class, and wrote in learning logs to keep track of their growing body of knowledge. Finally, they organized their findings and put them all together in seven coauthored chapters that tell "with facts, stories, pictures, poems and dreams the lives of most marine mammals from a kid's point of view" (Kids of Room 14, 1979, Preface, p. 9).

We share this extended example with you because it illustrates what we consider the epitome of good learning and teaching. The Kids of Room 14, through their project, enlighten us as to the possibilities and potentials of students who take charge of their own learning with the facilitative guidance of an excellent teacher.

Let us take a look at the project in terms of what it might offer English learners. As we do so, we want to illustrate that most of what you or I readily recognize as excellent teaching with first language speakers incorporates strategies that facilitate optimal learning for English learners as well. The key to success lies with finding ways for all students to participate and contribute to the learning enterprise, even if their English language competence is limited.

The marine mammals project, the type of project that could be used at all grade levels, provided several avenues of learning that we consider highly beneficial to English learners. First, the project emerged from the expressed interests of the students. Thus, it built on prior knowledge and, more important, on the curiosity and concerns of the students themselves. Second, the teacher and the class were able to generate a variety of ideas leading to field trips, providing direct experiences for learning about marine mammals. Third, the teacher herself guided students in processing and keeping track of the information they acquired through oral class discussions, individual written learning logs, and posing questions to further the learning process. Finally, when the class decided to put their findings and illustrations into a book, each chapter was written collaboratively by pairs or small groups of students. Students used process writing with peer response groups to elaborate and refine their writing, keeping in mind the question: "Will other students who have not had the same experiences understand everything we've learned about these most wondrous of animals?" To complement the text, some students made line drawings to illustrate the chapters. Poems and song lyrics were added from student journals and learning logs, giving depth of feeling to the book's overall informational message. In other words, a variety of writing and drawing was published, accommodating individual strengths. Within this type of project, all students can contribute, native and non-native English speakers alike. The theme cycle approach used by this teacher helped the students learn to select and organize the materials they needed in order to synthesize information for themselves and others and, most important, to become independent learners.

In summary, the marine mammals project incorporated six elements that create optimal content learning for English language learners:

1. Meaning and Purpose: The topic was meaningful to the students; they selected it and helped shape its development.
2. Prior Knowledge: Learning was built on prior knowledge and direct experience such as field trips.
3. Integration of Opportunities to Use Language and Literacy for Learning Purposes: Oral and written language were used to acquire knowledge and present it to others.
4. Scaffolding for Support: Scaffolds were provided, including group work, process writing, and direct experiences for learning.
5. Collaboration: Students collaborated to build knowledge and organize it for summarizing in a book.
6. Variety: Variety was built in at every step, with oral language, reading, writing, field trips, class discussions, guest speakers, and other avenues of learning provided.

Our Friends in the Water provides a good example of **Content-Based Instruction (CBI)** (Anderson, 1999; Snow, 2001), which integrates language learning opportunities with content instruction. The teacher provides multiple opportunities for extensive reading, student choice, and collaboration in projects (Stoller, 2002). Students are learning language with a great deal of comprehensible input as well as output (Krashen, 1982; Swain, 1985). Among the advantages of CBI are: (1) CBI employs English at a comprehensible level, facilitating understanding of subject matter and building language skills simultaneously; (2) CBI often makes use of authentic tasks centered around authentic material, increasing student engagement; and (3) CBI helps students learn appropriate grade-level content, thus providing a bridge to mainstream classes (Custodio & Sutton, 1998). You will find examples of CBI throughout this book.

An important assumption that we make in this book is that all language skills—listening, speaking, reading, and writing—are best developed when students are using those skills to achieve communication goals that are interesting and meaningful to them. This assumption holds true for both first and second language development. When students are involved in projects such as the marine mammals study, they integrate and practice an astounding number of important social, linguistic, and academic skills related to their own learning: They pose questions; gather data through reading, interviewing, and direct experience; discuss findings with peers; evaluate formats for presenting findings; organize and summarize information for oral, written, and multimedia presentation; and so on. Through the integrated use of these skills, further social, linguistic, and academic development takes place. Our concern with English language learners is to help them participate fully while stretching their language and literacy performance to their next developmental level.

In this chapter, then, we focus on assisting English learners in reading and writing longer, more complex material that becomes increasingly predominant in the upper-elementary grades, middle school, and high school.

By our definition, English learners who are reading and writing longer, more complex pieces in English are intermediate or advanced in English language proficiency. For these students, we offer a wide variety of strategies, scaffolds for support, to assist them as they pursue complex information and ideas relevant to their interests and purposes. The strategies may be used in conjunction with theme cycles or units or with single subject instruction in science, social studies, literature, or any other area of study. As the teacher, you may select from the strategies, as needed, to help an individual student, a small group, or the whole class.

If you have non-English speakers or beginners in your class, they are not likely to be reading and writing long, complex English stories or essays. Nonetheless, it is important to involve them as much as possible in your instruction, because their participation will promote both social integration and second language development—top priorities for newcomers. Sheltering your instruction will improve beginners' chances of understanding the general ideas of your instruction and will facilitate language development. However, for older beginners, sheltering alone will not provide full access to the complex information taught in the upper grades. Supplementary instruction in the students' primary language may be needed to preview and review complex concepts you are

317

> **INTERNET RESOURCE:** You might use the Peace Corps site and search "culture" http://www.peacecorps.gov/index.cfm to search for information and lesson plans on culture. After using the site and viewing its resources, create a lesson in which students can select a culture they are interested in and use the Peace Corps site to find information. Students could use K-W-L, or you might create your own format for their completion of the search. Our companion website has many other activities you might also explore: www.ablongman.com/peregoy4e.

covering in class. As we present various strategies in this chapter, we will highlight ways to involve beginners in your day-to-day instruction.

This chapter offers strategies you may select *before* and *during* reading to promote reading comprehension as well as strategies that integrate writing into the process of academic learning. First, however, we provide background information on key issues related to helping students read and write longer, more complex pieces as part of their academic learning. In particular, we review the concept of sheltered instruction (SDAIE), describe classroom applications of research on text structure and metacognition, and discuss ways to estimate the difficulty of a text for particular students.

318

WHAT DOES RESEARCH TELL US ABOUT READING AND WRITING ACROSS THE CURRICULUM FOR ENGLISH LANGUAGE LEARNERS?

As students move beyond the primary grades, they are expected to read and write about increasingly complex topics in increasingly sophisticated ways. In particular, they must move beyond pattern books and simpler stories to longer literary works and expository prose found in textbooks, magazine articles, encyclopedias, and newspapers. All students, including English language learners, can benefit from assistance in dealing with expository texts and complex literature, both in reading and in writing (Singer & Donlan, 1989). In addition, English learners may need assistance related to their English language knowledge (O'Malley & Chamot, 1990).

Research is limited on second language students' abilities to read, write, and learn from either expository or narrative texts. Instead, most research and discussion falls under the broader category of sheltered English instruction or SDAIE—instruction designed to be understandable to students with limited English proficiency and also appropriate to the students' ages and academic levels (Northcutt & Watson, 1986; Schifini, 1985). As noted earlier, sheltered instruction serves two purposes: (1) subject matter learning and (2) second language development related to academic work. In other words, sheltered instruction is both comprehensible and cognitively demanding in that content is not "watered down." Without primary language instruction, this goal is not easy to achieve when students arrive in the upper-elementary grades, middle school, or high school. However, for students with an intermediate knowledge of English, sheltered English instruction can be effective.

Sheltered instruction aims to facilitate both language and subject matter learning by building on students' prior knowledge, making use of concrete materials and direct experiences, creating opportunities for students to collaborate on learning tasks, and providing explicit strategies to help students use oral and written language for learning (Chamot & O'Malley, 1986). As you can see, our criteria for teaching English learners include all of these features. To these we add the use of thematically organized instruction, which provides a single, meaningful theme to which all reading, writing, and other learning efforts relate. However, sheltered instruction may be successfully implemented in traditional, single subject areas such as mathematics, science, and social studies (Chamot & O'Malley, 1986, 1992; Crandall, 1987; Northcutt & Watson, 1986; Schifini, 1985). In developing instruction, second language acquisition experts typically incorporate learning strategies that have proven successful with first language students, modified to meet the needs of English learners according to their English language proficiency and prior experience.

BACKGROUND INFORMATION ON STUDENTS' INTERACTIONS WITH TEXTS

Because this chapter focuses on helping students read longer, more complex texts, this section presents background information on some characteristics of longer texts and ways readers interact with them. We present research and theory on (1) *aesthetic* and *efferent* stances toward a text, (2) text structure in relation to comprehension and composition, and (3) metacognition. In addition, we discuss how to match students with texts they must use for academic purposes. These are rather complex topics, but they are important because they provide the basis for the reading and writing strategies recommended later.

Aesthetic and Efferent Interactions with Texts

Louise Rosenblatt, in presenting her transactional view of literature response, discusses two attitudes or stances readers may take when reading: efferent and aesthetic (Rosenblatt, 1978, 1984). **Efferent** comes from the Latin word *effere*, meaning "to carry away." When the reader takes an efferent stance toward a text, the central purpose is to carry away information, and this is what we commonly do with expository texts. When we read an article or essay, for example, our major concern is to carry away the information or argument the author is presenting. Rosenblatt defines **aesthetic reading** as aimed at experiencing or feeling a piece of writing. Readers usually set aesthetic purposes when reading literary texts; they are interested in the problems faced by the characters, in the way characters deal with the problems, and in identifying with the characters and situations of a story. Their primary concern is not to carry away information about a particular type of government or about biology, though that may occur.

To illustrate the two purposes, Rosenblatt offers a "pure" example of efferent reading: a mother reading the antidote on a bottle of poison after her child has swallowed from the bottle. The mother's only concern is carrying away the information that will save her child. To illustrate the aesthetic purpose, Rosenblatt suggests we imagine a father reading to his son from *Alice in Wonderland*. When the rabbit says, "I'm late, I'm late, for a very important date," the boy objects, "Rabbits can't tell time and rabbits can't talk." The father replies, "They do in this story!" The boy missed the aesthetic purpose of the story, taking instead an efferent stance, in which the textual information contradicted his knowledge of the real world (Rosenblatt, 1983). These purposes do not mean that a reader cannot gain aesthetic experiences from an essay or that a reader cannot carry away specific information from a story. They simply mean that the primary stance when reading essays and narratives is often different. As John Dewey once said, "Just because a China teacup is beautiful does not mean that it cannot have the pragmatic purpose of carrying tea" (Rosenblatt, 1983).

One of the first things readers must do when approaching a text is to know whether they are to take a largely aesthetic or efferent stance. As the teacher, you can facilitate student success with reading by stating explicitly what you expect students to gain from a text and what you want them to do with what they have read. This holds true for narrative as well as expository texts, whether the stance is aesthetic or efferent. Theme cycles offer the advantage that students set the purpose themselves and select written materials accordingly, with teacher guidance.

Effects of Text Structure on Comprehension and Memory

An important feature of longer, more complex expository texts is their organization or sequencing of ideas and arguments, often referred to as **text structure.** One familiar expository text structure frequently found in textbooks is the **attributive, or enumerative,** pattern, which states a main idea and then lists supporting details. In the attributive structure, words such as *first, second,* and *third* typically signal the organization of the list, and words such as *in addition, also,* and *moreover* may tie the list together. Three other expository text structures include **compare/contrast, problem/solution,** and **cause/effect.** All three of these differ from the basic narrative structure summarized by the someone/wants/but/so narrative sequence discussed in Chapter 7. These ways of organizing information and ideas are standard conventions that have evolved and become accepted as appropriate for English (Connor & Kaplan, 1987). There are other ways to structure arguments and ideas; in fact, what is considered appropriate text structure in other languages may differ from the patterns to which we are accustomed in English (Chu, Swaffer, & Charney, 2002). Our discussion focuses on English.

Awareness of text structure is important because research indicates that readers use their knowledge of text structure to store, retrieve, and summarize infor-

320

mation they have read (Meyer, Brandt, & Bluth, 1980). In other words, text organization has a profound effect on comprehension and memory (Bartlett, 1978; Meyer, Brandt, & Bluth, 1980). As students gain familiarity with text structure patterns like compare/contrast or problem/solution through reading and writing, the patterns form templates that permit predictions of the words and ideas to come, thereby facilitating comprehension. The template also helps students remember the information in the text by providing a conceptual net for keeping the information in mind. Moreover, when students become aware of different text structure patterns, they can use them to structure their writing. Helping students become aware of text structure will help them become more effective in both reading and writing. Study the structures in Figures 8.1 and 8.2 and determine what the structure *alone* can tell you about the content.

If you have had experience with cooking or baking, you probably identified Figure 8.1 as a recipe structure. You would also be able to guess that the title goes on the top line of the recipe, that ingredients go after the numbers, and that an explanation of how to do the recipe follows. If you had only the title, such as Chocolate Cake, you could guess even more based on the structure.

The structure in Figure 8.2 represents a business letter. Because you probably identified the structure, you know that the date goes on the upper right side, that the name and address are on the upper left, that the addressee's name follows, that the content is next, and that the person's signature is last. You can also guess that the tone of the letter will be formal.

These two examples illustrate how much information we can derive from structure alone. When we teach students the structure of our textbooks or any of

321

FIGURE 8.1   Structure Outline

_____

_____

_____

_____

_____

_____:

_____

_____

_____

_____

_____

_____

_____

_____

_____

_____

_____

_____

_____

322

FIGURE 8.2   Structure Outline 2

the readings we are using, we assist them with both understanding and remembering what they have read. Similarly, if students recognize a compare/contrast structure, they can begin to look for things that are alike and things that are different about a topic; in other words, knowledge of text structure can help us predict what will come in a text, monitor whether we are getting the information, and help us remember what we have read.

Although there are some pure forms of structure in texts, such as compare/contrast, an enumerative (list) pattern, and cause/effect, many texts use a combination of these forms. Thus we suggest that you determine and teach explicitly the structure of your own textbooks to your students. We also believe that probably the best strategies for teaching text structures are visual/spatial strategies. For example, you might use a structured overview (see Figures 8.7 and 8.8) for a text organized like a list, a Venn diagram for a compare/contrast structure, or a map for combinations of structures or for less identifiable structures. These visual/spatial strategies are discussed in detail in this chapter and in Chapter 9.

As you familiarize yourself with different text structures, you may call students' attention to the organizational patterns of their texts, thereby helping them read and remember more efficiently. Some research suggests that different cultures structure texts in rather different ways (Connor & Kaplan, 1987; Hinds, 1983a, b). Therefore, explicit explanations regarding the conventions of English text structure may be important for older English language learners who have reached substantial literacy development in their home language prior to immigration. In fact, explicit instruction on text structure is apt to be beneficial for most students, whether native or non-native English speakers.

Cohesive Ties/Signal Words. Another important aspect of text organization is the use of signal words and phrases, called **cohesive ties,** that indicate how arguments and ideas relate within paragraphs and across paragraphs and larger sections of text. Cohesive ties act as signposts to help the reader navigate the text. One way they help is by pointing out the overall structure of a text. For example, words such as *first, second,* and *third* signal to the reader that the author is providing sequenced ideas of similar weight to support a main idea. *Moreover* and *in addition* indicate equal ideas, whereas *nevertheless* and *nonetheless* indicate minimization or negation of previous statements (Halliday, 1975). Table 8.1 categorizes several cohesive ties according to their signpost function: time order, additive, cause/effect, conclusive, and minimization or negation of previous information.

Some cohesive ties can be very difficult for English learners to understand and use appropriately because of their abstract quality (Goldman & Murray, 1989, 1992). After all, cohesive ties do not refer to objects, people, actions, or concepts. Instead, they convey relationships between complex ideas expressed in phrases and clauses. To get a feeling for the difficulty they may present, try defining a few for yourself, such as *nevertheless, moreover,* and *notwithstanding.* Other cohesive ties are more concrete in meaning, such as *first, second, third,* and *finally.* One way to help older students comprehend cohesive ties is to provide a bilingual dictionary so that they can find corresponding terms in their native language. This solution is limited, however, because relational words often do not translate directly into other languages. However, dictionary translations provide one way to start. A more useful approach is to show students how to use cohesive ties in their own writing. In this way the student offers the meaning, and you help the student convey that meaning effectively through cohesive ties.

Students can use their knowledge of cohesive ties together with their knowledge of text structure to assist them in comprehending and remembering the

323

TABLE 8.1   Cohesive Ties

Time/Order	Additive	Cause/Effect	Conclusive	Changing
soon	in addition	as a result	consequently	nonetheless
when	moreover	because	in summary	despite
finally	also	since	therefore	however

information in a text. With these basic structures in mind, students will be ready for strategies such as mapping and DR-TA, which will assist them with learning from texts. Moreover, the same knowledge of text structure assists students with writing expository prose. By learning how authors organize information, students can begin exploring compare/contrast, list structures, cause/effect, and other structures in their own writing. Similarly, they can begin to use the same cohesive ties good writers use as signposts to guide their readers.

Headings and Subheadings. Headings and subheadings are another aspect of text structure that students can use to become more proficient readers. For example, students can use headings and subheadings to preview a text to gain a general sense of its content. Students can read headings to assist them in making predictions about the content of a text. Research indicates that middle school and older students often ignore headings entirely. However, students can enhance their comprehension by reading and using headings and subheadings (Bartlett, 1978). Thus, you will want to explain their usefulness to your students.

Teaching Text Structure: One Classroom. In teaching **text structure** for reading and writing, one teacher we know, Leticia Alvarez, places a drawing of a train, such as the one in Figure 8.3, on her bulletin board. Leticia explains that one

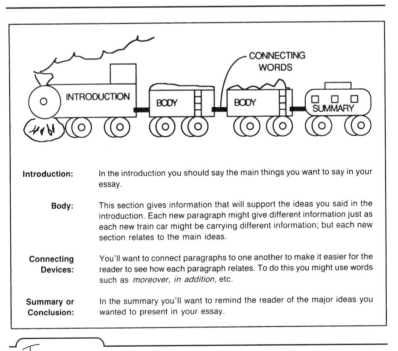

Introduction:	In the introduction you should say the main things you want to say in your essay.
Body:	This section gives information that will support the ideas you said in the introduction. Each new paragraph might give different information just as each new train car might be carrying different information; but each new section relates to the main ideas.
Connecting Devices:	You'll want to connect paragraphs to one another to make it easier for the reader to see how each paragraph relates. To do this you might use words such as *moreover, in addition,* etc.
Summary or Conclusion:	In the summary you'll want to remind the reader of the major ideas you wanted to present in your essay.

*F*IGURE 8.3   **Relating Essay Organization to a Train**

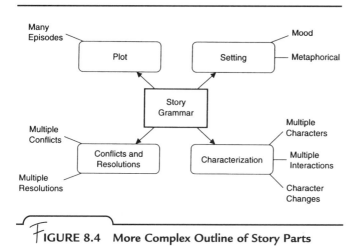

FIGURE 8.4   More Complex Outline of Story Parts

good structure for an essay is like a train. Each section of the train stands for an important part of the essay. For example, the engine of the train knows where it is going, just as the first paragraph of an essay tells the reader where the essay is going. The engine is linked to the car behind it, just as signal words or cohesive ties help link one paragraph to another in an essay. Similarly, each car in the train carries new cargo just as each new paragraph in an essay carries new information. Finally, the caboose in a train looks toward where we've been, just as the final paragraph in an essay tells readers where they have been. We have heard students refer to the train analogy while discussing one another's compositions, and we have heard them talk about the words they will use to link one paragraph to another. In a very concrete way, Leticia has taught her students how to develop very sophisticated essays. Later, she may teach them other structures to use for both reading and writing.

Literary Structure

As students progress through school, the stories they read will be longer and more complex than the patterned books and short narratives they encountered early on. Thus, a more sophisticated knowledge of literary structure may benefit students in understanding and remembering narratives. In Chapter 7, we shared the someone/wants/but/so outline as a simple structure young students could use to understand and retell simple stories, but a more detailed way to display narrative content becomes appropriate as students begin to read more complex stories (Boyle & Peregoy, 1991; Buckley & Boyle, 1981; Webster, 1998). The map in Figure 8.4 provides a more sophisticated template for summarizing the literary elements of such stories.

Discussion of Story Elements. To add depth to English learners' appreciation of literature, they need to know the basic elements of most stories: the setting, characters, conflict, and denouement. The **setting** is simply where the action takes place. In more complex narratives, the setting may change often and may even carry symbolic meaning such as good or evil. The **characters** (protagonists) are usually people or animals in the story. In longer narratives characters have time to develop and change, whereas in short stories characters often remain static. Thus, in longer stories we may ask students to look for changes made by characters. The **conflict** or problem usually consists of a situation the character is trying to resolve. In short narratives there is often only one conflict, but in longer narratives there may be many conflicts and problems to be solved. The solution or **dénouement** consists of the way the situation is resolved.

Metacognition and Learning from Text

Metacognition means thinking about thinking. In research on comprehension and problem solving, metacognition refers to the act of reflecting on one's own thought processes so as to consciously guide the outcome. In reading, metacognition includes the ability to monitor one's own reading processes, as well as the ability to take strategic steps to remedy the situation when one's reading does not make sense. Readers need to be aware of the demands of a reading task in order to make choices about the strategies they will use (Oxford, 2003). Metacognition is knowing when and how to use strategies to assist in comprehension and composition (Baker & Brown, 1984).

The strategies students need to know in studying texts, described in detail later, involve both retrieval and comprehension of information and remedying problems they may have with understanding texts. Specifically, students need to use strategies to preview texts, to ask questions, to preview headings and subheadings, and to organize information for memory. In addition, students need self-monitoring strategies to help them when they are having problems with achieving their goals in reading. These self-monitoring strategies include setting a purpose for reading, evaluating whether the purpose is being met, and revising goals or remediating their own interactions with texts. For example, students need to recognize that they may have to read a math text more slowly than a narrative text or that they need to recognize when they are not understanding a text. In the last decade there has been a great deal of concentration on the direct teaching of metacognitive strategies to help students recognize text structures, ask questions of texts, and recall information (Boyle & Peregoy, 1991; Nolte & Singer, 1985; Palincsar & Brown, 1984; Ruddell & Boyle, 1984, 1989).

Matching Students and Texts

In any class, students vary in their ability to read academic material independently. It is axiomatic among educators that variation among students increases with each grade level. Such variation is further accentuated when students vary in English language proficiency. Whether you are collecting materials for theme cycles or teaching a standardized curriculum, it is important to obtain a variety of resources to accommodate varying levels of reading ability and English language proficiency. For example, if your class is studying European exploration of the New World, it is important to supplement any textbook you may use with filmstrips, audiocassettes, and short, simple, illustrated articles on exploration of the New World. In addition, this topic calls for the use of maps, perhaps student-made, to post on the bulletin board. The supplementary materials offer a variety of ways for students to access information on the topic. In addition, they build background knowledge that may facilitate students' success in reading more difficult material.

One way to match students with texts, then, is to allow them to select from materials of varying difficulty. You will want to be available to encourage them to try more challenging texts when appropriate. At times, you may want to evaluate directly how your students handle written material from a textbook. **Readability formulas** will give a grade level for an expository text you are using; but because readability formulas are simply based on sentence and word length, they do not give an accurate measure of your students' ability to read a specific text. Similarly, we do not recommend using a **cloze procedure,** in which words are systematically left out of a text and the student tries to replace them; we find that the cloze procedure is extremely frustrating for second language learners and others and is not very predictive either. We recommend that you try the following procedure, the **group reading inventory (GRI),** if you want to get valid information about your students' ability to read your specific text.

Evaluating Students' Interaction with Text Using the Group Reading Inventory (GRI)

The group reading inventory (GRI) (Vacca & Vacca, 1989) allows you to evaluate students' reading based on your text and the kinds of assignments you require. Though intended for group administration, the GRI can also be adapted for individuals. The GRI has the advantage of assessing students on a typical reading of your text and allowing you to get immediate information on their interactions with your text. This information can be used to guide you in adapting your use of the text so that all students can be successful.

The first step in developing a group reading inventory is to choose a passage similar in content, length, and complexity to the readings you may require of your class. Next, select the key concepts you would want students to know after reading the passage. Determine the reading skill required to understand each concept. For example, the skill might be understanding vocabulary in context or identification of a main idea and its supporting details. Similarly, the skill might be to understand a cause/effect relationship or a compare/contrast relationship. Or you may want students to understand a graph or chart that illustrates an important concept in the selection you are using. Finally, make up a GRI based on the concepts and skills you have identified. An example of some concepts from a reading on the American Civil War and the derived GRI is presented in Figures 8.5 and 8.6.

The brief example of a GRI in Figures 8.5 and 8.6 is based on the key concepts identified in a chapter. In conjunction with your GRI, you might also ask students to outline the information in the chapter, using the headings and subheadings, or to write a short summary of the pages read. When the students have completed their GRI, you can evaluate their ability to interact with your text. You can determine how much time needs to be spent in discussing vocabulary terms or in modeling ways to determine main ideas using headings and subheadings. The GRI has the added advantage of being a study guide that students can use to develop purpose and monitor their own comprehension of the reading tasks in your class; it provides a scaffold for their reading. We recommend giving GRIs throughout the year as an ongoing informal evaluation procedure.

Concepts	Reading Skills
1. The North is industrialized and the South is agrarian	Compare/contrast the two sides Details of differences
2. Enumeration of differences from wars of the past	Details of differences Vocabulary terms
3. Involvement of different states in the war	Reading a chart and graph Extracting details and major ideas

FIGURE 8.5   Identified Concepts and Their Related Skills

Directions for Students: Read pages 32–37 in your book and answer the following questions:

Word Meanings: Briefly define or explain the meaning of the following words used in pages 32–37: (1) emancipation, (2) writ of habeas corpus, (3) border states, (4) blockade.

Comprehension—Compare/Contrast Relationships: Read pages 35–36 and answer the following questions:
1. How was the war different from wars of the past?
2. How were the life styles of the South and North different?
3. What advantages did the North have over the South in the war?
4. What states were involved on the North and South sides? Compare and contrast why the states *were* involved.

Details: Find the information for the following questions in pages 35–36:
1. Identify three labor-saving devices that helped make the North more wealthy than the South.
2. Give two examples of the Southern view of slavery.

FIGURE 8.6   Sample GRI Based on the Civil War

Evaluating Your Own Interaction with One Text. At this point, we would like you to try a brief exercise to evaluate your own efferent reading processes. Read the following passage and answer the questions following the passage without referring to the text (Right to Read Conference, 1972):

The Echmiadzin is a monastery in the Armenian S.S.R., in 40" 12' N., 44" 19' E., the seat of the Catholicus or primate of the Armenian church. It is situated close to the village of Vagarshapat, in the plain of the Aras, 2,840 ft. above the sea, 12 mi. west of Erivan and 40 mi. north of Mount Ararat. The monastery comprises a complex of buildings, surrounded by brick walls 30 ft. high, which with their loopholes and towers present the appearance of a fortress. Its architectural character has been considerably impaired by additions and alterations in modern Russian style.

On the western side of the quadrangle is the residence of the primate, on the south, the refectory (1730–35), on the east the lodgings for the monks, and on the north the cells. The cathedral is a small but fine cruciform building with a Byzantine cupola at the intersection. Its foundation is ascribed to St. Gregory the Illuminator in 302.

Of special interest is the porch, built of red porphyry and profusely adorned with sculptured designs somewhat of a Gothic character. The interior is decorated with Persian frescoes of flowers, birds, and scrollwork. It is here that the primate confers episcopal consecration by the sacred hand (relic) of St. Gregory; and here every seven years he prepares the holy oil which is to be used throughout the churches of the Armenian communion. Outside the main entrance are the alabaster tombs of the primates, Alexander I (1714), Alexander II (1755), Daniel (1806), and Narses (1857), and a white marble monument erected by the English East India company to mark the resting place of Sir John Macdonald Kinneir, who died at Tabriz in 1830 while on an embassy to the Persian court.

Questions to Be Answered without Referring to the Text:

1. What direction is Mount Ararat from the monastery?
2. What was the avocation of St. Gregory?
3. What are the five types of architecture mentioned in the passage?

Answers: 1. Southeast; 2. architect; 3. Romanesque, Gothic, Byzantine, modern Russian, Persian.

Did you answer correctly? If not, it may be because you did not know why you were reading the passage. If students don't know why they are reading a passage, they will not monitor their understanding appropriately, and they may remember unimportant details rather than key information. One of the ways teachers prepare students to read texts is by clarifying the purpose, pointing out what students must do with the information. For example, if we had asked you to read the questions prior to reading the passage, your purpose would have been clearly focused. Once students are prepared for a passage, they are ready to assess their own interactions with the text based on their purpose for reading. Finally, they will be able to organize key information for memory.

329

In summary, in this section we have discussed current theory and research that informs teaching decisions when students must read and learn from longer, more complex texts, both literary and expository. We described the difference between efferent and aesthetic stances toward a text; elaborated on a variety of narrative and expository text structures; explained how awareness of text structure facilitates effective reading and writing; and defined metacognition in relationship to students' monitoring and evaluating their own reading and writing. In addition, we discussed issues related to matching students and texts to maximize learning. All of these discussions provide the theoretical and practical underpinnings for the reading and writing strategies presented next.

STRATEGIES TO PROMOTE READING COMPREHENSION

Many students read texts passively, waiting for information to present and organize itself for them. Proficient readers, however, know what they are looking for, engage their background knowledge while reading, and monitor achievement based on their purpose (Boyle & Peregoy, 1991; Pearson & Johnson, 1978; Ruddell & Boyle, 1989). In other words, they are thoughtful about reading, using metacognitive processes every step of the way. Figure 8.7 depicts a variety of strategies to help students to become actively self-aware and proficient when reading for academic purposes. The strategies are grouped according to whether they

330

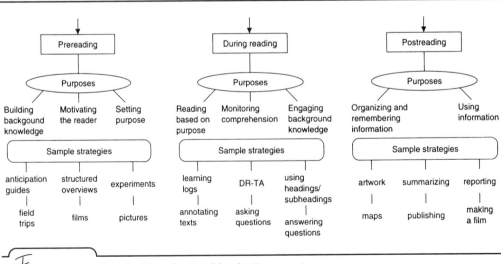

FIGURE 8.7   Model of Reading/Writing in Content Areas

are to be used before students read a text, during reading, or after reading. In the prereading phase, a purpose for reading is established and background knowledge is developed to enhance comprehension; during reading, readers monitor their comprehension based on purpose by asking questions of the text; in the postreading phase, students boost their memory through writing and organizing information. During all three phases, students are encouraged to be metacognitively aware of their reading. In addition, they are taught to use text structure to assist comprehension. Because vocabulary plays a key role in reading comprehension, vocabulary strategies are offered for all three phases.

In our previous chapters, we discussed different strategies for beginning and intermediate English language learners. For this chapter and the next one we drop this distinction, because the strategies used for both groups are virtually the same. This is not to say that beginning and intermediate English learners will benefit equally from the same instruction. In fact, the strategies generally require intermediate to advanced English language proficiency for students to participate fully and learn. However, if you have beginning English learners in your class, you can accommodate them in a variety of ways that will promote both language development and content learning. One way is to provide supplementary texts of varying difficulty along with audiovisual materials. Another way to accommodate beginners is to spend more time on a particular strategy or to combine strategies. Remember to choose strategies that (1) make use of pictures, graphs, dramatization, and other paralinguistic cues to meaning and (2) incorporate peer support to help beginners glean information from texts. These criteria ensure integration and involvement of newcomers. In addition, you may consider arranging assistance in the primary language from peers, paraprofessionals, and others, including yourself, if you speak the language. Primary language support for beginners has numerous benefits for communication, learning, and social-emotional adjustment.

PREREADING STRATEGIES: DEVELOPING MOTIVATION, PURPOSE, AND BACKGROUND KNOWLEDGE

The strategies we describe for the prereading phase serve several purposes. First, they motivate student interest and build background knowledge on the topic of the text the students are to read. Students may have little or no knowledge of the text topic, or they may have misconceptions about the topic that can be clarified during the prereading phase. In this way, students are better prepared to read an assigned or self-selected text (Hawkes & Schell, 1987; Herber, 1978). Second, during the prereading phase, students clarify their purpose for reading a particular text. If you have assigned the reading, you'll want to explain to your students why you have selected the material, what you expect them to gain from it, and what they are to do with the information later. In theme cycles, your students have selected their own purpose and already have in mind why they are seeking certain information. The third purpose of prereading strategies is to help students gain a general idea of the text's organization and content by perusing the headings, subheadings, table of contents, and so forth.

Direct and concrete experiences facilitate learning for anyone but are essential for English learners. Thus, if we are trying to teach about whales, the best way would be to visit the ocean when whales are present. If that is not possible, we could show a film about whales or make use of photographs and pictures. All of these are concrete experiences that enhance students' understanding of their reading about whales. The most important thing to give them, however, is a chance to develop their knowledge of a topic before they read about it, through such activities as class discussions, field trips, and films.

Teacher Talk: Making Purposes Clear

Were you ever in a class when the bell rang, and everybody was leaving, and the teacher shouted out, "Read chapter 5 and answer the questions at the back of the book for homework"? Even worse, were you ever simply told to read a chapter without having any idea what the chapter was about, or why you were reading it, or what you needed to know after reading the chapter? We have found that students are often unable to state why they are reading a text or what they are supposed to do with the information later. Lacking clear purpose, they are likely simply to read the words and forget about them.

As the teacher, you can prepare students for reading efficiently by using a few simple, straightforward techniques. One important technique, obvious as it may seem, is to state clearly to your students why you want them to read a particular passage and what they will do with the information later. Sometimes this only requires a few words, whereas at other times it may require a short talk, but we maintain that students should not be given an assignment without knowing its purpose and what they are expected to know when they have finished reading. Without this background, they will end up as you may have with the monastery assignment—not getting the point of the reading or remembering haphazardly. We maintain that no assignment should be made without making explicit what you expect of students after reading the text. One of the easiest ways to accomplish this is simply to tell students your expectations and provide them with the background knowledge they will need to get the information, whether it is efferent or aesthetic in nature.

Field Trips and Films

One of the best things you can do to build background knowledge and vocabulary on a topic is to take your class on a field trip where they will experience directly your topic of study. A visit to a primeval forest, a planetarium, a business or factory, a nursery, or a butcher shop builds students' schema for a topic. In addi-

332

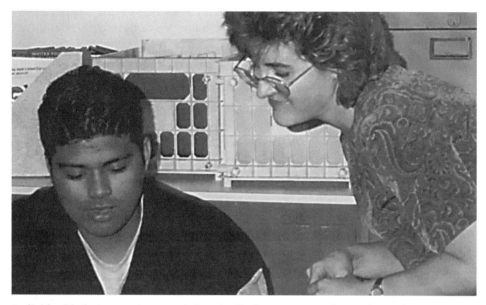

Individual help is sometimes needed to clarify the purpose and procedures of assignments.

333

tion to field trips, or in lieu of one, you can create excitement with a good film or videotape or even with simple pictures or transparencies. A good film involves students visually in a topic and contains narration that builds concepts and vocabulary. When English learners have a visual image of a subject that they carry to their reading, they will be better prepared to understand a text and much more motivated to endure a difficult one. In selecting films, it's important that you preview them to assess (1) how easy they will be for your English learners to understand and (2) how well they convey concepts visually that you want your students to acquire. The language complexity and narrational pace of most films are geared to native English speakers. One way to ensure comprehension of the film is to stop it at a crucial place to ask your students questions that clarify or underscore important points.

Simulation Games

Simulations re-create real-life experiences as closely as possible, just as the bridge-building project, mentioned in Chapter 3, involving "companies" in designing, building, and testing bridges, is a simulation of real-life bridge building. When students play the roles of senators and members of Congress, taking a bill from inception through various committees until it finally is voted on, they are recreating the realities of Congress. Simulations thus provide students with direct experience through role-play. As a result, simulations build background knowledge that will help students comprehend texts discussing how bills are passed. Therefore, simulations provide the appropriate background knowledge for students to understand difficult and abstract texts, and they also help motivate students to read.

Simulations may be of particular help to English learners because they provide direct experience for learning, thus engaging nonverbal channels of information. At the same time, the building of background knowledge verbally and nonverbally during simulations develops concepts and corresponding vocabulary in context. Thus, simulations may be especially helpful to students who have difficulty with complex texts. In the past, simulations were often used at the end of a unit of study, but current research on second language readers and others indicates the importance of building background knowledge prior to reading texts on new and unfamiliar topics (Carrell, 1984). Simulations offer a powerful way to do so.

Experiments

Another way to develop background knowledge as a prereading strategy is to involve students in experiments related to a theme or topic. For example, in a science unit on plants, students can experiment with growing plants. They may discover that roots will always grow down, seeking water and the earth, whereas shoots will try to reach the sunlight, even when the plants are placed upside down in a jar. Students can also chart the growth of carrots or potatoes, giving them different kinds of nutrients to test their effect. Students may keep journals, learning logs, or drawings to record growth for reporting later. Such experiments prepare students to read about plant growth, to use the knowledge acquired through their experiments, and to comprehend their texts better. Whether it is an experiment in science, an estimation project for mathematics, or an oral history project for social science, experiments and research build background knowledge for reading, provide motivation, and enhance comprehension.

Developing Vocabulary before Students Read a Text

All of the preceding strategies for building background knowledge also offer students concrete opportunities to acquire new vocabulary in the context of direct experiences through field trips, simulation games, and experiments. However, it is not possible to provide direct experiences for all vocabulary. Sometimes it is necessary to teach vocabulary separate from direct experience. Whenever possible, it is helpful to illustrate meanings with pictures or diagrams. In addition, it is helpful to teach semantically similar words in a way that shows how they are related, rather than simply presenting a list of words to be memorized. If, for example, you were teaching the *bow* of a boat, you would teach *fore, aft, mast,* and other nautical terms at the same time. This gives students a category or cognitive "net" to hold similar words and makes the words easier to remember. As we have stated before, when information is meaningfully organized, it is easier to remember.

One of the simplest ways to assist students with vocabulary before they read a text is to discuss critical terms before asking students to read. Another is to ask students to brainstorm or cluster around a familiar word to help them expand the word's meaning. For example, if students were going to read about the desert, you might ask them to think of all the words that relate to a desert. One class we observed came up with words such as *hot, wind, dry, sand, cactus,* and *scorpions.* The teacher wrote the words in a cluster on the board. The students also discussed each word so that they were prepared to read the text with a better understanding. In this case, the vocabulary activity activated important schema for their reading.

Another way to organize prereading information is to create a map or structured overview of a concept. In this case, the key word is placed in the center of the map, with supporting categories placed on extensions from the center. The map provides a context for understanding the word. For example, a map might have the word *giraffe* in the center. On the extensions might be such categories as "what the giraffes look like" or "food eaten by giraffes." Underneath the extensions would be details describing the category. In this way, students get a more complete view of what the category *giraffe* means before they read about it. In short, you might select key words or words you anticipate students might have difficulty with before they read the text. You will thus have a better assurance of their successfully engaging the text materials.

Structured Overviews

Structured overviews are visual displays of information, similar to flowcharts and maps, that provide readers with a basic outline of the important points in a book, chapter, or passage. Presented on an overhead projector, on tagboard, or on butcher paper prior to reading, structured overviews preview and highlight important information and interrelationships of ideas and corresponding vocabulary (Readence, Bean, & Baldwin, 1981). Similarly, by providing a hierarchy of ideas in a text, structured overviews give readers an idea of the relative importance of

335

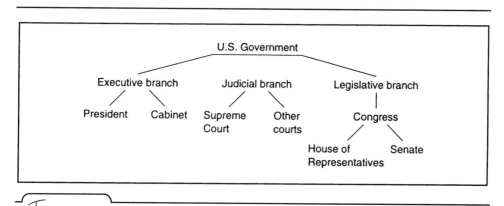

FIGURE 8.8   Structured Overview of U.S. Government

Directions: Consider the following questions, based on headings and subheadings from Chapter 8, before you read. Try to predict how the chapter will answer each of the questions and check your predictions when you read the chapter.

1. What is meant by prereading and during-reading instruction?
2. How are reading and writing used for learning in content areas?
3. What is the importance of text structure in content reading?
4. What can be done as a prereading exercise to prepare students to read a difficult text?
5. How can teachers assist students during reading?

FIGURE 8.9 Preview Guide for This Chapter

ideas and provide categories to assist comprehension and memory of key concepts. The structured overview in Figure 8.8 presents an organized scheme of the different parts of the U.S. government. Look at the overview to see how it might assist a student preparing to read a chapter on the U.S. government and how it might help a reader organize information.

Preview Guides

Preview guides can also help give students an overview of the important ideas in a text because they help them determine how to preview for reading (Vacca & Vacca, 1989). Typically, a preview guide shows students how to read the titles, headings, subheadings, and summaries in a book. By reading these, English learners gain a sense of a text's content and begin to set a purpose for their reading. By reading a summary, for example, your students become aware of what they should know before they begin reading a text. The preview guide in Figure 8.9 teaches students how to preview a chapter and assists them with setting a purpose and monitoring their comprehension.

Anticipation Guides

You can create anticipation guides to prepare students for a story or text. Anticipation guides motivate students and help them predict what will happen in a text (Ausubel, 1968; Holmes & Roser, 1987). A typical guide invites students to state an opinion or predict something about the main ideas or themes in a story or essay before they read it. After reading, students compare the views they held before and after reading.

The guide in Figure 8.10, based on *The Great Gilly Hopkins* (Paterson, 1978), illustrates how an anticipation guide both motivates students to read a passage or book and assists them with setting a purpose and monitoring for purpose during reading. Notice that the guide also provides learners with some background knowledge about the text they are about to read. Though we list anticipation

336

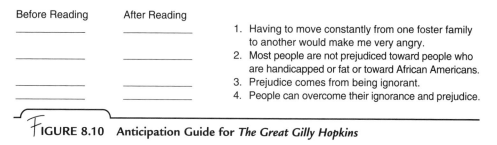

Directions: Before reading *The Great Gilly Hopkins* answer these questions, which stem from the book's experiences. After reading the book, answer the questions again to see if you still have the same opinions. Answer the questions: strongly agree, agree, agree somewhat, strongly disagree.

Before Reading   After Reading

_____   _____   1. Having to move constantly from one foster family to another would make me very angry.

_____   _____   2. Most people are not prejudiced toward people who are handicapped or fat or toward African Americans.

_____   _____   3. Prejudice comes from being ignorant.

_____   _____   4. People can overcome their ignorance and prejudice.

FIGURE 8.10   **Anticipation Guide for *The Great Gilly Hopkins***

guides under prereading, you can see that they provide support during and after reading as well.

In summary, prereading strategies build background knowledge, create motivation, and help students establish a purpose for their reading. Based on your view of what students need to be successful readers of a complex text, you may choose anticipation guides, preview guides, structured overviews, or less elaborate methods to assist students with comprehension. Finally, when students establish a purpose for reading, they are prepared to monitor their own interaction with a text. Self-monitoring assists students with assessing their own success rather than relying solely on the teacher to evaluate their interactions with a passage.

DURING-READING STRATEGIES: MONITORING COMPREHENSION

During-reading strategies help students monitor their comprehension based on the purpose they have set for reading (Leal, Crays, & Moetz, 1985). They need to ask themselves, "Did I find what I was looking for?" If they have a clearly set purpose, they will be able to determine their success while reading. In addition, they can use the structure of their texts to assist them with finding information based on their purpose. For instance, they can use headings and subheadings to ask questions they think will be answered in a passage. Thus, if they read a heading that says, "The Three Causes of the Civil War," they will know to look for three causes. If they only find two, they will recognize the need to reread. When students know what they are looking for and what they will be doing with the information later, they will be better able to evaluate their own reading. This **metacognitive** aspect is a key to comprehension (Anderson, 2002).

If English learners have not established a purpose for their reading, they will not be able to evaluate whether they have been successful readers. When they check their understanding based on the purpose they have set, then they are monitoring their comprehension. If the purpose for reading is to obtain a football score in the newspaper, they will know they have been successful when they have found the score. If, on the other hand, they are interested in who scored the touchdowns, they will be looking for different information and may scan the print differently. Thus, the purpose established for reading a chapter in your classroom will determine how the student will monitor his or her comprehension during reading.

Most of the during-reading strategies center around **questioning strategies** that you model or that build students' self-questioning abilities. These active comprehension strategies (Nolte & Singer, 1985) model questions for children (Stauffer, 1975), help them ask questions of each other (Palinscar & Brown, 1984), and teach self-questioning strategies after some background knowledge has been provided (Singer, 1978; Yopp, 1987). All of the following strategies attempt to model some form of **self-questioning** to assist readers in monitoring what they are learning as they read (MacDonald, 1986). We present several strategies that assist with purpose-setting and self-assessment.

Using Headings and Subheadings

Headings and subheadings not only help students establish specific purpose in reading but also guide students in monitoring comprehension during reading. Research shows that you can boost your students' comprehension and retention substantially if you simply make sure that they read the headings and subheadings and formulate questions about them (Meyer, Brandt, & Bluth, 1980). Students sometimes feel they can plow through a text more quickly if they don't bother to read headings. However, they will find that if they read the headings in texts, they will be able to *turn the headings into questions* and answer the questions when they read the text. For example, if a text heading states, "Three Environmental Dangers of Deforestation," students can create the question "What are the three environmental dangers?" or "What does deforestation mean?" The questions will create their purpose for reading, and they will know that if they only find two dangers in the subsequent paragraphs, then they will have to look for a third danger. By using headings in their reading, students can check whether they have been successful readers. This checking comprehension based on purpose is called **monitoring comprehension.** When you teach students how to turn headings into questions, you help them to monitor their understanding and become independent, successful readers.

Directed Reading-Thinking Activity (DR-TA)

In Chapter 7 we discussed another questioning procedure, DR-TA, in terms of narrative texts (Peregoy & Boyle, 1990a, b; Stauffer, 1975). DR-TA may also be used with expository text. Because expository texts normally contain headings and subheadings, it is sometimes easier to determine when and where to ask key

TEACHER: We're going to read an interesting article about the history of soap. What do you think we'll find in the article?

CHILDREN: "About different kinds of soap." "Like bubbles and watery." "Bars of soap."

TEACHER: One of the headings, you'll notice, says, "Cleaning before Soap." How do you think people got clean before soap?

CHILDREN: "They probably jumped in the river." "They didn't get very clean; they smelled." (*laughter*)

TEACHER: Another heading says, "Life without Soap." What do you think our lives would be like without soap?

CHILDREN: "Joey would smell." (*laughter*) "We'd all smell." (*laughter*)

TEACHER: When you read the article, see if your guesses about soap are like what the article says and make your own guesses using the other headings. Remember, if you're guessing you'll have your best chance of understanding what you're reading, even if your guesses are not always right.

FIGURE 8.11 **Edited DR-TA Transcript**

questions. When Lucinda Lim introduces DR-TA with expository text to her students, she uses the following steps. First, she models the procedure with a short reading. Next, she shows students how to create questions using headings and subheadings. She then asks students in groups to make up questions based on headings and answer them in their groups. Finally, she asks her students to report and compare their questions and answers. After some practice in groups, she asks them to use the procedure on their own. She often places beginning-level students in heterogeneous groups or places them with an advanced-level student to assist them with difficult reading. In this way, the advanced student, by clearly articulating the meaning of a text, gains a sophistication about it, while the beginning-level student gains access to a difficult text. Figure 8.11 is a brief edited transcript of Lucinda introducing DR-TA to her class with a text about the history of soap.

In this transcript, we can see that Lucinda has prepared her students to read the article on soap. First, she has activated their background knowledge about soap by simply asking some questions. Second, she has shown them how to anticipate and predict what an article might be about by using headings. She has also shown them that it is appropriate to make guesses about something they will read. Finally, she has prepared them to monitor their understanding. Thus, DR-TA combines aspects of prereading activities and questioning procedures to assist students' comprehension.

Vocabulary Strategies During Reading

Students often need strategies to help them comprehend unfamiliar words they may encounter while reading. Two strategies discussed by Tierney and Readence (2000) in their excellent resource book, *Reading Strategies and Practices: A*

Deborah and Theresa were happy because Ultima did many of the household _____ they normally did, and they had more time to spend in the attic and cut out an interminable train of paper dolls
which they dressed, gave names to, and most miraculously, made talk.

FIGURE 8.12   Excerpt from Bless me, Ultima (Anaya, 1972)

Compendium are contextual redefinition (Cunningham, Cunningham, & Arthur,
1981) and preview in context. Both strategies attempt to assist students with comprehending and acquiring vocabulary within the context of their reading. For convenience, we combine features from both strategies to suggest a way to help your
students use their background knowledge and the text context to gain a better
understanding of their reading. First, you select words you consider important to
the understanding of a particular passage. Next, you create several sentences using
the words to give your students a chance to predict the meaning of new words in
context. You might show students how to use the specific context of the words to
gain knowledge about them. For example, surrounding words can give clues to
meaning; headings or subheadings can hint at the meanings of words; or, often,
authors paraphrase technical words in common phrases to assure their readers'
understanding. When students become aware of the ways authors help them with
new vocabulary, they will be more successful in their interactions with texts. Using
some form of contextual vocabulary instruction gives students the capability of
becoming independent readers who can rely on their own use of strategies to gain
meaning from print.

Using Clustering to Develop Vocabulary in Context

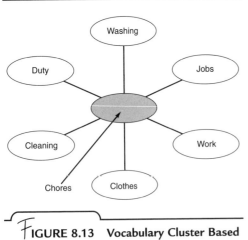

FIGURE 8.13   Vocabulary Cluster Based on Bless Me, Ultima

One way you can assist English learners with
developing their vocabularies through reading is
to teach them to guess a word's meaning by the
context of its use. One day while we were observing her class, Steffanie Marion used the novel the
students were reading to develop vocabulary. First
she placed a transparency page of the novel they
were reading, *Bless Me, Ultima* (Anaya, 1972), on
an overhead projector. She omitted vocabulary
words she felt the students might need help with
(Figure 8.12). Next, she asked them to guess what
word would fit in the first blank space. She placed
a circle on the board to represent the unknown
word and then surrounded it with students' encir-
cled guesses, as in Figure 8.13. When the students
had completed their guesses, she placed the word
used in the novel in the center circle in the cluster.

340

After the Louisiana Purchase, President Thomas Jefferson wanted to find out if the Missouri River went all the way through the United States to the Pacific Ocean. If it did, it would provide a possible trade route. To find out he sent Lewis and Clark on an expedition up the Missouri River to, he hoped, the Pacific Ocean. On this _____ Lewis and Clark took 48 men.

FIGURE 8.14   Social Science Passage about the Lewis and Clark Expedition

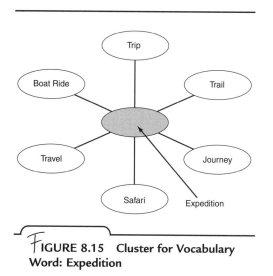

FIGURE 8.15   Cluster for Vocabulary Word: Expedition

Thus, she was able to point out the words in the cluster that were synonyms for the central word. Steffanie's strategy helped the students gain confidence in their guesses and developed their vocabulary further by giving them synonyms for a new and difficult vocabulary word. Steffanie doesn't use the strategy often, she says, but she finds it to be an excellent way to show how to generate the meaning of a new word by using context. In this way she provides students with a strategy that promotes independence in reading.

An example of an excerpt and cluster from a social science passage is shown in Figure 8.14 and Figure 8.15.

Jigsaw Procedure

Jigsaw, introduced in Chapter 3, is another group strategy for assisting comprehension of all students in a class (Johnson, Johnson, & Holubec, 1986). using jigsaw, teachers make students responsible for one another's learning, help them with identifying purpose and important concepts in a text, and assist them with reporting information gained. The steps for using jigsaw in a class are the following:

Step 1:   Place students in groups of three; each student has a number of 1, 2, or 3.

Step 2:   Students who are 1s become responsible for reading a certain number of pages in a text; likewise for numbers 2 and 3.

Step 3:   Students read the section for which they are responsible.

Step 4:   Groups of 1s, 2s, and 3s get together to form an "expert" group; they share information and decide how to report it back to their main or "base" groups (the groups consisting of the original 1, 2, and 3); 2s and 3s do the same.

Step 5:   1s report information to 2s and 3s in base groups; 2s and 3s do the same.

Step 6:   Some teachers like to have a brief whole-class discussion on the sections that they have read.

Using the jigsaw procedure, you place the responsibility for purpose setting, questioning, and comprehension monitoring on the shoulders of your students. Moreover, all students take responsibility for one another's learning. When students present information to their base group, they present ideas and answer questions about the text for which they are responsible. Similarly, when it is their turn to hear from other members, they will ask questions to clarify their own thinking. The approach, good for all students, is particularly useful for students who might otherwise struggle with content texts because of limited knowledge of English. They will be able to read, question, and understand on their own but will also be able to share their reading and understanding with other students in the "expert" groups. In addition, they will be assisted by other students in their base groups and tutored wherever necessary (Verplaetse, 1998). Because the jigsaw procedure makes each student in a base group responsible for the comprehension of all students in the group, English learners can rely on much more support than they might receive in many content classes. Through the constant negotiating of meaning and continuous use of oral language each day in class, students gain optimal access to comprehensible input for further language and concept development. Jigsaw provides all learners with a maximum amount of support for reading in the content areas. Although this support is provided mainly in the during-reading phase, it is also provided in the postreading phase because students are also asked to organize their information for reporting to their base groups after reading.

Learning Logs

Journals and learning logs are discussed more fully later, but we want to point out their utility now as an excellent metacognitive learning tool in the during-reading phase (Jaramillo, 1998). Learning logs require students to formulate questions about what they are learning or what might be difficult while they are reading (Calkins, 1994). Using learning logs, students may write specific notes concerning a passage in a text, a formula or experiment, or a period of history. As you review student logs, you can identify concepts that you may need to clarify. In addition, learning logs provide an excellent and natural way to evaluate a student's progress. Most important, learning logs provide students with a way to both assess their own learning and get help from you. One student's learning log shows how a student can create a dialogue of learning with the teacher:

JOSE: I don't understand about photosynthesis. How does the light make air? How do plants help us live and breathe?

TEACHER: This is a very difficult idea. Many students are having some difficulty with it, and I will be going over it tomorrow. We'll be going over it in groups where we'll share questions to help us make the ideas clearer. Then maybe it'll be clearer to everybody.

Summary

The prereading and during-reading phases of reading and writing across the curriculum are crucial. If students don't develop a clear purpose for reading, they will not be efficient content-area readers. In addition, they will not be able to monitor their comprehension if they aren't clear about what they should be learning. So the prereading phase of reading and writing across the curriculum prepares

343

Strategy \ Grade Level	K	1	2	3	4	5	6	7	8	9	10	11	12
Anticipation guides					→————————————————————→								
Cohesive ties					→————————————————————→								
DR-TA	→——→												
Essay structures						→——————————————————→							
Experiments	→——→												
Field trips	→——→												
Films	→——→												
Group reading inventory					→————————————————————→								
Headings/subheadings					→————————————————————→								
Jigsaw procedure					→————————————————————→								
Learning logs		→——————————————————————————————————→											
Preview guides					→————————————————————→								
Preview vocabulary		→——————————————————————————————————→											
Simulation games					→————————————————————→								
Story structure	→——→												
Structured overviews					→————————————————————→								
Teacher talk	→——→												
Text structure					→————————————————————→								

FIGURE 8.16 Grade Levels at Which Strategies May Be Used

students for the during-reading phase. The primary responsibility of students in the during-reading phase is to assess or monitor their comprehension based on their purpose for reading. During-reading strategies also help students keep track of information they may want to present later to others. As a final step, students must consider how they will organize the information so that it will be remembered. Although this chapter has been primarily concerned with helping students comprehend what they are reading, the next chapter, on postreading, focuses on helping students remember what they have understood. Learning requires not only comprehending but remembering.

In order to assist your students with content learning we have provided several strategies and listed their general grade-level use in Figure 8.16. As the chart shows, most of the strategies are initiated in the fourth or fifth grade and beyond. However, we recommend that you begin introducing purposeful content-area reading and writing in earlier grades and also introduce some of the strategies that will scaffold English learners' content reading. With this assistance, your students will be prepared gradually for success in later grades.

$\int$UGGESTIONS FOR FURTHER READING

344

Echevarria, J., Vogt, M. E., & Short, D. (2000). *Making content comprehensible for English language learners: The SIOP model.* Boston: Allyn and Bacon.

This is one of the best resources we know for helping teachers work with English language learners. We use this book ourselves to keep us on track when teaching and we have found the information invaluable for our students who are looking forward to working successfully in ELL classes. Chapters include the following: "Introducing Sheltered Instruction," "Indicators of Instruction: Building Background," "Comprehensible Input," "Strategies," "Lesson Delivery," and "Assessment." Every teacher should have this book.

Leu, D. (2003). Developing new literacies: Using the Internet in content area instruction. Retrieved on July 25, 2003, from http://web.syr.edu/~djleu/content.html

This article will appear in M. McLaughlin & M. E. Vogt (Eds.), *Creativity and innovation in content area instruction.* Norwood, MA: Christopher-Gordon. Simply put, if you want to use the Internet in your content-area teaching, this 18-page article will deliver all of the information you'll need.

Written by an expert on literacy and the Internet, the article contains excellent sites for literature, science, mathematics, social studies, and multicultural resources, and sites for specific cultures. The references alone will help any teacher working in content-area instruction. We highly recommend this resource.

Schmitt, N., & McCarthy, M. (Eds.). (2002). *Vocabulary: Description, acquisition, and pedagogy.* Cambridge: Cambridge University Press.

This comprehensive text on vocabulary contains a wide variety of articles including sections on vocabulary and description, vocabulary and acquisition, and the pedagogical context. Among the list of excellent articles, three we find especially interesting are "Written and Spoken Vocabulary," "On the Role of Context in First- and Second-Language Vocabulary," and "Current Trends in Teaching Second Language Vocabulary."

Seda, M. M., Ligouri, O. Z., & Seda, C. M. (1999). Bridging literacy and social science studies: Engaging prior knowledge through children's books. *TESOL Journal, 8*(3), 34–40.

This article provides a clear rationale for using children's literature to enhance the learning of middle school ESL students. It discusses the importance of prior knowledge for students reading in subjects such as history and shows how children's literature can help students build their schema to prepare them to read history texts. The authors give detailed examples of designing and implementing their program and provide examples of what they would do to improve the program. An excellent, thorough article.

Activities

1. Visit the classroom of a teacher who has been trained recently in content-area reading and writing or of a teacher who has a reputation of being the best teacher in the school and see what they do. How does the teacher prepare English learners and others to read a text? How does the teacher use writing in the class? What would you do differently based on information in this text? What would you do differently based on the success of the teacher you observed?

2. Try creating a group reading inventory (GRI) on a chapter you might teach. If you are already in the classroom, use the GRI with your class as a study guide and see how it guides your students' learning. Did it prepare them to be more efficient readers? Did it assist them with comprehension? Do you think a GRI will help students become more independent learners eventually or will they simply become dependent on the GRI as a scaffold for their learning? When is it appropriate to take the GRI away and ask students to develop their own questions for their reading?

3. Observe classrooms where teachers try to provide background information in such areas as social science or history for English learners who may have come from a country with a very different form of government or who may have a very different historical knowledge because of their country of origin. How does the teacher build such students' schema or background knowledge to help them better understand their text? Does this building of schema appear to work for most of the students? If not, what adaptations would you make to the teacher's lesson?

4. As there is a strong relationship between vocabulary knowledge and reading comprehension in content areas, visit content classes and see how teachers approach the teaching of content vocabulary. Do they use worksheets or do they seem to have developed some systematic approach to teaching vocabulary? Do the teachers organize the vocabulary to enhance memory and comprehension or do they simply give students lists or tell them what certain words mean? What kind of vocabulary instruction do you find most useful in the classrooms you observe?

5. If you were preparing a U.S. history lesson for second language learners, how would you develop their background knowledge, vocabulary, and approaches to reading a history text? What strategies discussed in this text or that you have observed in classrooms seem most useful? What scaffolding, SDAIE, or sheltering approaches would you use to enhance the students' learning? How would you teach students to become expert questioners of texts they are reading? How would you develop their confidence as readers?

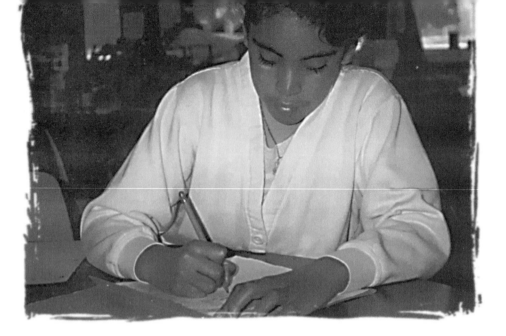

9

CONTENT READING AND WRITING: POSTREADING STRATEGIES FOR ORGANIZING AND REMEMBERING

In this chapter we discuss ways you can enhance students' comprehension and memory of what they have read in their texts. We discuss such questions as the following:

1. Why should we teach vocabulary in the postreading phase of content reading? What role does this instruction play in assisting students' memory?
2. What is the role of writing in content-area reading and writing?
3. Why are collaborative projects particularly valuable for second language content learners?
4. Why do thematic units enhance second language students' learning and memory in content-area classrooms?
5. How can we assess English language learners in content-area learning?

C lare Goldmark's students always develop projects to be presented at the end of specific units in her social science class. Although she provides students with a list of possible projects, she also encourages them to select a topic— within a unit on World War II, for example—that they are particularly interested in. Then she provides students with a model of how they will present the project to their classmates.

She organizes her class so that each group of about five students presents its topic to a cooperative panel of five classmates. The students are to use visuals, including films, maps, collages, or drama they have created, to describe their project, thereby sheltering their presentations. The panel's job is to ask friendly questions about the project so that all the class can learn more about their topic. This project/panel approach requires presenters to prepare, organize, and rehearse their lesson for the panel presentation; thus they must remember well what they have learned. In addition, because all of the students in the class are involved as both presenters of projects and panelists who must ask questions about the projects, the students are all active participants in the activity. This is especially important since research indicates that students in content classes are often left out in mainstream discussions, etc. (Harklau, 1994a; Harper & Platt, 1998). Clare says that the students show a remarkable memory not only for their own project information but for the information provided in other projects as well. These projects require her students to understand, rehearse, remember and present what they have studied.

347

POSTREADING STRATEGIES FOR STUDENTS

If students have developed background knowledge for a text, set a purpose for reading, and monitored their comprehension during reading, they must next organize the information so that they can remember what they have read. This is what Clare provides for her students with their project presentations. If content-area information is not organized in some way, it will not be adequately remembered (Bruner, 1960; Miller, 1956; Miller, Galanter, & Pribram, 1960). Thus, postreading activities help students organize and remember the information they have gathered in reading. The strategies discussed subsequently, such as semantic feature analysis, mapping, rehearsing, summarizing, and writing, will assist students with remembering important information.

Semantic Feature Analysis for Vocabulary Development after Reading

One method used for reinforcing important concepts and terms after reading is **semantic feature analysis,** which is a graphic method of listing and analyzing the essential traits or features that define members or examples of a particular category or concept. For example, given the category *pets,* one might list *dog, cat,*

CATEGORY: PETS					
	Features:				
	land	water	wings	legs	fur
Member:					
dog					
cat					
hamster					
fish					
parakeet					

FIGURE 9.1   **Chart for Semantic Feature Analysis of Pets**

hamster, fish, and *parakeet* as members. To analyze the essential traits or features of these pets, a list of traits, such as *land, water, wings, fur, legs,* and *fins,* must be generated. The final step in the semantic feature analysis is to create a chart and check the features that apply to each member of the category (Figure 9.1).

After the matrix is set up, students and teacher together check off the traits for each pet. In the process, vocabulary items are reinforced as categories are analyzed and explored. An additional step is to invite students to add other pets to the list for which the feature analysis was carried out. Students may also come up with other traits to analyze, such as whether the animals are carnivores, herbivores, or omnivores.

The semantic feature analysis can be especially helpful in illustrating abstract relationships among complex concepts, as shown in Figure 9.2 on government. After reading and studying about various forms of government, students may work in groups or as a class to list each type of government and establish a list of features such as freedom to assemble, the right to hold elections, the number of leaders, and so forth. Next, students fill in the chart, analyzing each type of government according to the traits listed in the chart. In this way, students are able to reinforce the meaning of words such as *oligarchy, monarchy, democracy,* and *dictatorship* while developing insights concerning similarities and differences among them.

Other visual strategies that help students assimilate special vocabulary are mapping, clustering, and structured overviews. Each of these strategies helps students expand their knowledge of new technical terms and understand them in the context of related terms, thus creating a kind of cognitive net for keeping the information in long-term memory. Briefly stated, vocabulary is best taught within

Type of Government	Elections	Freedom	Number of Leaders	Powers	Free to Assemble	Free Speech	Other
Monarchy							
Democracy							
Dictatorship							
Oligarchy							

FIGURE 9.2   **Chart for Semantic Feature Analysis of Government**

a meaningful context, whether you are learning words for a better understanding of government or a better understanding of literary writing. You will want to assist students with special vocabulary terms before they read, with strategies for understanding words during reading, and with strategies for consolidating their new vocabulary knowledge after they have completed a text. Because vocabulary knowledge plays a major role in reading comprehension, vocabulary strategies play a central role in our teaching.

Rehearsing to Organize and Remember Information

Rehearsing refers to the reformulation or presentation again of information to oneself or to others. Have you ever studied with someone else? If you have, you rehearsed the information you knew by sharing it with another person. When you repeated what you knew and listened to others present what they knew, you were rehearsing the information. Rehearsing information goes beyond simple memorization and repetition. Having an audience requires you to organize the information so that it is easier to understand. You can also rehearse information culled from a text by talking to yourself or repeating the information aloud. Rehearsing information, whether by repeating orally, paraphrasing in writing, or creating a map, is necessary for memory. Rehearsing requires a deeper level of processing than just reading and assuming that you will remember the information. The Venn diagram and the mapping strategy, presented next, facilitate rehearsal by organizing information visually and spatially to make it easier to access and recall.

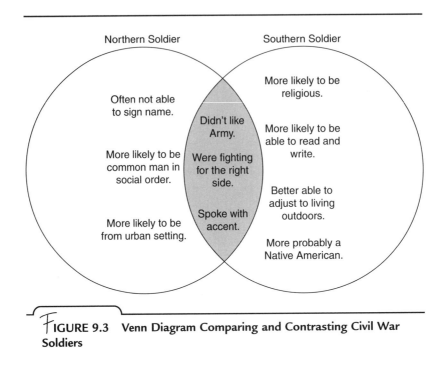

FIGURE 9.3   **Venn Diagram Comparing and Contrasting Civil War Soldiers**

Venn Diagrams

A Venn diagram (see Figure 9.3), represented by two interlocking circles, serves to illustrate similarities and differences between two novels, two periods in history, two characters, or any other pair of concepts. Where the circles intersect the two things being compared and contrasted are similar; where the circles are separate the things being compared and contrasted are different. The Venn diagram in Figure 9.3 illustrates some comparisons and contrasts students made between Northern and Southern soldiers during the Civil War. Venn diagrams can be used to compare and contrast characters in a novel, ideas, or historical situations, and they can become a prewriting diagram students can use when they write a compare/contrast essay of their own.

Mapping

Mapping is a powerful strategy for assisting students with organizing and remembering information. In addition, because maps are both spatial and visual, they assist second language readers with sharing information and their own visual interpretation of the information they have obtained from reading (Boyle & Peregoy, 1991; Boyle, 1982a, b, c; Buckley & Boyle, 1981; Ruddell & Boyle, 1989). A map may simply represent information using headings and subheadings as presented in a text, or it may synthesize the information according to the readers' deeper understanding of a text. Steps for developing a map are the following:

- Student places title in center of map and places headings on extensions from center.
- Student places information that he or she found under extension headings.
- When map is complete, student checks for important information and reviews map. If important information is missing, student places information under appropriate headings.
- Map is studied for a few minutes and is reviewed a few days later for memory. If student forgets something in map, he or she checks text for verification.

The map in Figure 9.4 on soap illustrates how one student developed a map using the headings and supporting details. The student was able to remember the information presented in the chapter "History of Soap" in some detail even a few weeks later.

The map in Figure 9.5 was developed by a group of students who had been studying the U.S. Constitution. After reading a chapter and developing a map such as the one on soap, the students attempted to develop a map that went beyond the information, showing relationships among the basic concepts discussed in the text (Boyle, 1982b). Their map on the Constitution (Figure 9.5) was their first attempt to synthesize the information they had derived from the activities in the class unit.

Maps help students organize key concepts in a text and their interrelationships. Mapping thus requires students to reconstruct information and organize it for memory.

FIGURE 9.4   Map of Chapter on Soap

352

$\mathcal{F}$IGURE 9.5   **Group Map Illustrating the U.S. Constitution**

In summary, the purpose of postreading strategies is to assist with under-standing and retention of important information. Most of the strategies, therefore, involve organizing or restructuring information in order to make it easier to remember. We have shared several strategies that assist with organizing and restructuring information, such as mapping, Venn diagrams, and semantic feature analysis. These strategies call for a deeper level of processing information because they require students to present information to others in a coherent manner. Next, we discuss writing in content areas.

WRITING AS A LEARNING TOOL ACROSS THE CURRICULUM

Writing is another powerful strategy that promotes discovery, comprehension, and retention of information (Calkins, 1994). In recent years, teachers have begun to use the writing process and its various phases as an integral part of their content-area classrooms. They have found that writing helps students clarify their thoughts and remember what they have learned. Similarly, you will find that you can evaluate and assist your students' learning by reading learning log entries, journals, and notebooks. Recent research has supported the use of writing in content areas by showing that students who write tend to understand more and remember more. We recommend that you ask English learners to write in logs and journals, to write in notebooks, to summarize and comment on their own learning, and to perform hands-on research projects that are reported in correct writing (Reppen, 1994/1995). We believe that journals and learning logs are an excellent way to begin involving students in writing in content areas, and we have found in our own research that even kindergartners can write in journals and evaluate their learning (Peregoy & Boyle, 1990a).

Journals and Learning Logs

We have recommended journals and learning logs for different purposes throughout this book. Table 9.1 illustrates the kinds of journals you can use in various content areas: dialogue/buddy journals, notebooks, learning logs, and response journals (Kreeft, 1984; Rupert & Brueggeman, 1986). In addition, the table notes the general purpose of each type of journal along with an example of its use in different content areas. Although the types of journals are not always mutually exclusive, they give you a feeling for the variety of roles journal writing can play in content areas.

In most cases, you will want to respond to the students' journal entries about once a week. As mentioned in our previous discussion of journals, your comments should concentrate on the content of the journals, not on grammar, punctuation, and spelling. For example, you might clarify a concept over which a student indicates confusion or you might simply give students support for their entries. Journals provide excellent opportunities for students to write daily, to develop fluency, to clarify ideas, and to monitor their own learning and to "become more aware" of their learning strategies (Oxford, 2003). Moreover, writing down information assists memory. You may remember a time when you made a grocery list but found when you entered the store that you had left it behind. Nevertheless, you remembered much of your list because you had written it down; writing had assisted your memory just as writing will assist your students' memory.

TABLE 9.1 Journal Writing in Content Areas

Journal Type and Purpose	Science	Language Arts	Mathematics	Social Science
Dialogue/Buddy: to share with another	Explain to teacher or to friend what is happening in class and what is understood	Share with another about a story or poem being read; share other aspects of class	Let teacher or friend know how class or assignments are going	"Discuss" information pertaining to topics in class
Notebook: to take notes to assist memory	Write down information pertaining to an experiment in class	Take down conversations overheard for use in a story to be written	Keep notes about math concepts	Write down key information discussed in class
Learning logs: to discuss and process information from class	Write down notes about what one understands in the class and about what might seem unclear	Write down key concepts from class such as definitions of concepts: setting, theme, characterization	Try to explain math concepts for oneself or perhaps for another; clarify or try to apply a new concept	Take notes on causes of Civil War or other key ideas; ask self to identify and clarify ideas
Response journals: to respond openly and freely to any topic	Respond to feelings about scientific experimentation or use of animals as subjects or biogenetics	Make any comments on characters or conflicts presented in a story being read	Respond to math in an interesting way, such as ask questions about why people who would never admit to being illiterate will seemingly brag about their math ignorance	Respond to politicians' handling of peace after World War I or about attitudes of pilgrims toward Native Americans

355

INTERNET RESOURCES: Dave's ESL Café contains over 3,000 links that deal with just about any topic you may be interested in: http://www.eslcafe.com/search/index.html Topics include literacy, writing, listening, pronunciation, vocabulary, and games. You might evaluate the site on your own, or with a student to see how well the site works for teacher and students. Also see our companion website for other resources: www.ablongman.com/peregoy4e.

Developing Topics and Student Self-Selection of Topics in Content Areas

We generally support the view that students, whenever possible, should select their own writing topics. That is, if your class is studying plants, students should be allowed to select topics that interest them within the context of plants. Additionally, if students are going to do research, they should select and shape their own topics for research. However, we also recognize that you may have important topics for students. When this is so, we recommend that you create **context-enriched topics,** which we define as topics that embed abstract concepts in real-life experiences, allowing students to use their own experiences as part of your assigned topic. The following examples should clarify this process.

Recently, we met a teacher, Joe Allyn, who wanted his students to know something about world economies. Instead of assigning his students to write a paper on the economy of Peru, Mr. Allyn gave them the following situation:

> You are a travel agent, and you intend to take a group of vacationers to a country. In order to attract enough people for the trip, you will need to prepare a brochure. In the brochure, you will explain the various sights and major cities. You will also need to advise people on how much money they will need and on the clothes they will take, based on the climate and the time of the year. Your travelers will also want to know the kinds of items they might buy and where the best buys are found. Finally, they will need to know how much to expect to pay for hotels, for meals, and what kinds of tips, if any, they should give to waiters. Your brochure should have an attractive cover and should contain any other pieces of information you feel travelers to your country should know. I will supply you with a model of such a brochure.

Joe let students pick a country, work in peer response and revision groups, and share research on the country with one another. He then had a travel day in which each group tried to entice their classmates to "travel" to their country; students used their brochures along with pictures and short films of the country.

The context-enriched topic Joe created has several advantages over traditional, assigned topics. First, the students selected their own country, which allowed some English learners to tell their classmates about their own country and culture. Second, they had an audience for their writing—other travelers and the students in their class. Third, they had a "real" assignment, one that people actually perform in the world. Fourth, the activity involves group collaboration and research. Finally, Joe gave students a model of an appropriate brochure. For English language learners, activities might range from doing research on their own home country to drawing pictures for the brochure to adding personal knowledge of travel in another country they may know well. Most traditional writing assignments can be changed into context-enriched assignments by allowing students to use what they already know to create something new.

Noel Anderson also offers context-enriched assignments when she asks her students to select a topic of their own or to use one of her suggested topics after reading a novel. Here is one context-enriched topic she gives to students as a possible writing assignment: "You are Tom Sawyer, and your raft has been carried away in a time warp. Select one of the situations below or create one of your own, and write a letter to Becky about what you experienced and what you think of your experience."

Writing Topic Ideas

1. You find yourself in the school cafeteria where the students are having a food fight.
2. You find yourself on the 50-yard line of the Super Bowl.
3. You find yourself in the middle of a crowd at a rock concert.
4. You find yourself in the middle of a class where the book *Tom Sawyer* is being discussed.
5. Select your own situation.

356

Noel finds that her students enjoy not only the topics she creates but also the ones they create for themselves, including some that are modeled after her own and others that are totally original. The opportunity to create their own situation instead of writing an abstract character sketch is particularly useful to English language learners because they can start with a familiar situation to use as background for explaining a less familiar character such as Tom Sawyer, for instance. These questions, furthermore, can be answered individually or in collaborative groups and can model for students questions they might wish to ask.

Photo Essays: Combining Direct Experience, the Visual Mode, and Writing

Photography has great potential for stimulating student interest in school projects, and it forms the basis of the photo essay, a method using visuals to organize thinking prior to speaking and/or writing (Sinatra, et al., 1990). In essence, students choose a topic for which they take a set of photographs, or they bring in photos already taken. Then they organize the pictures in a sequence that will support their discussion of the topic. After oral discussion, students write and publish their photo-illustrated essay. We have seen this approach used successfully at both the elementary- and secondary-school levels with students of varying English language proficiency.

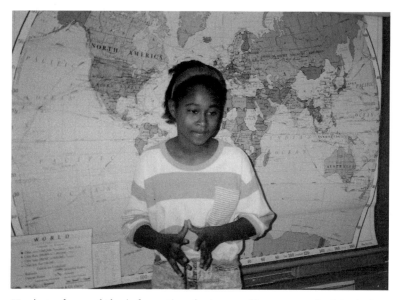

Having rehearsed the information during small-group work, this student is well prepared for her oral presentation on her home country, Haiti.

357

In Ms. Guadarrama's third-grade class, for example, children brought in photos of their families, including pictures of themselves. They organized their pictures on construction paper in the order they would tell about them during sharing time. Ms. Guadarrama and her assistant went around the room to listen to the children describe their pictures, helping them reorganize the pictures if necessary for sharing with the class. The students then pasted the pictures onto the paper and orally shared their stories with the entire class. The next day, they used their photo essays to organize the writing of their stories. The written story was then stapled beneath the photo essay, and the final products were posted around the room for everyone to look at and read. In this activity, the photos not only supported children's writing but also supported reading, as students took time to read each other's stories.

In Mia Taylor's sixth-grade class, students were invited to work in pairs to develop a photo essay related to their family, school, or neighborhood. Because Ms. Taylor often used whole-class photo essays as a follow-up after field trips, her students were familiar with the general idea. For the pair projects, Ms. Taylor asked her students to (1) choose a topic and brainstorm how they would develop their ideas through photography, (2) check with her to get approval for their topic and plan, (3) take the pictures, (4) organize their pictures into a storyboard, and (5) write the story, with the final product to be published complete with photo illustrations.

Students' photo essays addressed a variety of topics, including how to make tamales from scratch, a visual inventory of a shopping mall, and a day in the life of a laundromat operator. These photo essays were primarily organized around chronological or spatial sequences. In addition, the photo essay may be set up for classification, as was the case with a pair of students who photographed and analyzed different kinds of businesses in their neighborhood. The procedure also lends itself to thematic organization. Two girls, for example, prepared a photo essay on the problems of being 12 years old. In this case, the girls presented a photo of themselves in the center with the caption, "Problems with Being Twelve." They then presented a wheel of problems, with a photo attached to each spoke depicting problem areas: indecision over hair and makeup, too young to drive, boredom, too much homework, and so forth. The organization of the photographs thus offered a concrete form of semantic mapping.

In summary, the photo essay provides students of all ages and developmental levels with the opportunity to use direct experience and photography around a chosen theme. They are able to manipulate the pictures as a concrete way of organizing their ideas for writing. In the process, they use a great deal of visually supported oral language. Finally, they write the essay and produce an illustrated product for others to read.

Written and Oral Collaborative Research Projects

When entering Fernando Nichol's class, you will sense that he does things a little differently. All four walls of his classroom are covered with books, and, this year 3-by-3–foot airplanes are hanging from the high ceilings. In one corner, a

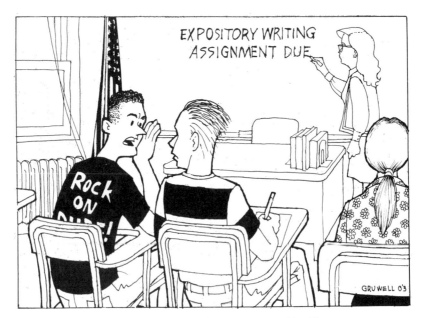

"That's what WE call suppository writing!"

rocking chair with a serape hanging over the back faces a large carpet. Each semester, Mr. Nichol's English learners use the books in his class to do research projects that require reading/writing and oral language use. They use his chair to present their findings to the rest of the class and use the tables around the classroom to work collaboratively on their research topics. Usually, while studying a general topic such as the Civil War, students select a subtopic such as the role of slaves, to explore more fully and share their findings with their peers. These written research projects involve collaborative reading and writing, and students need to be fairly proficient in English to be totally involved in them. Other teachers use oral history projects to engage students in research and sharing of knowledge.

Oral history projects involve students in selecting a topic of interest, researching the topic by reading and interviewing knowledgeable individuals, and reporting the information orally and in writing. For example, Lee Tzeng asks his students to select a topic that relates to what they are studying and to conduct an oral research project. In one case, students decided to do a project on World War II. They had read about the war in their class and had seen several related films. A number of students had relatives who had participated in the war, and they decided to interview their relatives and others in their own neighborhoods who could talk about their war experiences.

To get started on the project, students discussed the types of questions they wanted to ask and the purpose of their project. They determined that their purpose would be to get a personal view of the war and its aftermath. Next, they created questions and discussed how to conduct a good interview. Lee placed them in teams of three, with each member being responsible for one part of the interview: One would be responsible for asking questions, another would tape-record the interview and take notes, and the third person would think of some extra questions that might be asked at the end of the interview.

After completing interviews, students transcribed them. This required them to listen carefully and to work together on mechanics, spelling, and punctuation as they transcribed. After transcribing, they wrote a narrative describing the individual they had interviewed, using Studs Terkel's work as a model (Terkel, 1974). They then refined their written narratives in peer response and editing groups.

Next, each group created a chart with each individual's name and a summary of important elements from the interview. After finishing their charts, they examined them for categories or questions they might suggest. One category that emerged was racial discrimination in the army. One African American man, for instance, shared his experience of all-black troops who were headed by white captains. He said that he and his fellow troopers liked to slow down their work, acting as if they didn't understand the orders if the white captain treated them unfairly or without respect.

As a result of their initial analysis, the students began asking questions about different groups of soldiers. What was the effect of the war on African Americans as opposed to Japanese Americans, for example? What did this mean in terms of job availability for each group? How were Italian Americans and German Americans treated during the war? After students made these generalizations, they created a book about World War II that they disseminated to the people they interviewed as well as to others in the community. The oral projects represent one ideal type of research because students selected their own topics, decided on important questions, and carried out the topics on their own. In addition, students were involved in oral and written composing, transcribing, revising, and editing a research report on a relevant topic. When the students were ready to publish the results of their research, they could refer to the chart Lee Tzeng provided to assist them with clear interview reporting (see Table 9.2).

The oral interview topic just discussed was used for social science, but we have seen students perform the same kind of oral projects in math, science, and other areas. In mathematics, one class asked business people how math was used in their jobs and what aspect of math would be most important for students to know. Another class interviewed gardeners and nursery owners to gain information about plants. Wherever we have seen oral projects used, we have seen a great deal of enthusiasm from students and teachers alike. The projects tend to involve students at the deepest levels of oral discussion, critical thinking, reading, and writing. Moreover, they tie learning to real people, real problems, and real life. In so doing, they tend to override subject-matter boundaries, creating integrated knowledge across several traditional disciplines of study.

K-W-L, a Strategy That Fosters Thinking before, during, and after Reading

Some strategies combine elements of each of the three phases of content reading: before, during, and after. These strategies are particularly helpful in

TABLE 9.2   Elements of Good Reporting

Element	Description
Opening	At the very beginning state what your topic is and how you will develop it; e.g., state that you have interviewed World II veterans from different ethnic groups to learn about their different or similar experiences.
Background information	Give readers the background information they will need to know to understand your report. For example, explain the attitudes of Americans toward different ethnic groups at the time of the war. This might help explain why some troops were segregated from others or treated differently.
Reporting interviews	When reporting the interview of a specific person, give background information on the person that may be important to the reader's understanding of the interviewee. See Studs Terkel (1974) for examples.
Summarizing information	Use your interview charts to find categories of responses that might be similar or different among the interviewees. Remind the readers what your purpose was and state your findings.

teaching students overall methods for setting purpose, building background knowledge, and monitoring, organizing, and remembering information. K-W-L is such a strategy. **K-W-L** and **K-W-L Plus** provide a scaffolding structure for developing a research question and investigating it. *K, W,* and *L* stand for *Know, Want to Know,* and *Learn* (Ogle, 1986); the K-W-L Plus strategy simply adds mapping to Ogle's original K-W-L approach (Carr & Ogle, 1987). In the *Know* part of the strategy students can generate, in groups or individually, what they know about a topic; this step taps students' background knowledge and also gives you a chance to see what you may need to clarify in preparing students to read your text. In the *Want to Know* step students begin to think of questions concerning the topic; this step helps them generate a purpose for their reading and prepares them to monitor their comprehension. In the *Learned* step students list what they have learned. In the K-W-L Plus extension of the process, students organize what they have learned so they will be able to remember it. The K-W-L strategy helps students become responsible for their learning, assists them with becoming active learners, and provides them with a strategy they may use independently with practice. The worksheet in Figure 9.6 is used with the strategy to guide students through the process.

THEME STUDIES: PROVIDING A MEANINGFUL LEARNING CONTEXT

361

The theme study "Plants in Our World" described in this section illustrates how English learners can use oral and written language for learning academic material. Special attention is given to assuring a variety of ways students can participate. Ms. Carroll's class of fifth-graders has 29 students, including two

K (What I Know)	W (Want to Know)	L (Learned)

FIGURE 9.6 K-W-L Worksheet

newcomers and five intermediate English learners. The native languages of the English learners are Spanish, Russian, and Cantonese. Ms. Carroll has no aide, but a resource teacher provides all seven English learners with English language development on a pull-out basis.

The unit activities take place between 1:30 and 3:15 each afternoon, after sustained silent reading. Students have a 10-minute recess at 2:30. Ms. Carroll provides her students the time from 2:45 to 3:15 to complete any unfinished work. If they are caught up, they may read or choose a game with a friend. Students often use this time to complete projects undertaken during thematic instruction.

Introducing the Topic and Choosing Study Questions

Ms. Carroll has chosen to develop a unit of study on "Plants in Our World," a topic for which she is responsible according to the state science framework. She teaches this topic each year but with some variations, depending on her students' interests and curiosity. In accordance with her own philosophy and the state's guidelines, she makes sure all of her students have opportunities in the processes of scientific inquiry: observing, communicating, comparing events and objects, organizing information, relating concrete and abstract ideas, inferring, and applying knowledge. She is aware that these processes involve critical thinking and that as her English learners engage in these processes they will have opportunities to develop cognitive-academic English language skills. The careful and precise ways of thinking, talking, and writing about scientific data are fairly new to all her students, native and non-native English speakers alike.

In addition to making use of the inquiry approach to science, Ms. Carroll is concerned that certain basic information about plants be understood by all her students, as outlined in the state framework. In particular, she wants them to be able to describe the parts of a plant and how each functions to enable plant growth and reproduction. She also wants her students to know the basic needs of plants and to understand and appreciate how plants have adapted to various climate and soil conditions, leading to the remarkable diversity of plant life on earth. Throughout her science and social science curriculum, she weaves the philosophical thread of the interrelatedness among all living things and their environment.

This year for plant study, Ms. Carroll opened the unit by asking students to look around the room to see what was different. Several students pointed out that the room was decorated with potted plants—two ferns, an ivy plant, and a variety of cactus plants. Ms. Carroll then initiated a discussion on plants, inviting the class to name as many kinds of plants as possible. As students volunteered names of plants, she wrote them on a large piece of butcher paper. In this way, Ms. Carroll activated and assessed her students' background knowledge and started a vocabulary list developed in the context of class discussion of the topic.

Next, she asked the class to peruse the list and look for plants that were similar in some way and thus might be grouped together. She then created a map of the students' collective thinking, reproduced in Figure 9.7. Next, she invited the class to work in groups of four to discuss the question: What would our lives be

362

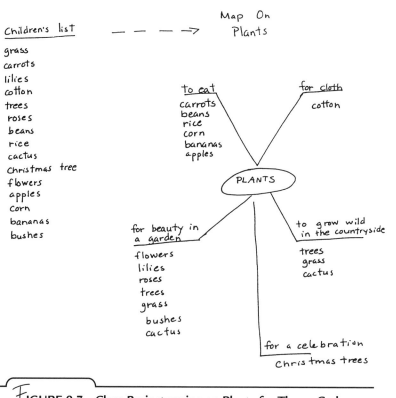

Children's list — — — —> Map On Plants

FIGURE 9.7   Class Brainstorming on Plants for Theme Cycle

like without plants? Students discussed the question for about 10 minutes and then shared their ideas with the whole class.

This introduction helped students focus on the general theme, plants. For those few students who were unfamiliar with the word *plant,* the oral discussion with mapping established the concept and its label. As students listed all the specific plants they could think of, the concept was elaborated and additional vocabulary was generated. For all students, the listing and categorizing activated background knowledge about plants to prepare them to discuss the question, What would our lives be like without plants? As students discussed this question, Ms. Carroll was able to get some ideas about what the students already knew about plants. For example, several groups suggested that our food supply would have to come from animals instead of plants. Then someone pointed out that some animals eat only plants, so they could not provide a food source if there were no plants. Another group mentioned the importance of plants for the air, but they didn't know what the effect would be if there were no plants. From this discussion, Ms. Carroll commented that her question had led to more questions than answers! She asked the students to help her list some study questions for the unit on plants. The class settled on the following questions, which were posted on the bulletin board.

1. How are plants used by people?
2. Plants give us so much. Do we give them something?
3. What kinds of plants grow in the rain forests?
4. What would the air be like without plants?

To get started on the first question, students were asked to make note of anything they used that day that came from plants. This was a homework assignment, and they were encouraged to ask family members to help them add to the list if possible. These lists would be compared the next day in class and posted on the bulletin board. Based on the lists, the class established six categories of things used by humans: food, clothing, medicine, shelter, tools/implements, and aesthetics. Students volunteered for study committees to specialize in finding out more about how plants are used in each category.

Ms. Carroll felt that the second and fourth questions could not be answered without first providing background information on plants, including how they grow and reproduce, what they need to survive, how they make food from sunlight and chlorophyll, and how they give off oxygen and other elements as by-products of photosynthesis. She explained to the class that they would be learning some basic information about plants that they could use to help them answer these questions.

For the third question, on the rain forests, Ms. Carroll foresaw rich learning possibilities extending beyond just plant life into the delicate balance among all earthly things, living and nonliving. A study of the rain forests would provide her students with a fine opportunity to understand and appreciate how plants adapt to their environment and how they form a part of a larger ecosystem, another topic designated for study in the state framework. She decided to leave the rain forest question for last, preparing her students for its complexities with direct study of plants in class and in the surrounding community. This would also give her some time to gather resources, as this was the first time she had undertaken a study of the rain forests. She explained her thinking to the students and asked them all to be on the lookout for information on rain forests in the form of news articles, television specials, or books they might come across in their research on plants. She established a small classroom corner for these resources and immediately began filling it with books, maps, and other materials that her students could peruse in their free time.

Organizing Instruction

To begin the study of plants, Ms. Carroll established two parallel projects for students to work on: (1) human uses of plants, with six research committees, and (2) plant observation and experimentation to lead to understanding of plant parts, functions, and life needs. Each research committee was to gather information on

364

its topic with the goal of sharing its findings through a poster display, including a short written report, pictures, and objects. Each group was given a section of classroom counter space or a table. The six displays would remain for two or three weeks to give everyone a chance to enjoy and learn from them, creating an impressive tribute to the gifts of the plant world.

For the first week of plant study, Ms. Carroll set up the following schedule:

Week 1: Introducing the Unit and Getting Started

Monday: Whole Class: Potting plants

Ask class what a typical plant needs in order to grow. List on chart.

Illustrate with simple drawings, pointing out plant parts and functions.

Set up experiments with groups of four or five, manipulating variables indicated by students such as water, plant food, sunlight, and soil.

Each group pots two identical plants and grows them under different conditions. Each day they will observe and record plant size, color, turgor, and other health signs in their science logs.

Tuesday and
Wednesday: Ms. Carroll meets with plant-use study groups to establish goals and plans to help them get started. She meets with three groups each day. While she meets with them, the other groups carry out activities she has set up for them at five science activity centers:

1. Parts of plant and functions: Drawing and labeling for journal

2. Herbs and spices: Classification by plant part; geography of where grown; history of uses and trade

3. George Washington Carver and his research on the many ways to use peanuts

4. Filmstrip on the life cycles of different kinds of plants: conifers, deciduous trees, wild grasses

5. Discussion, listing, and classifying of plants used for food. Group leader needed. List plants used for food. Classify according to plant part. Make a group chart to display the classification.

Thursday: Groups work on plant-use projects. Groups work at centers. Ms. Carroll is available to assist as needed.

Friday: Students take a field trip to the nursery to find out what kinds of plants are sold, who buys them, and how they are cared for.

During the first week of the unit, Ms. Carroll has followed a highly structured schedule to build basic background knowledge and get students launched in group study. During the subsequent weeks, students assume greater responsibility for independent work. Ms. Carroll adds several more plant-study experiments and reminds students to record results in their science logs. In addition, students work independently on their group projects. At the end of the third week, all six groups set up their poster displays. At this point Ms. Carroll reminds students of the questions they posed at the beginning of the unit. The class, satisfied with the amount of information they have accumulated on how people use plants, know that their rain forest interest will be studied next. However, their second and fourth questions have not yet been answered.

Ms. Carroll explains to the class that they have come up with good questions that require thinking about their current knowledge of plants. She also explains that these questions require using their imaginations to figure out some answers. She suggests that students talk in their groups and write down ideas to address the questions: What do we give plants? and What would the air be like without plants? She reminds her students that questions like these have many possible answers and that the students should use what they know about plants as the basis of their responses. The ideas generated by each group will be posted for each question.

Instructional Modifications for English Learners

Ms. Carroll has not changed the essence of her teaching style to accommodate her English learners. She has always organized instruction around topics and themes. However, in recent years, she has found ways to let students pose questions of their own and choose certain directions of study. These changes in her teaching, motivated by discussions with colleagues and occasional workshops, have aimed at improving instruction for all of her students. In addition, she now scrutinizes her teaching plans with an eye toward maximizing comprehension and participation among her English learners.

For the unit on plants, she used three strategies to this end. First, she introduced the topic with more sheltering than she might have if the students had all been native English speakers. For example, she made sure to have a variety of plants in the classroom on the first day of the unit to make her verbal reference to plants unmistakably clear. She did this specifically for the two non-English-speaking children in the class. She also made sure to illustrate some of the words she wrote on the board. These sheltering techniques, though unnecessary for many of her students, enriched her teaching and added interest for the entire class. The second strategy she used was collaborative grouping. She allowed students to cluster in interest groups around the plant-use categories. However, she balanced the groups in terms of number and social support for students with very limited English language knowledge. The two newcomers were placed in the same groups as their assigned buddy. Grouping was not adjusted for the intermediate-level students because they could communicate well enough to be successful in group work. In addition to checking for social support in group membership, Ms. Carroll assigned roles to each student for center activities, which were quite structured and would require students to work independently while she met with the study groups.

Ms. Carroll did not assign roles for the plant-use study groups. However, with her guidance the groups devised their own division of labor when she met with them during the first week of the unit. In so doing, Ms. Carroll utilized her third strategy, which was to make sure that within each task there were a variety of ways for students to participate and contribute. By meeting with the study groups one at a time, she was able to make sure that each student had an appropriate way to contribute to both knowledge building and knowledge sharing.

Developing the plant topic into theme studies provided students with several levels of learning. All students were given numerous opportunities to use oral language, reading, and writing for learning. The variety of whole-class and small-group tasks in conjunction with concrete materials and experimentation provided constant opportunities for concept development as well as language learning. Involvement in the scientific method offered opportunities to use such terms as *hypothesize, classify, predict,* and *conclude*. Moreover, in using such terms, students were involved in higher-level thinking processes. In addition to the rich learning opportunities through oral language use, the students made use of written language for a variety of functions. For example, all students kept careful observations of plant changes in their science learning logs for the four different experiments they conducted, including drawing and labeling plant parts and functions. They also read the directions and information sheets for carrying out the activities provided at the science centers. They wrote letters requesting pamphlets on the rain forests and thank-you notes to the nursery following their visit. In addition, they used textbooks, encyclopedias, and magazines to locate information on their plant-use topics.

In order to summarize the strengths provided by the thematic unit, let's take a look at how Yen, an advanced beginner/early intermediate English learner, participated in the plants unit. But first we will present a little background information about her. Yen arrived three years ago at the age of 7 and was placed in a first-grade class. Now 10 years old, she is in the fourth grade. Yen speaks Cantonese at home, as her family is ethnic Chinese from Vietnam. Though fluent in spoken Cantonese, Yen has had little opportunity to learn to write in her native language. However, her written English is fairly good, and she takes great pride in the appearance of her work. Given the choice, Yen likes to illustrate her writing with line drawings. Yen's oral English is adequate for most purposes. She understands Ms. Carroll's instruction and is aided by the sheltering techniques Ms. Carroll uses to make herself understood. At times, Yen herself is hard to understand, however, and she is often asked to repeat herself for clarification.

Ms. Carroll has taken a few special measures with Yen in mind. First of all, she has made Yen the buddy to a new Cantonese-speaking girl, Li Fen, and she has grouped them with two supportive advanced English speakers, Jerome and Linda,

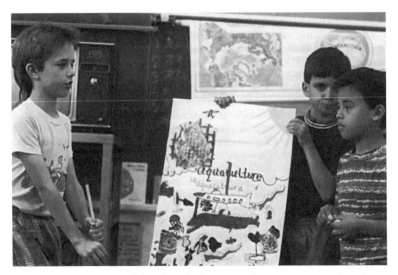

These boys have worked hard in their cooperative group preparing their oral and visual presentation, "Aquaculture," as part of the class theme cycle.

for the plant unit activities. Ms. Carroll has noticed that Yen's oral English gets better as she uses it on behalf of her newcomer friend, and, of course, Li Fen benefits from Yen's Cantonese explanations. At the same time, Ms. Carroll has made sure to place them with two advanced English speakers who will be receptive to their communication efforts.

Yen is readily able to do the majority of the activities required for the plant experiments and the science center activities. She draws, labels, records notes in her science log, and negotiates tasks with her group members. For her contribution to the poster display, she researched the topic of herbal remedies in Chinese medicine. She and Li Fen developed this topic together, at the suggestion of Ms. Carroll. They began by interviewing family members and looking for information in the encyclopedia. By providing a number of techniques combined with social support, Ms. Carroll has created an environment in which Yen can learn with others in the class. Because Yen has the opportunity to assist another child, she gains in self-esteem and advances in her own content learning.

Assessment

Assessment of reading and writing for academic learning is similar to assessment in writing and literature. Therefore, we will reiterate some basic, informal ways you can assess students, such as using portfolios, informal observation, and student self-assessment. However, the most important point we want to make here is that **all students, and especially non-native English speakers, should be assessed in a great variety of ways:** through work in groups and with partners; through participation in projects; through drawings, experiments, and oral talk; and through reading and writing (Huerta-Macias, 1995). If what you want to know is whether a student has learned about plants, you may find that some students can show you with drawings better than with essays, whereas others can perform science experiments meticulously showing a clear understanding of the content. Finally, always try to evaluate students' knowledge through their modalities of strength.

Portfolio Assessment

Whether you use a thematic unit or some other approach, there are many things you can evaluate beyond just whether students understand basic concepts or know the vocabulary of a content area. Using portfolio assessment throughout a unit, for instance, you can ask students to keep their work and evaluate it with you so that they know where they are and what they need to do. In their portfolios they keep their learning logs or other journals, as well as a record of an experiment they have performed, notes they took from oral interviews, and perhaps tapes or pictures they may have collected for a group publication (see Figure 9.8). All of these materials can then be evaluated with the students to determine their level of participation in your class. In addition to the portfolio assessment, your daily observations of students will help you evaluate their work (Gottlieb, 1995).

Selecting Materials for the Portfolio. When selecting materials for the portfolio, students are in charge of their own learning and must self-evaluate; however, you can assist students with becoming more aware of their best work (Smolen, Newman, Wathen, & Lee, 1995). Nevertheless, we have found that students are very capable of selecting their very best work for inclusion in the portfolio. In addition, you may wish to place all student tests, running records, and other observational materials in the portfolio in order to show students how far they have progressed throughout the year or semester. Moreover, in an ideal situation the portfolio would follow the student into the next year's classroom to give that teacher insights about the student's progress.

Evaluating Portfolios. You may also wish to set up an evaluation system for the grading of the portfolios. In the holistic scoring section in Chapter 6, we set up model papers with a trait analysis that gives students explicit information concerning excellent and poor papers and what their features are. You can also set up criteria for reading performance, which could consist of how many books students might read throughout certain periods of the year, how many response logs to books should be in the portfolio, and how they might be evaluated. We believe that students should have models of excellent, good, and fair work so that they

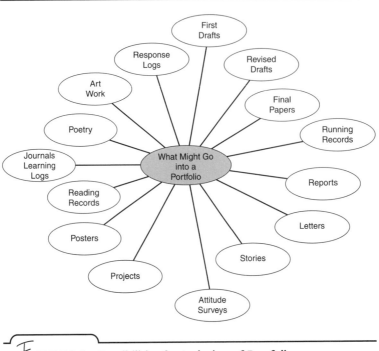

FIGURE 9.8   Possibilities for Inclusion of Portfolios

know what they are working toward. With these models students can evaluate themselves fairly; in fact, we find that when we set up clear criteria for evaluation students often evaluate themselves more critically than we do. If you need to give a specific grade for work in the portfolio, you may want to set up a point system. Some teachers place a scoring sheet in each portfolio that delineates the number of points for fair, good, or excellent papers. For example, an excellent paper might be worth 10 points, a good paper worth 8 points, and so on. Whatever fits your own teaching situation, we suggest that your system be explicit to your students and communicated to their parents clearly. In this way you can be assured of having the best chance for success. Finally, we think that just as each teacher has to work out a grading and management system that suits them, each teacher has to create a portfolio system designed to work for them.

Figure 9.9 gives an example of Lydia Martinez's portfolio checklist that helps her keep track of her students' progress. Note that every teacher's checklist will be different depending on the age of their students, the kinds of readings a teacher expects, the skill level of the students in the class, and the goals of the curriculum. At the end of this chapter we have listed resources we recommend if you wish to gain more knowledge about setting up and evaluating a portfolio assessment program. Finally, we find that classrooms using portfolio systems empower students

Student's Name: _____	

Reading Behaviors:
  * reads fluently
  * recognizes sight words
  * blends and digraphs
  * compound words
  * attends to punctuation	

Comprehension:
  * identifies main ideas or
    themes in fiction and
    nonfiction
  * makes predictions
  * monitors comprehension
  * sets purpose for reading
  * is able to summarize
    main ideas or themes in
    fiction and nonfiction	

Attitudes Concerning Reading:
  * selects books
  * reads during free-choice time
  * reads during
    Silent Sustained Reading
  * has favorite books or authors
  * responds in journals and
    during literature response time
  * clearly enjoys reading	

Other Areas Particular to the Student:	

FIGURE 9.9 Teacher's Chart for Keeping Track of a Student's Reading Progress

to take charge of their own learning and self-evaluation and to become more involved with their assignments.

In content instruction you might want to add presentations of both individual and group projects to the other reading and writing assessments in your students' portfolios. You may also add a performance assessment that evaluates how well students present the information they developed in a group project. Whatever you do with portfolio assessment you will want to have your students involved in selecting materials and determining forms of evaluation.

Using Multiple Measures for Assessment

With all students, but particularly with English learners, we recommend that you assess their participation in many different ways. For example, although there are exceptions, the speaking abilities of English language learners often surpass their ability to read and write. Therefore, if you assess them only through written exams, you will surely underestimate their capabilities and knowledge of the content you have taught. We have a friend who understands and speaks Italian fairly well and has participated in classes in which the language was used, but if her knowledge of what happened in these classes were assessed in writing only, she would probably fail miserably. If assessed orally or in reading, however, she would perform better. If given a chance to show her abilities with concrete materials, she might receive an "A" for exhibiting her knowledge. Students who may not be able to perform well on a written test may be able to show you through a scientific experiment, for example, that they understood the information at a very high level. If you do not assess students in many different ways, you will not find out what they really know.

SUMMARY

In the upper-elementary grades through high school, students must read and write longer, more complex texts. They must move from short, familiar stories and fables to longer chapter books containing a variety of characters involved in multiple problems, settings, and solutions. Students need strategies that will assist them with these longer narrative texts. Similarly, in curriculum areas such as history or science, students face texts that are longer, filled with new information, and structured differently from the short narrative texts with which they may be familiar from their earlier years of schooling. Therefore, students need special help in negotiating meaning in this new territory. In this chapter, we presented theory, research, and strategies to assist students in their journey.

Reading for academic learning involves reading to understand and remember. We presented strategies in Chapters 8 and 9 pertaining to three phases of the reading process: prereading, during-reading, and postreading. To be successful, *students must learn to set a purpose for reading, use their background knowledge, monitor their reading based on their purpose, and organize and remember what is important*. Strategies for all of these processes were presented within the context of real classrooms. We also described a variety of ways to use writing for learning across the curriculum, including journals, learning logs, and reports, as well as integrating writing into oral and written research projects.

The strategies chart in Figure 9.10 illustrates various grade levels at which we have seen the strategies used successfully. But as with the strategies shown throughout our book, these strategies are to be used at your discretion.

In addition to presenting a great variety of strategies in this chapter, we presented an example of a thematic unit that incorporates many of the strategies. In

Strategy / Grade Level	K	1	2	3	4	5	6	7	8	9	10	11	12
Brainstorming													→
Group mapping													→
Journals													→
Learning logs													→
Oral research projects													→
Mapping													→
Multiple assessment													→
Photo essays													→
Portfolios													→
Rehearsing													→
Semantic feature analysis													→
Student selected topics													→
Thematic units													→
Theme cycles													→
Written research project													→

FIGURE 9.10   Grade Levels at Which Strategies May Be Used

this way, we illustrated how to select and integrate strategies into the larger learning process in which students are actively engaged in acquiring information and insights to be shared with their peers in written research reports, oral presentations, and creative audiovisual works. In our example, we focused on the use of sheltering techniques, peer support, and oral and written language uses aimed at student learning.

Finally, we described assessment procedures, emphasizing multiple modes of assessment including portfolios, informal observation, and student self-assessment. Multiple modes of assessment help you to gain a complete picture of a student's progress and determine adjustments in your teaching approach. Most important of all, we reiterated that the best way to become an informed teacher is to watch and listen to the students in your classroom.

SUGGESTIONS FOR FURTHER READING

Armbruster, B. B. & Osborn, J. H. (2002). *Reading instruction and assessment: Understanding the IRA Standards.* Boston: Allyn and Bacon.
The IRA (International Reading Association) is the major international organization for all reading instructors. This book explains the reading instruction standards developed by the IRS. The book takes each reading standard, interprets its meaning, discusses research and other issues, and discusses what the standard means to a teacher. There are seven sections: (1) creating a literate environment, (2) word identification, vocabulary, and spelling, (3) comprehension, (4) study strategies, (5) writing, (6) assessment, and (7) recommendations. This is a very useful and readable text.

Chamot, A. U., & O'Malley, J. M. (1992). *The CALLA handbook: Implementing the cognitive academic language learning approach.* Reading, MA: Addison-Wesley.

The authors present their own approach to ELD content-based instruction. Their model is presented for content-based instruction along with a discussion of the characteristics of learning from different types of content texts. The emphasis throughout is on English language development, and the book contains numerous specific examples of how development can be embedded within content instruction and thematic instruction.

Feyton, C., Macy, M., Ducher, J., Yoshii, M., Park, E., Calandra, B., & Meros, J. (2002). *Teaching ESL/EFL with the Internet: Catching the wave.* Upper Saddle River, NJ: Merrill/Prentice Hall.

This book was written for teachers who want to "integrate technology into their teaching." The book contains chapters on listening, oral proficiency, reading skills and comprehension, writing skills, exploring culture, and assessment. Each activity has a teacher's guide, which consists of three steps: schema building, grouping, and postactivity. An excellent book for secondary teachers who have access to computers and the Internet.

Snow, M. A., & Brinton, D. M. (1997). *The content-based classroom: Perspectives on integrating language and content.* White Plains, NY: Addison Wesley Longman.

In this excellent edited text Snow and Brinton have brought together some of the most knowledgeable researchers and educators working with second language learners in content area instruction. Topics include theoretical underpinnings, K-12 instruction, postsecondary instruction, research, practical issues, and connections between content-based instruction and other teaching approaches. An introduction to the best thinking in the field.

374 ACTIVITIES

1. Observe how different teachers use writing in the content areas. What are the ways students write? What kind of prewriting activities do teachers use to make sure students will succeed in their assignments? Does the teacher respond to the students' writing? Do students respond to one another? Are the content-area writing activities authentic and meaningful? For example, do activities involve students in responding to their texts and asking and answering meaningful personal questions about topics?

2. Many students who have been "good" readers in the first few grades, where mainly very short stories are used, begin to have difficulty later with their content texts. Why do you think this is so? What are some possible differences between narrative and expository texts in terms of structure and content? What kinds of procedures or strategies can a teacher use to assist English learners with content reading? Since students are required to remember a lot of information out of their content texts, how will you help them remember what they have learned?

3. How do teachers use prereading, during-reading, and postreading activities to assist students with content reading? Do all teachers follow a prereading, during-reading, and postreading model? Some elementary teachers use a model they call "into, through, and beyond" instead of prereading, during-reading, and postreading. When you observe them, are they doing something different from the content model presented in this book? Do teachers you have observed assist students with text structure and with using headings and subheadings to create questions and a purpose for reading?

4. Develop a lesson in one content area—English, social science, or mathematics—and discuss how you will use the prereading, during-reading, and postreading model to teach the lesson. For example, what are the best prereading strategies for mathematics instruction or history instruction? What kinds of postreading activities can best assist students in remembering what they learned? Why would you use one strategy over another in a particular content area?

5. Visit a class that uses thematic units to integrate content areas and ask the teacher how a thematic approach might assist students in reading and remembering content materials. Observe for yourself the strengths and weaknesses of a thematic approach to instruction. For example, keep a checklist of your observations consisting of categories such as (1) time students spend reading or working on projects, (2) quality of ideas presented by students, (3) level of involvement in student groups, and (4) learning that appears to take place during the units. Evaluate your checklist and compare it with the quality of work in classrooms where a thematic approach is not used.

10

READING ASSESSMENT AND INSTRUCTION

In Chapter 3, we discussed the purposes of English learner assessment in terms of (1) identifying and placing students in language education support programs, (2) evaluating the effectiveness of such programs, and (3) assessing student learning and progress. In subsequent chapters we offered various ways to informally assess oral language, emergent literacy, reading, writing, and spelling in English. For each of these areas, we emphasized the importance of directly observing students as they engage in authentic, day-to-day learning tasks so that your assessment ties in directly with your instructional goals and teaching. We noted how important it is to make assessment continuous and ongoing as well as multidimensional, that is based on a variety of observations, in a variety of situations, using a variety of instruments. By observing students continuously over time, you gain a solid perspective on their progress. By making assessment multidimensional, you provide the student varied opportunities to demonstrate competence while giving yourself several information sources from which to construct a more accurate view of the student's abilities. Throughout this book we have also emphasized the benefits of engaging students in assessing their own learning. Students often understand aspects of their own development that would not otherwise come to light. Moreover, by engaging students in assessing themselves, they gain a more sophisticated understanding of their own reading, writing and learning processes. Finally, we have discussed why it is essential to consider the student's cultural, linguistic and other special characteristics and needs when collecting and evaluating information to inform instruction.

In this chapter, we return to the topic of assessment with two purposes in mind: (1) to provide an in-depth discussion of how to evaluate student reading through an informal reading inventory as one way to assess reading and (2) to illustrate how to consider information on oral language, reading, and writing to help you form a clearer picture of student abilities and to inform specific instructional choices. In this chapter, we will address the following questions:

1. What are some theoretical views of language proficiency and reading and how do they relate to assessment?
2. What are some of the ways we can informally assess student reading?
3. What is an informal reading inventory?
4. How can an informal reading inventory help us systematically evaluate students' reading development?
5. What is the meaning of the three reading levels: independent reading level, instructional reading level, and frustration reading level? How can we use these levels to inform our evaluation and instruction?
6. What are some instructional strategies for addressing students' assessed needs in reading?

377

*L*isa Charles, a student of ours, recently won the award as teacher of the year. We were curious about what she did to achieve this distinction. When we asked her, she was humble, stating only that she worked hard like other teachers in her district. But later in the semester she turned in a paper that illustrated her special dedication to students. In a case study, she described a student, Carlos, who seemed uninterested in reading and she described what she did to try to change his direction. First of all, she met with Carlos' parents, talked with them about reading to their child, and showed them how they could help Carlos with books she was able to give them. She also paired Carlos with a student who loved reading in a buddy reading situation. Finally, she enlisted the principal of the school to read to Carlos three times a week. Carlos gradually began to look at reading differently and became an enthusiastic beginning reader himself, progressing far enough that he became a buddy reader with another student who needed help at the end of the year.

Lisa identified a problem Carlos was having: valuing reading and perceiving himself as a reader. She then selected several strategies to assist him. Essentially, assessment is about identifying student strengths and needs and finding strategies to help students succeed where they didn't succeed before. You can't always expect the principal of your school to have time to read to one of your students; but you can think about your parents, your community, and your school as resources to assist you and your students. You can also use systematic ways to assess and assist your students in reading development, as we will show you in this chapter.

THEORETICAL APPROACH TO LITERACY ASSESSMENT

There can be no aspect of teaching that is more theoretically driven and value laden than assessment. When we assess our students, we must select those aspects of reading, writing and content learning that we believe are most important for students to know. Decisions about what and how to assess are dependent upon both your theoretical perspective and the values you hold. When teachers work together on grade-level, schoolwide or district-level curriculum development, discussions on assessment often become lively and heated. As these discussions yield to consensus, the process itself, difficult as it is, has great potential for clarifying your views and values on literacy and learning, while creating community, cohesion, and common purpose among you and your colleagues. Furthermore, when curriculum and assessment decisions are made schoolwide, students reap great benefits from the articulated consistency in instructional goals and assessment across the grades. Next we summarize our own views and values concerning language and literacy development as context for the remainder of this chapter on assessment.

Language Proficiency: Listening, Speaking, Reading, and Writing

In Chapter 4, we highlighted interrelationships among the four language processes: listening, speaking, reading, and writing. Because we believe that the strongest communicators are those who are effective users of both the oral and written word, and because we value both oral and written communication, we believe in setting goals for all students in listening, speaking, reading, and writing. In addition to these values and beliefs, we also hold a theoretical view concerning the interrelationships among the four language processes, and language proficiency in general. Our theoretical view holds that individuals possess a reservoir of *general language knowledge that is brought into play during any act of listening, speaking, reading, or writing.* Such knowledge consists of the grammatical conventions, vocabulary, and other linguistic elements of language as these work together to convey and comprehend meaning. In addition to certain general aspects of linguistic knowledge, each language process requires certain elements that are particular to it. Every time a student uses any one of the four language processes, the general language reservoir is exercised, creating a stronger base for subsequent efforts in listening, speaking, reading, and writing.

378

In addition to developing general aspects of language knowledge, considerable attention is necessary to help students become proficient in the special demands inherent in each of the four language processes, which is why as teachers we at times must focus specifically on assessing performance in reading, writing, listening, or speaking in ways that yield useful analyses to inform and guide instruction in each area. When we do so, we zero in on the student's strengths and needs in each area. On the other hand, when we place information on all four language processes in front of us, as in a portfolio, we can see the big picture of a student's language proficiency. Moreover, as we begin to look closely at the various performance samples in the portfolio, we can make comparisons across reading, writing, listening, and speaking that may help us better understand a student's strengths and struggles in oral and written language development. With this understanding, we are in a position to acknowledge and build on the strengths, while providing instruction to meet the student's learning needs. In this chapter, we focus primarily on reading assessment, due to its importance for all learning and because many non-native English speakers struggle to achieve facility in this important school and life skill. Thereafter, we provide case studies of individual students to illustrate how to glean information from the assessment processes we recommend. Throughout the chapter, we emphasize ways to use assessment information to guide instruction, as illustrated in Figure 10.1.

Figure 10.1 illustrates our view of assessment as an integral part of the instructional cycle. First, we *assess* to find a student's strengths and needs, then we *instruct* the student based upon these needs. As we teach, we *evaluate* and *adjust* our instruction based on how well the student is responding and learning. Finally, we *assess* the student's progress *again*. We repeat this cycle until the student is ready to move to more advanced material. Implicit in this approach are several assumptions about how students become better readers and writers. First, students become better at reading and writing by engaging in these processes daily, both independently and with teacher assistance. For example, journal writing and self-selected reading are two ways students apply their literacy abilities at their level of independence, while guided reading and student–teacher writing conferences are two ways to provide teacher assistance. When the teacher is on hand to assist, students work at their next level of development, that is, their zone of proximal development, which we discussed in Chapter 3. Thus, our second assumption about how students become better at reading and writing is that they are nudged to read and write texts

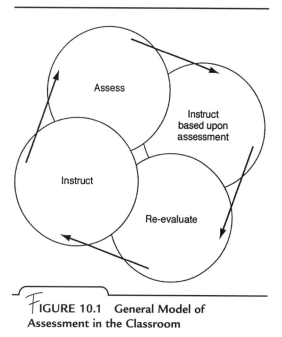

FIGURE 10.1   General Model of Assessment in the Classroom

that are a little difficult for them by virtue of such features as length, content, vocabulary, genre, text structure, and so forth. With teacher assistance, students can work through challenging texts successfully. To work effectively with students in their zones of proximal development, teachers need to have a clear view of general developmental progressions in reading and writing, such as those provided in the scales of reading and writing development at the end of Chapter 5. They also need to be able to analyze specific aspects of reading and writing in order to determine a student's strengths and needs. For example, we need to know what to do if a student is confusing the letter *d* with the letter *b*, what to do if a student consistently misses the main ideas in passages, and what will help a student remember what they've read or better organize what they have written.

In our view, students' learning needs are addressed through **scaffolding, modeling,** and **direct instruction** (Cazden, 1983). Scaffolding, a holistic approach, provides students help with reading or writing a text as a whole, supported by teacher assistance and modeling, as explained in Chapter 3. Scaffolding thus provides practice in coordinating all the complex aspects of comprehending or producing a text. Direct instruction involves explicit teaching of a particular skill or strategy aimed at improving a student's reading or writing and often includes teacher modeling of the skill or strategy as part of the lesson. Direct instruction may address reading and writing processes at any level, from phonics and spelling strategies to higher level critical thinking and composing strategies. In order for direct instruction to be effective, however, it is necessary to identify an area of need and teach to it.

We are reminded, for example, of a third-grader by the name of Ema. Each time Ema came to a compound word such as *baseball, football, booklist,* or *homework,* she was stymied. When we mentioned this to her teacher, a friend of ours, she told us that Ema would learn compound words on her own. Indeed, many children do intuit such things on their own. However, after several months, we noticed that Ema was still struggling with compound words. With her teacher's permission, we devised a simple mini-lesson showing Ema how compound words are made up of two smaller words put together. We gave her a list of compound words to practice with. After about ten minutes working on the list, she was able to recognize all the words by breaking them down into their constituent parts. Subsequently, Ema demonstrated her ability to apply the new strategy when reading stories to us. Through a little direct instruction with something she had struggled with for months, Ema was no longer stuck when she came to a compound word. Ema taught us that sometimes it is much more efficient to identify a skill that a student doesn't know and teach it directly. When a student applies that skill during actual reading or writing, what was once an isolated skill becomes a productive literacy strategy (Routman, 1995).

It is not often that a solution as simple as teaching compound words will solve a student's reading problems. More often a systematic, analytic approach to assessment is needed. Moreover, several assessment and instructional strategies may be required over a period of time before substantial progress can be measured. Addressing students' diverse learning needs may mean changing and adjust-

Reading Level	Instrument that might be used	What is tested	What might be learned
Beginning Readers: usually early grades, but can be later grades as well.	Running Records: As student reads, the teacher checks off words that student reads correctly and codes those student has trouble with.	Student reading fluency and ability to process print: decoding, syntax, use of context, etc.	Whether students have basic ability to recognize words automatically so that they can concentrate on comprehension.
Intermediate Readers: students who have learned how to read but may still be having difficulties with processing text.	Miscue Analysis: Student reads materials while you are listening or tape recording; words are coded by you and comprehension questions are asked or student recalls information.	Student strategies for processing print, possible difficulties with print, and comprehension of information as given in recall or answering questions.	What student knows or doesn't know based upon oral reading. Whether student is "barking at print" or actually comprehending.
Advanced Readers: readers who have basic ability to process print automatically and who focus on comprehension.	Comprehension Checks: looking at student's ability to understand both narrative and expository texts, e.g., GRI (Group Reading Inventory).	Student ability to comprehend materials at high levels, including, factual, inferential, and applicative.	Student's sophistication in reading various levels and genres of print.
Appropriate for all readers whether struggling or gifted.	Informal Reading Inventory (IRI): Using leveled reading passages and comprehension checks, you can establish reading levels of your students.	Student ability to comprehend and process text at Independent, Instructional, and Frustration levels.	How student is able to read and comprehend passages written at various grade levels.
Appropriate for all readers and writers.	Portfolio Assessment: Teacher and student together collect in a portfolio various examples of student reading and writing.	How students perceive their literacy ability, general progress.	How student has developed over time. How student perceives work. What might be done next to assist moving the student to the next level of development.

FIGURE 10.2   Reading Assessment of English Language Learners

ing our instruction many times. It certainly means that we must have a great many strategies on hand to assist students. All good teachers must be like Shakespeare's Cleopatra, commanding "infinite variety." Figure 10.2 summarizes some of the assessment techniques we have introduced in Chapters 7, 8, and 9. In addition, at the end of this chapter we recommend some valuable resources that will provide you with the variety you'll need to serve your students well. In the next section, we describe some ways to systematically and analytically assess student reading performance. We begin with a discussion of some elements of the reading process in English.

Looking Closely at the Reading Process in English

In order to assess a student's reading performance using a systematic and analytic approach, you need to have an idea of what proficient reading involves. Here we offer our view of proficient reading, that is, the reading process displayed when a mature reader reads a text closely and carefully, as we hope you are reading this one right now. By delineating various kinds of knowledge that go into the process of reading, we can assess and teach to those areas.

Proficient readers approach a given text, be it a newspaper, a recipe, or a novel, with a **purpose** in mind for reading it. Next comes attention to the print, with visual processing proceeding from left to right, from the top to bottom of the page, given that we are talking about reading in English. Processing the print involves **decoding** the words on the page, producing a mental or verbal equivalent. Fluent readers recognize most words almost instantly, using sound/symbol knowledge, grammar, and meaning cues as they decode. **Comprehension** initially requires processing word sequences as meaningful units at the phrase or sentence level in order to begin to construct meaning. Continued comprehension further requires not only understanding the sentences but also relationships among sentences as text meaning is reconstructed. Decoding, in our view then, provides the reader access to the words on the page, whereas comprehension requires the reader to process word meanings in the context of the grammatical relationships among the words in a phrase or sentence to arrive at the meaning. It is largely through the relationships of words to each other that English sentences convey meaning. You may have observed how some students read word by word, as if the words in the sentence were nothing more than a random list, sometimes called "barking at print." They have decoded the words without comprehension of the phrase or sentence. To get at the meaning, the reader must attend to the *words as meaningful language* in order to understand the ideas in the phrase or the sentence. When teachers ask a beginning reader to "read it again, but this time with expression," they are attempting to focus students on pulling meaning from phrases and sentences and expressing that meaning in their oral reading. For example, consider the sentence:

The frightened fox finally escaped the hunters by diving into its den.

A student who reads this sentence word by word might be able to say each word and even know the meaning of each word, but only by reading and understanding the words in relation to each other can the reader glean the meaning of the sentence as a whole, making it possible to visualize a fox chased by hunters, running in a panic, and narrowly escaping death. In order to get that far in comprehension, the reader must understand the meaning of the words in context. For example, the reader must comprehend the word *frightened* as modifying the word *fox*, while understanding *fox* as the subject whose action is conveyed by the verb *escaped*. The fact that the verb is in the past tense is very important here, as it lets the reader know that the fox is now safe, because he *did* escape, not that he *is escaping* or *will escape*. The adverb *finally* modifies the verb *escaped*, implying that the fox has been chased for quite some time. Another grammatical element to understand is the phrase, *by diving into its den*. This phrase elaborates upon the verb, telling the reader *how* the fox escaped. Readers understand these grammatical relationships implicitly as a result of knowing the language, *not* as a result of being able to state the grammatical rules as we have done here. Reading with compre-

382

> **INTERNET RESOURCE:** The ERIC site on assessment is so large that we've known people who entered it and never returned: http://ericae.net/intbod.stm. The site contains 30 pages of links on assessment ranging from Alternative Assessment to secondary education, to early childhood assessment, to test reviews and tests online. You might choose an area such as mathematics and science assessment and evaluate the site's usefulness. Or explore and assess the national results on reading, writing, or mathematics. There are hundreds of links here, most of them annotated. You might also want to see the companion website: www.ablongman.com/peregoy4e.

hension thus calls into play the reader's English language knowledge and is dependent upon the reader's ability to understand the specific morphology, syntax, and semantics of the language used in the text.

There is more to reading comprehension than decoding words and comprehending sentences. After all, most passages consist of at least several paragraphs structured in particular ways. Therefore, in addition to knowledge of decoding, syntax, and semantics, the reader's prior knowledge of the passage's content and familiarity with its genre and text structure play a major role in comprehension. Reading along, the reader needs to hold on to his or her ongoing interpretation of the meaning in order to elaborate, modify, and further build upon it, thereby keeping the interpretation going and growing. Reading is thus a complex, cognitive-linguistic process that depends upon the reader's ability to engage background knowledge, language knowledge, and memory while processing print. Reading is also a social process in that it involves communicative interaction between the author and the reader. In this view, text comprehension is simultaneously driven by the reader's purpose, prior knowedge, and ongoing interpretation as these interact with the continued decoding and comprehending of the print on the page to achieve communication. Finally, proficient readers monitor their own understanding as they read along to determine whether their interpretation makes sense and to make sure they are achieving their purpose for reading. This view of proficient reading, illustrated with a discussion of how a mature reader might read the brief passage below, provides the theoretical background for our approach to reading assessment.

> One of the most popular pets in today's homes is the cat. Cats were first tamed in Ancient Egypt probably around 3,000 B.C. The ancient Egyptians needed cats to keep rats and mice from eating their large stores of grain. The Egyptians grew to admire the cats for their strength, agility and superb hunting ability. They admired them so much that they not only kept them as pets, but also considered them sacred. They even mourned their cats when they died, embalmed them, and took their mummified bodies to a special temple for cats. Today's cats may not be considered sacred, but they are loved by their owners for many of the same traits admired by the ancient Egyptians.

Let us consider how a mature reader might process this brief expository text about cats. In this case, let us assume that the student has chosen to research her

383

favorite animal, cats, for which she will write a short report. The student's purpose for reading the text is to learn new information about cats and choose facts and ideas to include in her report. She brings prior knowledge of cats and their behavior, as she has a pet cat at home. However, she is unfamiliar with the ancient Egyptians. She will build upon her knowledge of cats as she reads and learns new information about cats in Ancient Egypt. Her prior knowledge, intrinsic interest and purpose for reading about cats bolster the effort it will take to construct new knowledge from her reading.

Our mature reader begins reading the first sentence, already automatic at reading left to right, top to bottom. As a mature reader, she is able to recognize every word in the first sentence. Decoding is fast and fluent. Notice, however, that to comprehend the subject of the sentence, conveyed by a phrase, she must process the **syntax** of the entire phrase "One of the most popular pets in today's homes." A few of the syntactic relationships that have to be understood include the way that the word *today's* modifies the word *homes* and the way the phrase "one of the most popular" modifies the word *pets*. Important relationships are conveyed by the prepositions *of* and *in* the prepositional phrases, "(one) *of* the most popular pets" and "*in* today's homes." To understand the sentence it is also necessary to know that the verb *is* indicates equivalence between the subject of the sentence, the long phrase we have just discussed, and the complement, "the cat."

In terms of **vocabulary,** some words that may be unfamiliar to our mature reader include *mourned, embalmed, mummified*. At the level of word formation, **morphology,** the reader needs to know the meaning of the plural marker -*s* as in *cats* and *homes*, while being able to distinguish it from the possessive marker *'s*, in *today's*. These elements of syntax and morphology can be a bit tedious to think about (and write about!). However, the discussion serves to illustrate how knowledge of English syntax and morphology is essential to getting at the meaning of the sentence. That is, understanding the meaning of a sentence requires not only knowing the meaning of the words and their different forms, but also understanding the relationships among the words conveyed by the syntax of the sentence. Thus, reading comprehension at the sentence level depends upon the reader's language knowledge.

In addition to our reader's purpose, prior knowledge, decoding ability and language knowledge, her familiarity with **written language features** helps her read the passage easily. One of the most important written language features is **text structure.** Our passage about cats displays paragraph structure, with an introductory topic sentence, elaborating information and concluding sentence. Our mature reader knows that she is reading an expository text, one that is written to convey information about cats. Her experiences with this genre of written text create expectations about the kind of content and text structure she will find in this passage. This familiarity assists her in comprehending and remembering the passage.

Finally, our mature reader must put the ideas together that are conveyed in the paragraph as a whole, using **cognitive** and **metacognitive processes.** One cognitive process is inferencing. For example, the reader must infer that the embalming of cats' bodies represents one way in which cats are treated as sacred.

384

That connection is not explicit in the text. Rather, it is an implicit connection that the reader must *infer* in order to fully understand the passage. Another cognitive process readers must use is memory. The reader must hold information in memory within and across sentences in order to build the meaning of the passage. The longer the passage, the more there is to remember and relate. This is where some **metacognitive strategies** are helpful. Our mature reader has a particular purpose in mind for reading: She will be writing a report. Her purpose helps her decide what is important to remember. One of her strategies in achieving her reading purpose is to make notes on ideas she might include in her report.

In summary, our view of the reading process highlights the importance of several components: purpose, prior knowledge, language knowledge, decoding ability, written text knowledge, and cognitive and metacognitive processes. Next we examine these components as they impact non-native English speakers as they work to become proficient readers in English.

Resources That Non-Native English Speakers Bring to English Reading

Keeping in mind this view of reading, there are three kinds of general information we need to know about our students as non-native English speakers before we even start assessing their reading performance—information that may shed light upon their efforts to read in English while indicating ways to assist them in becoming better readers. First of all, we need to know something about our students' life experiences, their interests, their aspirations. With this information, we are better able to make use of their prior knowledge and interests to provide purpose for reading and motivate their desire to read. Second, we need to have a general idea of how well they know English, given the key role of language knowledge in reading. Are they beginners in English? Intermediate? Advanced? With a general sense of a student's **English language proficiency** we will be able to gauge whether language knowledge is making comprehension difficult and we can guide students toward texts at an appropriate level of linguistic difficulty. Third, we need to find out about the student's prior literacy experiences, both in the primary language and in English. Students who are literate in the primary language are generally familiar with various purposes for reading and writing (Peregoy & Boyle, 2000). If they are proficient readers in their primary language, they have exercised the process of constructing meaning from text, a complex process in any language. Thus, they bring substantial **funds of knowledge** (Moll, 1994) specific to written language forms, functions and processes that they may build upon as they learn to read in English. Although much of their **primary language literacy** knowledge is generally helpful as students begin to read in English, there are at least two broad areas English learners need growth in: English language development and understanding the ways that English is portrayed in print, that is, its writing system. Knowing the writing system will permit them to decode the printed words, while knowing English will facilitate text comprehension as we explained in detail above. Students who read a logographic writing system such as Chinese face a different

385

Students who are literate in their primary language bring funds of knowledge about reading and writing that serve them well as they develop English literacy.

386

task from those who read an alphabetic writing system such as the one used for Spanish or French. Nonetheless, all students who are literate in their home language bring funds of literacy knowledge to build upon as they learn to read in English.

In addition to the general information about a student's prior knowledge, English language proficiency, and primary language literacy, there are several specific kinds of information to look for in relation to student performance on a particular passage. These specific kinds of information stem directly from the theoretical view of reading described above and relate to the student's ability to deal with this particular passage. Because we are now discussing a student's ability to read a passage, we are referring to students who are beyond the emergent literacy phase of development discussed in Chapter 5. Thus they are at least beginning readers with at least beginner to advanced beginner proficiency in English. In other words, at a minimum, they have sufficient decoding and comprehension abilities to understand a simple passage in English. Among the areas of knowledge we want to learn about are the student's background knowledge about the passage topic itself. If a student doesn't know anything about catalytic converters, for example, he or she might have difficulty with a passage on that topic. Closely related to background knowledge, vocabulary knowledge also plays an important role in comprehension. Perhaps the student knows what a catalytic converter is, but has never *heard* or *seen* the term before. Familiarity with **key content vocabulary** can make or break comprehension. Another important knowledge area to assess is the student's **word recognition** and ability to decode with ease and fluency. The more words a student recognizes immediately, the more fluent he or she will be at processing the language of the text and constructing meaning. The better students are at figuring out words they don't recognize on sight, the easier it will be for them to remain focused on the meaning. Thus, sight word knowledge and decoding strategies are important to assess.

In addition to evaluating background knowledge, vocabulary, and decoding, it is also necessary to find out how well the student understands the **syntax** and **semantics** of the text, as they process and relate the ideas across phrases, sentences and paragraphs. One area that can create difficulty, for example, is understanding the meaning of prepositional phrases, such as "under the tree," or "before returning to the party." Longer and more complex sentences are often difficult to understand because they require readers to comprehend and remember several complicated ideas at once, while mentally juggling the interrelationships among those ideas. Consider, for example, sentences such as the one at the beginning of this paragraph. This sentence connects ideas discussed in the previous paragraph and introduces the direction of the next discussion. Such sentences are more typical of written language than oral, and require facility in English as well as experience with written text.

Finally, as the student reads, you'll want to find out what strategies, including metacognitive strategies, he or she uses for comprehension of the passage. Does the student make good use of prior knowledge to comprehend? Does the student use text structure to aid comprehension and memory? Does the student slow down or reread complex texts, such as mathematics texts?

As a student reads, then, you are going to look at all of the above: background knowledge and vocabulary, word level skills such as decoding and sight word recognition, language knowledge, and comprehension strategies. With these in mind you can begin evaluating and helping students in their reading progress. Figure 10.3 synthesizes some major categories in reading, some of the things we'll want to know about each category, and examples of techniques we might use to evaluate each area.

What we want to look at	Some of the things we want to evaluate	How we evaluate
Background Knowledge	What the students know about passages they're reading; whether they engage their background knowledge when they read.	Through questioning and procedures such as guided reading, DR-TA, and IRIs.
Language Knowledge	Language knowledge includes such areas as prepositional phrases, anaphoric references, syntax, etc.	Through miscue analysis and comprehension assessment as students read connected text.
Word Recognition	Students' knowledge of sight words, decoding ability, and level of automaticity the student possesses.	Through procedures such as running records, miscue analysis, and Informal Reading Inventories.
Vocabulary	This category is related, of course, to the students' background knowledge. We want to know the extent of the students' vocabulary, including levels of knowledge such as denotation and connotation.	Students' use of vocabulary in speaking, reading, and writing as seen in daily classroom work, as seen in miscue analysis and in more formal tests you might give.
Comprehension	Students' ability to comprehend at different levels, including Independent, Instructional and Frustration levels. Students' ability to comprehend at factual, interpretive, and applicative levels	Through students' answering and asking questions at the various levels of comprehension. Through students' recall, learning logs, and other more informal techniques.

FIGURE 10.3   **What We Want to Assess with Readers**

ASSESSING READING USING AN INFORMAL READING INVENTORY

388

Throughout this book we have discussed assessment techniques you can use day to day in your classroom, including checklists, anecdotal observations, miscue analysis, running records, lists of published works, lists and notes on literature students read, writing samples, and teacher-made tests. When items such as these are collected, evaluated and placed in a portfolio, they provide a rich description of a student's overall language and literacy development. In this section, we share with you an assessment instrument, the informal reading inventory (IRI), to use when you need in-depth information on a student's reading processes, such as a new student or one for whom your day-to-day observations have left you uncertain as to individual strengths and needs. Results of the IRI are another source of information that you may add to the student's portfolio.

IRIs are often used by reading specialists who work with individuals and small groups of students identified as needing special help in reading. Classroom teachers who use IRIs with their students benefit in two ways. First, they gain in-depth information about each student's reading processes. Second, they benefit from knowing the principles and procedures involved, such as how to systematically collect information about students' reading over time; how to use grade-level materials such as word lists and grade-level passages to create benchmarks for students' progress; how to evaluate students' decoding and comprehension strategies; and how to evaluate what students need to progress to the next level of reading development. The IRI process itself can become a mental template that you use when listening to students read during day-to-day classroom activities and instruction. In other words, as you internalize the analytic process, you become a more acute observer and evaluator of student reading performance, even though you are not using the "official" procedure.

Using IRIs to Systematically Assess Students' Status and Progress

An informal reading inventory is a commercially available assessment tool, often published in a spiral-bound notebook format. IRIs include sets of passages of gradually increasing difficulty, usually designated as pre-primer through sixth grade level or beyond. By providing a general index of passage difficulty, IRIs offer you a way of determining how a student performs on material at increasing levels of difficulty. Following each passage is a set of comprehension questions for students to answer. The comprehension questions, usually both factual and interpretive questions, give you a good idea of how students make sense of texts of varying difficulty. Some teachers also like to ask students to summarize information to help them get a fuller picture of the student's reading comprehension. When they do this, they prepare an outline of the major points in the text they would expect to be included in a complete retelling. If a student leaves out a major point, you can probe by asking an open-ended question, such as "What happened at the end of the story?" or "What about the dream the boy had?" These questions prompt memory without giving the information in the text. Through probing questions, you can help students display their understanding of a passage while distinguishing lack of recall from lack of comprehension.

When conducting an informal reading inventory, you may tape-record as the student reads each passage aloud, summarizes it, and answers the comprehension questions. It is also possible to have students read the passages silently, and then to assess comprehension. However, oral reading provides you with information on decoding and comprehending that silent reading cannot. Either way, it is best to begin with a passage that you believe is relatively easy for your student, as this helps put the student at ease, bolsters confidence, and provides a chance to warm up. Next the student reads passages of gradually increasing difficulty. It's a good idea to have students read only two or three passages at one sitting, depending on their energy and enthusiasm for the task. If the student tires easily, you might want to spread the task out over a few days. The goal is to continue until you arrive at a passage level at which the student has difficulty. In this way you have tapped the ceiling (or plumbed the depths) of their reading proficiency on the IRI passages. In addition, by assessing a student with a challenging passage, you will obtain sufficient oral reading miscues to form the basis of a **miscue analysis** that will assist you in determining the student's reading strategies and potential learning needs.

After tape-recording the student to the highest passage level, you listen to the tape in order to analyze the student's oral reading performance. First, you code the miscues, or oral reading errors, using the system we provided in Chapter 7. Then you assess comprehension by evaluating the student's summary retelling or by checking their answers to the comprehension questions or both, if you have included both in your assessment. In this way, if the student has problems with the comprehension questions or in the retelling, you can look for patterns of miscues in the oral reading that might explain the comprehension difficulty. You can also look for general patterns of miscues to see what the student's strategies for reading are. For example, how does the student figure out an unfamiliar word? Does the student rely on letter/sound cues only or does he or she use a combination of letter/sound cues and context cues? Does the student self-correct? In this way you can get data on your students' relative reading level to help you determine the kind of instruction they may need—for example, in determining main ideas—to move up to the next level of reading development.

Using the results of the IRI, you can then create a strategy development plan for your students to help them become more competent readers. It can be very useful to discuss the IRI results with your students in individual conferences, commending them for their strengths, explaining growth areas you would like them to work on, and inviting input from the students themselves. When you do this, you make reading strategies and processes *explicit*, providing students both the concepts and the words used to talk about strategies good readers use. If you emphasize that your students are in charge of their own learning, and that you will be there to support their efforts, the reading conference will invite mutual commitment between teacher and student toward reading improvement. Informal reading inventories take some time, but they are well worth it for the data you will get on your students' reading capabilities. You can perform an IRI in about 50 minutes with most students and the information will help you every day in your instructional decision making.

Reading Levels Can Be Established Using Informal Reading Inventories

Reading specialists and others often refer to three levels of reading performance on a given passage: the Independent reading level, the Instructional reading level, and the Frustration reading level. Because the terms are used in conjunction with leveled passages—materials that have a designated grade level such as primer, tenth grade and so on—you can generalize cautiously as to the difficulty level of materials a student will be able to read independently, which materials will be appropriate for instruction, and which materials will probably be too difficult. When used flexibly and in combination with other assessment information, including your day-to-day observations, IRI results can be quite useful in helping you select both materials and strategies for instruction. In addition, IRI results can help you guide students in selecting materials for independent reading.

Procedures for Determining Independent, Instructional, and Frustration Levels

When you use published IRI's, you will find that they include simple formulas to apply to determine whether a student is reading a particular passage at the Independent, Instructional, or Frustration level. These formulas usually address word recognition and comprehension. For each passage, the IRI will tell you the number or percentage of word recognition errors, or miscues, that indicate Independent, Instructional, and Frustration levels on that passage. In addition, the IRI will tell you the number or percentage of missed comprehension questions that indicate each level. It's important to know that experts disagree slightly on these percentages. Furthermore, it is essential that you combine IRI results with other assessment measures including your own personal judgment to be most accurate in gauging each student's reading abilities. It is especially important for you to use your own judgment when interpreting IRIs with non-native English speakers because all the IRIs that we know of have been designed and tested with native English speakers. Therefore, the calculations used to determine Independent, Instructional and Frustration levels may very well differ for your English learners. The procedure is nonetheless appropriate and useful, as is the general information yielded by the miscue analysis and by the student's ability to deal with leveled passages. Your task will be to decide whether the passage is at the Independent, Instructional, or Frustration level for your student. Below we describe how these levels are usually calculated in the IRIs for native English speakers.

Independent Reading Level. When a student is reading at an Independent level, he or she is reading at a level that is relatively easy for him or her, a level at which the student requires little, if any, help from you. In numerical terms, if a student can read the material with roughly 98 percent word-recognition accuracy and with about 90 percent comprehension, they are reading at the Independent level. Comprehension is determined according to student performance on the retelling or on the comprehension questions for the passage or on a combination of the two. In an IRI, if students read narrative and expository passages at an Independent fourth grade level, you can have some confidence that they will be able to read other fourth grade materials with success.

Instructional Reading Level. At the instructional level, students' word recognition is about 95 percent accurate and comprehension is about 70 percent in an IRI or other assessment method using leveled materials. Students are able to read classroom materials at their instructional level when given your assistance. For example, you may do something as simple as developing a topic and building student background knowledge about marine mammals to help them read a passage on that topic. Or you may provide students with a study guide that helps them focus on key ideas in their reading.

Frustration Reading Level. When a student is reading at the Frustration level, he or she is having great difficulty with word recognition and comprehension. If students consistently have great difficulty with fourth grade passages, for example, you will probably want to consider using less difficult texts with them. At the Frustration level students are below 90 percent in word recognition and below about 70 percent in comprehension. In other words, this level is simply too difficult for the student, even with help.

Obviously, you don't want to use these percentages rigidly to make decisions about your students. Your students may be highly motivated and willing to work with difficult materials, enabling them to grapple successfully with reading materials you deem to be at their Frustration level. Similarly, they may bring a large amount of background knowledge to a passage you would otherwise consider too complex and therefore frustrating for them. These reading levels must be thought of as general guidelines, not as rigid, unchanging levels to be followed doggedly. Nevertheless, using these general guidelines can enhance your knowledge and teaching.

Sample Informal Reading Inventory

Throughout this chapter we will be using materials from one of the best reading inventories we know of, the *Qualitative Reading Inventory-II* (QRI-II) by Leslie and Caldwell (1995). This reading inventory has several features that we feel are important for all students, but especially for second language learners:

- The QRI-II contains word lists related to each passage provided to help you decide which passage to choose when assessing a student. Research suggests that good readers are able to read from word lists fluently and automatically. In addition, a student's performance on a word list is a quick way to gauge their reading level and start them on an appropriate-grade-level passage for the reading inventory.

- The QRI-II includes "concept questions" to ask *before* the student reads the passage. These questions assess student familiarity with the topic and understanding of selected vocabulary or phrases included in the passage. Students are then given the opportunity to make a prediction about what the passage will be about. The concept questions serve two extremely useful purposes. First, they give you important information on what the student knows about the topic; second, they give you an idea of student understanding of some of the words and phrases in the passage. If the student has trouble understanding the passage, you have some information on background and language knowledge specific to the passage that may help you determine the source of difficulty. The concept and prediction questions serve another purpose in that they key the student into the passage topic, activate prior knowledge, and get the student ready to read. The process thus scaffolds student comprehension. For non-native English speakers, in particular, this process is especially helpful both for the information it provides you and for the warm-up it provides the student.

- The QRI-II contains multiple narrative and expository passages at each grade level, from preprimer to junior high. This feature is very useful because students generally have more difficulty with expository passages than with narrative passages. This difficulty may result from the fact that narrative passages tend to be self-contained and relate information that is generally more familiar to readers and because expository passages have different text structures that may play a role in making a passage less familiar and more difficult: for example, expository structures such as problem/solution and compare/contrast among others.

392

- The QRI-II contains both explicit and implicit questions for checking student comprehension of a passage. Explicit questions are those for which answers are stated explicitly in the text while implicit questions require the reader to *infer* the answer from information which is not stated explicitly in the text.
- The QRI-II includes retelling as a comprehension measure to complement the information you obtain from student performance on the comprehension questions. A recall checklist is provided to help you determine how much of the passage information the student understood and recalled. We suggest open-ended probing questions to help students recall information they leave out of the retelling.
- The QRI-II miscue scoring counts only errors that interfere with comprehending the meaning of the passage. Thus repetitions and self-corrections are not counted as errors. Applying this scoring principle to English learners, non-native pronunciations are not counted as reading errors as long as comprehension is demonstrated, given that comprehension is the goal of reading, not pronunciation.

With this information, let's see how one teacher used and adapted an informal reading inventory to gauge her student's general reading abilities and strategies and to determine the student's Independent, Instructional, and Frustration reading levels. Figure 10.4, adapted from Leslie and Caldwell, illustrates categories in a score sheet to help you collect information about your student. The Concept Questions in Figure 10.4 tap into the student's prior knowledge about the passage which is about to be read. The total number of miscues gives you the accuracy of the student's reading so that you can estimate Independent, Instructional and Frustration levels of reading. In addition, there is a retelling sheet that helps you determine how well the student recalls the passage content after reading. Finally, there are comprehension questions to help you estimate the student's ability to understand the passage that has been read. Let's now look at one student's performance on an IRI.

Case Study of Lou Using an IRI. Lou is a 13-year-old Chinese bilingual eighth grader who speaks Mandarin at home with his parents. Lou's mother speaks no English, whereas his father speaks and reads some English. Both parents are literate in Chinese, and they frequently read newspapers, books, and magazines in Chinese. The family has been in the U.S. public school system for four years. Lou's teacher, Ms. Collins, noticed that Lou was having trouble reading material in her sheltered social studies/English language arts class. In class, Lou works well with his peers, using English effectively in most situations. However, he does not volunteer to participate in whole class discussions, nor is he eager to make formal presentations to the class. Based on her in-class observations, Ms. Collins rated Lou at a score of 18 on the SOLOM (see Chapter 4), with vocabulary and pronunciation his lowest areas, rating a 3 each. She rated him as a 4 on comprehension, fluency, and grammar. Based on SOLOM scoring, Lou is rated as upper Phase II, limited English proficient. In our terms he is an intermediate English language learner.

393

Concept Questions:

1. Who was Amelia Earhart? (3-2-1-0)
2. What are the dangers of flying a small Plane? (3-2-1-0)
3. What is an adventurer? (3-2-1-0)
4. What are women's rights? (3-2-1-0)
Score _____/12 (×100) = _____%

Prediction: _____

Number of Total Miscues
(Total Accuracy): _____

Number of Meaning Change Miscues
(Total Acceptability): _____

Total Accuracy		Total Acceptability
0−6 miscues _____ Independent _____		0−6 miscues
7−27 miscues _____ Instructional _____		7−14 miscues
28+ miscues _____ Frustration _____		15+ miscues
Rate: 263 × 60/ _____ seconds = _____ WPM		

Partial retelling sheet for Amelia Earhart Passage

Setting/Background
___ Amelia Earhart was an adventurer
___ during World I
___ she was a nurse
___ who had been hurt

Goal
___ She knew
___ that she must fly

Events
___ Earhart trained
___ to be a pilot

Resolution
___ Her plane disappeared
___ People searched
___ over the ocean
___ for a long time

A few sample comprehension questions:

1. What was Amelia Earhart's main goal? *Implicit:* to fly; to do challenging things
2. When Amelia Earhart first crossed the Atlantic in a plane, what was her role? *Explicit:* she was a passenger
3. Why do you think her plane was never found? *Implicit:* probably sank in the ocean; ocean was so big; plane was very small

FIGURE 10.4   Concept Questions and Partial Scoring Sheet for the QRI-II for Amelia Earhart Passage

Adapted from Lauren Leslie and Joanne Caldwell, *Qualitative Reading Inventory-2.* Published by Allyn and Bacon, Boston, MA. Copyright ©1995 by Pearson Education. Reprinted by permission of the publisher.

Ms. Collins decided to assess his reading, beginning with a third-grade-level passage, "A Trip to the Zoo," using her own judgment rather than giving him word lists to decide where to start on the IRI. Figure 10.5 illustrates how Lou read the passage. As we can see, Lou omitted some *-ed* endings which Ms. Collins determined didn't get in the way of his understanding the passage (Lou was able to

---

The Trip to the Zoo

jump

The day was bright and sunny. Carlos and Maria jumped out of bed and

dressed in a hurry. They didn't want to be late for school today. It was a special day

because their classes were going to the zoo. When they got to school, all of the

children were waiting outside to get on the bus. When everyone was there, the

second and third graders got on the bus and rode to the zoo. On the bus, the

talk   want

children talked about the zoo animals that they liked best. Joe and Carlos wanted to

want

see the lion, king of the beasts. Maria and Angela wanted to see the chimps. Maria

thought they acted a lot like people.

When they got to the zoo, their teachers divided the children into four groups.

One teacher, Mr. Lopez, told them if anyone got lost, to go to the ice cream stand.

Everyone would meet there at noon. Maria went with the group to the monkey house

where she spent a long time watching the chimps groom each other. She wrote

down all the ways that the chimps acted like people. Her notes would help her write

a good report of what she liked best at the zoo.

Carlos went with the group to the lion house. He watched the cats pace in

front of the glass. Carlos was watching a lion so carefully that he didn't see his

group leave. Finally, he noticed that it was very quiet in the lion house. He turned

around and didn't see anyone. At first he was worried. Then he remembered what

Mr. Lopez had said. He traced his way back to the entrance and found a map. He

followed the map to the ice cream stand, just as everyone was meeting there for

lunch. Joe smiled and said, "We thought that the lion had you for lunch!" (312 words)

FIGURE 10.5   Third-Grade Narrative Passage Read by Lou

Adapted from Lauren Leslie and Joanne Caldwell, *Qualitative Reading Inventory-2.*
Published by Allyn and Bacon, Boston, MA. Copyright ©1995 by Pearson
Education. Reprinted by permission of the publisher.

answer all of the comprehension questions accurately). But he did have trouble
with two words: *noticed,* which he pronounced *no-tiched* and he paused at the
word *remembered* for a second or two before figuring it out correctly. Ms. Collins
determined, therefore, that Lou read the third-grade zoo passage at the independent level. Next, she wanted to see how Lou would read a fourth-grade narrative passage.

Figure 10.6 illustrates Lou's performance on the fourth-grade narrative passage about Amelia Earhart. On the concept questions prior to reading the passage, Lou indicated that he didn't know anything about Amelia Earhart or what "an adventurer" was; thus, the information in the passage was basically unfamiliar to him. As shown in Figure 10.6, Lou read the passage making only six miscues, which means that he is reading this fourth-grade material at the independent level. Moreover, he correctly answered all of the comprehension questions on the passage and recalled most of the important information in the passage. Therefore, Ms. Collins concludes that Lou probably will be able to read other unfamiliar, narrative

---

Amelia Earhart

Amelia Earhart was an *a avent* adventurer and a pioneer in the field of flying. She did

things no other woman had ever done before.

During World War I, Earhart worked as a nurse. She cared for pilots who had

been hurt in the war. Earhart listened to what they said about flying. She watched

planes take off and land. She knew that she, too, must fly.

In 1928, Earhart was the first woman to cross the Atlantic in a plane. But

someone else flew the plane. Earhart wanted to be more than just a *Passage* passenger. She

wanted to fly a plane across the ocean herself. For four years, Earhart trained to be a

pilot. Then, in 1932, she flew alone across the Atlantic to Ireland. The trip took over

fourteen hours.

Flying may seem easy today. (However) Earhart faced many dangers. Airplanes

had just been invented. They were much smaller than our planes today. *mech* *mechan* Mechanical

problems happened quite often. There were also no computers to help her. Flying

Frigen *Frig* across the ocean was as frightening as sailing across it had been years before.

Earhart knew the dangers she faced. However, she said, "I want to do it because I want

to do it. Women must try to do things as men have tried. When they fail, their failure

must be a challenge to others."

Earhart planned to fly around the world. She flew more than twenty thousand

disa... *some* miles. Then, her plane disappeared somewhere over the huge Pacific Ocean. People

look searched for a long time. Finally, they gave up. Earhart and her plane were never

found.   (263 words)

FIGURE 10.6   Lou's Reading of Fourth-Grade Narrative Passage

Adapted from *Scott, Foresman Social Studies, Grade 4: Regions of Our Country and Our World* (Glenview, IL.: Scott, Foresman and Co., 1983), p. 83. Used with permission.

material written at a similar level of difficulty, that is, the fourth-grade level. However, his performance on the passage indicates that Lou has some difficulty with multisyllabic words such as *adventurer, frightening,* and *disappeared.* Even though he discussed *adventurer* with Ms. Collins before reading the passage, he still had difficulty recognizing the word and understanding it in the context of the passage. This difficulty with decoding and understanding multisyllabic words may cause trouble for him when he reads other content material containing such words.

Figure 10.7 illustrates Lou's performance on the fifth-grade narrative passage about Margaret Mead. Lou made 16 miscues on the passage that have affected the meaning, and this loss of meaning shows up when he misses half of the

---

Margaret Mead

Margaret Mead had always been interested in the ways of life of people from other lands. When Mead went to college, she took a class in anthropology. This is the study of how different people live. Mead decided to make this her career. She wanted to study primitive people before modern ways of living destroyed their culture.

Mead realized that living with a people is the only effective way to learn about them. She chose a village in Samoa to investigate. Several islands make up Samoa which is in the Pacific Ocean. Mead worked hard to prepare for Samoa. She studied languages like the Samoan language. She read everything she could about the Samoan people. She read about their food and how they built their homes. She read about their ceremonies, their past history, and their taboos. But she wanted to learn much more.

Finally Mead arrived in Samoa. At first life was difficult for her. She was alone. She was not fluent in the Samoan language. She lived in a house with no walls and no electricity or gas. It had no running water and no bathroom. One day she said to herself, "I can't go on," in Samoan. Then she thought that maybe she could continue after all. Mead became fluent in the Samoan language, and the people soon regarded her as one of the village. She listened to their talk, their jokes, and their gossip. They told her their problems. Mead felt that being a woman assisted her in learning more about the lives of these people. Instead of having to go on hunts with the men, Mead stayed with the women. She observed the children play and learned how food was prepared. She made efforts to get the older people to recount tales of the past.

Mead learned many things from the Samoan people. She always took notes and kept careful records. These notes were used to write her first book which was called Coming of Age in Samoa. It made her famous. Mead spent the rest of her life studying and writing about primitive ways of life that no longer exist today.

(357 words)

FIGURE 10.7 Lou's Reading of Fifth-Grade Narrative Passage

Adapted from *The People of Tiegs-Adams: People and Their Heritage* series, Copyright © 1983, Silver, Burdett & Ginn, Inc., p. 215. Used with permission.

comprehension questions on the passage. Ms. Collins has noted Lou's continued difficulty with multisyllabic words and also sees that this difficulty is leading to comprehension problems. She will work individually with Lou on these problems: first, by making a list of words that can be made from certain roots, such as *work, works, worked, working* and *faith, faithful, faithfulness*. Ms. Collins also plans to have Lou learn some prefixes and suffixes by playing a game that provides practice with them. In the meantime she knows that Lou is reading fifth-grade narrative material at the Frustration level. Next, she plans to see how Lou performs on an unfamiliar expository passage at the fourth-grade level.

Figure 10.8 illustrates Lou's reading of the fourth-grade expository passage concerning Saudi Arabia. Lou makes 13 errors that affect meaning while reading

398

Saudi Arabia is a large country. It is about the size of the United States east of the Mississippi River. But it is a country that has not one lake or river!

The capital is a city of both new and old. *[ca-pi-tal]* *[aircon]* There are air-conditioned buildings and high-rise apartments. *[higher]* There are also old buildings made of mud brick. Families often sleep on the roofs at night to escape the heat. They don't worry that it will rain.

Saudi Arabia has very dry, very hot weather. Where do people find water? They dig wells deep into the earth. The capital, a city of many people, is watered by many of these wells. *[ca-pi-tal]* *[water]*

Outside the capital lies the world's largest sand desert. Strong winds blow the sand. From the air, the sand dunes look like waves of a great tan ocean. *[du]* On the ground, the feel of sand covers everything. *[fill]* A few islands of palm trees spring up out of the desert. They mean only one thing, water. These islands of life are the oases of *[oses]* Saudi Arabia which form around the springs or wells. *[come from]* Many people live near the oases in low mud houses. They plant gardens and orchards and raise camels. *[orc]*

Many groups of people live on the desert itself. They are the Bedouin who *[Bed] [Be]* move from place to place in search of food and water for their animals. The Bedouin *[Bedon]* depend on camels and goats for milk and meat. They use the animals' hair to make *[Bedon] [boud]* rugs and cloth for tents. The Bedouin know no boundaries. The open desert has been their home for generations.   (265 words) *[generat]*

FIGURE 10.8   Lou's Reading a Fourth-Grade Expository Passage

Adapted from *Scott, Foresman Social Studies, Grade 4: Regions of Our Country and Our World* (Glenview, IL.: Scott, Foresman and Co., 1983), pp. 244–245. Used with permission.

the expository passage, and he misses two out of six of the comprehension questions. This indicates that he is reading at the instructional level in unfamiliar fourth-grade expository passages. He continues to exhibit difficulties with multisyllabic words and will have to continue work in this area.

Summary of Lou's Reading Abilities. Lou's IRI results suggest that he reads fourth-grade narrative passages at an Independent level and fourth-grade unfamiliar expository passages at the Instructional level. Given that he has been in the United States for only four years and has achieved an intermediate level of English proficiency, this level of reading progress is reasonable, and in fact he should be commended for it. Nonetheless, Lou needs to accelerate his literacy progress in order to achieve a performance level that will allow him to succeed later on in high school. Examining Lou's performance on the IRI, Ms. Collins noticed several strengths Lou brings to his reading. First, Lou reads fairly fluently due to a good sight vocabulary and he's able to decode simple unfamiliar words, such as *capital* in the Saudi Arabia passage. Second, Lou reads for meaning. He expects the passage to make sense.

Ms. Collins looks for patterns of recurring errors in Lou's reading. When students make errors over and over again, it is more likely that the errors represent an area the student needs help on, provided that the errors are important for reading comprehension. In Lou's reading, one of his recurring error patterns is the omission of the *-ed* endings on past tense verbs. Ms. Collins has to decide whether to work on this with Lou in his reading. In order to decide, she first examines whether the omission results in lack of comprehension. Does Lou understand that the passage is referring to something that happened in the past? She finds that he *does* understand, even though he did not pronounce the *-ed* ending. She concludes that this pronunciation error does not affect his reading comprehension. She decides not to concern Lou or herself with this oral pronunciation miscue. Ms. Collins has also noticed, however, that Lou leaves out the *-ed* on some verbs in his writing, which is generally fluent and grammatical. She therefore makes a note that she will work on the *-ed* ending *in his writing*, where it does make a difference. It will be a detail for Lou to check for when he edits his papers.

A different recurring error pattern that Ms. Collins notices is Lou's difficulty with multisyllabic words, such as *generations* in the Saudi Arabia passage and *anthropology, primitive, investigate,* and *ceremonies* in the Margaret Mead passage. This difficulty interrupts the flow of meaning and impedes Lou's comprehension. Difficulty with these multisyllabic words stems from Lou's lack of familiarity with the words themselves combined with his lack of knowledge about English word formation in the areas of compound words, prefixes, suffixes, and roots. Ms. Collins decides to intensify her work with Lou on vocabulary development and word study related to prefixes, suffixes, and roots. Word study of this type will address not only decoding but also word meanings. First, she will ask Lou to keep his own vocabulary self-collection journal (Haggard, 1986) in which Lou keeps a list of new words he comes across in his reading. From this list, Ms. Collins will work with Lou to develop lessons on prefixes, suffixes, and roots to promote his ability

399

to analyze and understand new words. She also plans to provide a computer program that will help him specifically in these areas. In addition, she will set up word games to play with other students who can benefit from similar practice.

Analyzing Lou's reading reminded Ms. Collins of how important it is to prepare all of her students for the reading they will do in class. As a result, she has decided to be more consistent in applying the prereading, during-reading and postreading strategies recommended in Chapters 7, 8, and 9. For her eighth-grade social studies content, it is clear to her that she needs to provide direct experiences, visuals, and graphic organizers to develop both concepts and vocabulary prior to asking students to read materials on their own. For vocabulary development in reading, Ms. Collins has decided to talk about and model strategies for figuring out new words through word analysis and context, something she had not done much of lately. Finally, Ms. Collins has decided to provide her students with 25 minutes per week of independent, self-selected reading time. During this time, she will conference quietly with individual students, listen to and informally assess their oral reading, discuss strategies to help them read, and find out more about their interests. She may also conference with them on their writing at this time. Such information will further inform her work with her students as individuals and as a group.

All of the IRI testing with Lou took Ms. Collins approximately 55 minutes. With the results of the IRI in mind, she will observe Lou in class during buddy reading, independent reading, and guided reading to discover whether the IRI results are corroborated or not. In addition, she will watch for improvement in the areas for which she has targeted instruction. Later, she may decide to conduct an IRI with Lou again to estimate his progress in reading development.

We chose to use the QRI-II to assess Lou's reading performance for the reasons we stated earlier. However, other informal reading inventories may be more useful to you if, for example, (1) you need passages that go beyond the preprimer to junior high levels found in the QRI-II; (2) you need passages in a language other than English to evaluate reading performance in another language, or (3) you want passages to evaluate both gifted and remedial students. We offer a list of other IRIs that address some of these needs.

A List of Commercial Informal Reading Inventories

Below is a list of some of the commercial reading inventories that you may find useful. We recommend that you go to your school district or county library to find these commercial inventories and evaluate them based on your own classroom needs. Of course, you can also develop your own inventory using classroom or reading program graded materials. You will also find that some reading programs will provide you with informal reading inventories that may be useful.

Bader, L. A. (1998). *Bader Reading and Language Inventory* (4th ed.). Upper Saddle River, NJ: Merrill.

Flynt, E. S. & Cooter, R. B. (1999). *English-Español Reading Inventory for the Classroom.* Upper Saddle River, NJ: Merrill.

Leslie, L., & Caldwell, J. (1995). *Qualitative Reading Inventory, II.* New York: Addison Wesley Longman.

Stieglitz, E. L., & Lanigan, V. (1996). *The Stieglitz Informal Reading Inventory: Assessing Reading Behaviors from Emergent to Advanced Levels* (2nd ed.). Portland, OR: Book News.

Woods, M. L., & Moe, A. J. (1998). *Analytical Reading Inventory: Comprehensive Assessment for all Students including Gifted and Remedial.* Upper Saddle River, NJ: Prentice Hall.

OTHER PROCEDURES FOR EVALUATING AND HELPING READERS

There are many other ways of evaluating English language learners in reading beyond what we have already discussed in earlier chapters and in this chapter. Below we list a few other methods that we think may be valuable to you in assessing student literacy. The strategies range from echo reading, which evaluates a student's oral language, syntax, and reading; guided reading, which assists students at the discourse level; ReQuest procedure, which evaluates and assesses students at the questioning and comprehension level; and two holistic procedures, silent sustained reading and read alouds, which motivate students to love reading and become lifetime readers. We begin with Echo Reading.

Linking Assessment and Instruction

Assessment, whether in reading, writing or any other subject, is only useful if the assessment results inform your instructional decisions. We mentioned earlier that your experience assessing students through an informal reading inventory can help you become a better observer of student reading performance during day-to-day classroom activities in which students read aloud. For example, if you pair your students to read aloud quietly to each other during buddy reading, you now have an opportunity to listen in and get an idea of how well the student reads, while making a mental note of areas that might lead to reading improvement, such as providing a mini lesson later on a particular strategy. Often you will find several students who need similar strategy instruction, leading to the formation of a small group in need of your direct assistance. This kind of group is relatively homogeneous in terms of students' reading development, and represents one kind of flexible grouping designed to meet students' learning needs. It is flexible in that the group is called together for a short time based on a particular, shared learning need. Guided reading, a teaching-learning format described below, is a small group instructional format that calls together several students who read at roughly similar levels.

Echo Reading

Echo reading is a process whereby the teacher reads a sentence and the student repeats or echoes the sentence. Although the procedure has not been researched with second language learners, you may wish to try it with your students. Specifically, echo reading is a method that assists you in discovering the level of syntax a child may possess. Interestingly, if a student is unable to repeat a sentence you have read to them, they will probably be unable to read the sentence. So you can use echo reading to gauge the oral language level of a student and to gain an estimation of what the student may be able to do with reading. This is especially helpful if you have an English language learner who is shy, quiet, or reluctant to speak and you are having difficulty finding his/her oral language abilities.

The procedure is fairly simple: First, explain the process to the student; that you are going to read sentences aloud and that their job is to repeat the sentence word for word; second, you'll read the sentence to the student and ask the student to repeat it; finally, as the student echoes the sentence, you'll record what the student has repeated.

We find it easiest to record using the same basic guidelines you would follow if you were doing a miscue analysis:

1. If the student has echoed the word correctly, don't do anything.
2. If the student substitutes or adds a word, write the word above the word or phrase where the substitution takes place.
3. Circle words left out in the student's version.

Follow other procedures discussed in the miscue analysis section to code the student's repetitions and make decisions about the student's English abilities accordingly. As in miscue analysis, if the student substitutes a synonym such as *table* for *desk*, you'll know that the student is echoing appropriately. On the other hand, if students have to omit many words in a sentence, they indicate that they are having difficulty with the syntax and may have trouble reading similar material. For example, one kind of omission is given below:

ORIGINAL SENTENCE: The boy went to the store and bought candy.
STUDENT'S ECHO: Boy went store and candy.

With the echo reading procedure, you can use your own classroom texts to see if students can echo sentences in them. If the student cannot repeat sentences correctly, you may want to carefully select materials the student can read. You could, for example, try pattern books or sentences with the student since they are usually easier to repeat and thus easier to read for second language students and others with less developed English syntax.

Guided Reading

Guided reading is a teaching strategy in which a small group of students is guided by the teacher through reading a text that is at the students' instructional reading level. The text may be narrative, expository or even poetic, but it must be a text that challenges students a bit. The teacher's role is to guide students toward reading strategies that will enable them to successfully comprehend the text. The strategies on which the teacher chooses to focus will depend upon the text itself, along with the strategy knowledge and learning needs of the students in the group. Usually, the guided reading group meets several times a week, if not daily. As a result, the teacher has plenty of time to observe students and gauge their reading abilities informally. During the guided reading session, the goal is to assist students in understanding what was read and responding to it personally and critically. Guided reading can be especially helpful to beginning English learners, but it is also very practical and useful for more advanced English language learners who are reading complex narrative and expository texts.

Guided reading is a powerful tool because it provides frequent opportunities for students to read challenging material in small groups with the support and guidance of the teacher. In this way, guided reading provides a scaffolding routine, a predictable routine with which students become comfortable and secure. Students know that the reading material will be somewhat difficult, but the teacher will be there to help them with it, and that is how they will become better readers. The teacher's job during guided reading will be to select reading material at gradually increasing levels of difficulty, "upping the ante," as we mentioned in our discussion of scaffolding in Chapter 3. In addition, the teacher must be prepared to observe students, assess informally, and then provide scaffolding, modeling and direct instruction that address student needs.

While guided reading may vary from one teacher to another, it usually includes several procedures that are similar to the DR-TA procedure that we presented in Chapter 7. These procedures are as follows:

1. You begin by introducing the story or other text, beginning with the title, author and illustrator, inviting students to make predictions about the text; this helps to create a purpose for reading. With younger children you may want to go through the pictures in the book, talking about the pictures and inviting predictions as to what the story will be about.

2. Based upon what they have seen of the story, students engage in a brief discussion about the story based on the title, the illustrations, the topic, and their expectations of what the story will be about.

3. Next, you ask students to read a portion or all of the text; with younger students you may want to read a few pages of the story before asking them to read the rest of the text. The text can be read either aloud or silently depending on your knowledge of the students' capabilities and your purpose.

4. If students read the text aloud in pairs or if you ask them to read aloud quietly to themselves, you can circulate around the group and help individuals solve problems they may have, such as identifying words, understanding punctuation, or understanding a word in a new context. You may have older, more proficient students read larger chunks of the text or story to discuss as a group, providing help and guidance as needed.

5. After reading the story, you will want to facilitate or guide the students to think about what they have read by asking students to share their own responses to the story, to discuss their favorite parts, or to discuss main ideas or themes in a story.

6. You may follow up the last phase of guided reading with a brief, explicit discussion of useful reading strategies for reading and understanding the selection just read. One way is to invite a student to tell how he or she figured out a particular word if you noticed the student applying a good strategy or one you have recently been teaching, such as the use of chunking, or decoding parts of a long word one part at a time. Another way is to provide a brief mini-lesson on an aspect of the text with which several children had difficulty: for example, understanding a simile such as "pretty as a picture." Other mini-lesson topics that might emerge include discussing the text structures, narrative or expository, based on the selection that was read.

7. Finally, following the guided reading lesson you may invite students to respond to a story by creating a puppet show or readers' theater or by responding in their literature response journals.

Figure 10.9, from the excellent book on guided reading by Fountas and Pinnell (1996) illustrates what the teacher and children do before, during and after guided reading. Although this book focuses on guided reading in the primary grades, guided reading is also a superb tool for upper grades, middle school, and high school. The main differences between younger and older learners relate to the topic, linguistic complexity and level of sophistication in the reading material used. Multiple benefits accrue during small group instruction using challenging material with teacher guidance, benefits for students of all ages and levels of language and literacy development.

Erlinda Quintanar uses guided reading with her English language learners to extend their background knowledge of a story, to expand their understanding of narrative structure, and to enlarge their repertoire of response. Using the Native American story "Coyote and the Star" from a collection of multicultural folktales she is using in her class, she develops her own approach to guided reading. Below is a synopsis of this appealing story:

> The story explains why coyote howls at the night sky. The reason is that coyote fell in love with a beautiful star which eventually took coyote into the sky. But coyote missed the earth and asked the star to let him go back down to earth; the star took him back to earth. But now coyote misses the star and howls his love for it.

Erlinda introduces and builds background knowledge about the story by reading the title and taking the children on a "picture walk" through the book.

ERLINDA: Class, the title of this story is "Coyote and the Star"; what do you think it'll be about?

SONIA: Coyote and a star in the sky.

CARLOS: How many stars coyote sees.

The Essential Elements of Guided Reading			
	Before the reading	During the reading	After the reading
Teacher	• selects an appropriate text, one that will be supportive but with a few problems to solve • prepares an introduction to the story • briefly introduces the story, keeping in mind the meaning, language, and visual information in the text, and the knowledge, experience, and skills of the reader • leaves some questions to be answered through reading	• "listens in" • observes the reader's behaviors for evidence of strategy use • confirms children's problem-solving attempts and successes • interacts with individuals to assist with problem solving at moment of difficulty (when appropriate) • makes notes about the strategy use of individual readers	• talks about the story with children • invites personal response • returns to the text for one or two teaching opportunities such as finding evidence or discussing problem solving • assesses children's understanding of what they read • sometimes engages the children in extending the story through such activities as drama, writing, art, or more reading
Children	• engage in a conversation about the story • raise questions • build expectations • notice information in the text	• read the whole text or a unified part to themselves (softly or silently) • request help in problem solving when needed	• talk about the story • check predictions and react personally to the story or information • revisit the text at points of problem solving as guided by the teacher • may reread the story to a partner or independently • sometimes engage in activities that involve extending and responding to the text (such as drama or journal writing)

405

ƒIGURE 10.9   The Essential Elements of Guided Reading

From: *Guided Reading: Good First Teaching for All Children* by Irene C. Fountas and Gay Su Pinnell. Copyright © 1996 by Irene C. Fountas and Gay Su Pinnell. Published by Heinemann, a division of Reed Elsevier, Inc., Portsmouth, NH.

OTHERS: *(various comments)*

ERLINDA: Those are good ideas.

ERLINDA: Let's look at the pictures and see what you think will happen in the story. [*She thumbs through the pictures with the children and stops at certain important pictures such as the one of coyote embracing the star in the sky and asks students what's happening in them. Then she reads the first two pages of the story to the children.*]

ERLINDA: Now I want you to read the rest of the story aloud to a buddy. I'll be right here so if you need any help, just raise your hand and ask me. [*She walks around the table, listens in on their reading, and takes notes on the children's reading strengths and needs*].

When the children have finished reading the story to one another, she asks them to briefly discuss with their buddy what they thought of the story and what their favorite parts were or who were their favorite characters. Then she asks the group of six students to discuss what they found in their talk with their buddy reader.

JUAN: I thought it was sad how coyote yells.
ERLINDA: Who else felt that way? [*Other children respond in similar ways*].
LON: I like the part when the star take coyote to the sky.
NGYEN: Me too.

The children continue, with Erlinda's help, answering questions and elaborating on the story and its outcome. After the 10-minute discussion Erlinda suggests that the children may wish to make a puppet show about the story and the children respond enthusiastically. The children begin gathering materials for the show and work together while Erlinda moves to another group that has been working on stories they are writing themselves. The children will present their puppet show to the rest of the class in two days when they are ready.

We have indicated that there are many variations on the guided reading approach depending upon the age and abilities of the students in your class. But the basic outline is similar: (1) the teacher builds some background knowledge before the story is read; (2) the story is read silently or aloud by the students; (3) the students discuss the story with the teacher facilitating the discussion; and (4) sometimes the teacher asks the students to do some kind of follow-up activity with the story such as writing in their literature response journals or performing the story. With these steps the teacher has guided her students through the story and modeled how one might go about reading any story.

In addition, she uses guided reading to assess the children's progress in reading and understanding stories, making a note of specific kinds of strategy instruction she might provide to improve their reading.

ReQuest Procedure

The purpose of the ReQuest procedure (Manzo, 1968) is to help students learn to develop their own questioning while reading to enable them to be better and more active comprehenders. ReQuest is usually used with students who are advanced enough in English literacy to read short texts. It is a good procedure for small group instruction, but may be used with the whole class. The basic elements of the procedure are relatively simple. You select appropriate material which will involve students in thinking and predicting. Next, you explain the purpose of the procedure to the students. As with most lessons, you'll want to prepare students for reading the text by building necessary background information and discussing difficult and important vocabulary in the text. Next, tell students that they will read a sentence or section of the text and then ask you a question. You will answer the question and then ask them a question about the next section. Your purpose here is to model good questions for the students and to help them with developing their own good questions. When answering the questions you and the students keep the text closed. After taking students through some of the text, you have them predict what will happen in the rest of the text and then let them read and monitor their predictions. After students have read the text, you might ask them to discuss and recall what they read and what they predicted. You might also have them summarize what they read in their learning logs. Through the ReQuest procedure you hope to build students' independent reading comprehension and develop confidence in their ability to actively understand and remember what they have read.

While the procedure above relates to older students, it can also be used with students in the primary grades (Legenza, 1974). We saw one second grade teacher, Lilly Chan, using the method with the book *Fortunately* (Charlip, 1997). First, she told children she was going to play a questioning game with them.

She explained that the rules of the game were simple: She would give an "answer," and their job was to ask a question to go with it. For example, she said, "If I say bat, you might ask, 'What do you hit a baseball with?' or 'What do you hold in your hands when it is your turn to hit in a baseball game?'" After some other examples and clarification, Lilly started the game:

LILLY: The answer is peanut butter. What's the question?
PHAM: What goes good with jam?
JOSE: What sticks to the roof of your mouth?
LEE: What is made out of stomped peanuts?

After naming other topics and developing questions, the children became relatively proficient and enthusiastic about asking questions. So Lilly told the students that she was now going to play the game using a story. They would read the first part of the story, ask a question of her, and she would answer. Then she would ask them a question and they would answer. To introduce the procedure to these young children, she selected a book that was predictable and had pictures that illustrate the action, *Fortunately, Unfortunately* (Charlip). The book has a pattern that repeats something fortunate and something unfortunate that happens. She explained that the word fortunately meant something good had happened and unfortunately meant something was not good. She also took time to explain that when *un-* was in front of a word it meant "not." She then read the first two lines of the book, asked the students to predict what would happen in subsequent pages and asked the students to read the following three pages on their own before asking her a question. She would read a line and ask the children a question. Finally, she had the children predict what would happen in the rest of the book and then read it. She finished with a brief discussion of the book.

When you use the ReQuest procedure with either younger or older students, you teach them to anticipate what a story is about, to develop questions that will help them understand the story better, and to predict what will happen next. Moreover, you show them how to be active learners.

Silent Sustained Reading

One strategy that may be the most important one to use with all readers is silent sustained reading. In a National Assessment of Educational Progress Report (2003) one of the most salient features of schools that scored high in reading nationally was simply more time spent reading. With silent sustained reading everybody in the school reads at the same time every day; with the principal, school secretaries and janitors sometimes joining in as well. Usually, a specific time is set aside for reading every day at a school; for example, everybody reads for a half hour immediately after lunch or recess. Students are usually allowed to select any kind of appropriate material for reading, including magazines or newspapers. They are not asked to report on their reading and your role is simply to read while the children are reading. During silent sustained reading there are to be no unnecessary interruptions; in other words, school announcements and other activities will not interrupt the activity. Silent sustained reading is based on several beliefs: (1) that reading is one of the most important things we can do in school, (2) that practice in reading is essential, and (3) that adults such as secretaries, principals, teachers, and others can model the value of reading for students and that this modeling plays an important role in motivating them to become lifelong readers.

Read Alouds

In addition to silent sustained reading, we can't emphasize enough how important it is to read aloud to students at all grade levels, K through 12. Through listening to selections read aloud to them, English learners can become interested in various genres: stories, poems, essays, articles, and more. As they listen, they will hear and hopefully come to enjoy the rhythm and cadence of the language in the selections you read aloud. Moreover, listening to read alouds introduces students to the conventions of written English. Let us note, however, that listening to read alouds is a very demanding task, especially for those new to the language. It is especially difficult to listen to a new language for extended periods of time without suffering from auditory overload: Students may just tune out. Thus it is important to consider the length of the selection, and to choose pieces for which students have at least some prior knowledge and for which you will be able to support comprehension through pictures, discussion and other sheltering assistance. In brief, we feel that two of the most important activities that take place in school are silent sustained reading, where students select and read their own materials, and read alouds where you carefully select books and materials that will illustrate the fun of good reading.

408

Summary

In this chapter on analytic reading assessment and instruction, we began with a theoretical discussion of language proficiency as including both oral and written language: listening, speaking, reading and writing. We then focused on reading *per se*. We chose this focus due to the important role of reading in school and beyond. As background for the discussion on reading assessment, we laid out our theoretical view of the reading process of mature readers. We then discussed what non-native English speakers bring to this process, especially in terms of background knowledge, language knowledge, word recognition, vocabulary and comprehension. Next we presented a detailed description of an informal reading inventory, which we illustrated with the oral reading performance of an eighth grade English learner. Finally, we showed how small-group instruction for students of similar reading abilities can address students' particular, assessed needs in ways that promote improvement and lead to independence in reading. To end the chapter, we highlighted the importance of reading aloud to students and providing them with daily opportunities to read materials of their own choosing without interruptions during silent sustained reading.

Suggestions for Further Reading

409

Brown, J. D. (Ed.). (1998). *New ways of classroom assessment.* Alexandria, VA: Teachers of English to Speakers of Other Languages.

This book, part of the New Ways series by TESOL, offers almost a hundred different strategies and approaches to classroom assessment in listening, speaking, reading, and writing. Short articles also include portfolio assessment, self-assessment, group assessment, and much more. If you don't like some of the approaches to assessment in the book, you're sure to find others you do like and will use.

Genesee, F., & Upshur, J. A. (2002). *Classroom-based evaluation in second language education.* Cambridge: Cambridge University Press.

This thorough book on classroom-based evaluation is well written, well organized, and reader friendly. It begins by introducing evaluation, discusses second language evaluation, provides a theoretical framework, and then moves to chapters on topics such as observation, portfolios and conferences, objective-referenced testing, choosing and devising tests, and interpreting tests. Each chapter begins with excellent preview questions and ends with discussion questions you could share with peers in class.

Huerta-Macias, A. (1995). Alternative assessment: Responses to commonly asked questions. *TESOL Journal, 5*(1), 8–12.

In this article, Huerta-Macias fulfills the promise of the title, answering common questions about alternative assessments such as validity, reliability, and objectivity. We recommend the article to anyone who is initiating alternative assessment or anyone who wants to explain it to others.

Hughes, A. (2003). *Testing for language teachers* (2nd ed.). Cambridge: Cambridge University Press.

The brief chapters discuss teaching and testing; kinds, validity, and reliability of tests and testing; stages of test development; and testing writing, oral ability, reading, listening, grammar and vocabulary, and overall ability. The book concludes with chapters on testing young learners and test administration. It is clearly written and organized to make it a user-friendly text for teachers.

Hurley, S. R., & Tinajero, J. V. (Eds.). (2001). *Literacy assessment of second language learners.* Boston: Allyn and Bacon.

This edited text contains articles by key educators and researchers on literacy assessment of second language learners. Articles include topics such as integrated perspectives, assessing acquisition, assessing comprehension and content area learning, and assessing biliteracy development. The articles discuss standardized and informal assessment, and one article assesses work with parents. A very interesting collection.

Leslie, L., & Caldwell, J. (2000). *Qualitative Reading Inventory III,* New York: Longman.

We would be remiss if we did not take special note of this excellent informal reading inventory. It has been praised by researchers and educators as a model for others who are developing inventories. Some of the highlights of this inventory are that it assesses background knowledge for passages being read; the word lists contain words from the actual passages; it provides both expository and narrative passages; and comprehension is assessed through both recall and questioning.

O'Malley, J. M., & Valdez Pierce, L. (1996). *Authentic assessment for English language learners: Practical approaches for teachers.* New York: Addison-Wesley.

This excellent and practical teacher-oriented text helps a teacher construct assessments in oral language, reading, writing, and content areas and helps teachers deliver a curriculum that meets the needs of English language learners. Chapters address moving toward and designing authentic assessment, portfolio assessment, oral language assessment, reading assessment, writing assessment, and content area assessment. The last chapter provides examples from the classroom. Each chapter begins with a discussion of the chapter topic, e.g., the nature of oral language, the nature of reading, etc., and follows with assessment techniques and ways to use assessment results for instruction.

410

Activities

1. Do a case study of one student. Use a published IRI to discover the student's reading level: Independent, Instructional, or Frustration. Also, discuss the student's strengths and weaknesses and what you would plan to do to assist the student. Be specific about the student's needs and your plan to assist him or her.

2. Assess a student and discover one thing that he or she is unable to do in reading. See if you can teach him or her that one thing. Use books recommended in this chapter to discover a variety of ways you might teach your student one useful strategy for reading that they didn't know before your intervention. Discuss your findings. Did your student learn something? How long did it take him or her to learn? Did learning it make a difference? Did it change him or her as a reader in some way? Did your student become more confident? What did you learn from this process?

3. Have someone administer an IRI with you as the reader. From this you can learn some of the inherent problems in trying to remember information in passages and trying to answer questions. Teachers should be aware that we all will miss questions of recall under the circumstances of reading a passage either aloud or silently. Are students missing questions because they didn't understand a passage or are they missing questions because they can't recall part of a passage? What might a teacher do to gain accurate information using a reading inventory?

4. Administer IRIs to two or three students using different commercial reading inventories. See whether the inventories yield the same or different results in terms of the students' reading levels: Frustration, Instructional, and Independent. Examine the different inventories to try to explain similar or different results.

5. Work in a group to make up an IRI of your own. Discuss the difficulties you had selecting passages and creating questions for the passages. Reflect on some commercial IRI's. Do the commercial IRI's have some weaknesses and strengths? What are they?

6. After you have looked over a few IRI's, develop criteria for helping a teacher select an IRI. What major features of an IRI are helpful? What should the passages in the IRI consist of and how would a teacher decide that one IRI is better than another for his or her students?

REFERENCES

Aardema, V. (1975). *Why mosquitoes buzz in people's ears*. New York: Dial.

Aardema, V. (1981). *Bringing the rain to Kapiti plain*. New York: Dial.

Aaronson, E. (1978). *The jigsaw classroom*. Beverly Hills, CA: Sage.

Abedi, J. (2001, Summer). Assessment and accommodations for English Language Learners: Issues and recommendations. *Policy Brief 4*. Los Angeles, CA: National Center for Research on Evaluation, Standards, and Student Testing, University of California.

Abedi, J., Leon, S., & Mirocha, J. (2001). *Impact of students' language background on standardized achievement test results: Analyses of extant data*. Los Angeles: National Center for Research on Evaluation, Standards and Student Testing, University of California.

Ada, A. F. (1988). The Pajaro Valley experience. In J. Cummins (Ed.), *Empowering language minority students* (pp. 223–238). Sacramento, CA: California Association for Bilingual Education.

Ada, A. F., & Zubizarreta, R. (2001). Parent narratives: The cultural bridge between Latino parents and their children. In M. de la Luz Reyes & J. Halcon (Eds.), *The best for our children: Critical perspectives on literacy for Latino students*. New York: Teachers College Press.

Adams, M. J. (1990a). *Beginning to read: Thinking and learning about print*. Cambridge, MA: MIT Press.

Adams, M. J. (1990b). *Beginning to read: Thinking and learning about print: A summary*. Urbana-Champaign: University of Illinois, Center for the Study of Reading.

Adams, M. J., & Bruck, M. (1995). *Resolving the "great debate."* American Educator. Washington, DC: American Federation of Teachers.

Afflerbach, P. (2002). The road to folly and redemption: Perspectives on the legitimacy of high stakes testing. *Reading Research Quarterly, 37*(3) 348–360.

Agor, B. (Ed.). (2000). *Integrating the ESL standards into classroom practice: Grades 9–12*. Alexandria, VA: Teachers of English to Speakers of Other Languages.

Ahlberg, J., & Ahlberg, A. (1981). *Peek-a-boo!* London: Puffin.

Allen, R. V. (1976). *Language experience in communication*. Boston: Houghton Mifflin.

Altwerger, B., & Flores, B. (1991). The theme cycle: An overview. In K. Goodman, L. B. Bird, & Y. Goodman (Eds.), *The whole language catalogue* (p. 95). Santa Rosa, CA: American School Publishers.

Ammon, P. (1985). Helping children learn to write in ESL: Some observations and hypotheses. In S. W. Freedman (Ed.), *The acquisition of written language: Response and revision* (pp. 65–84). Norwood, NJ: Ablex.

Ananda, S., & Rabinowitz, S. N. (2000). The high stakes of high stakes testing. West Ed Policy Brief. Retrieved August 14, 2003, from http://www.wested.org/cs/wew/view/rs/181

Anaya, R. (1972). *Bless Me, Ultima*. New York: Warner Books.

Anderson, N. (1999). *Exploring second language reading: Issues and strategies.* Boston: Heinle & Heinle.

Anderson, N. (2002). The role of metacognition in second language teaching and learning. ERIC Digest. Retrieved August 14, 2003, from http://www.cal.org/ericcll/digest/0110anderson.html

Anderson, R. C., Hiebert, E. H., Scott, J. A., & Wilkinson, I. A. G. (1985). *Becoming a nation of readers: The report of the commission on reading.* Washington, DC: National Institute of Education.

Antunez, B. (2002). Reading and English language learners. WFSU Reading Center. WFSU.org. Retrieved May 31, 2003, from http://readingrockets.org/wfsu/article/php?ID=409

Armbruster, B. B., & Osborn, J. H. (2002). *Reading instruction and assessment: Understanding the IRA Standards.* Boston: Allyn and Bacon.

Ashton-Warner, S. (1963). *Teacher.* New York: Simon & Schuster.

Atwell, N. (1984). *Writing and reading literature from the inside out.* Language Arts, 61, 240–252.

Au, K. (2000). A multicultural perspective on policies for improving literacy achievement: Equity and excellence. In M. L. Kamil, P. B. Mosenthal, P. D. Pearson, & R. Barr (Eds.), *Handbook of reading research: Volume III* (pp. 835–851). Mahwah, NJ: Erlbaum.

Au, K. H., & Jordan, C. (1981). Teaching reading to Hawaiian children: Finding a culturally appropriate solution. In H. Trueba, G. P. Guthrie, & K. H.-P. Au (Eds.), *Culture and the bilingual classroom: Studies in classroom ethnography* (pp. 139–152). Rowley, MA: Newbury House.

Auerbach, E. R. (1991). Toward a social-contextual approach to family literacy. In M. Minami & B. P. Kennedy (Eds.), *Language issues in literacy and bilingual/multicultural education* (pp. 391–408). Reprint Series No. 22. Cambridge, MA: Harvard Educational Review.

Ausubel, D. P. (1968). *Educational psychology: A cognitive view.* New York: Holt, Rinehart & Winston.

Bader, L. A. (1998). *Bader reading and language inventory* (3rd ed.). New Jersey: Merrill.

Baker, L., & Brown, A. L. (1984). Metacognition skills and reading. In P. D. Pearson (Ed.), *Handbook of reading research.* White Plains, NY: Longman.

Bakhtin, M. (1981). *The dialogic imagination.* Austin: University of Texas Press.

Baldwin, J. (1979/1998). If Black English isn't a language, then tell me, what is? In T. Perry & L. Delpit (Eds.), *The real Ebonics debate: Power, language and the education of African-American children.* Boston: Beacon Press. (Originally published in *The New Yorker,* 1979.)

Ballard & Tighe (1978). *IDEA oral language proficiency test.* San Rafael, CA: Ballard & Tighe.

Banks, J. A. (1991). *Teaching strategies for ethnic studies* (5th ed.). Boston: Allyn & Bacon.

Bartlett, B. J. (1978). *Top-level structure as an organizational strategy for recall of classroom text.* Unpublished doctoral dissertation, Arizona State University, Tempe.

Baugh, J. (1999). *Out of the mouths of slaves: African American Language and educational malpractice.* Austin: University of Texas Press.

Bauman, R., & Scherzer, J. (1974). *Explorations in the ethnography of speaking.* New York: Cambridge University Press.

Bear, D. R., Invernizzi, M., Templeton, S., & Johnston, F. (2003). *Words their way: Word study for phonics, vocabulary and spelling instruction* (3rd ed.). Upper Saddle River, NJ: Merrill/Prentice Hall.

Beck, I., McKeown, M., Omanson, R., & Pople, M. (1984). Improving the comprehensibility of stories: The effects of revisions that improve coherence. *Reading Research Quarterly,* 19, 263–277.

Becker, H. (2001). *Teaching ESL K–12: Views from the classroom* with commentary from Else Hamayan. Boston: Heinle & Heinle.

Bemelmans, L. (1939). *Madeline.* New York: Viking.

Berg, E. C. (1999). Preparing ESL students for peer response. *TESOL Journal, 8*(2), 20–25.

Bernardt, E. B. (2000). Second language reading as a case study of reading scholarship in the 20th century. In M. L. Kamil, P. B. Mosenthal, P. D. Pearson, & R. Barr (Eds.), *Handbook of reading research: Volume III* (pp. 791–811). Mahwah, NJ: Erlbaum.

Bertera, J., & Rayner, K. (1979). Reading without a fovea. *Science,* 206, 468–469.

414

Birch, B. (2002). *English L2 reading.* Mahwah, NJ: Erlbaum.

Boggs, S. (1972). The meaning of questions and narratives to Hawaiian children. In C. B. Cazden, V. P. Johns, & D. Hymes (Eds.), *The functions of language in the classroom.* New York: Teachers College Press.

Bolton, F. & Snowball, D. (1993a). *Ideas for spelling.* Portsmouth, NH: Heinemann.

Bolton, F. & Snowball, D. (1993b). *Teaching spelling: A practical resource.* Portsmouth, NH: Heinemann.

Bond, G. I., & Dykstra, R. (1967, Summer). The cooperative research program in first-grade reading instruction. *Reading Research Quarterly,* 2(4), 5–142.

Boyle, O. F. (1979). Oral language, reading and writing: An integrated approach. In O. Boyle (Ed.), *Writing lessons that work* (Vol. I, pp. 34–41). Berkeley: University of California/Bay Area Writing Project.

Boyle, O. F. (1982b). Writing: Process vs. product. In O. Boyle (Ed.), *Writing lessons II: Lessons in writing by teachers* (pp. 39–44). Berkeley: University of California/Bay Area Writing Project.

Boyle, O. F. (1982c). Cognitive schemes and reading in the content areas. In H. Singer & T. Bean (Eds.), *Proceedings of the learning from text conference* (pp. 106–114). Riverside, CA: UC Riverside Press.

Boyle, O. F. (1983). Mapping and writing. *Notes Plus.* Urbana, IL: National Council of Teachers of English.

Boyle, O. F. (1985a). Writing research: Present and future. *Quarterly for the Center for the Study of Writing,* 4(1), 3–7.

Boyle, O. F. (1985b). Writing research: Present and future. *The Quarterly of the National Writing Project.* Berkeley: University of California/Bay Area Writing Project.

Boyle, O. F. (1986). Teaching and assessing writing: Recent advances in understanding, evaluating, and improving student performance. *Quarterly of the Center for the Study of Writing,* 8(3), 36–43.

Boyle, O. F. (1987). *Holistic scoring procedures for essays.* New York: Cambridge University Press.

Boyle, O. F. (1990). *The magician's apprentice.* Unpublished manuscript, San Jose State University, San Jose, CA.

Boyle, O. F. (Ed.). (1982a). *Writing lessons II: Lessons in writing by teachers.* Berkeley: University of California/Bay Area Writing Project.

Boyle, O. F., & Buckley, M. H. (1983). Mapping and composing. In M. Myers & J. Gray (Eds.), *Theory and practice in the teaching of composition: Processing, distancing, and modeling.* Urbana, IL: National Council of Teachers of English.

Boyle, O. F., & Peregoy, S. F. (1990). Literacy scaffolds: Strategies for first- and second-language readers and writers. *The Reading Teacher,* 44(3), 194–200.

Boyle, O. F., & Peregoy, S. F. (1991). The effects of cognitive mapping on students' learning from college texts. *Journal of College Reading and Learning,* XXIII(2), 14–22.

Bradley, J., & Thalgott, M. (1987). Reducing reading anxiety. *Academic Therapy,* 22(4), 349–358.

Brinton, D. M., Snow, M. A., & Wesche, M. B. (1993). Content-based second language instruction. In J. W. Oller, Jr. (Ed.), *Methods that work: Ideas for literacy and language teachers* (2nd ed., pp. 136–142). Boston: Heinle & Heinle.

Bromley, K. (1989). Buddy journals make the reading-writing connection. *The Reading Teacher,* 43(2), 122–129.

Bromley, K. (1995). Buddy journals for ESL and native-English-speaking students. *TESOL Journal,* 4(3), 7–11.

Brown, J. D. (Ed.). (1998). *New ways of classroom assessment.* Alexandria, VA: TESOL.

Bruner, J. (1960). *The process of education.* New York: Vintage.

Bruner, J. (1978). The role of dialogue in language acquisition. In A. Sinclair, R. J. Jarvella, & W. J. M. Levelt (Eds.), *The child's conception of language* (pp. 44–62). New York: Springer-Verlag.

Buckley, M. H. (1981). *Oral language guidelines.* Unpublished handout from class.

Buckley, M. H., & Boyle, O. F. (1981). *Mapping the writing journey.* Berkeley: University of California/Bay Area Writing Project.

Burt, M., Dulay, H., & Hernandez-Chavez, E. (1975). *Bilingual syntax measure.* Orlando, FL: Harcourt Brace Jovanovich.

Busching, B. (1981). Reader's theater: An education for language and life. *Language Arts,* 58, 330–338.

415

Buswell, G. T. (1922). Fundamental reading habits: A study of their development. *Supplementary Educational Monographs, 21*. Chicago: University of Chicago Press.

Caldwell, K. (1984, February). *Teaching using the writing process*. Speech presented at the Bay Area Writing Project Workshop, Fairfield, CA.

California State Department of Education. (1994). *Building bilingual instruction: Putting the pieces together*. Sacramento, CA: Bilingual Education Office.

California State Department of Education (2002). *English-language development standards for California public schools: Kindergarten through grade twelve*. Sacramento, CA: Author.

California State Department of Education, Standards and Assessment Division (2003). *California English Language Development Test: CELDT Communications Assistance Packet for Districts/ Schools: Section II: CELDT Overview*. Retrieved on July 7, 2003, from http://www.cde.ca.gov/ statetests/celdt/resources/assistpkts2203.pdf

Calkins, L. M. (1994). *The art of teaching writing*. Portsmouth, NH: Heinemann.

Campbell, C. (1998). *Teaching second-language writing*. Boston: Heinle & Heinle.

Canale, M., & Swain, M. (1980). Theoretical bases of communicative approaches to second language teaching and testing. *Applied Linguistics, 1*(1), 1–47.

Caplan, R. (1982). Showing-writing: A training program to help students be specific. In G. Camp (Ed.), *Teaching writing: Essays from the Bay Area writing project*. Upper Montclair, NJ: Boynton/Cook.

Carle, E. (1986). *The very hungry caterpillar*. New York: Philomel Books.

Carle, E. (1984). *The very busy spider*. New York: Philomel Books.

Carr, W., & Ogle, D. (1987). K-W-L Plus: A strategy for comprehension and summarization. *Journal of Reading, 30*, 626–631.

Carrell, P. (1984). Schema theory and ESL reading: Classroom implications and applications. *Modern Language Journal, 68*(4), 332–343.

Carrell, P., Devine, J., & Eskey, D. (1988). *Interactive approaches to second language reading*. Cambridge: Cambridge University Press.

Carrell, P., & Eisterhold, J. (1988). Schema theory and ESL reading pedagogy. In P. Carrell, J. Devine, & D. Eskey (Eds.), *Interactive approaches to second language reading*. Cambridge: Cambridge University Press.

Cazden, C. (1983). Adult assistance to language development: Scaffolds, models and direct instruction. In R. Parker & F. Davis (Eds.), *Developing literacy: Young children's use of language* (pp. 3–18). Newark, DE: International Reading Association.

Cazden, C. (1986). Classroom discourse. In M. C. Wittrock (Ed.), *Handbook of research on teaching* (pp. 432–463). New York: Macmillan.

Celce-Murcia, M. (Ed.). (1991). *Teaching English as a second or foreign language* (2nd ed). Boston: Heinle & Heinle.

Celce-Murcia, M. (Ed.). (2001). *Teaching English as a second or foreign language* (3rd ed.). Boston: Heinle & Heinle.

Chall, J. (1983). *Learning to read: The great debate* (Rev. ed.). New York: McGraw-Hill.

Chall, J., & Snow, C. (1982). *Families and literacy: The contributions of out of school experiences to children's acquisition of literacy: A final report to the National Institute of Education*. Cambridge, MA: Harvard Families and Literacy Project.

Chamot, A. U., & O'Malley, J. M. (1986). *A cognitive academic language learning approach: An ESL content-based curriculum*. Rosslyn, VA: National Clearinghouse for Bilingual Education.

Chamot, A. U., & O'Malley, J. M. (1992). *The Calla handbook: Implementing the cognitive academic language learning approach*. Reading, MA: Addison-Wesley.

Chang, H. N.-L. (1990). *Newcomer programs*. San Francisco: California Tomorrow Immigrant Students Project.

Charlip, R. (1997). *Fortunately*. New York: Macmillan.

Chavez, R. (1990). The development of story writing within an IBM writing to read program lab among language minority students: Preliminary findings of a naturalistic study. *Computers in Schools, 7*, 121–143.

Chi, M. (1988). Invented spelling/writing in Chinese-speaking children: The developmental patterns. From *Dialogues in literacy research*,

416

thirty-seventh yearbook, National Reading Conference.

Chittenden, L. (1982). *Teaching writing to elementary children.* Speech presented at the Bay Area Writing Project Workshop, University of California, Berkeley.

Chomsky, N. (1957). *Syntactic structures.* The Hague: Mouton.

Chomsky, N. (1959). A review of Skinner's *Verbal Behavior. Language, 35,* 26–58.

Christian, D. (1994). *Two-way bilingual education: Students learning through two languages.* (Educational Practice Rep. No. 12). Santa Cruz, CA, and Washington, DC: National Center for Research on Cultural Diversity and Second Language Learning.

Chu, J., Swaffer, J., & Charney, D. (2002). Cultural representations of rhetorical conventions: The effects on reading recall. *TESOL Quarterly, 36*(4), 511–41.

Cisneros, S. (1994). *The house on Mango Street.* New York: Random House.

Clarke, L. K. (1989). Encouraging invented spelling in first graders' writing: Effects on learning to spell and read. *Research in the Teaching of English, 22,* 281–309.

Clay, M. (1975). *What did I write?* Portsmouth, NH: Heinemann.

Clay, M. (1979). *The early detection of reading difficulties.* Auckland, New Zealand and Portsmouth, NH: Heinemann.

Clay, M. (1982). *Observing young readers: Selected papers.* Exeter, NH: Heinemann.

Clay, M. (1989). Concepts about print: In English and other languages. *The Reading Teacher, 42*(4), 268–277.

Cohen, E. G. (1986). *Designing groupwork: Strategies for the heterogeneous classroom.* New York: Teachers College Press.

Cohen, E. G. (1994). *Designing groupwork: Strategies for the heterogeneous classroom* (2nd ed.). New York: Teachers College Press.

Collier, V. P. (1987). Age and rate of acquisition of second language for academic purposes. *TESOL Quarterly, 21,* 617–641.

Collier, V. P. (1987/1988). *The effect of age on acquisition of a second language for school* (Occasional Papers in Bilingual Education No. 2). Rosslyn, VA: National Clearinghouse for Bilingual Education.

Commission on Teacher Credentialing of the State of California. (1995, May). *California code of regulations: Guidelines for staff development programs for teachers of English learners.* Sacramento, CA: Author.

Connor, U., & Kaplan, R. B. (Eds.). (1987). *Writing across languages: Analysis of L2 text.* Reading, MA: Addison-Wesley.

Cooper, C. (1981, June). *Ten elements of a good writing program.* Speech presented at the Bay Area Writing Project Institute, University of California, Berkeley.

Crandall, J. (Ed.). (1987). *ESL through content-area instruction: Mathematics, science, social studies.* Englewood Cliffs, NJ: Prentice Hall.

Crandall, J. A., Dale, T. C., Rhodes, N., & Spanos, G. (1985, Oct.). *The language of mathematics: The English barrier.* Paper presented at the Delaware Symposium on Language Studies VII, University of Delaware, Newark.

Crawford, J. (1999). *Bilingual education: History, politics, theory and practice* (4th ed.). Los Angeles, CA: Bilingual Educational Services.

Crystal, D. (1987). *The Cambridge encyclopedia of language.* New York: Cambridge University Press.

Crystal, D. (1997). *The Cambridge encyclopedia of language.* Cambridge: Cambridge University Press.

Cullinan, B. (1989). Literature for young children. In D. S. Strickland & L. M. Morrow (Eds.), *Developing literacy: Young children learn to read and write.* Newark, DE: International Reading Association.

Cummins, J. (1979). Cognitive-academic language proficiency, linguistic interdependence, optimal age and some other matters. *Working Papers in Bilingualism, 19,* 197–205.

Cummins, J. (1980). The construct of language proficiency in bilingual education. In J. E. Alatis (Ed.), *Georgetown University roundtable on languages and linguistics* (pp. 76–93). Washington, DC: Georgetown University Press.

Cummins, J. (1981). The role of primary language development in promoting educational success for language minority students. In California State Department of Education (Ed.), *Schooling*

417

and language minority students: A theoretical framework (pp. 3–49). Los Angeles: Evaluation, Dissemination and Assessment Center, California State University.

Cunningham, J., Cunningham, P., & Arthur, S. (1981). *Middle and secondary school reading.* White Plains, NY: Longman.

Cunningham, P. (1995). *Phonics they use: Words for reading and writing* (2nd ed.). New York: HarperCollins College Publishers.

Custodio, B., & Sutton, M. J. (1998). Literature-based ESL for secondary school students. *TESOL Journal, 7*(5), 19–23.

Dahl, R. (1972). *Charlie and the chocolate factory.* New York: Puffin.

Daiute, C. (1985). *Writing and computers.* Reading, MA: Addison-Wesley.

Dale, T. C., & Cuevas, G. J. (1987). Integrating language and mathematics learning. In J. Crandall (Ed.), *ESL through content-area instruction: Mathematics, science, social studies.* Englewood Cliffs, NJ: Prentice Hall.

Day, R., & Bamford, J. (1998). *Extensive reading in the second language classroom.* Cambridge: Cambridge University Press.

De Avila, E., & Duncan, S. (1984). *Finding out and descubrimiento: Teacher's guide.* San Rafael, CA: Linguametrics Group.

Delgado-Gaitán, C. (1987). Mexican adult literacy: New directions from immigrants. In S. R. Goldman & K. Trueba (Eds.), *Becoming literate in English as a second language.* Norwood, NJ: Ablex.

Díaz, S., Moll, L., & Mehan, H. (1986). Socio-cultural resources in instruction: A context-specific approach. In *Beyond language: Social and cultural factors in schooling language minority children.* Los Angeles: California State Department of Education and California State University.

Díaz-Rico, L. T., & Weed, K. Z. (1995). *The crosscultural, language and academic development handbook: A complete K–12 reference guide.* Boston: Allyn and Bacon.

Dillard, J. L. (1972). *Black English: Its history and usage in the United States.* New York: Random House.

Dishon, D., & O'Leary, P. W. (1984). *A guidebook for cooperative learning: A technique for creating more effective schools.* Holmes Beach, FL: Learning Publications.

Dixon, C. N., & Nessel, D. (1990). *Language experience approach to reading and writing: LEA for ESL.* Hayward, CA: Alemany Press.

Dulay, H., & Burt, M. (1974). Errors and strategies in child second language acquisition. *TESOL Quarterly, 8,* 129–138.

Dulay, H., Burt, M., & Krashen, S. (1982). *Language two.* Oxford: Oxford University Press.

Duncan, S. E., & De Avila, E. (1977). *Language assessment scales.* Larkspur, CA: De Avila, Duncan and Associates.

Durkin, D. (1966). *Children who read early.* New York: Teachers College Press.

Dyson, A. (1982). The emergence of visible language: Interrelationships between drawing and early writing. *Visible Language, 16,* 360–381.

Echevarria, J., & Graves, A. (1998). *Sheltered content instruction: Teaching English-language learners with diverse abilities.* Boston: Allyn and Bacon.

Echevarria, J., Vogt, M. E., & Short, D. (2000). *Making content comprehensible for English language learners: The SIOP model.* Boston: Allyn and Bacon.

Edelsky, C. (1981a). *Development of writing in a bilingual program.* Final Report, Grant No. NIE–G–81–0051. Washington, DC: National Institute of Education.

Edelsky, C. (1981b). From "JIMOSALCO" to "7 naranjas se calleron e el arbol-est-triste en lagrymas": Writing development in a bilingual program. In B. Cronnel (Ed.), *The writing needs of linguistically different students* (pp. 63–98). Los Alamitos, CA: Southwest Regional Laboratory.

Eder, D. (1982). Difference in communication styles across ability groups. In L. C. Wilkinson (Ed.), *Communicating in the classroom.* New York: Academic.

Edwards, P. A. (1989). Supporting lower SES mothers' attempts to provide scaffolding for book reading. In J. B. Allen & J. M. Mason (Eds.), *Risk makers, risk takers, risk breakers: Reducing the risks for young literacy learners.* Portsmouth, NH: Heinemann.

Ehri, L. (1991). Development of the ability to read words. In R. Barr, M. L. Kamil, P. Mosenthal, & P. D. Pearson (Eds.), *Handbook of reading research: Volume II* (pp. 383–417). New York: Longman.

Ehri, L., & Wilce, L. (1985). Movement into reading: Is the first stage of printed word learning visual or phonetic? *Reading Research Quarterly, 20,* 163–169.

Ekwall, E. (1993). *Locating and correcting reading difficulties* (5th ed.). Columbus, OH: Charles E. Merrill.

Elbow, P. (1973). *Writing without teachers.* New York: Oxford University Press.

Elley, W., & Mangubhai, F. (1983). The impact of reading on second language readers. *Reading Research Quarterly, 19,* 53–67.

Ellis, R. (1994). *The study of second language acquisition.* Oxford: Oxford University Press.

Ellis, R. (1997). *Second language acquisition.* Oxford: Oxford University Press.

Emig, J. (1971). *The composing processes of twelfth graders.* Champaign, IL: National Council of Teachers of English.

Emig, J. (1981). Non-magical thinking: Presenting writing developmentally in schools. In C. H. Frederickson & J. F. Dominic (Eds.), *Writing: Process, development and communication* (pp. 21–30). Hillsdale, NJ: Erlbaum.

Enright, D. S., & McCloskey, M. L. (1985). Organizing the classroom to promote second language acquisition. *TESOL Quarterly, 19*(3), 431–453.

Enright, D. S., & McCloskey, M. L. (1988). *Integrating English: Developing English language and literacy in the multilingual classroom.* Reading, MA: Addison-Wesley.

Epstein, J. (1986). Parent involvement: Implications for LEP parents. In *Issues of parent involvement in literacy.* Proceedings of the symposium at Trinity College (pp. 6–16). Washington, DC: Trinity College, Department of Education and Counseling.

Ernst-Slavit, G., & Wenger, K. J. (1998). Using creative drama in the elementary ESL classroom. *TESOL Journal, 7*(4), 30–33.

Escamilla, K., Mahon, E., Riley-Bernal, H., & Rutledge, D. (2003). High-stakes testing, Latinos, and English language learners: Lessons from Colorado. *Bilingual Research Journal, 27*(1), 25–49.

Eskey, D. (2002). *Reading and the teaching of L2 reading. TESOL Journal, 11*(1), 5–9.

Faltis, C. J., & Hudelson, S. J. (1998). *Bilingual education in elementary and secondary school communities: Toward understanding and caring.* Boston: Allyn and Bacon.

Ferguson, C. A., & Heath, S. B. (Eds.). (1981). *Language in the U.S.A.* New York: Cambridge University Press.

Ferreiro, E., & Teberosky, A. (1982). *Literacy before schooling* (K. Castro, Trans.). Exeter, NH: Heinemann.

Ferris, D. (1995). Teaching students to self-edit. *TESOL Journal, 4*(4), 18–22.

Ferris, D. R. (2002). *Treatment of error in second language student writing.* Ann Arbor: University of Michigan Press.

Feyton, C., Macy, M., Ducher, J., Yoshii, M., Park, E., Calandra, B., and Meros, J. (Eds.). (2002). *Teaching ESL/EFL with the Internet: Catching the wave.* Upper Saddle River, NJ: Merrill/Prentice Hall.

Fillmore, C. (1968). The case for case. In E. Bach & R. T. Harms (Eds.), *Universals in linguistic theory* (pp. 1–68). New York: Holt, Rinehart & Winston.

Fitzgerald, J. (1995). English-as-a-second-language learners' cognitive reading processes: A review of research in the United States. *Review of Educational Research, 65,* 145–190.

Flavell, J. H. (1985). *Cognitive development* (2nd ed.). Englewood Cliffs, NJ: Prentice Hall.

Flores, B., Cousin, P., & Díaz, E. (1991). Transforming deficit myths about learning, language, and culture. *Language Arts, 68,* 370–379.

Flynt, E. S., & Cooter, R. B. (1999). *English-Español reading inventory for the classroom.* New Jersey: Merrill.

Fountas, I., & Pinnell, G. (1996). *Guided reading: Good first teaching for all children.* Portsmouth, NH: Heinemann.

Fradd, S., & McGee, P., with Wilen, D. (1994). *Instructional assessment: An integrative approach to evaluating student performance.* Reading, MA: Addison-Wesley.

Freire, P. (1970). *Pedagogy of the oppressed.* New York: Seabury Press.

Freire, P., & Macedo, D. (1987). *Literacy: Reading the word and reading the world.* South Hadley, MA: Bergin & Garvey.

Frith, U. (1985). Beneath the surface of developmental dyslexia. In K. E. Patterson, K. C.

419

Marshall, & M. Coltheart (Eds.), *Surface dyslexia: Neuropsychological and cognitive studies of phonological reading.* Hillsdale, NJ: Erlbaum.

Fromkin, V., Rodman R., & Hyams, N. (2003). *An introduction to language* (7th ed.). Boston: Thomson & Heinle.

Garcia, E. (1994). *Understanding and meeting the challenge of student cultural diversity.* Boston: Houghton Mifflin.

Garcia, G. (Ed.). (2003). *English learners reaching the highest level of English literacy.* Newark, DE: International Reading Association.

Gardner, H. (1995). Green ideas sleeping furiously. *The New York Review of Books. Vol. XLII, No. 5.* New York: Rea S. Headerman.

Gardner, J. (1983). *The art of fiction: Notes on craft for young writers.* New York: Vintage.

Gasparro, M., & Falletta, B. (1994, April). *Creating drama with poetry: Teaching English as a second language through dramatization and improvisation.* Washington, DC: ERIC Clearinghouse on Languages and Linguistics (ED 368 214).

Gee, R.W. (1999). Encouraging ESL students to read. *TESOL Journal, 8*(1), 3–7.

Genesee, F. (1984). *Studies in immersion education.* Sacramento, CA: California State Department of Education.

Genesee, F. (1987). *Learning through two languages: Studies of immersion and bilingual education.* Cambridge, MA: Newbury House.

Genesee, F., & Upshur, J. A. (2002). *Classroom-based evaluation in second language education.* Cambridge: Cambridge University Press.

Gentry, J. R. (1980). Early spelling strategies. *Elementary School Journal, 79,* 88–92.

Gersten, R., & Woodward, J. (1995). A longitudinal study of transitional and immersion bilingual education programs in one district. *The Elementary School Journal, 95*(3), 223–239.

Gesell, A. (1925). *The mental growth of the preschool child.* New York: Macmillan.

Gibbs, J. (1994). *Tribes: A new way of learning together.* Santa Rosa, CA: Center Source Publications.

Goldman, S. R., & Murray, J. (1989). *Knowledge of connectors as cohesive devices in text: A comparative study of native English and ESL speakers* (Technical Report). Santa Barbara: University of California.

Goldman, S. R., & Murray, J. (1992). Knowledge of connectors as cohesion devices in text: A comparative study of native-English and English-as-a-second-language speakers. *Journal of Educational Psychology, 84*(2), 504–519.

Goodenough, W. H. (1981). *Language, culture and society.* New York: Cambridge University Press.

Goodman, K. (1967, May). Reading: A psycholinguistic guessing game. *Journal of the Reading Specialist,* 126–135.

Goodman, K. S. (1973). *Miscue analysis: Application to reading instruction.* Urbana, IL: National Council of Teachers of English.

Goodman, K., & Goodman, Y. (1978). *Reading of American children whose language is a stable rural dialect of English or a language other than English* (Final Report No. C–003–0087). Washington, DC: National Institute of Education.

Goodman, K., Goodman, Y., & Flores, B. (1979). *Reading in a bilingual classroom.* Rosslyn, VA: National Clearinghouse for Bilingual Education.

Goodman, K. S., Goodman, Y. M., & Hood, W. J. (Eds.). (1989). *The whole language evaluation book.* Portsmouth, NH: Heinemann.

Goodman, Y. (1978). Kid watching: An alternative to testing. *Journal of National Elementary Principals, 57*(4), 41–45.

Goodman, Y. M., & Burke, C. L. (1972). *Reading miscue inventory manual: Procedure for diagnosis and evaluation.* New York: Macmillan.

Gottlieb, M. (1995). Nurturing student learning through portfolios. *TESOL Journal, 5*(1), 12–14.

Grabe, W. (1991). Current developments in second language reading research. *TESOL Quarterly, 25*(3), 375–406.

Grabe, W., & Stoller, F. (1997). Content-based instruction: Research foundations. In M. A. Snow & D. M. Brinton (Eds.), *The content-based classroom: Perspectives on integrating language and content* (pp. 5–21). White Plains, NY: Addison Wesley Longman.

Grant, C. (Ed.). (1995). *Education for diversity: An anthology of multicultural voices.* Boston: Allyn and Bacon.

Graves, D. (1983). *Writing: Children and teachers at work.* Portsmouth, NH: Heinemann.

Graves, D., & Hansen, J. (1983, February). The author's chair. *Language Arts, 60,* 176–183.

Grosjean, F. (1982). *Life with two languages: An introduction to bilingualism.* Cambridge, MA: Harvard University Press.

420

Gutierrez, K., Asato, J., Pacheco, M., Moll, L. C., Olson, K., Horng, K. L., Ruiz, R., Garcia, E., & McCarty, T. L. (2002). "Sounding American": The consequences of new reforms on English language learners. *Reading Research Quarterly, 37*(3) 328–347.

Gutierrez, K., Baquedano-Lopez, & Alvarez, H. (2001). Literacy as hybridity: Moving beyond bilingualism in urban classrooms. In M. de la Luz Reyes, & J. Halcon (Eds.), *The best for our children: Critical perspectives on literacy for Latino students.* New York: Teachers College Press.

Haggard, M. R. (1986). The vocabulary self-collection strategy: Using student interest and world knowledge to enhance vocabulary growth. *Journal on Reading, 29,* 634–642.

Hakuta, K. (1986). *Mirror of language: The debate on bilingualism.* New York: Basic Books.

Halliday, M. A. K. (1975). *Learning how to mean: Exploration in the development of language.* London: Arnold.

Halliday, M. A. K. (1984a). *Listening to Nigel: Conversations of a very small child.* Sydney, Australia: Linguistics Department, University of Sydney.

Halliday, M. A. K. (1985). *Spoken and written language.* Oxford: Oxford University Press.

Halliday, M. A. K. (1994). The place of dialogue in children's construction of meaning. In R.Ruddell, M. Ruddell, & H. Singer (Eds.), *Theoretical models and processes of reading* (4th ed.). Newark, DE: International Reading Association.

Hamayan, E. (1994). Language development of low literacy children. In F. Genesee (Ed.), *Educating second language children: The whole child, the whole curriculum, the whole community* (pp. 278–300). Cambridge: Cambridge University Press.

Hanf, M. B. (1971). Mapping: A technique for translating reading into thinking. *Journal of Reading, 14,* 225–230.

Harklau, L. (1994). ESL versus mainstream classes: Contrasting L2 learning environments. *TESOL Quarterly, 28*(2), 241–272.

Harley, B. (1986). *Age in second language acquisition.* London: Multilingual Matters.

Harley, B., Allen, P., Cummins, J., & Swain, M. (Eds.). (1990). *The development of second language proficiency.* Cambridge: Cambridge University Press.

Harper, C., & Platt, E. (1998). Full inclusion for secondary school ESOL students: Some concerns from Florida. *TESOL Journal, 7*(5), 30–36.

Harste, J. (1988). *Creating classrooms for authors: The reading-writing connection.* Portsmouth, NH: Heinemann.

Harste, J., Woodward, V., & Burke, C. (1984). *Language stories and literacy lessons.* Portsmouth, NH: Heinemann.

Hawkes, K. S., & Schell, L. M. (1987). Teacher-set prereading purposes and comprehension. *Reading Horizons, 27,* 164–169.

Heald-Taylor, G. (1987). Predictable literature selections and activities for language arts instruction. *The Reading Teacher, 41,* 6–12.

Healy, M. K. (1980). *Using student writing response groups in the classroom.* Berkeley: University of California/Bay Area Writing Project.

Heath, S. B. (1983). *Ways with words: Language, life and work in communities and classrooms.* New York: Cambridge University Press.

Heath, S. B. (1986). Sociocultural contexts of language development. In California State Department of Education (Ed.), *Beyond language: Social and cultural factors in schooling language minority students* (pp. 143–186). Los Angeles: Evaluation, Dissemination and Assessment Center, California State University.

Heath, S. B., & Mangiola, L. (1991). *Children of promise: Literate activity in linguistically and culturally diverse classrooms.* Washington, DC: National Education Association.

Heckleman, R. G. (1969). A neurological-impress method of remedial reading instruction. *Academic Therapy, 4,* 277–282.

Herber, H. L. (1978). *Teaching reading in content areas* (2nd ed.). Englewood Cliffs, NJ: Prentice Hall.

Herrell, A. (2000). *Fifty strategies for teaching English language learners.* Upper Saddle River, NJ: Merrill/Prentice Hall.

Hinds, J. (1983a). *Contrastive rhetoric: Japanese and English.* Edmonton, Calgary, Canada: Linguistic Research.

Hinds, J. (1983b). Linguistics and written discourse in particular languages: Contrastive studies: English and Japanese. In R. B. Kaplan (Ed.), *Annual review of applied linguistics, III* (pp. 75–84). Rowley, MA: Newbury House.

421

Hirvela, A. (1999). Collaborative writing instruction and communities of readers and writers. *TESOL Journal 8*(2), 7–12.

Hoban, R. (1960). *Bedtime for Frances*. New York: Harper & Row.

Holdaway, D. (1979). *The foundations of literacy*. Portsmouth, NH: Heinemann.

Hollingsworth, P. M. (1978). An experimental approach to the impress method of teaching reading. *The Reading Teacher, 313,* 624–626.

Holmes, B. C., & Roser, N. (1987). Five ways to assist readers' prior knowledge. *The Reading Teacher, 40,* 646–649.

Howard, K. (1990). Making the writing portfolio real. *The Quarterly of the National Writing Project and the Center for the Study of Writing, 12*(2), 4–6.

Hudelson, S. (1984). "Kan yu ret an rayt en ingles": Children become literate in English as a second language. *TESOL Quarterly, 18,* 221–238.

Hudelson, S. (1986). ESL children's writing: What we've learned, what we're learning. In P. Rigg & D. S. Enright (Eds.), *Children and ESL: Integrating perspectives* (pp. 23–54). Washington, DC: Teachers of English to Speakers of Other Languages.

Hudelson, S. (1987). The role of native language literacy in the education of language minority children. *Language Arts, 64,* 827–841.

Hudelson, S. (Ed.). (1981). *Learning to read in different languages*. Washington, DC: Center for Applied Linguistics.

Hudson, W. (1982). Essay writing for reluctant writers. In O. F. Boyle (Ed.), *Writing lessons II: Lessons in writing by teachers*. Berkeley: University of California Press.

Huerta-Macias, A. (1995). Alternative assessment: Responses to commonly asked questions. *TESOL Journal, 5*(1), 8–12.

Hughes, A. (2003). *Testing for language teachers* (2nd ed.). Cambridge: Cambridge University Press.

Hurley, S. R., & Tinajero, J. V. (Eds.). (2001). *Literacy assessment of second language learners*. Boston: Allyn and Bacon.

Igoa, C. (1995). *The inner world of the immigrant child*. New York: St. Martin's Press.

Irujo, S. (Ed.). (2000). *Integrating the ESL standards into classroom practice: Grades 6–8*. Alexandria, VA: Teachers of English to Speakers of Other Languages.

Jackson, S. L. (1980). Analysis of procedures and summary statistics of the language data. In B.J. Mace-Matluck (Ed.), *A longitudinal study of the oral language development of Texas bilingual children (Spanish-English): Findings from the first year*. Austin, TX: Southwest Educational Development Laboratory.

Jaramillo, A. (1998). Professional development from the inside out. *TESOL Journal, 7*(5), 12–18.

Johns, J. (1986). *Handbook for remediation of reading difficulties*. Englewood Cliffs, NJ: Prentice Hall.

Johns, J., & Lenski, S. (1994). *Improving reading: A handbook of strategies* (2nd ed). Dubuque, IA: Kendall-Hunt.

Johnson, C. (1955). *Harold and the purple crayon*. New York: Harper & Row.

Johnson, C. (1959). *Harold's circus*. New York: Harper & Row.

Johnson, D. W., Johnson, R. T., & Holubec, E. J. (1986). *Circles of learning: Cooperation in the classroom*. Edina, MN: Interaction Book.

Johnson, D., with Sulzby, E. (1999). Critical issue: Addressing the literacy needs of emergent and early readers. North Central Regional Educational Laboratory. Retrieved on July 20, 2003, from http://www.ncrel.org/sdrs/areas/issues/content/cntareas/reading/li100.htm

Jones, T. (2003). Favor asking and ESL. *TESOL Journal, 12*(2), 33–34.

Juel, C., Griffith, P., & Gough, P. B. (1986). Acquisition of literacy: A longitudinal study of children in first and second grade. *Journal of Educational Psychology, 78,* 243–255.

Kagan, S. (1986). Cooperative learning and sociocultural factors in schooling. In California State Department of Education (Ed.), *Beyond language: Social and cultural factors in schooling language minority students* (pp. 231–298). Los Angeles: Evaluation, Dissemination and Assessment Center, California State University

Kamil, M. L., Mosenthal, P., Pearson, P. D., & Barr, R. (Eds.). (2000). *Handbook of Reading Research: Volume III*. Mahwah, NJ: Erlbaum.

Karlsen, B., Madden, R., & Gardner, E. (1976). *Stanford diagnostic reading test*. New York: Harcourt Brace Jovanovich.

422

Kasper, L. N. (1995). Assessing metacognitive growth of ESL student writers. *TESL-EJ Foreign Language 1*(4), 1–12.

Katsiavriades, K. (2000). Language families. Retrieved on August 14, 2003, from http://www.krysstal.com/langfams.html

Kessler, C., & Quinn, M. E. (1984). *Second language acquisition in the context of science experiences.* Paper presented at the meeting of Teachers of English to Speakers of Other Languages, Houston, Texas. (ERIC Document Reproduction Service No. ED 248 713).

Kessler, C., & Quinn, M. E. (1987). ESL and science learning. In J. Crandall (Ed.), *ESL through content-area instruction: Mathematics, science, social studies* (pp. 55–88). Englewood Cliffs, NJ: Prentice Hall.

Kids of Room 14. (1979). *Our friends in the water.* Berkeley, CA: West Coast Print Center.

Kim, H., & Krashen, S. (1997). Why don't language acquirers take advantage of the power of reading? *TESOL Journal, 6*(3), 26–29.

Koch, K. (1970). *Wishes, lies and dreams: Teaching children to write poetry.* New York: Perennial Library.

Koskinen, P., Blum, I., Tennant, N., Parker, E. M., Straub, M. W., & Curry, C. (1995). Have you heard any good books lately? Encouraging shared reading at home with books and audiotapes. In L. M. Morrow (Ed.), *Family literacy: Connections in schools and communities.* Urbana, IL: International Reading Association.

Krapels, A. R. (1990). An overview of second language writing process research. In B. Kroll (Ed.), *Second language writing: Research insights for the classroom* (pp. 37–56). Cambridge: Cambridge University Press.

Krashen, S. (1981a). Bilingual education and second language acquisition theory. In California State Department of Education (Ed.), *Schooling and language minority students: A theoretical framework.* Los Angeles: Evaluation, Dissemination and Assessment Center, California State University.

Krashen, S. (1981b). The case for narrow reading. *TESOL Newsletter, 15*(6), 23.

Krashen, S. (1982). *Principles and practices in second language acquisition.* Oxford: Pergamon Press.

Krashen, S. (1993). *The power of reading.* Englewood, CO: Libraries Unlimited.

Krashen, S. D. (1984). Immersion: Why it works and what it has taught us. *Language in Society,12,* 61–64.

Krashen, S. D., & Terrell, D. (1983). *The natural approach: Language acquisition in the classroom.* Hayward, CA: Alemany Press.

Kreeft, J. (1984). Dialogue writing—Bridge from talk to essay writing. *Language Arts, 61,* 141–150.

Kroll, B. (Ed.). (1990). *Second language writing: Research insights for the classroom.* New York: Cambridge University Press.

LaBerge, D., & Samuels, S. J. (1976). Toward a theory of automatic information processing in reading. In H. Singer & R. B. Ruddell (Eds.), *Theoretical models and processes of reading.* Newark, DE: International Reading Association.

Labov, W. (1972). *Language in the inner city: Studies in the Black English vernacular.* Philadelphia: University of Pennsylvania Press.

Labov, W. (1981). *Logic of nonstandard English.* Speech given at University of California, Berkeley.

Lambert, W. (1987). The effects of bilingual and bicultural experiences on children's attitudes and social perspectives. In P. Homel, M. Paliz, & D. Aaronson (Eds.), *Childhood bilingualism: Aspects of linguistic, cognitive and social development* (pp. 197–222). Hillsdale, NJ: Erlbaum.

Lamme, L., & Hysmith, C. (1991). One school's adventure into portfolio assessment, *Language Arts, 68,* 629–640.

Laturnau, J. (2003). Standards-based instruction for English language learners. In G. G. Garcia (Ed.), *English learners reaching the highest level of English literacy* (pp. 286–305). Newark, DE: International Reading Association.

Leal, L., Crays, N., & Moetz, B. (1985). Training children to use a self-monitoring study strategy in preparation for recall: Maintenance and generalization effects. *Child Development, 56,* 643–653.

Legenza, A. (1974). *Questioning behavior of kindergarten children.* Paper presented at Nineteenth Annual Convention, International Reading Association.

423

Leslie, L., & Caldwell, J. (1995). *Qualitative Reading Inventory, II.* New York: Longman.

Leslie, L., & Caldwell, J. (2000). *Qualitative Reading Inventory, 3.* New York: Longman.

Lessow-Hurley, J. (2000). *The foundations of dual language instruction* (2nd ed.). New York: Addison-Wesley Longman.

Leu, D. (2003). Developing new literacies: Using the internet in content area instruction. Retrieved on July 25, 2003, from http://web.syr.edu/~djleu/content.html To appear in M. McLaughlin & M. E. Vogt (Eds.), *Creativity and innovations in content area instruction.* Norwood, MA: Christopher-Gordon.

Lightbown, P., & Spada, N. (1993). *How languages are learned.* Oxford: Oxford University Press.

Lindholm, K. J. (1990). Bilingual immersion education: Criteria for program development. In A.Padilla, H. Fairchild, & C. Valadez (Eds.), *Bilingual education: Issues and strategies* (pp.91–105). Newbury Park, CA: Sage.

Lindholm, K. J., & Gavlek, K. (1994). *California DBE projects: Project-wide evaluation report, 1992–1993.* San Jose, CA: Author.

Lindholm-Leary, K. (2001). *Dual language education.* Clevedon, England: Multilingual Matters.

Linquanti, R. (2001). *The redesignation dilemma: Challenges and choices in fostering meaningful accountability for English learners.* The University of California Linguistic Minority Research Institute Policy Report 2001-1. San Francisco, CA: WestEd.

Liu, J., & Hansen, J. G. (2002). *Peer response in second language writing classrooms.* Ann Arbor: University of Michigan Press.

Loban, W. (1968). *Stages, velocity, and prediction of language development: Kindergarten through grade twelve.* Urbana, IL: National Council of Teachers of English.

Loban, W. (1982). Personal correspondence.

Long, M., & Porter, P. (1985). Group work, interlanguage talk, and second language acquisition. *TESOL Quarterly, 18,* 207–227.

Los Angeles County Office of Education. (n.d.). *Sheltered English checklist.* Los Angeles, CA: Los Angeles County Office of Education.

Lowery, L. (1980). Speech at University of California, Berkeley.

MacDonald, J. (1986). Self-generated questions and reading recall: Does training help? *Contemporary Educational Psychology, 11,* 290–304.

Mace-Matluck, B. J. (1980). General characteristics of the children's language use in three environments. In B. J. Mace-Matluck (Ed.), *A longitudinal study of the oral language development of Texas bilingual children (Spanish-English): Findings from the first year.* Austin, TX: Southwest Educational Development Laboratory.

Mace-Matluck, B. J. (1981). General characteristics of the children's language use in three environments. In B. J. Mace-Matluck (Ed.), *A longitudinal study of the oral language development of Texas bilingual children (Spanish-English): Findings from the second year.* Austin, TX: Southwest Educational Development Laboratory.

Manzo, A. V. (1968). The ReQuest Procedure. *Journal of Reading, 12,* 123–126. Urbana, Illinois: International Reading Association.

Manzo, A. V., & Legenza, A. (1975). Inquiry training for kindergarten children. *Educational Leadership, 32,* 479–483.

Martin, B. (1967). *Brown bear, brown bear, what do you see?* New York: Holt, Rinehart & Winston.

Maslow, A. H. (1968). *Toward a psychology of being.* New York: Van Nostrand Reinhold.

Mason, J., & Au, K. (1990). *Reading instruction for today* (2nd ed.). Glenview, IL: Scott, Foresman.

McCauley, J., & McCauley, D. (1992). Using choral reading to promote language learning for ESL students. *The Reading Teacher, 45*(7), 526–533.

McCracken, R. A. (1971). Initiating sustained silent reading. *Journal of Reading, 14,* pp. 521–524.

McCracken, R. A., & McCracken, M. J. (1972). *Reading is only the tiger's tail.* San Rafael, CA: Leswig Press.

McKenna, M., & Robinson, R. (1993). *Teaching through text: A content literacy approach to content area reading.* White Plains, NY: Longman.

McKissack, P. (1988). *Mirandy and brother wind.* New York: Knopf.

McLaughlin, B. (1985). *Second language acquisition in childhood* (Vol. 2). Hillsdale, NJ: Erlbaum.

McLaughlin, B. (1987). *Theories of second language learning.* London: Arnold.

Mehan, H. (1979). *Learning lessons.* Cambridge, MA: Harvard University Press.

424

Merino, B., Legarreta, D., Coughran, C., & Hoskins, J. (1990). Interaction at the computer by language minority boys and girls paired with fluent English proficient peers. *Computers in the Schools, 7,* 109–119.

Meyer, B. J. F., Brandt, K. M., & Bluth, G. J. (1980). Use of top-level structure in text: Key for reading comprehension of ninth grade students. *Reading Research Quarterly, 16,* 72–103.

Meyer, L. (Ed.). (2000a). *Theory into Practice, 39*(4). Columbus: Ohio State University.

Meyer, L. (2000b). Barriers to meaningful instruction for English learners. *Theory into Practice, 39* (4), 228–236.

Michaels, S. (1979). *A study of sharing time with first grade students: Discourse narratives in the classroom.* Proceedings of the Fifth Annual Meeting of the Berkeley Linguistics Society, Berkeley, CA.

Miller, G. A. (1956). The magic number seven, plus or minus two. *Psychological Review, 63,* 81–97.

Miller, G. A., Galanter, E., & Pribram, K. (1960). *Plans and the structure of behavior.* New York: Holt, Rinehart & Winston.

Mills, H., O'Keefe, T., & Stephens, D. (1992). *Looking closely: Exploring the role of phonics in one whole language classroom.* Urbana, IL: National Council of Teachers of English.

Mohan, B. (1986). *Language and content.* Reading, MA: Addison-Wesley.

Moll, L. (1994). Literacy research in community and classrooms: A sociocultural approach. In R. R. Ruddell, M. R. Ruddell, & H. Singer (Eds.), *Theoretical models and processes of reading* (4th ed., pp. 179–207). Newark, DE: International Reading Association.

Moraes, M. (1996). *Bilingual education: A dialogue with the Bakhtin Circle.* Albany: State University of New York Press.

Morphet, M. V., & Washburn, C. (1931). When should children begin to read? *Elementary School Journal, 31,* 496–508.

Morrow, L. M. (1983). Home and school correlates of early interest in literature. *Journal of Educational Research, 76,* 24–30.

Morrow, L. M. (1993). *Literacy development in the early years: Helping children read and write* (2nd ed.). Boston: Allyn and Bacon.

Morrow, L. M. (Ed.) (1995). *Family literacy: Connections in schools and communities.* Newark, DE: International Reading Association.

Mullen, N., & Olsen, L. (1990). You and I are the same. In J. A. Cabello (Ed.), *California perspectives* (pp. 23–29). San Francisco: California Tomorrow.

Murphy, S., & Smith, M. A. (1990). Talking about portfolios. *The Quarterly of the National Writing Project and the Center for the Study of Writing, 12*(2), 1–3.

Murray, D. (1992). Language in the attic. In D. Murray (Ed.), *Diversity as resource* (pp. 1–17). Alexandria, VA: Teachers of English to Speakers of Other Languages.

Myers, M. (1980). *A procedure for writing assessment and holistic scoring.* Urbana, IL: National Council of Teachers of English.

Nagy, W. E. & Scott, J. A. (2000). Vocabulary processes. In M. L. Kamil, P. B. Mosenthal, P. D. Pearson, & R. Barr (Eds.), *Handbook of reading research: Volume III.* Mahwah, NJ: Erlbaum.

National Assessment for Educational Progress. (2003). Nation's Report Card. http://nces.ed. gov.nationsreportcard/reading/results2003/

National Commission on Excellence in Education (1983). *A nation at risk.* Washington, DC: U.S. Government Printing Office.

National Council of Teachers of Mathematics, Inc. (1989). *Curriculum and evaluation standards for school mathematics.* Reston, VA: Author.

Nieto, S. (1996). *Affirming diversity: The sociopolitical context of multicultural education* (2nd ed.). White Plains, NY: Longman.

Ninio, A. (1980). Picture-book reading in mother-infant dyads belonging to two subgroups in Israel. *Child Development, 51,* 587–590.

Ninio, A., & Bruner, J. (1978). The achievement and antecedents of labeling. *Child Language, 5,* 1–15.

Nolte, R., & Singer, H. (1985). Active comprehension: Teaching a process of reading comprehension and its effects on reading achievement. *The Reading Teacher, 39,* 24–31.

Northcutt, M., & Watson, D. (1986). *Sheltered English teaching handbook.* San Marcos, CA: AM Graphics & Printing.

Norton, B. (1997). Language, identity, and the ownership of English. *TESOL Quarterly 31*(3), 409–429.

425

Ochs, E., & Schieffelin, G. G. (1984). Language acquisition and socialization: Three developmental stories and their implications. In R. Shweder & R. LeVine (Eds.), *Culture theory: Essays on mind, self, and emotion* (pp. 276–322). Cambridge: Cambridge University Press.

Odlin, T. (1989). *Language transfer: Cross-linguistic influence in language learning.* Cambridge: Cambridge University Press.

Ogle, D. (1986). A teaching model that develops active reading of expository text. *The Reading Teacher, 39,* 564–570.

O'Hare, F. (1973). *Sentence combining: Improving student writing without formal grammar instruction* (Report No. 15). Urbana, IL: National Council of Teachers of English.

Oller, J., Jr. (Ed.). (1993). *Methods that work: Ideas for literacy and language teachers* (2nd ed.). Boston: Heinle & Heinle.

Olsen, L. (1998). *Made in America: Immigrant students in our public schools.* New York: The New Press.

Olsen, L., & Mullen, N. (1990). *Embracing diversity: Teachers' voices from California's classrooms.* San Francisco: California Tomorrow.

O'Malley, J. M., & Chamot, A. U. (1990). *Learning strategies in second language acquisition.* Cambridge: Cambridge University Press.

Ovando, C. (2003, Spring). Bilingual education in the United States: Historical development and current issues. *Bilingual Research Journal, 27*(1), 1–24. Retrieved on July 7, 2003, from http://brj.asu.edu

Ovando, C. J., Collier, V. P., & Combs, M. C. (2003). *Bilingual and ESL classrooms: Teaching in multicultural contexts* (3rd ed.). Boston: McGraw-Hill.

Oxford, R. L. (2003). Language learning strategies in a nutshell: Update and ESL suggestions. In J. C. Richards & W. A. Renandya (Eds.), *Methodology in language teaching: An anthology of current practice* (pp. 124–132). Cambridge, UK: Cambridge University Press.

Padolsky, D. (2002a). AskNCELA no. 1: How many school-aged English language learners (ELLs) are there in the U.S.? Retrieved on June 18, 2003, from http://www.ncela.gwu.edu/askncela/01leps.htm

Padolsky, D. (2002b). AskNCELA no. 8. How has the English language learner population changed in recent years? Retrieved on June 18, 2003, from http://www.ncela.gwu.edu/askncela/08leps.htm

Palinscar, A., & Brown, A. (1984). Reciprocal teaching of comprehension-fostering and comprehension-monitoring activities. *Cognition and Instruction, 1,* 117–175.

Pappas, C., Kiefer, B., & Levstik, L. (1990). *An integrated language perspective in the elementary school: Theory into action.* White Plains, NY: Longman.

Paterson, K. (1978). *The Great Gilly Hopkins.* New York: Avon/Camelot.

Pearson, P. D., & Johnson, D. (1978). *Teaching reading comprehension.* New York: Macmillan.

Peregoy, S. (1989, Spring). Relationships between second language oral proficiency and reading comprehension of bilingual fifth grade students. *Journal of the National Association for Bilingual Education, 13*(3), 217–234.

Peregoy, S. (1991). Environmental scaffolds and learner responses in a two-way Spanish immersion kindergarten. *Canadian Modern Language Review, 47*(3), 463–476.

Peregoy, S., & Boyle, O. (1990a). Kindergartners write! Emergent literacy of Mexican American children in a two-way Spanish immersion program. *Journal of the Association of Mexican American Educators,* 6–18.

Peregoy, S., & Boyle, O. (1990b). Reading and writing scaffolds: Supporting literacy for second language learners. *Educational Issues of Language Minority Students: The Journal, 6,* 55–67.

Peregoy, S., & Boyle, O. (1991). Second language oral proficiency characteristics of low, intermediate, and high second language readers. *Hispanic Journal of Behavioral Sciences, 13*(1), 35–47.

Peregoy, S., & Boyle, O. (1993). *Reading, writing, and learning in ESL: A resource book for K–8 teachers.* White Plains, NY: Longman.

Peregoy, S., & Boyle, O. (1999a). Multiple embedded scaffolds: Supporting English learners' social/affective, linguistic and academic development in kindergarten. *Kindergarten Education: Theory, Research and Practice, 4,* 41–54.

Peregoy, S., & Boyle, O. (2000). English learners reading in English: What we know, what we need to know. In L. Meyer (Ed.), *Theory into Practice, 39*(4), 237–247.

426

Peregoy, S. F., & Boyle, O. F. (1999b). Multiple embedded scaffolds: Support for English speakers in a two-way Spanish immersion kindergarten. *Bilingual Research Journal, 23*(2 & 3), 135–126.

Perfetti, C., Beck, I., Bell, L., & Hughes, C. (1987). Phonemic knowledge and learning to read are reciprocal: A longitudinal study of first grade children. *Merrill-Palmer Quarterly, 33,* 283–319.

Perry, T., & Delpit, L. (Eds.). (1998). *The real Ebonics debate: Power, language and the education of African-American children.* Boston: Beacon Press.

Peterson, A. (1981, June). *Working with the sentence.* Speech presented at the Bay Area Writing Project Workshop, Fairfield, CA.

Peterson, R., & Eeds, M. (1990). *Grand conversations: Literature groups in action.* New York: Scholastic.

Peyton, J., & Reed, L. (1990). *Dialogue journal writing with nonnative English speakers: A handbook for teachers.* Alexandria, VA: TESOL.

Philips, S. U. (1983). *The invisible culture: Communication in classroom and community on the Warm Springs Indian Reservation.* White Plains, NY: Longman.

Pica, T. (1994). Monitor theory in classroom perspective. In R. Barasch & C. Vaughn James (Eds.), *Beyond the monitor model: Comments on current theory and practice in second language acquisition.* Boston: Heinle & Heinle.

Pollard, J. (1985). *Building toothpick bridges.* Palo Alto, CA: Dale Seymour.

Position Paper. (1992). *TESOL Statement on the Education of K–12 Language Minority Students in the United States.* Alexandria, VA.

Purcell-Gates, V. (1988). Lexical and syntactic knowledge of written narrative held by well-read-to-kindergartners and second graders. *Research in the Teaching of English, 22,* 128–160.

Purcell-Gates, V. (1995). *Other people's words: The cycle of low literacy.* Cambridge, MA: Harvard University Press.

Raimes, A. (1983). *Techniques in teaching writing.* Oxford: Oxford University Press.

Raimes, A. (2001). *Exploring through writing: A process approach to ESL composition* (2nd ed.). Cambridge: Cambridge University Press.

Ratekin, N., Simpson, M., Alvermann, D., & Dishner, E. (1985). Why content teachers resist reading instruction. *Journal of Reading, 28,* 432–437.

Rayner, K., & Pollatsek, A. (1989). *The psychology of reading.* Englewood Cliffs, NJ: Prentice Hall.

Readence, J., Bean, T., & Baldwin, S. (1981). *Content area reading: An integrated approach.* Dubuque, IA: Kendall/Hunt.

Renandya, W. A., & Jacobs, G. M. (2002). Extensive reading: Why aren't we all doing it? In J. Richard & W. Renandya (Eds.), *Methodology in language teaching: An anthology of current practice.* Cambridge: Cambridge University Press.

Reppen, R. (1994/1995). A genre-based approach to content writing instruction. *TESOL Journal, 4*(2), 32–35.

Reyes, M. de la Luz, & Halcon, J. J. (Eds.). (2001). The best for our children: Critical perspectives on literacy for Latino students. New York: Teachers College Press.

Reynolds, J., Dale, G., & Moore, J. (1989). *How to plan and implement a two-way Spanish immersion program.* Sacramento, CA: California State Department of Education.

Reys, R., Suydam, M., & Lindquist, M. (1991). *Helping children learn mathematics* (3rd ed.). Englewood Cliffs, NJ: Prentice Hall.

Richard-Amato, P. (2003). *Making it happen: Interaction in the second language classroom* (3rd ed.). White Plains, NY: Longman.

Richards, J., & Renandya, W. (Eds.). (2002). *Methodology in language teaching: An anthology of current practice.* Cambridge: Cambridge University Press.

Rico, G. L., & Claggett, F. (1980). *Balancing the hemispheres: Brain research and the teaching of writing.* Berkeley: University of California/Bay Area Writing Project.

Right to Read Conference (1972). Out-of-print passage used in workshop, Anaheim, CA.

Rodriguez, R. (1982). *Hunger of memory.* New York: Godine.

Romaine, S. (1989). *Bilingualism.* Oxford: Blackwell.

Rosegrant, T. J. (1988). Talking word processors for the early grades. In J. L. Hoot & S. B. Silvern (Eds.), *Writing with computers in the early grades* (pp. 143–159). New York: Teachers College Press.

Rosenblatt, L. M. (1978). *The reader, the text, the poem.* Carbondale: Southern Illinois University.

427

Rosenblatt, L. M. (1983). The reading transaction: What for? In R. P. Parker & F. A. Davis (Eds.), *Developing literacy: Young children's use of language* (pp. 118–135). Newark, DE: International Reading Association.

Rosenblatt, L. M. (1984). *Literature as exploration* (3rd ed.). New York: Modern Language Association.

Rothstein-Fisch, C., & Greenfield, P. M. (2003). About the bridging cultures project. Retrieved on June 17, 2003, from http://web.wested.org/online_pubs/bridging/about_bc.shtml

Routman, R. (1995). *Invitations: Changing as teachers and learners* (2nd ed.). Portsmouth, NH: Heinemann.

Rowe, M. B. (1974). Wait time—Is anybody listening? *Journal of Psycholinguistic Research, 3,* 203–224.

Ruddell, R., & Boyle, O. (1984). *A study of the effects of cognitive mapping on reading comprehension and written protocols.* (Tech. Rep. No. 7). Riverside, CA: Learning from Text Project, University of California.

Ruddell, R., & Boyle, O. (1989). A study of cognitive mapping as a means to improve summarization and comprehension of expository text. *Reading Research and Instruction, 29,* 12–22.

Ruddell, R. B., & Ruddell, M. R. (1995). *Teaching children to read and write: Becoming an influential teacher.* Boston: Allyn and Bacon.

Rupert, P. R., & Brueggeman, M. A. (1986). Reading journals: Making the language connection in college. *Journal of Reading, 30,* 26–33.

Rylant, C. (1989). *When I was young in the mountains.* New York: Bantam Books.

Sampson, M., Allen, R., & Sampson, M. (1990). *Pathways to literacy.* Chicago: Holt, Rinehart, & Winston.

Samway, K. (1987). *The writing processes of nonnative English speaking children in the elementary grades.* Unpublished doctoral dissertation, University of Rochester, NY.

Samway, K. D. (Ed.). (2000). *Integrating the ESL standards into classroom practice: Grades 3–5.* Alexandria, VA: Teachers of English to Speakers of Other Languages.

Samway, K. D., & McKeon, D. (1999). *Myths and realities: Best practices for language minority students.* Portsmouth, NH: Heinemann.

Samway, K., Whang, G., Cade, C., Gamil, M., Lubandina, M., & Phomachanh, K. (1991). Reading the skeleton, the heart and the brain of a book: Students' perspectives on literature study circles. *The Reading Teacher, 45,* 196–205.

Sartre, J.-P. (1967). *The Words.* New York: Random House.

Saville-Troike, M. (1978). *A guide to culture in the classroom.* Rosslyn, VA: National Clearinghouse for Bilingual Education.

Scarcella, R. (1990). *Teaching language minority students in the multicultural classroom.* Englewood Cliffs, NJ: Prentice Hall.

Schieffelin, B. B., & Eisenberg, A. (1984). Cultural variation in children's conversations. In R. L. Schiefelbusch & J. Pickar (Eds.), *The acquisition of communicative competence* (pp.377–420). Baltimore: University Park Press.

Schifini, A. (1985). *Sheltered English.* Los Angeles: Los Angeles County Office of Education.

Schmidt, B. (n.d.). *Story mapping.* In unpublished manuscript, California State University, Sacramento.

Schmitt, N., & Carter, R. (2000). The lexical advantages of narrow reading for second language learners. *TESOL Journal, 9*(1), 4–9.

Schmitt, N., & McCarthy, M. (Eds.). (2002). *Vocabulary: Description, acquisition, and pedagogy.* Cambridge: Cambridge University Press.

Scieszka, J. (1989). *The true story of the three little pigs by A. Wolf.* New York: Viking Penguin.

Seda, M. M., Ligouri, O. Z., & Seda, C. M. (1999). Bridging literacy and social studies: Engaging prior knowledge through children's books. *TESOL Journal, 8*(3), 34–40.

Seigel, G. (1983). From speech given at Bay Area Writing Project, Berkeley, CA.

Selinker, L. (1972). Interlanguage. *International Review of Applied Linguistics, 10,* 209–231.

Sheets, R. H., & Hollins, E. R. (1999). *Racial and ethnic identity in school: Aspects of human development.* Mahwah, NJ: Erlbaum.

Shepherd, J. (1971). *Wanda Hicky's night of golden memories and other disasters.* New York: Doubleday.

Shultz, J., Erickson, F., & Florio, S. (1982). "Where's the floor?": Aspects of social relationships in communication at home and at school. In P. Gilmore & A. Glatthorn (Eds.), *Children in*

428

and out of school: Ethnography and education (pp. 88–123). Washington, DC: Center for Applied Linguistics.

Silva, T. (1990). Second language composition instruction: Developments, issues, and directions in ESL. In B. Kroll (Ed.), Second language writing: Research insights for the classroom (pp. 11–23). New York: Cambridge University Press.

Silverstein, S. (1974). Where the sidewalk ends. New York: Harper & Row.

Sinatra, R., Beaudry, J., Stahl-Gemake, J., & Guastello, E. (1990). Combining visual literacy, text understanding, and writing for culturally diverse students. Journal of Reading, 8, 612–617.

Singer, H. (1978). Active comprehension: From answering to asking questions. The Reading Teacher, 31, 901–908.

Singer, H., & Donlan, D. (1989). Reading and learning from text (3rd ed.). Hillsdale, NJ: Erlbaum.

Skinner, B. F. (1957). Verbal behavior. New York: Appleton-Century-Crofts.

Sloyer, S. (1982). Reader's theater: Story dramatization in the classroom. Urbana, IL: National Council of Teachers of English.

Smallwood, B. A. (Ed.). (2000). Integrating the ESL standards into classroom practice: Grades pre-K–2. Alexandria, VA: Teachers of English to Speakers of Other Languages.

Smitherman, G. (1986). Talkin' and testifyin'. Detroit: Wayne State University Press.

Smitherman, G. (1998a). "Dat teacher be hollin at us"—What is Ebonics? TESOL Quarterly 32(1), 139–143.

Smitherman, G. (1998b). Black English/Ebonics: What it be like? In T. Perry & L. Delpit (Eds.), The real Ebonics debate: Power, language and the education of African-American children. Boston: Beacon Press.

Smolen, L., Newman, C., Wathen, T., & Lee, D. (1995). Developing student self-assessment strategies. TESOL Journal, 5(1), 22–27.

Snow, C. (1977). The development of conversation between mothers and babies. Journal of Child Language, 4, 47–56.

Snow, C. (1983). Literacy and language: Relationships during the preschool years. Harvard Educational Review, 53, 165–189.

Snow, C. E., Burns, M. S., & Griffin, P. (Eds.). (1998). Preventing reading difficulties in young children. Washington, DC: National Academy Press.

Snow, M. A. (2000). Implementing the ESL standards for pre-K–12 students through teacher education. Alexandria, VA: Teachers of English to Speakers of Other Languages.

Snow, M. A. (2001). Content-based and immersion models for second and foreign language teaching. In M. Celce-Murcia (Ed.), Teaching English as a second or foreign language (3rd ed.). Boston: Heinle & Heinle.

Snow, M. A. & Brinton, D. M. (1997). The content-based classroom: Perspectives on integrating language and content. White Plains, NY: Addison-Wesley Longman.

Spolin, V. (1963/1983). Improvisations for the theater. Evanston, IL: Northwestern University Press.

Spradley, J. P. (1980). Participant observation. New York: Holt, Rinehart & Winston.

Stahl, S. (1992). Saying the "p" word: Nine guidelines for exemplary phonics instruction. The Reading Teacher, 45, 618–625.

Stauffer, R. G. (1970). The language-experience approach to the teaching of reading. New York: Harper & Row.

Stauffer, R. G. (1975). Directing the reading-thinking process. New York: Harper & Row.

Steinbeck, J. (1958). A teacher I remember. In Bay Area Reading Association Newsletter. Oakland, CA.

Stewig, J. (1981). Choral speaking. Who has the time? Why take the time? Childhood Education, 58(1), 25–29.

Stieglitz, E. L., & Lanigan, V. (1996). The Stieglitz informal reading inventory: Assessing reading behaviors from emergent to advanced levels.

Stoller, F. L. (2002). Project work: A means to promote language and content. In J. C. Richards & W. A. Renandya, Methodology in language teaching: An anthology of current practice. Cambridge: Cambridge University Press.

Strickland, D. S. & Morrow, L. M. (Eds.). (1989). Emerging literacy: Young children learn to read and write. Newark, DE: International Reading Association.

Sulzby, E. (1985). Children's emergent reading of favorite storybooks. Reading Research Quarterly, 20, 458–481.

Swain, M. (1985). Communicative competence: Some roles of comprehensible input and com-

429

prehensible output in its development. In S. M. Gass and C. G. Madden (Eds.), *Input in second language acquisition* (pp. 235–253). Rowley, MA: Newbury House.

Swain, M., & Lapkin, S. (1989). *Evaluating bilingual education: A Canadian case study.* Clevedon, England: Multilingual Matters.

Takaki, R. (Ed.). (1987). From different shores: *Perspectives on race and ethnicity in America.* New York: Oxford University Press.

Tatsuki, D. H. (1996). Games with a pronunciation focus. *TESOL Journal, 6*(2) 32–33.

Taylor, D., & Dorsey-Gaines, C. (1988). *Growing up literate: Learning from inner-city families.* Portsmouth, NH: Heinemann.

Taylor, M. D. (1976). *Roll of thunder, hear my cry.* New York: Dial.

Teachers of English to Speakers of Other Languages (1992). *TESOL statement on the education of K–12 language minority students in the United States.* Washington, DC: Author.

Teachers of English to Speakers of Other Languages (1997). *ESL Standards for Pre-K–12 Students.* Alexandria, VA: Author.

Teachers of English to Speakers of Other Languages (1998). *Mapping the assessment process: A framework for measuring student attainment of the ESL standards.* Alexandria, VA: Author.

Teachers of English to Speakers of Other Languages (2001). *Scenarios for ESL standards-based assessment.* Alexandria, VA: Author.

Teale, W. H. (1984). Reading to young children: Its significance for literacy development. In H. Goelman, A. A. Oberg, & G. Smith (Eds.), *Awakening to literacy.* Portsmouth, NH: Heinemann.

Teale, W. H., & Sulzby, E. (Eds.). (1986). *Emergent literacy: Writing and reading.* Norwood, NJ: Ablex.

Tease, K. (1995). *Literacy rich environments in the preschool and kindergarten classroom: A teacher handbook.* Unpublished master's paper.

Terkel, S. (1974). *Working.* New York: Pantheon.

Terrell, T. D. (1981). The natural approach in bilingual education. In D. Dolson (Ed.), *Schooling and language minority students: A theoretical framework.* Sacramento: California State Department of Education.

Tharp, R., & Gallimore, R. (1988). *Rousing minds to life: Teaching, learning and schooling in social context.* New York: Cambridge University Press.

Thomas, W., & Collier, V. (1997, December). *School effectiveness for language minority students.* National Clearinghouse for Bilingual Education (NCBE) Resource Collection Series, No. 9. http://www.gwu.edu/ncbepubs/resource/effectiveness/index.html.

Thomas, W., & Collier, V. (2002). *A national study of school effectiveness for language minority students' long-term academic achievement.* Santa Cruz: Center for Research on Education, Diversity and Excellence, University of California, Santa Cruz. http://www.crede.ucsc.edu/research/llaa/1.1_final.html.

Tiedt, P. L., & Tiedt, I. M. (1990). *Multicultural teaching: A handbook of activities, information, and resources* (3rd ed.). Boston: Allyn and Bacon.

Tierney, R. J., & Readance, J. E. (2000). *Reading strategies and practices: A compendium* (5th ed.). Boston: Allyn and Bacon.

Tinajero, J. V., & Calderon, M. E. (1988). Language experience approach plus. *Educational Issues of Language Minority Students: The Journal, 2,* 31–45.

Tomlinson, B. (1986). Using poetry with mixed ability language classes. *English Language Teaching Journal, 40,* 33–41.

Topping, K., & Wolfingdale, S. (Eds.). (1985). *Parental involvement in children's reading.* New York: Nichols.

Tragar, B., & Wong, B. K. (1984). The relationship between native and second language reading and second language oral ability. In C. Rivera (Ed.), *Placement procedures in bilingual education: Education and policy issues* (pp. 152–164). Clevedon, England: Multilingual Matters.

Trieman, R. (1985). Onsets and rimes as units of spoken syllables: Evidence from children. *Journal of Experimental Psychology, 39,* 161–181.

Trumbull, E., Rothstein-Fisch, C., & Greenfield, P. (2000). *Bridging cultures in our schools: New approaches that work.* West Ed Knowledge Brief. Retrieved June 17, 2003 from http://web.wested.org/online_pubs/bridging/about_bc.shtml.

430

Urzúa, C. (1987). "You stopped too soon": Second language children composing and revising. *TESOL Quarterly, 21,* 279–305.

Urquhart, S., & Weir, C. (1998). *Reading in a second language: Process, product and practice.* London: Longman.

Urzúa, C. (1992). Faith in learners through literature studies. *Language Arts, 69,* 492–501.

U.S. Office of Elementary and Secondary Education (2002). The No Child Left Behind Act, Executive Summary. Available at http://www. ed.gov/offices/OESE/esea/exec-summ.html

Vacca, R., & Vacca, J. (1989). *Content area reading.* Glenview, IL: Scott, Foresman.

Vacca, R., & Vacca, J. (1993). *Content area reading* (4th ed.). New York: HarperCollins College Publishers.

Valdez Pierce, L. (2003, March/April/May). Accountability and equity: Compatible goals of high-stakes testing? *TESOL Matters 13*(2). Alexandria, VA: Teachers of English to Speakers of Other Languages.

Valencia, S. W., & Wixson, K. K. (2000). Policy-oriented research on literacy standards and assessment. In M. L. Kamil, P. B. Mosenthal, P. D. Pearson, & R. Barr (Eds.), *Handbook of Reading Research: Volume III* (pp. 909–935). Mahwah, NJ: Erlbaum.

Varonis, E. M., & Gass, S. M. (1985). Non-native/non-native conversations: A model for negotiation of meaning. *Applied Linguistics, 6*(1), 71–90.

Vásquez, O. (1991). Reading the world in a multicultural setting: A Mexicano perspective. *The Quarterly Newsletter of the Laboratory of Comparative Human Cognition, 13,* 13–15.

Verplaetse, L-S. (1998). How content teachers interact with English language learners. *TESOL Journal, 7*(5), 24–28.

Vygotsky, L. S. (1962). *Thought and language.* Cambridge, MA: MIT Press.

Waddell, M., Esch, R., & Walker, R. (1972). *The art of styling sentences: 20 patterns to success.* New York: Barron's Educational Series.

Wallat, C. (1984). An overview of communicative competence. In C. Rivera (Ed.), *Communicative competence approaches to language proficiency assessment* (pp. 2–33). London: Multilingual Matters.

Webster, J. P. (1998). Semantic maps. *TESOL Journal, 7*(5), 42–43.

Weinborg, H. (Producer & Writer). (1989). *First things first* [videotape]. Pittsburgh, PA: Public Broadcasting, Inc.

Wells, G. (1986). *The meaning makers: Children learning language and using language to learn.* Portsmouth, NH: Heinemann.

Welty, E. (1983). *One writer's beginnings.* New York: Warner Books.

White, E. B. (1952). *Charlotte's web.* New York: Harper & Row.

White, E. M. (1985). *Teaching and assessing writing: Recent advances in understanding, evaluating, and improving student performance.* San Francisco: Jossey-Bass.

Wiesner, D. (1991). *Window.* New York: Clarion.

Wink, J. (2000). *Critical pedagogy: Notes from the real world* (2nd ed.). New York: Addison-Wesley Longman.

Wisniewska, I. (1998). Using games to get feedback. *TESOL Journal, 7*(6) 38–39.

Wong Fillmore, L. (1980). Learning a second language: Chinese children in the American classroom. In J. E. Alatis (Ed.), *Current issues in bilingual education: Georgetown University roundtable on languages and linguistics* (pp. 309–325). Washington, DC: Georgetown University Press.

Wong Fillmore, L. (1982). Instructional language as linguistic input: Second-language learning in classrooms. In L. C. Wilkinson (Ed.), *Communicating in the classroom* (pp. 283–296). Madison: University of Wisconsin Press.

Wong Fillmore, L. (1983, February). *Levels of language proficiency: The view from second language acquisition.* TESOL Forum Lecture presented at Teachers of English to Speakers of Other Languages, Austin, TX.

Wong Fillmore, L. (1985). When does teacher talk work as input? In S. Gass & C. Madden (Eds.), *Input in second language acquisition* (pp. 17–50). Rowley, MA: Newbury House.

Wong Fillmore, L. (1990). Latino families and the schools. In J. Cabello (Ed.), *California perspectives: An anthology from the immigrant students project.* San Francisco: California Tomorrow.

Wong Fillmore, L. (1991a). Second-language learning in children: A model of language

431

learning in social context. In E. Bialystok (Ed.), *Language processing in bilingual children* (pp. 49–69). Cambridge: Cambridge University Press.

Wong Fillmore, L. (1991b). When learning a second language means losing the first. *Early Childhood Research Quarterly, 6*(3), 323–346.

Wong Fillmore, L., Ammon, P., Ammon, M. S., DeLucchi, K., Jensen, J. A., McLaughlin, B., & Strong, M. (1983). *Language learning through bilingual instruction* (Second Year Report No. 400–80–0030). Washington, DC: National Institute of Education.

Wong, H. K., & Wong, R. T. (1998). *How to be an effective teacher: The first days of school.* Mountain View, CA: Harry K. Wong Publications.

Woods, M. L., & Moe, A. J. (1998). *Analytical reading inventory: Comprehensive assessment for all students including gifted and remedial.* Englewood Cliffs, NJ: Prentice Hall.

Wright, W., Betteridge, D., & Buckby, M. (2002). *Games for language learning: New edition.* Cambridge: Cambridge University Press.

Yang, D. (1992). Create a board game. *TESOL Journal, 1*(3), 35.

Yochum, N., & Miller, S. (1990). Classroom reading assessment: Using students' perceptions. *Reading Psychology: An International Quarterly, 11,* 159–165.

Yopp, R. (1987). *Active comprehension: Declarative knowledge for generating questions and procedural knowledge for answering them.* Unpublished doctoral dissertation, University of California, Riverside.

Zola, D. (1984). Redundancy and word perception during reading. *Perception and Psychophysics, 36,* 277–284.

Author Index

436

437

438

Subject index

440

441

442

445